Judging & (Re)Thinking European Union Law

Luca Prete • Leila Rezki
Editors

Judging & (Re)Thinking European Union Law

Liber Amicorum in Honour of Nils Wahl

Springer

Editors
Luca Prete
Chambers of First Advocate General,
Maciej Szpunar
Court of Justice of the European Union
Luxembourg, Luxembourg

Leila Rezki
Chambers of the President of the Court,
Koen Lenaerts
Court of Justice of the European Union
Luxembourg, Luxembourg

ISBN 978-3-032-13472-1 ISBN 978-3-032-13473-8 (eBook)
https://doi.org/10.1007/978-3-032-13473-8

This Springer imprint is published by the registered company Springer Nature Switzerland AG
The registered company address is: Gewerbestrasse 11, 6330 Cham, Switzerland

Nils Wahl

Preface

A tribute to Nils Wahl

'Please come in'. The phone call would be that short. We normally expected it within an hour of sending him the draft opinion or judgment that he had asked us to prepare. When examining cases, Nils Wahl always managed to be efficient and thorough at the same time. Even after many years of service, each time a new opinion or judgment took shape, he still shared our enthusiasm for having dealt with yet another case and having addressed — hopefully, in a sound and reasonable manner — all the legal issues which it raised. His energy and determination never faltered — no matter how many cases he had already handled in his time at the Court of Justice of the European Union ('CJEU').

Indeed, Nils' departure from the CJEU in 2024 marked the end of an eighteen-year career within that institution, during which he had the opportunity to exercise various judicial functions in the service of European justice. As President Lenaerts pointed out at the formal sitting held on 7 October 2024, Nils' career at the CJEU can be described as *exceptional* in that he is one of the few people at the institution to have 'known it all', having served as a judge at the General Court from 2006 to 2012, as an Advocate General at the Court of Justice from 2012 to 2019, and as a judge at the Court of Justice from 2019 to 2024.

As a Doctor of Law at *Stockholms Universitet*, Nils came to the General Court with a solid academic background as a Professor of European Law and a particular *penchant* for economic law and, above all, competition law. At the General Court, he quickly showed a remarkable ability to handle voluminous and highly technical files. With that experience as a 'first instance' EU judge, it was only natural that, when the possibility arose, Nils was appointed to the Court of Justice, where he could apply his skills and knowledge to a broader range of cases. As Advocate General, he strove to contribute in a constructive and valuable manner to the legal debate within the Court. This could only be achieved by delivering robust and thoughtful opinions that reflected his own views on the matter, regardless of whether it affected his chance of 'being followed' by the Court. Using an original metaphor, he once stated that an Advocate General is like a mine detection dog: very useful to the security forces regardless of whether it actually locates the mine.

Indeed, most of the time, the dog finds the mine or the explosive device, which can then be safely removed. On the rare occasion the dog fails to detect the mine, it will unintentionally — and, sadly, especially in the eyes of those who, like Nils, have great love for dogs — detonate the mine, thereby saving the minesweepers' life in a different manner. Similarly, the Advocate General usually identifies the correct solution for a case and thus assists the Court in coming to the correct interpretation and application of the relevant provisions of EU law. When the Advocate General does not manage, despite his or her best efforts, to convince the Court of a given solution, the opinion is no less useful, as it allows the Court to adopt a different approach in full knowledge of the arguments that can be raised against it. At times, Nils also enjoyed *spicing-up* his opinions with references to various sources, for example, unexpected legal documents (such as the Code of Hammurabi, providing an interesting precedent in a case on motor vehicles liability), controversial rulings (such as that of the US Supreme Court judgment in the 'Obamacare' case, when dealing with social security), literature (such as Publius Ovidius's *Ars Amatoria*, in a VAT case concerning horse racing stables) and mythological creatures (such as when he wrote that 'coming across a "true" *acte clair* situation [under the *CILFIT* case-law] would ... seem just as likely as encountering a unicorn'). The use of such references was never, however, an end in itself. For him, this simply served as a way of placing a legal dispute in a broader context. Interpreting the law is not an arid and technical exercise. Law is an expression of the culture, values and beliefs of a society at a given point in time. As an avid reader (including, for instance, of essays on history, economics and psychology), he often had additional perspectives to offer in given cases. Finally, as a judge at the Court of Justice, he was able to contribute even more directly to the Court's function of 'speaking the law'. He achieved this, in particular, by acting as Reporting Judge in a number of cases which raised fundamental issues in the fields of, inter alia, EU anti-trust and State aid control (in cases such as *World Duty Free II*, *Fiat*, *Towercast*, *Illumina* and *Apple*, to name but a few).

Nils' integrity, professionalism and sense of justice were particularly appreciated by his colleagues. In one of his opinions, he wrote, 'courts are guided, first and foremost, by procedural principles that ensure due process in each individual case. Those principles cannot be sacrificed in order to further a greater cause, as noble as it might be'. This passage says a lot about his view of the role of the judiciary, which must remain mindful of the principles of separation of powers and institutional balance. He often emphasised that the Court of Justice is a *court of law*. However, he was, of course, fully aware that in the rare cases when tension between law and justice arises, the two must be reconciled. That is why that passage does not offer an *exhaustive* picture of Nils' views on the matter, as it could obscure his willingness to 'move the lines' where appropriate and his strong aversion to blindly copying-and-pasting previous case-law into new legal decisions. Some findings may be correct and just in a given context, but they may not be equally so when taken out of that context and *ipso facto* transplanted onto a different set of legal and factual circumstances. As he wrote in his farewell speech, 'it is the content of a previous judgment seen in context that should be observed—not the *verbatim* citation of an isolated phrase'.

Undoubtedly, Nils has a strong personality. His ideas are always expressed with conviction and he never hesitates to convey them in a particularly direct and frank manner — regardless of whether discussing the case with the members of his cabinet in his private office, deciding the fate of a case in the deliberation room, or questioning counsel for the parties during a hearing. For some lawyers, the idiom 'being grilled' acquired all its true meaning after a Court hearing with Nils on the bench. Yet again, the external image of Nils may not be fully faithful to his real character. Those who were lucky enough, like us, to work alongside him for several years could also appreciate his taste for exchanging and comparing ideas, the simplicity with which he conducted discussions (punctuated by his great sense of humour), his readiness to change his initial stance when presented with different, more convincing views and, last but not least, his willingness to move things forward in compliance with the constraints imposed. On a more personal level, we greatly valued the respect and dignity with which he has always treated his collaborators, his Scandinavian 'coolness' and the friendly and harmonious atmosphere in his cabinet.

Numerous observers have — at conferences, at seminars or in publications — emphasised the important legacy he left, as a judge and Advocate General, especially in economic matters. However, it would be overly simplistic to limit the importance of his contribution to the development of EU law to that area alone. That is why we decided to divide this volume into three parts.

The *first part* deals with issues relating to competition law. Some of the contributions focus on issues that Nils addressed in cases he handled at the Court, such as the concept of 'State aid', the categorisation of practices under EU competition law, and the undertakings' rights of defence in competition procedures. In this context, certain papers discuss the opinions and judgments drafted under Nils's efficient and sharp pen in the following cases: *SKW, Deutsche Bahn*, *Cartes bancaires, AKKA/LAA, Intel*, and *MEO*. Other papers take a broader and more systemic approach to 'classic' issues of EU competition law, such as judicial review or private enforcement, and some even address somewhat existential questions on the current and future application of competition law in the European Union and beyond.

The *second part* concerns aspects of judicial proceedings confronted by Nils during his time on the *Plateau de Kirchberg*, either because they arose in cases before the Court or because they touched upon organisational and functional aspects of the institution's structure and inner workings. The chapters presented under this section are intended to provide food for thought for both practitioners and those interested in the dynamics of court proceedings. Certain contributions shed light on issues that are rarely explored in legal literature (such as the thorny issues surrounding the '*économie de moyens*', the definition of the contours of the review of legality, the role of the Registry and of the office of First Advocate General).

Finally, the *third part* addresses questions of EU law of a constitutional and administrative nature. Some of the contributions under this heading provide an opportunity to take stock of, or to advocate new perspectives on, some institutional or transversal questions of EU law — both in 'classic' areas of EU law (such as the internal market or the budgetary rules) and in more recent areas of activity (such as data protection or cybersecurity).

The present *Liber Amicorum* brings together contributions from current and former members and staff of the CJEU, esteemed academics and valued practitioners, who wish to show their admiration and friendship for Nils. It is, therefore, a small token of appreciation for his remarkable contribution to the development of EU law; a contribution which bears witness to his great ability to *judge* and, sometimes, '*rethink*' EU law.

As editors of this volume, we are very grateful to all the authors for their enthusiasm in contributing to this project. Above all, we would like to thank them for taking time out from their busy schedules, sharing original and stimulating ideas, and producing texts of the highest quality. We would also like to thank Marie-Claire Gresse (first assistant in Nils' cabinet for several years) who helped us put together this volume, Siofra Collins and Eileen Sheehan for the linguistic revision, as well as Dr. Brigitte Reschke, Dr. Peter Pushpanathan and everyone else at *Springer* for incorporating this *Liber Amicorum* into their editorial programme and ensuring smooth publication.

Luxembourg, Luxembourg — Luca Prete
Luxembourg, Luxembourg — Leila Rezki
June 2025

Disclaimer

All views expressed by the editors and contributors are strictly personal and should not be construed as reflecting the opinion of their institution, authority, body or firm.

Usual disclaimers apply.

Contents

Contributors

Stanislas Adam Référendaire, Court of Justice, Luxembourg, Luxembourg

Professor, Ghent University, Ghent, Belgium

Micaela Arias Domecq Special advisor, Comisión Nacional de los Mercados y la Competencia, Madrid, Spain

Carl Baudenbacher Professor Emeritus, University of St. Gallen, St. Gallen, Switzerland

Laura Melusine Baudenbacher President, Swiss Competition Commission, Bern, Switzerland

Carl Fredrik Bergström Professor, Uppsala University, Uppsala, Sweden

Andrea Biondi Advocate General, Court of Justice, Luxembourg, Luxembourg

Professor, King's College, London, London, UK

Michal Bobek Chamber President, Supreme Administrative Court of the Czech Republic, Brno, Czech Republic

Professor, Wien University, Wien, Austria

Formerly Advocate General, Court of Justice, Luxembourg, Luxembourg

Stefano Boni Référendaire, Court of Justice, Luxembourg, Luxembourg

Fernando Castillo de la Torre Director, Legal Service, European Commission, Brussels, Belgium

Benjamin Cheynel Référendaire, General Court, Luxembourg, Luxembourg

Jean-Philippe Christienne Référendaire, General Court, Luxembourg, Luxembourg

Francisco de Paula Roig Guerrero Case handler, Comisión Nacional de los Mercados y la Competencia, Madrid, Spain

Frederik De Ridder Legal officer, EFTA Surveillance Authority, Brussels, Belgium

Cani Fernández Vicién Chairwoman, Comisión Nacional de los Mercados y la Competencia, Madrid, Spain

Sven Frisch Member of the Luxembourg Competition Authority, Luxembourg, Luxembourg

Marie-Claire Gresse First assistant, Court of Justice, Luxembourg, Luxembourg

Barry E. Hawk Adjunct Professor of Law, Fordham University, New York, NY, USA

Lars Henriksson Professor, Stockholm School of Economics, Stockholm, Sweden

Pablo Ibáñez Colomo Professor, London School of Economics, London, UK

College of Europe, Brugge, Belgium

Niilo Jääskinen Judge, Court of Justice, Luxembourg, Luxembourg

Heikki Kanninen Judge, General Court, Luxembourg, Luxembourg

Maria Krausenboeck Référendaire, Court of Justice, Luxembourg, Luxembourg

Johannes Laitenberger Judge, General Court, Luxembourg, Luxembourg

Formerly Director-General, DG Competition, European Commission, Brussels, Belgium

Koen Lenaerts President, Court of Justice, Luxembourg, Luxembourg

Professor, Leuven University, Leuven, Belgium

William Lindsay-Poulsen Judge, Copenhagen City Court, Copenhagen, Denmark

Björn Lundqvist Professor, Stockholm University, Stockholm, Sweden

Luigi Malferrari Member of the Legal Service, European Commission, Brussels, Belgium

Lecturer, Europa-Institute, University of Saarland, Saarbrücken, Germany

SciencesPo, Strasbourg, France

Petros C. Mavroidis Professor, Columbia Law School, New York, NY, USA

Marie Meister Référendaire, Court of Justice, Luxembourg, Luxembourg

Gwenaël Muguet-Poullennec Référendaire, General Court, Luxembourg, Luxembourg

Damien J. Neven Professor, Geneva Graduate Institute, Geneva, Switzerland

Jorge Padilla Chair of EMEA practice, Compass Lexecon, Madrid, Spain

Senior Fellow, George Washington University, Washington, DC, USA

Savvas S. Papasavvas Vice-President, General Court, Luxembourg, Luxembourg

Jan Passer Judge, Court of Justice, Luxembourg, Luxembourg

Elina Paunio Référendaire, Court of Justice, Luxembourg, Luxembourg

Nicolas Petit Professor and Head of Department, European University Institute, Firenze, Italy

Giovanni Pitruzzella Judge, Corte Costituzionale, Rome, Italy

Formerly Advocate General, Court of Justice, Luxembourg, Luxembourg

Luca Prete Référendaire, Court of Justice, Luxembourg, Luxembourg

Leila Rezki Référendaire, Court of Justice, Luxembourg, Luxembourg

Fredrik Schalin Judge, Court of Justice, Luxembourg, Luxembourg

Pierre Schmitt Référendaire, Court of Justice, Luxembourg, Luxembourg

Andreas Scordamaglia-Tousis Référendaire, Court of Justice, Luxembourg, Luxembourg

Maciej Szpunar First Advocate General, Court of Justice, Luxembourg, Luxembourg

Thomas von Danwitz Vice-President, Court of Justice, Luxembourg, Luxembourg

Melchior Wathelet Professor, Leuven University, Leuven, Belgium

Formerly Judge and First Advocate General, Court of Justice, Luxembourg, Luxembourg

Wouter P. J. Wils Hearing Officer, European Commission, Brussels, Belgium

Visiting Professor, King's College, London, London, UK

Fabien Zivy Référendaire, Court of Justice, Luxembourg, Luxembourg

Competition Law

Export Yes, Import No: Reflections on Switzerland's Position in the European Single Market

Carl Baudenbacher and Laura Melusine Baudenbacher

The Swiss have always been good at numbers. Their reputation of being money minded has even preoccupied literary writers. *Jean Racine*, the master of classical French tragedy, coined the famous phrase "*Point d'argent – point de Suisse*".[1] This saying was an allegation to a period when Switzerland, lacking a peacetime army, sent its young soldiers to join the armed forces of foreign powers as mercenaries where they earned a reputation for greed. Zurich author *Conrad Ferdinand Meyer* wrote a wonderful poem about how the stingy *Pope Leo XIII* wanted to withhold the customary inaugural gift from the Swiss Guard when he took office, whereupon the guards threatened to auction off the Holy See.[2] And *Peter von Matt*, a renowned professor of literature at the University of Zurich, aptly remarked that unlike most other countries, Switzerland does not define itself outwardly by its culture. It rather behaves as a utilitarian enterprise and defines and presents itself from a market perspective.[3]

This approach to politics and economics has many advantages. Switzerland is doing well economically. The Swiss invented the debt brake, which they have

[1] *Liternaute.fr*, Point d'argent, point de Suisse, available on line.

[2] *Exgardisten Wallis*, Alte Schweiz, available on line.

[3] Das Kalb von der Gotthardpost. Zur Literatur und Politik der Schweiz, Munich 2012, 167 ff.

C. Baudenbacher (✉)
University of St. Gallen, St. Gallen, Switzerland
e-mail: carl.baudenbacher@baudenbacher.law

L. M. Baudenbacher
Swiss Competition Commission, Bern, Switzerland
e-mail: laura.baudenbacher@baudenbacher.law

L. Prete, L. Rezki (eds.), *Judging & (Re)Thinking European Union Law*,
https://doi.org/10.1007/978-3-032-13473-8_1

exported to other countries.[4] Ironically, a spectacle has recently taken place unfolding in economic law and politics in relation to Swiss avariciousness that is astonishing.

1 Endeavours to Curb Parallel Imports into Switzerland

1.1 A Bit of History

In 1995, the traditional cartel country Switzerland for the first time enacted a modern competition law aimed at protecting "effective competition". In substantive terms, the Cartel Act (or "CartA") is based on three pillars: A quasi-prohibition of agreements that eliminate or significantly restrict competition and are not justified by reasons of economic efficiency (Article 5); a prohibition of the abusive exploitation of a dominant market position by one or more companies (Article 7); and a merger control where the newly created Competition Commission ("ComCo") examines whether a merger establishes or strengthens a dominant market position that could eliminate effective competition. The notification thresholds were deliberately set high (Articles 9 and 10).

These reforms were accepted by Corporate Switzerland without much resistance for two reasons: First, ComCo was given insufficient tools to uncover cartels. Notably, the CartA 95 did not introduce a leniency programme. Second, the law did not grant ComCo the power to sanction at first infringement; the authority could only issue a fine if a previous cease and desist order had been violated.

2004 ushered in several reforms of the CartA: (i) ComCo was given the authority to fine perpetrators upon first infringement; (ii) a US-style leniency programme was introduced which has proven successful in practice;[5] and (iii) a new paragraph was added to Article 5 CartA which presumes the elimination of effective competition for vertical agreements on minimum or fixed prices as well as for vertical agreements in distribution contracts on the allocation of territories, insofar as sales into these by non-local distribution partners are excluded.

These changes were also accepted by the business community and its legal and economic advisors. Swiss competition law seemed to be developing largely in step with the EU and the EEA. Leading constitutional law scholars even noted that the relevant Article 96(1) of the Constitution did "not prohibit a prohibition legislation".[6]

The young ComCo struggled in the first years following the 04 revision. Many decisions were overturned by the courts on procedural grounds. During this time,

[4] C. Baudenbacher, 'Swiss Economic Law Facing the Challenges of International and European Law', ZSR 2012 II, 419 ff., 650 f.

[5] F. Hoffet, 'Zwanzig Jahre modernes Kartellgesetz. Bilanz und Ausblick aus Anwaltssicht', 1.07.2016, available on line.

[6] *See* ATF 143 II 297, cons. 5.3.4 with references.

the business community and its legal and economic advisors took no issue with the law or its application by the authority. However, after ComCo began implementing procedural improvements in the late 2000s, the courts increasingly upheld its decisions. This led to 180-degree shift of opinion in business circles and among certain legal and economic advisors, who suddenly claimed that ComCo's structure and the law it was applying were unconstitutional and violated the European Human Rights Convention.

An 2014 attempt to weaken competition law enforcement by pushing for a change to a prosecutorial enforcement system based on the US model failed.[7] Unfortunately for its supporters, their claims of unconstitutionality and human rights violations collapsed like a card house following the European Court of Human Rights' seminal *Menarini* judgment[8] and the EFTA Court's *Posten Norge* ruling,[9] which were taken over by the Swiss Federal Supreme Court.[10] It was certainly also not helpful to the proponents of weakened enforcement that the general trend in Europe is moving in the opposite direction, as the examples of Ireland, Belgium, and most recently Sweden show.[11]

1.2 The Motion **Français**

Following ComCo's successes in sanctioning parallel import bans and bid rigging cartels, the road construction industry formed an unholy alliance with sectors opposing free parallel imports (i.a. the car import and pharmaceutical industries) and resistance against ComCo grew. The circles concerned started to seek a change of the CartA to limit its application to the protection of interbrand competition; it should be possible to freely restrict intra-brand competition.

These efforts led to a parliamentary motion of a (in the meantime retired) member of the Council of States, the small chamber of Parliament, named *Olivier Français*, originally a Frenchman from Metz, Lorraine. On 13 December 2018, Mr. *Français* demanded that Article 5 of the Cartel Act be amended to require COMCO to conduct a full qualitative and quantitative market analysis for hardcore agreements, without exception, including the assessment of market shares and an examination of the actual enforcement of restrictions of competition.[12] It was clear that

[7] *See* L. M. Baudenbacher, 'Schweizer KG-Reform als europapolitischer Slalomlauf?', in: Jusletter of 30.05.2022, available on line.

[8] ECtHR, *A. Menarini Diagnostics S.r.l. v. Italy*, app. no. 43509/08.

[9] Case E-15/10, *Posten Norge v EFTA Surveillance Authority*, 2012 EFTA Ct. Rep., 246.

[10] ATF 139 I 72; cons. 2.2.2; see also Federal Administrative Court B-506/2010, *GABA*, cons. 6.3.1.

[11] O. Brook, B. Rodger, 'Comparative report: National judicial review of competition law enforcement in the EU and the UK', in: Rodger et al. (eds.), *Judicial Review of Competition Law Enforcement in the EU Member States and the UK*, 2024, pp. 3 et seq.

[12] Motion 18.4282, Die Kartellgesetzrevision muss sowohl qualitative als auch quantitative Kriterien berücksichtigen, um die Unzulässigkeit einer Wettbewerbsabrede zu beurteilen ("Motion

this "reform", would put Switzerland in clear opposition to the EU and its Member States and to the EEA and the EEA/EFTA States. A bit surprisingly, it was backed by the Swiss branch of the German competition lawyers' association, *Studienvereinigung Kartellrecht e.V.* ("*Studienvereinigung*"). This influential group has had smaller sub-sections in Austria and Switzerland for some time. In its submission to Parliament, *Studienvereinigung* Switzerland supported[13] the introduction of an effects-test for hardcore (price) cartels with the claim that this would bring Swiss competition in line with recent EU case law, notably the CJEU's rulings in *Cartes Bancaires*, *Budapest Bank*, and *UK Generics*.[14] The organisation's true goal, however, seemed a different one: vis-à-vis one of the leading Swiss economic journalists, *Hansueli Schöchli*, one of the competition lawyers interviewed pointed "to self-interest: discussions about the quantitative significance of agreements can prolong proceedings and generate additional fees for lawyers."[15]

The German mother organisation and the Austrian subgroup did not distance themselves from their Swiss section's claims. It cannot be ruled out that certain German and Austrian colleagues may have taken a liking to the idea of weaking their respective competition acts should their Swiss cohort succeed.

The critics of ComCO complained about two rulings by the Federal Supreme Court on parallel imports and a series of ComCo decisions on bid rigging in the road construction industry.

1.3 The Elmex *and* BMW *Cases*

1.3.1 Federal Administrative Court *Elmex*

On 19 December 2013, a five-judge chamber of the Federal Administrative Court (the first appeal instance) ruled that vertical agreements prohibiting passive sales to foreclose the Swiss market constitutet hardcore agreements that significantly impeded effective competition.[16] Quantitative considerations, such as market shares or market effects, are not required in such cases. Justification on grounds of efficiency remains possible but failed in this case. The Federal Administrative Court therefore confirmed the sanctions against the Elmex toothpaste manufacturer Gaba and its Austrian licensee Gebro in the amount of approximately CHF 5 million and CHF 10,000, respectively (today c. EUR 5,3 m and EUR 10,600).

Français"), submitted on 13.12.2018, available on line.

[13] Vernehmlassung zur Revision des Kartellgesetzes – Stellungnahme der Arbeitsgruppe, Schweiz der Studienvereinigung Kartellrecht e.V. of 11.03.2022, pp. 23–25, available on line.

[14] CJEU, Case C-67/13 P, *Cartes Bancaires*, EU:C:2014:2204; CJEU, Case C-228/18, *Budapest Bank*, EU:C:2020:265; CJEU, Case C-307/18, *Generics (UK)*, EU:C:2020:52.

[15] "Baukartelle haben ein politisches Nachspiel", Neue Zürcher Zeitung of 4.03.2022, available on line.

[16] B-506/2010, *Gaba* and B-463/2010, *Gebro*, referred to as the *Elmex* case.

1.3.2 Federal Administrative Court *BMW*

On 13 November 2015, the Federal Administrative Court, again sitting in a five-member formation, confirmed its *Elmex* judgment in the *BMW* case.[17] A contractual clause prohibiting dealers of BMW vehicles and spare parts in the EEA from exporting to countries outside the EEA, including Switzerland, was ruled an inadmissible vertical territorial agreement under Article 5 paragraph 4 CartA of the Cartel Act. The Court upheld the fine of CHF 156 million (today c. EUR 169 million).

A central question of both the *Elmex* and the *BMW* case concerned the territorial scope of Swiss competition law. Unlike EU competition law, the Swiss CartA explicitly lays down the effects principle in Article 2 para. 2:

> This Act applies to practices that have an effect in Switzerland, even if they originate in another country.

The court rejected a qualification of the effects principle in the sense of a special intensity of the effects and allowed simple effects to suffice. In doing so, it followed University of Zurich professor *Anton K. Schnyder*, a former Hamburg Max Planck Institute scholar.[18] According to *Schnyder*, relevant effects exist where the elements of the substantive norms are fulfilled to a degree that render them applicable.

1.3.3 Federal Supreme Court Gaba

On 28 June 2016, the Federal Supreme Court dismissed the appeal against the *Elmex* judgment.[19] It held that "*Art. 5 para. 1 CartA, which only speaks of 'significantly affecting' and does not distinguish between two levels of significance, only requires one level of significance [...].*" This could be of a quantitative or qualitative nature, whereby the "*quality to be achieved to determine the threshold for taking up the case remains the same overall in a case*". If the qualitative element is very significant, there is little need for a quantitative element and vice versa.

The Federal Supreme Court also followed the Federal Administrative Court's approach regarding the effects doctrine and confirmed its compatibility with public international law. If a particular effects-threshold were to be required to open a proceeding in an international case, a comprehensive substantive examination would have to already be carried out at this point, so that "*Art. 2 para. 2 CartA would secretly mutate into Art. 5 CartA*".

---

[17] B-3332/2012, *BMW*. LMB was directly involved in the *Elmex* and *BMW* cases at the Federal Administrative Court as a law clerk, drafting the judgment with the sitting president, partaking in the deliberations with an advisory vote, and signing the judgment with the president.

[18] A. K. Schnyder, in: Günter Hirsch/Frank Montag/Franz Jürgen Säcker [Hrsg.], Münchener Kommentar zum Europäischen und Deutschen Wettbewerbsrecht (Kartellrecht), Band 1: Europäisches Wettbewerbsrecht, München 2007 [hiernach Münchener Kommentar EuWettbR], Einleitung: Sachlicher, zeitlicher und räumlicher Geltungsbereich des Wettbewerbsrechts. Extraterritoriale Anwendung, para. 848 et seqq., 927 et seqq.

[19] ATF 143 II 297.

1.3.4 Federal Supreme Court *BMW*

On 24 October 2017, the Federal Supreme Court also dismissed the appeal against the Federal Administrative Court's *BMW* judgment.[20] We assume that the Supreme Court sat in a 5-member formation in this matter to indicate that its *Gaba* case law constitutes established practice.

Regarding the criterion of "significant impediment of effective competition" in Art. 5 para. 1 CartA, the Federal Supreme Court held: (i) the criterion constitutes a "de minimis clause" that allows the exclusion of minor cases; (ii) agreements that, according to the law, presumably eliminate "effective competition" will "generally" also significantly impede effective competition; and (iii) ComCo must not prove actual effects for such agreements; a "potential restriction of competition" is sufficient.

1.4 Bid Rigging in Road Construction

The Federal Administrative Court's *Elmex* and *BMW* rulings led to criticism from certain competition lawyers, some who had been directly involved in these cases. The negative comments increased following the Federal Supreme Court's *Elmex* ruling. Most practitioners, however, accepted the case law. Leading experts in the field—including the 'father' of the Cartel Act 95, former Ambassador *Marino Baldi*, and the then Vice-President and later President of ComCo, University of Zurich Professor *Andreas Heinemann*—unreservedly welcomed the *Elmex* judgment.[21] *Marino Baldi* aptly stated that the decisive course was set in the Federal Administrative Court's *Elmex* ruling.[22]

In this situation, the *Elmex* critics received support from an unexpected quarter: the construction lobby. In the Canton of Graubünden alone, around 40 companies had rigged over 1100 public and private construction projects with an estimated procurement volume of over CHF 300 million. 70–80% of the total value of construction projects in the north and south of the Canton were affected by the collusion. ComCo proved that the agreements existed and were implemented, which is what the law requires today. The fines have been confirmed at first instance.

Construction industry lobbyists in the Federal Parliament led by Messrs. *Français* and *Wicki* claimed that due to ComCo's enforcement practice, companies no longer

---

[20] ATF 144 II 194.

[21] A. Heinemann, Das Gaba-Urteil des Bundesgerichts: Ein Meilenstein des Kartellrechts, Zeitschrift für Schweizerisches Recht / Revue de droit suisse / Rivista di diritto svizzero / Revista da dretg svizzer (ZSR) 2018/1, 103 et seqq., available on line; M. Baldi, Nach dem GABA-Urteil zur Erheblichkeit von Wettbewerbsabreden, Aktuelle Juristische Praxis / Pratique Juridique Actuelle (AJP) 2017, 613 et seqq., available on line.

[22] M. Baldi, F. Schraner, 'Gaba-Urteil des Bundesverwaltungsgerichts als wettbewerbspolitischer Markstein', European Law Reporter, 2 2014, 62 et seqq., available on line.

dared to pursue pro-competitive cooperative ventures. Explanations by ComCo that cooperations with the aim of working more efficiently are allowed, but agreements on prices, quantities, territories, and customers are prohibited, fell on deaf ears. The president of the industry association "*BauenSchweiz*" ("ConstructionSwitzerland"), State Councillor *Hans Wicki*, personally took up the cause.[23]

2 Endeavours to Foster Swiss Exports

2.1 Swiss Industry Has Partial Preferential Access to the Single Market

The EU Member States and the three EEA/EFTA States Iceland, Liechtenstein, and Norway enjoy preferential access to the Single Market. A precondition for this is that a state is subject to so-called institutions, i.e. a supranational surveillance authority and a supranational court of law. For EU Member States, these are the European Commission and the CJEU; for the EEA/EFTA States the EFTA Surveillance Authority and the EFTA Court. Switzerland is linked to the EU by a network of sectoral agreements. Apart from the Air Transport Agreement,[24] under which Switzerland had to recognise the competence of the European Commission and the CJEU, these agreements are institution-free.

The EU granted Switzerland those institution-free agreements because there was a Swiss application for EU membership pending and the Federal Council (the Swiss Government) officially described accession as its goal. Swiss industry thus enjoys partial preferential access to the Single Market.

2.2 EU Demands Institutions

When it became clear that the political conditions for EU accession were lacking in Switzerland, the EU from 2008 onward regularly demanded that Switzerland agree to an institutionalisation of its agreements with the EU.[25] Since Bern was still pursuing the long-term goal of EU membership, it rejected the EU's offer to submit the bilateral agreements to the supervision of the EFTA Surveillance Authority and to the jurisdiction of the EFTA Court, including the right to nominate one representative each to the two bodies.

---

[23] Motion 21.4189, Untersuchungsgrundsatz wahren. Keine Beweislastumkehr im Kartellgesetz ("Motion Wicki"), submitted on 30.09.2021, available on line.

[24] Agreement between the European Community and the Swiss Confederation on Air Transport, OJ L 114 of 30.04.2002, p. 73.

[25] Draft Council conclusions on EU relations with EFTA countries of 5.12.2008, 16651/1/08.

Instead, the Federal Council opted for a submission of those agreements to the supervision of the European Commission and a monopoly on interpretation by the CJEU. Negotiations were conducted on this basis as of 2014. However, it eventually became clear that such a treaty would most probably be rejected in a referendum in Switzerland. The European Commission then offered Switzerland the model it had created for the post-Soviet republics of Armenia, Georgia, Moldova, and Ukraine as part of their respective association agreements with the EU: the formal authority to decide conflicts between the EU and one of these states should lie with an "arbitration panel" which, however, must request a binding interpretation decision from the CJEU on all matters involving EU law or treaty law with the same content.[26] This "Ukraine"-mechanism was also proposed to the United Kingdom after the 2016 Brexit vote of their electorate. The UK accepted it in the Withdrawal Agreement for a transitional period, but rejected it in the Trade and Cooperation Agreement, thus leaving the Single Market.[27] The CJEU is certainly an institution with a great reputation, but in matters of conflict between the EU and a third state it is the court of the other side. This has given rise to criticism in Switzerland.[28]

The Federal Council accepted the model with the pro forma arbitration panel on 20 December 2024.[29]

3 Inconsistency of the Main Supporters of the Motion *Français*

3.1 General

For years, the umbrella organisation of Corporate Switzerland, *economiesuisse*, and numerous members of parliament close to it have been warning of dire consequences if the Motion *Français* is not implemented.[30] One could have believed that Switzerland's economic future was at risk.

---

[26] See, for example, G. Van der Loo, *The EU-Ukraine Association Agreement and Deep and Comprehensive Free Trade Area*, 2016.

[27] Agreement on the withdrawal of the United Kingdom of Great Britain and Northern Ireland from the European Union and the European Atomic Energy Community2019/C 384 I/01, available here; Trade and Cooperation Agreement between the European Union and the European Atomic Energy Community, of the one part, and the United Kingdom of Great Britain and Northern Ireland, of the other part, available here.

[28] C. Baudenbacher, Institutionelle Aspekte des Rahmenabkommens 2.0, Kurzpapier zu Handen der WAK-Nationalrat, 12.02.2024, available on line.

[29] Federal Council takes note of substantive conclusion of Swiss–EU negotiations, available on line.

[30] *See*, e.g., economieuisse, Revision des Kartellgesetzes: Ein notwendiger Schritt für die gesamte Schweizer Wirtschaft, article of 24.09.2024, available on line; furthermore Umbrella Organisation of Swiss SME, Vernehmlassungsantwort Teilrevision Kartellgesetz (KG), 3.03.2022, available on line.

Simultaneously, many of these supporters are advocating for the conclusion of the Framework Agreement with the EU, arguing that Swiss export industry needs preferential access to the Single Market. They prioritize export freedom above all else. Partisans of this agreement are willing to accept the dynamic adoption of EU law, the factual surveillance of Switzerland by the European Commission, and an interpretation monopoly of the CJEU based on the model that the EU has designed for post-Soviet republics.[31]

The same business circles pushing for weaker competition law enforcement and the possibility to limit parallel imports thus also lobbied vigorously to maintain their freedom to export to the EU as cost-effectively as possible.

3.2 Contradiction to EU Law

Supporters of the Motion *Français* overlooked that weakening the CartA would not be welcomed in Brussels or the Member State capitals. In EU law, agreements on minimum and fixed prices as well as certain territorial restrictions are generally considered hardcore restraints, regardless of the market share of the businesses involved. Implementing the Motion *Français* would create a system that differs from the EU's on the most fundamental aspects and would weaken competition law enforcement in Switzerland. This would undermine the Federal Council's objective of creating a level playing field between the EU and Switzerland in competition law.[32] "Underenforcement" in Switzerland would not be without consequences.

It would be a mistake to think that Swiss businesses could operate in a vacuum if the CartA were watered down to give special treatment to hardcore cartels. If the Motion *Français* were to become law, it would also in particular favour companies with international operations. GABA was an international group producing toothpaste and oral hygiene products, and BMW is a global carmaker.

The EU applies its competition law if a restriction of competition initiated in Switzerland has an effect on its market. The list of cases in which Swiss companies have been fined is long. It started with the *Dyestuffs* Saga,[33] in which Swiss companies were fined for the first time. Other matters involving Swiss companies include

[31] *See*, e.g., economieuisse, Exportwirtschaft trifft Bundesrat: Es braucht bessere Rahmenbedingungen, article of 28.11.2023, available on line; Umbrella Organisation of Swiss SME, Konsultationsantwort: Entwurf des Institutionellen Abkommens (InstA) mit der Europäischen Union, 26.04.2019, available on line.

[32] Dispatch of the Federal Council of 23 November 1994 on the Cartel Act, BBl 1995 I 468, 529 et seqq.; Dispatch of the Federal Council of 7 November 2001 on the Cartel Act, BBl BBl 2002 2022, 2026 and 2051 et seq.; also Agreement between the European Community and the Swiss Confederation on Air Transport, OJ L114 of 30.04.2002, p. 73.

[33] Commission decision IV/26.267 of 24 July 1969 (*Dyestuffs*), OJ L195 of 7.08.1969, p. 11.

the *Vitamin* cartel,[34] the *District heating pipes* cartel[35] and the *Elevators and escalators* cartel.[36] In these cases, the European Commission has made it clear that it is prepared to close antitrust enforcement gaps outside the EU if there are effects on its market. The fines then go to Brussels while the damage remains for Swiss consumers and thus for the Swiss economy.

Perhaps the Swiss cartel friends have forgotten that serious restrictions of competition can only be sanctioned directly since the 2003 reform. The change of heart was mainly due to the Europe-wide *Vitamins* cartels where the Basel-based ringleader Hoffmann LaRoche had to pay almost half of the EUR 855 million fine imposed by the European Commission. Switzerland, whose consumers were also harmed, got nothing.[37]

3.3 Incompatibility with the Switzerland-EU Cooperation Agreement

One of the main objectives of the Agreement between the European Union and the Swiss Confederation on cooperation in the application of their competition laws of 17 May 2013 is the coordination of enforcement measures. The agreement was concluded "noting that the sound and effective enforcement of competition law is a matter of importance to the efficient operation of their respective markets, as well as to economic welfare of consumers of both Parties and trade between them" and "bearing in mind that the competition enforcement systems of the Union and of Switzerland are based on the same principles and provide for similar rules".[38]

In its 2012 dispatch, the Federal Council correctly pointed out that the agreement assumes a "comparable body of law" in Switzerland and the EU in the area of competition, and that any divergence could impair the proper functioning of the agreement. In technical jargon, this is referred to as a "level playing field". The negotiations on the Trade and Cooperation Agreement between the EU and the United Kingdom have shown that this point is a key concern for the Union. The EU has insisted on this principle vis-à-vis the UK, even though the country has left the single market.[39]

[34] Commission decision COMP/E-1/37.512 of 22 November 2001 (*Vitamins*), OJ L6 of 10.01.2003, p. 1.

[35] Commission decision 1999/60/EC of 21 October 1998 (*Pre-Insulated Pipes*), OJ L 24 of 30.01.1999, p. 1.

[36] Commission decision C(2007) 512 final of 21.02.2007 (Elevators and Escalators), OJ C75 of 26.03.2008, p. 19.

[37] Cited in fn. 34.

[38] Agreement between the European Union and the Swiss Confederation concerning cooperation on the application of their competition laws, OJ L347 of 3.12.2014, p. 3.

[39] C. Baudenbacher, 'Rebuilding Trust Between London and Brussels Will Not Be Easy', St. Gallen Symposium, available on line; I. Jozepa et al., 'The UK-EU Trade and Cooperation Agreement: Level playing field', 20 May 2021, available on line.

By contrast, Switzerland is a (partial) participant in the single market. The implementation of the Motion *Français* would impair the level playing field, and not in a secondary point, but in the handling of hardcore cartels.

Therefore, the US Supreme Court's ruling in *Leegin*,[40] which is often cited by advocates of restrained antitrust enforcement in Switzerland, is not relevant. The Supreme Court has ruled that vertical price agreements are not per se unlawful, but must be examined for negative effects according to the "rule of reason". This case law cannot be transferred to the EU without further ado, as the EU wants to protect its incomplete internal market from foreclosure by (horizontal and vertical) hardcore agreements. As mentioned above, the latter is also relevant for the relationship between the EU and Switzerland.

Since COMCO would no longer be able to enforce competition law in the same way as the EU Commission, the question would arise as to whether the EU is still interested in coordination. It is in particular unclear whether the Commission would continue to be willing to share information with COMCO if it had to assume that proceedings in Switzerland would not be conducted according to European standards.

3.4 *Contradiction to OECD 'Best Practices'*

An implementation of the motion could also contradict the OECD's best practices. The OECD recommends that its member states should treat hard-core cartels as illegal, regardless of whether there is evidence of actual adverse effects on the markets, and should design their laws, policies and enforcement practices to combat cartels in such a way that they ensure, in accordance with their legal framework, institutional structure and procedural guarantees, that hard-core cartels are stopped and deterred and that cartel victims are effectively compensated.[41]

If the motion were to be implemented, this would create a regime that deviates from these principles (for both vertical and horizontal hardcore agreements) and would lead to a weakening of cartel enforcement in Switzerland overall, thus going against the developments in other OECD member states.

[40] 551 US 877.

[41] Recommendation of the Council concerning Effective Action against Hard Core Cartels, available on line.

4 Is the Pendulum Swinging Back in the Motion *Français*?

4.1 Great Initial Optimism

At the beginning, the supporters of the Motion *Français* were highly optimistic. In discussions, one was told patronisingly that there was no way around a fundamental change to the CartA, but that in the end one would offer one's hand to a good Swiss compromise.

However, at times, it looked as if the trees would not grow into the sky. Not only the current leadership of ComCo spoke out clearly against the planned weakening of the CartA in essays and interviews. All previous presidents have also rejected the revision in an appeal that appeared in both German and French.[42]

4.2 Setback in the Council of States

When the revision came before the Committee for Economic Affairs and Taxation ("WAK") of the Council of States, the chief lobbyist of "ConstructionSwitzerland", State Councillor *Wicki*, presided over the Committee, and he shed all inhibitions. Despite all the efforts of his industry, there was a tie vote on the crucial issues, whereupon Mr. Wicki introduced his casting vote. We leave open the question of whether there was a case of bias here.

4.3 The National Council caves in

In principle, the pro-competition forces in the large chamber tend to be stronger than in the small one. There was therefore hope that the Motion Français would ultimately be defeated. In the end, however, the lobbyists succeeded in undermining the fight against cartels. The centuries-old corporatist reflex prevailed. In December 2025, the revised CartA was adopted by Parliament. The term "reform" should in our view be avoided. The new law is expected to enter into force in 2027.

[42] Kartellrecht: Die Weko-Präsidentin kämpft gegen eine Aufweichung – BILANZ (available on line at handelszeitung.ch); Kartellabsprachen nicht erleichtern, sagen frühere Weko-Chefs (available on line at nzz.ch); and La nouvelle loi sur les cartels constitue un risque pour la politique de la concurrence (avaiable onmine at Le Temps).

5 Conclusions

In antitrust law, the money-mindedness of certain circles in William Tell's country manifests itself in their endeavours to collect cartel rents. They do not shy away from obvious untruths or contradictions. Any reasonable observer realises that Mr Français and his fellow fighters were by no means interested in improving legal certainty, but in turning back the wheel of history. It is also astonishing that the advocates of weakening the Cartel Act were and are unable to recognise the contradictoriness of their arguments: You cannot simultaneously support the conclusion of a highly unilateral framework agreement with the EU and at the same time jeopardise the existing cooperation agreement in antitrust law. As far as the Swiss antitrust lawyers are concerned, the lack of regulatory awareness is surprising. One could modify Racine's proverb and state "Point d'Argent - Point d'Avocats Suisses". When the Cooperation Agreement with the EU was concluded in 2012, the danger that it could be jeopardised by ill-considered parliamentary motions was seen, but now that the scenario has arrived it is no longer remembered. It remains to be seen how the Federal Courts will react to the fact that the legislature has reined them in the fight against cartels. Should there be significant under-enforcement, the question will arise as to how powerful foreign competition authorities will react. It could then be that the Swiss consumers suffer the damage and others collect the fines. Whether Switzerland, in order to facilitate business for exporters, will accept the de facto monitoring by the European Commission and the CJEU's monopoly on interpretation is an open question.

EU State Aid Greatest Hits: How AG Nils Wahl Helped Shaping the Notion of State Aid in EU Law

Andrea Biondi

1 Introduction

I love lists. I draft lists on everything, and sometimes I go to the extremes of having "consolidated lists", which are the ultimate satisfaction. I must admit, I have compiled my own greatest hits of Advocate General ('AG') Opinions on EU State aid law, along with a consolidated one on the notion of aid as provided in Article 107(1) TFEU. In the latter, a very prominent position (even in numerical terms) is taken by the Opinions of AG Wahl (as he then was): selectivity of fiscal measures in *Dirk Andres*,[1] the engaging *Eventech*,[2] the notion of State resources in *Achema*,[3] selectivity again in *Orange*[4] and *Commission v MOL*,[5] among many others. All truly valuable Opinions for at least two reasons: first, AG Wahl attempted to introduce an extra element of "formal legal certainty" within the definition of EU State aid. This may sound odd, as Article 107(1) has been there since the Treaty of Rome and the subject of countless jurisprudential interpretations. Still, the precise contours of the notion of aid are proving to be elusive for many reasons (and not all ascribable to

[1] Opinion in *Andres (insolvency of Heitkamp BauHolding) v Commission*, C-203/16 P, EU:C:2017:1017.

[2] Opinion in *Eventech*, C-518/13, EU:C:2014:2239.

[3] Opinion in *Achema and Others*, C-706/17, EU:C:2019:38.

[4] Opinion in *Orange v Commission*, C-211/15 P, EU:C:2016:78.

[5] Opinion in *Commission v MOL*, C-15/14 P, EU:C:2015:32.

A. Biondi (✉)
Court of Justice of the European Union, Luxembourg, Luxembourg
e-mail: Andrea.Biondi@curia.europa.eu

L. Prete, L. Rezki (eds.), *Judging & (Re)Thinking European Union Law*,
https://doi.org/10.1007/978-3-032-13473-8_2

jurisprudential hesitations). At the same time—second reason—his *opus* is a very clear case for a rigorous reaffirmation of the centrality of State aid control within the EU market regulation system. All done in a short, concise style, devoid of any pompous theoretical reconstructions. Such contributions, especially in the current geopolitical scenario, are by all means not a small feat. Nils Wahl's influence in shaping up the operation of State aid control goes of course much further than his Opinions, as his time in Kirchberg comprises two stints as judge first at the General Court and later at the European Court of Justice. As *deliberees* are, of course, to be kept confidential, this contribution will mostly dwell on the years 2012 to 2019, when Mr. Wahl was the Swedish AG.

2 Not Everything Is a State Aid Measure

2.1 The Notion of State Aid According to the Court of Justice's Case Law

The whole discipline of State aid, as masterfully defined in Articles 107 and 108 TFEU—two provisions immune to the many successive Treaty reforms—encompasses one of the fundamental principles of European integration: the fight against State protectionism. Article 107(1) TFEU enshrines the principle that State aid is incompatible with market integration. As the Court of Justice has repeatedly clarified, this provision is intended "*to prevent trade between Member States from being affected by advantages granted by public authorities which, in various forms, distort or threaten to distort competition by favouring certain undertakings or the production of certain goods products. [...] Article 107(1) TFEU does not distinguish between measures of State intervention by reference to their causes or their aims but defines them in relation to their effects*".[6] Article 108 TFEU introduces a further "EU law distinctiveness" entrusting enforcement to a supranational institution, the European Commission. Despite being given such a cornerstone position, State aid rules are often misunderstood. They are either perceived as an excessive bureaucratization of economic choices, constraining businesses by imposing excessive red tape, or, at the other side of the spectrum, as reducing the possibility of pursuing national welfare related goals. Both criticisms have something in common: the *fear* that if State aid rules are applied too extensively they could end up transforming any form of State intervention in the economy into a violation of EU law. These are, in reality, very partial interpretations and reconstructions, as the prohibition imposed on Member States is "neither absolute nor unconditional":[7] first and foremost

[6] Judgment of 14 July 2016, *Germany v Commission*, T-143/12, EU:T:2016:406, para 74,108 and case law cited; and judgment of 25 March 2015, *Belgium v Commission*, T-538/11, EU:T:2015:188, para 62 and 80 and case law cited.

[7] Judgment of 22 March 1977, *Steinike & Weinlig*, 78/76, EU:C:1977:52, para 8.

because the second and third paragraphs of Article 107 TFEU cover, respectively, aid that is "automatically compatible" and aid that "may be declared compatible", thus balancing freedom of movement and protection of competition in the single market with State interventions necessary to achieve objectives that the EU legal system deems worthy of protection.

As for Article 107(1) TFEU, in order for a measure to fall within the notion of aid, the following four conditions must be met: a national measure (i) should involve State intervention, *i.e.*, carried out through State resources; (ii) should be capable of affecting trade between Member States; (iii) must distort or threaten to distort competition; (iv) must grant a selective advantage to its beneficiary. Case law is consistent in holding that these conditions are cumulative. Here lies one of the most obvious but fundamental tenets of the whole EU control system: not every State measure of economic policy adopted by a Member State constitutes aid, but only those that meet the conditions set forth in the Treaty itself. Once again, only when all four conditions are satisfied does the overall effect threaten the integrity of the EU market and become capable of distorting competition. Of course, it would be disingenuous to simply pretend that, in terms of regulatory model, the EU State aid rules could be considered as *neutral.* Hence the importance of the market operator principle in imposing on States a specific obligation not to discriminate against private operators while also serving as a reminder that, when the State decides to enter the market, it is subject to its rules. "*Put simply, the private operator test is a tool that the Commission uses to determine whether there is an economic advantage, one of the necessary features of State aid*".[8]

Despite such an inevitable "attraction" towards market liberalization, boundaries need to be drawn. There are two ways of limiting a possibly excessive application of EU State aid rules. The first is an *ex ante* assessment to determine whether there are activities performed by the State claimed to be in the general interest that can be therefore sheltered from the full force of privatization of State functions that a process of supranational market integration inevitably entails. Such an *ex ante* approach has been recently widened by the Court of Justice that found State aid law inapplicable to several State activities considered to be non-economic[9] even in cases dealing with legal monopolies.[10] This approach then tends to deny *a priori* the application of EU law, leaving Members States a wide margin of manoeuvring. The other approach tends instead to consider EU law as relevant but inapplicable in terms of the scale of appreciable distortions of competition and impact on trade.

---

[8] Opinion of AG Wahl in *Commission v Frucona Košice*, C-300/16 P, EU: C: 2017:331, para 47.

[9] Judgment of 27 April 2023, *Casa Regina Apostolorum Della Pia Società delle Figlie di San Paolo v Commission*, C-492/21 P, EU:C:2023:354, para 70.

[10] Judgment of, 6 October 2021, Joined Cases C-174/19 P and C-175/19 P *Scandlines Danmark ApS, Scandlines Deutschland GmbH v European Commission, Kingdom of Denmark, Föreningen Svensk Sjöfart, Naturschutzbund Deutschland (NABU)*, EU:C:2021:801.

2.2 AG Wahl and a Very British Case

To attempt to explain the previous ruminations, let us take the "effect on trade/distortion of competition" criteria under Article 107(1) TFEU—the so-called negative conditions—as their satisfaction is apparently way too easy. The Court of Justice's case law indeed has consistently held that, as far as the effect on competition is concerned, it is sufficient to prove that when financial aid is granted by a State this strengthens the position of an undertaking compared with other undertakings competing in intra-EU trade.[11] With regard to the effect on trade, the Court's acquis is consistent in refusing to apply any threshold or percentage below which it may be considered that trade between Member States would be unaffected.[12] Consistent with its case law on free movement, the Court has essentially held that any restriction, even minor, should be prohibited.[13] One of the most comprehensive critiques—or you could say *explanation*—of such a case law comes from AG Wahl's Opinion in a rather quirky and very British case. The *Eventech* case[14] dealt with the question of whether reserving the use of bus lanes for black cabs only (other than buses, of course) could have been considered as a State aid measure. One of the most contentious issues was whether the use of the bus lane for black cabs could distort competition and/or have an effect on trade. In his Opinion, Wahl (hinting that black cabs and pre-booked taxis were in a comparable situation and that some form of advantage could be established) made several interesting points. First, he argued that when the advantage has not been granted to a single or significantly limited number of undertakings, an automatic application of distortion of competition/effect on trade would not necessarily work. Further, he argued that what the Court really means is that the *possibility* of an effect on inter-State trade could not be excluded. Thus, "*it is not for no reason that, by the language it typically uses in these types of cases, the Court usually errs on the side of caution*".[15] Still, such a cautious presumption is indeed a presumption that can therefore be rebutted as to avoid transforming it into an irrebuttable presumption. The Court in its judgment recurred, to borrow Wahl words, *to the time-tested, cautiously worded formula* and held, despite its local character, that it is not impossible that the bus lane policy might affect inter--State trade. Still, echoes of the Opinion of AG Wahl seem to reverberate in the case law. For instance, in *Congregación de Escuelas Pías Provincia Betania v Ayuntamiento de Getafe* on the question of whether a tax exemption granted to the Catholic Church had an effect on intra-EU trade, AG Kokott observed in her Opinion that the fact that the Catholic Church possessed '*numerous properties*', which were

[11] Judgment of 17 September 1980, *Philip Morris Holland v Commission*, 730/79, EU:C:1980:209.

[12] Judgment of 24 July 2003, *Altmark Trans and Regierungspräsidium Magdeburg*, C-280/00, EU:C2003:415.

[13] Judgment of 1 April 2008, *Government of the French Community and Walloon Government*, C-212/06, EU:C:2008:178.

[14] Judgment of 14 January 2015, *Eventech*, C-518/13, EU:C:2015:9.

[15] Opinion of AG Wahl in *Eventech*, C-518/13, EU:C:2014:2239, para 82.

all capable of enjoying the tax exemption would seem to satisfy the effect on trade requirement.[16] The Court, instead, called the national court to verify a possible application of the *De Minimis* Regulation—a regulation that sets out the basis upon which small amounts of public aid given to an undertaking would not count as State aid—in the case at stake, and to seek the assistance of the European Commission if necessary. Interestingly, the Court's attitude towards the State Aid *De Minimis* Regulation[17] has very much developed. Initially, arguments based on the *De Minimis* Regulation were brutally dismissed,[18] whilst the Court now refers to the Regulation as an instrument with the objective "*to reduce the administrative burden on undertakings*".[19] Further, the Court requires national courts to provide "factual details" to enable the Court to assess whether an effect on trade can be actually established.[20] Thus, although it is reasonable for the Court to still rely on market behaviour presumptions, these presumptions can of course be rebutted if no factual or exclusionary effect can be demonstrated. Such an approach is, in my view, preferable as it anchors the State aid analysis on market-related considerations, instead of overemphasising characteristics of the national systems in question—such as its social objective, or the level of supervision by the State—to exclude *ex ante* the application of EU State aid law.[21]

3 Not Every Tax Is a State Aid

3.1 The Selectivity Criteria in the Area of Taxation

Speaking of essential State functions: taxation, naturally. Over the years, AG Wahl has been indeed often confronted with the application of the selectivity criteria. Once a nearly dormant criterion, now the pinnacle of every State aid litigation. As to complicate things further, the learned AG became embroiled in one of the most complex questions: the selectivity of national fiscal measures.

---

[16] Opinion of AG Kokott in *Congregación de Escuelas Pías Provincia Betania*, C-74/16, EU:C:2017:135, para 85.

[17] Commission Regulation (EU) 2023/2831 of 13 December 2023 on the application of Articles 107 and 108 of the Treaty on the Functioning of the European Union to *de minimis* aid (OJ L, 2023/2831, C/2023/9700).

[18] Judgment of 3 March 2005, *Heiser*, C-172/03, EU:C:2005:130, para 34.

[19] See *inter alia* judgment of 28 October 2020, *INAIL*, C--608/19, EU:C:2020:865 para 41.

[20] Judgments of 30 April 2009, *Commission v Italy and Wam*, C-494/06 P, EU:C:2009:272, para 55; and of 7 April 2022, *Autonome Provinz Bozen*, joined Cases C-102/21 and C-103/21, EU:C:2022:272, para 55. See also judgment of 19 October 2022, *Ighoga Region 10 and Others v Commission*, T-582/20, EU:T:2022:648.

[21] Judgment of 11 June 2020, *Commission and Slovak Republic v Dôvera zdravotná poisťovňa*, joined Cases C-262/18 P and C-271/18 P, EU:C:2020:450.

Within the "fight against protectionism" State aid framework, the application of the selectivity criteria becomes crucial. This criterion should constitute the dividing line between general measures of horizontal economic policies (no aid) and those that instead confer a specific advantage to an undertaking or a class of undertakings (aid). In cases of general measures, the difficulty is in distinguishing the measures that benefit the economy as a whole—that is, those intended to favour all activities that have the potential for positive spillover effects on a plurality of enterprises and sectors are therefore outside the scope of the aid rules—from those that are instead sectoral interventions or merely remedy market failures and must qualify as aid. According to the definition contained in the Communication on the notion of State aid, selectivity can be categorized as either *de jure* selectivity, which results directly from a *prima facie* discrimination, and the more insidious *de facto* selectivity that "*can be established in cases where, although the formal criteria for the application of the measure are formulated in general and objective terms, the structure of the measure is such that its effects significantly favour a particular group of undertakings*".[22]

The definition of the notion of selectivity is thus *per se* not an easy exercise. It becomes even more arduous in the area of taxation. The reasons are rather obvious: in an ideal world, taxation should serve primarily as a means of revenue generation for public expenditures and should be generally unrequited—that is to say, collected not in exchange for a specific thing but as to benefit an entire collectivity. In practice, taxation serves a multitude of purposes, from income redistribution to international competiveness, debt management, and, alas, in some cases, fiscal gifts to gain political traction. Whilst of course feudal arbitrary taxation is definitively out of fashion, taxation is thus *per se* an exercise in policy making based on the need to make a choice (what to tax, how to tax, which rates to apply and so on). In general, tax systems should be guided by the principle of tax fairness, which requires, on the one hand, that individuals and legal entities with the same ability to pay be taxed equally and, on the other hand, that the proper redistribution of resources, carried out by the State, succeeds in fostering a well-functioning market, even if the administration must often then still bear a cost in terms of efficiency. In addition, governments often use tax instruments in order to increase the development of certain activities, to increase production, or to encourage investment (tax breaks and incentives and so on). Thus, when it comes to State aid, to borrow the words of another State aid specialist, AG Kokott, "*the examination of such selectivity in the tax legislation of the Member States presents considerable difficulties*".[23] An extra effort to establish selectivity needs to be undertaken as "*tax advantages are granted in the context of a tax system to which, as a general rule, undertakings are permanently and inevitably subject. Tax systems include differentiations in many different ways, the purpose of those differentiations being, as a rule, simply to ensure that the tax*

[22] Commission Notice on the notion of State aid as referred to in Article 107(1) of the Treaty on the Functioning of the European Union (OJ 2016 C 262, p. 1), para 5.2.1.

[23] Opinion of AG Kokott in *ANGED*, C-233/16, EU:C:2017:852, para 76.

achieves the precise objective it pursues".[24] There are of course cases where the "fiscal" nature of the measure does not pose too much trouble as it may simply cover a *de jure* discrimination. For instance, in *Escuelas Pías Provincia Betania,* the Court simply held that an exemption from local tax normally payable by all taxpayers who carried out the construction works, enjoyed by the Catholic Church, conferred a clear advantage to the Church. Thus, the Spanish legislation providing for such an exemption had to be classified not as "*a general measure applicable without distinction to all economic operators but [...] rather a measure that is prima facie selective*".[25] The selectivity test applied by the Court was based on a comparison between undertakings carrying out exactly the same economic activities. Therefore, the derogation from the general system of taxation had to be considered a selective measure. Moving to general tax measures, the "classic" principle elaborated by the Court in this particular domain is that "*the appropriate criterion for establishing the selectivity of the measure at issue consists in determining whether that measure introduces, between operators that are, in the light of the objective pursued by the general tax system concerned, in a comparable factual and legal situation, a distinction that is not justified by the nature and general structure of that system* ".[26] The necessary and sufficient element is therefore always found by the Court in the fact that, irrespective of its form or the regulatory technique used, a given tax measure has the effect of placing the recipient undertakings in a more advantageous situation than other undertakings. According to the Court, "*a condition for the application or the receipt of tax aid may be grounds for a finding that that aid is selective, if that condition leads to a distinction being made between undertakings despite the fact that they are, in the light of the objective pursued by the tax system concerned, in a comparable factual and legal situation, and if, therefore, it represents discrimination against undertakings which are excluded from it*".[27] Such a stance has generally been interpreted as confirming a particularly broad interpretation of the concept of selectivity, in the sense that all measures derogating from a tax regime and involving any form of different treatment are—according to the Court—to be regarded as selective and, therefore, as State aid. In reality, the kind of analysis that the case law requires is much more complex and nuanced. The line drawn by the Court on the selectivity of fiscal measures is actually zigzag shaped. With specific reference to taxation, the Court explained that in order to classify a tax measure as selective, the ordinary or normal tax system applicable in the Member State concerned must be identified (*step one*). Next, it must be shown that the tax measure at issue derogates from that ordinary system, in so far as it differentiates between operators who, in the light of the objective pursued by that system, are in a comparable factual and legal situation *(step two).* If that is so, it must be verified whether

[24] *Id.*, para 80.

[25] Judgment of 27 June 2017, *Congregación de Escuelas Pías Provincia Betania*, C-74/16, EU:C:2017:496, paras 69 and 70.

[26] Judgment of 21 December 2016, *Commission v World Duty Free Group and Others*, C-20/15 P and C-21/15 P, EU:C:2016:981, para 60.

[27] *Id.*, para 86.

the differentiation is justified to the extent that it derives from the nature or general structure of the system of which the measure forms part *(step three)*. The Court further elaborated that for a tax to be selective it should be shown to *derogate* from the ordinary or 'normal' tax system applicable in the Member State concerned, thereby introducing, through its actual effects, differences in the treatment of operators, although the operators who qualify for the tax advantage and those who do not are in a comparable factual and legal situation in the light of the objective pursued by that Member State's tax system.[28]

Each of the steps needs a bit of an elaboration so let us get some support from AG Wahl's Opinion in *Dirk Andres*, a rather complex case concerning the compatibility with EU State aid rules of German legislation. This legislation, under certain conditions, allowed a company in financial difficulties to carry forward tax losses despite changes in its shareholder structure. On the question of the identification of the general system of reference, he very candidly acknowledges that such a determination is indeed arduous: "*in contrast to other types of aid schemes, determining with precision such a common, generally applicable system is replete with uncertainty in the context of taxation. Keeping in mind the complexities of any tax system and the variables involved in determining the tax burden of undertakings, it seems impossible to know with certainty what the 'normal situation' is*".[29] If one looks at the many fiscal aid cases the Court has dealt with since then, it is impossible not to agree. Still, some kind of guidance has gradually emerged.[30] For instance, in the celebrated (by some) *Apple* judgment in which Wahl was juge rapporteur, the Court first made it clear that the satisfaction of this first criterion is of the utmost importance so much as that an error made in that determination necessarily vitiates the whole of the analysis of the condition relating to selectivity.[31] Secondly, the Court explained that the identification of the reference framework "*must follow from an objective examination of the content, the structure and the specific effects of the applicable rules under the national law of that State*".[32] The Court is walking a tigh trope here.

On the one hand, by stressing the need for an "objective" examination, it reaffirms that as direct taxation is a national competence, the analysis on whether a fiscal measure can be in breach of EU law must be strict and based on the national system, and not on a concept that is extraneous or non-existent within that national tax system.[33] Especially in its recent case law, the Court has been very careful in

---

[28] *Id.*, paras 57 and 67.

[29] Opinion of AG Wahl in *Andres*, cited above, para 101.

[30] *Id.*; see also judgment of 6 October 2021, *World Duty Free Group and Spain v Commission*, C-51/19 P and C-64/19 P, EU:C:2021:793.

[31] Judgment of 10 September 2024, *Commission v Ireland and Apple Sales International*, C-465/20 P, EU:C:2024:724, para 79.

[32] Judgment of 19 September 2024, *United Kingdom and Others v Commission (Taxation of profits of CFCs)*, joined Cases C-555/22 P, C-556/22 P and C-564/22 P, EU:C:2024:763, para 95.

[33] See the very sharp criticisms of Commission decisions expressed by the Court in C-562/19 P, *Commission* v *Poland* EU: C: 2021:201, para 38 and 39; and C-596/19 P, *Commission* v *Hungary*,

reaffirming the importance of preserving the power of Member States to decide on their fiscal priorities, albeit still operating within a European framework. Thus, in *Fiat Luxembourg* the Court—paradoxically relying on a precedent in an area of EU exclusive competence: VAT—[34] held that the determination of the basis of assessment and the taxable event is an expression of "*the principle of legality of taxation, which forms part of the legal order of the European Union as a general principle of law, requiring that any obligation to pay a tax and all the essential elements defining the substantive features thereof must be provided for by law, the taxable person having to be in a position to foresee and calculate the amount of tax due and determine the point at which it becomes payable*".[35]

On the other hand, "*the structure and the specific effects of the applicable rules*"[36] is a definition broad enough as to be able to catch measures that are not only in breach of EU law but are an arbitrary deviation from the national legal system itself. Thus, an entire tax system designed to circumvent State aid control would still be incompatible with EU law,[37] as would specific measures that are arbitrary and do not respect the structure or logic of a national reference system.[38] As anticipated by AG Wahl in *Dirk Andres*, "*an approach that seeks to identify the entire body of rules that influence the tax burden weighing on undertakings [...] is warranted. It ensures that the selectivity of a tax measure is assessed against a framework that includes all relevant provisions, and not against provisions that have been carved out artificially from a broader legislative framework*".[39]

The identification of a general system of reference is indeed a necessary tool but does not sort out all the issues related to fiscal aid. It can work out in dealing with rules that establish the tax base, the subjects of taxation, and on these a "novella" intervenes that derogates from their application. However, there are more complex cases in which it is practically impossible to find a benchmark, as in the case of an *ad hoc* tax. For instance, in *Paint Graphos*[40]—yet another famous tax related case concerning the taxation regime under Italian rules applicable to cooperative societies—the identification of the reference system was identified laconically by the Court in the general corporation tax regime, but only for a very specific reason, namely that the taxable base for the cooperatives concerned was determined in

EU: C: 2021:202 paras 44 and 45.

[34] Judgment of 8 May 2019, *Związek Gmin Zagłębia Miedziowego*, C-566/17, EU:C:2019:390, para 39.

[35] Judgment of 8 November 2022, *Fiat Chrysler Finance Europe v Commission*, joined Cases C-885/19 P and C-898/19 P, EU:C:2022:859, para 97.

[36] Judgment *United Kingdom and Others v Commission (Taxation of profits of CFCs)*, cited above, para 95.

[37] Judgment of 15 November 2011, *Commission and Spain v Government of Gibraltar and United Kingdom*, joined Cases C-106/09 P and C-107/09 P, EU: C: 2011:732.

[38] Judgment of 30 May 2024, *Autoridad Portuaria de Bilbao v Commission*, C-110/23 P, EU:C:2024:441.

[39] Opinion of AG Wahl in *Andres*, cited above, para 109.

[40] Judgment of 8 September 2011, *Paint Graphos and Others*, C-78/08 to C-80/08, EU:C:2011:550.

exactly the same way as for other types of companies, that is according to the amount of net profits resulting from the company's activity at the end of the tax year. The Court's analysis moves however to the second step: the difference in treatment when the taxable income earned by the cooperatives concerned was exempt from corporate tax. Said cooperatives thus benefited from a tax break that profit-making societies could not access. Likewise, in the *Lippe-Ems* case, the Court—once it had established that the objective of the tax was merely to generate tax revenues that must in particular contribute, in the context of a budgetary manoeuver, "*in accordance with the polluter pays principle, to a reduction in the burden entailed for the Federal budget*" arising from the necessary clean-up of radioactive waste—stated that electricity production obviously cannot be found to be "*in a factual and legal situation that is comparable to that of the production method based on nuclear fuel, as only that method generates radioactive waste arising from the use of such fuel*".[41] The second step thus becomes essential. Where the general system of reference is looser, the comparison between undertakings needs to be specific and detailed. In this regard, the Court has shown that it knows how to penetrate national tax systems with panache and confidence. To take the example of the *Paint Graphos* case discussed above, the Court ruled that cooperatives "*conform to particular operating principles which clearly distinguish them from other economic operators*".[42] This statement, borrowed mainly from EU sources such as Regulation 1435/2003 on the European Cooperative Society,[43] is based on criteria that apply only to cooperative societies and not to those with shared capitals. These include conditions of admission, withdrawal and exclusion of members, liquidation, redistribution of assets, and so on. A series of factual and legal differences led the Court to conclude that the differential tax treatment reserved for cooperatives was not to be considered as a selective measure when these companies operate in the exclusive economic interest of their members and have a special, personal—rather than purely commercial—relationship with their members, in which they actively participate and are entitled to an equitable sharing of the economic results. It should also be restated that in "ordinary cases", outside the preliminary reference context, it is the Commission's task to prove the effect of possible discrimination between undertakings. Such an examination must be carried out "*in a rigorous and sufficiently reasoned manner in order to enable full judicial review*",[44] in particular as to the similarity of the situation of the operators benefiting from the measure and that of the operators excluded from it. Thus, while the Commission cannot be required to identify precisely a category of undertakings with specific characteristics which benefit exclusively from

[41] Judgment of 4 June 2015, *Kernkraftwerke Lippe-Ems*, C-5/14, EU:C:2015:354, para 78 and 79.

[42] Judgment *Paint Graphos and Others*, cited above, para 55.

[43] Regulation (EC) No 1435/2003 of 22 July 2003 on the Statute for a European Cooperative Society (SCE).

[44] Judgment of 6 October 2021, *Prosegur Compañía de Seguridad v Commission*, C-55/19 P, EU:C:2021:797, para 49.

the measure at issue[45] it must nevertheless be established in practice that the measure is capable of creating an advantage for certain undertakings.[46]

A final note on the second step is also necessary: if a narrower approach is adopted in cases of *ad hoc* taxes, the policy reasons behind the introduction of such a measure invariably comes to the fore. In this context, the Court has shown some degree of "generosity" towards Member States, especially when the objective pursued at national level seems to be in conformity with EU policies. For instance, in the area of environmental protection or promotion of green electricity, the Court accepted to look at possible objective reasons as to why a certain differentiation did occur. In *ANGED*, the Court was asked whether a Spanish regional tax calculated on the surface occupied by a sales area could have been considered either a State aid, as it conferred an advantage to small undertakings, or an as obstacle to the freedom of establishment for large companies. The Court accepted to look into the specific reasons that, according to the Spanish government, justified the introduction of the *ad hoc* tax: that is to say the territorial and environmental impact that a concentration of large establishments can cause and the need to modernise retail infrastructures and the urban space. The Court concluded that there was no selectivity as small and large undertakings were not in a comparable situation in the light of those objectives.[47] Likewise, in a case on lower rate tax that applied differently on the use of inland waters for the production of electricity in inter-community river basins, the Court reiterated first that it fell within the tax competence of the Member States to designate bases of assessment and to spread the tax burden across the various factors of production and economic sectors, and secondly that a criterion for taxation connected to the source of production of electricity (water) should not entail a discrimination, allowing a Member State to apply a tax only to electricity producers using water as the source of electricity production.[48]

3.2 *Justifying Selective Measures?*

The last step of the selectivity test is as follows: a measure derogating from the reference system is not selective if it is justified by the nature or general scheme of the system. There are two questions: the first is to determine whether the Court intended to introduce further possible justifications for a measure that is indeed aid, and if so, it is then necessary to understand what they are; the second is on the burden of proof. Regarding the first point, the Court has never specifically defined the scope of application but has gradually clarified that a selective tax rule may

[45] See Opinion of AG Wathelet in Joined Cases *Commission v Banco Santander and Santusa*, C-20/15 P and C-21/15 P, EU:C:2016:624, in particular paras 7 and 10.

[46] Judgment of 4 June 2015, *Commission v MOL*, C-15/14 P, EU: C: 2015:362, para 60.

[47] Judgment of 26 April 2018, *ANGED*, C-233/16, EU: C: 2018:280, para 55.

[48] Judgment of 7 November 2019, *UNESA and Others*, C-105/18 to C-113/18, EU: C: 2019:935, paras 68 and 69.

nevertheless be justified if it follows directly from the guiding or basic principles of the tax system. Thus, for example, the Court has "accepted" as a justification the need to combat tax fraud or tax evasion, the need to take account of specific accounting obligations, good administrative management, the principle of tax neutrality, the progressive nature of income tax and its redistributive logic, the need to avoid double taxation or the objective of optimising the recovery of tax debts.[49] On the other hand, "external" objectives that are not inherent to the system itself cannot be invoked. The distinction between internal and external objectives is crucial, in that obviously the third stage of the test cannot be interpreted as a kind of authorisation for Member States to introduce or justify aid measures. Such reasons can and must be invoked at the level of the examination of compatibility under Articles 107(2) and 107(3) TFEU. Thus, the purpose of adapting to the liberalisation regime or the economic reorganisation of companies in crisis should be, for instance, considered "external".[50] However, as once again suggested by AG Wahl in *Dirk Andres,* the "tax related" reasons are often hard to separate from other objectives that the State pursues through taxation; "*in other words, reasons that in the Court's taxonomy are intrinsic to the tax system are inseparably linked to objectives that have a broader societal context*".[51] The Court's case law suggests some flexibility. In the *British Aggregates*[52] and *Commission v. Netherlands*[53] cases, while classifying the measures as selective, the Court clearly considered the protection of the environment as a worthy end; equally, in *Paint Graphos*, the social purpose of cooperatives was also considered relevant. However, these ends cannot be considered as true justifications, only as differentiations within a system of reference. A parallel can be drawn with the jurisprudence on Article 110 TFEU concerning indirect taxation on products, one of the few Treaty provisions that do not provide the possibility for Member States to justify a possible breach. The Court has consistently held that—notwithstanding the prohibition of discrimination—it is possible for a Member State to establish a differentiated system of taxation for certain products, even similar products, "*on the basis of objective criteria, such as the nature of the raw materials used or the production processes employed*".[54] However, such "differentiations" are compatible with EU law only if they pursue objectives that are also compatible with the Treaties and secondary legislation and if their modalities are such as to avoid any form of direct or indirect discrimination against imports from other Member States or protection in favour of competing national products.[55] Similarly, in the field of aid, differentiations are possible, but only if the specific modalities of application

[49] Judgment *Paint Graphos* cited above, para 69 and 70; and judgment *P Oy*, cited above, paras 27 et seq.

[50] Judgment of 28 June 2018, *Andres (insolvency of Heitkamp BauHolding) v Commission*, C-203/16 P, EU:C:2018:505.

[51] Opinion of AG Wahl in *Andres,* cited above, para 185.

[52] Judgment of 22 December 2008, *British Aggregates v Commission*, C-487/06 P, EU:C:2008:757.

[53] Judgment of 8 September 2011, *Commission v Netherlands*, C-279/08 P, EU:C:2011:551.

[54] Judgment of 2 April 1998, *Outokumpu*, C-213/96, EU: C: 1998:155, para 30.

[55] *Id.*

comply with the principle of equality—in this case proportional: the same to the same and the different to the different.

The other issue to be addressed is that of the burden of proof. The Commission must of course prove the existence of a selective measure, whereas the burden of proof for the existence of a justification would seem to be on the Member State. According to the Commission, it is up to the Member States to introduce and enforce *"appropriate control and monitoring procedures to ensure that the derogations are consistent with the logic and general scheme of the tax system,"* and not only to demonstrate that the derogations are *"proportionate and do not go beyond what is necessary to achieve the legitimate objective being pursued, in that the objective could not be attained by less far-reaching measures"*.[56] The Court indeed reaffirmed that once it has established the *a priori* selective nature of a measure, *"it is for the Member State which has introduced such a differentiation between undertakings in relation to charges to show that it is actually justified by the nature and general scheme of the system in question*".[57] Requiring States to bear an "additional" burden of proof in order to prove the non-selectivity of a State measure, one that has already been deemed as such by the Commission, seems to make their task rather burdensome. Indeed *"a de facto irrefutable assumption that tax measures found to be a priori selective are, in reality, selective"*.[58]

4 A Very Personal Conclusion

The analysis above has attempted to show that the "fears" of an exorbitant application of State aid rules are unjustified. I know that my new job is to deliver *des conclusions*, but let me instead try to offer a very personal opinion (pun intended). When I accepted to contribute to this *Liber Amicorum*, little did I know that, just a few months later, I would find myself listening to President Lenaerts' farewell speech for Judge Wahl. Minutes later, I took my oath to become Advocate General at the Court. Looking at the magnitude of Nils Wahl's contribution to the development of EU State aid law, it is something to be scared of. Yet, at a historical moment in which, emergency after emergency, the whole system of State aid control is subject to so many criticisms and its future is somehow uncertain, it is of great comfort that I can always consult my EU State aid greatest hits.

---

[56] Commission Notice on the notion of State aid, cited above, point 140.

[57] Judgment of 29 April 2004, *Netherlands v Commission*, C-159/01, EU: C: 2004:246, para 43.

[58] Opinion of AG Wahl in *Andres*, cited above, para 187.

Predicting the Future: Evidential Basis for Prospective Assessments in EU Merger Control

Fernando Castillo de la Torre

1 Introduction

The recent *CK Telecoms* saga has put issues of evidence and proof at the centre of litigation in EU merger control. The saga was closed by the judgment of the Court of Justice,[1] but a few other recent judgments have also shed light on several aspects of the evidentiary assessment of mergers.[2] In the following pages, I intend to recapitulate on this recent case-law, while also reflecting on some issues of principle about how evidence is (and should be) assessed.

The substantive legal test in the context of EU merger review is that of "significant impediment of effective competition" ("SIEC").[3] The Commission must not only prove its case when it intends to prohibit a merger (i.e., where it finds a SIEC). It must prove its case where it intends to find no SIEC because the burden of proof runs "both ways". The Commission is not required to comply with a higher standard

[1] C-376/20 P, *Commission* v *CK Telecoms UK Investments*, EU:C:2023:561. At the time of writing the proceedings after the case was referred to the GC are still pending (T-399/16 RENV).

[2] T-584/19, *thyssenkrupp v Commission*, EU:T:2022:386 (upheld on appeal: C-581/22 P, *thyssenkrupp v Commission*, EU:C:2024:821); T-251/19, *Wieland-Werke v Commission*, EU:T:2022:296; T-312/20, *EVH v Commission*, EU:T:2023:252 (*EVH I*) (upheld on appeal, C-464/23 P, C-465/23 P, C-467/23 P, C-468/23 P and C-470/23 P, *EVH and Others v Commission*, EU:C:2025:478); T-53/21, *EVH v Commission*, EU:T:2023:834 (*EVH II*); T-58/20, *NetCologne v Commission*, EU:T:2024:813; T-64/20, *Deutsche Telekom v Commission*, EU:T:2024:815; T-69/20, *Tele Columbus v Commission*, EU:T:2024:816.

[3] Article 2 of Council Regulation (EC) No 139/2004 of 20 January 2004 on the control of concentrations between undertakings (the Merger Regulation or "EUMR") (OJ 2004 L 24, p. 1).

F. Castillo de la Torre (✉)
Legal Service, European Commission, Brussels, Belgium
e-mail: Fernando.CASTILLO-DE-LA-TORRE@ec.europa.eu

L. Prete, L. Rezki (eds.), *Judging & (Re)Thinking European Union Law*, https://doi.org/10.1007/978-3-032-13473-8_3

of proof in relation to decisions prohibiting concentrations than in relation to decisions approving concentrations.[4] Issues of evidence are crucial in merger control and often constitute the focus of litigation (which is an opportunity for merging parties to "relitigate the facts"). Yet, while the Commission's guidelines on horizontal and non-horizontal mergers contain a lot about the elements that may be relevant in the assessment (what the Commission "must prove", so to say), there is little on evidentiary matters as such.[5]

One key notion which has animated debates is that of "standard of proof". To me, while this expression is often used in the case-law,[6] and any prospective (predictive) assessment must be based on sound epistemic grounds (and therefore also on evidence), it is difficult to apply a notion of "proof" as such in this context. Merger review is not about ascertaining the truth about something that happened.[7] Rather, it involves estimating a probability about whether something will happen in the future.[8] So, the assessment involved could be rather described as "proving a probability" (of SIEC) so to say. In my view, the intellectual exercise is about making a reasonable (i.e. epistemically justified) predictive estimate, based on the best available qualitative and quantitative evidence that can be obtained within tight deadlines. The future is estimated based on a combination of evidence (typically about the market and competition therein today) and rational inferences projected into the future based on logical reasoning, economic insight, and experience.

The reality when observing the process in practice is that the overwhelming majority of mergers are unproblematic. The first task is therefore to apply simple proxies to identify those which may be problematic (typically, market shares and levels of concentration). Much of the information for this first selection is typically submitted in the notification form, but in those early stages, the case-teams should identify the types of data that may be available and needed to analyse the markets.

---

[4] *Commission* v *CK Telecoms*, note 1, paras 73–74.

[5] By contrast, the 2023 US Merger Guidelines contain Section 4 on "*Analytical, Economic, and Evidentiary tools*". At global level, the ICN Merger Working Group has developed guidance which includes useful indications on evidentiary matters, see *ICN Recommended Practices for Merger Analysis* and the *Merger Investigative Techniques Handbook*.

[6] In French (the working language of EU Courts) the terms used are not always the same, even in the same judgment, and they are probably more nuanced. It is sometimes "*niveau de preuve*", but also "*exigences de preuve*" (compare *Commission* v *CK Telecoms*, note 1, paras 63, 64, 74, 77–79, on the one hand, and 73 and 88, on the other), the latter expression also probably capturing other dimensions of the evidence, such as what the case-law refers to as "quality". In *EVH v Commission (I) (GC)*, note 2, the French term "*exigences de preuve*" is translated as "*standard of proof*" (paras 49–50) and "*evidential requirements*" (para. 197).

[7] While proving events of the past is also done in conditions of uncertainty, we tend to believe that there is a "true" version of events. Having said this, much of the analysis of capability to produce restrictive effects under a "by effects" analysis in Articles 101 and 102 TFEU is also prospective (about the capacity at the time when the conduct is implemented), even if it is applied to past conduct.

[8] I assume here that what is relevant in this context is an internal conception of probability (as opposed to an external one). To be clear, saying that evidence is probabilistic says nothing about whether those probabilities can or should be reduced to, or expressed in terms of, numbers.

Evidence/information is instrumental, and the Commission must try to identify and test plausible market definitions and competitive assessment/theories of harm, to focus the enquiry (i.e. to identify "candidate" theory or theories).[9] The use of economics in merger control is not limited to conducting empirical analysis. Economics is now embedded within merger control as it provides the conceptual framework to analyse the functioning of the markets and to assess merger effects.[10]

2 Merger Control as a Complex Economic Assessment

Merger control often involves "complex economic assessments". When reviewing such assessments, the EU judicature may only annul if there is a manifest error of assessment. It checks whether the evidence put forward is factually accurate, reliable and consistent, whether that evidence contains all the relevant data that must be taken into consideration in appraising a complex situation, and whether it is capable of substantiating the conclusions drawn from it.[11] The threefold test tries to capture three different aspects of the assessment. First, the quality of the evidence relied upon by the deciding authority, requiring the EU Courts to review the existence of "*factually accurate, reliable, and consistent*" evidence. Second, the test captures elements of "*completeness*", somewhat more quantitative, when it mentions that the evidence shall contain "*all the information that must be taken into account in order to assess a complex situation*". Third, the assessment whether that evidence is "*capable of substantiating the conclusions drawn*" from it is relational in nature. On this last aspect, the case-law has not provided that the conclusion must derive from that evidence beyond any reasonable doubt, but only that the evidence must be "*capable of substantiating*" it. The test allows a finding that is justified by the evidentiary record, while not excluding that another reasonable person could draw a

[9] For example, if we are examining a proposed merger between two of several undertakings selling differentiated products to many consumers, a natural investigative focus would be on possible unilateral (non-coordinated) effects. Relevant economic evidence would be the extent to which product offerings of the merging parties are the first and second choices for consumers: e.g. collecting data to determine historic substitution patterns in response to changes in relative prices, or internal documents, such as surveys conducted by the merging parties (or others in the industry) in their normal course of business.

[10] See, contribution of the EU in OECD (2012), "Economic Evidence in Merger Analysis: Key findings, summary and notes", *OECD Roundtables on Competition Policy Papers*, No. 126, OECD Publishing, Paris, p. 245. To be clear, the expression "theory of harm" is not entirely "neutral" as it has been conceptually associated to some views of what "harm" is (i.e. to "consumer welfare"). I personally find the expression more useful for merger control than for the enforcement of Articles 101 and 102 since logically in order to know what evidence must be obtained in a limited period of time, one must have an "anti-competitive story" that evidence will prove or disprove. However, such "harm" need not be limited to a narrow view of "consumer harm". The disagreements on whether a theory of harm is "solid" or not do not often relate to its evidentiary strength, but to the definition of the relevant harm and the purpose of the rule.

[11] This test was first formulated in C-12/03 P, *Commission v Tetra Laval*, EU:C:2005:87, para. 39.

different conclusion based on the same evidence.[12] Predictive assessments are those where more variability is generally to be expected.[13]

Finding an error may not be enough to annul the decision. The EU judicature examines whether a deficiency in the examination by the Commission has, or at least may have, an impact on the outcome.[14] For example, in *Commission v CK Telecoms*, the Court of Justice (ECJ) upheld one of the Commission's grounds of appeal because the General Court (GC) failed to carry out an overall examination of whether it could be considered that the Commission had demonstrated to the requisite legal standard the existence of a SIEC, in light of: (i) the outcome of its examination of CK Telecoms' arguments at first instance concerning some of the relevant circumstances; and (ii) the other relevant circumstances that formed part of the Commission's overall analysis and that, since they were not challenged, could therefore be regarded as established.[15] In *Orlen*, the Court of Justice recalled that

[12] F. Castillo de la Torre and E. Gippini Fournier, *Evidence, Proof and Judicial Review in EU Competition Law*, Second Edition, Elgar Publishing, 2024, paras 2.188 and 6.072, with further references. For then Advocate General Wahl a decision by a judge ensures sounder outcomes provided the reviewing entity is "*at least as knowledgeable as the decision making authority in the relevant field*" (N. Wahl, "The Role of the Court of Justice in Ensuring Compliance with Fundamental Rights in Competition Cases since the Lisbon Treaty" in J. Derenne and M. Merola, *The Role of the Court of Justice of the European Union in Competition Law Cases*, Bruylant, 2012, pp. 267–276, 271). What the judge can and should undertake is "*to verify that the facts invoked by the Commission are ascertained, pertinent, sufficient and capable of substantiating the conclusions drawn by the Commission*" (ibid.). See also, on the intensity of judicial review of complex economic assessments, Opinion of Advocate General Emiliou in C-389/21, *European Central Bank v Crédit Lyonnais*, EU:C:2022:844, paras 50, 58 and 62. In merger control, see *thyssenkrupp v Commission (GC)*, note 2, paras 615, 617–618, where the GC finds the Commission's prospective assessment "*coherent and very plausible*" and therefore concludes that it meets "*the requisite legal standard*" (see also, referring to whether the Commission's findings are "not plausible", paras 188, 488, 512, 546). In *CK Telecoms* the ECJ also refers to "*the plausibility of the various consequences such a concentration may have*" (*Commission* v *CK Telecoms*, note 1, para. 78). The case-law increasingly refers to varying degrees of "plausibility" as standard in some contexts, while the meaning of such qualification is not entire clear, in particular the distinction between "plausibility, and "possibility" or "probability". For example, T-1077/23, *Bytedance v Commission*, EU:T:2024:478, refers to a "*high degree of plausibility*" (para. 71). For a discussion of the different meanings of "plausible", see C. Dahlman, "What does it mean to be "Plausible"?" (2024) *Quaestio Facti - International Journal of Evidential Legal Reasoning*, 7, pp. 1–12.

[13] D. Kahneman, O. Sibony, C. R. Sunstein, *Noise – A Flaw in Human Judgment*, 2021, Harper Collins, which tellingly explain that "*forecasts are noisy*" (p. 6, see also chapter 21).

[14] Castillo de la Torre/Gippini Fournier, note 12, paras 1.101 and 6.083-083.

[15] *Commission* v *CK Telecoms*, note 1, paras 269–270. In some cases, the evidentiary record still allows the judges to make an overall assessment and determine if the error is fatal for the outcome. Some decisions may be based on a body of evidence that largely exceeds what would be required to discharge the burden of proof, and therefore a gap or error should not be fatal. In other cases, what remains of the case is so limited that it is simply not possible to reconsider the case *ex novo*. The *Intel II* judgment of the ECJ appears to belong to the latter category (C-240/22 P, *Commission* v *Intel*, EU:C:2024:915, paras 339–343). In my view, there can also be a difference, in the outcome of judicial review, between committing an error in assessing a point that was effectively the basis of the Commission's findings and assessing the impact of the failure to take into account a point that was effectively not (properly) assessed. By considering what remains of the case the judges are

"the existence of a manifest error of assessment cannot correspond to the presence of a mere irregularity or omission on the part of the Commission, since a certain degree of seriousness, capable of calling into question the validity of the analysis which the Commission carried out, must be reached".[16]

3 Investigative Tools and Sources of Evidence

The scope and depth of the evidential enquiry varies greatly. In some cases, evidence may be abundant from the very beginning, as many of the relevant elements are readily available to the notifying party, even if the Commission will still gather additional data and the views of other market participants. In other cases, the notifying party may lack (or may be less willing to provide) industry-wide information. It is not uncommon for the Commission to have to carry out a "market reconstruction".

Merger control involves different analytical tools, rather than a single methodology. The investigative tools to obtain evidence are the same as under Regulation 1/2003, and the Commission's investigation is mainly conducted in the form of written requests for information.[17] Information is typically requested at least from the customers and competitors of the parties to the transaction but, depending on the needs of the case, the case team may request information from the suppliers of the

not substituting their assessment for that of the Commission, but exercising the function of judicial review by determining if the error is relevant for the outcome, as they routinely do in other contexts. When some pieces of evidence have been discarded as inadmissible, the EU judicature still examines if remaining evidence is enough to prove the relevant point (T-191/98, T-212/98-T-214/98, *Atlantic Container Line and Others v Commission*, EU:T:2003:245, para. 338; T-379/10 and T-381/10, *Keramag and Others v Commission*, EU:T:2013:457, para. 264). In T-321/05 *AstraZeneca* v *Commission,* EU:T:2010:266, paras 182 and 196–197, one error and one "*lacuna*" did not affect the "soundness" of the conclusions of the Commission. See also *EVH v Commission (I) (GC)*, note 2, para. 351: "*[t]he Court must also, in the course of its review, consider whether any possible omissions on the part of the Commission are capable of calling into question its finding that the present concentration does not raise serious doubts as to its compatibility with the internal market*" (see, approvingly on appeal, *EVH v Commission (I) (ECJ)*, note 2, paras 187, 190 and 214–215).

[16] C-255/22 P, *Orlen* v *Commission*, EU:C:2024:790, para. 115. The fact that the applicant must adduce arguments and evidence in its application is not a reversal of the burden of proof, but a procedural rule in judicial review, see *EVH v Commission (I) (ECJ)*, note 2, para. 212, and Opinion of Advocate-General Medina in C-541/23 P, *Polwax v Commission*, EU:C:2025:360, paras 25–29.

[17] Such requests include simple requests for information ("RFI") pursuant to Article 11(2) and decisions requiring the supply of information pursuant to Article 11(3). The Commission may also interview any natural or legal person who consents to be interviewed (Article 11(7) EUMR). Information may be requested also from the governments and authorities of the Member States (Article 11(6) EUMR). Other investigative tools may be used depending on the needs of the case. These include agreed visits to the premises of the undertakings concerned ("site visits"), external studies, as well as unannounced inspections under Article 12 and 13 EUMR.

parties to a concentration as well from as any other third parties.[18] Where needed, the case team may also request additional information from the parties to the transaction, including requesting them to reply to sets of questions and to provide the Commission with a selection of their internal documents.

Yet, the dynamics under merger review are very different from antitrust, since the notifying party is interested in getting the authorisation and it is far more "motivated" to rely promptly and comprehensively to all requests from the Commission. While part of information provided will have an element of advocacy, as opposed to an unbiased description of events or information, it is very rare to encounter the delaying tactics that often occur when an undertaking is under investigation for breach of Articles 101 or 102 TFEU.

The types of evidence the enquiry will gather are also common to any investigative procedure. First, the Commission will rely not only on pre-existing documents which can be internal to the undertakings (and will typically have a higher probative value, as we will see) but also on existing reports on industry-wide trends.[19] Second, the Commission will also look for "raw" data, such as data at retail level, in case for example of consumer products, or bidding data. Third, evidence may take the form of descriptions of different competitively relevant conditions or views of market participants (sometimes on hypothetical questions). Evidence that appears to reflect a subjective element (e.g. an element of opinion, or the hypothetical reaction to a hypothetical question) will not be discarded, even if its probative value may be lower.

4 The Nature of Prospective Analysis: Proof v (Epistemically Justified) Estimates

Once accepted that any analysis of the future can only be probabilistic, the next question is "how probable" such effects must be. This is presented often as an issue of "standard of proof", where the subject of the proof is a probability (and not a "fact").

While it has been uncontroversial that it is inappropriate to apply a "beyond reasonable doubt" standard since it would make almost impossible to prohibit a merger, in the understanding that there are few things which can be said with certainty about

[18] In an "in depth" investigation (phase II), the Commission will typically send a RFI in the form of a questionnaire as a mass sending to various third-party market participants in the early stages of Phase II investigation (in *Essilor/Luxottica*, the Commission sent questionnaires to around 42,000 opticians), and it may further send more targeted requests to individual third parties or the parties to the transaction at any stages of Phase II investigation. The RFI in Phase II is typically more focused and detailed than the RFI sent out in Phase I.

[19] A variety of sources collects industry data (trade statistics or collections of individual price transactions). Such data generally has the advantage of being readily available to the parties and presented in a consistent way, and thus constitute a natural source for descriptive statistics of the industry in which a merger takes place.

the future, the judgment of the GC in *CK Telecoms* applied a standard of "strong probability" that intended to be more demanding than the standard of "more likely than not" that could be drawn from previous case-law.[20] The Grand Chamber of the Court of Justice closed the debate in July 2023 and ruled that the standard of proof is "more likely than not", or, in other words, a "balance of probabilities".[21]

This conclusion was drawn from "*the symmetrical structure of Article 2(2) and (3) of Regulation No 139/2004*" and "*the prospective nature of the Commission's economic analyses when conducting the review of concentrations*". Indeed, the latter will not suffice to establish a "balance of probabilities" standard since the prospective nature does not exclude a standard of "strong" probability, which would be somewhere below a "beyond reasonable doubt" standard.[22]

Having a symmetrical standard may *prima facie* facilitate decisions since standards such as "strong probability" or expressed in percentages would be, in my view, less operational. We do not tend to be good at assigning a figure to a given probability.[23] Verbal expressions of uncertainty and probability are common in decisions and judgments, but no less problematic.[24] Yet, while we may have different views of what "strong" means, we may be marginally better at ascertaining if one

[20] T-399/16, *CK Telecoms UK Investments* v *Commission*, EU:T:2020:217. In *thyssenkrupp v Commission (GC)*, note 2, the GC already took some distance from the GC judgment in *CK Telecoms* (paras 278–280).

[21] *Commission* v *CK Telecoms*, note 1, para. 87. In separate judgments, the GC has ruled that the standard of proof is *"identical"* for decisions adopted under Article 6 and 8 of the EUMR (T-79/12, *Cisco Systems and Messagenet* v *Commission*, EU:T:2013:635, para. 46, and such standard of proof is being "*more likely than not*", para. 47; see also *EVH v Commission (I) (GC)*, note 2, paras 48–52). Therefore, the notion of "*serious doubts*" (which is considered an "*objective notion*", *Cisco Systems and Messagenet* v *Commission*, para. 49) appears be part of the substantive criterion, and not of the standard of proof.

[22] Some authors consider that even a "strong probability" standard is "*more than the economic analysis can deliver*" (G. Monti, "Article: EU Merger Control After the Grand Chamber's Judgment In Commission v. CK Telecoms Investments", (2024) 47 *World Competition*, Issue 1, pp. 11–32, 16).

[23] Studies have shown that people's intuitive (estimative) numeric probabilities are poorly calibrated and show "overconfidence" (see, *inter alia*, D.A. Moore, E.R. Tenney, E. R., U. Haran, (2015) "Overprecision in Judgment", in G. Wu and G. Keren (Eds.), *Handbook of Judgment and Decision Making*, Wiley, pp. 182–212).

[24] There is ample literature on the difficulties to express uncertainty or probability in numerical terms, and how humans prefer verbal statements about probabilities, as they are richer and more flexible (they allow for the use of verbs, adjectives, nouns and intensifiers) and convey also other dimensions, such as directionality (drawing attention to the outcome's occurrence or non-occurrence) (see K. Teigen, "Dimensions of uncertainty communication: What is conveyed by verbal terms and numeric ranges", *Current Psychology* (2023) 42:29122–29137; M. Juanchich, and M. Sirota, "Do people really prefer verbal probabilities?", *Psychological Research* (2020) 84:2325–2338). At EU level, the use of such verbal statement of probabilities is rendered more complex because judgments are available in many different languages, and different linguistic versions often convey slightly different nuances. More research would be useful on the language the EU judicature uses to express uncertainty and probability (see also note 12 on the use of some terms).

story is more convincing than another. The "relative plausibility" approach[25] may suit well to conceptualise the evidentiary debates in mergers. Traces of such conceptual approach may be captured by the wording in *CK Telecoms,* where the Court of Justice refers to "*the plausibility of the various consequences such a concentration may have, in order to identify those which are most likely to arise*".[26]

One must bear in mind that the case-law may set out a different standard in some other contexts of merger control. In the context of the assessment of commitments, while the test for occurrence of a SIEC is still the same, the implementation of the commitments as such is subject to a higher standard, that of *certainty* that the proposed commitments "*will be able to be implemented and that they will be sufficiently workable and lasting*".[27] In other words, the Commission must be certain that the commitments as such are sufficiently workable and lasting, while the balance of probabilities applies regarding whether that commitment, whose workable and lasting implementation is sufficiently certain, is adequate to remedy a SIEC.

The Court of Justice has also developed a difference between the "quality" of the evidence and the "standard of proof". The latter remains the same whatever the type of case and factual situation. However, in *Tetra Laval* the Court of Justice first referred to the requirement of "convincing" evidence, which it categorised as part of the "quality" of the evidence.[28] *CK Telecoms* further elaborated on this distinction,[29] and restated that while some theories of harm may be more complex (and may require "proof" of different dimensions and "more evidence in support" so to say), the standard of proof remains the same.[30] To the extent that this reflects the existence of some "priors" regarding some types of mergers, we will discuss about it below.

As regards the "quality" of the evidence required, the case-law has tried to define it, mainly through adjectives.[31] The Court of Justice ruled in *CK Telecoms* that the

---

[25] The "relative plausibility" theory explains the process as involving reasoning put to the effort of deciding the relative plausibility of the parties' various explanations of the evidence (see M. Pardo and R. J. Allen, "Juridical Proof and the Best Explanation", 27 *Law & Philosophy* 223 (2008). The debate between relative plausibility and probabilistic approaches has kept the experts on evidence law quite busy over the last 15 years.

[26] *Commission* v *CK Telecoms*, note 1, para. 78.

[27] See *thyssenkrupp v Commission (GC)*, note 2, para. 792 (see also paras 822–823 on the need of analysis of the "long-term" viability and competitiveness of the divested business); *Deutsche Telekom v Commission*, note 2, paras 377–379, and *Tele Columbus v Commission*, note 2, para. 380.

[28] The ECJ explained in *Tetra Laval* that by referring to "*convincing evidence*", the GC "*by no means added a condition relating to the requisite standard of proof but merely drew attention to the essential function of evidence, which is to establish convincingly the merits of an argument or, as in the present case, of a decision on a merger*" (*Commission v Tetra Laval*, note 11, para. 41). This sentence captures that it is about updating the *subjective* probability of the decision-maker.

[29] *Commission* v *CK Telecoms*, note 1, paras 76–77.

[30] *Commission* v *CK Telecoms*, note 1, paras 78–79.

[31] Schauer has referred to the "tyranny of adjectives" in the evidence discourse (F. Schauer, *The Proof: Uses of Evidence in Law, Politics and Everything Else*, Harvard University Press, 2022, 51). The number of adjectives which the case-law uses is increasing. The use of the adjective "*convincing*" in *Tetra Laval* was already the subject of some debate at the time (see note 28 above). In *Wieland-Werke* the GC used several ones at the same time: "*a set of reliable, substantiated, consis-*

body of evidence must be "*sufficiently cogent and consistent*".[32] The word "sufficiently" is quite important in this context since the lack of full consistency in the body of evidence is often relied upon by those challenging Commission decisions in this area. The reality is that it is not uncommon (and may even be inevitable in complex cases given the viewpoints of market participants are likely to diverge) that evidence is a bit mixed—some evidence will point in a certain direction, other evidence may go in a different direction—and may support multiple plausible narratives. Requiring a high degree of cogency would *de facto* mean requiring a high probability: if all evidence points towards a SIEC, then one can assume that a SIEC is not just more likely than not, but very probable. In cases where evidence is mixed, the Commission must then have a closer look at the evidence and weigh the probative value of those different items (see Sect. 7 below). However, the quality of evidence is also related to the weight of evidence, that will increase when further enquiries aiming at considering all relevant elements and information are made (see Sect. 9 below).

The Court of Justice also clarified in *CK Telecoms* that efficiencies cannot be assumed and the burden of proof is on the parties. Neither the Merger Regulation, nor the Implementing Regulation,[33] nor the Horizontal Merger Guidelines refer to a category of "standard" efficiencies, nor do they establish a presumption that all concentrations give rise to such efficiencies. To acknowledge that all concentrations give rise to "standard" efficiencies would amount to creating a presumption, and therefore a reversal of the burden of proof, in respect of a particular category of efficiencies, whereas that burden is borne by the undertakings.[34] In the same way as the Commission cannot just prohibit a merger relying on a prior assumption relating to some categories of mergers (Sect. 6 below), merger control does not have any prior assumption about efficiencies, which have to be demonstrated in each case. We have no space here to fully assess the consequences of these statements, but it is enough to point out that the debate about efficiencies shows the multidimensional

tent, relevant and sufficient items of evidence" (*Wieland-Werke v Commission*, note 2, para. 48). In the context of Articles 101 and 102 different adjectives are used to convey this qualitative element of the evidence: "*tangible*" and "*case-specific*" (C-333/21, *European Superleague Company*, EU:C:2023:1011, para. 130). Capacity to restrict competition must be both "*intrinsic*" (C-413/14 P, *Intel v Commission*, EU:C:2017:632, para. 140) but also contextual (the Commission must consider the "legal and economic context") (Castillo de la Torre/Gippini Fournier, note 12, para. 2.171).

[32] *Commission* v *CK Telecoms*, note 1, paras 75, 87. The fact that the case law refers to "*cogent*" and "*consistent*" evidence and to the "*great care*" the Commission must show is the result of the complexity which any prognosis implies, but such complexity works both ways, and C-413/06 P, *Bertelsmann and Sony Corporation of America* v *Impala*, EU:C:2008:392, para. 50 does not limit those qualities to decisions prohibiting a concentration.

[33] Commission Regulation (EC) No 802/2004 of 21 April 2004 implementing Regulation No 139/2004 (OJ 2004 L 133, p. 1, and corrigendum OJ 2004 L 172, p. 9), as amended by Commission Implementing Regulation (EU) No 1269/2013 of 5 December 2013 (OJ 2013 L 336, p. 1).

[34] *Commission* v *CK Telecoms*, note 1, paras 241 and 243.

nature of the weighing of the evidence and creates further ground for disagreements on the forecasts.[35]

The confidence of the decision-maker on the prospective analysis may influence also the time frame. Predictions cannot reasonably go too far into the future. There has been a debate in some recent cases about the time frame of analysis. *CK Telecoms* refers to a "*foreseeable time frame*".[36] In *EVH (I)* the GC had to examine allegations that the Commission should have examined the effects in a more distant future. The GC recalled that Commission's appraisal "*must be carried out solely on the basis of the matters of fact and law existing at the time of notification of that transaction, and not on the basis of hypothetical factors the economic implications of which cannot be assessed at the time when the decision is adopted*".[37] As a result, and this was the main operational added value of this judgment, "*the Commission is expected to carry out an assessment of the effects of the concentration over a period the maximum duration of which cannot exceed – with a sufficient degree of certainty – the time frame within which certain events may occur. The further into the future the event to be foreseen, the greater is the uncertainty as to whether it will occur. From that point of view, the Commission cannot be required to carry out a prospective analysis on the basis of elements of which it is not able to envisage, within a reasonable margin of error, the long-term effects*".[38] On the facts of the case, the GC ruled that the Commission did not have information allowing it to carry out a prospective analysis based on a period longer than the one which it chose, namely three to five years from the notification of the concentration.[39]

One must bear in mind, however, that in the context of the assessments of commitments, the case-law has sometimes referred to whether commitments will prevent a SIEC in the "*relatively near future*",[40] what may create a dissonance between different steps in the analysis, insofar as *EVH (I)* suggests that the Commission may

---

[35] Thomas is critical of this part of the judgment, as he considers that lack of offsetting efficiencies should be part of the theory of harm (S. Thomas, "Structure and Enforcement of the SIEC Test – Analyzing the CK Telecoms Judgment of the Court of Justice", ZWeR 4/2023, pp. 446, 469–470). Monti opines that the ECJ's fears "*are overstated*" (Monti, note 22, at 25). Ultimately, as Monti puts it, the two judgments show a different economic vision, that of the GC, where "*markets perform best when left to themselves*" and that of the ECJ which "*values the role of merger control and sees real risks that certain mergers may result in lasting damage to competition*" (Monti, note 22, at 22).

[36] *Commission* v *CK Telecoms*, note 1, para. 82.

[37] *EVH v Commission (I) (GC)*, note 2, paras 232–233.

[38] *EVH v Commission (I) (GC)*, note 2, para. 234. Events in the more distant future are not, by definition, less certain. For example, if it is certain that in two years certain laws will enter into force that will ensure entry of competitors, whereas the state of competition until then is less certain. It is therefore not impossible to imagine scenarios where there could more certainty about a later period than about the immediate future. The approach was endorsed on appeal (*EVH v Commission (I) (ECJ)*, note 2, paras 140–152 and in particular para. 151).

[39] *EVH v Commission (I) (GC)*, note 2, para. 235.

[40] See, *inter alia*, *thyssenkrupp v Commission (GC)*, note 2, para. 792; T-430/18, *American Airlines* v *Commission*, EU:T:2020:603, para. 118; *NetCologne v Commission*, note 2, para. 364.

go beyond the "*relatively near future*" if it is "*able to envisage, within a reasonable margin of error, the long-term effects*" of the merger. In my view, the life cycle of different sectors may be different, and it is not excluded that conditions of assessment may slightly vary, also regarding the time frame. In sectors with long cycles (e.g. between investment decisions and impact on the market) or where innovation is examined, the time frame may be longer. What is relevant is not the time as such, but whether the evidence is reliable enough to make the long-term prediction ("*within a reasonable margin of error*", as the GC now puts it). Moreover, the language in some judgments of the GC requiring that the SIEC "*is the direct and immediate effect of the concentration*" as part of the "merger specificity" may also create tensions, if is to be interpreted as capturing a time dimension (see Sect. 5 below).

Finally on this point, we must bear in mind that a prediction, however epistemically justified it may be, remains a prediction. While the EU has set up a system that is aimed at getting the best reasonable estimate about the future, evidence will be inevitably incomplete (on this see Sect. 9 below), and some future events will not be entirely predictable. The fact that, in some cases, the future does not turn out to be as predicted in the decision is certainly something from which the decision-maker should draw lessons (i.e. check if something relevant was missing from the assessment) in order to make more accurate assessments in the future. However, it is inevitable that the future will not always turn out to be as predicted, whatever the efforts put into making predictions, and "occasional mistakes" do not necessarily reveal a systemic flaw.[41]

Since the "standard of proof" is a balance of probabilities, it is inherent in the system that some mergers which are authorised will end up being harmful, since the system is not based on a "precautionary principle".[42] Unlike regulatory environments that weigh some interests (health, for example) more than others (economic benefits, for example), the EU legislature does explicitly recognise the benefits of mergers[43] and creates a symmetrical system. Moreover, whereas a system where the standard of proof is very high (typically premised on the presumption of innocence) reflects a trade-off where certain errors are less desirable than others,[44] the

[41] If one were to find that absolutely no authorised merger turned out to be harmful, my intuition would be that probably the decision-maker is systematically not applying a balance of probabilities approach, but a "lower" one.

[42] If four mergers are authorised considering a probability of only 30% that each of the mergers is harmful, it is quite possible that at least one of them will be harmful. This is not something that the system is supposed to avoid at all costs, since it is not based on a "precautionary principle". Actually, evidence of events that happened after the decision that may appear to be inconsistent with the content of the decision will be discarded in judicial review, since it cannot affect the legality of the decision (*thyssenkrupp v Commission (GC)*, note 2, para. 972; *NetCologne v Commission*, note 2, para. 157).

[43] See, e.g., recital 4 EUMR: mergers are "*to be welcomed to the extent that they are in line with the requirements of dynamic competition and capable of increasing the competitiveness of European industry, improving the conditions of growth and raising the standard of living in the Community*."

[44] Typically, in a criminal context type 1 and 2 errors are not given the same weight. The legal system gives a higher value to avoiding wrong convictions than to avoiding wrong acquittals. It is

symmetric system of EU merger review does not operate in the same way and tries to evenly distribute error costs.

5 Causation and Counterfactual ("Merger Specificity")

A SIEC must be caused by the merger: in the merger jargon, changes must be "merger specific". As the case-law has put it: "*the Commission compares the competitive conditions that would result from the notified merger with the conditions that would have prevailed without the merger*".[45] Normally, this means a comparison with the situation *ex ante*, at the time of the merger, but the Commission may take into account changes in the market that can be reasonably predicted and not caused by the merger.[46] Under certain circumstances, the Commission may ignore the situation at the time of the merger if it reflects steps already undertaken by the parties in view of the merger. If future changes in the market would have happened independently of merger, the outcome is not "merger specific".[47] And if some harmful conduct was theoretically possible even before the merger, the Commission, if it is to prohibit the merger on the basis of such event, must demonstrate why such conduct is more likely to arise following the concentration.[48]

However, things are not always black or white. Admittedly, in some cases a SIEC was simply inconceivable before because, for example, in a vertical merger, in the absence of vertical links pre-merger, any foreclosure strategy was neither possible nor profitable. In such cases the merger renders possible what was not possible, as it enables a certain course of conduct. But that is not yet enough, since the future conduct must not only be possible, but (sufficiently) probable. In other cases, the future event was possible, but the merger increases the probability: it renders probable what was simply possible.[49] Some recent judgments appear to reflect that

an open question whether this may lead, in the context of the enforcement of Arts 101 and 102 TFEU, to underenforcement. The presumption of innocence is applicable, but the "correction" to this is that the legal standard as such is not premised on certainty about effects of the conduct (Castillo de la Torre/Gippini Fournier, note 12, paras 1.067–1.070).

[45] *EVH v Commission (II)*, note 2, para. 356. On merger specificity see also *NetCologne v Commission*, note 2, paras 202–206.

[46] Guidelines on the assessment of horizontal mergers under the Council Regulation on the control of concentrations between undertakings (OJ 2004 C 31, p. 5; the "HMG"), para. 9 (likely entry or exit). This is also the case when the target is a failing firm destined to exit the market anyway.

[47] *EVH v Commission (I) (GC)*, note 2, paras 359–363 (see, on appeal, *EVH v Commission (I) (ECJ)*, note 2, paras 193–195).

[48] *EVH v Commission (II)*, note 2, paras 351–353, 375–385, a certain theory of harm was unlikely since, if such strategy was profitable, the parties would have already implemented it.

[49] There is a wealth of literature on the difference between deterministic and probabilistic conceptions of causation. See, for example, F. Schauer and B. A. Spellman, 'Probabilistic Causation in Law', (2020) 176 *Journal of International and Theoretical Economics*, 4–17. The authors explain that "*predictive conceptions of causation are typically about types and not about tokens – about*

causation is about an increase in probability,[50] where the "but for" scenario is not one where, absent the merger, there is certainty that a SIEC would not happen, but one where such SIEC would not be sufficiently likely.[51]

The GC has required in some judgments that the SIEC "*is the direct and immediate effect of the concentration*".[52] Interestingly, that language has never appeared in the case-law of the Court of Justice. The Commission drew the Court of Justice's attention to this inconsistency in the proceedings on appeal in *CK Telecoms*, and the judgment on appeal does not take over that language. In general, such language, if narrowly construed, does not appear to sit well with the case law that, in the context of the standard of proof, has clarified that the complexity of the theory of harm does not affect the standard of proof, even if such complexity may make it more difficult for such standard to be met. The Court of Justice has not ruled out that the effect of the concentration may be indirect or distant.[53] To the extent that the immediacy of effects concerns the time frame for the analysis (since otherwise it would appear not to add anything to the expression "direct"), it is not clear why such effects are only relevant if they happen in the immediate future (see Sect. 4 above).

---

classes and not about particulars – and are accordingly probabilistic rather than deterministic" (at 5). What counts is whether the conduct makes the effect more probable, not whether an observed effect is caused by the conduct. Under this approach, the counterfactual is not about whether the observable market development would happen absent the conduct, but whether absent the conduct, the market development would be less likely.

[50] *EVH v Commission (II)*, note 2, paras 352, 418.

[51] See also HMG, para. 39, which refers to a situation where "*a merger may also make coordination easier, more stable or more effective for firms, that were already coordinating before the merger*". In such case coordination becomes more probable, but such coordination was possible before. Admittedly, not any (negligible) increase is enough since the impediment to competition must be "significant".

[52] *CK Telecoms* v *Commission*, note 20, para. 114; see also more recently, in *NetCologne v Commission*, note 2, para. 194: a SIEC which would stem from future decisions by the merged entity "*may only be regarded as a direct and immediate effect of the concentration if that future conduct is made possible and economically rational by the alteration of the characteristics and the structure of the market caused by the concentration*" (*NetCologne v Commission*, note 2, paras 194 and 202). Therefore, if conduct was already possible in the past, a SIEC is not the "direct and immediate" effect of the merger (paras 200–212, and *Tele Columbus v Commission*, note 2, para. 225).

[53] If sufficiently solid evidence exists, there is no reason in principle to disregard such indirect or distant effects. Admittedly, the complexity of a theory of harm often derives from several chains of cause and effect, which implies that the Commission's case may be more difficult to prove, but this cannot be interpreted as implying that the Court of Justice has excluded that such indirect causation may be demonstrated in a given case, even if it may make it more difficult to prove the SIEC.

6 Priors and Presumptions

Any prospective analysis necessarily relies, as a starting point, on generalisations and working assumptions (priors) about the likely effect of some type of mergers.[54] These assumptions will help identify the evidence that will be necessary to refine the appropriate assessment.

Under a (Bayesian) view of "belief" decisions-makers hold beliefs with varying degree of subjective probability and update them as they encounter new evidence. The same cognitive process is at play here, but a merger cannot be prohibited before searching for additional information. While uncontroversial mergers can be authorised in phase I, even the most *prima facie* harmful of mergers requires a full enquiry to confirm that the merger is indeed harmful. This reflects the somewhat ambivalent effects a merger may have. Even in horizontal mergers, focusing only on the loss of inter-partes competition could almost systematically lead to a prohibition (at least in oligopolistic markets), if anything else (e.g. rivals' reaction or efficiencies) is ignored.

As a simple thought experiment to illustrate the process, let's assume that there is robust evidence to affirm that two out of three mergers of a certain type have led to a SIEC in the past. In the absence of specific evidence, one can then assume that there is therefore a 66% probability of a SIEC and the Commission should prohibit any merger of that type.[55] But that is not enough. The obligation (not simply the option) of the authority is to get further evidence to corroborate the probability, i.e. to check whether the merger is the one (out of three) that is not problematic. The Commission cannot just say "*since 66% of mergers of this type are problematic, I will prohibit, on balance, any merger of this type*". It must show that *the specific merger* is problematic. This is, in a way, logical: an important dimension of the evidence is its weight,[56] and relying on priors only would amount to taking decisions based on weak evidence.[57] The EU judicature's references to the "quality" of the evidence that we saw above must, in my view, be understood in this way.

---

[54] This is background information that takes often the form of "*non-case-specific beliefs about how the world works with which a fact-finder approaches the task of adjudication*" (D. Nance, *The Burdens of Proof: discriminatory power, weight of evidence, and tenacity of belief*, Cambridge University Press, 2016, 97). On evidentiary tools as being primarily based on generalisations of different type see Castillo de la Torre/Gippini Fournier, note 12, pars 2.078–2.092, and A. Kalintiri, 'Analytical Shortcuts in EU Competition Enforcement: Proxies, Premises and Presumptions', *Journal of Competition Law and Economics*, 16(3) 392–433.

[55] In that case, one could prohibit all mergers belonging to that category since in each case the probability would higher than 50%.

[56] I refer here to the Keynesian weight, see Castillo de la Torre/Gippini Fournier, note 12, para. 1.031 (with further references) and D. Nance, "Weight of Evidence" in *Philosophical Foundations of Evidence Law*, C. Dahlman, A. Stein and G. Tuzet (eds), OUP, 2021, 123–136.

[57] As Thomas points out, "*it is (still)necessary to distinguish between the measurement of the probability on the one hand, and the reliability and robustness of the body of evidence to reach a conclusion on the probability on the other*" (Thomas, note 35, 450). It is more epistemically justified to prohibit a merger on the basis of a 60% probability of it producing a SIEC, based on weightier

The case-law does acknowledge that priors matter. In *Bertelsmann and Sony* the Court of Justice considered that conglomerate mergers are normally unproblematic and mentioned the "*complexity of a theory of harm*" as relevant factor.[58] To prohibit a merger of that type, the Commission will have to "fight" against that prior, so to say. Conversely, it will be probably easier to convince the GC that a "3-to-2" merger is problematic, and the amount of additional evidence needed to confirm that view will be probably more limited. If the Commission is to authorise that merger it must also rely on particularly good evidence against the prior that type of merger has generally a greater potential to give rise to competition concerns. Yet, an investigation will have to be carried out, and the Commission cannot just rely on a prior.

Whether the evidential dynamics can be taken a step further and "structural presumptions" can be used is another matter. The use of structural presumptions in antitrust enforcement continues to animate debates, reflecting different views on their relevance, application and accuracy when assessing potential anticompetitive practices.[59] The presumption is more than just a prior in that it will more conclusively shift the evidential burden of proof to the notifying party. Absent any evidence to the contrary, the Commission can prohibit the merger. By contrast, a prior will simply represent the background knowledge against which any new and case-specific evidence will be examined, and, as such, it may not necessarily shift the evidential burden of proof, even if it may do it in some cases.[60] Some authors consider that too many mergers are authorised[61] and have been advocating for the use of "structural presumptions". These presumptions would establish, for example, that all mergers above certain thresholds should be prohibited unless the merging parties can prove that merger-specific efficiencies will be shared with consumers and yield tangible welfare gains.[62]

Beyond substantive issues, the articulation of such presumptions in today's practice, and as the law stands today (in particular, the "need for speed" inherent in the Commission's investigations), is not obvious, since if a presumption is presented only in a statement of objections deep into a Phase II investigation, and the notifying party tries to rebut a presumption, it may be too late to start obtaining evidence very

evidence, than on the basis of a 80% probability based on much lighter evidence, since in the latter scenario any additional evidence may significantly alter the probability, whereas in the former the body of evidence will be more resilient to any change in the informational base.

58 C-413/06 P, *Bertelsmann and Sony Corporation of America* v *Impala*, EU:C:2008:392, para. 51.

59 See OECD (2024), *The use of structural presumptions in antitrust*, OECD Roundtables on Competition Policy Papers, No. 317, OECD Publishing, Paris.

60 On the difference between the legal burden of proof and the evidential burden of proof, see Castillo de la Torre/Gippini Fournier, note 12, paras 1.032–1.037.

61 According to a recent meta-study of existing retrospectives of approved mergers, prices went up in 52% of the cases (A. Stöhr, "Price Effects of Horizontal Mergers: A Retrospective on Retrospectives", 2024 *Journal of Competition Law & Economics*, 20 (1–2), pp. 155–179).

62 F. Lancieri and T. Valletti, "Towards an Effective Merger Review Policy: A Defence of Rebuttable Structural Presumptions", *George J. Stigler Center for the Study of the Economy & the State Working Paper*, No. 345.

late in the process.[63] Moreover, if to avoid that problem the Commission tries to obtain evidence early on just in case the notifying party tries to rebut a presumption, the presumption may have limited impact in practice. Yet, if such presumption is embedded as a "decision rule" (as rule of evidence in the case-law's language), it may help the decision-maker to prohibit in borderline cases (and arguably even beyond), where, once the enquiry is completed, and after the notifying party has tried to discharge its own burden to provide case-specific evidence that the anticipated effects will not occur, there is some degree of indecision as whether to make the call one way or the other.[64]

In this context, I am uneasy about a recent trend to stress the importance of "case-specific" evidence. While gathering specific evidence is absolutely necessary and inherent in the obligation to carry out an "in depth" analysis for problematic mergers, it may end up leading to a sort of "base rate neglect", a well-documented cognitive bias: the risk is that when the decision-maker in a competition case examines only the situation at hand, omitting to consider prior guidance, experience, assumptions (you name it), it will take the wrong decision, as it will tend to underestimate the probability.[65] If priors correspond to most instances, the amount of specific information required to depart from that prior must correspond to a level that that would allow the decision-maker to deviate significantly from the background information. Therefore, if the information is not sufficiently conclusive to allow deviation from the generalisation, the structure of a prospective rule should rather direct the decision-maker to stick to the prior in case of "doubt" or a "close call". Such approach would have in my view a good epistemic justification.

7 Principles for Evidence Assessment and Probative Value

The criteria for assessing evidence (probative value) in merger control are the same as in any other area of EU law. The principle is one of unfettered evaluation of the evidence, that relies on epistemic reasons, not pre-determined legal rules. Yet, unfettered does not mean arbitrary and some limiting principles exist. The quality of forecasts in general depends on assessing all evidence with an open mind,[66] what is captured, in legal terms, by the reference in the case-law on merger control to a duty

[63] In practice, such rebuttal may also be provided in the notification form, once the notifying party is aware in advance that a structural presumption is applicable.

[64] This is the normal characterisation of the legal burden of proof, which directs the decision-maker when evidence is inconclusive (Castillo de la Torre/Gippini Fournier, note 12, para. 1.032).

[65] While the decision-maker must consider "all relevant circumstances", this should not be an invitation to ignore any "priors", and the "all" must very prominently include such priors or working assumptions.

[66] Engaging with opposing views, updating forecasts based on updated information, and caring about base rates, has been shown to improve the quality of forecasts, see Kahneman/Sibony/Sunstein, note 13, 262–270, with further references.

of care, and diligent and impartial examination.[67] While the judicial enforceability of such principles may be difficult in each specific case, they should prominently guide decision-making and they explain the existence of internal checks and balances.[68] Moreover, the duty to state reasons ensures that the decision is rationally justified.[69]

Despite the trend towards using more quantitative tools (some of them will be briefly referred to in the following section), it is settled case-law that there is no hierarchy between qualitative (e.g. internal documents, descriptive replies to request for information) and quantitative evidence, and the latter is not more probative than the former.[70] The GC ruled recently that, in the instant case, there was no obligation to carry out "*sophisticated market studies*",[71] and sound assumptions may be enough: "*simple economic and commercial realities*" or "*basic rational and economic considerations*".[72] Ultimately, what counts is the credibility of the piece of evidence,[73] and accordingly it is not surprising that internal documents have been consistently held to be particularly reliable.[74]

The decision-maker usually faces a body of evidence that may not be entirely consistent. Since evidence will rarely be uniform, there must be a "weighing" or

---

[67] *Commission v Tetra Laval*, note 11, para. 42; T-240/18, *Polskie Linie Lotnicze 'LOT'* v *Commission*, EU:T:2021:723, para. 87; *EVH v Commission (II)*, note 2, para. 186.

[68] One open issue which would deserve further research is how cognitive biases of individuals influence decisions of bodies or entities where a vast number of individuals intervene in shaping the decision. While one can reasonably expect that officials handling a case could be influenced by some cognitive biases, there are guardrails in the system (typically different layers of review by officials independent of the case team) that will try to critically review the evidence and infuse more objectivity into the system. At one point, the bias may not be so much cognitive, but rather institutional, as matters of policy or perception may influence the outcome. Comparable biases may apply to judges and courts when they decide.

[69] On the importance of the duty to state reasons when assessing evidence, Castillo de la Torre/Gippini Fournier, note 12, paras 1.038–044.

[70] *Wieland-Werke v Commission*, note 2, paras 227–228, 306, 346.

[71] *thyssenkrupp v Commission (GC)*, note 2, para. 283, "*no need for sophisticated market studies*".

[72] *thyssenkrupp v Commission (GC)*, note 2, 283, 296–297. Later in the judgment the GC confirmed points 32 to 35 of the HMG: when market conditions are such that competitors of the merging parties are unlikely to increase output following a price increase, the merged entity would have an incentive to raise prices. Increase in output is unlikely when competitors face binding capacity constraints (para. 614). The GC considered that these are not mere assumptions but sound economic analysis (para. 619).

[73] *Wieland-Werke v Commission*, note 2, para. 346.

[74] Also when defining markets, see *thyssenkrupp v Commission (GC)*, note 2, para. 182; *Wieland-Werke v Commission*, note 2, paras 48, 117, 162, 305, and *EVH v Commission (II)*, note 2, para. 269. In *Wieland-Werke*, the GC regarded as reliable the content of annual reports. While it acknowledged that "*any company naturally tends to present itself in the best possible light in its annual report or on its website, which are available to the public, it cannot, without risking causing harm to its credibility and image, present therein incorrect analyses concerning the decisive factors for success on that market which it has identified and which direct its business strategy, or statements of its largest customers which do not correspond to the image that they have of their business partner*" (*Wieland-Werke v Commission*, note 2, para. 179).

"prioritising" of the evidence.[75] What ultimately counts is the proper overall assessment of that evidence by the Commission, and such assessment must be autonomous.[76] The applicant in court will only succeed if the weighing of the different pieces of evidence in the file is unjustified, to the point of not being capable of supporting the Commission's case.[77] Or, as another judgment puts it, the sole fact that, in the context of a Commission decision based on a body of evidence, some indicia are prioritised and others discounted does not suffice to call into question the lawfulness of that decision, when the choices made by the Commission, in that regard, are adequately justified.[78] It is important to consider that, in merger control, an overall assessment often requires two types of weighing. One type of weighing refers to the credibility of the piece of evidence in proving the existence of the relevant point, whereas the second one is more substantive and refers to the weight the specific point is to have in the overall assessment.[79]

Part of this assessment is the "weighing of credibility" ("*relative credibility*" as the GC puts it in *Wieland-Werke*).[80] The interests of the sources of information are relevant. Accordingly, statements by merging parties are normally less credible than those of third parties; but, between third parties, customers may be more credible than competitors that may have an interest in the merger being authorised or

[75] *Wieland-Werke v Commission*, note 2, para. 47. To be clear, this is about considering some evidence more credible (or relevant to prove the point) than some other evidence. This is not about the (Keynesian) weight of the body of evidence as a whole (note 56). Even under Bayesian approaches one problem may be that there is disagreement on the direction in which a given piece of evidence points. This may imply some weighing where Bayesian methods may prove their limits (see, on this point, J. Farrell, "*Looking at More Evidence in Antitrust*", *Network Law Review*, Spring 2023 (https://www.networklawreview.org/farrell-evidence/).

[76] The GC stressed in *Wieland* that the Commission must carry out an "*autonomous assessment*". While, in that context, "*the opinion of market participants constitutes an important source of information, it cannot bind it, especially since it is generally not uniform*" (*Wieland-Werke v Commission*, note 2, para. 47, referring to further case-law). On how the views of competitors on potential competition may ultimately be outweighed by more objective indicia, including the merging parties' own internal documents and statements on investment criteria, see *Deutsche Telekom v Commission*, note 2, paras 138–154 (on potential competition) and 283–284 (weighing Vodafone's reply to the statement of objections and Tele Columbus own statements, where the Commission also relied on Tele Columbus "own figures", implicitly indicating that such figures weigh more than simply statements by same company); *Tele Columbus v Commission*, note 2, paras 146–147 and 160–164.

[77] *Wieland-Werke v Commission*, note 2, paras 165, 611–618. See also Opinion of Advocate-General Medina in C-541/23 P, *Polwax v Commission*, EU:C:2025:360, paras 31–32.

[78] *Wieland-Werke v Commission*, note 2, para. 120; T-342/07, *Ryanair* v *Commission*, EU:T:2010:280, para. 108; *EVH v Commission (II)*, note 2, para. 173; *Deutsche Telekom v Commission*, note 2, para. 58.

[79] As Farrell puts it: "*one might distinguish between disagreements on how to weigh evidence on a particular topic or aspect of the overall inquiry versus disagreements on how to weigh the dimensions of the inquiry*" (Farrell, note 75).

[80] See *Wieland-Werke v Commission*, note 2, paras 163, 325 and 651.

prohibited.[81] A statement provided to the Commission by a third-party in the context of a market test of commitments will be more reliable than a statement provided by that third-party to the parties (and later communicated to the Commission by the parties).[82] Being in a better position to make statements about competitively relevant information (immediacy or directness) is also a relevant factor.[83]

While often applicants tend to consider that the Commission has "ignored" some evidence that was favourable to their case, the GC has ruled that the mere fact that the Decision ultimately is not influenced by that evidence does not mean that the Commission has "ignored" (or disregarded) it but simply that the Commission did not consider it sufficiently convincing or relevant.[84]

What about "character evidence", in the sense of proof of past misconduct? In general, in merger control decision-makers and courts take into account past conduct to predict future conduct.[85] Proof of past unlawful conduct is normally not relevant when it is about proving a quasi-criminal case (the simple fact that someone infringed the law in the past is no evidence that it infringed the law in a later case), but it is relevant to make predictive assessments.[86]

---

[81] *Wieland-Werke v Commission*, note 2, paras 163–164 (comparing replies of industrial customers v competitors), 325, 329, 611, 651. See, in particular, para. 164: "*while the competitors could, as the case may be, benefit from [prices increases], by claiming the activities divested by the applicant in its implementation of the proposed commitments or by following the price increases orchestrated by the applicant in that segment*" (similarly, para. 329),

[82] See *thyssenkrupp v Commission (GC)*, note 2, paras 857–863.

[83] For example, the opinion of competitors about their technical capabilities to produce all types of rolled products and that of their industrial customers on the same subject constituted information that is more direct and reliable than the opinion of equipment manufacturers on the use that their customers might make of their machines. Those customers were better able to evaluate their own technical limitations (*Wieland-Werke v Commission*, note 2, para. 52).

[84] *thyssenkrupp v Commission (GC)*, note 2, paras 105, 224, 250, 255, 367, 391, 433, 490, 512, 546, 585, 590, 626, 676, 682, 717, 721; *Wieland-Werke v Commission*, note 2, paras 47, 91–92, 440, 545.

[85] See, to this end, *NetCologne v Commission*, note 2, para. 212. If the merging parties have not undertaken a given course of conduct in the past, it will be more difficult to prove that they will engage in such course of conduct if the competitive conditions do not change.

[86] Schauer, note 31, chapter 12 ("The Relevance of the Past to the Present"), making the point that prospective assessments necessarily take into account past conduct, both in everyday life and in the courtroom. The examination of whether the parties may later engage into unlawful conduct and whether the unlawfulness of such conduct may affect the probability of its occurrence was examined in *Tetra Laval* and *General Electric*, see *Commission v Tetra Laval*, note 11, paras 74–78; T-210/01, *General Electric* v *Commission*, EU:T:2005:456, para. 73. See also, more recently, on whether Articles 101 and 102 may affect whether exclusivity agreements will be concluded in the future, *Deutsche Telekom v Commission*, note 2, paras 332–334.

8 Economic Tools and Evidence

Merger investigations often use economic tools and models.[87] The SSNIP test ("small but significant and non-transitory increase in price"), critical loss analysis, and correlation analysis, may be used for market definition.[88] The level of concentration is typically examined by first having a look at the HHI index (Herfindahl-Hirschman index). Merger simulations[89] or UPP-type exercises (upward pricing measures) are also often used.[90] This list is not exhaustive and the informative value of these tools critically depends on the reliability of the inputted data. Moreover, they are to be used in combination with other types of evidence, as each one tool may not be sufficient by itself to draw solid conclusions.

Event analysis is also a preferred type of "direct" evidence when conditions for such analysis are present: actual market conduct, how variables evolve (or have evolved) in response to particular events (e.g. shock analysis),[91] or direct evaluation of competitive constraints (when one can compare outcomes in scenarios where the main difference is whether parties compete against each other or not).

Some of these techniques have been examined in the case law. It is settled case-law that there is no obligation to carry out a SSNIP test in the context of market definition.[92] The GC has upheld the Commission's use of "natural events" (in support of market definition) in *AstraZeneca*,[93] has discarded studies if their assumptions are not supported by facts of the case,[94] and has also ruled that the evidentiary value of price correlation analyses is limited when it comes to showing that different products or regions form part of the same relevant market.[95] The case-law contains some

[87] For an overview, see the ICN document, *The Role of Economics and Economic Evidence in Merger Analysis* (an update of Chapter 4 of the *Merger Investigative Techniques Handbook*), and the contribution of the EU in OECD, note 10, pp. 245–260. See also D. Gore, S. Lewis, A. Lofaro, F. Dethmers, F., *The Economic Assessment of Mergers under European Competition Law*, Cambridge University Press, 2013, pp. 43–147 (empirical techniques for market definition) and 176–250 (techniques for assessment of competitive constraints between the parties) and C. Jones and L. Weinert (eds.), *EU Competition law, Volume II - Mergers and Acquisition, Book One*, third edition (2021), Elgar Publishing, pp. 391–399.

[88] See, OECD, note 10, pp. 24–26. In EU law, see Jones and Weinert, note 87, pp. 233–252, making a difference between "indirect" and "direct" evidence of substitutability.

[89] For a comparative and somewhat critical view of merger simulations, see OECD, note 10, pp. 32–39.

[90] OECD, note 10, pp. 39–44.

[91] Shock analysis involves looking at past shocks to an industry, such as input cost shocks, new product entry and so on, and trying to understand if the response of the industry to the shock tells us anything about competitive interactions.

[92] *thyssenkrupp v Commission (GC)*, note 2, paras 74–77, and case-law referred to therein.

[93] *AstraZeneca* v *Commission*, note 15, paras 200–222.

[94] *EVH v Commission (I) (GC)*, note 2, para. 308.

[95] *thyssenkrupp v Commission (GC)*, note 2, paras 241–248.

language about the appropriateness of market surveys as an investigative tool,[96] while setting out the conditions under which they become more reliable.[97]

The quality of empirical economic analysis (and therefore, its probative value) is based on well-known criteria. Good empirical analysis used in a merger inquiry should be based on clear economic theory which implies testable propositions. The analysis should test these propositions in a transparent and, ideally, intuitive manner. The analysis should be replicable so that it can be properly tested (i.e. the analysis must be falsifiable). Assumptions must be consistent with the facts of the industry, data should be fit for purpose, and the results should be robust (sensitivity to small changes in data or changes in methodology).

In the EU, the Commission has adopted "Best Practices" on the submission of economic evidence[98] to ensure quality and transparency and avoid 'black boxes'. Interestingly, in *UPS (damages)* the GC confirmed that the Commission made certain errors in applying the Best Practices (which were given some sort of binding effect).[99] However, the GC added that the econometric model was only one of the factors taken into consideration for the purposes of assessing the proposed transaction. It also recalled the limits of quantitative analysis: "*however useful it may be in refining the understanding of the functioning of the markets affected by the proposed transaction, a quantitative analysis based on an econometric model, by its very nature, cannot generally constitute the only evidence in support of an incompatibility decision. Any model is based on simplifications of reality, as the Commission rightly points out in point 12 of the Best Practices. That limitation*

---

[96] *thyssenkrupp v Commission (GC),* note 2, para. 131.

[97] *EVH v Commission (I) (GC)*, note 2,: "*in order to determine the correct sample size for a market study, account must be taken of, first, the size of the population among which the survey is to be conducted, second, the confidence level, which is the percentage indicating the degree of certainty with which the population will choose a response between two given values, and, third, the margin of error, which is the percentage indicating the extent to which the survey results are likely to reflect the opinion of the general population*" (para. 216). In the instant case, the GC considered that the Commission could not be reasonably criticised (paras 217–218).

[98] Best practices for the submission of economic evidence and data collection in cases concerning the application of Articles 101 and 102 TFEU and in merger cases ("the Best Practices"), SEC(2011) 1216 final of 17 October 2011, accompanying the Commission notice on best practices for the conduct of proceedings concerning Articles 101 and 102 TFEU (OJ 2011 C 308, p. 6).

[99] T-834/17, *UPS* v *Commission*, EU:T:2022:84, para. 215*:"[T]he Commission did not comply with its own rules of best practice, since it relied on a non-standard method based on untested and unverified assumptions, without examining the robustness of its results and the sensitivity of the model, or revealing to the parties those choices and the reasons which might justify them. ...*". However, those errors did not constitute sufficiently serious breaches of EU law to be capable of giving rise to non-contractual liability on the part of the EU. In that regard, the GC stated that, even though the Commission used, in disregard of its own rules, an econometric model that departs significantly from standard economic practice, it enjoyed considerable discretion in defining that model (*UPS* v *Commission*, note 99, paras 211–216). The Commission did not rely exclusively on that econometric model, but also carried out a general analysis of the characteristics of the market in question, highlighting the nature and characteristics of that market and the consequences flowing from the proposed transaction.

inherent in the modelling technique means that econometric studies have probative value which cannot be equated with substantive evidence of a fact".[100]

Increasingly, the transaction terms are subject to scrutiny. If the purchase price exceeds the acquired firm's stand-alone market value this may indicate sometimes hat the acquiring firm is paying a "premium" because it expects to be able to benefit from reduced competition[101] or, in other words, the acquiring firm is imputing anti-competitive rents into the evaluation.[102]

9 Need for Speed and Completeness of the Enquiry

One important dimension that confers weight to the evidential basis for the prognosis is evidential completeness. Yet, there are important constraints on how complete the investigation can be, as there are strict time-limits to be complied with. The time factor ("need for speed", as the case-law has often put it) has an impact on depth and completeness of enquiry. In a nutshell, the soundness of the decision hinges on what evidence the Commission can realistically obtain under tight deadlines.

Case-law has positively considered time-constraints. There is no duty to systematically verify all information provided by notifying parties (or in general all information the Commission receives), as there are tight deadlines to decide and sanctions in case of incorrect and misleading information, and accordingly "*the procedure for the control of concentrations is based, of necessity and to a certain extent, on trust*".[103] There is no need to force all participants to reply to a market test (sending

[100] *UPS* v *Commission*, note 99, para. 216.

[101] 2023 US Merger Guidelines, section 4.1.

[102] Lancieri/Valletti, note 62.

[103] *EVH v Commission (II)*, note 2, paras 185–193; *Tele Columbus v Commission*, note 2, paras 144–145. Also stressing the possibility of fines for incorrect or misleading information, *thyssenkrupp v Commission (GC)*, note 2, para. 862; *Deutsche Telekom v Commission*, note 2, para. 153. The GC recalled in *EVH (II)* that there is no legal provision prohibiting the Commission from relying on information provided by the parties to the concentration themselves in the administrative procedure or, to the contrary, requiring it to conduct its own market investigation independently of the information provided by the parties to the concentration. In view of need for speed and the tight deadlines the Commission "*cannot be required, in the absence of evidence indicating that the information provided is inaccurate, to carry out checks in respect of all the information it receives*". The GC added that "*[a]lthough the diligent and impartial examination which the Commission is obliged to carry out in the context of that procedure does not permit it to base itself on facts or information which cannot be regarded as accurate, the abovementioned need for speed presupposes, however, that it cannot itself verify down to the last detail the authenticity and reliability of all the information it receives, since the procedure for the control of concentrations is based, of necessity and to a certain extent, on trust*" (para. 186, referring also to T-240/18, *Polskie Linie Lotnicze 'LOT'* v *Commission*, EU:T:2021:723, para. 87). Fines remain a serious threat, as the Commission in the past has imposed sanctions to notifying undertakings after the merger was finally approved. The Commission fined Sigma-Aldrich (€7.5 million in 2021) for hiding an innovation project during a review of its takeover of Merck, General Electric (€52 million) for negli-

reminders instead of binding requests will normally suffice).[104] It is not uncommon that the response rate to questionnaires is not particularly high, but the fact that a large part of the addressees does not respond a questionnaire does not diminish credibility of those who did reply.[105] The need for speed also justifies not providing translations of questionnaires and the generally short deadlines for replies.[106] There is no need for new investigations, if the Commission already has consistent, reliable and relevant body of evidence.[107]

In other words, the body of evidence does not need to be "*perfect*".[108] While, in general, the more information, the more accurate the estimate will be, if additional information will not significantly alter the estimate, the Commission is not required to seek it out proactively.[109] Having too much evidence may even unnecessarily expand opportunities for confusion or error.[110] The need for speed will also influence the conclusiveness of the assessment: the analysis may not take a final position on some matters when the outcome of the merger review will not be impacted by the position the Commission might have adopted on those matters.[111]

---

gently providing incorrect information during its takeover of LM Wind in 2019, and Facebook (€110 million) for providing misleading information during the review of its purchase of WhatsApp.

[104] *thyssenkrupp v Commission (GC)*, note 2, para. 955, and *thyssenkrupp v Commission (ECJ)*, note 2, para. 380.

[105] *Wieland-Werke v Commission*, note 2, para. 162.

[106] *EVH v Commission (II)*, note 2, paras 222–224.

[107] *Wieland-Werke v Commission*, note 2, para. 119. Some 20 years ago the GC examined in *General Electric* the necessary trade-offs between the timetable laid down by the EUMR and adverse effects on the conditions under which all the parties to the proceedings must work. It held that the gain in terms of the speed of the proceedings as a whole was regarded by the legislature as justifying those sacrifices, particularly in order to take account of the commercial interest of the merging parties in completing their proposed merger as quickly as possible. In those circumstances, the parties to a notified transaction may invoke the shortness of the periods allowed to them in the context of those proceedings only inasmuch as those periods are disproportionate to the duration of the proceedings as a whole (T-210/01, *General Electric* v *Commission*, EU:T:2005:456, paras 701–703).

[108] *Wieland-Werke v Commission*, note 2, para. 143. In that case the "*best guesses*" of the undertaking directly concerned constituted "*the most reliable evidence*" that the Commission "*could actually obtain*" on the relevant point.

[109] On optimal decision-making (and possible stopping rules), I. Horowitz, "A Bayesian View of Post-Acquisition Evidence and Antitrust" (1977) 22 *Antitrust Bull* 757; F. Becker and S. Salop, "Decision Theory and Antitrust Rules", (1999) *Antitrust Law Journal* 67(1), 41–76; A. I. Gavil and S. Salop, "Probability, Presumptions and Evidentiary Burdens in Antitrust Analysis: Revitalizing the Rule of Reason for Exclusionary Conduct", (2020)168 *U. Pa. L. Rev.* 2107.

[110] Farrell, note 75. This is in particular the case where there is disagreement about the weighing of the evidence: "*that kind of disagreement on relative magnitudes of opposite-sign evidence opens the door for directional disagreements about the likelihood ratio to be assigned to a given "body" (multiple "pieces") of evidence.*"

[111] The Commission may leave open certain findings, such as market definition, if the outcome does not change depending on alternatives: *EVH v Commission (II)*, note 2, paras 323–324 (on geographic market definition); T-58/20, *NetCologne v Commission*, EU:T:2024:813, paras 282–283 (on product market definition); *EVH v Commission (I) (GC)*, note 2, paras 294–295 (whether the

10 Conclusion

I have briefly explored some issues of principle regarding the evidentiary process when carrying out prospective assessments in the context of merger control, in the light of the most recent case-law. Inferences based on evidence gathered during the investigation are typically used in order to confer sound epistemic grounds to the final decision. The legal obligation to carry out an in-depth review in all cases of possible prohibition pursues the objective of ensuring the soundness of that assessment. In turn, the EU judicature will check whether the decision contains a reasonable estimate (i.e. epistemically justified, but not necessarily the only conceivable one considering the evidence), based on the best available evidence that could be actually obtained within tight deadlines. It is not about having the "perfect" evidence or estimate, but one that is "good enough", depending on the circumstances, to make a call.

undertaking is dominant or not). The Commission must provide reasons as to why the assessment is not affected (T-58/20, *NetCologne v Commission*, EU:T:2024:813, para. 282).

Closing the Gap? The Commission's Powers of Inspection After *Deutsche Bahn*

Gwenaël Muguet-Poullennec and Benjamin Cheynel

He would certainly deny it,[1] but, for those who were able to observe him in hearings, read his opinions or appreciate him during his 18 years spent at the General Court ('GC') and the Court of Justice ('CJ'), the recipient of this *Liber Amicorum* often brought to mind the titular and formidable figure of action films: the One-Man Army.[2]

In order to illustrate such feats of strength, the temptation is great to return to cases like *Cartes Bancaires*, *Intel* or *Illumina*,[3] in which he played an instrumental part as Advocate General or Reporting Judge. However, rather than evoking well-known blockbusters, appreciated by the public and critics alike, we decided to focus instead on the slightly more confidential, but no less daring, *Deutsche Bahn*,[4] where a simple "I do not believe it"[5] was enough to announce the end of the judgement under appeal. In our view, this case remains a good example of how the Commission's

[1] He did deny it. In his farewell speech, given at the CJ, Judge Nils Wahl argued emphatically and convincingly for the triumph of the collective wisdom over the individual vision and emphasized the fact that "being a judge is not a solitary exercise".

[2] According to the Wiktionary, a One-Man Army is "a single person who performs a task typically performed by a group". Interestingly, Wikipedia also refers to One Man Army and the Undead Quartet, a Swedish band that played a fusion of melodic death metal and thrash metal.

[3] Judgments in *CB v Commission*, C-67/13 P, EU:C:2014:2204 (*Cartes Bancaires*), in *Intel v Commission*, C-413/14 P, EU:C:2017:632 (*Intel*) and in *Illumina and Grail v Commission*, C-611/22 P and C-625/22 P, EU:C:2024:677 (*Illumina*). Advocate General Wahl's Opinions in *Cartes Bancaires* (EU:C:2014:1958) and in *Intel* (EU:C:2016:788). He was also (Judge) Rapporteur in *Illumina*. As an internal equivalent to the Internet Movie Database (IMDb), which provides information about films, as well as their cast and crew, "EURêka", one of the databases run by the Research and Documentation Directorate of the CJ, mentions 20 "doctrines notes" for *Cartes Bancaires*, 30 for *Intel*, and already 6 for *Illumina*.

[4] Judgment in *Deutsche Bahn and Others v Commission*, C-583/13 P, EU:C:2015:404 (*Deutsche Bahn*) with the Opinion of Advocated General Wahl (EU:C:2015:92). Eureka mentions 12 "doctrine notes" on this case. As regards the Opinion in Deutsche Bahn, see also Chapter 16 of the present volume.

[5] Opinion in *Deutsche Bahn*, para 59.

G. Muguet-Poullennec (✉) · B. Cheynel
Court of Justice of the European Union, Luxembourg, Luxembourg
e-mail: Gwenael.Muguet-Poullennec@curia.europa.eu; Benjamin.Cheynel@curia.europa.eu

L. Prete, L. Rezki (eds.), *Judging & (Re)Thinking European Union Law*,
https://doi.org/10.1007/978-3-032-13473-8_4

power to inspect business premises is limited by fundamental rights like the right to privacy or the right to an effective judicial remedy.

In *Deutsche Bahn*, the CJ held that the presence of post-inspection judicial review, capable of offsetting the lack of prior judicial authorization, constitutes a fundamental guarantee in order to ensure the compatibility of an inspection measure with the right to privacy.[6] As observed by the Advocate General in his Opinion in this case, effective ex post judicial review dealing with all issues of law and fact provides an adequate level of protection.[7] In this context, we will begin this contribution by recalling, in a sort of retrospective coupled with flashbacks, the former and current case law on inspection decisions. We will also plead for the judicial or legislative recognition of a direct and timely action making it possible to challenge promptly and effectively not only an inspection decision but also the conduct or results of an inspection when it goes beyond its scope. In such a way, it would be possible to "close the gap" that still exists between EU competition law, as applied on the *Kirchberg Plateau*, and the importance given to effective judicial protection by the Strasbourg Court or certain Member States aiming for the best possible balance between competing interests.

1 Retrospective

Effective law enforcement versus right to privacy. In his Opinion in *Deutsche Bahn*, the Advocate General only needed a few paragraphs to explain what is at stake when an enforcement authority like the Commission decides on its own to order an inspection.[8] On the one hand, he emphasized that legal protection against unjustified searches of private homes by enforcement authorities constitutes one of the principles marking the divide between societies based on the rule of law and other, more repressive, forms of government. On the other hand, he recalled that, even communities ruled by law, such as the EU, recognize that public authorities need effective investigative powers in order to pursue suspected infringements.

[6] *Deutsche Bahn*, para 32. Both Article 7 of the Charter of Fundamental Rights of the European Union ('Charter') and Article 8 of the Convention for the Protection of Human Rights and Fundamental Freedoms, signed in Rome on 4 November 1950 ('ECHR') protect the right to the inviolability of private premises, also known as the right to privacy because it also includes correspondence.

[7] Opinion in *Deutsche Bahn*, paras 38 to 40.

[8] Opinion in *Deutsche Bahn*, paras 1 to 4. See also, paras 61 and 62, which refer to the wide investigative powers of the Commission under Regulation 1/2003, exercised on the basis of no (or little) ex ante judicial control, the fact that an inspection decision is decided in practice by DG Competition alone and the serious implications of a competition infringement for the undertakings concerned. This led the Advocate General to observe in para 63 that, "because those powers are so extensive, the discretion so ample and the decision-making subject to so few (judicial and administrative) prior controls, it is for the EU Courts to ensure that the rights of the undertakings involved in an investigation are fully respected.

Legislation therefore needed to strike a balance between the right to privacy, and in particular its implied right to be protected against unjustified searches, and the need for effective law enforcement. Initially, the need for effective law enforcement took precedence over the right to privacy. It was only little by little that case law defined and enforced the limits of public intrusion into business premises, first in words, then in actions.

The end tends to justify the means. In order to detect agreements, decisions or concerted practices prohibited by Article 101 TFUE or abuses of a dominant position prohibited by Article 102 TFUE, the Commission has the essential power to conduct inspections of business premises.[9] Article 20 of Regulation 1/2003 currently defines this power,[10] initially conferred by the Council on the Commission as early as 1962 in Article 14 of Regulation 17.[11]

Thus, the Commission may legally conduct all necessary inspections of undertakings and associations of undertaking in order to carry out its duties regarding EU competition law infringements. Among the different investigative tools listed in Chapter V of Regulation 1/2003, such as sector inquiries, requests for information and agreed-upon interviews, the inspection of business premises is certainly the most intrusive and, after the request for information, the one most commonly used. When the Commission considers it can count on the cooperation of the inspected undertaking, it can conduct an inspection upon production of a written authorization.[12] In most cases, however, the Commission will use a stricter procedure and order by decision the undertaking to submit to an inspection.[13]

In practice, an inspection generally takes place at the early stage of an investigation. Its goal is to substantiate the suspicions or information gathered by or communicated to the Commission. This is particularly important, as an inspection always require a specific subject matter. The Commission would not order an inspection if it was not searching for something in particular. In an inspection,

[9] Article 21 of Regulation 1/2003 also allows for the inspection of other than business premises "if a reasonable suspicion exists that books or other records related to the business and to the subject-matter of the inspection, which may be relevant to prove a serious violation of Article 101 TFUE or Article 102 TFUE, are being kept".

[10] On the Commission's powers of inspection, see Commentary of Article 20, by A. De Moncuit, M. Jaspers & C. Moriarty, in K. Dekeyser, C. Gauer, J. Laitenberger, N. Wahl, W. Wils & L. Prete (eds), *Regulation 1/2003 and EU Antitrust Enforcement, A Systematic Guide*, Wolters Kluwer, 2023.

[11] EEC Council: Regulation No 17: First Regulation implementing Articles 85 and 86 of the Treaty. OJ 13, 21.2.1962, pp. 204–211. English special edition: Series I Vol. 1959-1962 p. 87.

[12] See, Article 20(3) of Regulation 1/2003.

[13] See, Article 20(4) of Regulation 1/2003: "Undertakings and associations of undertakings are required to submit to inspections ordered by decision of the Commission. The decision shall specify the subject matter and purpose of the inspection, appoint the date on which it is to begin and indicate the penalties provided for in Articles 23 and 24 and the right to have the decision reviewed by the Court of Justice. The Commission shall take such decisions after consulting the competition authority of the Member State in whose territory the inspection is to be conducted" ("inspection decisions", also known as dawn raid inspections). Our contribution will only focus on this type of decisions.

officials and other authorized accompanying persons are empowered to enter any business premises to do the following.[14] First, they can examine any book or other record related to the business, irrespective of the medium on which they are stored, and take or obtain in any form copies of or extracts from such books or records (the "search and seizure power"). Second, they can seal any business premises and books or records for the period and to the extent necessary for the inspection (the "power to seal premises or records"). Third, they may ask any representative or member of staff for explanations on facts or documents relating to the subject matter and purpose of the inspection and record the answers (the "power to record interview"). Inspected undertakings risk significant penalties if they obstruct or fail to comply with an inspection decision[15] and, if the Commission finds that an undertaking opposes this decision, it may require and count on the necessary assistance of the police or an equivalent enforcement authority.[16]

Progressive definition of limits. Broadly speaking, when adopting Regulation 1/2003 the Council took care to emphasize that this law respects the fundamental rights and observes the principles recognized in particular by the Charter.[17] However, questions and doubts about the compatibility of the EU legal framework on inspections with fundamental rights remained, as it was not then clear if undertakings benefited from the protection conferred on individuals by the right to privacy.[18]

On the one hand, in *Hoechst* and *Dow Benelux*, which preceded the adoption of Regulation 1/2003,[19] the CJ specifically refused to acknowledge that the right to privacy covered not only the private dwellings of individuals but also the professional premises of legal entities. In particular, the CJ held that the protective scope of Article 8 of the ECHR, according to which "Everyone has the right to respect for his private and family life, his home and his correspondence", was concerned with "the development of man's personal freedom and may not therefore be extended to

---

[14] See, Article 20(2) of Regulation 1/2003, which extended the original inspection powers provided initially to the Commission by Article 14 of Regulation 17 in relation to business premises. The changes included the ability to seal business records as well as the codification of the power to request explanations of any staff- member of the undertaking and to record the answers.

[15] Article 23(1)c), of Regulation 1/2003 allows the Commission to impose a fine not exceeding 1% of the total turnover in the preceding business year on an undertaking which, intentionally or negligently, produces books or other records in incomplete form or refuses to submit to an inspection decision. Article 24 also provides for periodic penalty payments in order to compel an undertaking to submit to an inspection decision.

[16] See, Article 20(6) of Regulation 1/2003.

[17] Recital 37 of Regulation 1/2003.

[18] See, for instance, P. Berghe, A. Dawes, "Little Pig, Little Pig, Let Me Come In", in Evaluation of the European Commission's Powers of Inspection in Competition Cases, (2009) ECLR 407; D. Théophile, I. Simic, Legal Challenges to Dawn Raid Inspections under the Principles of EU, French and ECHR Law, (2012) JECLAP 512; or, more recently, N. Jalabert-Doury, "Peut-on concevoir qu'en 2002, les entreprises n'aient toujours pas de recours effectif contre le déroulement des inspections de la Commission?", in *Laurence Idot, Concurrence et Europe, Liber Amicorum*, vol. 1, Concurrences (2022).

[19] Judgments in *Hoechst v Commission*, 46/87 and 227/88, EU:C:1989:337 (*Hoechst*) and in *Dow Benelux v Commission*, 85/87, EU:C:1989:379 (*Dow Benelux*).

business premises".[20] Such a solution may be surprising as the Advocate General proposed for his part, as the Commission did in its pleadings, "that it should be expressly accepted that there is at Community level a fundamental right to the inviolability of business premises".[21] Adopted when Europe was beginning its reunification around the values shared by a community ruled by law, these judgments could be compared on this point to offbeat silent and monochrome films, outdated by contemporary developments.

On the other hand, according to the same case law and because the legislative framework provided sufficient protection against "arbitrary or disproportionate intervention" by the Commission, the CJ also held that the power to inspect business premises of undertakings reasonably suspected of having infringed competition rules did not infringe other fundamental rights.[22] Indeed, since *National Panasonic* in 1980 and later *Hoechst* and *Dow Benelux* in 1989, the CJ has stated a series of principles that remain to these days useful for assessing inspection decisions.[23] In these cases, the CJ indicated that several conditions for the exercise of the search and seizure power granted to the Commission guarantee the rights of the suspected undertaking. First, the CJ stated that the suspected undertaking, which may appeal the inspection decision, has also a right to legal representation during the inspection and can claim the benefit of the privileged nature of correspondence between lawyer and client.[24] Second, the CJ also emphasized the fact that EU competition law requires the Commission to specify the subject matter and purpose of its investigation. For the CJ, that requirement to state the reasons upon which an inspection decision is based is fundamental, not merely in order to show that the investigation is justified, but also to enable the suspected undertaking to assess the scope of its duty to cooperate while at the same time safeguarding its rights of defense.[25] Third, the CJ emphasized the fact that, in order to carry out an investigation when it cannot count on the cooperation of the suspected undertaking, the Commission must adopt an inspection decision and may even, as a precautionary measure, request the necessary assistance of the police or of an equivalent enforcement authority. Therefore, in a situation where the suspected undertaking refused to cooperate, either voluntarily or by virtue of an obligation arising under an inspec-

---

[20] *Hoechst*, paras 17 and 18, *Dow Benelux*, paras 28 and 30.

[21] Opinion of Advocate General Mischo in *Hoechst* (EU:C:1989:73), paras 103 and 104.

[22] The rights mentioned in this case law were the protection against arbitrary or disproportionate intervention and the rights of defense. For the first one, see *Hoechst*, para 19, with a reference to judgment in *Acciaierie San Michele and Others v High Authority*, 5/62 to 11/62 and 13/62 to 15/62, EU:C:1962:46. For the second one, see *Hoechst*, para 14, with a reference to judgment in *Nederlandsche Banden-Industrie-Michelin v Commission*, 322/81, EU:C:1983:313, para 7.

[23] Judgment in *National Panasonic v Commission*, 136/79, EU:C:1980:169 (*National Panasonic*).

[24] *Hoechst*, para 16, with a reference to judgment in *AM & S Europe v Commission*, 155/79, EU:C:1982:157. An inspected undertaking has a limited right to the confidentiality of communications with its legal advisers, on condition that they are independent and authorized to practice in one of the Member States and that the communications in issue concern the exercise of the undertaking's rights of defense.

[25] *Hoechst*, para 29.

tion decision, the Commission has to respect the relevant procedural guarantees laid down by national law to obtain this assistance.[26] In this regard, should the applicable national rules require authorization from a judicial authority in order to use coercive measures during an inspection, the competent national court is entitled to carry out a review of the "authenticity" of the Commission's decision and to decide whether the coercive measures envisaged are neither arbitrary nor disproportionate.[27] Nonetheless, in such review, the national court cannot question the "necessity" of the measure or ask for access to the file, although it can seek "further explanations" from the Commission, especially as regards the "reasonable suspicion" prompting the inspection.[28]

Remaining challenges. This case law gave rise to some criticism on two main aspects. In the first place, in comparison with the provisions applicable in certain Member States, like France or Germany,[29] the Commission's power to decide and carry out inspections without having to request prior judicial authorization may seem excessive or not sufficiently justified against the highest standards expected from a community ruled by law. In the second place, in view of the case law of the Strasbourg Court on the implementation of fundamental rights enshrined in the ECHR ('ECtHR'), it is possible to ask whether the position adopted by the CJ in *Hoechst* and *Dow Benelux* remains tenable.

2 Flashbacks

Since Judge Nils Wahl's arrival at the Court of Justice of the European Union ("CJEU" or "EU Courts") in 2006, inspection litigation has developed in three main directions representative of a kind of "nouvelle vague" more in tune with the times. First, the GC has introduced an in-depth ex post judicial review of the inspection decision, verifying the existence and reality of the suspicions mentioned therein.[30] Second, following this development, *Deutsche Bahn* clarified the conditions under which it was possible to guarantee effective judicial protection for legal entities whose business premises are searched in the absence of prior review of the inspection decision. Third, the GC also addressed the conditions applicable to an action

[26] *Hoechst*, paras 30 to 35.

[27] Judgment in *Roquette Frères*, C-94/00, EU:C:2002:603 (*Roquette*), para 52. See, also, Article 20(8) of Regulation 1/2003.

[28] *Roquette*, paras 61 and 62, and Article 20(8) of Regulation 1/2003.

[29] For a description of the French or German law on inspections at that time, see Opinion in *Hoechst*, paras 56 to 60, 69 and 70.

[30] Judgment in *Nexans France and Nexans v Commission*, T-135/09, EU:T:2012:596, affirmed by judgment in *Nexans and Nexans France v Commission*, C-37/13 P, EU:C:2014:2030 (*Nexans*).

for annulment, when what is at stake is not the inspection decision as such, but an act adopted during the inspection itself.[31]

Nexans: On 28 January 2009, the Commission notified to Nexans, one of the main European electric cable manufacturers, a decision by which Nexans had to submit immediately to an inspection of its business premises.

In the inspection decision, the Commission stated that it had received information that electric cable suppliers, including Nexans, were participating or had participated in agreements and/or concerted practices in relation to "the supply of electric cables and material associated with such supply, including, amongst others, high voltage underwater electric cables, and, in certain cases, high voltage underground electric cables". This decision also provided further indications on the suspected infringements. According to the information received by the Commission, they involved "the offering of concerted bids in public tenders, client attribution, as well as the illegal exchange of information relating to the supply of those products", since 2001 at the latest and probably with a global reach.

In its appeal before the GC, Nexans requested in particular the annulment of the inspection decision because its scope was overly broad and vague. The examination of this claim by the GC remains illustrative to this day of the intensity of the judicial review carried out by the judge on the object and purpose of a decision ordering an inspection.

- **the Commission has to state its suspicions in the inspection decision:** In *Nexans*, the GC recalled first that, according to the above-mentioned case law, the obligation on the Commission to specify the subject matter and purpose of the inspection, expressly provided for by Article 20(4) of Regulation No 1/2003, is a "fundamental requirement". Indeed, this provision allows the undertaking, which is required to submit to an inspection, to understand why the investigation of its business premises is justified. This in turn will allow the suspected undertaking both to assess the scope of its duty to cooperate and to safeguard its rights of the defense.[32] In this regard, the GC held also that, although the Commission is not required to communicate to the recipient of an inspection decision all the information at its disposal concerning the suspected infringements, or to make a precise legal analysis of those infringements, it must nonetheless clearly indicate the suspected facts which it intends to investigate.[33]
- **the GC must satisfy itself that there are reasonable grounds for the suspicions:** In this context, the GC held that its power to review a decision ordering an inspection allowed it to ensure that it was not arbitrary and thus relied on facts

[31] Judgment in *Akzo Nobel Chemicals and Akcros Chemicals v Commission*, T-125/03 and T-253/03, EU:T:2007:287, affirmed by judgment in *Akzo Nobel Chemicals and Akcros Chemicals v Commission and Others*, C-550/07 P, EU:C:2010:512 (*Akzo*).

[32] *Nexans*, GC, para 39.

[33] *Nexans*, GC, para 42. In this paragraph, the GC used the terms "presumed infringement" or "presumed facts". However, as in EU competition law cases involving sanctions it seems more appropriate to presume the innocence of the suspected undertaking until proven guilty, we will use the terms "suspected infringement" or "suspected facts" (see, for instance, *Nexans*, CJ, para 18).

capable of justifying an inspection. The GC further emphasized in this regard that the objective of an inspection is to enable the Commission to gather the necessary documentary evidence to check the actual existence and scope of a given factual and legal situation concerning which it already possesses certain information. Therefore, in the course of its judicial review, the GC must satisfy itself that there exist "reasonable grounds"[34] for suspecting an infringement of the competition rules by the undertaking concerned.[35] At this stage, the GC sought to reconcile the different trends illustrated by previous case law to emphasize the need for the Commission to set out in the inspection decision, at a minimum, the essential characteristics of the alleged infringement. For instance, although the Commission is not required to delimit precisely the market covered by its investigation at the inspection stage, it must nevertheless identify the sectors covered by the alleged infringement with which the investigation is concerned with a sufficient degree of precision.[36]

– **in its review, the GC may examine the elements available to the Commission:** *Nexans* demonstrates the concrete nature of the judicial review carried out by the GC on the existence of reasonable grounds capable of establishing the suspicions mentioned in the decision to justify the inspection of business premises. Indeed, in order to fulfill its role, the GC requested from the Commission the communication of the various pieces of evidence at its disposal, which enabled it to establish these suspicions and to decide to conduct an inspection of business premises. Such review, which usually requires the use of measures of organization of procedure, is frequent in practice and we are convinced it has become the norm.[37] In this case, following the examination of the various elements submitted by the Commission, the GC decided to annul partially the inspection decision. Indeed, as the Commission had no reasonable grounds in its file concerning "electrical cables other than high voltage underwater and underground cables and the material associated with those cables" mentioned in the inspection decision, it should

[34] According to the French version of *Nexans*, the authentic version in this case, this notion of "reasonable grounds" refers to "indices suffisamment sérieux" which translates word for word to "sufficiently serious evidence".

[35] *Nexans*, GC, para 43.

[36] *Nexans*, GC, para 45.

[37] On the basis of the doubts raised by the applicants as to the scope of their inspection decision, a judicial review of the elements available to the Commission took place in *Nexans* (T-135/09), *České dráhy* (T 325/16) and in the associated cases, *Casino, Guichard-Perrachon* (T 249/17), *Les Mousquetaires* (T-255/17) and *Intermarché Casino Achats* (T-254/17). In the past, the GC concluded that an inspection decision was not arbitrary on the sole basis of the reasons set out in this decision, without it being necessary to examine the indicia in the Commission's possession when it was adopted (see Judgment in *Orange v Commission*, T-402/13, EU:T:2014:991, paras 89 to 93). In our view, such a solution would now fall short of what is expected of the GC, particularly since *Deutsche Bahn* emphasized that it is the presence of a post-inspection judicial review that makes it possible to compensate for the absence of prior judicial review and to ensure compatibility of the inspection decision with fundamental rights.

not be allowed to conduct an inspection to gather evidence involving these products.[38]

Deutsche Bahn: In 2011 the Commission adopted three decisions, each ordering an inspection of the premises of Deutsche Bahn and several of its subsidiaries, including DB Energie and Deutsche Umschlagegesellschaft Schiene-Straße ("DUSS"), active mainly in the German and European rail transport sector.

In the first inspection decision, notified on 29 March 2011, the Commission stated that it had received information on the potentially unjustified preferential treatment accorded by DB Energie to other Deutsche Bahn subsidiaries in the form of a rebate system for the supply of electric traction energy ("the first suspected infringement"). In the course of this inspection, the Commission's officials found documents relating to DUSS, which the Commission considered might indicate the existence of further anti-competitive conduct ("the DUSS documents"). Based on suspicions arising from the DUSS documents, the Commission adopted another inspection decision, notified on 31 March 2011, while the first inspection was still in progress. The second inspection decision concerned suspected competition infringements by DUSS, through the strategic use of infrastructure managed by Deutsche Bahn ("the second suspected infringement"). Subsequently, the Commission adopted an additional inspection decision, notified on 26 July 2011, in relation to the second suspected infringement.

Deutsche Bahn and its subsidiaries brought actions against the Commission before the GC for annulment of the three inspection decisions because they infringed, among other rights or principles, their rights to privacy or to effective judicial protection or their rights of defense. The GC dismissed those actions in their entirety[39] and the unsuccessful applicants then lodged an appeal before the CJ.[40] The answers provided in *Deutsche Bahn* and its related Opinion will help to clarify one of the most debated question about the compatibility of the EU legal framework on inspections with fundamental rights, that of the absence of prior judicial authorization when the Commission orders an undertaking to submit to an inspection. *Deutsche Bahn* will also provide useful guidance on the limits that bind the Commission during an inspection.

- **post–inspection judicial review offsets the lack of prior judicial authorization:** Before the CJ, the appellants claimed that, according to the right of privacy provided for in Article 7 of the Charter and Article 8 of the ECHR, an inspection of its business premises required prior judicial authorization and could not solely

[38] *Nexans*, GC, paras 62 to 94.

[39] Judgment in *Deutsche Bahn and Others v Commission*, T-289/11, T-290/11 and T-521/11, EU:T:2013:404.

[40] At this stage, an appeal against a judgment of the GC brought before the CJ (*pourvoi*) is limited to points of law. If the appeal is admissible and well founded, the CJ sets aside the judgment of the GC under appeal. Where the state of the proceedings so permits, the CJ may itself give judgment in the case. Otherwise, it refers the case back to the GC, which is bound by the decision given by the CJ on the appeal.

by decided by the Commission. In its answer, the CJ recalled first that the fundamental right to the inviolability of "the home" is a general principle of EU law, now expressed in Article 7 of the Charter, which corresponds to Article 8 of the ECHR.[41]

Referring to the case law of the ECtHR, the CJ noted that if this protection may extend to certain commercial premises, an interference by a public authority could go further for professional or commercial premises or activities than in other cases.[42] More specifically, the CJ held that the case law of the ECtHR mentioned by the appellants was not as conclusive as alleged because either it concerned another provision than Article 8, such as Article 6, or took into consideration other important factors. Indeed, as the GC pointed out in the judgment under appeal, the lack of prior judicial authorization is only one factor among others for the ECtHR in its assessment under Article 8 of the ECHR and a post-inspection review covering both questions of fact and questions of law may counterbalance its absence.[43]

Within the EU legal framework, the CJ therefore stated that the GC was right when it held that several safeguards protect against arbitrary interference by the Commission when it adopts an inspection decision.[44] In this respect, as it is the case for the ECtHR, the CJ considered that the presence of a post-inspection judicial review, capable of offsetting the lack of prior judicial authorization, provides an adequate level of protection to ensure the compatibility of an inspection decision with the fundamental right of privacy.[45] Indeed, the review done by the EU Courts allows for an in-depth review of the law and of the facts, based on the evidence adduced before them. Moreover, if the GC or the CJ annuls an inspection decision, the Commission may not use any documents or other evidence obtained in the course of that investigation, and if it does, the decision on that infringement might, in so far at it is based on such evidence, be annulled by the EU Courts.[46] The CJ used

[41] *Deutsche Bahn*, para 19.

[42] *Deutsche Bahn*, para 20, with references to judgments of the ECtHR, *Niemietz v. Germany* (CE:ECHR:1992:1216JUD001371088), and *Bernh Larsen Holding AS and Others v. Norway* (CE:ECHR:2013:0314JUD002411708).

[43] *Deutsche Bahn*, paras 21 to 26, with references to judgments of the ECtHR, *Société Colas Est and Others v. France* (CE:ECHR:2002:0416JUD003797197), *Société Métallurgique Liotard Frères v. France* (CE:ECHR:2011:0505JUD002959808), *Société Canal Plus and Others v. France* (CE:ECHR:2010:1221JUD002940808), *Harju v. Finland* (CE:ECHR:2011:0215JUD005671609) and *Heino v. Finland* (CE:ECHR:2011:0215JUD005672009). See also, Opinion in *Deutsche Bahn*, paras 29 to 39.

[44] *Deutsche Bahn*, para 28. The five safeguards mentioned by the GC in its judgement were: (i) the statement of reasons on which an inspection decision is based; (ii) the limits imposed on the Commission during the conduct of inspection, such as legal professional privilege or legal assistance; (iii) the impossibility for the Commission to carry out an inspection by force; (iv) the intervention of national authorities; and (v) the existence of a post-inspection judicial review.

[45] *Deutsche Bahn*, para 32, with a reference to judgment of the ECtHR, *Delta Pekárny a.s. v. the Czech Republic* (CE:ECHR:2014:1002JUD000009711). See also, Opinion in *Deutsche Bahn*, para 40.

[46] *Deutsche Bahn*, para 34, and Opinion in *Deutsche Bahn*, para 40.

the same reasoning to reject the second ground of appeal alleging the violation of the appellants' right to effective judicial protection, as provided for in Article 47 of the Charter or Article 6(1) of the ECHR. In the present case, by contrast with the situations judged in the ECtHR cases cited by the appellants, it was possible to challenge the inspection decisions immediately, without having to wait for the final decision on the suspected infringements, and the actions for annulment could call into question both points of facts and points of law.[47]

– **on documents "found by chance":** The appellants were more successful with another claim, in which they alleged that the DUSS documents were not "found by chance", as the GC stated in the judgement under appeal. Rather, they considered that the search and seizure of this set of documents were the result of a "fishing expedition", in which the Commission used an inspection decision to enter the business premises in order to find documents unrelated to the suspected infringement mentioned in this decision. For them, it was important to note in this regard that the Commission acknowledged that it specifically briefed its officials, immediately before the first inspection, on the existence of a third party complaint against DUSS. In this context, the applicants claimed that the irregular seizure of the DUSS documents infringed their rights of defense. The CJ agreed.

In terms of principles, the CJ held, as it had previously, that the fundamental requirement provided for in Article 20(4) of Regulation No 1/2003 that an inspection decision states its subject matter is necessary to show to the inspected undertakings that the inspection is justified and to enable them to safeguard their rights of defense.[48] This requirement guarantees that, as stated now in Article 28(1) of Regulation No 1/2003, information collected during an inspection shall be used only for the purposes for which it was acquired. Therefore, the reasons stated in the inspection decision circumscribe the powers conferred on the Commission's officials and a search and seizure may only concern documents coming within the scope of the subject matter of the inspection. The Commission would seriously endanger the rights of defense if it could rely on information unrelated to this scope.[49] However, the CJ also recalled that, as was clarified in *Dow Benelux*, there is one exceptional possibility to seize and use information falling outside the scope of the inspection decision. This exception covers the situation where the relevant information is "found by chance" during an inspection, which means that this information was not specifically searched for but was obtained incidentally during the search covered by the inspection decision. In such situation, a new investigation could start based on this information even if it was unrelated to the scope of the first suspected infringement. For the CJ, to bar the Commission from doing so would constitute an unjustified hindrance to the Commission in the accomplishment of its task of ensuring compliance with EU competition law and identifying

[47] *Deutsche Bahn*, paras 41 to 49, and Opinion in *Deutsche Bahn*, paras 45 to 52.

[48] *Deutsche Bahn*, para 56, with references to *Roquette*, para 45, and *Nexans*, para 34.

[49] *Deutsche Bahn*, paras 57, 58 and 60, with a reference to *Dow Benelux*, paras 17 and 18.

infringements of Articles 101 TFEU and 102 TFEU.[50] In the event of a legal dispute on this, it will nevertheless be for the Commission to demonstrate to the EU Courts that it satisfied the conditions for the application of this exception.[51]

Contrary to what the GC had judged, the CJ found that the information given to the Commission's officials, prior to the conduct of the first inspection, that there was another complaint against Deutsche Bahn concerning DUSS, was not necessary to help them understand the scope of the first suspected infringement. That prior information, which was not part of the general background information on the case but rather pertained to the existence of a separate complaint, was thus unrelated to the subject matter of the first inspection decision. Accordingly, the lack of reference to that complaint in the description of the subject matter of that inspection decision infringed the obligation to state reasons and the rights of defense of the undertaking concerned.[52] Moreover, the CJ noted that the fact that the Commission adopted the second inspection decision whilst the first inspection was underway demonstrates the importance of the information gathered during that inspection in triggering the second inspection and, later, the third inspection. In those circumstances, the CJ upheld the third ground of appeal and set aside the judgment under appeal. The CJ decided to give final judgement in the matter and to set aside the second and third inspections decisions on the ground of infringement of the rights of defense.[53]

Akzo: On 12 February 2003, the Commission notified to Akzo the decision by which this undertaking had to submit immediately to an investigation aimed at seeking evidence of possible anti-competitive practices.

During the inspection, Akzo's representatives informed the Commission officials that legal professional privilege ("LPP"), which covers communications between lawyers and their clients, was applicable to certain documents falling within the scope of the inspection. Following a discussion, the investigating team decided that it would briefly examine the documents in question, with a representative of the applicants at its side. After this cursory examination, the Commission officials decided to copy and place in a sealed envelope those documents for which they were not in a position to reach a final conclusion on the spot as to whether the documents should be privileged ('Set A'). The Commission officials also decided to copy and place directly in the file the documents for which LLP did not apply according to their analysis ('Set B').

On 17 February 2003, Akzo's representatives sent the Commission a letter setting out the reasons why, in their view, LPP protected the documents in Set A and Set B. The Commission then informed Akzo that these arguments were not sufficient to show that LPP was applicable to the documents in question. However, the Commission pointed out that Akzo could submit observations on this provisional conclusion within two weeks, after which the Commission would adopt a final

[50] *Deutsche Bahn*, para 59, with a reference to *Dow Benelux*, para 19.

[51] See Opinion in *Deutsche Bahn*, para 93.

[52] *Deutsche Bahn*, paras 61 to 64.

[53] *Deutsche Bahn*, paras 70 and 71.

decision. Akzo submitted these observations in the context of its first appeal, seeking the annulment of the inspection decision (Case T-125/03). On 8 May 2003, the Commission adopted a decision rejecting the claim of LPP in the context of an investigation regarding the documents of Sets A and B. In a second appeal, Akzo sought the annulment of this decision (Case T-253/03). *Akzo* is often cited in case law in relation to the content of LPP and its implementation, because it takes up and extends the solutions previously established by the CJ in its judgment of 18 May 1982, AM & S Europe v Commission (155/79). We would like however to mention *Akzo* from another perspective, that of the procedural and substantive treatment given to the two appeals brought by Akzo, to the extent that this allows a better understanding of the essential distinction which exists in EU law between the inspection decision and the conduct of the inspection.

- **an action against an inspection decision cannot challenge the conduct of the inspection:** In *Akzo*, the GC declared inadmissible the appeal against the inspection decision (Case T-125/03), because the acts which adversely affected the inspected undertaking, namely the acts refusing the protection granted by the alleged LPP, were adopted during the course of the inspection.[54] Indeed, under settled case law, the lawfulness of an act must be determined in the light of the matters of law and fact existing at the time when the decision was adopted and that acts subsequent to a decision cannot affect its validity. Therefore, an undertaking cannot plead unlawfulness of the investigation procedures to support claims for annulment of the measure on the basis of which the Commission carries out that investigation.[55] Such a solution could have placed Akzo in a delicate position had it not also filed another appeal challenging some aspects of the conduct of the inspection.
- **the conditions required to challenge some aspects of the conduct of an inspection:** Unlike the appeal filed against the inspection decision, the appeal filed against the decision of May 8, 2003 rejecting the claim of LPP was examined on the merits by the GC.[56] Indeed, according to the case law, such appeal is admissible without having to wait for the final decision on the substance of the infringement if the contested measures, despite their adoption during a preparatory procedure related to this investigation, nevertheless immediately affect the interests of the applicant by bringing about themselves a distinct change in its legal position.[57] Therefore, to recognize the admissibility of such an appeal, the GC took into consideration several key aspects, which, although they are particu-

[54] *Akzo*, GC, paras 45 to 57.

[55] *Akzo*, GC, para 55 with references to *Dow Benelux*, para 49.

[56] To be more specific, as specified by the GC, the second appeal was also against the informal decisions taken during the inspection, when the Commission's officials decided to briefly examined the documents, to place some of them in a sealed envelope and to place others directly in the file. See *Akzo*, GC, paras 48 to 53.

[57] *Akzo*, GC, para 55 with references to judgement of 11 November 1981, *IBM v Commission*, 60/81, EU:C:1981:264, paras 9 to 11.

larly present in a situation involving the protection conferred by LPP, appear likely to be applicable by analogy to other situations.[58] First, the GC noted that the decision whereby the Commission rejected, in the course on an inspection, the requests made by the inspected undertaking to benefit from LPP in order to prevent the seizure of some documents, produced legal effects that are definitive in nature and independent of any final decision on the substance of the infringement. Second, the GC observed that the possibility to bring an action against a final decision on the substance of the infringement does not provide the applicant with an adequate degree of protection of its rights. Indeed, it is possible that the administrative procedure will not result in a decision finding that an infringement has been committed. Moreover, in any event, such action would not provide the undertaking with the means of preventing the irreversible consequences resulting from improper disclosure of documents protected under LPP. Third, the GC considered that the contested measures brought to an end a special procedure and thus constituted acts capable of being challenged by an action for annulment, coupled, if need be, with a request for interim relief.[59]

3 Potential End Clap

At this stage of our contribution, one might wonder what the case law of the EU Courts relating to the Commission's inspection powers could score on a kind of "Tomatometer". From our point of view, we would have no hesitation to say this case law is "fresh"[60] when it involves an inspection decision. However, we would be more reserved and probably display a gray faded tomato on cases related to the conduct of an inspection, as we consider that, with the exception of *Akzo* and some other indications trailing in other cases, we do not have enough reviews to generate a rating on a kind of Tomatometer.[61]

A "fresh" case law on inspection decisions. In our view, as it stands, the case law involving an inspection decision responds satisfactorily to the needs of both the Commission and the inspected undertaking. In the current circumstances, we are of the opinion that the EU Courts fulfill their "obligation to properly balance competing interests for the benefit of society as a whole".[62]

In terms of principles, the fundamental right of privacy is now solidly enshrined in provisions that have supra-legislative rank, whether it is the Charter, a binding

[58] *Akzo*, GC, paras 46 to 48.

[59] *Akzo*, GC, paras 46 to 48.

[60] On rottentomatoes.com, an American review-aggregation website for film and television, when at least 60% of reviews for a movie or TV show are positive, it is considered "Fresh" and a red tomato is displayed.

[61] Alternatively, on rottentomatoes.com, if a title has not been released yet or there are not enough reviews to generate a Tomatometer score, a gray faded tomato is displayed.

[62] See, Judge Nils Wahl, farewell speech given at the CJ.

source of EU lawn, or the ECHR, a reference and inspiration tool always useful within the EU system. Since *Hoechst*, the CJ has also repeatedly stated that the protection of persons, both natural and legal, against arbitrary or disproportionate intervention by the public authorities in the sphere of those persons' private activities constitutes a general principle of EU law.[63]

In practice, the Commission has demonstrated in the past its ability to act with independence and professionalism, as guardian of the Treaties, without taking into account other interests. As an enforcement authority for EU competition law, the Commission also knows that the sole purpose of an inspection is to gather the necessary documentary evidence to check the actual existence and scope of a situation concerning which the Commission already possesses certain information.[64] The case law has clearly determined what is required of the Commission in an inspection decision, so that it can obtain the information needed to confirm its suspicions and to demonstrate the existence of a practice prohibited by Article 101 or 102 TFEU. In the same way, with such inspection decision, the undertaking is in a position to assess the scope of its duty to cooperate whilst at the same time safeguarding its rights of defense. The undertaking has also the possibility of asking the GC, as soon as possible, to verify that reasonable grounds for the suspicions mentioned in the inspection decision do exist to justify the intrusion into its business premises. In this regard, the examination of the cases judged by the EU Courts since *Nexans* tends to demonstrate the reality and the intensity of the judicial review, which, although if it occurs after the adoption of the inspection decision, remains consistent in our view with the principle of effective judicial protection.

A gap to close on cases related to the conduct of an inspection. As mentioned previously, there is a difference—a gap—between the ECHR system and EU law.

In situations where the inspected company, ordered to submit to an inspection, faces coercive measures in the event of opposition, the ECtHR prescribed the existence of an "effective remedy" to allow for judicial review, both in fact and in law, not only of the legality of the inspection decision, but also of the conduct of the inspection. The ECtHR also clarified that to be effective, such judicial control needs to be "certain", to "intervene within a reasonable time" and, in the event that an irregularity has already taken place, to provide an appropriate remedy.[65] An effective remedy was also required in a situation where the inspected undertaking, even though it was ordered to submit to an inspection, could oppose it but would then be

---

[63] See, for instance, judgment of 6 October 2020, *État luxembourgeois (Right to bring an action against a request for information in tax matters)*, C-245/19 and C-246/19, EU:C:2020:795, para 57. See also judgement of 14 February 2008, *Varec SA v Belgian State*, C-450/06, EU:C:2008:91, para 48 ("[…] It follows from the case-law of the ECtHR that the notion of "private life" cannot be taken to mean that the professional or commercial activities of either natural or legal persons are excluded […]".

[64] See *National Panasonic*, para 13 or 21, and *Roquette*, para 55.

[65] See judgments of the ECtHR, *Ravon and Others v. France* (CE:ECHR:2008:0221JUD001849703, para 28), *Société Canal Plus and Others v. France* (cit., para 40), *Compagnie des gaz de pétrole Primagaz v. France* (CE:ECHR:2010:1221JUD002961308, para 28); *Vinci constructions and GTM Génie civil et services v. France* (CE:ECHR:1999:0504DEC004093598, paras 78 and 79).

fined for obstruction.[66] In essence, this case law pleads for effective judicial review as soon as something important happens during an inspection that could require a court to rule on the legality of the related implicit or explicit act of the enforcement authority.

Within the EU framework, as it is apparent since *Dow Benelux*, everything that happens after the adoption of an inspection decision has no effect on the legality per se of such decision. What effective remedy would then be available if a significant event occurred during an inspection? For instance, if documents are seized[67] in an inspection that are apparently unrelated to either suspicions mentioned in the inspection decision (like in *Nexans*) or suspicions mentioned in another, subsequent, inspection decision (like in *Deutsche Bahn*), or do not involve LPP (like in *Akzo*), the inspected undertaking has few options to contest the legality of such measure. The main option, usually available, is to wait for the final decision on the suspected infringement of Article 101 or 102 TFEU to claim then before the GC, in the event that this decision used the documents in question, that their seizure was illegal for the above-mentioned reason.[68] Realistically speaking, this scenario is less than optimal, as it requires quite some time to allow the Commission to complete its investigation, from the earlier stage of the inspection to the final stage of its decision. There is also no certainty for the inspected undertaking that such final decision, referring specifically to the documents in question, will materialize. Other available options are not always appropriate. For instance, the undertaking may oppose the seizure of the documents in question, therefore obstructing the inspection, and be fined for that according to Article 23(1) of Regulation 1/2003. It would then be possible for the fined undertaking to appeal this decision before the GC, alleging that the obstruction was justified by the need to protect its right of privacy. Such a procedure seems burdensome and reverses the burden of proof: from a situation in which the Commission has to show that it is justified to infringe the right of privacy, the undertaking has now to demonstrate that its right of privacy prevails. Moreover, it is difficult to consider that, in order to have access to a judge, the inspected undertaking must violate its legal obligation to submit to an inspection decision and expose itself to the sanction attached.[69] Alternatively, if the inspected company considers that an illegal conduct of the Commission during the inspection caused it to

[66] See judgment of the ECtHR, *Delta Pekárny a.s. v. the Czech Republic* (*cit.*, para 87).

[67] In our example, we are referring to documents materially seized, that is to say documents put in the file as evidence and thus leaving the private sphere of the inspected undertaking. We are not referring to documents that were looked upon, even cursorily, in the context of the search and then considered unrelated to the subject matter of the inspection decision or to documents falling under the protection of LPP even after a discussion on the scope of this protection with the Commission.

[68] See, for instance, *Dow Benelux*, para 49, or judgment of 20 April 1999, *Limburgse Vinyl Maatschappij and Others v Commission*, T-305/94 to T-307/94, T-313/94 to T-316/94, T-318/94, T-325/94, T-328/94, T-329/94 and T-335/94, EU:T:1999:80, para 414.

[69] Interestingly, the CJ held that, in order to exercise the right to an effective remedy enshrined in Article 47 of the Charter, the person who holds the right cannot be compelled to infringe a legal rule or obligation or to be subject to the penalty attached to that offence [see judgment of 6 October 2020, *État luxembourgeois cit.*, para 66.

suffer harm such as to cause the EU to incur liability, it may choose to bring an action against the Commission for non-contractual liability. A remedy of that kind is not part of the system for the review of the legality of acts of the EU which have legal effects binding on, and capable of affecting the interests of, the applicant, but it is available where a party has suffered harm on account of unlawful conduct on the part of an institution.[70] However, in order to succeed the applicant must meet rigorous conditions[71] and, even in this case, it will only obtain compensation and not the nullity of the contested seizure and its consequences.

In such situations, paying attention to the method exposed by Judge Nils Wahl in his farewell speech,[72] we would argue that the time is ripe to recognize the possibility to challenge directly and promptly the way an inspection actually unfolds if it compromises an undertaking's right to privacy. The EU Courts could acknowledge such action in a specific case.[73] The EU legislature could also take advantage of the current modernization of the rules set out in Regulation 1/2003 to allow this type of judicial review. Indeed, as was already observed by Advocate General Pitruzella, *Akzo* constitutes merely the application to a specific case of settled case law. Under this case law, any measure that produces binding legal effects such as to affect the interests of an applicant by bringing about a distinct change in his legal position may be subject to an action for annulment under Article 263 TFEU. Therefore, as he deduced, "any act by the Commission occurring within the course of an inspection and satisfying that definition is, in principle, an act open to challenge by an action for annulment". Advocate General Pitruzella went further by stating that, in his view, a right of action against a decision by which the Commission explicitly or implicitly rejects the opposition raised by the inspected undertaking to the seizure of certain documents should be afforded not only where that opposition is based on LLP, as in *Akzo*, but also in other cases. In this regard, he specifically mentioned the

[70] See *Nexans*, GC, para 133, with a reference to judgment of 12 September 2006, *Reynolds Tobacco and Others v Commission*, C-131/03 P, EU:C:2006:541, paras 82 and 83.

[71] See, for instance, judgment of 15 January 2015, *Ziegler and Ziegler Relocation v Commission*, T-539/12 and T-150/13, EU:T:2015:15, para 94.

[72] To summarize his inspiring speech, Judge Wahl's views were that the role of a judge is and should always be to apply the law; that having said that he was aware that EU law contains on occasions more gaps than substance and that "formalism", meaning trying to understand the intended meaning of legislative texts, was his preferred option where there was no law to apply. Regarding formalism, Judge Wahl emphasized the facts that, over the years, the CJEU has developed an extensive case law; that observing older precedents foster coherence and predictability and that established jurisprudence should not be changed lightly. In this regard, he also wisely noted that a too extensive use or adherence to previous case law will eventually stifle the law's development, which in turn will lead it straight to irrelevance. To conclude this balanced and nuanced intervention, he observed that proper use of precedents leads in turn to an incremental development in sync with the more general development of what is now the EU.

[73] Besides *Akzo*, previously discussed, it is interesting to refer to the judgment of 6 October 2020, *État luxembourgeois*, *cit.*, para 44. In this judgment, the CJ held that "the right to an effective remedy may be invoked on the basis of Article 47 of the Charter alone, without there being a need for the content thereof to be made more specific by other provisions of EU law or by provisions of the domestic law of the Member States".

case of documents protected on the basis of the private life of the members of staff of the inspected undertaking, a situation accepted by the GC in the judgment under appeal. He also cited the case where it was argued that the duration of the inspection had gone beyond a period deemed reasonable or that the documents fell outside the subject matter of the inspection.[74]

By analogy with the reasoning used in Akzo, it might be possible to consider that a contested seizure of documents, placed in the file as evidence despite an opposition, puts an end to a "separate special procedure", the one applicable to the search and seizure power of the Commission during an inspection. According to this procedure, Commission officials are empowered to take or obtain in any form copies or extracts of any book or record relating to the business of an undertaking ordered to submit to an inspection if this seizure respects the fundamental right of privacy. Therefore, when an inspected undertaking invokes its right of privacy to oppose the seizure of documents because they allegedly fall outside the subject matter of the inspection, the act by which the Commission rejects this opposition produces significant and immediate legal effects. First, as pieces of evidence, the Commission may now use the documents placed in its file for the purposes of the investigation mentioned in the inspection decision. Second, as grounds for new suspicions validly seized in the context of an inspection, the Commission may use them alternatively for the purposes of other investigations. Third, the Commission may also decide to transmit these documents to national competition authorities in order for them to open their own investigations on the related and suspected anticompetitive conduct. In this regard, the possibility to wait for the final decision of the Commission on the infringement of Article 101 or 102 TFEU in order to allege a violation of the right of privacy during the inspection does not seem sufficient to provide adequate protection. On the one hand, the administrative procedure may not result in a final decision. On the other hand, the action for annulment of the final decision, if there is one, does not provide the applicant with the means of preventing the effects that would result from irregular knowledge of documents protected by the fundamental right of privacy. In this context, we can consider the issue of seizing or sealing electronic documents hosted in a third country (on a dedicated server or in the cloud). However, this issue calls into question not only the validity of the Commission's decision (taken during the inspection) to seize or seal these servers, but also its very competence to adopt such a decision, particularly when the question arises as to the accessibility of these servers from the premises of the inspected undertaking.

For those reasons, in order to allow for an effective judicial review fully in line with the ECHR, we believe it would be beneficial for all stakeholders to recognize the existence of such action when it is required. Indeed, the applicant would have an adequate and specific remedy, the Commission would be able to ensure that the documents seized could form the basis of a finding of an infringement despite the

[74] Opinion of Advocate General Pitruzzella, in Case C-682/20 P, *Les Mousquetaires and ITM Entreprises SAS v Commission* (EU:C:2022:578), paras 67 and 68.

opposition of the inspected undertaking, and the EU courts would be able to assess the particular problem arising from the conduct of the inspection. The effectiveness of the Commission inspections would not be impaired. On the contrary, such inspections would offer enhanced protection for the inspected undertaking and therefore reinforce the legitimacy required to justify any public intrusion in the private sphere. This also appears to be the conclusion reached by Advocate General Medina in her second opinion in the joint cases Imagens Médicas Integradas and Others case (pending). She suggests that "Article 8 of the Charter should be interpreted as not precluding legislation of a Member State pursuant to which, in the course of an inspection at the premises of an undertaking carried out as part of an investigation into an infringement of Article 101 or 102 TFEU, the national competition authority seizes emails whose content relates to the subject matter of the inspection without prior judicial authorisation, provided that [...] adequate and effective safeguards against abuse and arbitrariness, in particular in the form of an ex post facto judicial review of the measures at issue, both during and at the end of the investigation procedure".

Extraterritorial Objects and Effects: Advocate General Wahl in the EFTA Court

Frederik De Ridder

1 Introduction

When working in the Chambers of Advocate General Wahl, one of my tasks was to give presentations to groups of visitors on what an Advocate General ('AG') does. The short answer is that Advocates General write independent Opinions ('AG Opinions') on cases before the Court of Justice of the European Union ('CJEU') renders its judgment. One of the visitors would inevitably ask what value AG Opinions add to the judgment. The discussions that ensued gave me a unique perspective on the atypical role the Advocate General plays in the decision-making at the CJEU.

Whereas an AG Opinion is linked to an individual CJEU case, the reach of AG Opinions is not limited to that case. Often, an Opinion remains a relevant source of interpretation of EU law. Sometimes, Opinions lead a life of their own. Due to the close links between EU and EEA law, AG Opinions inform and influence the EFTA Court, up to being cited in the latter's case law. This way, AG Opinions produce effects beyond the EU legal order strictly speaking.

The present contribution will document two of the many marks AG Wahl has left on the case law of the EFTA Court and, consequently, on the development of EEA law. In *Ski Taxi*,[1] the EFTA Court relied on the Opinion of AG Wahl in *Cartes*

[1] Judgment of the EFTA Court of 22 December 2016, *Ski Taxi*, E-3/16.

F. De Ridder (✉)
EFTA Surveillance Authority, Brussels, Belgium
e-mail: Frederik.DeRidder@eftasurv.int

L. Prete, L. Rezki (eds.), *Judging & (Re)Thinking European Union Law*,
https://doi.org/10.1007/978-3-032-13473-8_5

Bancaires[2] to nuance the CJEU case law on the notion of by object restriction of competition. In *Scanteam*,[3] the EFTA Court relied on the CJEU judgment in *Intel*,[4] where the CJEU, encouraged by AG Wahl's Opinion,[5] explicitly adopted a qualified effects criterion to determine the application of EU competition law to conduct which is not implemented in, but only produces effects on the internal market.

The present contribution is structured in four parts. First, I will briefly recall the two-pillar structure of the EEA Agreement, and its objective to extend the EU's internal market to Iceland, Norway, and Liechtenstein. That objective requires a homogeneous interpretation of EU law incorporated into the Agreement, leading to a judicial dialogue between the CJEU and the EFTA Court. Second, I will recall the different roles of the Advocate General. Third, I will analyse through two case studies the influence of the Opinions of AG Wahl on the EFTA Court. Finally, I will make some concluding remarks, supporting the creation of the function of Advocate General at the EFTA Court.

2 The EEA Agreement and the EFTA Court

The Agreement on the European Economic Area (EEA Agreement)[6] is an association agreement between the EU and its Member States on the one hand, and Norway, Iceland, and Liechtenstein (the EEA EFTA States)[7] on the other. The objective of the Agreement is to extend, as much as possible, the EU's internal market to the EEA EFTA States.[8] Whereas the text of the Agreement contains provisions which reflect the provisions of the EU Treaties setting out, for example, the fundamental freedoms and the competition rules, secondary EU legislation is made applicable to the EEA EFTA States through a system of incorporation in the 22 Annexes to the Agreement.[9]

Lawyers familiar with EU law know that it does not suffice to copy the text of legislation in national law to create uniform rights and obligations. To avoid the same provision receiving a different interpretation or application from one EU Member State to the other, national courts can ask the CJEU questions for a

[2] Opinion of AG Wahl of 27 March 2014, C-67/13 P, *CB* v *Commission*, EU:C:2014:1958.

[3] Judgment of the EFTA Court of 16 July 2020, *Scanteam*, E-8/19.

[4] Judgment of the CJEU of 6 September 2017, *Intel* v *Commission*, C-413/14 P, EU:C:2017:632.

[5] Opinion of AG Wahl of 20 October 2016, C-413/14 P, *Intel* v *Commission*, EU:C:2016:788.

[6] OJ 1994 L 1, p. 3.

[7] Switzerland is also member of the European Free Trade Association (EFTA) but did not ratify the EEA Agreement. Norway, Iceland, and Liechtenstein are therefore the EFTA States that have also ratified the EEA Agreement, or the "EEA EFTA States".

[8] Article 1 EEA.

[9] See F. De Ridder, 'L'Espace économique européen: comment assurer l'homogénéité avec le droit de l'Union', in *Journal du droit européen*, 2023, pp. 289–293.

preliminary ruling when they are applying EU law.[10] Moreover, the CJEU rules on infringement cases brought by the Commission against the EU Member States for failure to fulfil obligations.[11] The Treaties' surveillance mechanism allows for mutual trust among the Member States, economic operators and citizens that everyone is playing by the same rules.

As far as Norway, Iceland, and Liechtenstein are concerned, neither the CJEU, nor the Commission, have competence to oversee the implementation and application of EEA law. To allow for a similar surveillance mechanism, the EEA EFTA States set up the EFTA Surveillance Authority (ESA) and the EFTA Court through the Surveillance and Court Agreement (SCA). Like the Commission for the EU Member States, ESA is competent to pursue infringement proceedings against the EEA EFTA States. The EFTA Court is competent to rule on requests for advisory opinions brought by the national courts and tribunals of the EEA EFTA States, like the preliminary rulings of the CJEU,[12] and to rule on the infringement cases brought by ESA.[13]

An analogy that has become commonplace to illustrate this institutional setup is that the EEA Agreement sets up a single internal market with two institutional pillars: the EU pillar on the one hand, and the EFTA pillar on the other.

The glue that keeps the two pillars together is the principle of homogeneity, which guarantees a uniform (or 'homogeneous') interpretation and application of EU law incorporated into the EEA Agreement. Recitals 4 and 15, and Article 6 of the EEA Agreement, as well as Article 3 SCA, provide that the EFTA Court and ESA need to interpret the provisions of the EEA Agreement in the same way as the CJEU interprets the corresponding provisions of EU law. This uniform interpretation of EEA law has a dimension both at the level of the Contracting Parties to the EEA Agreement and at the level of the individual, by guaranteeing "*equality [...], reciprocity and [...] an overall balance of benefits, rights and obligations for the Contracting Parties*",[14] as well as "*equal treatment of individuals and economic operators as regards the four freedoms and the conditions of competition*".[15] Therefore, by virtue of the principle of homogeneity, an EEA EFTA State can be equated to an EU Member State for the purposes of legislation incorporated in the EEA Agreement.[16]

The CJEU and the EFTA Court must interpret and enforce a common set of rules, EU law incorporated into the EEA Agreement, in a homogeneous fashion. This institutional set up strikes a balance between legal integration and autonomy of the

[10] Article 267 TFEU.

[11] Article 258 TFEU.

[12] Article 34 SCA.

[13] Article 31 SCA.

[14] Recital 4 EEA.

[15] Recital 15 EEA.

[16] See, in comparison to the association agreement with Türkiye, judgment of the CJEU of 18 December 2014, *UK Council*, C-81/13, EU:C:2014:2449, para 58.

EU and EEA legal orders. Direct oversight of EEA law by the CJEU in the EEA EFTA States would have threatened the independence of the EEA EFTA States, whereas interpretation of EU law by judges from the EEA EFTA States, for example in a unified EEA Court, would have threatened the autonomy of the EU legal order.[17]

In two recent judgments, the CJEU and the EFTA Court have unveiled the constitutional foundation to the principle of homogeneity. In *Ruska Federacija*, the CJEU held that extending the internal market to the EEA EFTA States, which requires a uniform interpretation of the EEA Agreement, is justified by the "*special relationship between the European Union, its Member States and the [EEA] EFTA States, which is based on proximity, long-standing common values and European identity*", recalling the second recital of the preamble to the EEA Agreement.[18] The EFTA Court followed suit in its judgment in the *A* v *B* case.[19] The two Courts therefore agreed that the objective of homogeneity is not just a consequence of the mutual obligations and benefits of the Contracting Parties to the EEA Agreement, but justified by the fact that the EEA EFTA States share (at least some of) the core values of the European project.[20]

As AG Kokott has pointed out extrajudicially, the two-pillar set up requires a strong dialogue between the jurisdictions that interpret and apply the rules.[21] *Ruska Federacija* and *A* v *B* demonstrate how the CJEU and the EFTA Court actively engage in this dialogue, but the dialogue also extends to the European Court of Human Rights ('ECtHR'). Fundamental rights form part of the general principles of EEA law, and the judgments of the ECtHR are important sources for the EFTA Court to determine the scope of these fundamental rights.[22] Moreover, the judicial dialogue extends to the national courts and tribunals, which are the ordinary courts within the EU/EEA legal orders to implement EU/EEA law, and which are connected with the CJEU or EFTA Court through preliminary ruling procedures.[23]

A web connecting national and supranational courts emerges, establishing a "*complete system of legal remedies and procedures*".[24] This web presents, J. Kokott and D. Dittert wrote, "*a unique opportunity of judicial dialogue between judges*

[17] See, to that effect, K. Lenaerts and S. Adam, "The Foundations of the EFTA Court, Looking Back at the Two EEA Opinions of the Court of Justice", in EFTA Court (ed.), *The EFTA Court: Developing the EEA over Three Decades*, Hart Publishing, 2024, pp. 3–19.

[18] Judgment of the CJEU of 2 April 2020, *Ruska Federacija*, C-897/19 PPU, EU:C:2020:262, para 50. For a commentary of the case, see H.H. Fredriksen and C. Hillion, "The 'special relationship' between the EU and the EEA EFTA States - free movement of persons in an extended area of freedom, security and justice: Ruska Federacija v. I.N.", *Common Market Law Review*, 2021, N° 58(3), pp. 851–876.

[19] Judgment of the EFTA Court of 12 December 2024, *A* v *B*, E-15/24, para 68.

[20] See, to that effect, K. Lenaerts and S. Adam, (no 17), p. 12.

[21] See, to that effect, J. Kokott and D. Dittert, "European Courts in Dialogue", in EFTA Court (ed.), *The EEA and the EFTA Court: Decentred Integration*, Hart Publishing, 2014, pp. 43–52.

[22] EFTA Court, *A* v *B*, (no 19), para 50.

[23] Opinion of the CJEU of 8 March 2011, Opinion 1/09, *Agreement creating a Unified Patent Litigation System*, EU:C:2011:123, para 69.

[24] See, by analogy, judgment of the CJEU in *Inuit*, C-583/11 P, EU:C:2013:625, para 92.

from different legal and cultural backgrounds, with a view to finding widely accepted solutions for common legal problems".[25] Writing extrajudicially about the influence of the Charter on EEA law, AG Wahl used the term "*judicial cross-fertilisation*".[26]

However, full harmony, or harmonisation, is impossible.[27] The central judicial instances of each system, the CJEU, the EFTA Court, and the ECtHR, will always have to strike the right balance between uniformity and diversity, "*in particular where highly ideological questions, choices of society, cultural issues or matters of national identity are concerned*".[28] In the EEA legal order, the risk of divergences in the interpretation of EEA rules is the price to pay for legal autonomy within the two pillars.[29]

Of particular interest for this contribution is the string of the web that connects the CJEU and the EFTA Court. As we will see in what follows, the Advocates General play a pivotal role in establishing and strengthening that connection.

3 The Role of the AG

According to Article 252 TFEU, the Advocate General "assists" the CJEU by making reasoned submissions on individual cases. These Opinions are read in open court and published on the Court's website, after the hearing in the case but before the CJEU renders its judgment. In the Opinion, the Advocate General suggests to the CJEU how they would solve the legal issues raised by the case. The Opinion is typically more elaborate on facts and reasoning than the final judgment. The Opinion is purely advisory: the CJEU is not bound by the Opinion when it renders its subsequent judgment in the case and does not even have to answer or acknowledge the arguments raised by the Advocate General.

Before becoming an Advocate General himself, Professor Bobek distinguished six ways in which the Advocates General "assist" the CJEU: (i) framing the case and the legal arguments used, (ii) controlling the reporting judge, by keeping a second pair of eyes on procedural and substantive questions, (iii) researching and summarising the state of the case law, the academic debate, and other sources of law, (iv) innovating, by suggesting further developments of the case law, rising above the individual case, (v) testing the acceptability of a legal opinion, by providing a

---

[25] See, to that effect, J. Kokott and D. Dittert, (no 21), p. 51.

[26] N. Wahl, 'Uncharted Waters: Reflections on the Legal Significance of the Charter under EEA Law and Judicial Cross-Fertilisation in the Field of Fundamental Rights', in EFTA Court (ed.), (no 21), pp. 281–298.

[27] "*It is an inherent consequence of such a system that from time to time the two courts may come to different conclusions in their interpretation of the rules.*" Judgment of the EFTA Court of 8 July 2008, *L'Oreal Norge*, E-9/07 and E-10/07, para 28.

[28] See, to that effect, J. Kokott and D. Dittert, (no 21), p. 48.

[29] K. Lenaerts and S. Adam, (no 17), p. 12.

definitive, but non-binding reasoning for the case, and, finally, (vi) explaining and, where necessary, dissenting with the case law of the CJEU.[30]

Professor Bobek concluded that Advocates General play an integral and useful role in the CJEU's functioning. Most recently, the usefulness of the position of Advocate General has been implicitly confirmed by the decision to revive the function at the General Court, on the occasion of the transfer of the competence for preliminary rulings in certain fields to that Court.[31]

At present, there are no Advocates General in the EFTA Court. In 2011, the EFTA Court suggested creating the function of Advocate General. Whereas the EEA EFTA States did not follow up on that proposal at the time, it recently has been picked up again by commentators.[32]

Despite having no AGs itself, the EFTA Court occasionally refers to AG Opinions in its case law. Moreover, Advocates General also refer to EFTA Court case law in their Opinions, making these Opinions a gateway for EFTA Court case law into the CJEU's jurisprudence.[33] Advocates General therefore bridge the gap between the two Courts, contributing to homogeneity. In the remainder of this contribution, I will demonstrate through two case studies how AG Wahl's Opinions have helped shaping the development of EEA law.

4 *Cartes Bancaires*, *Ski Taxi*, and by Object Restrictions of Competition

4.1 Facts and Background to Ski Taxi

Case E-3/16 *Ski Taxi ea.* v *Norway* concerned an agreement between two taxi companies in a region outside Oslo. The companies jointly participated in tenders organised by a hospital for patient transport services. According to the Norwegian Competition Authority ("NCA"), the joint participation in the tender process had as its object the restriction of competition. Therefore, the NCA fined the taxi companies, and saw no need to prove that the competition had also produced anticompetitive effects.[34]

[30] M. Bobek, 'A Fourth in the Court: Why are there Advocates-General in the Court of Justice?', *Cambridge Yearbook of European Legal Studies*, issue 14, 2011–2012, pp. 529–561.

[31] Article 49a of the Statute of the CJEU and Article 31a of the Rules of Procedure of the General Court.

[32] G. Butler, 'Reform of the Judicial Architecture of the EFTA Pillar of the EEA', in EFTA Court (ed.), (no 17), pp. 83–85.

[33] See, for example, P. Mengozzi, 'The Advocates General and the EFTA Court' and V. Skouris, 'The Role of the Court of Justice in the Development of the EEA Single Market', in EFTA Court (ed.), (no 21), pp. 10–12 and 53–61.

[34] EFTA Court, *Ski Taxi*, (no 1), paras 5–20.

The NCA decision was challenged in the national courts and the case made its way to the Norwegian Supreme Court, which had doubts about the interpretation of Article 53 EEA, the equivalent to Article 101 TFEU in the EFTA Pillar. The Norwegian Supreme Court referred three questions to the EFTA Court, enquiring what legal test it needed to apply to determine whether an agreement between undertakings was restrictive of competition by object.

The CJEU's judgment in *Cartes Bancaires* was 2 years old at the time. Up until that judgment, the CJEU and the General Court had progressively widened the notion of restrictions of competition by object. In *Cartes Bancaires*, the General Court had ruled that that notion could not be interpreted restrictively, and that, for an agreement to restrict competition by object, it simply had to be capable of restricting competition in the particular case, having regard to the specific legal and economic context.[35] That judgment of the General Court was appealed, and the judgment upon appeal is widely seen as the judgment that reversed the trend.[36]

In *Cartes Bancaires*, the CJEU held that restrictions by object had to be interpreted restrictively.[37] In that regard, the CJEU followed the Opinion of AG Wahl, which, in essence, argued that a restriction by object constituted an exception to the general rule according to which the authority enforcing the competition rules must demonstrate the anticompetitive effects of the agreement.

In point 56 of the Opinion, AG Wahl suggested a legal test to determine whether conduct was restrictive by object in the following terms:"*[o]nly conduct whose harmful nature is proven and easily identifiable, in the light of experience and economics, should [...] be regarded as a restriction of competition by object, and not agreements which, having regard to their context, have ambivalent effects on the market or which produce ancillary restrictive effects necessary for the pursuit of a main objective which does not restrict competition.*" The AG suggested that only "*conduct entailing an inherent risk of a particularly serious harmful effect*" or "*conduct in respect of which it can be concluded that the unfavourable effects on competition outweigh the pro-competitive effects*" would be marked as a restriction by object. The test would only be met when "*experience based on economic analysis shows that a restriction is constantly prohibited.*"[38]

In other words, economic analysis by, and enforcement experience of, national competition authorities, the Commission and ESA, as well as litigation before the national and EU/EEA Courts would have allowed the objective definition of conduct that is always restrictive of competition.[39] This means that progressively it would have been possible to define an open-ended list of conduct that is in all

---

[35] Judgment of the General Court of 29 November 2012, *CB* v *Commission*, T-491/07, EU:T:2012:633, paras 124 and 125.

[36] R. Whish and D. Bailey, *Competition Law*, 11th edition, OUP, 2024, pp. 131–133.

[37] Judgment of the CJEU of 11 September 2014, *CB v Commission*, C-67/13 P, EU:C:2014:2204, paras 57 and 58.

[38] Opinion of AG Wahl in *CB*, (no 2), point 55.

[39] *Ibid.*, point 79.

instances prohibited.[40] The proposal by the Advocate General reduced the importance of the "economic and legal context" of the agreement, which might, if applied too extensively, have come down to an assessment of the anticompetitive effects, thereby blurring the distinction between "by object" and "by effect".[41]

The CJEU did not adopt this test in its judgment. Instead, the CJEU ruled that, to qualify an agreement as restrictive by object, "*regard must be had to the content of its provisions, its objectives and the economic and legal context of which it forms a part. When determining that context, it is also necessary to take into consideration the nature of the goods or services affected, as well as the real conditions of the functioning and structure of the market or markets in question. In addition, although the parties' intention is not a necessary factor in determining whether an agreement between undertakings is restrictive, there is nothing prohibiting the competition authorities, the national courts or the Courts of the European Union from taking that factor into account.*"[42]

4.2 The EFTA Court's Assessment in Ski Taxi

It is against this background that the EFTA Court had to interpret Article 53 EEA in *Ski Taxi*. As mentioned before, the objective of homogeneity results in a presumption that Article 53 EEA and Article 101 TFEU are to be construed in the same way.[43]

The EFTA Court repeated the judgment of the CJEU in *Cartes Bancaires* when it held that regard must be had to the content of the agreement's provisions, its objectives and the economic and legal context of which it forms part, the nature of the goods and services, the functioning and structure of the market and potentially, the parties' intention.[44]

The EFTA Court continued by echoing AG Wahl's Opinion in *Cartes Bancaires*, according to which the consideration of the economic and legal context of an agreement to identify an anticompetitive object must clearly be distinguished from the demonstration of anticompetitive effects, to avoid blurring the distinction between "by object" and "by effect" restrictions.[45]

Going back to the judgment of the CJEU, the EFTA Court held that the "*concept [of restriction of competition by object] must be interpreted restrictively in the sense that it can be applied only to certain types of coordination between undertakings*

---

[40] By object restrictions cannot be contained in an exhaustive list, see *ibid.*, point 68. For an attempt of such a list on the basis of current case law, see R. Whish and D. Bailey, (no 37), p. 136–139. For a recent contribution on this matter, see Opinion of AG Emiliou of 15 May 2025, C-133/24, CD Tondela , EU:C:2024:364, points 23-45.

[41] Opinion of AG Wahl in *CB*, (no 2), point 44. See also EFTA Court, *Ski Taxi*, (no 1), para 58.

[42] CJEU, *CB*, (no 37), paras 53 and 54.

[43] EFTA Court, *L'Oreal Norge*, (no 27), para 27.

[44] EFTA Court, *Ski Taxi*, (no 1), paras 56 and 57.

[45] *Ibid.*, para 58.

which reveal a sufficient degree of harm to competition that it may be found that there is no need to examine their effects [...]."

However, the EFTA Court added, with specific reference to point 56 of the Opinion of AG Wahl, that "*[o]nly conduct whose harmful nature is easily identifiable, in the light of experience and economics, should be regarded as a restriction of competition by object.*" The assessment whether conduct is harmful by nature cannot go as far as a full examination of its actual or potential effects, nor can it amount to assessing the pro- and anticompetitive effects.[46]

4.3 Commentary

By putting emphasis on the notion of "experience and economics", absent in the judgment in *Cartes Bancaires*, the EFTA Court diverged from the CJEU's case law. Some commentators have however stated that this reference might not have been intentional and note that the EFTA Court's interpretation of by object restrictions in *Ski Taxi* is in line with CJEU case law.[47]

Ski Taxi therefore raises some uncertainty around the notion of by object restrictions in the EFTA Court's case law. Regardless of whether it was the EFTA Court's intention to interpret Article 53 EEA differently, this gives me an opportunity to discuss the challenges that divergent interpretation pose to homogeneity.

In its case law on homogeneity, the EFTA Court has acknowledged the possibility that differences in scope and purpose might under specific circumstances lead to a difference in interpretation between EU and EEA law.[48] In those circumstances, the EFTA Court typically provides reasons for its divergent interpretation. The *Scanteam*-case provides an example. In that case, the EFTA Court did not follow the CJEU's restrictive interpretation of what constitutes a national "court or tribunal" which can refer questions for a preliminary ruling under Article 267 TFEU. In *Banco de Santander*, the CJEU had held that administrative appeals boards that were not sufficiently independent, were not "courts or tribunals" for the purposes of Article 267 TFEU.[49] By consequence, requests for preliminary rulings referred by such bodies are inadmissible. Confronted with that case law in *Scanteam*, the EFTA Court recalled that, whereas homogeneity also applies to procedural rules, questions referred to it by administrative appeal boards can still be admissible under Article 34 SCA, the equivalent in EEA law to Article 267 TFEU. It justified its divergent

[46] *Ibid.*, paras 61 and 66.

[47] R. Gjendemsjø, 'Article 53 [Agreements, decisions and concerted practices]', in Arnesen, Fredriksen ea. (eds.), *Agreement on the European Economic Area, a Commentary,* C.H. Beck, Hart, Nomos and Unversitetsforlaget, 2018, pp. 536–537.

[48] EFTA Court, *L'Oreal Norge*, (no 27), paras 21 and 27.

[49] Judgment of the CJEU of 21 January 2020, *Banco de* Santander, C-274/14, EU:C:2020:17.

interpretation with reference to the "*constitutional and legal traditions of the EFTA States*", in which administrative appeal boards play an important role.[50]

However, in *Ski Taxi*, the EFTA Court did not explain why it referred to the AG Opinion instead of sticking to the CJEU judgment. The case seems part of a line of case law, including *LO* and *Holship*,[51] where the EFTA Court has referred to AG Opinions to put different accents than the CJEU. In *LO* and *Holship*, which concern the position of collective bargaining agreements under Article 53 EEA, the EFTA Court took, according to some commentators, a stricter approach than the CJEU in *Albany*,[52] which might sit uneasily with the principle of homogeneity.[53]

As mentioned above, divergent case law is symptomatic of the trade-off between uniformity and autonomy in the EEA legal order. By referring to points in AG Opinions which have not been followed by the CJEU, the EFTA Court engages in the judicial dialogue on the development of EEA law.

The judicial dialogue on the notion of by object restriction has continued since *Ski Taxi*. AG Bobek cited the Opinion of AG Wahl and the judgment in *Ski Taxi* in his Opinion in *Budapest Bank*.[54] In the judgment in that case the CJEU ruled that there must be sufficiently reliable and robust experience for the view to be taken that conduct is, by its very nature, harmful to the proper functioning of competition.[55] However, in subsequent cases, the CJEU seems to have nuanced that point. In *Servier*, with specific reference to AG Wahl's Opinion in *Intel*, the CJEU ruled that "*[i]t is in no way necessary that the same type of agreement has already been censured by the Commission in order for [conduct] to be considered to be restrictive of competition by object*."[56] The CJEU has therefore confirmed that whereas prior decisional experience can be relevant to establish the harmful nature of conduct, it is by no means a necessary condition.[57]

---

[50] EFTA Court, *Scanteam*, (no 3), paras 45 and 46.

[51] Judgments of the EFTA Court of 22 March 2002, *LO*, E-8/00, and of 19 April 2016, *Holship*, E-14/15.

[52] Judgment of the CJEU of 21 September 1999, *Albany*, C-67/96, EU:C:1999:430.

[53] P. Wennerås, 'Article 6—Homogeneity', in Arnesen, Fredriksen ea. (eds.), (no 47), pp. 220–234.

[54] Opinion of AG Bobek of 5 September 2019, *Budapest Bank*, C-228/18, EU:C:2019:678, footnote 21.

[55] Judgment of the CJEU of 2 April 2020, *Budapest Bank*, C-228/18, EU:C:2020:265, point 76.

[56] Judgment of the CJEU of 27 June 2024, *Servier*, C-201/19 P, EU:C:2024:552, paras 129 and 144. See also judgments of the CJEU of 25 March 2021, *Generics*, C-588/16 P, EU:C:2021:242, para 79; *Lundbeck*, C-591/16 P, EU:C:2021:243, paras 130–131; and *Sun*, C-586/16 P, EU:C:2021:241, para 86.

[57] This also seems to align with point 79 of the Opinion of AG Wahl in *CB*, (no 2), which held that "*experience is a perfectly relevant point of reference [to establish a sufficient degree of harm]. 'Experience' must be understood to mean what can traditionally be seen to follow from economic analysis, as confirmed by the competition authorities and supported, if necessary, by case-law.*" In its Guidelines on the applicability of Article 101 [TFEU] to horizontal co-operation agreements (C(2023) 3445 final, 1 June 2023), the Commission considers, at point 24, that conduct can be categorised as restrictions by object on the basis of sufficiently reliable and robust experience, or

Looking at *Ski Taxi* in the context of the development of the notion of by object restriction, the judgment therefore fits neatly in the movement towards a more restrictive reading from *Cartes Bancaires* to *Budapest Bank*. To avoid going too far in that movement, the CJEU has nuanced that case law more recently.

Since *Ski Taxi*, the EFTA Court has not had the opportunity to rule on the interpretation of Article 53 EEA. Homogeneity requires that, in its interpretation of Article 53 EEA, the EFTA Court pays due account to the judgments of the CJEU on the interpretation of Article 101 TFEU.[58] Sometimes, this leads the EFTA Court to explicitly overrule or distinguish its previous case law to align with more recent judgments of the CJEU. The EFTA Court did so to align with the CJEU in the *L'Oréal* case, despite the fact that "*[b]oth sets of arguments [of the EFTA Court in its prior case law, and of the CJEU which contradicted that EFTA Court case law] are equally valid in a [Union] law context and an EEA law context*".[59] In other words, the EFTA Court was not convinced its prior interpretation was legally wrong, but it saw the importance of aligning with the CJEU to ensure legal certainty and homogeneity in the EEA. Indeed, divergences in case law might foster legal uncertainty. In that regard, K. Lenaerts and S. Adam write that "*if [divergent interpretation] would materialise too frequently, this could have harmful impacts on citizens' – and businesses' – confidence in the EEA in the long term.*"[60]

After 50 years of EU competition law, the case law on the notion of by object restrictions has still not fully crystalised.[61] The saga demonstrates that it requires a confrontation of different views and opinions, none of which are necessarily wrong, to arrive to a balanced outcome. The CJEU, its Advocates General, and the EFTA Court will continue to nurture that judicial dialogue.

on the basis of the specific characteristics of the agreement, from which it is possible to infer its particular harmfulness for competition.

[58] Article 3(2) SCA.

[59] EFTA Court, *L'Oreal Norge*, (no 27), para 30.

[60] K. Lenaerts and S. Adam, (no 17), p. 19.

[61] R. Whish and D. Bailey, (no 36), p. 128. See also L. Prete, M. Scholz, 'The Object/Effect dichotomy', in K. Dekeyser, C. Gauer, J. Laitenberger, N. Wahl, W. Wils and L. Prete (eds), *Regulation 1/2003 and EU Antitrust Enforcement – A Systematic Guide*, Wolters Kluwer, 2023, pp. 83–89.

5 *Scanteam*, *Intel*, and the Extraterritorial Application of EEA Law

5.1 The Judgment in Scanteam

The *Scanteam*-case raised the question whether the Public Procurement Directive[62] applies to procurement by a foreign mission of an EEA EFTA State in a third country.

Scanteam, a consultancy, contested the award decision of a contract for consultancy services by the Norwegian Embassy in Luanda before the Norwegian Complaints Board for Public Procurement. That Board was unsure whether the procurement fell under the geographical scope of the national legislation transposing the Procurement Directive and referred a question for an advisory opinion to the EFTA Court.

On the substance, the EFTA Court recalled that legal acts incorporated into the EEA Agreement apply in principle to the same area as the EEA Agreement. However, the geographical scope of the EEA Agreement does not preclude EEA law from having effects outside the territory of the EEA. To that effect, the EFTA Court reasoned by analogy to the judgment of the CJEU in *Intel*,[63] that competition law applies to conduct adopted outside of the EEA which would have "*foreseeable, immediate and substantial effects*" in the EEA.[64]

Procurement will therefore necessarily come within the scope of the EEA Agreement if it is "*sufficiently closely linked to the EEA*". Such sufficiently close link can be demonstrated by factors such as the language of the procurement, language requirements in the contract, the law applicable to the procurement procedure or the awarded contract, the location of the review body or courts having jurisdiction, domestic registration requirements, the publication of a contract notice within the EEA, or the fact that a procurement procedure has been designed to engage economic operators in the EEA.[65]

Considering this answer, the EFTA Court found it not necessary to rule on the argumentation of the Norwegian Government, according to which the territorial scope of the EEA Agreement as defined by Article 126 EEA differs between the EFTA States and the EU Member States.[66]

---

[62] Directive 2014/24/EU of the European Parliament and of the Council of 26 February 2014 on public procurement, OJ 2014 L 94, p. 65.

[63] CJEU, *Intel*, (no 4), paras 40–65.

[64] EFTA Court, *Scanteam*, (no 3), paras 65–66.

[65] *Ibid.*, paras 68–73, and operative part.

[66] *Ibid.*, para 73.

5.2 Commentary

In *Scanteam*, the EFTA Court refers to the judgment in *Intel*, not the Opinion of AG Wahl. However, the report for the hearing shows that the argument relating to the application of EEA law to the procurement was raised by the French Government, with specific reference to the AG Opinion in *Intel*.[67] Indeed, in that Opinion, AG Wahl provided a remarkable and convincing balancing exercise of the interests at stake when applying EU law to facts which have occurred outside of the territory of the EU.

For the present purposes, it is worth recalling that the Commission fined Intel, a computer chip producer, for an abuse of dominant position. Intel argued before both the General Court and the CJEU that none of the alleged anticompetitive conduct was implemented in the EEA, and that the Commission therefore did not have jurisdiction over this conduct.[68]

AG Wahl saw the case as an opportunity to clarify previous case law on the territorial scope of EU competition law. The applicability of the competition rules is beyond doubt for conduct implemented in the EU. In addition to that implementation criterion, AG Wahl however argued that the CJEU should explicitly adopt a qualified effects criterion: the competition rules should also be applied to conduct which produces qualified, or sufficiently significant, effects on the internal market. Such effects cannot be too remote or purely hypothetical. AG Wahl recalled that there were over 100 national or supranational authorities worldwide that claim jurisdiction over anticompetitive practices. An over-reach of EU competition rules would risk encroaching upon the sovereign interests of other States and be legally and practically difficult to enforce. It would also considerably increase the overlaps in the jurisdictions of different States or polities and thereby create great uncertainty for undertakings and increased risks of conflicting rules (or judgments) applying to the same conduct.[69] The CJEU in essence followed the Opinion on this point.[70]

Interestingly, the considerations of AG Wahl on the concomitant application of competition law allow me to draw a parallel with the judicial dialogue within the EEA. As I have explained above, the concomitant application of the same rules leads to risks in relation to consistency and homogeneity. This applies to competition rules, but also to EU and EEA law more generally. Only if all interlocutors show sufficient restraint and effectively listen to each other, is the dialogue maintained.

---

[67] The report for the hearing is available on the case page on the EFTA Court's website.

[68] CJEU, *Intel*, (no 4), para 32.

[69] Opinion of AG Wahl in *Intel*, (no 5), points 280–306.

[70] CJEU, *Intel*, (no 4), para 49. The CJEU referred to the "qualified effects test" instead of "criterion". See also R. Wish and D. Bailey, (no 36), pp. 554–555; and L. Prete, 'On Implementationm and Effects: The Recent Case-law on the Territorial (or Extraterritorial?) Application of EU Competition Rules', in *Journal of European Competition Law & Practice*, 2018, pp. 487–495.

A second parallel I can draw here, is with the argument of the Norwegian Government regarding the reduced geographical scope of the EEA Agreement compared to the EU Treaties, which the EFTA Court explicitly left unanswered in *Scanteam*.

The scope of EU law is decided by functional, in addition to geographical criteria. Most notably, EU law applies in the exclusive economic zone and on the continental shelf in the fields where the Member States exercise sovereign powers.[71]

Article 126(1) EEA defines the geographical scope of the EEA Agreement by reference to the territories of the EFTA States,[72] whereas Article 52 of the Treaty on the European Union (TEU) does not use the term "territory" to define the scope of the EU Treaties.[73] The Norwegian Government deducts from the different terminology that it was the intention of the Contracting Parties to differentiate between the geographical scope of the EU Treaties and the EEA Agreement. In line with public international law, the term "territory" connotes the geographical area over which a State exercises sovereignty: the land, territorial waters, and air space. The use of the term in Article 126 EEA would therefore, consciously in Norway's view, exclude the continental shelf, the exclusive economic zone, and the fishery zones of the EEA EFTA States from the scope of the EEA Agreement.[74]

ESA has addressed the issue multiple times, for example in cases where Norway refused oil platform workers social security protection. In 1999, ESA issued a reasoned opinion, arguing that, like in EU law, the geographical scope of the EEA Agreement must be defined in a functional manner. ESA referred to the EEA Agreement's objective of homogeneity, the duty of loyal cooperation laid down in Article 3 EEA and reciprocity of rights and obligations of the contracting parties to the EEA Agreement.[75] Before the case could be referred to the EFTA Court, the Norwegian Government adapted its legislation and ESA closed the case.[76] At the time the present contribution was being finalised, a request for advisory opinion concerning an offshore worker made its way to the EFTA Court. In its forthcoming

---

[71] Judgments of the CJEU of 20 October 2005, *Commission* v *UK*, C-6/04, EU:C:2005:626, para 117, and of 17 January 2012, *Salemink*, C-347/10, EU:C:2012:17, para 35.

[72] "*The Agreement shall apply to the territories to which the Treaty establishing the European [Union] is applied and under the conditions laid down in that Treaty, and to the territories of Iceland, the Principality of Liechtenstein and the Kingdom of Norway.*"

[73] "*The Treaties shall apply to the Kingdom of Belgium, the Republic of Bulgaria, [etc.]*"

[74] EEA Committee report to the Ministry of Foreign Affairs reviewing Norway's experience under the EEA Agreement, *Norge og EØS: Utvikling og erfaringer*, 2024, NOU 2024:7, pp. 64–65. Other arguments supporting these views are derived from the wording of the free trade agreement with Norway that preceded the EEA Agreement, a detailed reading of Article 126(1) EEA in light of other provisions of the Agreement, and the subsequent practice after concluding the agreement, see, F. Arnesen, 'Article 126 [Territorial application of the EEA Agreement]', in Arnesen, Fredriksen ea. (eds.), (no 47), pp. 945–953.

[75] ESA Decision of 24 September 1999 no 233/99/COL, Doc No 99/6990-D (ESA document database number 159181). See also ESA Decision of 11 November 1999 no 269/99/COL (Letter of Formal Notice), Doc No 99–7991-D (ESA document database number 159960).

[76] ESA Decision of 10 October 2001 no 297/01/COL, Doc No 01-7100-I.

judgment in case E-6/25, the EFTA Court might therefore provide more clarity on the interpretation of Article 126 EEA.

Despite this legal disagreement, Norway applies EEA law to many activities outside its territorial waters. For example, Norway has applied for an exemption from the Utilities Procurement Directive in relation to the exploration and the extraction of crude oil and natural gas on the continental shelf,[77] notified State Aid measures to ESA for offshore wind farms,[78] and submitted a notification to ESA concerning carbon capture and storage (CCS) activities on its continental shelf.[79] However, Norway's position seems to be that it applies EEA law voluntarily to activities on the continental shelf which nevertheless, formally, it maintains fall outside of the geographical scope of the EEA Agreement.[80]

Another way of looking at these issues is that, the Norwegian Government implicitly accepts that there is value in applying the legislation to activities outside the territorial waters of Norway. The CCS Directive aims to achieve a high level of protection of the environment and trust in this technology.[81] Applying it has value because any environmental incident in a CCS storage site off the Norwegian coast will have environmental effects which will be prejudicial to Norway first and foremost. Similarly, applying EEA social security coordination legislation to employees working on oil platforms guarantees the attractiveness of the sector and legal certainty for its employees.

To come back to *Scanteam*, I agree with other commentators that, even though the EFTA Court has not directly interpreted Article 126 EEA, it has adopted, in essence, an effect-based, or functional approach to the substantive scope of the EEA Agreement, where substantive EEA law is applied to conduct that takes place in areas which might be argued as being outside the territorial scope of the EEA Agreement, to ensure its effectiveness. Whereas the EFTA Court did not rule on Article 126 EEA in *Scanteam*, it limited the consequences of a potential difference in geographical scope.[82] By analogy to what AG Wahl pointed out in his Opinion in

[77] ESA Decision No 178/13/COL of 30 April 2013 exempting the exploration and the extraction of crude oil and natural gas on the Norwegian Continental Shelf from the application of Directive 2004/17/EC of the European Parliament and of the Council coordinating the procurement procedures of entities operating in the water, energy, transport and postal services sectors (Norway) (OJ L 249, 19.9.2013, p. 16–30). Directive 2004/17 has since been replaced by Directive 2014/25.

[78] ESA Decision No 194/23/COL of 19 December 2023, Doc No 1331624.

[79] See ESA Report on the Implementation of Directive 2009/31/EC on the Geological Storage of Carbon Dioxide, Document No 1406720.

[80] "*The geographical scope of the EEA Agreement is not a legal obstacle if, following a specific assessment, Norway wishes to assume specific EEA obligations outside its territory.*" Freely translated from the Committee report, (no 74), pp. 64–65.

[81] Article 1 of Directive 2009/81 of the European Parliament and of the Council of 23 April 2009 on the geological storage of carbon dioxide (OJ 2009 L 140, p. 114).

[82] O.J. Einarsson, 'On the Margins, The Case Law of the EFTA Court Regarding the Scope of the EEA Agreement', in EFTA Court (ed.), (no 17), pp. 260–262.

Intel, to decide otherwise would make it too easy to circumvent EEA law obligations.[83]

5.3 Concluding Remarks

Cartes Bancaires and *Intel* demonstrate the usefulness of Advocates General at the CJEU. The solid Opinions of AG Wahl empowered the CJEU to confidently clarify the notion of restriction by object and to adopt the qualified effects criterion for the application of competition law to conduct that is not implemented in but only creates effects on the internal market.

Ski Taxi and *Scanteam* demonstrate how the echo of the AG Opinions can be heard on the other side of the Kirchberg, the plateau in Luxembourg on which both Courts are located. Through the EEA Agreement, and amplified by the judicial dialogue, that echo can be heard well beyond Luxembourg, even in Iceland, Norway, and Liechtenstein. The cases demonstrate how the EFTA Court uses AG Opinions to develop EEA law, and to inform the interpretation of the EEA Agreement.

As mentioned, the EFTA Court previously asked the EEA EFTA States to create the function of Advocate General at the EFTA Court. At the time, the States did not follow up on that proposal. Nonetheless, this idea merits reconsideration.

The fact that not one, but two Courts guarantee the uniform interpretation of the EEA Agreement, increases the risks of divergent interpretation of the common rules. It is precisely in these situations that Advocates General provide added value: they can assess the risks, opportunities, or justification of possible divergence, or test its acceptability. In addition, they can provide an extra pair of eyes and an extra pen to the three judges of the EFTA Court who must shoulder all the cases.[84] Finally, like in the CJEU, they can provide a non-partisan assessment of the arguments presented by the parties, and complement or contextualise them. In my view, the extra voice of the Advocate General at the EFTA Court would therefore not increase the risk of divergent case law, but rather strengthen the judicial dialogue and thereby help realise the homogeneity objective of the EEA Agreement.

---

[83] Opinion of AG Wahl in *Intel*, (no 5), point 291.

[84] From 2014 to the end of 2023, the EFTA Court registered 170 cases. In 2024 alone, however, the EFTA Court registered a record 32 cases. That trend continued in 2025. Commentators have argued that the small bench makes the EFTA Court "*extremely vulnerable to being undermined*", see G. Butler, 'Reform of the Judicial Architecture of the EFTA Pillar of the EEA', in EFTA Court (ed.), (no 17), p. 81.

An Early Case of the Interplay Between the DMA and EU Competition Law: The Spanish Booking.com Case

Micaela Arias Domecq, Cani Fernández Vicién, and Francisco de Paula Roig Guerrero

1 Introduction

Until fairly recently, the prevailing view was that digital markets should remain largely unregulated, as their dynamic nature was thought to encourage self-regulation. Intervention, be it through antitrust or via economic regulation, was considered to hinder innovation.

However, this consensus has shifted. Concerns have grown that antitrust law has not been applied with sufficient effectiveness to digital markets, allowing digital companies to entrench their market power and restrict competition.[1] Similarly, the acknowledgement that there are market failures in digital sectors, where network effects and extreme economies of scale and scope often lead to winner-takes-all or winner-takes-most dynamics, have paved the way for imposing ex ante economic regulation on digital players.

On the one hand, the EU's Digital Markets Act ('DMA') marks a major departure, introducing an ambitious ex ante regulatory framework that applies asymmetric obligations to online digital players with considerable economic power. On the other hand, in recent years we have seen a firmer application of competition law to

[1] See e.g. J. Cremer *et al.*, *Competition policy for the digital era*, European Commission 2019 (available online); J. Furman *et al.*, *Unlocking digital competition, Report of the Digital Competition Expert Panel* CMA 2019; F. Jenny, *Competition law enforcement and regulation for digital ecosystems: Understanding the issues, facing the challenges and moving forward*, Concurrences, 2021.

M. Arias Domecq · C. Fernández Vicién (✉) · F. de Paula Roig Guerrero
Comisión Nacional de los Mercados y la Competencia, Madrid, Spain
e-mail: micaela.arias@cnmc.es; cani.fernandez@cnmc.es; francisco.roig@cnmc.es

L. Prete, L. Rezki (eds.), *Judging & (Re)Thinking European Union Law*,
https://doi.org/10.1007/978-3-032-13473-8_6

digital players, both globally and within the EU.[2] This dual framework raises new questions around their compatibility and interplay.

This contribution examines how competition law and the DMA intersect and reinforce each other in addressing the specific economic challenges digital markets pose. First, it analyses the framework under which both regulations may apply to a given conduct. Second, it focuses on their complementary nature. Third, it describes the Spanish antitrust Booking.com case and assesses how the anticompetitive conducts sanctioned in that case may fit into the DMA. Finally, this contribution concludes that the concurrent application of competition law and the DMA is not only feasible but desirable, as each framework brings a unique set of tools and goals. By leveraging both approaches, public authorities can more effectively address the challenges that market power in digital sectors poses for consumer welfare.

2 The Concurrent Application of Sector Regulation and Competition Law

Articles 101 and 102 TFEU, as well as their national equivalents, fully apply to the conduct of regulated undertakings. This has been consistently upheld by EU courts regarding classical regulated industries like telecommunications and energy. Indeed, the case law has clearly established that antitrust prohibitions are applicable to conduct that is permitted by sectoral regulation.[3]

The ruling by the Court of Justice of the European Union in Case C-117/20 (*bpost*)[4] provides further support for the concurrent application of sector regulation and competition law by clarifying in which circumstances imposing sanctions on the same undertakings for the same facts under parallel antitrust and sector specific proceedings does not violate the *ne bis in idem* principle. First, the proceedings must pursue different legal interests. Second, the rules must make it possible to predict what conduct is liable to be subject to a duplication of proceedings and that there will be coordination between the two competent authorities. Third, the two sets of proceedings have to be conducted in a sufficiently coordinated manner and fourth, the overall penalty must be proportionate to the seriousness of the offence.

In this regard, simultaneous application of the DMA and competition law would, in principle, not infringe the *ne bis in idem* principle as long as (i) each framework pursues a different objective, (ii) the conduct that could be investigated under both

[2] See e.g. EU cases AT. 39740 (Google Shopping), AT. 40099 (Google Android) AT. 40462 (Amazon Market Place), AT.40437 – Apple – App Store Practices (music streaming), and Facebook *Bundeskartellamt*'s case (Case B6-22/16).

[3] See Judgments in *Telefónica v Commission*, T-336/07 EU:T:2012:172, paras 327-337 and 339; in *Telefónica v Commission*, C-295/12 P, EU:C:2014:2062; and in *Deutsche Telekom v Commission*, C-280/08, EU:C:2010:603.

[4] Judgment in *bpost v Autorité belge de la concurrence*, C-117/20, EU:C:2022:202. See also Judgment in *Nordzuker*, C-151/20, EU:C:2022:203.

regimes is clear and (iii) the DMA includes built-in coordination mechanisms specifically designed to align DMA and competition enforcement.

As to the objectives pursued by each framework, while competition law protects undistorted competition in all markets, the DMA is aimed at preserving contestability and fairness exclusively in digital markets.[5] This complementarity is reflected in Article 1(6) DMA, which explicitly states that the DMA is applied "*without prejudice to the application of Articles 101 and 102 TFEU*" and their equivalent national rules.[6]

In addition, Article 1(7) DMA imposes a general cooperation obligation on the European Commission and Member States and Article 38 DMA mandates cooperation and coordination between the European Commission, which enforces the DMA as well as Articles 101 and 102 TFEU, and national competition authorities.[7] These mechanisms seek to ensure that the DMA and competition law enforcement are coordinated, mutually reinforcing, and applied in a streamlined, complementary manner across the EU.

3 Complementary Characteristics of the DMA and Antitrust Law

The complementary nature[8] of the DMA and Article 102 TFEU is further illustrated by their different regulatory design and the specific tools they employ to achieve their objectives. In what follows, these are briefly explored.

3.1 Scope of Application

Article 102 TFEU applies to any undertaking with a dominant market position, regardless of the sector in which it operates. It does not contain a closed list of prohibited conduct that can be deemed abusive but rather establishes a broad prohibition on abuse of dominance, covering any conduct by a dominant firm that harms

[5] Article 1.1. DMA states that its purpose is "*to contribute to the proper functioning of the internal market by laying down harmonised rules ensuring for all businesses, contestable and fair markets in the digital sector across the Union where gatekeepers are present, to the benefit of business users and end users.*"

[6] Also reflected in recitals 10-12 of the DMA.

[7] In addition, recital 91 of the DMA addresses cooperation and coordination.

[8] V. Robertson, 'The complementary nature of the Digital Markets Act and the EU antitrust rules', Journal of Antitrust Enforcement, 2024, 12, 325–330. M. L. Tierno Centella, F.J. Ripoll Vázquez, I. Álvarez Fernández del Vallado, La interacción de la política de competencia con la regulación de mercados digitales: una visión desde España, Concurrences, 2024.

competition, regardless of the specific form it takes. In a nutshell, competition law is applied horizontally to all undertakings operating in all sectors of the economy.

In contrast, the DMA only applies to undertakings that have been designated as "gatekeepers" by the European Commission[9] in relation to a set of limited pre-defined services (the so-called core platform services). Gatekeepers are large digital platforms that serve as a crucial intermediary between businesses and consumers, providing core platform services such as online search engines, app stores, and social networking services. As this contribution went to press seven gatekeepers have been designated by the European Commission.[10] This design ensures that the DMA focuses on platforms with systemic market impact, while Article 102 TFEU retains broad applicability across other undertakings.

The DMA establishes a predefined set of obligations and prohibitions in Articles 5 to 7, often referred to as the "blacklist," that gatekeepers must follow to ensure fair and open market conditions.[11] These rules prohibit certain practices that have been identified as harmful to competition and consumer choice in digital markets and are deeply rooted in the application of antitrust rules to digital markets. For instance, gatekeepers are forbidden from engaging in self-preferencing, such as ranking their own products or services higher than those of rivals on their platforms. They are also barred from restricting interoperability, limiting access to data generated by business users, and blocking users from accessing services outside the platform's ecosystem. By setting clear ex ante prohibitions, the DMA aims to prevent behaviours commonly observed in digital markets, ensuring that gatekeepers operate fairly and transparently, allowing for greater contestability and innovation.

3.2 Decentralized vs Centralized Enforcement

Article 102 TFEU operates through a decentralized enforcement structure,[12] where both the European Commission, the courts and national competition authorities (NCAs) in EU member states have the power to investigate and address abuses of dominance that may affect trade between Member States within their jurisdictions. This decentralized model allows for a tailored response to anticompetitive conduct

---

[9] See Article 3 DMA.

[10] Alphabet Inc. (Google), Amazon.com Inc., Apple Inc., ByteDance Ltd. (TikTok), Meta Platforms, Inc. (Facebook, Instagram), Microsoft Corporation, and Booking.com. The designation decisions are available on line.

[11] Article 5 DMA includes a list of core obligations for gatekeepers, such as the prohibition of price parity clauses that are self-executing. Article 6 outlines obligations that may require additional clarification or adaptation to specific context, such as data portability or interoperability obligations. Article 7 mandates that gatekeepers offering messaging and communication services ensure interoperability with similar services from other providers.

[12] Council Regulation (EC) No 1/2003 of 16 December 2002 on the implementation of the rules on competition laid down in Articles 81 and 82 of the Treaty ('Regulation 1/2003').

across diverse national markets, leveraging local insights and expertise to ensure effective enforcement. Moreover, to ensure consistency, the European Commission relieves NCAs of their competence if the Commission initiates its own proceedings. In contrast, the sole enforcer of the provisions set out in the DMA is the European Commission.[13] Although empowered NCAs may conduct investigations into possible non-compliance by gatekeepers, only the European Commission can open proceedings and enforce the regulation. This centralized approach aims to provide consistency and uniformity in the application of the DMA across the entire EU, ensuring that digital platforms are subject to the same regulatory standards regardless of the member state in which they operate.

3.3 *Ex Post Vs Ex Ante*

Article 102 TFEU aims to deter anticompetitive conduct with an ex post approach, addressing abuses that exploit or entrench dominance after they have occurred. Interim measures may provide a certain degree of flexibility in this respect as they may be implemented during an ongoing antitrust investigation when there is a risk of significant and immediate damage to competition that may be difficult to reverse if action is delayed until the final ruling.

Conversely, the DMA applies ex ante, with a forward-looking approach that pre-empts a set of previously defined conduct that is likely to inhibit market entry or expansion. The prohibitions outlined in the DMA are informed by prior antitrust cases, which have demonstrated in practice that such behaviours are detrimental to overall welfare and offer limited scope for justifiable efficiencies. Consequently, these precedents provide a robust basis to conclude that the same practices will similarly undermine fairness and contestability within the digital markets' framework.

[13] See recital 91 and Article 38(7) DMA which reads as follows: '*Where it has the competence and investigative powers to do so under national law, a national competent authority of the Member States enforcing the rules referred to in Article 1(6) may, on its own initiative, conduct an investigation into a case of possible non-compliance with Articles 5, 6 and 7 of this Regulation on its territory. Before taking a first formal investigative measure, that authority shall inform the Commission in writing. The opening of proceedings by the Commission pursuant to Article 20 shall relieve the national competent authorities of the Member States enforcing the rules referred to in Article 1(6) of the possibility to conduct such an investigation or end it where it is already ongoing. Those authorities shall report to the Commission on the findings of such investigation in order to support the Commission in its role as sole enforcer of this Regulation.*'

3.4 *Burden of Proof*

In competition law the burden of proof rests with the enforcement authority,[14] which must demonstrate to the requisite legal standard that the undertaking in question has engaged in conduct constituting an abuse of its dominant position. This entails proving on a case-by-case basis that the undertaking is dominant and that a given conduct has been capable of restricting competition. However, undertakings may show that the conduct under investigation was objectively justified or that it produces efficiencies that counterbalance, or even outweigh, the negative effect of its conduct on competition.[15]

In contrast, the DMA imposes pre-defined boundaries, it provides legal certainty and reduces the need for prolonged investigations. This streamlined framework enables the European Commission to act without the lengthy procedural requirements typical of antitrust cases, where authorities must gather extensive evidence to demonstrate an infringement. Additionally, the DMA's built-in obligations eliminate the need for a case-by-case analysis of the conduct, focusing instead on preventing problematic behaviours from occurring in the first place. Consequently, enforcement under the DMA should be more direct and expedient, providing faster regulatory responses in digital markets. Thus, the burden of proof is reversed[16] as it is for designated gatekeepers to explain how they aim to comply with the DMA obligations.[17]

3.5 *Flexibility*

The broad language in Article 102 TFEU enables it to encompass emerging behaviours that may not have been anticipated when the legislation was drafted. This adaptability allows authorities to effectively use this tool to preserve competition as business models and market strategies change. In fast-evolving digital markets, the inherent flexibility of Article 102 is especially valuable, as it can adapt to both economic and technological developments without requiring legislative amendments.

Conversely, the DMA prohibits only specific practices explicitly outlined in Articles 5 and 6. These articles set forth a fixed list of obligations and prohibitions for gatekeepers, targeting conduct that has been clearly identified as harmful to market contestability and fairness. However, recognizing that digital markets are dynamic, the DMA empowers the European Commission to modify and expand these obligations through delegated acts if market conditions change. This

[14] Article 2 Regulation 1/2003.

[15] Judgment in *Servizio Elettrico Nazionale*, C-377/20 EU:C:2022:379, paras 44–46.

[16] P. Ibáñez Colomo, 'The Draft Digital Markets Act: A Legal and Institutional Analysis', Journal of European Competition Law & Practice, 2021, Vol. 12, No. 7.

[17] See Article 8.1 DMA.

mechanism allows the DMA to address emerging challenges, but it does so through regulatory adjustments.[18]

3.6 *Deterrence and Redress*

Antitrust law exerts a significant deterrent effect by not only addressing anticompetitive conduct but also actively working to restore competitive conditions and provide mechanisms for compensating parties harmed by such behaviour. Through its sanctions and corrective measures, competition law dissuades dominant firms from engaging in practices that would distort competition. In cases where a violation has been established, antitrust sanctions can include structural or behavioural remedies that restore competitive dynamics within the market. Furthermore, by facilitating claims for damages, antitrust enforcement enables those adversely affected by anticompetitive actions to seek redress, thereby reinforcing its preventive and corrective roles. This dual approach of fining harmful conduct, restoring market balance and establishing redress mechanisms strengthens the law's impact on fostering fair competition and safeguarding consumer welfare.

In contrast, the DMA adopts a preventive approach aimed at ensuring that digital markets remain fair and contestable. The DMA imposes clear obligations on gatekeepers to prevent the emergence of clearly defined practices and empowers the European Commission to impose fines if these obligations are not complied with. While this approach fosters a fairer market environment, it lacks the remedial and compensatory dimensions inherent in antitrust enforcement, underscoring the distinct yet complementary roles of both frameworks.

4 The Spanish Antitrust Case Against Booking.Com

An antitrust case against Booking.com B.V. (Booking.com) by the Spanish competition authority (CNMC) serves as an early illustration of the issues arising from the simultaneous enforcement of EU competition law and the DMA.

On 29 July 2024 the CNMC issued a decision fining Booking.com for breaching Article 102 of the TFEU and its equivalent under Spanish law.[19] This decision was adopted shortly after the European Commission had designated Booking Holdings Inc., parent company of Booking.com, as a gatekeeper under the DMA in relation to Booking.com's online intermediation service.

[18] See recital 77 and Articles 12 and 49 DMA.

[19] A comprehensive summary in English of the decision and the full text of the decision in Spanish are available on CNMC's website.

In order to explore the interplay between EU competition law and the DMA in this case, it is first necessary to provide a short summary of the practices that were deemed anticompetitive in the afore-mentioned Spanish antitrust decision.

This decision found that Booking.com held a dominant position in the provision of hotel intermediation services by OTAs in Spain from at least 2019 to the date of the decision. For reaching this conclusion, the CNMC took into account Booking.com's market shares (70–90%, during that period), and the high barriers to entry and expansion in that relevant market, which include (i) indirect network effects, (ii) the role of data generated within the platform and its interaction with network effects, and (ii) the high fixed costs related to marketing in order to compete in the market and the advantages associated with being the first mover.

The decision then sets out the reasons for considering that Booking.com had committed two abuses of its dominant position, one exploitative of hotels and another exclusionary of other OTAs competing against Booking.com in order to attract hotels to their platforms.

As regards the exploitative abuse of hotels, the decision considers that it is a single and continuous infringement consisting of three anticompetitive conducts:

- First, the simultaneous placing by Booking.com in contracts with hotels located in Spain, of two clauses:
  - a narrow price parity clause, whereby hotels cannot set a lower retail room price in their direct online channel than in Booking.com,
  - another clause allowing Booking.com to unilaterally lower the room price set by the hotel in Booking.com's platform.
- Second, hotels located in Spain must accept the following terms in the contract governing the relationship between Booking.com and them (contract known as *General Delivery Terms* -GDTs-): the English version of the GDTs as binding, the Dutch legal system as the law governing the GDTs, and the jurisdiction of the courts of Amsterdam, the Netherlands, in case of disputes arising in connection with the GDTs.
- Third, a lack of transparency in the information provided by Booking.com to hotels on the impact of the Preferred Partner, Preferred Partner Plus and Genius Programs[20] on their position in the default results ranking provided by Booking.com on its website, and on the resulting additional number of hotel visits and bookings on Booking.com.

In order to establish that these practices amount to unfair trading conditions under Article 102 of the TFEU (and its equivalent under Spanish law), the CNMC follows a three-step test that shows that these conditions are (i) imposed by a dominant undertaking on its trading partners, (ii) unfavourable or detrimental to the interest of

[20] These programs, which are optional for hotels, allow a better positioning (or visibility) of hotels in Booking.com's default ranking of results in exchange of (i) a higher commission for Booking.com (Preferred Partner, Preferred Partner Plus programs) or (ii) the hotel setting a lower price of certain rooms in Booking.com (Genius program).

trading partners or of third parties, including consumers, and (iii) not necessary for achieving a legitimate objective or in any event not proportionate.

Regarding the exclusionary abuse of other OTAs wishing to attract hotels, the decision considers that it is a single and continuous infringement consisting of two anticompetitive conducts:

- First, the use of the number of bookings a hotel has had in Booking.com in order to rank results by default; and
- Second, the use of the profitability a hotel has entailed for Booking.com (under the criteria known as *performance score*) in order to join and remain in the Preferred Partner Program and Preferred Plus Partner Program, which are very popular among hotels because they lead to a better positioning in Booking.com's default search ranking of results.

Given the novelty of the exclusionary conducts examined in the case, the CNMC follows the general three-step procedure in order to establish their exclusionary nature, that is, (i) conduct departing from competition on the merits, (ii) capability to produce exclusionary effects, and (iii) lack of objective justification.

The main reason given in the decision for finding both conducts exclusionary is that they lead hotels not to offer better trade terms (price or room availability) in other OTAs competing with Booking.com; otherwise, hotels risk being demoted in the default result ranking of Booking.com, with the ensuing loss in bookings in this platform. The following quote from the market study on the distribution of hotel accommodation in the EU (section 3.2.13 and, in particular, p. 59) attests the importance hotels place on how OTAs rank them[21]:

> hotels argue that ranking and visibility are indirect, but very significant, incentives (or disincentives) used by OTAs to actively influence hotels' pricing or room availability on OTAs

Apart from fining Booking.com for both infringements, the decision also imposes behavioural remedies on Booking.com in order to guarantee the removal of the five anticompetitive conducts that are sanctioned in the decision.

5 The Possible Coverage of the Antitrust Infringements of the Spanish Booking.com Case Under the DMA

Pursuant to Article 3(3), first subparagraph of the DMA, on 1 March 2024, Booking Holdings Inc. notified the European Commission that Booking Holdings Inc., together with all legal entities directly or indirectly controlled by Booking Holdings Inc., potentially met the DMA thresholds laid down in Article 3(2) DMA in relation

[21] This study COMP/2020/OP/002 was commissioned by the Directorate-General for Competition of the European Commission. It focused on the activity of hotels in certain Member States, Spain among them, for the period 2017-2021.

to the core platform service consisting of the online intermediation service provided by its subsidiary Booking.com.[22]

On 13 May 2024 Booking Holdings Inc. became the seventh firm to be designated a gatekeeper under the DMA by the European Commission, as it presumptively satisfied the requirements set out in Article 3(1) DMA, once having met the quantitative thresholds laid down in Article 3(2) DMA.[23] The designation decision listed the online intermediation service provided by Booking.com as a core platform service which is individually an important gateway for business users to reach end users.

As a result of this designation, Booking Holdings Inc. had to comply with all the obligations provided for in Articles 5, 6 and 7 DMA, in relation to its designated core platform service, as from 14 November 2024. On this date Booking Holdings Inc. published a report on its compliance with the DMA, explaining in detail the compliance solutions adopted for each of the relevant DMA obligations,[24] together with an audited report on its consumer profiling techniques.[25] This was followed by a public workshop on 25 November 2024 held by the European Commission so that interested parties could ask for clarifications and give feedback on the proposed compliance solutions.[26]

In order to analyse the possible coverage of the antitrust infringements of the Spanish Booking.com case by the obligations of the DMA affecting the online intermediation service provided by Booking.com, it is useful to recall the letter of Article 1(7) DMA, which states that

> National authorities shall not take decisions which run counter to a decision adopted by the Commission under this Regulation. The Commission and Member States shall work in close cooperation and coordinate their enforcement actions on the basis of the principles established in Articles 37 and 38.

In principle, the potential inclusion of the practices sanctioned by the CNMC under Articles 5, 6 and 7 DMA can be ruled out as the period of the infringements in the Spanish antitrust decision does not coincide with the date from which Booking.com had to comply with the DMA obligations. While the Spanish antitrust decision covered a period ranging from 2019 to the date of the issuing of the decision (29 July 2024), Booking.com had to comply with the DMA obligations from 14 November 2024. Thus, there is no room for overlap in any practice that may be covered both by the Spanish antitrust decision and the DMA. Moreover, it is worth noting that the CNMC opened its formal antitrust proceedings against Booking.com on 5 October

[22] Article 2, point (2), subpoint (a), of the DMA lists online intermediation services as one of the categories of CPSs within the meaning of that Regulation. Article 2, point (5), of Regulation (EU) 2022/1925 defines ‘online intermediation services’ by cross-referring to Article 2, point (2), of Regulation 2019/1150, which sets the requirements a service must meet in order to be considered an online intermediation service.

[23] Booking.com had been preceded by Alphabet, Amazon, Apple, ByteDance, Meta and Microsoft.

[24] The public version of this compliance report is available on the DMA website.

[25] A non-confidential version of this consumer profiling report is available on the DMA website.

[26] According to the public information made available by the European Commission on line.

2022, well before Booking Holdings Inc. was designated a gatekeeper under the DMA in relation to the online intermediation service provided by its subsidiary Booking.com.

Nevertheless, from a theoretical point of view, it is worth scrutinising whether the Spanish antitrust decision contains infringements which may coincide with prohibitions or obligations for gatekeepers in the DMA. This analysis becomes even more pertinent if Booking.com's statements after the CNMC's decision are taken into account. In particular, Booking.com stated that the DMA was "*the right forum to discuss and assess the majority of these issues* [covered by the antitrust decision], *presenting an opportunity to agree on solutions that apply across Europe, rather than country by country, as the CNMC is doing.*[27]"

One relevant difference between the Spanish Booking.com case and Booking.com's designation under the DMA is that the latter covers all kinds of online intermediation services provided by Booking.com (accommodations, flights, car rentals, public transport, airport taxis, attractions, and other forms of travel) while the Spanish antitrust decision concerns itself exclusively with hotel accommodation (but not short-term rentals).

The most obvious DMA obligation affecting Booking.com's business model is the ban on parity clauses (Article 5.3 DMA). Before being subject to this obligation, Booking.com had in place, in contracts with hotels across the European Economic Area (EEA), narrow parity clauses preventing them from offering better room conditions in their online direct channels (e.g. hotel website) than in Booking.com.[28] In June 2024 Booking.com announced its decision to remove parity obligations with hotels based in the EEA starting from 1 July 2024, before the expiry of the six-month period from which it had to become compliant with the DMA's obligations after its gatekeeper designation.

As regards this DMA obligation, there is no contradiction between the DMA and the Spanish antitrust decision. The Spanish antitrust decision finds exploitatively abusive vis-à-vis hotels the simultaneous placing in contracts with hotels of both the narrow price parity clause and the clause allowing Booking.com to unilaterally lower the room price set by the hotel in Booking.com's platform. Thus, the Spanish antitrust decision does not contain a direct pronouncement on the validity of the narrow price parity clause in isolation.

Given this exploitative abuse by Booking.com, the Spanish antitrust decision decided to impose on Booking.com a behavioural remedy consisting on the removal of one of the above mentioned clauses, to the discretion of Booking.com.

As previously mentioned, just before the adoption of the CNMC decision, Booking.com announced that as 1 July 2024 it would abandon the parity clause

---

[27] Comments by Booking.com cited in *MLex* (available on line).

[28] This clause was not effective in some countries of the EEA (Austria, Belgium, France, Italy and Portugal), where they had been banned following national legislation. In addition, Booking.com had dropped the clause in Germany following a decision from the national competition authority which sanctioned wide and narrow price parity in Booking.com's contracts with hotels, a decision which was subsequently upheld by the German Supreme Court.

from its contracts with hotels in the EEA, as part of its plan to comply with the DMA, so, as a matter of fact, complying with the DMA made compliance with this behavioural remedy automatic for Booking.com. Moreover, it is worth noting that the DMA would have removed the existence of this particular anticompetitive conduct had the Spanish antitrust decision decided to open this case when the DMA obligations were effective for Booking.com.

The second exploitative abusive conduct addressed in the Spanish Booking.com decision concerns the imposition, on hotels located in Spain, of (i) the English version of the GDTs as binding, (ii) the Dutch legal system as the law governing the GDTs, and (iii) the jurisdiction of the courts of Amsterdam, the Netherlands, in case of disputes arising in connection with the GDTs. One may consider if this conduct infringes the obligation established in Article 5(6) DMA, which states that

> The gatekeeper shall not directly or indirectly prevent or restrict business users or end users from raising any issue of non-compliance with the relevant Union or national law by the gatekeeper with any relevant public authority, including national courts, related to any practice of the gatekeeper.

However, it is rather doubtful that the content of this obligation includes the aforementioned exploitative conduct. The DMA obligation speaks of restricting the possibility of raising any issue of non-compliance with the relevant Union or national law by the gatekeeper. Its interpretation should be made in combination with Recital 42 del DMA, which says that

> *To safeguard a fair commercial environment and protect the contestability of the digital sector it is important to safeguard the right of business users and end users, including whistleblowers, to raise concerns about unfair practices by gatekeepers raising any issue of non-compliance with the relevant Union or national law with any relevant administrative or other public authorities, including national courts. For example, it is possible that business users or end users will want to complain about different types of unfair practices, such as discriminatory access conditions, unjustified closing of business user accounts or unclear grounds for product de-listings. Any practice that would in any way inhibit or hinder those users in raising their concerns or in seeking available redress, for instance by means of confidentiality clauses in agreements or other written terms, should therefore be prohibited.* This prohibition should be without prejudice to the right of business users and gatekeepers to lay down in their agreements the terms of use including *the use of lawful complaints-handling mechanisms, including any use of alternative dispute resolution mechanisms or of* the jurisdiction of specific courts in compliance with respective Union and national law. *This should also be without prejudice to the role gatekeepers play in the fight against illegal content online.* (emphasis added)

In contrast, the exploitative abusive conduct sanctioned by the CNMC deals with private conflicts stemming from the interpretation of the GDTs, which govern the commercial relationship between Booking.com and accommodations. In particular, according to the CNMC decision (paragraph 595), the terms imposed by Booking.com on hotels that the CNMC found exploitatively abusive just make more costly for hotels based in Spain the prospect of exerting their rights before a court, but, in our opinion, do not restrict the ability of hotels of raising issues related to Booking.com practices that may not comply with the relevant Union or national law. For this reason, we believe that the letter of Article 5(6) DMA does not cover this specific anticompetitive conduct.

The third exploitative abusive conduct sanctioned by the CNMC considers the lack of transparency in the information provided by Booking.com to hotels with respect to the expected number of additional bookings and visits a hotel has had o may have on Booking.com's platform as a result of its participation in the Preferred Partner, Preferred Partner Plus and Genius Programs. The DMA does not contain any obligation related to this practice: while the relevant obligations in the DMA deal with pure data, the lack of transparency mentioned before involves calculations with data stored by Booking.com (i.e., estimations of additional bookings and visits to the hotel in Booking.com) that the CNMC deems that Booking.com is able to provide to hotels.

As regards the exclusionary abuse sanctioned by the CNMC, it covers Booking.com policies[29] compelling hotels to offer lower room prices or greater room availability in Booking.com rather than in other competing OTAs, in exchange for greater visibility in Booking.com's default search ranking. A close reading of the DMA obligations shows that these exclusionary practices are not neatly covered by DMA obligations and thus prosecuting them under EU competition law would not run counter to the letter of the DMA.

Consequently, for the reasons detailed before, in our view, the DMA would not be the appropriate policy instrument to assess the specific antitrust issues sanctioned in the Spanish antitrust decision.

In addition, it is worth mentioning that, from a procedural point of view, the complementarity between EU competition law and the DMA manifested itself in the application of the mechanisms of cooperation and coordination between the European Commission and national competent authorities enforcing competition rules as regards their enforcement actions, envisaged in Article 1(7) DMA.[30] As the CNMC publicly acknowledged in connection with the handling of the Spanish antitrust investigation, "*there has been coordination with the European Commission*" and "*due consideration with the Commission*". As a result of this coordination and due consideration, the CNMC pointed out that the European Commission "*has considered this is not going to be enforceable under the DMA or we* [the CNMC] *are better placed to deal with it under competition rules*".[31]

Therefore, the Spanish Booking.com case provides a practical instance of the complementarity between the DMA and EU competition law, confirming the view that EU antitrust law remains highly relevant for addressing anticompetitive practices by a gatekeeper that are not prohibited under the DMA. The complementarity

[29] As previously explained, these policies are: (i) the use of the number of reservations a hotel has had in Booking.com, as criteria used for ranking results by default, and (ii) the use of the profitability a hotel has entailed for Booking.com, as a requirement for being able to participate in the Preferred Partner and Preferred Plus Partner Programs.

[30] Article 38 of the DMA delineates the principles that must guide this cooperation and coordination.

[31] Comments cited at MLex (available on line).

of goals between the DMA and EU competition law is further illustrated by the nature of the practices sanctioned in the Spanish Booking.com case, which, as it has been shown, covers both exploitative abuses (which would be related to the goal of "*fairness*" pursued by the DMA) and exclusionary abuses (in turn, related to the aim of ensuring "*contestability*" also contained in the DMA).

6 Conclusion

The EU's regulatory stance toward digital markets has evolved, recognizing the limitations of relying exclusively on ex post antitrust enforcement in fast-moving, innovation-driven sectors.

The DMA and Article 102 TFEU together form a balanced approach, where sector-specific obligations on gatekeepers prevent systemic issues, and the abuse of dominance prohibition deters dominant undertakings from engaging in conduct that would distort competition. Moreover, they have complementary roles in reigning in digital market power as the DMA protects fairness and contestability by imposing clearly defined obligations on gatekeepers and competition law uses responsive enforcement under a horizontal and flexible framework to prevent conduct that may restrict competition. There is of course a trade-off between speed and flexibility[32] that is inherent to the design of each tool. While the nimble wording of Article 102 TFEU enables it to adapt to evolving market realities, the case by case approach typically translates into lengthier proceedings.

As previously argued, the Spanish Booking.com case exemplifies the benefits of this approach, showing how both frameworks can work together to tackle anticompetitive behaviour while promoting fair access in digital markets. As digital platforms continue to grow in scale and influence, this dual framework may become central to maintaining fair and competitive digital markets in the EU.

[32] F. Chirico, 'Digital Markets Act: A Regulatory Perspective', Journal of European Competition Law & Practice, 2021, Vol. 12, No. 7.

Antitrust and Competition Law: Enforcement Cycles in the US and EU

Barry E. Hawk

1 Introduction

This paper offers a perspective of the histories of EU and U.S. competition law and policy different from common perspectives published in the literature and aired at International Competition Network's ('ICN') conclaves and other meetings among competition agencies. For example, the commonly accepted history of U.S. antitrust enforcement emphasizes "antitrust schools" like the triumphant Chicago School and its emphasis on consumer welfare and price effects. Indeed, U.S. antitrust history often is viewed as a Hegelian progression from a potpourri of political, social and economic goals to the narrower economics concept of consumer welfare adopted in the late 1970s, a telos that continues to dominate U.S. antitrust analysis—although it has been increasingly challenged in the last several years with more aggressive antitrust enforcement directed at mergers and dominant positions of large tech or digital platform firms. The U.S. academic emphasis on antitrust schools is not shared by EU commentators to the same extent, although ordoliberals might differ.

What are missing in the "school" approach to U.S. antitrust history are electoral politics, changes in economic facts and concerns, developments in economic theory—in addition to legal process concerns in the U.S.—as factors shifts in enforcement. Two general conclusions are offered. First, U.S. enforcement is more volatile and subject to electoral swings than EU enforcement. Second, the influence on procedural and substantive law from political appointment of judges is greater in the U.S. than in the EU.

B. E. Hawk (✉)
Fordham University, New York, NY, USA
e-mail: bhawk1@fordham.edu

L. Prete, L. Rezki (eds.), *Judging & (Re)Thinking European Union Law*,
https://doi.org/10.1007/978-3-032-13473-8_7

2 U.S. Antitrust Law and Policy

The history of U.S. antitrust law and policy is more like Vico than Hegel. Enforcement of U.S. antitrust law has been cyclical, with periods of relative action and inaction. This can be put into five periods: Trustbusting (1890 to 1920), Hibernation (1920 to 1937), Expansion (1937 to 1970s), Retrenchment (1980 to 2021) and Renewal (today).[1]

2.1 *Trustbusting (1890 to 1920)*

After a slow start, Sect. 2 was used by Presidents Theodore Roosevelt and William Howard Taft to successfully break up large firms whose dominant positions were often achieved through horizontal acquisitions and mergers—like Standard Oil and American Tobacco. This is known as the "trust-busting era." But not everyone at the time was satisfied. Progressives like Louis Brandeis demanded even more action against large firms. The election of Woodrow Wilson led to creation in 1914 of a new statute prohibiting "unfair methods of competition." But the war in Europe blunted any Progressive crusade against monopoly. Indeed, Progressive demands for vigorous enforcement against large firms had little influence on antitrust enforcement until four years ago.

2.2 *Hibernation (1920 to 1937)*

In 1920, trustbusting came to an abrupt end when the Supreme Court rejected the government's request to break up U.S. Steel for unlawful monopolization. Antitrust law challenges of monopoly—and the antimonopoly tradition—went into hibernation during the good times of the Roaring Twenties. And cooperation—not competition—was the aim of U.S. economic policy during Franklin Roosevelt's first term (1933–1937).

2.3 *Expansion (1937 to 1970s)*

In 1937, the pragmatic president shifted U.S. economic policy from business cooperation to competition. The change in course reflected the view that the Depression and slow economic recovery resulted from domination of industry by a small

[1] See B. E. Hawk, *Monopoly in America*, 2020.

number of large firms. This initiated an era of aggressive and often successful antitrust challenges to dominant firms and mergers, an era that lasted into the 1970s.

With increased funding and executive support, the Justice Department ('DOJ') under Thurman Arnold initiated industry-wide investigations of large firms. Arnold's policy was "to hit hard, hit everyone and hit them all at once." In the construction industry alone, the DOJ divided the nation into ten districts and by the end of the year grand juries were sitting in 11 major cities that ultimately produced 99 criminal actions and 22 two civil actions. Arnold estimated that the antitrust actions saved consumers over $300 million in building costs (or over $ 5 billion in 2020 dollars).

Continuing into the late 1960s, the government successfully challenged many dominant firms and mergers—the latter with market shares and concentration ratios far below later government Merger Guidelines. For example, in *Brown Shoe* the Supreme Court condemned a merger involving a combined horizontal market share and vertical foreclosure under 10%.[2] The Court later declared that "possible economies cannot be used as a defense to illegality."[3] During the expansionary period, the DOJ'S and the court's aggressive interpretation of antitrust law was described as the inhospitality tradition, that is, they were said to express inhospitality toward efficient business conduct.

2.4 Retrenchment (Late 1970s to 2021)

The era of condemnation of mergers with trivial combined market shares, monopolization actions against successful large firms and per se rules on vertical (distribution) agreements came to an end in the late 1970s. Except for the breakup of AT&T in 1982, government challenges to monopoly were sparse between 1980 and 2020, certainly when compared with the trustbusting and post-war expansionary periods. The most important government case was the DOJ's successful action against Microsoft in the late 1990s concerning self-preferencing, coercive tying and bundling to prevent or deter nascent rivals from gaining a foothold in the market for operating platforms which Microsoft dominated.[4] However, remedies were limited to those specific practices and no divestiture was required. As to merger enforcement, a series of Merger Guidelines—based mostly on developments in economic theory—considerably relaxed substantive standards as compared with court decisions of the expansionary era. The courts generally accepted the more relaxed standards.

For the first two decades in this century, it is fair to generalize that the two U.S agencies (DOJ and the Federal Trade Commission) under both Republican and

---

[2] *Brown Shoe Co. v. United States*, 370 U.S. 294, 346 (1962).

[3] *FTC v. Procter & Gamble Co.*, 386 U.S. 568, 580 (1967).

[4] *U.S. v. Microsoft Corp.*, 253 F.3d 34 (D.C. Cir. 2001).

Democratic administrations continued a cautious approach in bringing monopolization and merger cases—at least compared with previous periods.

2.5 *Renewal (2021 to Present)*

This all changed when President Biden was elected. U.S. antitrust enforcement was considerably strengthened in 2021 with the appointments of Jonathan Kanter as Head of the DOJ Antitrust Division and Lina Khan as Chairman of the FTC. Both federal agencies, as well as state antitrust authorities, initiated a number of monopolization cases and merger challenges, particularly in digital platform and other high-tech markets. We are living in a different antitrust world today than four years ago.

3 Reasons for the Cycle of U.S. Enforcement

There are four reasons or factors in the enforcement cycle of dramatic shifts in antitrust enforcement:

1. developments in economic theory
2. changes in facts (economic conditions)
3. political support and electoral politics
4. legal process concerns

This contrasts with the EU where changes in the role of economic analysis and economic conditions have been far more important than politics or legal process concerns.

3.1 *Developments in Economic Theory*

Economic theory, as it continued to develop throughout the twentieth and twenty-first centuries, gradually increased its role in antitrust law over the decades. For example, economic theory played a far more important role in the post-1945 expansionary period than in the earlier trustbusting period. Developments in economic theory also were significant factors in shifting from expansion to retrenchment in the 1970s. In the 1950s, economic theory supported aggressive antimonopoly enforcement, notably structuralist theories holding that market structure (concentration and monopoly) leads to harmful market performance (higher prices, less output and lower quality goods or innovation). In the early 1970s the underlying assumptions of the structuralists were rejected and economists emphasized the importance of efficiencies and criticized antitrust law's inattention to business justifications.

This unquestionably influenced both the agencies and the courts to take a more tolerant view of dominant firms and mergers.

Developments in economic theory have clearly influenced merger enforcement. The antitrust authorities have continued to refine merger reviewing standards to reflect developments in economic theory and changes in market conditions like production technologies or innovation. Non-structural factors have been added to merger analysis and structural presumptions have been modified.

Linked to developments in economic theory, the retrenchment era ushered in a new set of related assumptions (a new worldview or *weltanschauung*): (1) efficiencies explain most business arrangements; (2) market power self-corrects and competition is robust; (3) governments (including courts) are less capable than markets to address perceived competition problems; and (4) the risks of false positives are greater than risks of false negatives. These assumptions have been increasingly challenged as many economists began to challenge the focus on short term prices and the inattention to historical concerns about exclusionary or foreclosure effects on competitors. Critics cite the failure to consider longer-term business strategies like raising rivals' costs and strategic behavior in markets with network effects.

What about "consumer welfare"—a buzzword in contemporary competition policy around the world. Since the 1970s, consumer welfare analysis has dominated U.S. antitrust law—to the apparent exclusion of a variety of political and social concerns underlying the original antitrust movement, which generated the state antitrust laws and then the Sherman Act in the first place.[5]

Debates about "consumer welfare" can be more academic than practical. Definitions of "consumer welfare" are secondary to the main question: what exactly is required to prove an antitrust violation or claim. For example, a "static" analysis requires proof of effect on present (or past) prices, output or product quality/innovation. A "dynamic" analysis focuses on proof of (predicted) effect on future prices, output or product quality/innovation. U.S. courts—as well as the authorities—consider proffered economic evidence and arguments, generally with no attempt to place those theories in an academic category. Schools are more for the classroom than the court room or agency office.

Moreover, schools are not purely economic theories. The Chicago School was part of a broader intellectual movement that expressed confidence in markets and scepticism in government with an emphasis on efficiencies and focus on price effects. Ordoliberalism is more a political economy theory than a branch within mainstream economics.

[5] See B. E. Hawk, *Antitrust and Competition Laws*, 2020.

3.2 Changes in Facts/Economic Conditions (and Assumptions)

Changes in economic conditions—changes in the facts—are also important in understanding enforcement cycles. One example is the comparison of the post-war expansionary period and the later retrenchment period. The competitive position of U.S. firms had improved significantly by 1945. U.S. firms were relatively free from foreign competition, given the still existing trade barriers to entry and the economic weakness of potential foreign competitors. A reasonable assumption was that any market power enjoyed by U.S. firms would persist. And the success of U.S. firms after 1945 reduced the risks that aggressive enforcement might chill innovation or other procompetitive behaviour.

By the end of the 1970s, however, entry of foreign competitors into U.S. markets strongly suggested relaxation of the previous assumption that market power persists without antitrust law intervention. The retrenchment era assumption held that markets (and monopolies) tend to self-correct, making antitrust intervention necessary in only rare circumstances of market failure. That assumption led to more tolerant legal rules for mergers and for dominant firm conduct—such as predatory pricing and refusals to deal.

Economic conditions have significantly changed again with the internet and digital revolutions. As in the past, changes in facts go together with changes in economic theory. Often the facts come first and theoreticians then reflect on the new facts to develop new theories. This has certainly been the case with antitrust economics.

3.3 Political Support and Electoral Politics

Executive support and congressional funding were critical in both the trustbusting era and the expansionary era, as well as in the present period since 2021. Their importance cannot be exaggerated. For example, the strong political support of the Administrations of both Roosevelts and Lyndon Johnson contrasts with the more tolerant view of monopoly and mergers begun in the Administrations of Ronald Reagan and George W. Bush.

Electoral outcomes offer a different perspective to the conventional explanation that rests on changes in "antitrust schools." For example, Franklin Roosevelt restarted the antitrust engine primarily for pragmatic reasons. Roosevelt expressed his general pragmatism in 1932: "It is common sense to take a method and try it. If it fails, admit it frankly and try another. But above all, try something."[6] In his first term, Roosevelt tried business cooperation and not competition to halt the Depression; when that failed, in 1937 he shifted to tough antitrust enforcement. The ultimate result was the most aggressive antimonopoly period since the Administration

[6] Roosevelt, Franklin Delano (1933). Looking forward. John Day. p. 141.

of his cousin. The policies of the Biden Administration—which embraces Progressive views on antitrust enforcement—is the most recent example of the importance of political electoral shifts in U.S. enforcement. Attempted shifts in antitrust enforcement policy initiated by new administrations are not always successful, at least in the short run. For example, the Reagan administration's attempt to persuade the Congress and the courts to abandon a per se ban on resale price maintenance failed.

What about popular support for antitrust enforcement? In my view, popular support less clearly correlates with aggressive enforcement. To be sure, popular support was an important motivator during the trustbusting era of Teddy Roosevelt. But popular support was far less visible for the aggressive antitrust enforcement after 1945. And popular concerns about large firms and concentration did not elect President Biden, although complaints about price gouging and large corporate misbehaviour are topics of the 2024 electoral campaign that could well affect enforcement.[7]

What about political appointment of judges? Do Republican-appointed "conservative" judges favour business and "liberal" Democratic-appointed judges favour the government and private complainants? A tentative conclusion is that this was not a frequently voiced concern until the last two decades. Supreme Court antitrust decisions do not clearly evidence a stark division along partisan lines to the same extent as constitutional law cases. However, political partisanship cannot be entirely excluded. In tThe Supreme Court's 2018 decision in *Amex*[8] five conservative judges selected economic models that favoured the defendant, and four liberal judges selected economic models that favoured the plaintiff. Whether or not this reflects political divisions, the decision in *Amex* shows that we remain far removed from an algorithmic application of economic principles that produce clear administrable legal rules even in restraint of trade cases, let alone more complex monopolization cases.

3.4 Legal Process Concerns

Concerns about litigation costs, administrability of legal rules, the capability of jurors and judges to fully understand complex facts and economic theories, and the magnitude of chilling effects on investment and efficiency-enhancing conduct when legal rules are overly broad were critical factors in narrowing application of U.S. antitrust law during the retrenchment period. The greater emphasis on legal process concerns to narrow antitrust law in the U.S.—compared with the EU—may reflect U.S. courts' concerns about private antitrust action.

[7] Popular complaints about price gouging and price spikes commonly led to increased enforcement of laws of forestalling and hoarding in pre-industrial times. See B. E. Hawk, *Antitrust and Competition Law*, 2020, pp. 12–81.

[8] *Ohio v. American Express Co.*, 585 U.S. 316 (2018).

4 EU Cycles of Competition Law and Policy

Let me briefly turn to EU enforcement of competition law and policy since 1962, a period far shorter than the more than a century of U.S. enforcement since 1890. Although there certainly have been changes in EU competition law and policy since 1958, those changes are not as dramatic or as politically influenced as the enforcement cycles in the United States. Changes in EU enforcement appear more like trends that occurred over time rather than the kind of sudden changes seen in U.S. enforcement policy. Moreover, changes in the EU can be more clearly attributed to developments in economic theory and changes in economic conditions than to electoral politics or legal process concerns.

I suggest three periods of EU enforcement based on the increasing resort to economics in the formulation and application of Articles 101 and 102: (1) Formative period (1962 to 1990); (2) Middle period (1990 to 2003), and (3) Current period (2003 to present).

4.1 1962 (Regulation 17) to 1990 (ECMR)

The early decades of EU competition law and policy were marked by the necessity to build an effective enforcement system. Priorities were initially given to the overarching Treaty goal of market integration. It is not the case, however, that the Treaty goal of competition was neglected. Restrictive practices and dominant firm conduct were assessed under a competition analysis that often (but not always) reflected developments in mainstream economic theory. Economic analysis was employed by both the Commission and the Courts. The most notable example was the Court's 1972 judgment in *Continental Can*[9] which certainly compares favourably with the quality of economic analyses of U.S. judgments of the same period. Counsel for the parties put forth sophisticated economic arguments to which the Court of Justice responded in its opinion. Many observers and EU commentators argued, however, that the Commission and Court relied on either non-economic ideas (*vide* ordoliberal) or outdated economic theories. This criticism often centered on vertical restrictions, intellectual property licenses and dominant firm conduct. There were few economists with advanced degrees working in DG-IV/Competition Directorate before 1990 and it is fair to say that—generally speaking—developments in economic theory did not play the same role in the EU than they did in the U.S.

---

[9] Judgment in *Europemballage Corp. & Continental Can Co. v. Commission,* 6/72, EU:C:1973:22.

4.2 1990 (ECMR) to 2003 (Regulation 1/2003)

This all changed with the introduction of the Merger Regulation in 1990, and the creation of the Merger Task Force. Economists, notably seconded from authorities like the BKA and the U.S. Federal Trade Commission, began to play an important (and praised) role in EU competition enforcement. Perhaps to oversimplify and unduly humanize the situation, over the next decade economists and economic analysis gained significant influence that ultimately changed the rules under Article 101, particularly concerning vertical restraints and intellectual property. Developments in economic theory were reflected in Commission decisions and Court judgments, much like they were in the U.S.

During the same period, the Commission significantly increased application of the rules on state aid and member state interventions into markets. Of course, member state political support (particularly from the British and Germans) was critical. This more aggressive enforcement of existing Treaty rules came more from political pressure from member states than developments in economic theories. This raises a larger point. Of course, political events (like the dissolution of the USSR) and member state attitudes toward markets were important for competition policy. But in contrast to the dramatic shifts in antitrust enforcement resulting from electoral politics in the United States, political influence on EU enforcement has always been far more nuanced and—at least to this observer—less volatile (and less visible). For example, the abandonment of the notification system and its replacement in 2003 did not result from changes in the Commission, the Council of Ministers or the member state governments.

Let's turn to the present period of EU competition law, a period characterized by an even greater acceptance of economic analysis.

4.3 Regulation 1/2023 to Present

Much of the period since adoption of Regulation 1/2003 has been devoted to the issue of the appropriate mix of law and economics. Under both EU competition law and U.S. antitrust law, rules have changed to reflect developments in economic theory, as well as the growing acceptance of conventional economic analyses in the EU where debate has been framed in terms of legal formalism versus effects rules. This is illustrated by the shift away from the notion of economic freedom of the trader as an operative principle of competition law to a more conventional economics-oriented effects analysis. In both the EU and the U.S., economic freedom to trade supported an aggressive application of competition law that condemned practices like vertical price and non-price restraints with little or no inquiry into competitive effects. Both jurisdictions eventually responded to criticism that the legal rules were overly broad and failed to reflect developments in economic theory and experience which required a more tolerant position. Though later than the U.S., the EU shift from legal formalism to effects analysis correlates with the increasing role of economics and economists in the enforcement of EU competition law.

There is an important difference between the EU and U.S. developments. Although both jurisdictions shifted to more tolerant rules because of changes in economic theory, the U.S. shift also was motivated to some extent by concerns about false positives and systemic costs, particularly arising in the context of private actions. The EU courts have not voiced similar concerns, perhaps because of the relative paucity of private actions.

There is another difference between EU and U.S. developments. The EU and U.S. shift in legal standards have come at different speeds. Changes in U.S. rules can be abrupt, as with the Supreme Court overturning well-established precedent in one swoop in *GTE Sylvania*[10] and then in *Leegin*.[11] The development came more gradually in the EU, shifting from formalistic legal analysis to a more conventional economics-oriented effects analysis. That evolution in the EU also came earlier for restrictive vertical agreements under Article 101 than for abuses of dominant position under Article 102. The judgment in *Intel I* is the best example.[12]

In conclusion, economic currents constitute the principal force in cycles of competition law enforcement. Both the EU and U.S. rivers flow in the same direction, albeit at different speeds. The EU river has tended to go in the same direction. But the rapids are higher in the U.S. where new Administrations change course more suddenly when their perception of antitrust policy changes the river's course on the other side of the Atlantic.

[10] *Continental T.V., Inc. v. GTE Sylvania, Inc.*, 433 U.S. 36 (1977).

[11] *Leegin Creative Leather Products, Inc. v. PSKS, Inc.*, 551 U.S. 877 (2007).

[12] Judgment in *Intel Corp. v. Commission*, C-413/14 P, EU:C:2017:632, which, in that respect, largely follows the Opinion of AG Wahl in the case (EU:C:2017:632).

Excessive Pricing and the Elusive Concept of Exploitative Abuse

Lars Henriksson

1 Introduction and Background: The Notion of Unfairness in EU Competition Law

Ever since Article 86 of the EEC was introduced, there has been persistent uncertainty related to the true meaning of what was to become Article 102 (a) TFEU, according to which it may be an abuse to directly impose *unfair* purchase or selling prices or other unfair trading conditions. In other words, it addresses the situation when a dominant undertaking is overcharging its trading partner for products sold, or, conversely, undercharging trading parties for products purchased. Although the antitrust effects of such mirror images are arguably different because the alleged abuse would take place higher or lower in the distribution chain and it may not manifest itself in the same way amongst end consumers when the results of the pricing behaviour inevitably trickle down through distribution chain.[1] To simplify for the purpose of this Article, it is illustrative to focus on the situation when a dominant undertaking charges an excessive price. At the outset, the adjectives 'unfair' and 'excessive' says very little about where to draw a distinct line between high, but lawful, prices and those that are so high that they are unreasonably high or excessive and thereby unfair.

[1] To the antitrust effects of purchasing power, see I. Herrera Anchustegui, *Buyer Power in EU Competition Law*, Bergen, diss. 2017.

L. Henriksson (✉)
Stockholm School of Economics, Stockholm, Sweden
e-mail: Lars.Henriksson@hhs.se

L. Prete, L. Rezki (eds.), *Judging & (Re)Thinking European Union Law*,
https://doi.org/10.1007/978-3-032-13473-8_8

This author has earlier made futile attempts to find the answer to this question more than two decades ago,[2] only to be fiercely—but justifiably—challenged by the very person to whom we now give our praise in this book. Knowing him, he would probably not view it that way, but rather as a constructive and straightforward dialogue on a subject that interested him. If so, I would now in hindsight agree. The thrust of his critique was simply amplified by the acuity of his arguments. Being on the receiving end of his scrutiny of my dissertation, it was still daunting, but most likely one of the greatest learning experiences that I have experienced. For this, I owe him a deed of gratitude that I will probably not be able to repay. Wahl's impressive sharpness and insightfulness and legal wisdom has undoubtedly set its lasting mark on the application of EU law. It has been especially gratifying to read his opinions in his role as Advocate General with the CJEU. It was therefore not a surprise that when he was given opportunity, he wrote a long awaited, well formulated and most interesting opinion on the matter of unfair prices.[3] Against that backdrop, I'd like to offer my thoughts on the question at hand.

1.1 The Beginnings of Unfairness in Competition Law

The ordoliberal heritage in EU competition law appears obvious when exploitative abuses are to be assessed. Unlike the U.S. Sherman Act, however, which concerns attempts to monopolise markets, the EU counterpart abuse of dominance has a broader meaning and application encompassing not only exclusionary conduct but also undue exercise of the market power stemming from the dominant position. The ordoliberal theoretical command towards dominant firms to act *as if* they were facing fierce competition (Ger. 'Wettbewerb als ob')[4] fits theoretically well with the notion of unfairness. Nonetheless, it has always been fraught with difficulties to find an adequate, clear, and administrative workable definition or criteria to what more precisely amounts to an excessive price within the meaning of competition law. That fact alone makes it doubtful whether any rule or method would be able to meet even low standards of legal certainty, which in turn exacerbates the dilemma associated with clarifying an inherently elusive concept. This is, however, not to say that excessive prices do not exist or that they cannot be viewed as problematic. On the

[2] L. Henriksson, *Rätten till priskonkurrens – i marknadsdominans*, diss. MercurIUS 2003, and N. Wahl, *anm. av Henriksson, L., Rätten till priskonkurrens – i marknadsdominans*, JT 2003–2004 pp. 675 ff. Further regarding the legal assessment of excessive pricing and unfair prices in contract law, see L. Henriksson, 'Om oskäliga priser', Juridisk Tidskrift 2006/2007, pp. 566–591.

[3] AG Wahl Opinion in case C-177/16, *Autortiesību un komunicēšanās konsultāciju aģentūra / Latvijas Autoru apvienība v Konkurences padome (AKKA/LAA)*, EU:C:2017:286. See also, extra-judicially, N. Wahl, 'From Greek Olive Oil to Latvian Music: is there any such thing as unfair prices?", 1 May 2018, *Concurrences* N. 2–2018, Art. N. 86617.

[4] See D., J., Gerber, *Law and Competition in Twentieth Century Europe: Protecting Prometheus*, Oxford, 2003, p. 252.

contrary, the undue exercise of monopoly power and exploitation of consumers and customers are conducts that arguably are the very raison-d'être of antitrust rules. Nevertheless, the question remains of whether it is possible—or desirable—to combat the causes or the symptoms as an antitrust problem. Other measures like addressing barriers to entry or simply ex ante regulation could perhaps be better suited to address the underlying market problem. Some would argue that both are important tools, but, if so; the challenge remains of how to properly define what constitutes unjustified exploitation and which market conduct can be accepted.

1.2 The Overall Problem of Reconciling Article 102 a) TFEU with Economic Theory

Returning to the subject-matter of excessiveness, the main demur to the methods I discussed in my earlier works on excessive pricing was in essence this; the theoretically highest imaginable price that can be charged on a monopoly market is the monopoly price. Monopoly is the extreme form of dominance, which is per se is not prohibited—only the abuse thereof. So, if the monopoly in theory could normally be expected to generate the monopoly price—it could then be argued that condemning that price as being excessive would also entail indirectly condemning the monopoly itself? It remains hard to rebut that assertion at the outset. Unquestionably, the monopoly price is generally speaking always to some extent excessive—after all, that is the very reason to why legislators either endeavour to introduce competition, or if that is not possible to regulate prices, e.g., on markets of natural monopolies. Still, Article 102 a) TFEU does make unfair prices unlawful. So, we are left with a legal ban that, without doubt, is very hard to apply even in theory.

Case law on excessive prices outside commercial situations when it has been used as a tool in exclusionary strategies[5] or on markets with de facto monopolies where little competition can be expected challenge the dominant position remains scarce. Particularly, there has been some cases on the exploitative abusive conduct related to pricing of licenses from copyright collection societies, where the conditions on downstream markets have been affected.[6]

[5] Cf. Judgment in *General Motors Continental NV v Commission*, 26–75, EU:C:1975:150, where an excessive price for issuance of a certificate of conformity was used with the effect to curb intra-community trade. Also, in Judgment in *British Leyland Public Limited Company v Commission*, 226/84, EU:C:1986:421, a similar practice was under scrutiny by the court.

[6] See Judgments in *Ministère public v Jean-Louis Tournier*, 395/87, EU:C:1989:319; *François Lucazeau and others v Société des Auteurs, Compositeurs et Editeurs de Musique (SACEM) and others*, 110/88, 241/88 and 242/88, EU:C:1989:326; and *Kanal 5 and TV 4 (Kanal 5)*, C-52/07, EU:C:2008:703.

2 Early Days: The First Formulated Test for Excessive Prices

The first test for exploitative abuse in the form of excessive pricing was articulated in the *United Brands* case[7] that concerned a more traditional market for sales of goods.

The case essentially concerned United Brands Company's (UBC) pricing of bananas across member states of the community. UBC was held to have abused its dominant position on the banana market by charging discriminatory and excessive prices to its customers.[8] Although the ECJ eventually found UBC to have abused its dominant position by discriminatory prices, the matter of excessive prices was also addressed by the court. At the heart of the problem was the fact that UBC charged prices in inter alia Denmark that were considerably higher than the prices charged in, e.g., Ireland. As a dominant undertaking on the banana market—could that fact alone be regarded as an abuse by way of an exploitative behaviour and as an expression of charging unfair prices within the meaning of competition law?

The Commission argued in *United Brands* that UBC's prices were excessive in relation to the *economic value* of the bananas. More precisely, there was a considerable price difference between member states and bearing in mind that even the lowest prices yielded a profit, the higher prices then had to be regarded as abusive—seemingly without regard to the underlying cost structure or terms of delivery for supplying the bananas. Also, compared to unbranded bananas, UBC's prices were 20–40 per cent higher whilst UBC's competitors were still operating such prices at a profit. In view of the Commission, this accentuated the abusive nature of the dominant undertaking's pricing scheme and a reduction of the prices by 15 per cent appeared appropriate. UBC held the argument to be unintelligent claiming that profit levels were not unreasonably high and that there were substantial differences in the terms of cost structures, seasonal variations of prices etc. across member states.

2.1 Establishing a Benchmark: The Notion of Economic Value

In finding criteria for excessive prices, the court essentially started in *United Brands* by reiterating the first example of abuses enshrined in Article 86, namely that the imposition by a dominant undertaking or directly or indirectly of unfair purchase or

[7] Case 27/76, *United Brands Company and United Brands Continentaal BV v Commission (United Brands)*, EU:C:1978:22.

[8] The ECJ has in later case law used the expression 'exorbitant' prices in parallel to excessive prices. The adjectives still appear synonyms and although other expressions can also be used, they all have in common that they address the situation where the dominant firm is charging prices that are objectively too high. Cf. judgment in *Société civile agricole du Centre d'insémination de la Crespelle v Coopérative de la Mayenne (Centre d'insémination de la Crespelle)*, C-323/93, EU:C:1994:368, para. 19.

selling prices is an abuse [now Article 102 (a) TFEU]. However, very little guidance was available regarding what constituted an 'unfair selling price' at the time of the judgment in 1978.

As a general remark, the ECJ held that it would be advisable to ascertain whether the dominant undertaking had made use of the opportunities arising out of its dominant position in such a way as to reap trading benefits which it could not have reaped absent the dominant position and subject to normal and sufficiently effective competition.[9] In principle, this alternative price charged under hypothetical competitive conditions could be viewed as the benchmark price, although it would not necessarily follow that the difference alone between the actual price and the hypothetical could make the actual price unlawful. In broad terms, however, this is echoing the ordoliberalist theoretical approach to competition policy of 'Wettbewerb als ob', namely the overarching principle that monopolists should be forced to trade at conditions that would have applied under perfectly competitive conditions to better reflect the notion of *Leistungswettbewerb* (competition on the merits).[10]

Although intuitively understandable as a general starting point, such a principle offers no more precision compared to the wording of Article 102 TFEU and does not answer the question of how high a price should be to become abusive, and not even how the benchmark should be calculated to assess a given price level. The court agreed in *United Brands* with the Commission on the principal standpoint that charging a price which has no *reasonable relation to the economic value* of the product supplied would be an abuse.[11] That stance triggers, in turn, two major questions: (a) when does the relationship become 'unreasonable/excessive/exorbitant', and (b) what constitutes an 'economic value'; is that economic value synonymous with the hypothetical, alternative, price mentioned above as the benchmark?

2.2 *The Stepwise Approach to Establishing Excessive Prices*

To establish the existence of an excessive price, the court relied in *United Brands* on a stepwise approach. The court held that the excess in relation to the economic value could in fact be objectively determined [sic!] if it first were possible to make a comparison between the selling price for the products and its costs of production, i.e. disclosing the profit margin. The legal test for abusively high prices, i.e. excessive or exorbitantly high prices established by the ECJ was in then end somewhat confusing. First, the court required that it should be demonstrated that the calculated

[9] Judgment in *United Brands*, para. 249. Later case law has confirmed this principle starting point in judgment *Kanal 5*, para. 27.

[10] Cf. Gerber, op. cit.

[11] Judgment in *United Brands*, para. 250.

profit level was excessive, and, if so; whether the *price* imposed—not the profit incurred—was unfair either *in itself or when compared to competing products.*[12]

Consequently, the true meaning of the notion of excessiveness or unfairness was not addressed; the price could be abusive because if it is unfair. Still, the judgment said very little about how to calculate an unreasonable profit (the 'excess'), and the reader was left in the dark on the matter of what the economic value actually is and how much a price—or profit—may justifiably deviate from this theoretical benchmark. The stepwise approach entailed an apparent problem of sequencing; first the profit level should 'excessive', and, secondly, the price should be 'unfair' either in itself or when compared to other competing products. Neither of these criteria were, however, clarified in further detail.

2.3 Excessive Nature of Profits

The first step involves establishing an excessive profit level. The difficulties of establishing whether a profit level is excessive should not be overlooked. At the outset, no undertaking should be indirectly forced to operate at losses in order to reduce a purported excessive price level. Neither should an undertaking be forced to operate at unsustainably low profit levels. Otherwise, this may generate other antitrust concerns insofar the terms may generate predatory effects vis-à-vis the dominant undertaking's competitors. It must therefore reasonably be acceptable that prices afford the undertaking an acceptable margin to cover its costs. Long-term fully allocated costs of the undertaking and a satisfactory return on capital should be covered, whilst considering the needs of consumers, the competitive market situation, including the prices of the other undertakings, and the need to prevent predatory pricing behaviour should be taken into account.[13]

What amounts to a normal or satisfactory profit level is possible to ascertain without greater difficulty. In corporate finance or valuation, e.g., it is commonplace to calculate the risk-adjusted cost of capital (debt and equity) necessary for a particular company, often expressed as the key ratio WACC (weighted average cost of capital), which reveals the hurdle rate a company should meet to objectively satisfy the required rate of return on investments. For the purpose of antitrust proceedings, this would then be relevant to consider in setting a minimum profit level, i.e., the return on capital that would be any investor would require with regard to risk associated with the investment.

Still, the question remains what measurement of deviation upwards from this floor should be regarded as excessive under law. There is no not exact guidance on

[12] Judgment in *United Brands*, para. 252. An unfair profit level can naturally stem either from an exorbitantly high price or a disproportionate and wrongful allocation of cost to the product in question. Cf. judgment *Centre d'insémination de la Crespelle*, para. 21.

[13] Cf. Judgment in *Ahmed Saeed Flugreisen and Others v Zentrale zur Bekämpfung unlauteren Wettbewerbs*, 66/86, EU:C:1989:140, para. 43.

the metrics of deviation to satisfy this first step and thereby triggering the second step laid down by the court. Comparing prices at this step would say very little about the excessive nature of a profit level and is essentially something that should be done in the second step. Again, the first step merely concerns establishing an excessive profitability of the dominant undertaking. There should therefore be a substantial deviation from what can be regarded as normal profits in order for the actual profit to be viewed as excessive. Regrettably, this does not bring much clarity to the analysis of what amounts in addition to 'excessiveness'.

In defence of the stepwise approach, and although it appears somewhat confusing, a profit level should normally only be excessive if the income generated a pricing scheme that entails exorbitantly high prices. Still, the price could not reasonably be exorbitant if the dominant undertaking was operating at losses. The first step of the analysis is therefore merited—otherwise the analysis would be reduced to assessing prices without regard to cost structures.

AG Wahl underlined in his opinion in *AKKA/LAA* that any test, method, screening, or criteria for excessive prices face some grave difficulties.[14] Firstly, no test have ever been devised to be generally applicable and instead they are highly dependent on the particular settings and circumstances in individual cases. Costs for production may indeed be very difficult or complex to ascertain, and especially in pricing of intellectual property rights such as copyrights the cost of production may prove senseless to scrutinise because it has very little to do with pricing of licenses. Secondly, there is no universal standard for measuring costs for a product supplied. Although international accounting standards such as IFRS or US GAAP may be indicative of a certain cost level, decisions on pricing may be entirely disconnected from financial statements and reporting. Allocation of costs, accrual of incomes and timing issues may very well be different than that which is required for financial reporting and taxation purposes, in turn implying that the notion of profit is not always a straight-forward issue and that different profit levels may therefore not be adequately comparable across industries or between companies. Different markets, both product markets and geographic markets, may display considerable differences and features in terms of cost levels, taxes and demand characteristics, rendering comparisons between markets inadequate for antitrust purposes. If comparisons are to be made, corrections and adjustments for differences are unavoidable. All in all, these caveats result in a great uncertainty and low precision of the benchmark, and with regard to basic requirements related to legal certainty this would make authorities reluctant or at least very careful to venture into this from of abuse.[15]

[14] AG Wahl Opinion in *AKKA/LAA*, C-177/16, EU:C:2017:286, paras. 36–42.

[15] Although competition law in not part of the core area of criminal law, it has a similar character bearing in mind the potential severe penalties, The European Court of Human Rights held in *A Menarini Diagnostics S.R.L. v. Italy* (CE:ECHR:2011:0927JUD004350908, §§ 38–45), that administrative fines imposed in cartel proceedings could be regarded as 'criminal' within the meaning of Article 6(1) ECHR. See also AG Kokott, who underlined in *Schenker & Co. and Others* that "... regard must be had in antitrust law to certain principles stemming from criminal law

According to AG Wahl, the methodological weaknesses could perhaps be remedied by combining different methods. This could be likened with several strands of in themselves weak evidence that viewed together would make a finding of abuse stronger. Still, as AG Wahl underlines, that does not make the individual tests stronger. In fact, if combining several tests they also need to be independent of each other.[16] Pricing decisions are most often based on a number of factors and circumstances that are dependent on one another and may indeed display interdependencies and covariations. If so, tests or methods may also rely on the same variables. Furthermore, the combination of them may be weaker than viewed separately; a factor with low probability depending on another low probability would, taken together, yield a combined ever lower probability. Therefore, not only is it necessary to adjust for differences under the underlying market structure, but also to assess whether the tests employed display interdependencies.

2.4 The Comparison of Relevant Prices

Next, the final step in the analysis is to assess whether the actual price charged is excessive *in itself* or when compared to other prices. To establish a price as unfair in itself without connection to a proper benchmark appears meaningless and not surprisingly such findings in case law are scarce. Perhaps it could be argued, as AG Wahl discussed in *AKKA/LAA*, that as in *Merci* or *Grüne Punkt* not delivering anything is return for a price could be viewed as abusive.[17] However, it appears to be considerably better to handle such cases under contract law or as form of tying, when applicable. Refusal to deliver anything in return for remuneration paid would render any price excessive if one were to pursue that line of reasoning. Therefore, whether those cases add anything to the conundrum of when a price is unfair in itself when the dominant firm actually delivers something is doubtful. The same applies, as mentioned above in *General Motors* or *British Leyland,* that when high prices—exorbitant as they very well may be *perceived*—are used as instruments to pursue an exclusionary strategy—the antitrust concern in such cases are not the exploitation, but rather the foreclosure of competitors. Later case law also indicates that rates for, e.g. licensing of copyrighted works, may amount to an abuse if the dominant undertaking employs imprecise pricing methods that do not correspond to actual use of the intellectual property concerned, when alternative and more precise

which can ultimately be traced back to the rule of law and the principle of fault." (Opinion in C-681/11, EU:C:2013:126, para. 40).

[16] AG Wahl Opinion in *AKKA/LAA*, paras 43–45.

[17] Cf. Judgments in *Merci Convenzionali Porto di Genova v Siderurgica Gabrielli*, C-179/90, EU:C:1991:464, para. 19; and in *Der Grüne Punkt v Commission*, C-385/07 P, EU:C:2009:456, para. 146. See also AG Wahl Opinion in *AKKA/LAA*, para. 122.

calculation methods are readily, technically, and economically available that would better and precisely achieve the in itself legitimate aim of collecting royalties.[18]

The other alternative once the profit level has been deemed excessive is then to compare the price with other relevant prices charged either by the dominant firm itself or by its competitors.[19] This matter was dealt with by the court in 2017, following a request for preliminary ruling and the CJEU then revisited the issue of excessive prices in *AKKA/LAA*.

The collective management organisation for copyrights to musical works in Latvia, AKKA/LAA, had allegedly charged unfairly high prices for licenses for public performance of musical works on behalf of copyright holders. Based upon a comparison of prices/rates in neighbouring countries, adjusted to the purchasing power parity index (PPP index), the Latvian Competition Council concluded that the rates were excessive and thus amounted to an abuse of dominance. On appeal before the Latvian Supreme Court, Administrative Cases Division, the court decided to stay the proceedings and refer questions to the CJEU for preliminary ruling. Among other uncertainties, the court had doubts about the method employed to determine the unfair nature of the prices. However, instead of asking for a general method to determine unfairly high prices, the questions referred concerned the legality of the method employed by the Competition Council.

With regard to the referred questions there is therefore at the outset a risk that the ruling in *AKKA/LAA* could become too casuistic, and that the abusive nature of exploitative practices may only be partly determined. The referred questions to the CJEU also primarily concerned the second step of the test in *United Brands*, i.e., the appropriateness of method of comparing prices.

Still, in view of the CJEU, abuse *might* generally lie in the imposition of a price which is excessive in relation to the economic value. In this regard, the court then reiterated, the original general method laid down in *United Brands* insofar it entailed first to establish whether the profit level is excessive, and if so, whether the price is either unfair in itself or when compared with competing products.[20] Again, the court reiterated that other methods exist to determine such prices, although no such alternative tests or methods were explored by the court. Unfortunately, yet understandably, the court did not recognize the challenges associated with relying on single method or test as explicitly underlined by AG Wahl and the need in most cases to

[18] Judgment in *SABAM*, C-372/19, EU:C:2020:959, paras 52–53.

[19] In early case law the ECJ underlined that sale price of a protected product may be regarded as a factor to be taken into account in determining the possible existence of an abuse, although a higher price for the patented product as compared with the unpatented product does not necessarily constitute an abuse—see judgment in *Parke, Davis & Co. v Probel and Others*, 24/67, EU:C:1968:11. The court later developed this reasoning by stating that a proprietor of protective rights in respect of an ornamental design may lawfully call for a return on the amounts which he has invested in order to perfect the protected design, judgment in *CICRA and Others v Renault*, C-53/87, EU:C:1988:472, para. 17.

[20] Judgments in *AKKA/LAA*, para. 36, and in *United Brands*, para. 253.

combine different methods to minimise the risk for false positives and false negatives.

If the Court had indeed highlighted the challenges and inherent weaknesses of any method designed to determine an excessive or exorbitantly high price, such a finding might have been perceived as an indirect way of saying that Article 102 (a) TFEU in the form of exploitative abuse does exist, at least in theory, but cannot be practically applied in almost any setting. In practice, that would be essentially indistinguishable from a finding that exploitative abuses do not exist. Admittedly, that would be going too far with regard to existing case law, and the court cannot deny the existence of elements in primary EU law and therefore not deprive such provisions of their application. An altogether other matter is whether a provision lend itself to be practically applicable in individual cases.

2.5 General Criteria for Comparing Prices

AG Wahl underlined in *AKKA/LAA* that it is primarily a matter for the adjudicating court to determine the correctness of a method of comparison employed, although any comparison would have to be made according to criteria that are *objective, appropriate and verifiable*. The court agreed and held that it is appropriate to compare the rates under scrutiny with those applicable in neighbouring Member States as well as with those applicable in other Member States adjusted in accordance with the purchasing power parity index (PPP index),[21] The selection of Member States must, however, been done in accordance with objective, appropriate and verifiable criteria and that the comparisons must be made on a consistent basis. In that respect, it was also held permissible to compare the rates charged in one or several specific user segments if there are indications that the excessive nature of the fees affects those segments.[22] With regard to the question of which markets could be used for comparison, the court held that the selection criteria may include, amongst others, consumption habits and other economic and sociocultural factors, such as GDP per capita and cultural and historical heritage. Again, it is for the adjudicating court to assess the relevance of the criteria applied in the case in the main proceedings, whilst considering all the circumstances of the case.[23]

The ruling in *AKKA/LAA*, which confirmed AG Wahl's opinion on the correctness of the methodology for making comparison, has made the matter of comparison requirements clearer and has narrowed the scope of comparison only to those prices that are objectively relevant to compare, and which can be verified over time.

[21] Purchasing power parities (PPPs) are indicators that measure the rates of currency conversion that are designed to equalise the purchasing power of different currencies, by way of eliminating the differences in price levels between countries. See 'Purchasing power parities (PPP)' on OECD's website.

[22] AG Wahl Opinion in *AKKA/LAA*, paras 51 and 60–68.

[23] Judgment in *AKKA/LAA*, para. 41.

Naturally, these criteria along with the selection criteria for suitable markets to compare opens up for considerable litigation of what should be deemed as comparable markets, and what shall be regarded as objective, appropriate and verifiable. In *AKKA/LAA*, the pricing concerned rates of licenses to copyrighted works and as such the comparison concerned more or less identical products across states that, adjusted for PPP, were indeed truly comparable. Those rather clear circumstances may not exist in other industries or relevant markets.

After relevant comparable prices have been identified it remains ascertain the how much the difference shall be to be regarded as unfair, or in other words; above what threshold shall the difference between the rates compared be regarded as *appreciable*[24] and, therefore, *indicative* of an abuse. The CJEU has still not established any clear criteria in that regard, but the short answer is that difference must be *significant* and *persistent*.[25] Again, this was based on AG Wahl's opinion. The two-fold requirement has perhaps not been so explicitly articulated in case law but is still consistent with earlier rulings. The requirement of significance was already articulated in *Tournier* and *Lucazeau* as the difference should be appreciably higher. The novelty in *AKKA/LAA* was the added requirement of persistency. Temporary or episodic high prices cannot be sufficient for an indication of abuse.[26] Instead, fluctuating prices with periodically higher and lower prices can very well be an expression of a functioning market as result of market forces drives high prices to a more competitive level. The significant high prices must therefore persist for certain length of time.[27]

Now, having formulated and specified the criteria, the question till remains on *how* significant and *how* persistent the difference must be to justify a finding of abuse. Naturally, the higher the difference is and the longer period it lasts, the easier it may be to arrive at such a conclusion. Even so, this question remains unanswered and thereby we are no closer to a workable, clear and foreseeable legal rule for abusively high prices. Over the last five decades, one adjective has largely been added to another, whilst not introducing any higher degree of clarity.

In contrast to earlier case law on excessive prices, it is also clear that the methods employed—subject to being practically workable—would not lead to a firm and

---

[24] Judgment in Case C-351/12, *OSA*, EU:C:2014:110, para. 92.

[25] AG Wahl Opinion in *AKKA/LAA*, paras 61 and 106–108, para. 61. See also judgments in *Tournier*, 395/87, EU:C:1989:319; and in *Lucazeau and Others v SACEM and Others,* joined cases 110/88, 241/88 and 242/88, EU:C:1989:326. The dual requirement makes the United Brands test more in line with economic reality. The AG made in this respect direct references to E. Paulis, 'Article 82 EC and Exploitative Conduct', in C-D. Ehlermann, M. Marquis (eds.), *European Competition Law Annual 2007: A Reformed Approach to Article 82*, Hart Publishing, 2007; and B. Lyons, 'The Paradox of the Exclusion of Exploitative Abuse, in the Pros and Cons of High Prices', in *Konkurrensverket*, 2007, p. 65.

[26] Judgment in *AKKA/LAA,* para. 56.

[27] See e.g. judgment in *General Motors v Commission*, 26/75, EU:C:1975:150, where the Commission had considered five cases of high prices during a period between 15 March to 31 July the same year. This was however only an occasional activity during a relatively short period, and it could not be considered an abuse. See paras 16–20.

non-rebuttable finding of abuse—only to an *indication* of abuse. In practice that entails a reversal of the burden of proof towards the dominant undertaking to justify the pricing scheme under scrutiny. In *AKKA/LAA* the court underlined that was for the copyright management organisation holding a dominant position to show that its prices were fair by reference to *objective factors* that had an impact on management expenses or the remuneration of rights holders.[28] What facts and circumstances that are necessary and sufficient to demonstrate in terms of justifying a prima facie excessive price is, however, a matter for another article.

Whether the ECJ in *United Brands* intended to actually offer true practical guidance on what legally constituted excessive prices remains to date uncertain. The court did not, however stop short of this unaccommodating definition and avowed that other ways may be possible to establish abuse and asserted that economic theorists had not failed to think up several of selecting the rules for determining whether the price of a product is unfair.[29] That finding is, however, disturbingly unsubstantiated because the court has yet to say something more tangible about what those theories were or who had formulated them. The theories were, and still are, illusively scarce if they even exist at all for the purpose of establishing exploitative abuse under EU competition law.

2.6 The Elusive Nature of Economic Value

A complicating factor in establishing excessive prices is that the concept of 'economic value' does not have any foundation in established economic theory in capacity of a proper benchmark for antitrust purposes.[30] Broadly, the economic value of an assets can be viewed as the ability of that asset to generate income in the future. As such, it is presumably directly linked to, and dependent on, the nature of demand for the product in question. At the time of formulation something of a novation in law. Of particular interest to this question is that earlier decisional practice by the Commission has addressed just this conundrum. First, in *GT Link*, the ECJ underlined that levying port duties may amount to an abuse if the duties were unfair in relation to the economic value.[31] Later, the Commission dealt with precisely this

---

[28] Judgment in *AKKA/LAA,* para. 61. To that effect, see also judgment in *Servizio Elettrico Nazionale and Others*, C-377/20, EU:C:2022:379.

[29] Judgment in *United Brands*, para. 253. Reiterated in the judgment in *AKKA/LAA*, p. 37.

[30] Economists and philosophers have battled with this question for millennia dating back to Aristotle and Plato and, scholastic writers such as Thomas Acquinas, Adam Smith and Joseph Schumpeter. See OECD, *Excessive Prices*, Roundtables on Competition Policy, N° 121, DAF/COMP(2011)18, 2012. On the matter of economic value, the OECD's secretariat concluded in their report that "the passage is of interest as it points to the fundamental question of the appropriate benchmark for assessing whether prices are unfair, unjust or excessive that remains unresolved till this day." (p. 27).

[31] Judgment in *GT-Link v De Danske Statsbaner*, C-242/95, EU:C:1997:376, paras 39 and 46.

legal issue in the cases *Scandlines*[32] and *Sundbusserne.*[33] The companies were operating ferry services between Denmark and Sweden. Both cases essentially concerned the charging of harbour tariffs in the Swedish port of Helsingborg that were considerably higher than almost identical services in the Danish port of Helsingør on the other side of the Öresund strait between Denmark and Sweden. The Commission rejected a cost-plus approach to calculate the economic value and underlined that demand factors must be included in establishing the economic value.

> "The demand-side is relevant mainly because customers are notably willing to pay more for something specific attached to the product/service that they consider valuable. This specific feature does not necessarily imply higher production costs for the provider. However it is valuable for the customer and also for the provider, and thereby increases the economic value of the product/service".[34]

This in turn naturally makes it even theoretically very difficult to establish any deviation from the economic value; the price cannot be held unreasonable if it corresponds to what the buyer is willing to pay for the product. If so, the price imposed merely reflects, or is identical to, the economic value whereby the price cannot sensibly be regarded as abusive because it cannot be disproportionate in relationship to the economic value.

AG Wahl acknowledged the Commission's general stance in *AKKA/LAA* that a high price may pertain to customers' demand. In the eyes of customers, the economic value may therefore.

> … be higher than the benchmark price. Again, there may be a variety of reasons for that: for instance, the goods or service in question may be (or be merely perceived to be, perhaps for reasons relating to advertising or branding investment costs) of superior quality. Some features of the product or service may be regarded as particularly valuable by customers (or certain groups of customers), in spite of the fact that they are not reflected on the cost side. In those cases, the additional benefits or advantages provided to customers justify a higher mark-up over costs."[35]

In *SABAM*, the Court held that it may be particularly difficult to determine in an objective manner the specific elements which are not related to the musical works performed and, therefore, to the service of the collective management company. The same applies when trying to quantify the economic value and the downstream effects or royalties charged.[36]

---

[32] Case COMP/A 36.568/D3 – Scandlines Sverige AB v Port of Helsingborg.

[33] Case COMP/A36.570/D3 – Sundbusserne v. Port of Helsingborg.

[34] Case COMP/A 36.568/D3 – Scandlines Sverige AB v Port of Helsingborg, para. 227.

[35] Opinion in *AKKA/LAA*, p. 128.

[36] Judgment in *SABAM*, C-372/19, EU:C:2020:959, para. 45. The wide scope of the notion of economic value as encompassing also the value generated downstream and thereby demand factors also follow from article 16 of Directive 2014/25/EU: "Rightholders shall receive appropriate remuneration for the use of their rights. Tariffs for exclusive rights and rights to remuneration shall be reasonable in relation to, inter alia, the economic value of the use of the rights in trade, taking into account *the nature and scope of the use of the work and other subject-matter*, as well as in relation to the *economic value of the service provided* by the collective management organisation. Collective

This should not, however, be interpreted as the economic value always corresponds to the actual price. Still, although the economic value may in theory be lower than the actual and persistent price, demand factors do matter, and this may indeed have decisive importance to the resolving difficulty of whether the deviation from the benchmark is large enough to amount to an abuse.

With the regard to the difficulties reviewed above, shall the test laid down in *United Brands* be viewed as an expression of ignorance of the economic theories in objectively determining abusive prices? No, it could not reasonably be presumed that the court failed to grasp the inherent and grave difficulties associated with formulating a general objective legal rule for establishing abuse in the form excessively high prices. Also, rules on abuse of dominance does indeed include an example of unfair prices, which could not be overlooked by the court. All the same, would the court have been able to objectively formulate a definition of the notions of fairness and reasonableness? Those concepts are after all relative by their very nature. There is naturally no universal definition of what is 'objectively fair'.

Still, the formulated test became by all standards so general and unattainable that it would be most difficult to put to general use by the courts. Perhaps this was deliberately so. This is not to say that high prices can never be anticompetitive, and a number of antitrust cases have dealt with such pricing behaviour, however the main concern in those cases were not *exploitative* as such. The scarcity of EU case law on exploitative abuse does mirror the outcome in U.S. antitrust law, although ostensibly for different reasons. In the EU, the practical problems of establishing such abuses appears to explain the few cases, whereas in the U.S. there is a different principled stance to excessive prices.

3 U.S. Antitrust Law: A Comparison Regarding Excessive Prices

One of the dividing lines between EU competition law and U.S. Antitrust law is the view on exploitative behaviour as a matter of antitrust concern in general. In *Trinko,*[37] excessive pricing in the telecom industry was brought up by a claimant as a violation of antitrust law.

The case concerned purported supplementary antitrust liability in the telecom industry of the local exchange carrier (LEC), Verizon. Pursuant to the U.S. Telecommunications Act of 1996 an incumbent LEC was obligated to share its telephone network with competitors, including the duty to provide access to

management organisations shall inform the user concerned of the criteria used for the setting of those tariffs." [emphasis added]. Directive 2014/26/EU of the European Parliament and of the Council of 26 February 2014 on collective management of copyright and related rights and multi-territorial licensing of rights in musical works for online use in the internal market (OJ 2014 L 84, p. 72).

[37] *Verizon Communications, Inc. v. Law Offices of Curtis V. Trinko, LLP*, 540 US 398 (2003).

individual network elements on an "unbundled" basis. Verizon's interconnection agreement was approved by the New York Public Service Commission (PSC), and its authorization to provide long-distance service was approved by the Federal Communications Commission (FCC). Both approvals specified the methods which its operations support systems obligation would be met. Competitive LECs then complained that Verizon had violated that obligation, prompting the PSC and FCC to open parallel investigations, which resulted in the imposition of financial penalties, remediation measures, and additional reporting requirements on Verizon in accordance with the Telecom Act. Subsequent to this, however, Trinko, a local telephone service customer of AT&T, filed a class action alleging, inter alia, that Verizon had filled rivals' orders on a discriminatory basis as part of an anticompetitive scheme to discourage customers from becoming or remaining customers of competitive local exchange carriers (LECs) in violation of § 2 of the Sherman Act.

Several matters of law were dealt with in *Trinko, first* whether the existence of a detailed regulatory scheme shielded regulated companies from antitrust scrutiny by the doctrine of implied immunity. However, a saving clause in the Telecom Act stated that nothing in that act should be construed to modify, impair, or supersede the applicability of any of the antitrust laws. *Secondly*, the market behaviour of Verizon did not qualify as a refusal to deal within the meaning of *Aspen Skiing,*[38] which itself already was viewed by the court to be at or near the outer boundary or Section 2 liability and the court was explicitly reluctant to expand application of Section 2 of the Sherman beyond the point laid down in *Aspen Skiing*. Also, the matter of access to service was undisputed because this was required under the Telecom Act, similar to the EU local loop unbundling requirements[39]. Neither did the court endorse the essential facilities crafted by lower courts in this case. *Thirdly*, the Court underlined that in addition to monopoly power on the relevant market an offence under Section 2 of the Sherman Act requires the "the willful acquisition or maintenance of that power as distinguished from growth or development as a consequence of a superior product, business acumen, or historic accident."[40]

The court underlined that the mere possession of monopoly power, and the concomitant charging of monopoly prices, is not only *not unlawful*; it should even be viewed as an important element of the free-market system. Essentially, it would be illogical to punish the monopolist for enjoying the fruits of the legal endeavours by way of growth by merit that results in a privileged market position.[41] U.S. antitrust law therefore ascribes high importance to creating and maintaining appropriate incentives for undertakings to invest and grow. The Court held that

[38] *Aspen Skiing Co. v. Aspen Highlands Skiing Corp.*, 472 U. S. 585.

[39] See Regulation (EC) No 2887/2000 of the European Parliament and of the Council of 18 December 2000 on unbundled access to the local loop, OJ 2000 L 336, p. 4 (repealed first by Directive 2009/140/EC and then implicitly repealed by the Recast Directive (EU) 2018/1972).

[40] See *United States v. Grinnell Corp.*, 384 U. S. 563, 570–571 (1966).

[41] See also Justice Hands also underlined that "[t]he successful competitor, having been urged to compete, must not be turned upon when he wins", *U.S. v Aluminum Co. of America* et al., 148 F.2d 416 (2nd Cir. 1945).

> [t]he opportunity to charge monopoly prices—at least for a short period—is what attracts "business acumen" in the first place; it induces risk taking that produces innovation and economic growth. To safeguard the incentive to innovate, the possession of monopoly power will not be found unlawful unless it is accompanied by an element of anticompetitive *conduct.*[42]

This marks a fundamental difference between Section 2 of the Sherman Act and Article 102 TFEU. Abuse of dominance, and the examples thereof enshrined in Article 102 TFEU, does not formally exclude exploitative behaviour from its sphere of application. The U.S. counterpart, on the other hand, focuses already by virtue of its wording on what be viewed as primary line antitrust injury, i.e. harm to competitors or competition in general. In the EU, this is traditionally referred to as exclusionary abuse.

In *Trinko,* the U.S. Supreme court also dealt with the difficulties for antitrust authorities associated with objectively establishing a correct market price, quality and other contract terms, and how ill-suited authorities are to act as central planners. In recognising the shortcomings of any antitrust authority's ability to mirror or even replace the market's capabilities to generate an efficient outcome there are considerable dangers associated with the over-enforcement or false positive (so called type 1-errors). This may, according to the Supreme court, at the very least result in lessening the incentives for the monopolist, the rival or even to invest in economically beneficial facilities. More generally, the Sherman Act:

> … [d]oes not restrict the long recognized right of [a] trader or manufacturer engaged in an entirely private business, freely to exercise his own independent discretion as to parties with whom he will deal.[43]

Regardless of implications of type 1 errors, the Supreme court earlier underlined the problems associated with monitoring and controlling pricing as being "beyond practical".[44] The court therefore was in *Trinko* very unwilling to indirectly impose upon antitrust agencies an ongoing detailed price surveillance task.[45]

The same concerns voiced in *Trinko* were also highlighted by AG Wahl in *AKKA/LAA*; calculating the profit levels is indeed a complex and uncertain task to undertake and the cost for false positives tend to outweigh the costs of under-enforcement. Further, the uncertainty enshrined in this analysis triggers serious concerns related to legal certainty—especially bearing in mind the near criminal nature of antitrust

[42] *Verizon Communications, Inc. v. Law Offices of Curtis V. Trinko LLP*, 540 US 398 (2003), at 407.

[43] *United States v. Colgate & Co.*, 250 U. S. 300, 307 (1919).

[44] *Brooke Group Ltd. v. Brown & Williamson Tobacco Corp.*, 509 U. S. 209, 223 (1993).

[45] To this effect, the Supreme Court made a direct quote in *Trinko* to professor Areeda who concluded that "[n]o court should impose a duty to deal that it cannot explain or adequately and reasonably supervise. The problem should be deemed [irremediable] by antitrust law when compulsory access requires the court to assume the day-to-day controls characteristic of a regulatory agency". See P. Areeda, 'Essential Facilities: An Epithet in Need of Limiting Principles', Antitrust Law Journal, Vol. 58, No. 3, Developments: 1989 (1989), p. 853.

sanctions. Also, the enforcement system in the EU has never intended to be—or is equipped to undertake—a price regulation role.[46]

4 Concluding Remarks

Bearing in mind the wide-ranging difficulties associated with finding a clear, foreseeable and administrable legal test for excessive prices under Article 102 (a) TFEU, it appears natural that very few cases emerge outside industries where the undertaking holds a privileged or protected dominant position, e.g., as a result of regulation, natural monopoly that can be expected to last and not realistically be challenged by market forces. Cases on excessive prices are often associated with such markets that display comparable prices and steady price levels over time. Nonetheless, these circumstances would normally also give rise to calls for ex ante regulation instead of applying competition law ex post. On markets where excessive prices most likely would be possible to establish, it could be argued that a better way to deal with problem at hand would be to regulate the market. However, in doing so it may prove just as difficult to strike a fair balance between the market control and allow for necessary investments and create efficiency incentives over time. Many such markets like energy, and telecom, have already been regulated and sometimes deregulated, leaving a dwindling sphere of application for exploitative abuse as it stands to today.

Another way of dealing with the issue would be to introduce liability not for abuse of dominance, but for abuse of *relative* market power beyond the concept of dominance. Whether that is a welcome development for competition law in the EU, or just a matter of unfairness under contract law, is an altogether different matter and ultimately the legislator's prerogative to decide on. Also, whether more regulation and heavier regulatory burden enhances productivity and efficiency is far from clear. Nevertheless, it should be borne in mind that competition law—and application thereof—should not reasonably contribute to create a market order where companies are disincentivised to grow or being punished when dominance is the result of competition on the merits.[47]

---

46 See AG Wahl Opinion in *AKKA/LAA*, paras 103–105.

47 Justice Hand underlined in *Alcoa* already in 1945 that antitrust law according to the brocard *finis opus coronat* did not aim to denounce the results of the market behaviour that the legislation was designed to protect in the first place, even if consumers were subjected to the negative effects of e.g. a monopoly. See *U.S. v Aluminum Co. of America* et al., 148 F.2d 416 (2nd Cir. 1945).

The Categorisation of Practices in EU Competition Law

Pablo Ibáñez Colomo

1 Introduction

Categories are indispensable in any legal discipline worthy of the name.[1] Competition law is not an exception. As a field, it shows that categories are necessary when drawing the line between lawful and unlawful conduct and, more generally, as a means to ensure the appropriate functioning of the system. Articles 101 and 102 TFEU lack a well-defined, finite scope of application. 'Abuse' and 'restriction of competition' are open-ended concepts without an operational meaning. They need to be broken down into smaller, administrable building blocks so that they can apply in concrete scenarios. Categories are best seen as these building blocks, which plug the gap between the vague wording of the provisions and the specific issues raised by individual cases. In practice, enforcement revolves around them. The notion of abuse, for instance, is rarely ever usefully discussed in the abstract. More often than not, it is addressed by reference to the various categories ('predatory pricing', 'exclusive dealing', 'refusal to deal' and so on) that have emerged over time. Article 101 TFEU is not any different in this regard.

Categories may be a necessity in a legal system. It does not follow from this fact, however, that every approach to the categorisation of conduct is sound and workable over the long run. If they are not defined with care—or are based on criteria that turn out to be inadequate—categories will prove to be unsustainable. For as long as they

[1] W.P.J. Wils, 'The Judgment of the EU General Court in Intel and the So-Called More Economic Approach to Abuse of Dominance' (2014) 37 World Competition 405, 432.

P. Ibáñez Colomo (✉)
London School of Economics, London, UK
e-mail: P.Ibanez-Colomo@lse.ac.uk

L. Prete, L. Rezki (eds.), *Judging & (Re)Thinking European Union Law*,
https://doi.org/10.1007/978-3-032-13473-8_9

apply, moreover, they are likely to negatively affect the legal regime in several ways. The incorrect categorisation of conduct can be a source of enforcement errors and inconsistencies in decision-making. Specifically, it may lead to suboptimal outcomes, in the sense that it can result in both the overenforcement and the underenforcement of the law. Similarly, it favours the uneven treatment of conduct, in the sense that flawed categories do not treat like behaviour alike and, conversely, may treat fundamentally different conduct in the same way. For the same reason, they may make it impossible to anticipate the outcome of legal proceedings.

The fundamental conclusion to be drawn from the above is that the careful categorisation of conduct is one of the fundamental tasks that courts must perform when interpreting and applying competition law provisions. This contribution makes several points in relation to this idea. To begin with, it defines and explains the pivotal role of categories in the system. It focuses on Articles 101 and 102 TFEU, but the lessons drawn could be easily extended to other areas of EU law Second, it discusses the two main approaches that could be followed to the categorisation of conduct: one that is formal and another one that is substantive (or substance-based). It notes, in this regard, that economic analysis is not only not inimical to this exercise but can greatly contribute to the creation of sound categories. The piece moves, third, to the analysis of the Court's approach and of the techniques it uses to address and correct frictions and inconsistencies over time.

2 The Role of Categories in EU Competition Law

2.1 Defining Legal Categories

A legal category can be defined as a device that makes it possible to identify, in the abstract, various types of comparable practices and differentiate it from other conduct. The category cartel, for instance, brings together, without the need to engage in any sort of case-specific analysis, a range of practices that are assumed to share the same nature, aims and effects (in the sense that they involve collusion among competitors, lack redeeming virtues and can be safely presumed to have a net negative impact on competition), irrespective of the way in which it manifests itself (that is, regardless of whether cartel conduct is attained by means of price-fixing, market sharing or the restriction of output). Similarly, tying (to mention a practice that can be caught by Article 102 TFEU) comprises a family of practices whereby a firm makes the sale of one product (the so-called tying product) conditional upon the acquisition of a different one (the tied product), whether the mechanism used is contractual or technical instead.

Typically, a category is intimately associated with the legal treatment of the practices that come under its umbrella. The categorisation exercise, in other words, will sometimes determine whether a given practice is presumptively lawful, presumptively unlawful or demands a case-by-case analysis of its actual or potential effects on competition. Legally qualifying an agreement as a 'cartel', for instance, implies that it is restrictive of competition by its very nature within the meaning of Article 101(1) TFEU and, in addition, that it is exceedingly unlikely to meet the conditions of Article 101(3) TFEU.[2] Conversely, the fact that a rebate scheme amounts to a 'simple quantity rebate linked solely to the volume of purchases' means, by extension, that it is presumptively lawful under Article 102 TFEU.[3] The same is true, as far as Article 101(1) TFEU is concerned, of 'purely qualitative' selective distribution systems that meet the conditions laid down in *Metro I*.[4]

In other instances, a case-by-case evaluation will be necessary to determine the lawfulness of a practice falling within a given category. For example, an agreement characterised as a 'pay-for-delay' arrangement is not necessarily in breach of Article 101(1) TFEU (or Article 102 TFEU). Depending on the circumstances, it may restrict competition by object, it may have restrictive effects on competition or may even fall outside the scope of the prohibition altogether if it is deemed to amount to a genuine intellectual property settlement.[5] Accordingly, the categorisation exercise will only the starting point of the legality assessment as far as this practice is concerned. The same is true where conduct is characterised as a refusal to deal within the meaning of the *Bronner* doctrine.[6] This practice is not abusive by its very nature. It is only caught by Article 102 TFEU in 'exceptional circumstances', to be assessed in light of the criteria laid down in the case law.

2.2 Why Legal Categories Are Used

Legal categories make up the backbone of EU competition law and practice. Textbooks, as much as the European Commission's (hereinafter, the 'Commission') soft law instruments,[7] are structured around them. Categories, however, are not mere academic constructs. The Court relies on them frequently and explicitly.[8] This feature of the case law should not come as a surprise. Abstracts discussions about the notion of restriction of competition within the meaning of Article 101(1) TFEU

---

[2] N. Dunne, 'Characterizing Hard Core Cartels Under Article 101 TFEU' (2020) 65 Antitrust Bulletin 376.

[3] Judgment in *Post Danmark*, C-23/14, EU:C:2015:651, paras 27–28.

[4] Judgment in *Metro SB-Großmärkte v Commission*, 26/76, EU:C:1977:167.

[5] Judgment in *Generics (UK) and Others*, C-307/18, EU:C:2020:52.

[6] Judgment in Bronner, C-7/97 EU:C:1998:569.

[7] See for instance the Guidelines on vertical restraints (OJ 2022 C 248, p. 1) and the Guidelines on the applicability of Article 101 of the Treaty on the Functioning of the European Union to horizontal co-operation agreements (OJ 2023 C 259, p. 1).

[8] Just to mention some examples, the Court talks expressly about selective distribution, as exemplified in *Metro I* (n 4); franchising (judgment in *Pronuptia de Paris*, 161/84,EU:C:1986:41); cartels (see in this sense judgment in *CB v Commission*, C-67/13 P, EU:C:2014:2204, para 51); and refusal to deal (judgment in *Slovak Telekom v Commission*, C-165/19 P, EU:C:2021:239).

or about the notion of abuse under Article 102 TFEU only acquire a concrete, operational meaning when applied in the context of the various categories into which potentially anticompetitive conduct is broken down. It is not a secret, for instance, that concepts such as 'competition on the merits' are incapable of providing meaningful guidance to draw the line between lawful and unlawful behaviour in individual scenarios.[9] Efforts to develop overarching tests that apply across the board have proved to be equally fruitless.[10]

It is against this background that one can try and make sense of the various functions that categories fulfil in the EU legal order. In a discipline like competition law, to begin with, categories are an indispensable tool to navigate and manage the complexities of business life. Firms implement countless strategies and variations thereof. Technological change means that these strategies change frequently, and often unpredictably. The system would be unworkable if each practice (and/or each iteration thereof) were subject to ad hoc treatment. Categorisation makes it possible to group practices together and approach them in the same way. *Coty* is useful to illustrate this idea. The clause at stake in that case—a ban on the use of online marketplaces by selective distributors—was a contractual adjustment to the rise of e-commerce and, specifically, to a challenge that does not arise in the brick-and-mortar world. The Court approached the issue not by examining the legality of the clause in the abstract, but rather by ascertaining whether it could be seen as a 'qualitative requirement' within the meaning of the *Metro I* doctrine (introduced well before the development of e-commerce).[11]

Categorisation is valuable, second, insofar as it makes it possible to put the experience acquired by courts to effective use. It is, in a sense, a technique that allows courts to crystallise the lessons learnt without the need to rehearse them in individual cases (and, more importantly, without the need to engage in case-specific assessments). This function became apparent in *Cartes Bancaires*.[12] The Court pointed out that experience shows that price-fixing in the context of a cartel arrangement, which lacks any redeeming virtues, can be safely presumed to be a source of allocative inefficiency (manifested, inter alia, in the price, quantity and quality of goods and services). When it comes to the application of Article 101(1) TFEU, therefore, it may be 'redundant' to require evidence of the actual or potential effects of cartels on competition.[13] In the same vein (and equally importantly in practice), evidence about the absence of such effects (or about the pro-competitive aims allegedly

[9] For an extensive analysis of this question, see P. Ibáñez Colomo, 'Competition on the merits' (2024) 61 Common Market Law Review 387.

[10] For an overview of these tests and their limits, see R. Nazzini, *The Foundations of European Union Competition Law: The Objective and Principles of Article 102*, Oxford University Press, 2011. For an attempt to craft a unifying test of abuse, see judgment in *Servizio Elettrico Nazionale and* Others, C-377/20 EU:C:2022:379.

[11] Judgment in *Coty Germany*, C-230/16, EU:C:2017:941.

[12] *CB* (n 8).

[13] Ibid, para 51.

pursued by the parties to the cartel) can be summarily dismissed on the back of the experience acquired.[14]

There is a third reason why categories—and the legal tests with which they are associated—contribute to the effective application of competition law provisions. Articles 101 and 102 TFEU are intended to authorise conduct that is on the whole pro-competitive and to prohibit practices that have a net negative impact on competition. However, engaging in an unstructured, 'all-things-considered'[15] case-by-case balancing exercise would be demanding and prohibitively resource-consuming. Against this background, the categorisation of practices makes it easier for courts and authorities to ensure that the system is administrable, all while remaining reasonably accurate. While structured approaches that rely on pre-defined pigeonholes are inevitably a source of enforcement errors (they lead by definition to both under- and overenforcement), bringing together like practices under the same umbrella (and associated conditions to assess their lawfulness) minimises them.

This idea is best illustrated in light of several examples. Consider, first, the conditions laid down by the Court in *Metro I*, whereby purely qualitative selective distribution systems fall outside the scope of Article 101(1) TFEU. The presumptive lawfulness of any restraints that are necessary and proportionate for the operation of this distribution method strikes the right balance between accuracy and administrability if one considers, first, that the protection of the brand image of a product is not inherently restrictive of competition (and that it is, in fact, a legitimate aim); and, second, that suppliers would be unlikely to rely on third-party resellers if they were unable to protect the said brand image. It is equally reasonable to apply the same template to any emerging restraints pursuing the same aim. These include, for instance, the clause at issue in *Coty*.

Consider, second, refusal to deal as a category. As already pointed out above, it is only in 'exceptional circumstances', to be determined in light of the criteria laid down in *Bronner*, that such conduct amounts to an abuse of a dominant position. The high bar set by the Court reflects the difficulty of balancing short-term rivalry (which a duty to deal would promote) and long-term competition (which would be enhanced by allowing firms to exploit their property as they see fit). The legal test applying to refusals is based on the idea that, generally speaking, it is preferable to favour the latter over the former and therefore that the legal system should have a built-in bias against compelling firms to deal with rivals with which they have chosen not to deal.[16] Once created, the category dispenses courts and authorities with the need to engage in any complex assessments about the desirability of intervention in new cases revolving around access to an input or infrastructure.

[14] Ibid. On experience, see also judgment in *Budapest Bank and Others*, C-228/18, EU:C:2020:265.

[15] Expression borrowed from J. Lindeboom, 'Formalism in Competition Law' (2022) 18 Journal of Competition Law & Economics 832.

[16] *Slovak Telekom* (n 8).

2.3 The Importance of the Appropriate Design of Legal Categories

Categories can only fulfil their function in the system if they are carefully and adequately designed. This means, first and foremost, crafting categories so that like practices are treated alike and, conversely, so that different practices are treated differently. Legal frictions, tensions and arbitrage seem inevitable where the inadequate characterisation of conduct leads to a mismatch between the category and its content. Actors in the system (claimants, defendants and authorities) would have every incentive to exploit this mismatch in an opportunistic manner. Suppose that two practices that are essentially similar in their nature, aims and potential effects are treated as two separate categories, and that one of them is subject to a stricter legal test than the other. In such a scenario, the attention and energy of all actors in the system would be diverted away from the fundamental underlying issues to focus instead on semantic discussions around the appropriate pigeonholing of conduct.

The inadequate design of legal categories can also be a source of legal uncertainty. Suppose that there is a new practice that has never been scrutinised by a court or authority. If the scope of categories has not been properly crafted, it may be difficult for firms to anticipate the legal treatment to which the new practice is subject. In such a scenario, there may be two or more competing and equally plausible approaches. Similarly, inadequate design can be a source of unfettered discretion, if not arbitrariness. Where the scope and boundaries of categories have not been properly defined, the categorisation exercise may lack an ex ante rationale. As a result, decisions about the legal treatment to give to new conduct may rely, in effect, on nothing other than the preferences (or needs) of the decision-making body. For the same reason, the categorisation may fluctuate from one case to another, thereby fuelling legal uncertainty.

3 Approaches to the Categorisation of Practices

3.1 Formal and Substantive Approaches

One can distinguish between two broad approaches to the categorisation of conduct: a formal and a substantive one.[17] Under the first of the approaches, the formal features of practices would be the determinant factor. For instance, agreements would be categorised as inherently restrictive of competition (within the meaning of Article 101(1) TFEU) based on whether they provide for clauses involving, among others,

[17] For an extensive discussion of this question, see P. Ibáñez Colomo, 'Form and substance in EU Competition Law' (2023) 46 World Competition 401.

price-fixing, market sharing or the restriction of output.[18] Similarly, conduct would be categorised as abusive under Article 102 TFEU depending on whether it takes one form or the other. Thus, the award of, say, rebates would fall within the scope of the prohibition where it is formally conditional upon exclusivity, and it would be lawful where it is contingent on the volume supplied instead.[19]

The alternative approach is one that places less of an emphasis on the way in which conduct is formally manifested and more on its substantive dimension. Focusing on the latter means, in concrete terms, paying attention to the nature of the practice, the objective aims it pursues and the (positive and negative) impact on competition it is capable of having. Following this approach means, first, that two practices that share the same formal features are not necessarily (or not always) categorised in the same way. For instance, a cooperation arrangement whereby two or more firms acquire inputs together from their suppliers (which by definition involves the joint determination of prices) may not always be categorised in the same way. There may be circumstances where it is categorised as a purchasers' cartel[20]; and other instances where the behaviour would be more appropriately treated as a joint purchasing agreement.[21]

By the same token, second, a substantive approach means that formally different conduct may sometimes be categorised in the same way. For instance, practices aimed at restricting intra-EU trade would not be treated differently depending on the mechanisms formally relied upon to re-erect barriers to the flow of goods and services within the Union. Accordingly, the legal category would comprise not just clauses expressly banning the import and/or export of products,[22] but any behaviour pursuing the same objectives and achieving essentially the same effects. The latter includes, just to mention some examples, the implementation of a dual pricing mechanism aimed at disincentivising exports (or make them less profitable).[23] It would also include the use of technical devices to prevent retailers from using the Internet to reach customers outside their allocated territory (such as the re-routing of online traffic to other retailers[24]).

---

[18] The most illustrious example of this approach can be found in R. Whish and D. Bailey, *Competition Law* (10th ed., Oxford University Press 2021).

[19] See in this sense judgment in *Hoffmann-La Roche v Commission*, 85/76, EU:C:1979:36, paras 89–90, and the discussion that follows below.

[20] See for instance *Raw Tobacco—Spain* (Case COMP/C.38.238/B.2) Commission Decision of 20 October 2004; and *Ethylene* (Case AT.40410) Commission Decision of 14 July 2020.

[21] See for instance judgment in Case *DLG ('Gøttrup-Klim')*, C-250/92 EU:C:1994:413.

[22] See for instance judgment in *Miller International Schallplaten v Commission*, 19/77 EU:C:1978:19.

[23] Judgment in *GlaxoSmithKline Services and Others v Commission and Others*, C-501/06 P, C-513/06 P, C-515/06 P and C-519/06 P, EU:C:2009:610.

[24] Guidelines on vertical restraints (n 7), para 206.

3.2 Relative Advantages and Disadvantages of Each Approach

The formal approach to the categorisation of conduct presents several obvious advantages. To begin with, it makes the categorisation exercise straightforward (at least prima facie). A single variable would be sufficient, in and of itself, to decide how a particular practice is to be classified. For the same reason, this approach comes across, at least superficially, as easy to administer. The form of the practice alone would shed light on its legal treatment. For instance, the mere fact that a group of competitors has decided to engage in price-fixing (or market sharing, or the coordinated restriction of output) would mean that the conduct can be categorised as a cartel and, by the same token, that it can be deemed unlawful by its very nature within the meaning of Article 101(1) TFEU. Similarly, the fact that a dominant supplier demands exclusivity from its customers would be deemed sufficient, in and of itself, to establish an abuse to the requisite legal standard. One may argue (as some commentators have[25]) that formalism has the advantage of legal certainty. The focus on a single factor means that the economic operators are aware of what is permitted and what is not.

Some of the potential drawbacks of a formal approach are immediately apparent. To begin with, the ease with which the categorisation exercise can be undertaken necessarily comes at the expense of accuracy. By focusing exclusively on the form of the practice and leaving out of the analysis contextual considerations, the approach can lead to both the under- and overenforcement of Articles 101 and 102 TFEU. Coming back to the examples mentioned above, it is not necessarily the case that all forms of price-fixing among competitors amount to cartel conduct. There are, in fact, abundant examples showing that it would not be appropriate to treat the joint determination of prices as inherently anticompetitive always and in every circumstance.[26] Conversely, it is well understood that cartels take different firms and can even be concealed as superficially pro-competitive arrangements.[27] To the extent that they do, an exclusive focus on the form of the conduct is likely to lead to underenforcement (if practices are wrongly assumed to have a net positive impact on competition) or at least to a suboptimal use of resources (if an analysis of effects is undertaken where it would not have been necessary).

Other drawbacks do not spring to mind immediately but may have equally important consequences in practice. This approach is unlikely to live up to its promise of administrability and certainty. The opposite, in fact, may be the outcome

[25] See for instance B. Wardhaugh, *Competition, Effects and Predictability: Rule of Law and the Economic Approach to Competition*, Hart Publishing, 2020.

[26] See in this sense the Guidelines on horizontal co-operation agreements (n 7). See also judgments in *Tournier*, 395/87, EU:C:1989:319. Joined Cases 110/88, 241/88; and in *Lucazeau and Others*, EU:C:1989:326, which concerned the joint determination of prices in the context of the collective licensing of copyright.

[27] This is a common theme in Guidelines on horizontal co-operation agreements (n 7), where the Commission warns that cartel conduct can sometimes be concealed behind, inter alia, a joint production or a research and development agreement.

of relying, exclusively or primarily, on the form of a practice. The main reason why uncertainty may be an unintended consequence of formalism has to do with the fact that business conduct rarely ever takes the same form. Along the lines of what has already been pointed out, business strategies frequently mutate over time; it is not unusual that firms find new, ingenious ways to achieve a particular objective. They may do so for several reasons, sometimes as a means to circumvent a prohibition; in other instances, as an adaptation to the changing economic and/or technological landscape. A formal approach is inherently unable to adjust to these changes.

In a similar vein, the limits that are inherent to the formal approach may make it difficult for economic actors to anticipate the legal treatment of emerging conduct. Suppose that a dominant supplier avoids making the award of rebates conditional upon exclusivity, but achieves, in effect, the same result by different means (that is, by incentivising its customers to purchase its products exclusively from it). Such a scenario may be a source of uncertainty if a formal approach were to be followed. One could reasonably argue, on the one hand, that the circumvention of an exclusivity obligation should be categorised in the exact same way. Such a conclusion, however, would not just expose the limits of the formal approach; it would also be a source of legal uncertainty. Once the scope of the category is expanded to cover both exclusivity obligations and other practices having the same effect, it may not be obvious to define or anticipate the boundaries of the prohibition.

The drawbacks of formalism are the advantages of the substantive approach, and vice versa. Because the latter does not pay particular attention to the form of business strategies, but to their nature, aims and potential (positive and negative) effects, it can seamlessly adjust to novel conduct and variations on existing practices. It would be irrelevant, for instance, that cartel conduct is implemented in a new way (for instance, by formally presenting it as a pro-competitive arrangement), or that technology gives rise to challenges that had not been foreseen when the original doctrines were introduced (as was true, for instance, in the context of the *Coty* case). Focusing on the aims and impact of the practice means, in addition, that the categorisation exercise is more likely to lead to accurate outcomes. The more the emphasis is placed on contextual factors, the less likely enforcement errors become.

On the other hand, the need to consider a broader range of factors means that the categorisation exercise will necessarily be less straightforward and more resource-consuming under a substantive approach. For the same reason, it may prove more difficult to administer and may be more prone to errors. Where contextual factors are relevant at the categorisation stage, the potential for disagreements among actors in the system is likely to be higher. This is so, in particular, where the factual scenario with which courts and authorities are confronted is a new one. To mention a concrete example, the online marketplace ban at issue in *Coty* was not approached in the same way by national courts and authorities (both prior to the Court ruling and its immediate aftermath). Some national judges categorised it as restraint inherent in the operation of a selective distribution system (and as such presumptively lawful); others, as a restrictive of competition by its very nature.[28]

3.3 *Economic Analysis and the Categorisation of Practices*

The rise of economic analysis has been one of the most significant developments of the past two decades in EU competition law.[29] One question that has been frequently discussed in the literature relates to whether the use of economic tools is inimical to, or at odds with, the use of categories. It is not difficult to see why one may argue that it may not be easy to reconcile economic analysis with an exercise that is essentially legal in nature. The former is typically assumed to favour a strictly case-by-case analysis of practices, whereby their lawfulness is established in light of their actual or potential impact on a given measure of welfare.[30] From this perspective, how the practices are categorised (or whether the measure is categorised at all) would be far less relevant than their effects in the specific economic and legal context in which they are implemented. What would matter, rather than the label that is attached to them, is whether there is an internally coherent theory of harm and whether the available evidence is consistent with it.[31]

This view, however reasonable, is not accurate. More precisely, it does not reflect the only way in which economic analysis can inform the legal assessment of conduct. While it is true that some economists might be naturally inclined to favour the unstructured, case-by-case welfare balancing of the pro- and anticompetitive effects of practices, others are acutely aware of the features and needs of the legal system. The latter are aware, in particular, of the importance of providing structure and certainty to economic actors[32] and appreciate the role and value of categories in achieving these goals. What matters, from these economists' perspective, is that categories are meaningful and faithfully capture the nature, aims and potential effects of the conduct under consideration. Economic tools can assist the categorisation exercise in a number of ways. Formal analysis is useful to shed light on the objective rationale underpinning conduct. It is particularly helpful when it reveals that intuitions

[28] For an overview, see M. Reisinger, 'Asics vs Coty: Competitive effects of selective distribution systems in light of diverging court decisions' *Competition Policy International* (May 2018).

[29] For an extensive overview, see Chapter 2 in P. Ibáñez Colomo, *The New EU Competition Law*, Hart Publishing, 2023.

[30] C. Ahlborn and J. Padilla, 'From Fairness to Welfare: Implications for the Assessment of Unilateral Conduct under EC Competition Law', in C-D. Dieter Ehlermann and M. Marquis (eds), *European Competition Law Annual 2007: A Reformed Approach to Article 82 EC*, Hart Publishing, 2008.

[31] H. Zenger and M. Walker, 'Theories of Harm in European Competition Law: A Progress Report', in J. Bourgeois and D. Waelbroeck (eds), *Ten years of effects-based approach in EU competition law: State of play and perspectives*, Bruylant, 2012.

[32] This is a point emphasised in Ahlborn and Padilla (n 30).

about the potential aims of a practice are misguided, or overly simplistic. These tools are equally helpful when providing an idea about the instances where behaviours can be expected to harm competition. For instance, economic analysis provides support for the proposition that cartels can be safely presumed to be a net source of negative effects in virtually every instance.[33] Conversely, it shows that many, if not most, unilateral practices implemented by dominant firms are known to be capable of having both pro- and anticompetitive effects, which means that it is necessary to evaluate, case-by-case, whether the former outweighs the latter, or vice versa.[34]

4 The Categorisation of Practices in the Case Law

4.1 The Dominance of the Substantive Approach

By and large, the Court has favoured substance over form when categorising conduct. More often than not, judgments take it as given that the form of a practice is not determinant in and of itself. Where it appears that a business strategy is a variation on an existing one (or that it has an equivalent object and effect), the legal treatment will not vary. This point is perhaps more effectively illustrated in light of some examples. Take practices aimed at limiting intra-EU trade, which, as explained above, are presumptively restrictive of competition irrespective of their effects. The Court's treatment of these practices has not varied depending on the technique used to prevent market integration. Thus, the EU courts have administered the rule in the same way to explicit export prohibitions spelled out in a contract[35] and to more subtle techniques having the same object and effect (such as the use of dual pricing mechanisms[36] or an outright ban on online sales[37]). Similarly, cartel conduct will be categorised as such irrespective of whether it is manifested as price-fixing, the coordinated restriction of output or as a collective boycott instead[38]; and, similarly, irrespective of whether it occurs on the supply or the purchasing side. Conversely, not every cooperation involving price-fixing or market sharing has been categorised as a cartel.

The evolution of the case law suggests that the nature of the practice and the issues it raises are the crucial factors when categorising conduct. Consider, in this

---

33 See the point already made above in light of *CB* (n 8), para 51.

34 Economic Advisory Group on Competition Policy, 'An economic approach to Article 82' (July 2005).

35 *Miller* (n 22).

36 *Glaxo Spain* (n 23).

37 Judgment in *Pierre Fabre Dermo-Cosmétique*, C-439/09, EU:C:2011:649.

38 Judgment in *Nederlandse Federatieve Vereniging voor de Groothandel op Elektrotechnisch Gebied v Commission*, C-105/04 P, EU:C:2006:592.

sense, the Court's analysis in *Google Shopping*. A prominent discussion in the case revolved around whether the conduct in issue (which involved the discrimination in favour of the dominant firm's affiliate and against rivals of the latter) should be characterised as a refusal to deal. The categorisation of the practice had major consequences for the outcome of the case. As pointed out above, a refusal to deal is only abusive in 'exceptional circumstances', which are to be established in light of a set of notoriously stringent conditions.[39] The General Court followed a formal approach and held that these conditions are only relevant where the factual scenario corresponds to the one at stake in *Bronner*—that is, where there is a 'request' followed by a 'refusal'.[40]

The Court, on appeal, focused on substantive issues instead, and this in line with the position already expressed in *Slovak Telekom*.[41] Thus, the categorisation of a practice does not depend on whether there is, formally speaking, a refusal in the strict sense of the word, but on whether the case raises the sort of issues that were at stake in *Bronner* and that explain the rationale behind the 'exceptional circumstances' doctrine. The crucial factor, under this approach, is whether a finding of abuse would interfere with the firm's freedom of contract and with its right to property (that is, where the firm would be compelled to deal with rivals with which it has chosen not to deal).[42] In the specific circumstances of the *Google Shopping* case, the Court noted that the infringement could be brought to an end in several ways, that the Commission, in its decision, did not specify a particular one, and, finally, that some of the potential remedies did not necessarily entail the imposition of a duty to deal.[43]

One of the consequences of the substantive approach embraced by the Court is that undertakings may not rely on the form of an agreement to escape a finding of infringement (or to change the legal test against which the legality of the practice is evaluated). It is irrelevant, in this sense, that a particular practice is (generally speaking or in the abstract) pro-competitive. Similarly, the fact that the parties to an agreement chose to categorise it in a particular way is equally immaterial. These questions became apparent in the *Servier* saga. Formally speaking, the undertakings had concluded a set of settlements and licensing agreements which, they argued, sought to bring to an end the dispute between them. The Court noted, however, that this fact did not preclude a finding that the agreements in question were akin, in terms of their nature, aim and effects, to a cartel. Specifically, it held that 'the fact that an agreement takes a legal form which is in principle legitimate' is not, 'in itself, decisive in determining whether the agreement gives rise to an infringement of Article 101(1) TFEU'.[44]

---

[39] *Bronner* (n 6).

[40] Judgment in *Google and Alphabet v Commission*, T-612/17, EU:T:2021:763, para 232.

[41] *Slovak Telekom* (n 8).

[42] Ibid, para 51.

[43] Judgment in *Google and Alphabet v Commission (Google Shopping)*, C-48/22 P, EU:C:2024:726.

[44] Judgment in *Commission v KRKA*, C-151/19 P EU:C:2024:546, para 395.

4.2 Addressing the Vestiges of the Formal Approach

While it seems unquestionable that the substantive approach has been consistently followed when categorising practices, it is possible to discern in the case law some examples of formalism. Arguably, the most prominent vestige of formalism is the doctrine pursuant to which exclusivity agreements and loyalty rebates (that is, rebates conditional upon exclusivity) are presumptively abusive within the meaning of Article 102 TFEU. This doctrine dates back from the days of *Hoffmann-La Roche*, where the Court introduced a *summa divisio* between the said practices, on the one hand, and volume rebates (deemed presumptively lawful), on the other.[45] It did not take long before it became apparent that this divide does not provide the basis for an operational and predictable framework. The drawbacks of formalism, outlined in the preceding section, all became apparent in the aftermath of *Hoffmann-La Roche*.

To begin with, business realities are much more complex than suggested by the *summa divisio* introduced in *Hoffmann-La Roche*. In line with the observations made above, a predictable consequence of the mismatch between formalistic categories and the reality of business transactions is that the former may be unable to provide meaningful guidance about the legal treatment of conduct that does not fall squarely within the pigeonholes defined in the case law. This limit of formalism was manifested early on, in *Michelin I*.[46] This case concerned the award of rebates that were neither conditional upon exclusivity nor conditional upon the volume supplied. Instead, they were contingent on meeting an individualised sales target. The Court addressed this limit by ruling that, in the specific circumstances of the case, the scheme was, in substance, equivalent to one formally conditional upon exclusivity.

In other words, the Court addressed the drawbacks of formalism in by embracing, at least in part, a substantive approach. The aftermath of *Michelin I* was, however, unsatisfactory, and this for several reasons. The judgment effectively created three categories of rebate schemes: loyalty rebates, deemed abusive, volume rebates, deemed lawful and, finally, 'third category' schemes requiring a case-by-case evaluation. This tripartite categorisation was summarised by the General Court in its first-instance ruling in *Intel*.[47] The first concern with this hybrid (simultaneously formal and substantive) approach was that the scope of the 'third category' remained unclear. In the landmark cases that followed *Michelin I*, namely *British Airways* and *Michelin II*, the Commission sought to address this uncertainty by making the case-by-case analysis revolve around whether the rebates under consideration were 'loyalty-inducing' (or 'fidelity-building').[48]

---

[45] *Hoffmann-La Roche* (n 19), paras 89–90.

[46] Judgment in *Nederlandsche Banden Industrie Michelin v Commission*, 322/81, EU:C:1983:313.

[47] Judgment in T-286/09 *Intel v Commission*, EU:T:2014:547, paras 75–78.

[48] *Michelin* (Case COMP/E-2/36.041/PO) Commission Decision 2002/405/EC [2002] OJ L143/1, paras 226–239; and Virgin/British Airways (Case IV/D 2/34.780) Commission Decision 2000/74/

The fundamental issue with the Commission's solution is that rebates, by their very nature, have a 'loyalty-inducing' or 'fidelity-building' effect. The point of any such scheme, after all, is to provide incentives to increase the amounts purchased from the supplier. Accordingly, the Commission's test could, in effect, turn every rebate scheme into a presumptive abuse (and this insofar as it can be construed, always and everywhere, as being 'loyalty-inducing').[49] This risk became apparent in the aftermath of *Michelin II*. Unlike previous ones, the case concerned, in part, the award of rebates that were neither conditional upon exclusivity nor contingent on meeting an individualised target. Such rebates varied depending on the volume supplied, and a standardised grid applied equally to all customers. It would be reasonable to assume, against this background, that the scheme was lawful. The Commission, however, reached the opposite conclusion, and the General Court dismissed the action against the decision.[50] The lack of clarity about the scope of the 'third category' that followed the first-instance ruling in *Michelin II* exposed the legal uncertainty to which formalism gives rise. So much so, in fact, that it forced the Commission to rethink its overall approach to the enforcement of Article 102 TFEU.[51]

A second reason why the hybrid, tripartite categorisation proved problematic both in theory and practice relates the fact that it introduced stark differences in the legal treatment of rebates even though these are not warranted. The Court's approach, in other words, opened a gap between the law, on the one hand, and the reality to which it applied, on the other. Contrary to what rulings like *Michelin I* and *Michelin II* suggested, formal differences between rebate schemes are not indicative of fundamental differences in terms of their nature, aims and potential (pro- and anticompetitive) effects. Regardless of whether rebates formally demand exclusivity or revolve around a standardised, volume-based grid, they are a response to the same commercial issues and can give rise to concerns in the same circumstances.[52] As eloquently put by Advocate General Wahl, differences between these strategies are 'of degree rather than kind'.[53] For the same reason, the stricter treatment of exclusivity obligations is not just difficult to defend in the abstract, but unsustainable over the medium to long run.

EC [2000] OJ L30/1. Judgment in *British Airways v Commission*, C-95/04 P, EU:C:2007:166, paras 77 and 90.

[49] D. Waelbroeck, 'Michelin II: A Per Se Rule Against Rebates by Dominant Companies?' (2005) 1 Journal of Competition Law & Economics 149.

[50] Judgment in *Michelin v Commission*, T-203/01, EU:T:2003:250.

[51] The process would start with the study submitted by the Economic Advisory Group on Competition Policy (n 34) and would culminate with the adoption of the Guidance on the Commission's enforcement priorities in applying Article 82 of the EC Treaty to abusive exclusionary conduct by dominant undertakings (OJ 2009 C 45, p. 7).

[52] This is a point that economic analysis would go to confirm. See in this sense Economic Advisory Group on Competition Policy (n 34).

[53] Opinion of Advocate General Wahl in *Intel v Commission*, C-413/14 P EU:C:2016:788, para 105.

The way in which the Court has progressively addressed the drawbacks of formalism is instructive of the approach it follows, generally speaking, when addressing frictions in the case law. It proceeded in two clear steps. To begin with, the Court responded to the legal uncertainty around the boundaries of the 'third category' by introducing a meaningful analytical framework revolving around the actual or potential effects of such schemes on competition. By doing so, it made the lack of clarity about the boundaries of the 'third category' far less relevant in practice. The analysis moved away from such formal boundaries to focus on the impact of the schemes in the markets in which they are implemented. The framework was laid down in *Post Danmark II*.[54] The Court identified two factors to consider in the assessment. First, the nature and operation of the rebates.[55] In this sense, the judgment reflects the acknowledgement that not all schemes are created equal (there is a difference, for instance, between rebates calculated over a three-month period and those evaluated over a one-year period). Second, the impact of the rebates on the relevant market, in light of factors such as the coverage of the rebate scheme and the prevailing conditions of competition.[56]

In the second place, the appeal judgment in *Intel*[57] created a legal gateway across categories, which blurred the actual consequences of the divide between loyalty rebates and other schemes. Even though the Court reaffirmed the principle whereby loyalty rebates are abusive by their very nature, it introduced a clarification, according to which an analysis of the effects is necessary whenever the undertaking puts forward 'supporting evidence' in the context of the administrative procedure showing that the practice, in the relevant economic and legal context, is incapable of restricting competition.[58] In *Unilever*, the Court confirmed that the legal gateway is also applicable where outright exclusivity obligations—as opposed to loyalty-based schemes—are at stake.[59] The consequence of *Intel* is that the analysis actually conducted by authorities will not vary depending on the formal features of the rebates, thereby embracing, for all practical purposes, the substantive approach to the categorisation of practices.

5 Conclusions

Categorisation is, and will remain, a necessity in EU competition law. Economic analysis is not inherently at odds with this reality. In fact, it can contribute to the exercise by ensuring that like practices are treated alike and that new conduct is

[54] Judgment in *Post Danmark*, C-23/14 EU:C:2015:651.

[55] Ibid, para 29.

[56] Ibid, paras 30–40.

[57] Judgment in *Intel v Commission*, C-413/14 P, EU:C:2017:632.

[58] Ibid, paras 138–139.

[59] Judgment in *Unilever Italia Mkt. Operations*, C-680/20 EU:C:2023:33.

categorised adequately. In this same vein, a conclusion that follows from this piece is that the incorrect categorisation of conduct is a source of legal uncertainty. In addition, it can be expected to favour opportunistic conduct: potential contradictions, as much as the absence of clear boundaries can be easily exploited by the various actors in the system as a means to seek the legal treatment that best serves their interests. In particular, disputes revolving around formalistic divides are likely to divert the attention away from the fundamental issues raised by the practices under consideration to focus on irrelevant or adjacent questions instead.

A second conclusion that stems from the analysis above is that formalistic approaches to the categorisation of practices are not just likely to lead to legal uncertainty. One can expect them to prove unworkable over the medium to long run. The case law on rebates, where the formalistic (and unrealistic) divide between loyalty-based and volume-based schemes gave rise to considerable confusion for decades (until the Court all but abandoned it in *Intel* and *Unilever* that is), exemplifies this point particularly well. This saga is also illustrative of the techniques developed in the case law to remedy the undesirable consequences of formalism. By creating a legal gateway in *Intel*, the Court ensured that, in practice, like practices would be treated alike. It is not a surprise, against this background, that the appeal judgment in *Google Shopping* did not follow the General Court's formalistic approach and embraced a substantive one instead.

Even though the Court has expressed a consistent preference for substance over form, and in spite of the fact that the latter does not lead to optimal and sustainable outcomes, the temptation to rely on formalism is likely to persist in the foreseeable future. One should not ignore, in this regard, that it promises an administrable, straightforward approach to the categorisation of practices. If anything, the decentralised application of Article 101 and 102 TFEU, with the resulting rise in private enforcement, can be expected to create an environment in which formalistic approaches are likely to be favoured. For instance, it is more likely than not that claimants in private disputes will express a preference for an interpretation of Article 101(1) TFEU pursuant to which every form of price-fixing, irrespective of the context, is akin to a cartel and therefore prohibited by its very nature. Whether the case law remains resilient to this shift in enforcement patterns remains to be seen.

Further Reflections on a Judicial (and Administrative) Architecture in Support of an "Even More Efficient" Approach to EU Competition Law

Johannes Laitenberger

1 Introduction

Early in 2020, Nils Wahl suggested that I participate in the project of editing a systematic guide to Regulation 1/2003[1] on the implementation of the rules on competition laid down in the current version of the treaties in Arts 101 and 102 TFEU and the Union's antitrust enforcement more generally. We agreed on a layout that complemented an article-by-article commentary of the regulation by reflections of a diversity of antitrust enforcement actors on their perspective on the law and its implementation. Editing this book[2] was an intellectual privilege and pleasure, not in the least because of the exchanges with Nils Wahl and the other editors on the different contributions. It has kept alive and deepened my interest in the systemic reflection on the past, present and future of the Union's competition law. At a time when my move from the European Commission's Directorate-General of

The text has been written in a personal capacity and reflects solely the views of the author. Under no circumstance can it be attributed to the General Court of the European Union or any other institution. The author expresses his gratitude to James Kröger, Legal Secretary at his Private Office, for invaluable contributions to and comments on the draft. The manuscript was finalized in February 2025.

[1] OJ 2003 L 1, P. 1.

[2] K. Dekeyser, C. Gauer, J. Laitenberger, N. Wahl, W. Wils, L. Prete (eds.), *Regulation 1/2003 and EU Antitrust Enforcement: A Systematic Guide*, Wolters Kluwer, 2023.

J. Laitenberger (✉)
Judge, General Court, Court of Justice of the European Union, Luxembourg, Luxembourg
e-mail: Johannes.Laitenberger@curia.europa.eu

L. Prete, L. Rezki (eds.), *Judging & (Re)Thinking European Union Law*,
https://doi.org/10.1007/978-3-032-13473-8_10

Competition to the General Court meant that I was excluded for some time from the ongoing work on antitrust enforcement, working on the book offered a precious opportunity to keep up to speed with developments.

One reflection, triggered by the contribution of Marc van der Woude, the General Court's President, on the perspective of the General Court on EU competition procedures,[3] relates to the judicial architecture of the Union courts in competition cases. In his contribution, Marc van der Woude made a case to activate the competence foreseen by Art. 256 (3) TFEU, according to which the Statute of the Court of Justice can lay down the General Court's jurisdiction to hear and determine preliminary reference questions, with respect to EU competition law.[4] Whilst such a transfer of jurisdiction was ultimately not taken up by the proposal and subsequent decision to activate Art. 256 (3) TFEU for the first time in the Union's legal history, as briefly described below, this does not necessarily mean that the matter has been closed for the foreseeable future. To paraphrase a well-known German football manager: "After the reform is before the reform".[5] It does not take much power of foresight to predict that the debate on the Union's judicial architecture will remain in flux,[6] the same being true for the design of the procedural and substantial aspects of EU competition law, which are undergoing a modernization process.

This contribution will reflect on this momentum of evolution by examining the case for a further alignment of the judicial powers conferred on the EU courts in the field of EU competition law. Changes to the architecture of judicial review of EU competition law however cannot plausibly be conceived without having regard to the constraints defined by the normative and administrative framework of EU competition law enforcement. The following reflections will therefore also consider the case for changes to primary and secondary EU competition law as well as to the way the Commission assesses and applies economic evidence. These reflections are essentially motivated by the author's diagnosis that EU competition law enforcement is in need of an "even more efficient" approach[7] that strikes a balance between administrability and predictability and thus eventually allows for speedier court proceedings that contribute to a coherent interpretation of EU competition law.

---

[3] M. van der Woude, 'The EU Competition Procedure from the Perspective of the General Court', in Dekeyser, Gauer, Laitenberger, Wahl, Wils, Prete (eds.), *supra*, pp. 857–863.

[4] M. van der Woude, *supra*, pp. 862–863.

[5] Sepp Herberger: „Nach dem Spiel ist vor dem Spiel.", as quoted in the selection of football quotes published on the website of the German first league, the Bundesliga.

[6] See the obligation to report on the implementation of the transfer of preliminary references to the General Court enshrined in Art. 3 (2) of Regulation 2024/2019. As regards the transfer, see also the contribution in Chapter 26 of this voulme.

[7] See also J. Laitenberger, J. Kröger, 'Towards an "even more efficient" approach?', ZEuP 3/2023, pp. 621–637.

2 Recent Reforms of the General Court

The predecessor of what eventually became the General Court was established by Council Decision 88/591 of 24 October 1988[8] as the Court of First instance of the European Communities ('CFI'). The establishment of the CFI aimed foremost at improving the judicial protection of individual interests, whilst enabling the Court of Justice to concentrate its activities on its fundamental task of ensuring uniform interpretation of Community Law.[9] For the purpose of this contribution, it is worth reminding that the CFI's jurisdiction was initially limited to certain classes of actions which required an in-depth examination of often complex facts, such as in particular disputes between the Communities and their civil servants and actions challenging the implementation of the competition rules.[10] It is fair to say that the CFI was established as a partially specialised competition tribunal. Only in 1993, Council Decision 93/350 of 8 June 1993[11] turned the CFI into a more general court by extending its jurisdiction to hear and determine, in first instance, all actions for annulment brought by natural or legal persons.

The Treaty of Nice[12] introduced the possibility for the Council to create judicial panels to hear and determine at first instance certain classes of action or proceeding brought in specific areas. Consequently, the CFI was endowed with the jurisdiction to hear and determine appeals on points of law against decisions given by such judicial panels. By Decision 2004/752 of 2 November 2004,[13] the Council established the first and so far only specialised panel serving as the European Union Civil Service Tribunal.

In 2015, Regulation 2015/2422[14] initiated a wider reform of what had become the General Court with the Treaty of Lisbon. That reform aimed to meet the increasing workload of the General Court by gradually increasing the number of judges at the General Court from one to two judges per Member States until 1 September 2019. This increase of the number of judges of the General Court was accompanied by the transfer back to the General Court of jurisdiction at first instance in disputes between the Union and its servants under article 270 TFEU, which led to the dissolution of the EU Civil Service Tribunal in 2016.[15] While Regulation 2015/629 invited the Court to reflect on the further establishment of specialised chambers and/or other structural changes,[16] the General Court opted for a partial specialisation via the introduction of partially specialised chambers dealing either with EU civil

[8] OJ 1988 L 319, p. 1.

[9] Recitals 4 and 5 of Council Decision 88/591.

[10] Article 3, paragraph 1, of Council Decision 88/591.

[11] OJ 1993 L 144, p. 21.

[12] Article 225a.

[13] OJ 2004 L 333, p. 7.

[14] OJ 2015 L 341, p. 14.

[15] Regulation 2016/1192 of 6 July 2016 (OJ 2016 L 200, p. 137).

[16] Article 3, paragraph 1, of Regulation 2015/2422.

service disputes or intellectual property disputes.[17] However, no further specialisation was envisaged, neither in the form of specialised chambers for competition disputes or the establishment of a specialised competition court.

Another adjustment of the judicial architecture concerned the possibility to bring an appeal before the Court of Justice in cases which have already been considered twice, initially by an independent board of appeal, then by the General Court. For such cases, Regulation 2019/629[18] amended the Statute of the Court of Justice. An appeal brought against a decision of the General Court concerning a decision of an independent board of appeal of certain offices and agencies of the Union shall not proceed unless the Court of Justice first decides that it should be allowed to do so because it raises an issue that is significant with respect to the unity, consistency or development of Union law.[19]

Finally, the most recent reform of the judicial architecture as put in place by Regulation 2024/2019[20] might be the most consequential. It makes use, for the first time, of the possibility provided for in Article 256 (3), first subparagraph, TFEU to transfer to the General Court jurisdiction to hear and determine questions referred for a preliminary ruling under Article 267 TFEU, in specific areas. This transfer to the General Court of part of the jurisdiction to give preliminary rulings should enable the Court of Justice to devote its resources to examining the most complex and sensitive preliminary ruling requests, often of a constitutional nature.[21]

The transfer of jurisdiction to give preliminary rulings is limited to six clearly defined and separable areas of law. These have already originated a substantial body of case law of the Court of Justice capable of guiding the General Court. At the same time, they continue to generate a sufficiently high number of preliminary ruling cases so as to have a real impact on the workload of the Court of Justice.

The areas of law thus identified are: (a) the common system of value added tax; (b) excise duties; (c) the Customs Code; (d) the tariff classification of goods under the Combined Nomenclature; (e) compensation and assistance to passengers in the event of denied boarding or of delay or cancellation of transport services, and (f) the system for greenhouse gas emission allowance trading.

Notwithstanding the transfer to the General Court of jurisdiction to give preliminary rulings in these specific areas of law, the Statute explicitly foresees that the Court of Justice retains jurisdiction to hear and determine requests for a preliminary ruling that raise independent questions relating to the interpretation of primary law, public international law, general principles of Union law or the Charter of Fundamental Rights of the European Union. This underlines the character of the Court of Justice as the "supreme" court of the EU judicial system. The General

[17] See also the Report provided for under Article 3(1) of Regulation 2015/2422, p. 12.

[18] OJ 2019 L 111, p. 1.

[19] Article 58a of the Statute of the Court of Justice.

[20] OJ L, 2024/2019, 12.8.2024.

[21] Recitals 3 and 4 of Regulation 2024/2019.

Court is, essentially, entrusted with the task of ensuring the judicial review of EU administrative and regulatory law.

3 A transfer of Jurisdiction to the General Court to Give Preliminary Rulings on Competition Matters?

The case to activate Art. 256 (3) TFEU was largely motivated by the increasing workload of the Court of Justice,[22] coupled with the conviction that the General Court had in the meantime developed both the capacity and the expertise to deal with specific references for preliminary rulings.[23] This necessarily triggers the question of whether further areas could be subject to the transfer of jurisdiction in case the first transfer will not sustainably mitigate the pressure on the Court of Justice's workload, namely other areas of law characterized by factual, technical and scientific complexity, including economic complexity, of which competition law is a prime example. Hence, the continued relevance of the proposal in that sense put forward in our aforementioned book by Marc van der Woude.

He points out that this would align the power to interpret Articles 101 and 102 TFEU with the power to control the legality of the decisions adopted by the Commission on the basis of Regulation 1/2003. More importantly, "[i]n answering preliminary reference questions by national courts, the General Court could rely on its own practical experience and ensure consistency between Articles 101 and 102 TFUE".[24] In doing so, the General Court would indeed establish itself as the "antitrust court of the EU" as it had been conceived by the early legislator when adopting Council Decision 88/591 establishing the Court of First Instance.

At the same time, Marc van der Woude rightly singles out certain disadvantages of such an extended transfer of powers, e.g. as regards its acceptance by the highest courts of the Member States. However, acceptance of such transfer of jurisdiction also depends on the quality and the usefulness of the answers given to the national courts allowing for legal certainty and administrability in the implementation of EU competition law. The proposal therefore deserves further consideration, even if its

[22] See notably recital 2 of Regulation 2024/2019.

[23] More generally on the reform and its implementation, see, inter alia, J. Martín y Pérez de Nanclares. 'La reforma del Tribunal de Justicia de la Unión Europea: La rupture de un tabú' (2024) Reviste Española de Dereche Europeo, p. 21; R. Mastroianni, 'Il trasferimento delle questioni pregiudiziali al Tribunale: une riforma epocale o un salon el buio?', (2024) Quaderni AISDUE 3, 1; N. Mundhenke, 'Modernisierung des europäischen Verfahrensrechts – Ein praxisorientierter Überblick', EuZW 2024, p. 950; W. M. Kühn, 'Die bevorstehende Reform des Gerichtssystems der Europäischen Union', EuZW 2023, p. 925; J. Laitenberger, N. Lauer, 'Die Reform des Gerichts der Europäischen Union – Stand und Perspektive', NZKart 2023, p. 4 (8 f.); D. Sarmiento, 'On the Road to a Constitutional Court of the European Union: The Court of Justice after the Transfer of the Preliminary Reference Jurisdiction to the General Court' (2023) Croatian Yearbook of European Law and Policy VII.

[24] M. van der Woude, *supra*, p. 863.

future uptake will depend on the concrete experience with the General Court's track record on handling the preliminary references now entrusted to it. This includes a reflection on further structural changes that might be required to implement the proposal and to strengthen the General Court's role as the antitrust court of the EU. Two aspects might be singled out for the purpose of this contribution.

4 A More "Legislative" Approach to EU Competition Law

First, the interpretation of EU competition rules by way of preliminary ruling generally involves an interpretation of EU primary law. Substantive EU antitrust law is essentially contained in Art. 101 and 102 TFEU.[25] Their wording, unchanged since the treaties of Rome, is deliberatively open, thus requiring the enforcers and ultimately the Union courts to fill out the lack of normative detail by way of interpretation. One might thus consider that the interpretation of EU antitrust law inevitably bears a risk of affecting the unity and consistency of Union law in the meaning of Art. 256(3), third subparagraph, TFEU simply because it amounts to an interpretation of primary law. Also, it should be reminded that the transfer of jurisdiction to give preliminary rulings to the General Court has been limited to specific areas that are densely regulated by secondary legislation, not at least because of their very technical nature. According to Article 50b, subparagraph 2, of the revised Statute, the Court of Justice retains jurisdiction to hear and determine requests for a preliminary ruling that raise independent questions relating to the interpretation particularly of primary law. Under the status quo, this standard could raise a significant caveat regarding a transfer of jurisdiction to give preliminary rulings on Art. 101 and 102 to the General Court. However, a transfer of jurisdiction to give preliminary rulings might be facilitated by the enactment of substantive competition law in secondary legislation. Such secondary law could in turn be interpreted by the General Court by way of preliminary rulings.

In another contribution, I have raised the question to what extent changes to the present set of competition rules can or even should be operated through secondary legislation.[26] While some voices seem to suggest that the legitimacy and coherence of EU competition enforcement limit the scope for the development of secondary

[25] The situation is slightly different with respect e.g. to merger control where the substantial "SIEC" test is enshrined in secondary legislation (see Art. 2, para. 2 and 3, of Regulation 139/2004 of 20 January 2004 on the control of concentrations between undertakings). However, given the delimitation between the competencies of the European Commission and its Member States in the field of merger control, as enshrined in the secondary legislation, merger control does not normally give rise to requests for preliminary rulings. A special case is the "Towercast" jurisprudence of the Court of Justice, which confirms that a concentration with a non-Community dimension may be subject to an ex-post control by the national competition authorities and by the national courts on the basis of the prohibition of abuse of a dominant position enshrined in Art. 102 TFEU (see judgment in *Towercast*, C-449/21, EU:C:2023:207).

[26] J. Laitenberger, J. Kröger, *supra*, p. 621.

competition law[27] or even advocate for an even broader constitutional basis for competition law enforcement,[28] ongoing reflections on the modernization of EU competition law might give pause for further thought. At the time of writing, the European Commission is considering a methodological shift from defining enforcement priorities to issuing guidelines on exclusionary abuses that are binding on the Commission in the exercise of its discretion in accordance with the principle of equal treatment.[29] This shift is an expression of the Commission's quest to implement a "dynamic and workable effects-based approach"[30] to abuse of dominance. It is however striking that the debate on abuse of dominance—arguably the most intense debate in the EU competition community since the inception of Regulation 1/2003—has not really given rise to a more comprehensive reflection on the role of legislation. In contrast, at the Member State level, it is ordinary legislation that is tasked to reconcile the needs for administrability, legal certainty and openness towards evolving economic theory when defining and implementing legal standards of EU competition law.[31] The debate, as reflected by the draft guidelines, seems to focus on two actors, the Commission and the EU courts, which engage in a "Popperian" approach of trial and error or verification and falsification of findings in individual cases. While such an approach is of course indispensable and presents undeniable merits, it also comes with costs in term of duration and legal certainty. The "Intel saga"[32] might be the most extreme illustration of the difficulties to reach a lasting synthesis in good time through the repeated confrontation of thesis and antithesis in a single case. The—so far—final judgement of the Court of Justice came around 25 years after the original complaint originated the European Commission's case.[33]

Nils Wahl, in one of his last public statements before retiring as a judge, was quoted as diagnosing that the Union courts are on a 'slippery slope' when it comes to holding the antitrust enforcers to a consistent and coherent legal standard.[34] This

---

[27] See H. Schweitzer, S. de Ridder, 'How to Fix a Failing Art. 102 TFEU', JECLAP 1/2024, p. 22.

[28] T. Jaeger, 'Zukunft des EU-Wettbewerbsrechts: Signale der Konferenz, Reformbedarf und Optionen', EuZW 2022, p. 642 (p. 644 f.).

[29] See judgment in *Dansk Rørindustri and Others v Commission*, C-189/02 P, C-202/02 P, C-205/02 P à C-208/02 P et C-213/02 P, EU:C:2005:408, paras 209 and 211.

[30] European Commission, Policy Brief 2023/1, A dynamic and workable effects-based approach to abuse of dominance.

[31] See as one example the legislative history of Germany's "Gesetz gegen Wettbewerbsbeschränkungen" (GWB) since its first enactment in 1957, in a historical parallel to the EU competition rules, K. Ost, 'The EU system and the German system', in Dekeyser, Gauer, Laitenberger, Wahl, Wils, Prete, *supra*, p. 941 ff.

[32] In chronological order: judgments in *Intel v Commission*, T-286/09, EU:T:2014:547; *Intel v Commission*, C-413/14, EU:C:2017:632; *Intel Corporation v Commission*, T-286/09 RENV, EU:T:2022:19. See also G. Monti, 'Rebates after the General Court's 2022 Intel judgment' (2023) Common Market Law Review 60 (1), pp. 107 ff.

[33] Judgment in *Commission v Intel Cooperation*, C-240/22 P, EU:C:2024:915.

[34] MLex, Wahl warns of EU court's 'slippery slope' on antitrust abuses and effects (12 September 2024).

might also be due to the absence of pre-defined standards and protocols for structured tests based on state-of the art economic. As pointed out by Pablo Ibáñez Colomo, structured tests are a crucial element in reconciling effective enforcement, legal certainty and a meaningful judicial review.[35] Also Rupprecht Podszun reminds us that the pursuit of a more economic approach "cannot break the institutional restrictions of a legal system" and "cannot give the status of normativity to economic theories or models through case-law", as such normativity is achieved by the legislative process which obviously can (and should) be informed by economics.[36] There could thus be a case for an expanded role of secondary legislation in defining predictable and workable tests as well as clear evidential and procedural standards that nevertheless would allow for the flexibility needed to adapt to evolving economic theory and increasingly complex reality.[37]

Such flexibility and adaptability is commonly achieved via delegated legislation adopted under Art. 290 TFEU that concretizes the legal standards defined be the secondary legislator. The current legal set-up however confines the legislative powers in the field of competition law, in substance, to Art. 103 TFEU, which not only diverges from the ordinary legislative procedure, but also confines the scope for secondary legislation to the type of measures listed, albeit in a non-exhaustive manner, in its paragraph 2. This design encroaches on the ability of Art. 103 to serve as the sole legal basis for the adoption of substantive legal tests guiding the Commission in its enforcement activates under Art. 101 and 102 TFEU. Changes to Art. 103 TFEU, including its alignment to the ordinary legislative procedure, could however contribute to facilitate and encourage the recourse to secondary competition legislation on which then the General Court might be empowered to give preliminary rulings.

This could all the more be of interest since the more recent jurisprudence contains references that appear to align the interpretation of Art. 102 TFEU with the structure of Art. 101 TFEU, notably with respect to the notion of "infringement by object" and the efficiency defence.[38]

It might therefore be useful to explore to what extent the method of block exemption regulations currently employed under Art. 101 TFEU only could also pave a way to a more efficient enforcement of Art. 102 TFEU and—consequently—an opening for secondary law requests that could potentially be dealt with by the General Court.

---

[35] P. Ibáñez Colomo, 'The (Second) Modernization of Article 102 TFEU', JECLAP 2/2023, p. 12.

[36] R. Podszun, 'The Role of Economics in Competition Law' (2018), EuCML 57 (56 f.).

[37] See J. Laitenberger, J. Kröger, *supra*, p. 634.

[38] See judgments in *European Superleague Company*, C-333/21, EU:C:2023:1011, paras 131, 186, 201 and 202; *International Skating Union v Commission*, C-124/21 P, EU:C:2023:1012, para. 128. See also P. Ibáñez Colomo, 'Article 101 and 102 TFEU must be interpreted consistently': Superleague and the EU system of undistorted competition, blog post 25.3.2024, chillingcompetition.com.

5 The General Court as a Second-Tier Forum of Independent Examination of Competition Decisions

Second, the proposal of a transfer of the jurisdiction to give preliminary rulings on competition matters to the General Court could indeed contribute to an alignment of judicial powers as the interpretation and the validity check of Commission decisions would be concentrated within one and the same jurisdiction. However, such an alignment would remain imperfect given that, in the current judicial set-up, the judgments and orders rendered by the General Court in first instance in response to an application for annulment under Art. 263 TFEU can be appealed to the Court of Justice. The ultimate legality check therefore remains with the Court of Justice in case of an appeal. If the jurisdiction to give preliminary rulings would be transferred to the General Court, the desired alignment of powers would therefore not fully materialize in case of appeal.

This raises the question if there is a case to advocate for a further adjustment of the judicial architecture inspired by the mechanism foreseen in Article 58a of the statute. As pointed out above, for cases which have already been subject to an independent examination by a board of appeal of one of the bodies or agencies listed in Article 58a,[39] the General Court gives indeed final judgment, unless the Court of Justice decides that an appeal should be allowed to proceed because it raises an issue that is significant with respect to the unity, consistency or development of Union law.

Boards of appeal are independent bodies that are typically attached to an EU agency. They are composed both of legal and scientific experts. Their aim is "to fill an apparent gap in judicial review that results from epistemic uncertainty and administrative discretion in certain areas".[40] These areas are characterized by factual, technical or scientific complexity as well as empirical and normative uncertainty in the light of which the executive branch is required to define and apply its legal standards. Accordingly, the mechanism provided for in Article 58a of the Court's statute applies in particular to decisions of the independent boards of appeal of agencies such as the EUIPO, the ECHA, the ACER or the ESMA.[41]

One might argue that competition law is not fundamentally different and qualifies as such area of law, given its heavy reliance on economic insight as applied to

---

[39] European Union intellectual Property Office, Community Plant Variety Office, European Chemicals Agency, European Union Aviation Safety Agency, European Union Agency for the Cooperation of Energy regulators, Single Resolution board, European banking Authority, European Securities and Markets Authority, European Insurance and Occupational Pensions Authority, European Union Agency for Railways.

[40] M. Krajewski, 'Judicial and Extra-judicial Review: The Quest for Epistemic Certainty', in Chamon, Volpato, Eliantonio (eds.), *Boards of Appeal of EU Agencies*, Oxford University Press, 2022, p. 273.

[41] See more in detail G. Hesse, ‚Der Zugang zum Höchstgericht – Filtermechanismen in der österreichischen Verwaltungsgerichtsbarkeit und in der europäischen Gerichtsbarkeit', Abschnitt III, in: FS Thienel (forthcoming).

individual cases involving factual and technical complexity and the difficulties for both the executive and the judiciary to reach epistemic certainty when defining and applying the appropriate legal standard.

Moreover, the examination of an administrative decision by an independent board of appeal allows for a clear set out of the factual and legal grounds, which ultimately puts the EU judicature in a position to concentrate on its core responsibility, i.e. a legality check of the executive.[42]

In that regard, it should be recalled that judges serving at the Union Courts and deciding ultimately on matters of EU competition law are not selected because of their economic, but their legal expertise, which is assessed in the so-called "255-committee". Moreover, a system of judicial review governed by the rule of law cannot and should not rely on the degree of ultimately accidental education of judges on economic matters.[43] At the same time, while "material provisions of anti-competitive conduct need to remain in the grip of normativity, i.e., [of] legally-trained judges",[44] it would amount to a denial of reality to reject the importance of economic analysis in the application of legally defined standards in a specific case.

It is therefore worth reflecting on adding to the administrative and judicial architecture an intermediate layer of independent examination of competition decisions adopted by the Commission by an independent board of appeal type of body composed by legally and economically trained experts.[45] Their decisions could then be subject to a full legality review by the General Court without necessarily allowing for an unrestricted appeal to the Court of Justice. This being said, Art. 105 TFEU has entrusted the Commission—i.e. the college of commissioners—as the institution of the EU tasked with the enforcement of EU competition law. The establishment of an independent body of appeal with a mandate to overturn the Commission's decision or a "blanket" delegation of the Commission's ultimate decision-making competence in competition matters to such a body would appear at odds with the institutional balance enshrined by the treaties. The same is true for the establishment of an independent body entrusted with the enforcement of EU competition law outside of the Commission. As it stands, the "Meroni" jurisprudence of the Court of Justice[46] is not compatible with "outsourcing" the Commission's discretionary prerogatives to another body. Even though the Court of Justice has paved the way towards further agencification under the TFEU provided that the delegated powers are precisely delineated and amenable to judicial review,[47] Art. 105 TFEU would seem at odds with a wholesale transfer of EU competition law enforcement

---

[42] Judgment in T-735/18, *Alquind v ACER*, ECLI:EU:T:2020:542, para 29.

[43] J. Laitenberger, J. Kröger, *supra*, p. 628.

[44] R. Podszun, *supra*, p. 60.

[45] See in that sense also I. Forrester, 'A Scot's Account of Judicial Review: From Commercial Solvents to Google', WuW 2024, pp. 625–626.

[46] Judgment in *Meroni v High Authority*, 10/56, EU:C:1958:8.

[47] Judgment in *United Kingdom v Parliament and Council*, C-270/12, EU:C:2014:18, paras 42 and 53.

prerogatives to a body outside of the Commission.[48] At the same time, a purely internal arrangement of review within the European Commission would not change the ultimate legal nature of the Commission's decision and hence not qualify for the direct application of the present Art. 58a of the statute given the lack of a first tier independent examination.

One can of course not completely exclude a rekindling of the discussions on a change of the treaties foreseeing changes facilitating such developments or even the establishment of an independent EU competition authority. In the meantime, a more pragmatic approach could however consist in engaging in a reflection on how the current administrative set-up within the Commission could be completed to allow for an even more structured and materially independent way of assessing and applying economic evidence in a specific case in the administrative procedure. Such an approach would go beyond the current administrative practice of tasking the Chief Economist's team of the Commission's Directorate-General of Competition with giving economic guidance and organizing in-house "devil's advocate" panels on particularly complex cases.[49] A dedicated process ensuring wholly independent advice and input on economic evidence in the European Commission's decision-making process could at least help to underpin the General Court's review with increased economic epistemic certainty.

Here again, the experience from other areas characterized by scientific and technical complexity might serve as inspiration. The European Chemicals Agency (ECHA) is supported by the Committee for Risk Assessment when assessing the risks of substances to human health and environment in the framework of the REACH regulation[50] and by the Committee for Socio-Economic Analysis when assessing the socio-economic impact of a given regulatory measure to be adopted by ECHA or eventually the Commission.[51] Similar committees support the decision making process of other EU agencies.[52] They are fora that allow for an exchange of different scientific opinions. Divergences of such opinions are addressed and solved following the rules of internal procedure of the respective committee. Thus, the "Popperian" back and forth of trial and error is anticipated, so that it does not need to dominate the further debate in front of the courts. In fact, such procedural

---

[48] M. Chamon, 'Granting powers to EU decentralised agencies, three years following *Short-selling*' (2018) ERA-Forum 597 (598 f.).

[49] For the role of the Chief Economist in DG COMP see S. Albaek, P. Régibeau, in Dekeyser, Gauer, Laitenberger, Wahl, Wils, Prete (eds), *supra*, pp. 807 ff.

[50] Regulation (EC) No 1907/2006 of the European Parliament and of the Council of 18 December 2006 concerning the Registration, Evaluation, Authorisation and Restriction of Chemicals (REACH), establishing a European Chemicals Agency, amending Directive 1999/45/EC and repealing Council Regulation (EEC) No 793/93 and Commission Regulation (EC) No 1488/94 as well as Council Directive 76/769/EEC and Commission Directives 91/155/EEC, 93/67/EEC, 93/105/EC and 2000/21/EC (OJ 2006 L 396, p. 1, corrigendum OJ 2007 L 136, p. 3).

[51] See Art. 76, para. 1, lit. c) and d) of the REACH Regulation.

[52] See for example the Committee for Medicinal Products for Human Use and the Committee on Orphan Medicinal Products and established as parts of the European Medicines Agency under Regulation No 726/2004 (OJ 2004 L 136, p. 1).

complements to the administrative proceedings would allow for a certain form of pre-structuring of subsequent judicial proceedings regarding the Commission's decision ensuring thus a more informed judicial review.

Whilst such an approach would still fall short of an arrangement allowing for the application of Art. 58a of the statute in its present form, it could nevertheless decisively mitigate the concerns over a "scattered landscape" emerging from a General Court competence to hear and determine requests for preliminary references on competition law coupled with the continued existence of a right to appeal General Court judgements on direct actions in competition law to the Court of Justice.

6 Conclusions

The proposal of an alignment of powers in the judicial architecture with regard to EU competition law is an important one as it comes at a time of a discussion on the modernization of EU competition law and the quest for a dynamic and workable effects-based approach, which creates legal certainty and allows for an effective judicial review in respect of the institutional balance between the legislative, executive and judicial branches of the EU.

The material and institutional framework governing EU competition law being essentially enshrined in primary law, such an alignment appears to go beyond a "mere" adaptation of the statute of the Court of Justice and might be difficult to implement without changes to that framework and in particular changes to Art. 103 and 105 TFEU.

More than 70 years after the first adoption of competition rules by the ECSC Treaty and more than 60 years after the enshrinement of what is today Art. 101 and 102 TFEU by the treaties of Rome, the time may however have come to think more fundamentally and more boldly on fixing something that is not broken so that it may hold for further decades to come—an intention, I believe, that has also inspired Nils Wahl's significant and far-reaching contribution to the development of EU competition law in his roles as judge at the General Court and as advocate general and judge at the Court of Justice.

Should I Stay or Should I Go? Restrictions by Object, by Effect, and Their Application to Football Transfer Rules

Petros C. Mavroidis and Damien J. Neven

1 Introduction

The Diarra judgment[1] was yet another watershed in the ongoing saga of CJEU decisions questioning the legality of regulatory interventions by the world (FIFA) and European (UEFA) football governing bodies. The Court outlawed the transfer-system of professional football players which it held constituted a restriction by object. FIFA has moved back to the drawing board but has only produced an interim regime so far. We believe that it does not fully address the concerns that the CJEU has expressed. We advance a few thoughts that could hopefully inspire those entrusted with the regulation of the next regime so as to ensure that the new regime will correspond to the wishes of the EU judges.

The question before the Court concerned the rights of a player (Lassana Diarra) who had terminated his contract with Lokomotiv Moscow (a Russian professional club) allegedly without just cause when seeking his transfer abroad. He had been sanctioned by the competent FIFA body, the DRC (Dispute Resolution Center), and this decision was confirmed by a CAS (Court of Arbitration for Sport) panel. The

For helpful discussions, we are indebted to H. Horn, P. Ibañez Colomo, M. Maduro, A. Sykes, S. Szymanski, S. Weatherill, J. Weiler, J. Zglinski, as well as seminar participants at NYU on 12 November 2024.

[1] Judgment in *FIFA*, C-650/22, EU:C:2024:824.

P. C. Mavroidis (✉)
Columbia Law School, New York, NY, USA
e-mail: pm2030@columbia.edu

D. J. Neven
Geneva Graduate Institute, Geneva, Switzerland
e-mail: damien.neven@graduateinstitute.ch

L. Prete, L. Rezki (eds.), *Judging & (Re)Thinking European Union Law*,
https://doi.org/10.1007/978-3-032-13473-8_11

player subsequently introduced a complaint on the same issue before a Belgian civil court[2] and his dispute with his former club found eventually its way before the Luxembourg court.

Unlike what happens when labor contract is terminated in other profession, unless a player is at the end of his contract, there is an obligation for the acquiring club to pay a transfer fee to the original club.[3] Absent agreement on the amount, the transfer of the player might be jeopardized, thereby, depriving football players of better opportunities to ply their trade elsewhere.[4]

This case is also significant as it is the last in a series of disputes between the Sports Governing Bodies (SGB), FIFA and UEFA (Union Européenne de Football Association), and their stakeholders (football clubs and/or—players) that has been submitted for adjudication before civil courts in Europe, and eventually the CJEU. Taken together, these judgments provide a new framework for the conduct of these SGB.

The remaining part of the paper is organized as follows. In Sect. 2, we first describe the aspects of the FIFA transfer system that were at stake in the *Diarra* dispute. Section 3 discusses the opinion of Advocate General ('AG') Szpunar. Section 4 focuses on the judgment. In Sect. 5, we discuss the immediate consequences of the judgment for the transfer system, as well as the appropriate standard for damages in the context of a very simple model. Section 6 offers some concluding remarks.

2 The Legal Framework and Practice of the FIFA Transfer System

Following the Bosman ruling,[5] a player can move from one club to another at the end of his contract. A player can also unilaterally terminate his contract (without compensating the old club) if he has "just cause" to do so.[6] Finally, he can also leave his old club while under contract, but in this case, the club interested in his services

[2] There is no *res judicata* (Claim preclusion), as the Court does not share its prerogative to interpret EU law with no other judicial body. In its recent judgment in *International Skating Union v Commission* (C-124/21 P, EU:C:2023:1012, paras 184–204) ('*ISU*'), the CJEU clarified that questions regarding the interpretation of EU law must be submitted exclusively to the CJEU, or to courts that has the right to submit a request for preliminary ruling to the CJEU. The CAS is not such court, see N. Wahl, L. Prete, 'The Gatekeepers of Article 267 TFEU: On Jurisdiction and Admissibility of References for Preliminary Rulings' (2018) CML Rev, 511.

[3] This is the consequence of the notorious judgment in *Bosman*, C-415/93, EU:C:1995:463. There is one exception to this rule for young players who sign their first professional contract, the result of the judgment in *Olympique Lyonnais*, C-325/08, EU:C:2010:143.

[4] The commercial importance of the issue cannot be overstated. According to seemingly well-informed estimates the twenty highest spending clubs have paid 23,029,000,000 euros in the last five seasons (2019–2023). See information available on line on football-observatory.com.

[5] Supra, n. 4.

[6] We explain the concept of "just cause" as understood in FIFA statutes later on.

must agree on a transfer fee with the player's old club. The *Diarra* case concerns this situation in which a player terminated his contract allegedly without just cause so that a transfer fee was required for the transfer to take place. Article 17 of FIFA's transfer regulation (RSTP)[7] entitled "Consequences of Terminating a Contract Without Just Cause" provides that if a player has terminated his contract without just cause and moved to a new club:

- The player and the new club are jointly and severally liable to compensate the old club;
- Sporting sanctions will be imposed on the player if the breach of contract occurred during the "protected period"—essentially the first 3 years of a contract;[8]
- Sporting sanctions will be imposed to the (acquiring) club if it has incited a player to sign a new contract:
  - There is a rebuttable presumption that the acquiring club has egged on the player to abandon his old club and sign a new contract with it;
  - If not rebutted, the acquiring club will be banned from signing new players during two consecutive transfer seasons.[9]

The title of Article 17 can be misleading as the scope of this provision extends beyond instances of termination without just cause. According to the Commentary on the RSTP[10] (pp. 169 et seq.), Article 17 applies to two distinct sets of circumstances, namely: (i) when a party has terminated the contract without just cause; and (ii) when a party has seriously breached its obligations so that the other party is entitled to terminate the contract with just cause.

In essence, what determines whether a party has just cause, is the conduct of the other party. If, say, a club breaches its obligation towards a player, the player will have just cause to terminate the contract and, in this case, the old club will have to compensate the player. Conversely, in the absence of a breach of obligation by the

[7] RSTP stands for Regulation on the Status and the Transfer of Players. This regulation was adopted by FIFA on 22 March 2014.

[8] According to Definition 7 of the RSTP, "protected period" is defined as follows: a period of three entire seasons or three years, whichever comes first, following the entry into force of a contract, if such contract was concluded prior to the 28th birthday of the Professional, or to a period of two entire Seasons or two years, whichever comes first, following the entry into force of a contract, if such contract was concluded after the 28th birthday of the Professional.

[9] There are two transfer seasons in football, a long one every summer, and a shorter one during January each year.

[10] This is a FIFA publication (available on line). Its legal value is discussed in the Commentary itself, which notes that (p. 8): "the Commentary has once again become a basic tool for the FIFA Football Tribunal, its main stakeholders and CAS ... Considering the ever-evolving regulatory changes and jurisprudence of the FIFA Football Tribunal, the Commentary does not represent a formal position of the FIFA Football Tribunal on the FIFA Regulations on the Status and Transfer of Players (the Regulations). However, it is fair to say that it is indispensable to have insight into a set of regulations that has increased in technical and material complexity in recent years, and to get a better understanding of its application". It is consistently cited by sports tribunals (FIFA bodies and the CAS, Court of Arbitration for Sport) and its impact in practice cannot be overstated.

Table 1 How does Article 17 RSTP function?

	Duty to compensate	Sporting sanctions
Club good faith, Player terminates contract	Player and new club compensate the old club—**No Just cause**	Player and new club may be sanctioned
Club delinquent, Player terminates contract	Old Club compensates the player—Just Cause	No sporting sanctions
Player good faith, Club terminates contract	Old Club compensates the player—**No just cause**	No sporting sanctions
Player delinquent, Club terminates contract	Player compensates the old club Just cause	Player sanctioned

old club, a player who terminates his contract will do so without just cause, and, in this case, the player and the new club will have to compensate the old club (Table 1).

The presence or absence of just cause is thus central for the outcome of a dispute.

2.1 Understanding Just- and Unjust Cause

Termination with just cause by a player is regulated in Articles 14 and 14bis of the RSTP. Article 14bis discusses a very specific case of just cause, namely the non-payment of two-month salaries. In this case, a player has just cause to terminate his contract. Besides this specific circumstance, Article 14 does not define "just cause" per se but circumscribes its scope: 'Any abusive conduct of a party aiming at forcing the counterparty to terminate or change the terms of the contract shall entitle the counterparty (a player or a club) to terminate the contract with just cause'.

This provision leaves it to the discretion of adjudicators to decide what constitutes "abusive behavior". The FIFA Commentary to Article 14 cautions that it is simply not the case that every violation of contractual terms amounts to "abusive behavior":[11]

Whether just cause exists shall be established in accordance with the merits of each particular case. Behaviour that is in violation of the terms of an employment contract still cannot justify the termination of a contract for just cause. However, should the violation persist over a long time or should many violations be cumulated over a certain period of time, then it is most probable that the breach of contract has reached such a level that the party suffering the breach is entitled to terminate the contract unilaterally.

The type and frequency of violation thus matters. The non-payment (or delayed payment) of one salary (e.g., the absence of trend/pattern) would not be sufficient to trigger "just cause" for the player (assuming of course, that it is not periodically repeated). In certain circumstances, a (repeated) refusal to pay even part of the salary

[11] The Commentary (pp. 132 et seq.) includes various instances where CAS panels held the view that they were facing "abusive behavior".

has also been considered just cause for termination.[12] CAS jurisprudence has on occasion echoed the case law of the Swiss Federal Tribunal, in that only material breaches of contract can be considered as triggering a "just cause" for terminating a contract.[13] The jurisprudence of the Swiss Federal Tribunal stands for the proposition that an employment contract may be lawfully terminated when the "fundamental" terms and conditions which formed the basis of the contractual arrangement, are no longer respected (ATF 101 Ia 545). Lack of respect of auxiliary terms and conditions, conversely, could not be relied on as "just cause" for lawfully terminating a contract.

A judge has some discretion to decide whether a particular term/condition is "fundamental". Adjudicators will be first inspired by existing case law: the payment of remuneration agreed and/or the obligation of the club to provide players with appropriate conditions to practice their profession have been consistently considered as conditions of "fundamental" nature. A unilateral or unexpected change in the status of an employee, which is not related to either company requirements or to the organization of the work or even to a failure of the employee to observe his/her obligations has also been considered just cause for termination.[14]

From a procedural perspective, for a party to be allowed validly to terminate an employment contract, it is often required that it has provided the other party with adequate notice, in order for the latter to have had the opportunity to comply with its own obligations. By way of a typical illustration, a CAS Panel has held that: '... a prerequisite for terminating because of late payment is that the Appellant should have given a warning. This follows from the principle of good faith ... the Appellant must – before he terminates the Contract – let the Respondent know firstly that he is complaining that the Respondent's conduct is not in accordance with the Contract and secondly that he is not prepared to accept such breaches of contract in future (CAS 2006/A/1180)'.[15]

When a CAS panel is required to assess whether a valid reason exists for unilateral contract termination: (i) only a sufficiently serious breach of contractual obligations by one party to the contract qualifies as just cause for the other party to terminate the contract; (ii) the breach is considered sufficiently serious when there are objective circumstances that would render it unreasonable to expect the employment relationship between the parties to continue; and (iii) the termination of a contract should be an action of last resort.

Two requirements must be met for just cause to exist. First, a substantive requirement consisting of non-payment of two consecutive salaries; or a breach of a

[12] A. Staehlin, Kommentar zum Schweizerischen Zivilgesetzbuch, Obliagtionenrecht, V 2c, Der Arbeitsvertrag, Art. 319–362 OR, Zurich 1996, N 27 ad Art. 337 CO; Brunner, Bühler, Waeber, Bruchez, *Commentaire du contrat de travail*, Lausanne 2010, N 7 ad Art. 337 CO.

[13] CAS 2006/A/1062; CAS 2006/A/1100; CAS 2006/A/1180; CAS 2007/A/1210; CAS 2008/A/1447.

[14] Unpublished judgments of 7 October 1992 in SJ 1993 I 370, of 25 November 1985 in SJ 1986 I 300 and of 16 June 1981 in case C.40/81.

[15] There are circumstances though, where no reminder and no warning were deemed necessary, i.e. in a case when it is clear that the other side does not intend to comply with its contractual obligations.

fundamental term/condition embedded in the contract; or a pattern of violations which renders the continuation of the employment relationship in good faith unreasonable for the party giving notice. Second, a procedural requirement, that is, the obligation of the party with just cause terminating the contract, to furnish its contractual partner a written notice to this effect.

2.2 *Procuring the International Transfer Certificate (ITC)*

In the absence of an agreement between the old and the new club, if a player is bound by a contract, the association of the old club is supposed to refuse to issue an ITC certificate when the player moves to another country.

Article 9 of the RSTP, entitled "International Transfer Certificate" (ITC), states in its §1: 'Players registered at one association may only be registered at a new association once the latter has received an [ITC] from the former association. The ITC shall be issued free of charge without any conditions or time limit. Any provisions to the contrary shall be null and void. The association issuing the ITC shall lodge a copy with FIFA. The administrative procedures for issuing the ITC are contained in Annexe 3, Article 8 … of these regulations.'

Annex 3 to the RSTP, entitled "Transfer matching system", includes Article 8 which covers the "Administrative procedure governing the transfer of professionals between associations":

> 8.1 Principles
>
> 1. Any professional player who is registered with a club that is affiliated to one association may only be registered with a club affiliated to a different association after an ITC has been delivered by the former association and the new association has confirmed receipt of the ITC. …
>
> …
>
> 8.2 Creating an ITC for a professional player
>
> …
>
> 3. Upon receipt of the ITC request, the former association shall immediately request the former club and the professional player to confirm whether the professional player's contract has expired, whether early termination was mutually agreed or whether there is a contractual dispute.
>
> 4. Within seven days of the date of the ITC request, the former association shall …:
>
> (a) deliver the ITC in favour of the new association and enter the deregistration date of the player; or
> (b) reject the ITC request and indicate … the reason for rejection, which may be either that the contract between the former club and the professional player has not expired or that there has been no mutual agreement regarding its early termination.
>
> …
>
> 7. The former association shall not deliver an ITC if a contractual dispute on grounds of the circumstances stipulated in Annexe 3, Article 8.2, paragraph 4(b) has arisen between the former club and the professional player. In such a case, upon request of the new association, FIFA *may* take provisional measures in exceptional circumstances. … Furthermore, the professional player, the former club and/or the new club are entitled to lodge a claim with FIFA in accordance with Article 22. *FIFA shall then decide on the issue of the ITC and on*

> *sporting sanctions within 60 days*. In any case, the decision on sporting sanctions shall be taken before the delivery of the ITC. The delivery of the ITC shall be without prejudice to compensation for breach of contract. (emphasis added)

Hence, the new club can still request a provisional ITC from FIFA. In practice, FIFA has authorized the player's registration on numerous occasions. But, and this is a key point for the legal assessment of the consistency of Article 17 RSTP with EU law, the conditions under which, FIFA might or might not grant the ITC are not specified.

After FIFA has decided on sporting sanctions and has issued the certificate, the amount of compensation that should be paid to the old club becomes a matter of negotiation and/or litigation. The FIFA regulation thus does not in practice go as far as preventing players from moving. The question however, is whether the combination of the transfer fee, the (possible) sanctions imposed, and the uncertainty regarding FIFA's conduct (will it issue or not the requested ITC?) deter transfers. In particular, even if players and the new club can anticipate that, if they fail to agree on a transfer fee, the player will be allowed to move (and without sporting sanctions outside the protected period), the outcome of the dispute in front of CAS regarding the transfer fee might still discourage transfers. As discussed below, the wide range of possible outcome from CAS ruling might create different expectations in this respect and explain why clubs do not settle ex ante.

It is also worth noting that, paradoxically, international transfers are easier than transfers between clubs belonging to the same national federation. Assume a professional player wants to move between two clubs belonging to the same federation. The federation will (typically) not issue a registration if the old club maintains that the player is under contract. As no ITC is necessary for the transfer of a player between two clubs, Article 8.11.8 of Annex 3 is not germane to this move. Consequently, FIFA will not have the opportunity to by-pass the refusal of the national federation.

2.3 *Deciding on Compensation and Sporting Sanctions*

Article 17 has been invoked dozens of times before the CAS in litigations that focused on this issue. The FIFA Commentary on the RSTP includes a lengthy discussion (some forty pages) of practice under Article 17. Practice makes it clear that while payment of compensation has always been ordered, sporting sanctions have been seldom imposed. Furthermore, the amount of compensation due has not been consistently calculated using a consistent methodology.

2.3.1 Calculating the Amount of Compensation

The objective of compensation is clearly stated in the FIFA's commentary (p. 173, op. cit.): 'The aim of compensating the damaged party should always be to arrive at an amount of compensation that adequately compensates for the damage suffered. The process of calculating compensation due for a contractual breach must not lead to the injured party obtaining benefits or gain that compensates it over and above the harm it sustained because of the unlawful behaviour of the other party.[16]

This provision clarified that the damage is not assessed in terms of what the liable party has gained (restitution damages) but in terms of the loss that the injured party has suffered. Thus, the statutory aim is not inconsistent with the aim of putting the old club in the situation where it would have been had the unlawful act not happened and the contract had been completed (expectation damages).[17] The quantification of the term "damage suffered" in practice holds the key in this context. The assessment of the benefit that the old club could expect depends on the options that are considered and in particular whether the opportunity cost of a legal transfer is taken into account.

Note first that *when the compensation fee has been contractually agreed* (either in the form of liquidated damages or by including a buy-out clause), CAS jurisprudence has consistently held that only proportional clauses will be upheld (see for example, CAS 2017/A/5242 Esteghlal Football Club v. Pero Pejic). This case law begs the question of the benchmark for assessing proportionality. Should the comparator be the value of the contract (remuneration of the player) or the commercial value of the player? Relevant case law reflected in the Commentary on RSTP indicates that proportionality is calculated by using the remuneration of the player by the old club as comparator.

Following a recent amendment of the relevant statutes, compensation to a player (Article 14bis)[18] will be based on the provisions of a CBA (collective bargaining agreement) negotiated by employers' and employees' representatives at domestic level in accordance with national law, assuming one exists. CBAs take precedence over the FIFA statutes.

When the compensation fee has not been contractually agreed, then the amount of compensation must be calculated according to the various "objective" criteria mentioned in the body of Article 17 of RSTP, namely:

- the remuneration and other benefits due to the player under the existing contract and/or the new contract;
- the time remaining on the existing contract up to a maximum of 5 years;

[16]The aim thus stated does not appear in the body of Article 17. Since however, the FIFA is the author of this provision, it authentically reflects the target that the means committed in Article 17 aim to pursue.

[17]Note that expectation damages in principle do not lead to inefficient breaches (breach only occurs, if at all, if the value under the new contract exceeds the value under the old contract). Nevertheless, as observed by Szymanski (2024a), this assumes that the original contract has been efficient.

[18]Article 14bis was added to Article 14 of RSTP. Article 14 regulates compensation due in case of termination of contract with just cause. Because of the scope of Article 17 of RSTP as already explained above, this provision is relevant to our discussion.

- the fees and expenses paid or incurred by the former club (amortized over the term of the contract), and also
- whether the contractual breach falls within a protected period.

CAS case law[19] suggests that the list is not exhaustive and adjudicators can add other "objective" criteria at their discretion. They rarely, if ever, do so.[20] Sports adjudicators will routinely calculate compensation due paying particular heed to the time remaining on the existing contract (respecting the statutory norm to avoid extending it beyond five years). Fees and expenses paid or incurred by the former club[21] will be taken into account, as will mitigation compensation. Were a plaintiff to submit a dispute to CAS, then more often than not arbitrators will pay little heed to choice of law by the parties and apply FIFA law instead (and Swiss law accessorily). Sports specificity has been used to adjust amount due especially if player owes sums in only a handful of cases.

Two (hard to reconcile) decisions that are referred to in the relevant literature as the "Webster" and the "Matuzalem" decisions (named after the players involved in the two disputes)[22] are at the antipodes of the CAS jurisprudence regarding the calculation of the compensation fee. In the "Webster" award, the compensation to the old club was calculated based exclusively on the residual value of the contract that had been prematurely terminated, namely the wages (say W) that would have had to be paid (per year) until the end of the contract. The price initially paid by the old club gives a lower bound to the gross incremental value (say V, also per year) that it was expecting when the contract was signed (as the club would not have agreed on a salary in excess of the gross contribution of the player). As the club will no longer have to pay the wage to the player, the compensation (W) might make the club better off. If say, the player had negotiated a wage (W) corresponding to his incremental value to the club (V), the club will obtain a rent (relative to the counterfactual, in which the net benefit was 0) equal to the wage, which is also equal in this case to the incremental contribution the player. The rent will decrease in inverse proportion

[19] 2018/A/6037 & 6043 Bangkok United FC v. Mohanad Abdulraheeem Karrar and Mohanad Abdulraheeem Karrar v. Bangkok United FC.

[20] In lex-sportiva parlance, remuneration and other benefits due to the player under the existing contract and/or the new contract is known as the principle of "positive interest". This principle suggests that the amount of compensation should serve one function: the injured party should be placed back to the position that it would have been, had the breach of contract not occurred. See P. A. Czarnota, 'FIFA Transfer Rules and Unilateral Termination Without "Just Cause"' (2013) Berkeley Journal of Entertainment and Sports Law, 2: 1–47.

[21] For instance, if a club has misbehaved so that a player has left with just cause and the old blub needs to compensate the player, the compensation will take into account periods in which there is an overlap in contracts. The compensation will be reduced by the amount the player has received from the new club during the overlap.

[22] CAS 2007/A/1298 Wigan Athletic FC v. Heart of Midlothian, CAS 2007/A/1299 Heart of Midlothian v. Webster & Wigan Athletic FC, CAS 2007/A/1300 Webster v. Heart of Midlothian. 325 CAS 2008/A/1519 FC Shakhtar Donetsk (Ukraine) v. Mr Matuzalem Francelino da Silva (Brazil) & Real Zaragoza SAD (Spain) & FIFA, CAS 2008/A/1520 Mr Matuzalem Francelino da Silva (Brazil) & Real Zaragoza SAD (Spain) v. FC Shakhtar Donetsk (Ukraine) & FIFA.

with the wage that the player had negotiated. If the player had negotiated a wage equal to the next best alternative at the time (say A), in the counterfactual the club would have obtained (V-A). The proposed compensation will only give him A—a net reduction in his net benefit as long as (V-A > A) or A > V/2.

According the Webster approach, the relevant counterfactual (the situation in which the club would have been in the absence of early termination) is (implicitly) the rent that the club would have obtained ex ante. This is one possible benchmark for the definition of expectation damages (using the expectations at the time at which the initial contract was signed). The previous discussion makes it clear however that except for the very special case in which W = V/2, the Webster approach does not put the club in the situation in which it would had been in terms of expected rent if the contract had been honored. It also follows that the old club will have much to gain from the transfer if the player had originally obtained a large share of its contribution to the club.

In "Matuzalem", the player's (lost) transfer value was considered to be an element of the damage suffered since this value alone reflected the "economic reality". Whereas in Webster the CAS panel limited itself to the criteria included in the body of Article 17, the Matuzalem panel interpreted the embedded criteria in light of the overarching objective (as understood in the Commentary on RSTP). The CAS panel took into account the commercial value of the player (and not only the value of his contract as captured by his previous wage) in order to calculate the amount of compensation due. Specifically, the CAS assessed the value of the player from the transfer fee that a new club would have been willing to pay and the salary that the new (acquiring) club was prepared to pay him.[23] What the CAS used in this case, was an estimate of the gross contribution of the player to the new club.[24] To explore the difference with Webster, denote as VN the gross contribution of the player to the new club (this contribution may only become apparent as the talent of the player may have been revealed during his time at the old club). If the contribution to the new club is higher than his initial contribution to the old club (VN > V),[25] it follows that (since the initial wage is no greater than the initial contribution), damages based on

[23] The player moved to Zaragoza but was then loaned to Lazio. The CAS uses the transfer fee that Lazio had indicated they would have been willing to pay at the end of the loan and annualized the fee (the fee was negotiated in the context of a three years contract). The CAS added the average wage of the player (per year) in Zaragoza and Lazio. The case also added another 600 K Euros, because of sports specificity. The justification for this is not entirely clear but it seems to be related to the fact that the player acted in bad faith, see Czarnota, *supra*.

[24] Or at least a lower bound for that amount, assuming that the new club would have not obtained any rent with a package—sum of transfer fee and the players wages—equal to the contribution of the player.

[25] This condition ensures that together the player and the new club have a willingness to pay in excess of the maximum rent accruing to the old club. It is however not sufficient to ensure that the transfer is attractive for the old club—as the value of the player for the old club may also have increased between the initial contract and the time of early termination. It is however necessary to make the transfer attractive to both the old club and the player.

the gross contribution to the new club have to be higher than damages based on salary of the play in the old contract (as in Webster).

According to the approach in Matuzalem, the relevant counterfactual is no longer the expectation of rents at the time of initial contract but the expectation of rents that could have been obtained from a transfer at the time of the early termination that the old clug would have agreed to. This is a different benchmark for expectation damages (where expectations are defined by the options available at the time of the early termination).

However, the Mathuzalem benchmark is not an estimate of the opportunitys that the old club may have been deprived off as it does as it ignores the opportunity cost of the player. The player will only move if the damage does not exceed its incremental value. What the old club can extract is only the incremental value of the player, namely its gross value in the new club less the compensation that he already obtains.

Finally, it is worth recalling that the player and the new club are jointly and severally liable for the compensation to the old club, as this is a feature that the ECJ will find objectionable.[26]

2.3.2 Sporting Sanctions

As mentioned above, sanctions may still be imposed on the player if the transfer occurs during the protected period and on the club is it cannot show that it has not incited the player to move. The sporting sanction is a ban on registering any new players, either nationally or internationally, for a maximum of two entire and consecutive registration periods and seems to have been imposed on a number of cases. The maximum sporting sanction to be imposed on a player in the event of termination without just cause during the protected period is four-month ban on playing in official matches, extending to six months where there are "aggravating circumstances". FIFA adjudicating bodies have imposed the more severe sporting sanction on a player only sparingly.

2.4 Partial Conclusion

The analysis above suggests two interim conclusions:

- The outright prohibition of transfers embedded in Article 9 of the RSTP for players under contract, does not totally hold in practice. A request to FIFA might lead

[26] Subsequent CAS practice did not decidedly take position in favor of one or the other standard. In fact, in De Sanctis, a CAS panel opted for a slightly different standard: it calculated the compensation due based on the replacement value (e.g., the amount of money that the original club paid to replace the departing De Sanctis) augmented by a sum corresponding to sports specificity, see Czarnota, *supra*. While this standard is reminiscent of Matuzalem, it is not identical to it.

to an interim ITC to be issued, while the new club and the player remain liable to pay compensation to the old club. In other words, the old club might be de facto forced to see its player go even against its will;[27] whether such transfers are effectively deterred depends on how compensation is determined by the CAS.

- The amount of compensation due to the old club has been calculated inconsistently in practice:
  - the "Webster"-approach can be seen as involving expectation damages in relation to the expected rents at the time at which the initial contrat was signed. However, by taking to the wage of the player as a measure of compensation, will not in general provide damages commensurate with expected rents.
  - the "Matuzalem"- benchmark can be seen as involving expectation damages when the expected rents are those at the time of the breach. However, it does provide an appropriate proxy for expectation damages as it fails to take into account the opportunity cost of the player. The "Matuzalem" damages will be larger than expectation damages at the time of the breach.

Before turning to the judgment, a brief comment on what could be the rationale for the FIFA regulation may also be useful: the rationale might be considered in the analysis of legitimate objectives by the Court. Contractual stability has been recognized as a legitimate objective by EU Courts in the *Lethonen* case (C-176/96). In this case, the CJEU upheld the legitimacy of restricting the periods during which athletes can be transferred between clubs. This can be presumably rationalized in terms of the potential disruption to competitions that would be caused by important changes in the composition and strengths of the teams during the season. There may however be other justifications for restricting player contracts in relation to the discovery of talent and training, which were recognized as legitimate objectives in *Bosman* and *Olympique Lyonnais*. Even though the restriction on transfers, and associated transfer fees in those cases were not considered proportionate, a transfer system could be designed to meet this condition.

3 The Opinion of AG Szpunar

AG Szpunar found that Article 17 of the RSTP violates both Articles 45 and 101 of TFEU. In this section, we only consider the opinion of the AG with respect to Article 101as it is potentially the most consequential (as unlike violations of Article 45, violations of Article 101 by object cannot be justified by legitimate objectives). The operative part of AG Szpunar's Opinion that we focus on runs as follows (para.88): 'Article 101 TFEU must be interpreted as precluding rules that have been adopted

[27] Building a football team is also a mastery of network externalities and it is doubtful that ready-made replacements are available in the market. Furthermore, other clubs knowing the "new" need of the old club might be incentivized to increase the price of their own players that the old club might be eyeing as replacement for its departed player.

by an association responsible for organising football competitions at world level and implemented both by that association and by its member national football associations, providing that a player and a club wishing to employ him or her are jointly and severally liable in respect of the compensation due to the club whose contract with the player has been terminated without just cause and providing that an association to which a player's former club belongs is entitled not to deliver the international transfer certificate required if the player is to be employed by a new club, where there is a dispute between that former club and the player, if it is established, first, that those decisions by associations of undertakings are liable to affect trade between Member States and, second, that they have either as their object or their effect the restriction of competition between professional football clubs, unless, in the second of those scenarios, it is demonstrated, through convincing arguments and evidence, that they are both justified by the pursuit of one or more objectives that are legitimate and strictly necessary for that purpose'.

The key passage where AG Szpunar details his views on the nature of the violation is included in paras 52–56:

> Article 17 of the RSTP provides that, as soon as a player has terminated a contract without just cause, compensation must be paid and severe sporting sanctions kick in. Moreover, under Article 8.2 of Annexe 3 to the RSTP, such a player will not receive the ITC enabling a club to field him or her.
>
> In other words, the consequences of a player terminating a contract without just cause are so draconian that it is highly unlikely that a player will go down this route. The contested provisions are designed in such a way as to have a deterrent effect and send a chill down each player's spine. The same applies with respect to clubs potentially interested in luring players into new opportunities while the latter are in a running contract. The 'price tag' for such an operation would be extremely high.
>
> Thus, by their very nature, the contested provisions limit the possibility for players to switch clubs and, conversely, for (new) clubs to hire players, in a situation where a player has terminated his or her contract without just cause. As expressly recognised by the Court, the recruitment of talented players constitutes 'one of the essential parameters of the competition in which football clubs may engage', making players the most important 'factor of production' for clubs.
>
> In so doing, the contested provisions, by limiting clubs' ability to recruit players, necessarily affect competition between clubs on the market for the acquisition of professional players.
>
> These elements are strong indications that there is a restriction of competition by object. Obviously, there are other situations in which players can change clubs and be recruited. This, however, does not mean, as the Commission implies in its observations, that there is no restriction of competition by object. In a situation where a contract is terminated without just cause, competition is, under the contested provisions, designed to come to a halt. I do not see how this cannot be equated with a restriction of competition by object.

Hence, AG Szpunar finds that the FIFA regulation affects both the opportunities offered to players and the competition between clubs. Even though this is not made explicit, the AG thus considers both the labor market (in which some trades are discouraged) as well the output market in which the clubs compete (the market in which the club produce a performance). The AG accepts the legitimacy of contractual stability (paras 64 et seq.). It is not the objective sought by Article 17 that he objects to. It is the manner in which compensation will be calculated that leads him to his conclusion (para. 67): 'The payment of compensation for termination of contract without just cause can be considered to be reasonably necessary for obtaining the objective of contractual stability. However, the calculation of that compensation must be such that the amount owed by the party to whom the lack of just cause is attributed does not exceed what can reasonably be considered necessary to compensate the other party for the damage suffered as a result of the breach of contract and to deter – in this case the player – from terminating the contract without just cause'.

Immediately thereafter, in para. 68 AG Szpunar further explains why the liability of the new club constitutes a restriction under EU competition law. In his view the FIFA regulation, will: 'go beyond what is necessary to pursue the legitimate objective, in a situation in which the new club has played no role in the termination of the contract. The presumption contained in Article 17.4 of the RSTP that the new club has induced the player to commit the breach appears draconian, since I do not see how the new club can prove its 'innocence'. While one may argue, as do FIFA and the Commission, that it is possible to derogate from the application of Article 17.2 of the RSTP, with the DRC having the power to restrict the application of the principle of joint and several liability, I am of the opinion that affording such discretion to the DRC does not provide the necessary legal certainty for players and clubs, as everything hinges on the viability and expeditiousness of a procedure which appears difficult to ascertain'.

This formulation is odd. The AG seems to deduce the existence of a restriction of competition from the observation that the measure goes beyond what is necessary to meet a legitimate objective. Nevertheless, from an analytical perspective, the issue of whether the challenged measure is likely to have anti-competitive effect and the extent to which it contributes (and is necessary) to meet the legitimate objective are orthogonal to one another. Indeed, the fact that the legitimate objective cannot serve as justification for a finding that the challenged measure constitutes a restriction by object confirms that the nature of the restriction needs to be assessed before the invocation of a legitimate objective can be considered.

AG Szpunar further did not review FIFA practice in detailed manner. His opinion sheds no light on the frequency of clubs succeeding to rebut the presumption embedded in Article 17.4. It is a conjecture. In para. 69, he adds: 'FIFA may, at the request of the new club and in exceptional circumstances, adopt provisional measures. Again, however, these elements appear to me to be too tenuous so as to come to the conclusion that they are necessary for the attainment of contractual stability'.

We now turn to the Judgment.

4 The Judgment of the Court of Justice

In what follows, we first describe the judgment (Sects. 4.1 and 4.2) before assessing it in Sect. 4.3.

4.1 *Article 45 TFEU*

The Court found that this provision had been violated because of:

- The combination of three distinct factors, namely: (i) the amount of monetary compensation involved in transfers; (ii) the fact that the players and acquiring club incurred joint and several liability for its payment; and (iii) the (rebuttable) presumption that the acquiring club was presumed to have incited the players to quite the old club;
- The fact that the ITC might not be delivered in case of litigation between the player and the old club.

A violation of Article 45 TFEU can be however be justified (Article 45.3). The Court advanced two lines of thought in this respect. First, it held that contrary to FIFA's suggestion, the protection of players does not come under its mandate. Still, it did not definitively rule on this score, because anyway the RSTP (the challenged measure) does not appropriately serve this objective (para. 99). The regularity of competitions on the other hand is part and parcel of the FIFA competence (para. 102). The composition of teams is integral part of the endeavor to pursue this objective. The Court left it to the referring court though (Mons, Belgium) to assess whether the means (Article 17 RSTP) are proportional to the targeted objective (regularity of competitions). But even though the Court recognized that it is for the Belgian court to pronounce on this question, it still went ahead and put forward a few observations on this matter:

- It criticized the absence of precise criteria to calculate the amount of compensation due (paras 105 et seq.)
- The law of the country involved, one of the criteria mentioned in the body of Article 17 RSTP, has never been applied in practice;
- Sport specificity, the other criterion mentioned, is way too imprecise to serve as benchmark for the calculation of compensation;
- The rebuttable presumption of inciting the player to leave has not been applied in systematic manner.

One can reasonably conclude that, even though it remains for the Belgian court to decide on the proportionality of means to ends, the Court gave a rather strong indication that, in its view, the implementation of FIFA regulation raised concerns in terms of proportionality.

4.2 *Article 101 TFEU*

The Court found that Article 17 RSTP constitutes a restriction by object (which entailed that it did not have to assess the effects of this provision in practice, para. 125). The Court reminded that a measure is considered a restriction by object if its sufficiently harmful to competition so that an assessment of its effects is not warranted. By the way of illustration, the Court indicated that horizontal agreements like price cartels, and/or agreements to exclude competitors should be considered restrictions by object (paras 127–128). How did all this apply to Article 17 RSTP then?

The Court first explained its methodology (para. 130). It stated that it would examine: (1) the content of the challenged measure (restriction); (2) the legal and economic context where it operated; and finally, (3) the objective pursued.

With respect to the first criterion, the Court underscored (paras 135 et seq.): (i) the high amount that needed to be paid in the form of compensation for a player to be allowed to leave his club, which acted as factor deterring a move; (ii) the discrepancy resulting from the fact that for an intra-federation transfer (like those from one Belgian club to another) to take place, only the amount corresponding to the remainder of the contract needed to be paid; (iii) that in case of litigation between the (departing) player and the club, the ITC would not be issued; (iv) that the new club was severally liable for the payment of the compensation alongside the player, and rebuttably at fault for having incited him to move; and (v) all of the above were considered factors as dissuading transfers;

As to the second criterion, the Court held (paras 143 et seq.): (i) that protecting the regularity of competitions was a plausible objective; (ii) that the stability of teams (contracts) was inherent element of the overall objective; (iii) but that the FIFA regime effectively amounted to non-poaching of players and thus could lead to market segmentation; and (iv) the Court thus insinuated that the FIFA transfer system was disproportional to the (legitimate) objective that it aimed to achieve;

As to the third criterion, the Court concluded that (paras 152 et seq.): (i) FIFA was targeting poaching of players under contract; (ii) wanted to preserve contractual stability (the intermediate objective) in order to serve stability in the composition of teams which is an element inherent in guaranteeing regularity of competitions; and (iii) in doing that, it made it practically impossible for players to leave their employer without just cause (better remuneration does not count as just cause).

4.3 *Discussion*

We first discuss the findings of the Court regarding free movement, before turning our attention to the findings regarding the consistency of Article 17 with the EU competition law.

4.3.1 Article 45 TFEU

There is an issue with respect to the applicability of Article 45 in this case as it involves a transfer between a club outside of the EU and a club within it, and Article 45 only applies to transfers within the EU. It appears that Diarra has had offers from other EU clubs but potential transfers to these clubs would only amount to an EU transfer if Diarra had been registered with Mons (or another EU club) after Moscow. The Court does observe that Diarra is resident in Paris. However, it is not clear that this matters to qualify the transfer as intra-EU. The Court is not explicit on these issues and it seems that the case can be made that the application of Article 45 may have been stretched.

Recall that the Court accepted that FIFA could invoke regularity of competitions in order to justify the measure, and left it to the Belgian court to decide on this course. It hinted rather forcefully though, that FIFA would have to address both the lack of precise criteria to quantify the amount of compensation, as well as the presence of the rebuttable presumption that acquiring clubs have incited the move. These are two areas where FIFA will be looking for an overhaul of the current Article 17 RSTP, if it wants to maintain its core elements.

Arguably, FIFA has some leeway. A test of proportionality involves two legs. The first leg (necessity) involves an assessment of whether there is a less restrictive means to achieve the legitimate objective and whether the rules go beyond what is necessary to achieve the objective. The second leg (that is left for the national court to consider) involves an assessment of the benefits from reaching the legitimate objective in relation to the magnitude of the restrictions of competition. Still, the formulation of ends prejudges the choice of means. Other things equal, a very demanding threshold (ends) will have a bearing on the alternatives that could possibly be used to achieve it. FIFA, one would imagine, could go down this road to limit the scope of judicial review.

In any event, even if FIFA could design a regulation such that it would not infringe Article 45 because it is justified by the pursuit of legitimate objectives, it would face a different hurdle under Article 101 TFEU.

4.3.2 Article 101 TFEU

In considering whether the FIFA regulation involves a restriction by object, in §147 the Court held:

As regards, in the third and last place, the objective aim which the rules at issue in the main proceedings seek to attain from a competition standpoint, it follows from the preceding considerations that, irrespective of the subjective intention or the legitimate objectives that may have inspired or have been pursued by the entity which adopted them, those rules must be considered to be intended to ensure that, apart from the case of players whose employment contracts were terminated for just cause or terminated by common agreement with their former club, it becomes extremely difficult, having regard to the legal, financial and sporting risks which that would entail, for professional football clubs to compete for access to the essential resources which players already under contract are, by unilaterally recruiting a player employed by another club or a player whose contract is alleged to have been terminated unilaterally without just cause, as such recruitment can take place only through a transfer negotiated between the former club and the new club.

The Court confirmed the substance of the assessment by the AG that the FIFA regulation affects competition between clubs to the extent that it limits the opportunities for attracting key assets. This formulation also confirms that the assessment of whether there is a restriction of competition is not affected by intentions or the legitimate objective that it may pursue ("indépendamment de l'intention subjective ou des objectifs légitimes" in the original text in French). This finding confirms that the issue of whether there is a restriction is orthogonal to the issue whether a legitimate objective can justify it. In this respect, the Court does not introduce the same confusion as the AG did.

Even if para. 147 is clear, it is a little disturbing that in the previous paragraphs (paras 144-145) the Court discusses the legitimate objective of ensuring contractual stability and the proper organization of competition in the context of what is supposed to be an analysis of anti-competitive effects. In the same spirit as AG Szpunar (but less obviously so), the Court considers whether the restrictions are proportionate to meet the legitimate objective as informing the existence of a restriction by object (see in particular para. 145 in which the Court suggests that labor laws would be sufficient to meet the legitimate objective).

It is perhaps inevitable that, in assessing facts (say whether an agreement is very likely to distort competition), a decision maker will find it useful to consider whether there is a credible alternative explanation for the practice in terms of pursing a legitimate objective. Indeed, in *Cartes Bancaires* (C-67/13P, paras 67 et seq.), the leading case when it comes to discerning what a "restriction by object" is, the Court followed a similar approach.

Further, para. 135 is hard to understand. There the Court observes the discrepancy between Article 17 RSTP and the Belgian law. Its point is that in intra-Belgian transfers the new club might be asked to pay at most the remaining value of the contract. It is hard to understand why this is mentioned in the first place? Article 17 RSTP does not apply to domestic transfers. In addition, member states of the EU have the competence to regulate sport (Article 165 TFEU). Well then, what if Belgium when doing so, had adopted a law stating that transfers of players under contract will be sanctioned only if the buying club was prepared to pay 3 times the value of the contract of the transferred player. It can do as much, as sport is a matter of national competence. Article 165 TFEU leaves no one in doubt in this respect, and Article 45 TFEU does not even enter into consideration, as a regime along these lines does not affect intra-EU movement of production factors.

In our view, the reason why the FIFA regime (Article 17 of the RSTP) amounts to a restriction by object is quite straight-forward. This provision exercises a deterrent effect against mobility which is both very likely and significant in magnitude (so it "reveals in itself a sufficient degree of harm to competition" according the test in "Cartes Bancaires").[28] The only potential attenuating circumstance is FIFA discretion to issue the ITC. But the conditions under which discretion will be exercised

[28] Judgment in *CB v Commission*, C-67/13 P, EU:C:2014:2204, and Opinion of AG Wahl, EU:C:2014:1958.

are simply not mentioned in the body of Article 17 of the RSTP. This is an important circumstance for the Court, in line with its judgment in *Superleague*.

At any rate, since the Court found that the FIFA transfer system amounts to a restriction by object, the only option for FIFA to justify their regulation is to look for an efficiency defense under Article 101.3 TFEU.[29] This involves a high standard. Standard case law suggests that four conditions must be cumulatively met for the party raising this defense to prevail: (i) the measure must contribute to improving production/distribution of goods; (iii) consumers must receive fair share of resulting benefits; (iii) the restrictions imposed must be essential in achieving these objectives; and (iv) the agreement must not eliminate competition in substantial elements of this production.

Even though it is still for the Belgian court to decide this issue, a very detailed analysis will be required.

5 What Lies Ahead?

The judgment has thus outlawed the main provision regulation the transfer of players without just cause. The FIFA has decided to initiate a dialogue will all stakeholders[30] to outline a possible reform and in the meantime FIFA has decided to suspend all disciplinary measures envisaged in Art 17.[31] In this section, we first discuss how transfers will be conducted while a new regulation is developed (Sect. 5.1). We then briefly discuss the level of damages that may be appropriate (Sect. 5.2) in a very simple framework.

---

[29] Note the tension between the *Wouters* (C-309/99, EU:C:2002:98) and the *Superleague* judgments. In the former case, the CJEU followed a different order of analysis than in the latter. In *Wouters* the Court asked at the outset whether the challenged measure was pursuing a legitimate objective, and whether the means employed were proportionate to the ends pursued. Having responded in the affirmative on both counts, the Court decided that the challenged measure was escaping the purview of Article 101.1 TFEU. The Court did not distinguish between restrictions by object and/or effect. Successful invocation of a legitimate objective led the Court to find that the challenged measure was not coming under the ambit of Article 101.1 TFEU. In the Super-League conversely, the Court followed a more "orthodox" approach. It first asked whether the challenged measure qualified a restriction of competition, and if so, whether the restriction could be characterized as "by object" or "by effect". It would examine possible justifications only after it had found that the challenged measure violated indeed Article 101.1 TFEU. If yes, a legitimate objective could be invoked only to justify a restriction by effect. Conversely, an efficiency defense (Article 101.3 TFEU) can always be raised against both types of restriction. Consequently, *Superleague* is definitely a reduction when compared to prior case law: a legitimate objective can from now on only justify a restriction by effect. It follows then, that we should expect from now on that the order of analysis adopted in *Superleague* will be followed in future practice. For the potential invocation of a legitimate objective is lawful only after a challenged measure has been characterized a restriction by effect.

[30] Information available on FIFA website.

[31] Private communication from the FIFA secretariat.

5.1 Transfers in the Absence of a New Regulation

Assume that a player wishes to leave without good cause, and that the two clubs (original, acquiring) cannot agree on a transfer fee. If FIFA implements the Diarra judgment in good faith, it will issue the ITC (International Transfer Certificate). The player, the old, and the new club will then have to submit their dispute regarding the level of transfer fee to a dispute resolution mechanism.

Litigation could take place in front of a civil court in Europe (and eventually in front of the Luxembourg Court) or the CAS (Court of Arbitration for Sport). The old club might prefer to litigate in front of the CAS, in particular if it anticipates that the CAS will follow the Matuzalem jurisprudence, which involved the payment of expectation damages at the time of the breach. As discussed above, this benchmark is more favorable to the old clubs than other benchmarks used by CAS, and it has not been explicitly ruled out by the CJEU.

The new club and the player may however decide not to comply with the ruling. The risk of doing so is limited as FIFA will not be imposing sanctions for non-compliance as the legal basis (Article 17 RSTP) has been rescinded.

There is also a risk that the CAS judgment may not be ultimately enforceable. CAS awards in principle can be enforced globally according to the New York Convention on the Recognition and Enforcement of Arbitral Awards.[32] However, their enforcement could be denied in Europe if awards conflict with European public order.

In its recent *ISU* judgment, the CJEU (paras 184–204) clarified that questions regarding the interpretation of EU law must be submitted exclusively to the CJEU, or to courts that have the right to submit a request for preliminary ruling to the CJEU. The CAS is not such court. In addition, FIFA is very unlikely to contribute to enforcement by threatening clubs and players unwilling to abide by CAS awards, with sporting or monetary sanctions as a result of its decision to stop enforcing these aspects of Article 17 of RSTP. In addition, in her opinion on the dispute between Seraing and FIFA,[33] AG Capeta found that CAS rulings should not be considered as Res Judicata. Hence, it is likely that litigation may end up in front of a civil court.

A European civil court might be more likely to interpret the Diarra judgment as imposing a lower threshold on the impediments to the transfer of players, and thus lower damages, balancing the interest of the player's freedom to move and need to compensate the old club in favor of the former. Indeed, even though the practice varies across member states, damages in case of termination of wage contracts amount to a modest multiple of weekly wages (rather than the wage until the end of the contract as in Webster). Hence, it is worth considering the possible consequences of lower damages on the remuneration of players and their mobility.

In the following section, we develop a simple model to analyze the consequences of a reduction in damages on player mobility and remuneration. In the context of

---

[32] Available on line.

[33] Opinion of Advocate General Ćapeta in *Royal Football Club Seraing*, C-600/23, EU:C:2025:24.

this model, the level of damage is an exogenous parameter. We model the pre-Diarra world as one in which either the Webster or the Matuzalem benchmarks for damages are enforced. We then analyze the consequences of lowering the damages, as civil courts would be expected to enforce lower damages.

5.2 *The Appropriate Level of Damages*

Consider the simplest possible model in which alternative benchmark for damages can be assessed. Assume that are there are two clubs interested in signing one player. There are two seasons (periods). The contribution of the player to both clubs for the first period, t_1, is observed at the beginning of the period. To simplify exposition, assume that in the first period the value of the player to club 2 is 0 and the value of the player to club 1 is equal to 1. The value of the player for the second period (t_2) in the first club is known in advance and is the same as in the first period.[34] However, the value of the player in club 2 in the second period is a random variable with two discrete values ($0 \ or \ v \geq 1$). Specifically, there is a probability p that the value of the player in the second period is equal to v and hence is higher than the value of the player in the initial team. There is a realization of this random variable at the beginning of the second period. The probability p and the value the player could have in the second club in the second period are common knowledge. This is the simplest framework in which there may be an incentive for the player to move at the end of the first period.[35]

Employment contracts involve a fixed wage for the two periods.[36] We assume that the player has full bargaining power,[37] or equivalently that he makes a "take it or leave it" offer to clubs such that he extracts the entire expected gross surplus that

[34] The assumption that the value of the player in the first club in the second period is known in advance is not central for the reasoning. While the value of the player to both club in the second player could be random, what matters to analyse transfers is that the value of the player in the second club in the second period is higher than the value in the first club, with some probability. This can be achieved by assuming that only the value to the second club is random.

[35] Note that in this framework, the Coase conjecture [see also S. Rottenberg, 'The Baseball Player's Labor Market' (1956) Journal of Political Economy, 64: 242–258] such that outcomes are efficient (so that in the event in which the value of the Player is higher in the second club he would always move) and the allocation of property rights only affects the distribution of rents, does not apply. This is the case because the expectation that damages will be awarded by CAS in case of termination restricts the set of outcomes that can be implemented. In other words, CAS effectively allows the old club to tax transfers.

[36] In addition, we assume that the contract in the first stage cannot made contingent on the value that the player could have in the second period in the second club (for instance because v is not verifiable for the first club).

[37] S. Szymanski, 'The End of the Transfer System (?)' (2024), European Competition and Regulatory Law Review (2024) Vol. 8, Iss. 3, pp. 156–170.

the club can obtain from the employment (the proposed wage over the horizon of the contract is thus equal to the gross expected surplus of the club).[38]

The contract can be terminated by the player[39] after the first period subject to the payment of damages (D).[40] In this set up, there are two possible instances in which the player may want to terminate a contract, namely, (i) when he has initially signed a contract with club 1 and its value in club 2 turns out to be equal to v in the second period, and (ii) when the player has signed a contract with club 2 and terminates the contract if the value in club 2 turns out to be equal to 0. We assume that probability that the player has a high value in the second period in the second club as well as the magnitude of this value (*p and v*) are such that club 2 will not be able to attract the player in the first period.[41] Denote w_1 as the wage per period that is negotiated between the player and club 1. This wage will be determined by what club 1 anticipates will happen in period 2 and in particular will depend on whether in the event in which the value if the second club is higher, the damages will be such that the player will find it attractive to move.

5.2.1 Damages and Endogenous Termination

We solve the model by backward induction and first consider what happens in the second period. If the value of the player in the second club is 0, the player will have no incentive to move. However, if his value is equal to v, the player could make a take it or leave it offer to the new club for a (single period) wage in the second period equal to v.

In order to move, the player should obtain a net remuneration with the new club (gross wage less damage compensation to the old club) in excess of the fixed wage that he can obtain under the contract with the old club (so that $v - D - w_1 \geq 0$).

In the second period, when the valuation is equal to v, there are two possible outcomes. The damages and the contractual wage are either such that the player has an incentive to move, or such that he is deterred from moving. If the damages (and

[38] This assumption is not essential to characterize the decision to transfer. The distribution of the surplus between the player and the club will however affects the characterization of the different benchmarks for damages.

[39] We assume that the clubs cannot terminate the contracts—or equivalently that the damages in case of termination by the club is prohibitive.

[40] Hence, we assume that if a compensation is due, the player is liable to pay it. The issues of who (the player or the new club) is liable for the compensation cannot be discussed independently of who has the bargaining power for the second period. Having assumed that the player has the whole bargaining power, making the player liable is an efficient arrangement.

[41] A sufficient condition for this is that $pv + (1 - p) < 2$. It can be shown that if the player signs with clubs 2, an upper bound to his payoff is the payoff that he obtains if he terminates the contract in case value is not realized in the second period. At the same time, the payoff that the player obtains when he does not terminate the contract is a lower bound to this payoff when he signs with club 1. The condition guarantees that the lower bound for the contract with club 1 is higher than the upper bound of the contract with club 2.

the contractual wage in club 1) are so high (in relation to v) so that the player does not find it attractive to move, the initial wage contract will be such that the player obtains the entire surplus accruing to the old club over two periods, so that $w_1^{NT} = 1$ (where the superscript *NT* refers to the case of No Transfer)

If damages are such that the player will find it attractive to move, the old club will anticipate that with a probability p the player will move, and consequently it will not pay a second period wage but will obtain damages. Denote $w_1^T(p,D)$ as the wage that the player can obtain in this case.

The surplus of club 1 in this case is written

$$S_1 = 1 - w_1^T + (1-p)(1-w_1^T) + pD$$

Such the club 1 obtains the value from the player and ays the wage in the first period as well as in the second period if the value of the player in the second club is low so that he does not move and obtains damages if the value is high that he moves. The wage is thus

$$w_1^T = \frac{2 + p(D-1)}{2-p}$$

Interestingly, in this regime (where termination takes place) the wage obtained from the old club (as part of the initial contract) increases with the level of damages. This arises because in the event of termination the old club obtains a higher payment, so its overall surplus increases and the player can extract this in the initial contract negotiation. The initial wage also increases with the probability that the value will be higher with the other club in the second period. As the surplus of club 1 increases with the damages, it also increases with the probability that the damage is obtained. As one would expect, when there is no damage ($D = 0$), the wage set in period 1 is the same whether or not the player moves in the second period ($w_1^T(D=0) = w_1^{NT}$) and it wage in case the player moves is higher for positive levels of damages (as the player extracts part of the damage in the ex ante negotiation).

To sum up, in the first period, the player will make a take of leave it offer either for a wage such that that he (and the club) anticipates that he will terminate the contract in the event in which he obtains a higher value in the other club ($w_1^T(D)$) or a wage such that he anticipates that he will not move (w_1^{NT}). When the potential value of the player v and the damages D are such that the player would terminate the contract in the event in which the player obtains this value and is offered a wage that extract the surplus from the club, club 1 and the player enter into a contract with the wage w_1^T. The player prefers this wage as it yields a higher payoff ; in the first period, $w_1^T(D) \geq w_1^{NT}$ so that the player is better off and in the second period, since the player finds it attractive to move, he obtain a payoff higher than $w_1^T(D)$. If the condition for the termination of the contract in the second period is not met (so that

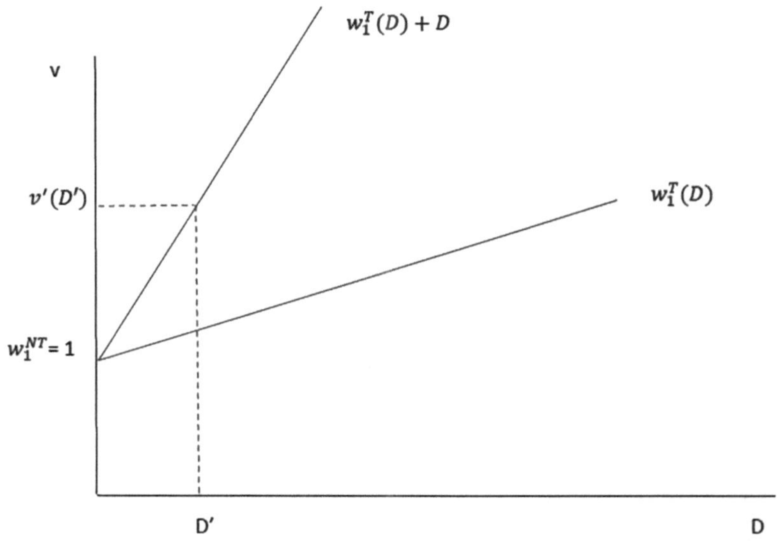

Fig. 1 Contract termination as a function of damages and player value

the player would not move given v, D and a wage that that extract the surplus from the club), the player and club enter into a contract with the wage w_1^{NT} (the club will only accept this contract)

The analysis can be represented graphically (see Fig. 1). The potential value of the player is on vertical axis and the damages on the horizontal axis. The wage when there is no termination is equal to 1. The wage in case of termination is equal to the wage in the absence of termination when damages are equal to zero and it increases with the level damages. For any level of damage, one can identify the range of potential values of the player for which termination takes places. These are the value which exceed the sum of w_1^T and D. One can also identify the lowest value for the potential value of the player for which termination would take place ($v'(D)$) for any D.

5.2.2 Damages and Endogenous Termination Under the CAS Damage Benchmarks

Alternatively, one can characterize, for any v, the range of damages for which termination takes places, and consider whether the damages routinely granted by CAS (in particular according to the Webster and Matuzalem benchmarks) would deter termination and discuss how the Diarra judgment will affect terminations.

Consider first the Webster and Matuzalem damages. The Webster damages are equal to the initial wage (at least in this framework). With $D = w_1$ the player will thus move if $v - 2\,w_1 \geq 0$. It is easy to check that in this case the initial wage only dependent on p ($w_1^T = \frac{2-p}{2(1-p)}$). This also implies that a necessary condition for termination to take place under the Webster standard is the value of the player in the new club is in excess of twice the value in the old club. As p approaches zero from above, the required ratio of the value in new club to the initial value in the old club approaches 2, so that for higher values of the probability the requires value of the player in the new club is in excess of two.

The Matuzalem damage is equal to v (at least in this framework). Since the player move if $v - D - w_1 \geq 0$, with $D = v$, the player will never move.

Hence, it appears that the CAS benchmarks deter either all or a range of terminations. Civil courts are however likely to apply lower damages in a post-Diarra world, influenced by the letter and the spirit of the Diarra judgment. As mentioned above, even though the practice varies across member states, damages in case of termination of wage contracts amount to a multiple of weekly wages (rather than the wage until the end of the contract as in Webster). Hence, it is likely that with lower damages likely to be applied by civil courts, player's mobility will be enhanced.

5.2.3 Player Remuneration

Let us now consider the remuneration of players and how it could be affected by a relaxation of the damage benchmark following the Diarra judgment. We characterize the pre-Diarra world as one in which the Matuzalem benchmark is enforced.

When damages are so high that termination is deterred, the player obtain a fixed wage contract $w_1^{NM} = 1$, i.e. a total remuneration equal to 2 (independently of v).

In the absence of damages, the fixed wage contract will involve a payment $w_1^M(p,D) = 1$. The remuneration of the player is equal to its value in the old club (1) because the old clubs does not get any income (nor expense) in the case of termination by the player. In this case, the player will move as long as $v > 1$, i.e. the player will move for all possible realizations of v.

The overall expected remuneration of the player is equal to $w_1^M(p,D) + (1-p)w_1^M(p,D) + pv - pD$. The first term relates to the remuneration in the first period, the second term relates to the remuneration in the second period if the higher value is not realized (no early termination) and the third term relates to the remuneration in case of termination and move to the second club and the last term is the damage.

In the absence of damages, the remuneration is equal to $(2 - p) + pv$. This remuneration exceeds the remuneration that the player obtains when he is deterred, whatever the value of v. The benefit from being allowed to terminate the contract also increases with the value in the new club. Players that achieve a higher value obtain a higher benefit.

Hence, in the context of this model, relative to a situation with full deterrence of termination (as in Mathuzalem), with no damage, all players will benefit.

So far, we have compared the remuneration of the player with full deterrence with its remuneration when there is no damage. One can also compare the remuneration with full deterrence with the remuneration with positive damage but damages falling short of the level inducing deterrence. There are two opposite effects: on the one hand, an increase in damages will increase the remuneration of the player in the first period as well as in the second period if the higher value (in the second club) is not realized; on the other hand the level of damages reduces the remuneration in the second period if the higher value in the second club is realized.

One can check that the player remuneration in excess of the remuneration obtained with full deterrence is independent of the level of damages and increases with the value of the player in the second club. The ex-ante remuneration is independent of the level of damages because the player can extract in the original contract a higher remuneration which exactly compensates for the damages that he expects to pay if the higher value is realized.

Hence, as damages increases from 0, there is a threshold in the value of the player in the new club below which players will be deterred from terminating the contract (see Fig. 1). Players that find it attractive to terminate the contract obtain a higher remuneration ex ante than the remuneration that they obtain under full deterrence.

In the context of this model, the only component of welfare ex ante is player remuneration (as the clubs make no rent). If the former FIFA system (at least with the Matuzalem standard) is associated with full deterrence, a relaxation will make players better off and increase welfare. In addition, if a positive level of damages is maintained (for reasons outside the model), it will change the distribution of welfare among players. The fate of players with less potential will not change while the situation of those with more potential will improve.

This very simple model should only be seen as providing an extreme benchmark as it does not provide a satisfactory treatment of potential sources of efficiencies stemming from the discouragement of player mobility. As mentioned above, the provision of incentives for the discovery and training of talent is one of the main justification for contract stability (and has been recognised by the Court as a legitimate objective). In the context of our model, damages are not required in order for players to be hired in the first place (and thus to allow for experimentation that might reveal its talent). The matter may be different for instance in the presence of fixed cost hiring of players or in the presence of external effects among players in the club in which they operate. In addition, our model focuses on the relation between players and abstract from the competition between clubs. As mentioned above, another possible justification for contract stability may arise from its contribution to competitive balance. These issues need to be further researched and one can only speculate about the consequence of a reduction in damages following Diarra judgment in particular for the training and discovery of players.

At the outset, it is not clear that that the transfer system leads to a significant redistribution between clubs of different sizes. Hoey et al.[42] compare the distribution of revenues across clubs; they find that large clubs have negative net transfer

[42] S. Hoey, T. Peeters, F. Principe, 'The transfer system in European football: A pro-competitive no-poaching agreement?' (2021) International Journal of Industrial Organization, 75, 1–18

earnings while small and in particular midsize clubs are net earners. However, their main finding is that transfers do not fundamentally change the distribution of revenues across clubs. In addition, they also find that while there is some evidence that clubs with younger squads are smaller, it is unclear whether clubs with younger squads get more transfer revenues.

This evidence should be interpreted carefully as it does not compare the distribution of club revenues with and without the transfers system. It only shows that net transfers in the current systems do not fundamentally change the distribution. Still, it suggests that the significance of the transfer systems should not be exaggerated, in particular as a source of revenues for clubs with younger squads. The significance of the role of the transfer system for the discovery of talent and training of young players should thus not be taken for granted.[43]

6 Conclusions

This paper has reviewed FIFA's transfer regulation and the Diarra judgment. The Court has, in our view, rightly concluded that the regulation involved a restriction by object under Article 101, given that the likelihood and significance of the distortions that it involves in particular in the (output) market in which the clubs compete. It is perhaps a concern however that the way in which the Court (and the AG) reached this conclusion may not have identified the nature of the restriction of competition independently from the question of whether the regulation may have pursued a legitimate objective. In principle, following the *Cartes Bancaires* judgment, whether an agreement involves a restriction of competition by object should be assessed independently of whether it may have pursued a legitimate objective. Conflating the two issues might lead to errors in the assessment, for instance a conclusion that an agreement does not involve a restriction by object because it is also pursuing a legitimate objective or a conclusion that it does because it does not have any redeeming feature in terms of the pursuit of a legitimate objective.

There may perhaps also be a concern in relation of the analysis of the legal and economic context, as the Court did not analyze the enforcement of the FIFA regulation. If it has done so, it would have found that FIFA routinely allowed the transfer of players by issuing international transfer certificates, thereby alleviating some of the restrictive effect of the regulation on transfers.

The paper has also provided a first analysis of the benchmark for damages adopted by the CAS, as such damages have not been outlawed by the judgment. We conclude that the two main benchmarks (Webster and Matuzalem) do not put the club in the situation in which it would have been in the absence of termination

[43] The training and solidarity payments also transfer revenues to smaller clubs and clubs that undertake training. The amount involved are however relatively modest. For example, solidarity payments between UEFA clubs only amounted to 177.2 million euros during 2022–2023. See information available on UEFA website.

without just cause. The Webster benchmark focuses on the cost incurred by the club rather than the benefit that could be anticipated. The Matuzalem benchmark does not capture the lost opportunity of undertaking a lawful transfer at the time of the early termination.

We develop a simple model of contracting between clubs and players in which improved opportunites over time might lead to the termination of a contract and a move by a player to assess the effect of the Diarra judgment. We show that a reduction of the damages from the current standards and in particular the Matuzalem standard, would trigger more frequent moves but also changes the distribution of welfare in favor of players with greater potential.

Even if the current regulation could in principle be amended, the Court has observed (para. 99, see above) that the protection of workers is not covered by FIFA statutes and that FIFA has not been granted any mission in this respect by public authorities.[44] One can thus wonder about alternative arrangements in the context of the usual institutions entrusted with a mission to regulate labor markets involving in particular trade unions. The emergence of collective bargaining agreement for players, that are quite common in the USA, unlike Europe is a distinct alternative. Interestingly, the CJE has excluded arrangements similar to collective bargaining from the scope of antitrust rules. In its well-known Albany exception, it took the view that agreements between trade unions and firms " seeking jointly to adopt measures to improve conditions of work and employment trade unions should not be subject to competition rules".[45]

In the Court's view, applying competition rules to collective agreements would undermine the social policy objectives inherent within such agreements. Hence, it would necessary for a potential CBA to pursue explicit objectives of social policy.

In addition, one can wonder whether the "Albany" exception will apply to restrictions by object (given that legitimate objectives do not). From an economic perspective, there is a distinction between the agreement in which the Albany exception has been applied and those in which the *Wouters* exception has been applied. The latter tend to refer to situations in which participation in the agreement has to be mandatory to ensure its existence. This is the case for instance of pension schemes that involve a redistribution across members. If participation is not mandatory, the scheme will unravel as those who anticipate having a net contribution will leave. The agreements considered under the *Wouters* exception do

[44] Para. 99 « en premier lieu, s'agissant de la protection des travailleurs, il convient de faire observer, d'une part, que celle-ci ne relève pas de l'objet de la FIFA, tel que défini par ses statuts, et, d'autre part, que cette association de droit privé ne s'est pas davantage vu confier de mission particulière en ce domaine par les pouvoirs publics ».

[45] Judgment of 21 September 1999, *Albany*, C-67/96, EU:C:1999:430, para. 59 reads: "It is beyond question that certain restrictions of competition are inherent in collective agreements between organisations representing employers and workers. However, the social policy objectives pursued by such agreements would be seriously undermined if management and labour were subject to Article 85(1) of the Treaty when seeking jointly to adopt measures to improve conditions of work and employment." The judgment does not quite say that trade unions are performing economic activities in this respect, but this is effectively what it implies.

not have that property. Hence, there is a differentiating factor and the argument could be made that the Court has only ruled out the possibility of invoking the “regulatory” ancillary restraints. Cases of objective necessity (or commercial ancillary restraints, as AG Rantos called them in *Superleague*, such that the product could not exist in the absence of the restriction) may possibly not have been ruled out in the same way.

A couple of additional issues merit attention. First, one can wonder whether the specific discipline on the quasi-regulator that the Court imposed on SGBs (in its ISU and ESLC judgments) would apply to the regulation of transfers and what this discipline might entail. What has triggered the imposition of this specific discipline inspired by Article 106 is arguably the existence of a conflict of interest such that UEFA would be included to restrict entry to protect its commercial interest. There no obvious direct conflict of interest for FIFA in the regulation of transfers but the poor governance of FIFA (and its ability to defend particular interest) may still be relevant in this respect.

Second, the judgment appears to be incomplete with respect to restrictions in the transfer market that only concern domestic transfers. The RSTP applies to international transfers only and by sanctioning its Article 17, the Court ruled that the FIFA system of international transfers is not in compliance with Articles 45 and 101 TFEU. The former has identical scope with that of RSTP: it applies to movement of workers from one member state to another The latter however, is relevant also for intra-state behaviour, provided that trade between the member states is affected and provided that the market constitutes a substantial part of the EU market.

Hence, it would seem provisions equivalent to Art 17 RSTP which may apply by virtue of domestic law might also infringe Article 101. It would have been useful for the Court to clarify this possibly in in the form of an obiter dictum.

7 Post Scriptum

In January 2025, following the Diarra ruling of the CJEU, FIFA amended Article 17 RSTP. Apparently, the FIFA amendment is an interim framework, meaning that eventually FIFA would enact a permanent regime. For now, the interim regime applies. The main innovation is that compensation for transfers should be calculated based on the “positive interest” principle. What does this principle entail? In simple terms, this principle is akin to lost revenue for clubs. In other words, an arbitral tribunal/court, in case of disagreement between the selling and the buying club, should ask what would the stream of revenue flowing to the selling club be if the player had been sold at arm’s length?

Additionally, the amendment removed the presumption that the acquiring club had induced the player to move. Interference (inducement) needs to be proved by the party making the claim to this effect. Joint liability as a result of this amendment, will be imposed only if say the old club has managed to provide the requisite evidence that the acquiring club has actively interfered and induced the player to breach his contract. The old club cannot object to the issuance of the ITC (International Transfer Certificate) either.

Are these changes enough to placate the CJEU? It is doubtful, to say the least. Recall that the ruling in Diarra was that the combination of high transfer fees, automatic presumption of inducement and sporting sanctions was major hindrance to the movement of players. While FIFA has addressed the second grounds, and possibly (but it remains to be seen in practice, the third as well), it has taken no step to address the first, and probably most important grounds for the CJEU finding in Diarra that Article 17 RSTP was contravening EU law.

Appendix

In this appendix, we derive a sufficient condition for the player to prefer to contract with club 1. As shown above, a lower bound to the surplus of the player if the contracts with clubs 1 is the payment that he receives if he does not terminate the contract after the period. The equilibrium wage in this case is $w_1^* = 1$ and the overall surplus of the player over two period is equal to 2. Hence we find a conditions which guarantees that the surplus of the player if he contracts with club 2 is less than 2.

We first consider the surplus of the player if he enters into a contract with club 2 and does not terminate the contract after the first period. The surplus of the club 2 assuming that the player does not terminate the contract at the end of the first period (if it turns out that its value is 0) is written

$$S_2 = pv - 2w_2$$

The only revenue from the club arises in the case in the player turns out to be valuable but he pays the fixed wage in both periods. The initial wage is $w_2^{NT} = \dfrac{pv}{2}$.

We then consider the surplus of the player if he finds it attractive to terminate the contract after one period. In this case the surplus of club 2 is written :

$$pv - w_2^T - pw_2^T + pv + (1-p)D$$

In this case the club pays the player in the first period, keeps the player (and pays his wage) with probability p if the value of the player is equal to v and obtains damages if the player leaves (with probability $(1 - p)$).

If the player leaves, he will obtain a wage equal to 1 for the second period in club 1; hene, we have that the player terminates the contract is $1 - D - w_2^T > 0$ and

$$w_2^T = \frac{pv + (1-p)D}{1+p}$$

where the wage is increasing with damages.

The remuneration of the player (per period) in this case is written

$$\frac{1}{2}\left(\frac{pv+(1-p)D}{1+p}(1+p)+(1-p)(1-D)\right)=\frac{pv}{2}+\frac{(1-p)}{2}$$

where the first term relates to the wage obtained in the first period as well as in the second period if the high value is realised, and the second term relates to the remuneration in the second period in case in which the high value is not realised. This remuneration need to be less than 1 in order to ensure that contracting with club 2 is not attractive (i.e. $(pv + (1 - p) < 2$, as reported in footnote 38).

What Is an Exploitative Abuse?

Jorge Padilla

1 Introduction

Article 102(a) of the Treaty on the Functioning of the European Union ("TFEU") states that a dominant undertaking abuses a dominant position if it directly or indirectly imposes unfair purchase or selling prices or other unfair trading conditions. Such practices are considered "exploitative" abuses, since they result in a direct loss of consumer welfare, in contrast to "exclusionary" abuses, which result in a loss of consumer welfare indirectly, as a result of foreclosure of competition.

Nils Wahl has provided important insights on the concept of exploitative abuse.[1] Wahl's opinions on excessive pricing during his tenure as Advocate General of the European Court of Justice ("CoJ") are generally cautious. He emphasizes the need for clear evidence when alleging excessive pricing, warning against over-intervention by competition authorities. In his view, excessive pricing cases amounting to price

Thanks to S. Vryna for constructive comments and suggestions. Jorge represents clients who have an interest in the issues discussed in this paper. Jorge was involved on behalf of Spotify in Case AT.40437—Apple. However, this paper has not been sponsored by any company.

[1] Judgment in *Autortiesību un komunicēšanās konsultāciju aģentūra/Latvijas Autoru apvienība*, C-177/16, EU:C:2017:689 (*AKKA/LAA*). This case involved allegations of excessive pricing by AKKA/LAA, a copyright management organization in Latvia. AG Wahl's Opinion (EU:C:2017:286) highlighted the complexities of defining excessive prices and suggested a cautious approach to intervening in cases of exploitative abuse. See also judgment in *Post Danmark*, C-23/14, EU:C:2015:651 (*Post Danmark II*). Although primarily focused on exclusionary abuse, Wahl's opinion emphasized the need for a rigorous analysis of the actual or potential effects of a dominant firm's behavior, signaling that blanket assumptions of harm in cases of high pricing could lead to regulatory overreach. As regards the Opinion in *AKKA/LAA*, see also Chapter 8 of this volume.

J. Padilla (✉)
Compass Lexecon, Madrid, Spain
e-mail: JPadilla@compasslexecon.com

L. Prete, L. Rezki (eds.), *Judging & (Re)Thinking European Union Law*,
https://doi.org/10.1007/978-3-032-13473-8_12

regulation may deter investment and innovation, especially given the difficulties in establishing when a price is "excessive" and the potential risks of distorting market dynamics.

Wahl's opinions focus on excessive prices, which is unsurprising given that most of the case law on Article 102(a) concerns excessive pricing cases. Yet, unfair terms and conditions within the meaning of Article 102(a) are not limited to excessive prices. A dominant undertaking may exploit trading parties through several other, non-price, unilateral practices, such as forcing them to acquire products or services for which they have no need or to pay for services they are not receiving.[2]

The case law on unfair trading terms other than excessive pricing cases is sparse. Prior to *Apple,*[3] the case law indicates that specific trading terms are regarded as abusive on the basis of a two-stage test based on "indispensability" and "equity" or, alternatively "necessity" and "proportionality".

This test has been recently revisited and clarified in *Apple*, where the Commission has stated that trading conditions are unfair and thus abusive, if they are: (i) imposed by a dominant undertaking on its trading partners, (ii) unfavourable or detrimental to the interests of that undertaking's trading partners or their consumers, and (iii) not necessary for the achievement of a legitimate objective or in any event not proportionate for that purpose.[4] *Apple* represents the first attempt by the Commission to consolidate the case law on non-price exploitative abuses into a clearly articulated legal test, and prompts *inter alia* an interesting debate on causation in non-price exploitative abuses.

Apple has argued that the Commission should be required to show a causal link between the existence of a dominant position and the ability to impose the terms in question.[5] It further argues that the Commission should be obliged to benchmark the conditions imposed by the dominant undertaking against the conduct of other players, who do not have a dominant position. The Commission disagrees.

In this essay, we seek to answer the following questions:

- First, is it necessary to posit and prove, to the requisite standard, a causal connection between dominance and the ability to impose the terms in question?
- Second, should the Commission be required to benchmark the conditions imposed by the dominant undertaking against the conduct of other players, who do not have a dominant position?
- Third, should the Commission be required to show that those terms are harmful by virtue of the undertaking's dominant position?

[2] Judgment in *BRT and Société belge des auteurs, compositeurs et éditeurs*, 127/73, EU:C:1974:25 (*SABAM*). See also judgments in *Lucazeau and Others*, 110/88, 241/88 and 242/88, EU:C:1989:326; *Tournier*, 395/87, EU:C:1989:319; *GVL v Commission*, 7/82, EU:C:1983:52; *Sacchi*, 155/73, EU:C:1974:40; *Basset*, 402/85, EU:C:1987:197; and *Duales System Deutschland v Commission*, T-151/01, EU:T:2007:154. See also Commission decisions in *GEMA* (OJ 1971 L 134, p. 15), and *GEMA II* (OJ 1972 L 166, p. 22).

[3] Case AT.40437 – Apple – App Store Practices (music streaming), available on line.

[4] Apple, para. 529.

[5] Apple, para. 532.

- And, fourth, should the Commission be required to show that those terms, if necessary for the achievement of a legitimate objective, are not proportionate as a result of the undertaking's dominant position?

The existing case law, while sparse, provides unambiguously affirmative answers to the third and fourth questions. The case law answers to the first two questions are less clear-cut. Nonetheless, the more recent rulings of the Union Courts confirm the view that a practice that would be unobjectionable in normal circumstances may, nonetheless, constitute an abuse if undertaken by a dominant firm, thus suggesting a negative answer for the first two questions.

Moving from case law to economics provides limited guidance: our review of the Ordo-liberal and Neo-classical economic literature also provides conflicting answers to the first two questions.

Fortunately, when we apply the well-known Error-Cost framework,[6] we obtained unambiguous answers. We show that, as a matter of economics, from an error-cost perspective:

(a) the Commission *should not* be required to show a causal link between the existence of a dominant position and the ability to impose the terms in question;
(b) the Commission *should not* be required to benchmark the conditions imposed by the dominant undertaking against the conduct of other players, who do not have a dominant position;
(c) the Commission *should* be required to show that those terms are harmful by virtue of the undertaking's dominant position; and
(d) the Commission *should* be required to show that those terms, if necessary for the achievement of a legitimate objective, are not proportionate as a result of the undertaking's dominant position.

Answers (a), (b) and (d) provide economic back-up for the case law as interpreted above. Answer (c) implies that, to establish causation in law, the Commission is not required to show a causal link between the existence of a dominant position and the ability to impose the terms in question. Rather, what it needs to show is that the conduct in question *when undertaken by a dominant firm* is capable of causing harm. That is, showing causation in law does not require showing a link between dominance and conduct. Causation in law is established when the causal link in fact (the relationship between conduct and effect) exists because of the dominant position.

[6] See R. A. Posner, 'An Economic Approach to Legal Procedure and Judicial Administration' (1973) Journal Legal Studies, 2, 399; F. H. Easterbrook, 'The Limits of Antitrust' (1984) Texas Law Review, 63(1), 1–40; C. F. Beckner III, S. C. Salop, 'Decision Theory and Antitrust Rules' (1999) Antitrust Law Journal, 67, 41; K. N. Hylton, M. Salinger, 'Tying Law and Policy: A Decision-Theoretic Approach' (2001) Antitrust Law Journal, 69, 469; S. C. Salop, 'An Enquiry Meet for the Case: Decision Theory, Presumptions, and Evidentiary Burdens in Formulating Antitrust Legal Standards' (2017) available on ssrn.com; and J. Padilla, 'Decision Theory and Legal Process in EU Competition Law', in Dekeyser, Gauer, Laitenberger, Wahl, Wils, Prete (eds), *Regulation 1/2003 and EU Antitrust Enforcement: A Systematic Guide*, 2023, Chapter 24.

2 An Overview of the Case Law before *Apple*[7]

This section reviews the few cases prior to *Apple* that address unfair contractual terms other than excessive pricing. As noted in the Introduction, the basic test emerging from these cases is that a trading practice is regarded as unfair and abusive if it is not necessary to achieve a legitimate objective and, even if necessary, if it is disproportionate, in the sense that the legitimate objective pursued by the dominant firm could be pursued through less harmful means.

2.1 *Tetra Pak II*

Tetra Pak II represents a comprehensive review by the Commission and EU Courts of a series of onerous contractual conditions governing the lease, purchase, and use of machines and consumables offered by a dominant carton manufacturer.[8] The Commission (confirmed by the EU Courts on appeal) objected to (a) an absolute right of control over the equipment configuration, which prohibited the buyer from adding accessories to Tetra Pak's machine, making modifications to the machine, and adding or removing anything to or from it, and from moving the machine; (b) clauses which gave Tetra Pak the exclusive right to maintain and repair equipment, the exclusive right to supply spare parts, and an obligation on the user to inform Tetra Pak of any improvements or modifications to the equipment and to grant Tetra Pak ownership of any resulting intellectual property rights; (c) clauses requiring the transfer of ownership or use of equipment, including the need for the customer to obtain Tetra Pak's agreement before selling or transferring the use of the equipment, reserving to Tetra Pak the right to repurchase the equipment at a pre-arranged fixed price, and the need to ensure that any subsequent vendor also assumed the same obligations; (d) long leases ranging from three years to nine years; and (e) clauses allowing Tetra Pak to impose a penalty over and above the usual damages and interest clauses on any leaseholder who infringed any of its obligations under the contract. The Commission's decision in *Tetra Pak II,* while not clearly articulating a legal test for what constitutes unfair trading terms, finds several of Tetra Pak's onerous terms to be unfair *inter alia* due to having "no connection with the purpose of the previously signed sales contract" and "in view of the effect […] on the very essence of the right of ownership".[9] The General Court's ruling in *Tetra Pak* already contains elements of the "necessity" and "proportionality" analysis articulated in *Apple.*[10]

---

[7] See R. O'Donoghue, J. Padilla, *The Law and Economics of Article 102 TFEU*, 3rd ed., Hart Publishing, 2020), chapters 14 and 16 for a more detailed review of the relevant case law until 2020.

[8] Tetra Pak II, OJ 1992 L 72/1, on appeal judgment in *Tetra Pak v Commission*, T-83/91, EU:T:1994:246, confirmed by judgment in *Tetra Pak v Commission*, C-333/94 P, EU:C:1996:436.

[9] Tetra Pak II, OJ 1992 L 72/1, para. 123.

[10] 'In those circumstances, it is clear that the tied-sale clauses and the other clauses referred to in the Decision *went beyond their ostensible purpose* and were intended to strengthen Tetra Pak's dominant position by reinforcing its customers' economic dependence on it. Those clauses were

2.2 *AAMS*

Another important reference is *AAMS*.[11] AAMS, a body forming part of the financial administration of the Italian State, engaged in the production, import, export and wholesale distribution of manufactured tobacco products. The Commission found the following clauses in AAMS's distribution contracts to be unfair and abusive: (a) a time limit for the introduction of new cigarette brands onto the Italian market (i.e., a bi-annual limitation); (b) a limit on the number of new brands allowed on the Italian market; (c) maximum monthly limits of cigarettes allowed on the Italian market; (d) very restrictive terms for the increase in monthly limits; (e) an unnecessary obligation to affix the Italian State monopoly abbreviation on each package; and (f6) quality controls that were wholly unnecessary.

The usefulness of these two precedents is, however, somewhat limited by the fact that the vast majority of the terms used by Tetra Pak and AAMS were onerous in the extreme, and most of the clauses in question were not only exploitative but also exclusionary.

2.3 *SABAM*

While the CoJ's preliminary ruling in SABAM does not directly address the causality question, it reveals that, already in 1974, the CoJ had articulated the fundamental elements of exploitative abuse contained in Apple.

The ruling related to terms imposed by a collecting society on its artist members. The CoJ confirmed that it may be abusive for an undertaking which enjoys a *de facto* monopoly for the management of copyrights to (a) demand the global assignment of all copyrights without drawing any distinction between specific categories of such rights or (b) demand assignment of an artist's present and future rights and continue to exercise these rights for five years following the withdrawal of that artist from the collecting society.

In doing so, the CoJ articulates that exploitative abuses entail, at their core, a balancing exercise between interests. More specifically, to the extent that the dominant company is seeking to protect a legitimate objective[12] the authority must apply a proportionality test—i.e., does the impugned conduct "exceed the limit absolutely

therefore *wholly unreasonable in the context of protecting public health*, and also *went beyond the recognized right of an undertaking in a dominant position to protect its commercial interests*. [...] Whether considered in isolation or together, they were unfair.' Case T-83/91, Tetra Pak v Commission [1994] ECR II-755, para. 140 (emphasis added).

[11] Amministrazione Autonoma dei Monopoli di Stato, OJ 1998 L 252/47, upheld on appeal in judgment in *AAMS v Commission*, T-139/98, EU:T:2001:272.

[12] In *SABAM* the CoJ recognises the legitimate objective of protecting the rights of individual creators against major exploiters and distributors of musical material.

necessary for the attainment of this object", to understand whether the conduct may be "inequitable", such that it unfairly encroaches upon the commercial freedom of the dominant company's trading partner.[13]

By analogy, this analytical framework is well-established in fundamental rights jurisprudence in both EU law and the European Convention of Human Rights, *where, the principle of proportionality* is the methodological tool used *to resolve conflicts between fundamental rights and* other *competing rights or interests*.[14]

2.4 GEMA Statutes

GEMA Statutes[15] is also instructive as, despite the Commission finding the disputed trading terms to be compatible with competition law, it made a number of observations that assist in understanding the underlying principles applying to non-price exploitative abuses.

GEMA, a German copyright collection society had added a clause to its statutes providing that the assignment of rights to GEMA precluded the beneficiary from making grants either directly or indirectly of a share of their revenue to parties who had entered into collective agreements with GEMA, or with other collecting societies, where said parties, when using the GEMA repertoire, would "favour unjustifiably" certain works of the beneficiary. The reason for this clause was to prevent discrimination if the user directly or indirectly (i.e., via an intermediary (e.g. a subsidiary)) shared in the GEMA member's royalties for the work used.

The Commission applied the same balancing approach as in *SABAM,* noting that the decisive test is whether GEMA's impugned terms exceeded the limits absolutely necessary (indispensability) for effective protection and whether they limited the trading partner's freedom no more than need be (equity) i.e., a clause would be abusive if it was not indispensable or it was indispensable but excessive (inequitable).[16]

In this case, the Commission found GEMA's terms to fulfil both conditions as (a) it was indispensable that GEMA should have joint, uniform control of the rights assigned to it and that non-discrimination was essential, since GEMA's membership also included users of music in the guise of publishers, whose interests often do not coincide with those of authors and (b) GEMA acted proportionately, since it restricted itself to prohibiting the beneficiaries from granting shares of royalty revenues to users only where the purpose was to favour certain works of the

[13] See judgment in SABAM, *supra*, paras 8, 11 and 15 ("encroach unfairly upon a member's freedom to exercise his copyright").

[14] Article 52(1) of the EU Charter of Fundamental Rights. See *inter alia* K. Lenaerts, P. Van Nuffel, *EU Constitutional Law,* Oxford University Press, 2021, pp. 683–684.

[15] Case IV/29.971- GEMA statutes, OJ 1982 L 94/12 (GEMA Statutes).

[16] GEMA Statutes, paras. 36 and 44–45.

beneficiaries (i.e., activation of the impugned clause required evidence of unjustified discrimination and was not applicable in all cases).[17]

2.5 *DSD*

The legal test was further clarified in *DSD*,[18] where the Commission found that DSD had abused its dominant position in the market for the organisation, collection, and recycling of sales packaging in Germany, because it charged licence fees in circumstances where its service was not actually used. More precisely, the fees did not vary with the amount of packaging that was actually processed through DSD's system, the consequence being that the users could not arrange to have part of their packaging collected under a different system without having to make a double payment for the same quantity of packaging. This pricing scheme was thus regarded as both exploitative and exclusionary.

The Commission adopted a two-stage test. It first considered whether the clause was central to the object of the contract. Then, it considered whether it was proportionate, in the sense that the harm arising from the conduct goes beyond what is needed to pursue the legitimate objective pursued by the dominant firm.[19]

The General Court confirmed the Commission's decision, stating that "an undertaking abuses its dominant position where it charges for its services fees which are disproportionate to the economic value of the service provided."[20]

2.6 *More Recent Cases*

In *Sequential Use of Coupons*,[21] the Commission considered whether a standard airline ticket contract term that required the sequential use of coupons in flight travel constituted an unfair contract term contrary to Article 102(a). The Commission concluded that it did not, because the clause at issue was necessary to allow airlines to efficiently price discriminate between users who wanted a cheaper, indirect flight, and those who were willing to pay more for a direct flight which, in turn, increased competition among airlines and benefited consumers.

[17] GEMA Statutes, para. 52.

[18] DSD, OJ 2001 L 166/1, confirmed on appeal in the judgment in Case T-151/01, *Der Grüne Punkt- Duales System Deutschland* (see *supra*); and then in the judgment in *Der Grüne Punkt - Duales System Deutschland v Commission*, C-385/07 P, EU:C:2009:456.

[19] Case COMP D3/34493, DSD, OJ 2001 L 166, p. 1, para. 112.

[20] Judgment in Case T-151/01, *Der Grüne Punkt- Duales System Deutschland GmbH* (*supra*), para. 121.

[21] Case COMP/A.38763/D2, Sequential Use Of Coupons, communication pursuant to Article 7(1) of Commission Regulation (EC) 773/2004, 14 July 2005 (on file with authors).

In *Kanal 5*,[22] the Swedish courts asked whether linking the payment for the right to make available music in television broadcasts to a proportion of the channel's revenue from those programs in which copyright material could be unfair. The CoJ indicated that the method of calculation was not abusive within the meaning of Article 102(a),[23] since the payment was proportionate overall to the quantity of musical works protected by copyright actually broadcast or likely to be broadcast and there was no other commercially viable method allowing the use of those works and the audience to be identified more precisely.

3 The Legal Test in *Apple*

In its recent decision in *Apple*, the Commission concluded that certain terms and conditions governing the use of Apple's App Store by developers of music streaming software applications (apps) on Apple's smart mobile devices running on the iOS operating system were exploitative. Those terms and conditions, known as the Anti-Steering Provisions, prohibited music streaming service providers from informing consumers on iOS about alternative (and often cheaper) subscription possibilities existing outside of music streaming apps on iOS (*e.g.*, on the developer's own website), and from allowing iOS users to exercise an effective choice between alternative subscription possibilities.

3.1 The Commission's Interpretation of the Case Law

The Commission applied the following legal test, based on its reading of the relevant case law. Paragraph 529 of the Commission's decision in *Apple* states:

> It can be inferred from the case law that, in essence, to be qualified as unfair under Article 102(a) of the Treaty and thus abusive, trading conditions must be: (i) imposed by a dominant undertaking on its trading partners, (ii) unfavourable or detrimental to the interests of that undertaking's trading partners or of third parties, including consumers, that are affected by the trading conditions imposed by the dominant undertaking, and (iii) not necessary for the achievement of a legitimate objective or in any event not proportionate for that purpose, in that they go beyond what is strictly necessary to achieve it.

Paragraph 530 then states that to find the imposition of unfair trading conditions abusive, the Commission is not required to "consider whether the object or effect of the dominant undertaking's activities was to restrict competition between undertakings within the internal market".

---

[22] Judgment in *Kanal 5 and TV 4*, C-52/07, EU:C:2008:703 ('*Kanal 5*').

[23] *Kanal 5*, ibid., para. 41.

3.2 Apple's Arguments

Apple argued that the Commission's legal test is incorrect. *Inter alia* according to Apple's interpretation of the case law, the Commission should "show a causal link between the existence of a dominant position and the ability to impose the terms in question" (para. 532).

Apple sustained that "the requirement of such a causal link is needed to distinguish exploitative and exclusionary abuses as well as to preserve the effectiveness of the requirements set by the Court of Justice for showing that the terms and conditions at issue are at least capable of foreclosing equally efficient competitors" (para. 533).

Apple further argued that the Commission is "obliged to benchmark the conditions imposed by the dominant undertaking against the conduct of other players, who do not have a dominant position, in order to be able to find an exploitative abuse". According to Apple, certain trading conditions can only be regarded as abusive if they are "manifestly more disadvantageous to business partners than they would be in a competitive market" (para. 535).

3.3 The Commission's Response

The Commission rejects Apple's arguments on *causality* by stating that the case law establishes that the Commission does not need to prove a specific causal link between the dominance and the content of those unfair trading conditions to find the direct or indirect imposition of unfair trading conditions abusive (para. 537).

The Commission maintains that "the position of economic strength which follows from a dominant position … enables that undertaking to impose trading conditions on its trading partners". And it is precisely the power conferred by the dominant position that "constitutes the specific link between the dominant position and the conduct in question, irrespectively of whether other non-dominant undertakings may use similar trading conditions" (para 538).

The Commission disagrees with Apple that the causal link between the dominant position of the undertaking concerned and the conduct in question is required to distinguish exploitative from exclusionary abuses (para 546). According to the Commission,

Firstly, "exclusionary abuses do not take precedence over exploitative abuses" (para. 547).

Secondly, showing that the imposition of unfair trading conditions is exploitative "does not require the demonstration that the conduct of the dominant company is liable to foreclose competitors" (para. 547).

Thirdly, the Commission is not required to show that "the conditions imposed on the trading partners be necessarily unfair vis-à-vis those trading partners, as they could be unfair also vis-à vis third parties, including consumers, that are affected by the conditions in question" (para. 549).

Fourthly, "once the Commission has shown that a given conduct gives rise to an exploitative abuse … it is not required to also assess whether the conditions for finding an exclusionary abuse are met" (para. 550).

The Commission also rejects the obligation to benchmark the conduct of the dominant undertaking arguing that (a) the benchmarking approach is specific to excessive pricing cases and, in any event, (b) the Commission has no obligation to undertake a benchmarking exercise even in excessive pricing cases (para. 544).

As regards Apple's claims on the need for a *counterfactual* analysis, the Commission states Even if similar unfair conditions can be requested by non-dominant companies, they can still lead to an abuse if they are imposed by a dominant undertaking which has a special position of economic strength giving it the power to behave independently of its customers (for instance because it is an unavoidable trading partner), and therefore—according to the established case law—has a special responsibility under Article 102 of the Treaty (para. 545).

Finally, concerning Apple's claims on *materiality*, the Commission maintains that certain trading conditions imposed by a dominant undertaking can be qualified as unfair if they are "appreciably and not insignificantly detrimental" to the interests of the trading partners or third parties, including consumers, without having to show that they have "an unacceptable impact" (para. 553).

4 Causation in Article 102

To assess the controversy between Apple and the Commission as regards causality, we first need to distinguish between two different notions of causality: *causation in fact* and *causation in law*.

There does not seem to be much dispute about the Commission's need to posit and prove, to the requisite standard, a causal relationship between the impugned conduct and its (at least potential but not hypothetical) effect. Indeed, in *Apple*, para. 529, the Commission acknowledges such a requirement when it states that to be deemed abusive, the trading conditions must cause harm to the dominant undertaking's trading partners or consumers.

The disagreement between Apple and the Commission concerns the requirement to posit and prove, to the requisite standard, a causal connection between dominance and the ability to adopt the conduct in question. Apple maintains that the Commission must establish a relationship between Apple's dominance and its use of the Anti-Steering Provisions or, otherwise, the impugned conduct cannot be regarded as an abuse of a dominant position.

Apple's position appears to be that there is no *causality in law* and, therefore, no special responsibility unless the impugned conduct is the result of the dominant position. Or, alternatively, that to establish causality in law the Commission needs to show *causation in fact* between dominance and conduct and also *causation in fact* between conduct and effects.

The Commission disagrees. Indeed, the Commission adopts a different view of causation—the Commission supports that it is by virtue of its dominant position, which makes it an unavoidable trading partner, that Apple can "impose" conditions on its trading partners, including unfair conditions, and that this is a sufficient link between dominance and abuse.[24] In other words, the Commission appears to be that it is enough to show the causal link between conduct and effect exists because of the dominant position to justify the special responsibility of the dominant firm.

4.1 The Case Law

Our reading of the early case law identifies statements that could support one or the other position.[25] On the one hand, in *Hoffman La Roche* the CoJ said: "The interpretation suggested by the applicant that an abuse implies that the use of the economic power bestowed by the dominant position is the means whereby the abuse has been brought cannot be accepted."[26]

Likewise, in *Continental Can*,[27] the CoJ stated that it was possible to abuse a dominant position without actually exercising or relying on market power. It is an abuse for a dominant undertaking to strengthen its position by taking over a rival. Lastly, in *Astra Zeneca,* the General Court ("GC") said: "an abuse of dominant position does not necessarily have to consist in the use of economic power conferred by a dominant position".[28]

On the other hand, in *United Brands,* the CoJ refers to the dominant undertaking taking advantage of its market power to extract rents from its customers.[29] In *Tetra Pak II*, the CoJ held that Article 102 TFEU "presupposes a link between the dominant position and the alleged abusive conduct," although this is not necessarily an observation related to causation, as the question the Court was seeking to answer was whether an abuse could be carried out in a non-dominant market that was very closely related to the dominant market.[30]

---

[24] Apple, paras. 538 and 545.

[25] R. Whish, D. Bailey, *Competition Law,* 11th ed., Oxford University Press, 2024, p. 220. See also O'Donoghue, Padilla, supra, pp. 316–320.

[26] Judgment in *Hoffmann-La Roche v Commission*, 85/76, EU:C:1979:36, para. 91, cited in judgment in *AstraZeneca v Commission*, T-321/05, EU:T:2010:266, para. 267.

[27] Judgment in *Europemballage and Continental Can v Commission*, 6/72, p. 225.

[28] Judgment in *AstraZeneca*, *supra*, para. 354.

[29] Judgment in *United Brands and United Brands Continentaal v Commission*, 27/76, EU:C:1978:22, para. 249 (The dominant firm uses its position to "reap trading benefits that it would not have reaped if there had been normal and sufficient effective competition.").

[30] Judgment in Case C-333/94 P, *Tetra Pak International SA v Commission*, *supra*, para. 27. R. Whish, D. Bailey, op. cit., *supra*, p. 220.

4.1.1 The Notion of Imitation in Recent Exclusionary Cases

Much more recently, in *Servizio Elettrico Nazionale*, the CoJ stated that "a practice that a hypothetical competitor – which, although it is as efficient, does not occupy a dominant position on the market in question – is unable to adopt, because that practice relies on the use of resources or means inherent to the holding of such a position"[31] cannot constitute *competition on the merits* or *normal competition* and, therefore, it is potentially abusive.

The Court added "The relevance of the material or rational impossibility for a hypothetical competitor, which is as efficient but not in a dominant position, to imitate the practice in question, in order to determine whether that practice is based on means that come within the scope of competition on the merits, is clear from the case law on practices both related and unrelated to prices".[32]

The implication of these statements seems to be that a practice that can be "imitated" by a non-dominant hypothetical competitor, which is as efficient, falls outside of the *special responsibility* of a dominant firm under Article 102 TFEU and, therefore, cannot be regarded as abusive. However, it is not clear that these statements can be interpreted as establishing a principle that *any* practice which a non-dominant but as-efficient hypothetical competitor *can* implement falls outside the *special responsibility* of a dominant company and is, therefore, unobjectionable if applied by a dominant company.

Indeed, *inter alia* in *Google Shopping* the EU General Court confirmed that "within the scope of Article 102 TFEU, a dominant undertaking is subject to certain restrictions that do not apply to other undertakings, and a practice which would be unobjectionable in normal circumstances may constitute abuse if engaged in by a dominant undertaking".[33]

Reconciling these seemingly inconsistent statements requires clarifying what is understood by "imitation" in the context of the above-mentioned exclusionary cases. To illustrate our thinking, consider the following example.

Suppose a dominant company ties a ubiquitous tying product *A* with a tied product *B*, and its non-dominant rival for the tied product *B* can offer this product together with product *C*, which is a substitute, albeit a much inferior one, to product *A*. In a formalistic sense, the non-dominant firm is able to imitate the dominant firm's tying strategy. Yet, if product *C* is a very poor substitute for product *A*, the non-dominant firm's bundle *(C,B)* is no match for (and thus no replica of) the dominant firm's bundle *(A,B)*. Because the non-dominant firm cannot replicate the commercial appeal of the dominant firm's bundle, its imitation strategy is ineffective.

---

[31] Judgment in *Servizio Elettrico Nazionale and Others*, C-377/20, EU:C:2022:379, para. 78.

[32] Id., para. 79.

[33] Judgment in *Google and Alphabet v Commission (Google Shopping)*, T-612/17, EU:T:2021:763, para. 613, citing the Opinion of Advocate General Kokott in *Post Danmark*, C-23/14, EU:C:2015:343, and judgment of 16 March 2000, *Compagnie maritime belge* v Commission, C-395/96 P and C-396/96 P, EU:C:2000:132, para. 131.

It follows from the example that we should not interpret the notion of "imitation" formalistically when interpreting the case law. For the purpose of assessing competition on the merits, a non-dominant firm is said to be able to imitate the dominant firm's strategy (or conduct) *only if* its response is capable of preserving its status as an effective competitor.

4.1.2 A.2. Benchmarking in Exploitative Cases

The Court's case law on exploitative abuses does not require, as a condition for finding an abuse, the dominant company's behaviour to be benchmarked against the behaviour of non-dominant companies in the same or other markets or by the same dominant undertaking at different points in time or in other geographic markets by the same dominant undertaking. Indeed, in *United Brands*, the CoJ states that "[t]he questions therefore to be determined are whether the difference between the costs actually incurred and the price actually charged is excessive, and, if the answer to this question is in the affirmative, whether a price has been imposed which is either unfair in itself <u>or</u> when compared to competing products. *Other ways may be devised* — and economic theorists have not failed to think up several — of selecting the rules for determining whether the price of a product is unfair." The Court thus indicates that comparisons are one of many ways that an authority can deploy to assess whether a price is excessive.[34] This logic is followed in *Kanal 5*, where the CoJ does not require benchmarking of the dominant company's conduct.[35]

Indeed, in his Opinion in *AKKA/LAA*, Nils Wahl noted in relation to the method for determining that a price is excessive "It can be safely stated that, at the current stage of legal and economic thinking, there is no single method, test or set of criteria which is generally accepted in economic writings or across jurisdictions for that purpose. Different authorities as well as lawyers and economists have suggested a number of methods of analysis (as well as a variety of criteria, tests or 'screens') to that end. [...] In the first place, none of those methods can be used in all circumstances, since their suitability (and, at times, the very possibility of applying them) depends very much on the specific features of each case."[36]

Indeed, in non-price exploitative abuses, the suitability of benchmarking the dominant company's terms against terms applied by companies in competitive markets comes further into question. Even in the pricing context comparators present risks as "[m]arkets are rarely so homogenous that a meaningful comparison can be made immediately and automatically."[37] These risks present themselves even more so when seeking appropriate comparators to use in relation to non-price unfair terms. Contrary to prices, contractual terms cannot be easily and reliably compared.

[34] Judgment in *United Brands*, paras. 49-50. Emphasis added.

[35] Judgment in *Kanal 5*, para. 29.

[36] *AKKA/LAA*, Opinion, paras. 36–37.

[37] *AKKA/LAA*, Opinion, paras. 39.

Even terms that may superficially appear similar to the dominant company's terms (e.g., in the *Apple* example terms described as 'anti-steering' or 'anti-circumvention' clauses) can prove fundamentally different in practice, thus being unsuitable comparators that increase the risk of false negatives. They can differ in core aspects such as their intensity, frequency and consistency of enforcement (for instance, it is our understanding that for years, Google had included anti-steering provisions in app developers' distribution contracts with the Play Store, which were not in practice enforced or at least not consistently enforced).

4.2 The Ordo-liberal School

The conflicting state of the existing case law compels us to consider other sources of authority. Our first stop is the ordo-liberal school of thought, since "fairness" as a competition law goal was imported into EU competition law from ordo-liberalism.

Ordo-liberalism was developed in Germany in the 1930s and 1940s, as a compromise between the centrally planned economy and the unregulated market. Ordo-liberals were convinced of the virtues of a competitive economy, but competition is only beneficial in markets where no firm has the power to coerce the conduct of other firms or their customers. That is, when "[t]he price is not forced upon the market by way of a market strategy but is taken from the market".[38]

Like today's Brandeisians, the ordo-liberals saw competition as having not only an economic but also an important political dimension: "Competition is by no means only an incentive mechanism but, first of all an instrument for the deprivation of power … The most magnificent and most ingenious instrument of deprivation of power in history."[39]

In an ordo-liberal system, competition policy would break up "avoidable monopolies" and regulate "unavoidable monopolies". The basic principle for that regulation was the principle of "behaviour analogous to competition", reflected in the "as if" approach: "The aim of monopoly legislation and monopoly supervision is to ensure that the bearers of economic power behave as if complete competition prevailed. The behaviour of the monopolists should be 'analogous to competition'."[40]

For the ordoliberals, therefore, firms with market power or enjoying a dominant position should be required to act "as if" they operated in competitive markets—i.e. "as if" they had no market power and therefore could not impose on their trading partners detrimental conditions. But if their special responsibility is therefore limited to act as if they had no market power, then they cannot be required to go beyond

[38] W. Eucken, 'The Competitive Order and its Implementation', 1949, reprinted in 2(2) Competition Policy International 222, 2006, p. 230.

[39] Id., p. 244.

[40] Id., p. 241.

what a firm without market power would do in order to maximize, or alternatively to increase, consumer welfare.

4.3 Neoclassical Economics

Our second stop in the search for clarity is "neoclassical economics".[41] Neoclassical economists maintain that (a) the ultimate goal of competition law is the maximization of consumer welfare, and (b) market power is not a problem *per se*.

Because of (b), dominant companies do not need to behave "as if" they lacked market power to comply with the competition laws. But that also means that they cannot defend their conduct by mere reference to competitive benchmarks. It needs to be aligned with (long-run) consumer welfare or, otherwise, it is infringing the law.

To explain this logic, let us consider the competitive character of a given conduct *C* undertaken by a dominant firm. This conduct affects consumers' welfare in two different ways. First, it restricts consumer choice and thus exposes consumers to e.g. higher prices or lower quality services. Second, it allows the dominant firm to offer a better service to its customers. Thus, in principle, the net effect of conduct *C* on consumer welfare could be either positive or negative.

Suppose conduct *C* is also implemented in other markets by firms *without* market power. The inference that results from this observation is that the net effect of conduct *C* on consumer welfare is positive in these competitive markets. Otherwise, some firms would have abandoned conduct *C* to steal the business of their rivals. In other words, competition would have compelled firms to get rid of conduct *C*.

However, this "factual inference" cannot be extrapolated automatically to the market where the dominant firm operates. This is because, while the positive effect of the conduct may be similar across markets with different degrees of concentration, that is unlikely to be true for the negative effects of the conduct. And, while conducts with a net negative effect are competed away in competitive markets, that is not the case in markets where a firm can act independently of its competitors, customers and consumers. This is all the more so the case in markets where there is a super-dominant player or a player who is a monopolist and by definition an unavoidable trading partner.

Thus, to determine whether conduct *C* is exploitative, benchmarking that conduct against the behaviour observed in competitive markets is of limited use. The fact that conduct *C* is also observed in competitive markets does not imply that the net effect of such a conduct when applied by a dominant company (not to mention a monopolist) in a market is positive.

Because such a factual inference is unjustified, the benchmarking exercise cannot justify a presumption of legality, even if that were rebuttable. That is, it is not enough for a dominant company to behave "as if" it had no market power, the

[41] J. Padilla, "Neoclassical Competition Policy Without Apology", 2022, available on ssrn.com.

special responsibility of dominant firms from a neoclassical perspective can only be discharged when its conduct is aligned with (long-run) consumer welfare.

4.4 Summary

Is it necessary to posit and prove, to the requisite standard, a causal connection between dominance and the conduct in question? As we have explained above, the case law is confusing, though on balance it seems to suggest that a practice which would be unobjectionable in normal circumstances may constitute abuse if engaged in by a dominant undertaking. Unfortunately, our review of the economic literature has not allowed us to go beyond these statements. This is why we provide further analysis in what follows. Our findings below are consistent with the interpretation of the case law above.

5 Applying the Error Cost Framework

Ultimately, the discussion about the requirement to posit and prove a causal relationship between dominance and conduct is a discussion about the scope of the special responsibility of dominant firms.

For the ordo-liberals, for example, firms enjoying a dominant position should be required to act "as if" they did not have market power. Thus, to conclude that a given conduct is exploitative, it is imperative to show that such conduct must exploit a dominant position—i.e. it should make "no economic sense" absent dominance.

For the neoclassicals, instead, firms enjoying a dominant position should be required to act in alignment with the customers and consumers, which may require them to behave differently than their competitive counterparts. That is, the conduct may be exploitative even if it makes no economic sense in the absence of a dominant position if, when undertaken by a dominant firm, it results in consumer harm.

In this section we explain why the neoclassical answer is correct from the viewpoint of the error-cost framework.

5.1 The Error Cost Minimization Principle

Consider a complaint filed with the Commission by company *P* (the "Plaintiff") against company *D* (the "Defendant"). Company *P* alleges that company *D* has infringed competition law by abusing a dominant position.

The job of the Commission during the administrative proceedings is to produce a decision {infringement, no infringement} by assessing the Plaintiff's complaint and the Defendant's defence, considering the available evidence. In the context of exploitative abuses, the ultimate goal of the Commission is to eliminate the exploitation and, hence, the harm to consumers inflicted by unfair trading practices.

In reaching a decision, the Commission can make two types of error: it may conclude that the Plaintiff is right when it is not (a Type I error) or that the Defendant is right when it is not (a Type II error). Each of these errors involves a cost—i.e. a loss of consumer welfare. Thus, as Judge Easterbrook explained,[42] to achieve its ultimate goal, a competition agency should choose the decision that minimizes the expected cost of error. The Commission should find that company *D* infringed the competition laws when error costs are minimized by an infringement decision, and vice versa.

5.2 Applying the Framework

This framework can also be used to adjudicate between those that maintain that the Commission should be required to posit and prove a causal connection between dominance and abuse and those that disagree with this proposition. Or, what in our view is the equivalent question: whether the Commission should be required to benchmark the conditions imposed by the dominant undertaking against the conduct of other players, who do not have a dominant position.

As discussed in section IV.C, benchmarking a given conduct by a dominant undertaking with the behaviour observed in competitive markets is not helpful to ascertain whether it is potentially exploitative and, on the contrary, may lead to incorrect inferences. It is not helpful because the fact that a conduct is not observed in competitive markets does not imply that the net effect of the conduct *C* is necessarily negative and, therefore, exploitative, in the market where the dominant undertaking operates.

Consider, for example, the case of excessive prices. Prices in a perfectly competitive market for a homogeneous good will be given by marginal costs. Prices for that good in a contestable market—i.e. one with free entry and free exit—exhibiting economies of scale will equal average total costs. Yet, the fact that the prices set in a market for a differentiated product are driven by demand factors (i.e. factors other than costs) does not imply that those prices are not competitive. Furthermore, the law does not require dominant firms to price at cost. The only prices that are regarded as abusive are those which bear no relationship with the economic value of the product and service (and, with the exception of scholastic philosophers and Marxists, everyone accepts that value and cost are not the same).

More importantly, the competitive benchmarking exercise may lead the Commission to conclude that the practice is not abusive when in fact it is—i.e. to incur a Type II error. The reason being that, as we explained in section IV.C, the fact

[42] Easterbrook, op. cit.

that a conduct is observed in competitive markets does not imply that its *net* effect on consumer welfare when adopted by a dominant firm in the market is positive.

5.3 Implications for the Causation Controversy

We conclude, therefore, that the Commission *should not* be required to benchmark the conditions imposed by the dominant undertaking against the conduct of players operating in competitive markets. This in turn implies that the Commission *should not* be required to show a causal link between the existence of a dominant position and the ability to apply the terms in question. The dominant company can exploit consumers even if it exhibits behaviour also exhibited by as firms without market power. That is, even if the conduct in question can be implemented in practice in the absence of a dominant position.

6 Causation in Law in Exploitative Cases

It follows from the above that the requirements to establish causation in law in exploitative cases need not be those in exclusionary cases. In exclusionary cases, the harm caused by the abusive conduct is *indirect*. That is, the conduct first causes a distortion of the competitive process by foreclosing or marginalising competitors, and then that distortion of competition causes consumer harm.

Thus, the Commission first needs to prove that the conduct distorts the competitive process, which it does by showing that the dominant firm is not competing on the merits. This in turn requires the Commission to show that no as-efficient competitor in a non-dominant position would have the ability or the incentive to engage in a similar conduct and protect its independence status as an effective competitor.[43] (Causation in fact I.) Then, the Commission needs to show that the conduct is capable of producing anticompetitive effects (i.e. higher prices, lower quality, less innovation) and, hence, harm consumers. (Causation in fact II.)

In short, in exclusionary cases, the Commission establish causation in law by establishing two factual causal links: (i) the conduct of the dominant firm departs from competition on the merits because it cannot be "imitated",[44] and (ii) the change in market structure brought about by conduct of the dominant firm is capable of causing anticompetitive effects.

Instead, in exploitative cases, the harm caused by the abusive conduct is *direct*: it is the conduct, rather than the change in the conditions of competition, that harms

[43] See judgment in *Servizio Elettrico Nazionale*, *supra*, para. 78.

[44] See the discussion on the appropriate interpretation of the notion of "imitation" in the case law in Sect. 4.1.1. above.

consumers. Thus, the Commission only needs to show that the conduct in question is capable of causing harm *when undertaken by a dominant firm*. That is, causation in law follows from a single causal link in fact: there is a relationship between conduct and effect when the conduct is undertaken by a dominant firm.

7 Concluding Remarks

In this paper we have argued that in cases involving allegations of unfair trading conditions under Article 102(a) TFEU, (a) the Commission *should not* be required to show a causal link between the existence of a dominant position and the ability to impose the terms in question; (b) the Commission *should not* be required to benchmark the conditions imposed by the dominant undertaking against the conduct of other players, who do not have a dominant position; (c) the Commission *should* be required to show that those terms are harmful by virtue of the undertaking's dominant position; and (d) the Commission *should* be required to show that those terms, if necessary for the achievement of a legitimate objective, are not proportionate as a result of the undertaking's dominant position.

Arguably, the test in *Apple* can be misused to transform every exclusionary case where the Commission fails unable to show foreclosure into an exploitative case. We disagree for the following reasons. First, the conduct of a dominant firm may cause harm even if it does not result in the exclusion or marginalisation of rivals. Second, while under the *Apple* test there is no need to show that the detriment to the dominant firm's trading partners is capable of producing exclusionary effects, it is still necessary to show harm to them or to their consumers. This is clear from the implementation of the test in *Apple*, where the Commission established that the impugned conduct, though imposed on its trading partners, did restrict consumer choice and, therefore, was likely to result in higher prices or lower quality by virtue of Apple's monopoly power.

Recent Developments in the Case Law of EU Courts on Competition Law, in the Wake of the *Superleague* Judgment

Jan Passer, Pierre Schmitt, and Fabien Zivy

1 Introduction

In the past 2 years, numerous judgments by the Court of Justice of the European Union have clarified fundamental issues of EU competition law, notably in the field of the digital economy[1] and in relation to the powers of European and national competition authorities in the area of merger control.[2] In this short contribution, we will focus on one such judgment, delivered on 21 December 2023 in the *Superleague* case.[3] In this judgment, which deals with the implementation of competition rules in the context of professional sports, the Court, sitting in the Grand Chamber, delivered, more broadly, what is known as a "recap" judgment.

The Court had previously made use of this method on a few occasions, particularly in the field of personal data protection.[4] In such areas, where the case law may

[1] See for instance the judgment in *Google and Alphabet v Commission*, C-48/22 P, EU:C:2024:726 ('Google Shopping'), in which the Court upheld the fine of €2.4 billion imposed on Google for abuse of its dominant position by favoring its own comparison shopping service.

[2] See the judgment in *Illumina and Grail v Commission*, C-611/22 P and C-625/22 P, EU:C:2024:677, in which the Court - following the Opinion of Advocate General Emiliou (EU:C:2024:264) - held that the Commission is not authorised to encourage or accept referrals of proposed concentrations without a European dimension from national competition authorities where those authorities are not competent to examine those proposed concentrations under their own national law.

[3] Judgment in *European Superleague Company*, C-333/21, EU:C:2023:1011 ('*Superleague*').

[4] See, for instance, judgment in *La Quadrature du Net and Others*, C-511/18, C-512/18 and C-520/18, EU:C:2020:791.

J. Passer · P. Schmitt (✉) · F. Zivy
Court of Justice of the European Union, Luxembourg, Luxembourg
e-mail: Jan.Passer@curia.europa.eu; Pierre.Schmitt@curia.europa.eu; Fabien.Zivy@curia.europa.eu

L. Prete, L. Rezki (eds.), *Judging & (Re)Thinking European Union Law*,
https://doi.org/10.1007/978-3-032-13473-8_13

be relatively old, abundant, and/or frequently evolving, issuing a "recap" judgment allows the Court to provide a comprehensive, consistent, and updated view of the law as it stands. At the same time, and as importantly, it can offer an opportunity to unify possibly diverging case law, clarify important legal issues, or, if necessary, restate principles. The Court did so in *Superleague*. Unlike two other judgments delivered on the same day and also concerning sports, *International Skating Union*[5] and *Royal Antwerp*,[6] *Superleague* is therefore not only, and perhaps not primarily, a judgment on sports law, even though its impact on that sector is obviously significant. It is, above all, a judgment intended to serve as an updated point of reference regarding Articles 101 and 102 TFEU, although there are certainly several important or technical issues that it does not address, such as the implementation of Article 102 TFEU in the context of the Internet (addressed in the recent *Google Shopping* case[7] and also at the heart of currently pending cases such as the *Alphabet*[8] case), or rebates (covered in the recent *Intel II* judgment[9]), the issue of essential facilities (on which the Court shed new light in several recent cases), or ancillary restraints (discussed in the recent *Booking* judgment[10]).

This short contribution will discuss and contextualise the main findings of this landmark judgment, as well as present a number of more recent judgments in which Articles 101 and 102 TFEU have been central.

2 Article 101 TFEU: Clarifications on the Content and Operation of the Notion of "Anti-Competitive Object"

In *Superleague*, the Court focused on three main aspects of Article 101 TFEU.

First, the Court recalled that in order to fall within the prohibition laid down in Article 101(1) TFEU, an agreement must have "as its object or effect" the prevention, restriction, or distortion of competition within the internal market.[11] It also emphasised that this condition is alternative in nature. While this may seem obvious, some recent judgments delivered by chambers of five judges, such as *Generics*[12] or *HSBC*,[13] had been interpreted as attenuating this alternative nature, allowing the actual or potential effects of a practice to be considered when examining its object,

[5] Judgment in *International Skating Union v Commission*, C-124/21 P, EU:C:2023:1012.

[6] Judgment in *Royal Antwerp Football Club*, C-680/21, EU:C:2023:1010 ('*Royal Antwerp*').

[7] *Supra*, n. 1.

[8] C-738/22 P, *Google and Alphabet v Commission*, currently pending.

[9] Judgment in *Commission v Intel Corporation*, C-240/22 P, EU:C:2024:915 ('*Intel II*').

[10] Judgment of 19 September 2024, *Booking.com and Booking.com (Deutschland)*, C-264/23, EU:C:2024:764.

[11] Para. 158.

[12] Judgment in *Generics (UK) and Others*, C-307/18, EU:C:2020:52 ('*Generics*').

[13] Judgment in *HSBC Holdings and Others v Commission*, C-883/19 P, EU:C:2023:11.

to the extent necessary to "double-check" its seriousness. In *Superleague*, the Court explicitly ruled out that this could be the case. More specifically, after recalling that it is appropriate to examine "first" the object of the conduct in question, the Court added that if, after that examination, the conduct proves to have an anti-competitive object, it is "in no way necessary to examine, a fortiori, to demonstrate" its effect on competition, whether positive or negative, and whether actual or potential. These are rather categorical terms.

Since then, this clarification has been taken up and further developed in a judgment delivered by a chamber of five judges, including the President of the Court, in *Commission v Servier and Others*.[14]

To be clear, this does not mean that we should return to a form-based, abstract, or otherwise superficial analysis of the existence (or absence) of an anti-competitive "object". Quite the contrary, in the *Superleague* case, the Court repeated the axiom that the notion of an "anti-competitive object" should be construed and applied "strictly". Therefore, this requirement, which is the cornerstone of the Court's historic (dating back to the 1960s) case law, and which has been most famously reiterated in the *Cartes Bancaires* judgment[15] (in which the Court followed the inspiring and strongly principled Opinion of Advocate General Wahl), after having been, seemingly, somewhat forgotten in some decisions of the European Commission or even in some judgments of the General Court, remains "good law"—and, we would add, is more important than ever. In other words, this axiom is crucial from a legal perspective and should also be of equal importance in practical terms, i.e., in the practice of the European Commission and national competition authorities.

In practice, this means that the analysis of the "legal and economic context" in which a practice or agreement occurs should be performed with great care and without prejudice. It is true that the Court has stated on some occasions that for cartels and similarly egregious practices, the analysis of their context can be limited to what is absolutely necessary[16] and cannot serve as a justification.[17] As the Court has repeatedly stated, economic experience teaches us that such practices are particularly harmful to competition and without redeeming qualities. This situation, we believe, explains why the Court holds that, in presence of such practices (an only such practices), the contextual analysis required by Article 101 TFEU may be limited. However, for practices other than cartels, the analysis of their context should include all relevant legal and economic parameters, as recalled in both the *Cartes Bancaires* and *Superleague* judgments. From this perspective, the requirement is essentially the same as the one expressed by the Court in its *Intel I* judgment in relation to Article 102 TFEU.[18]

---

[14] Judgment in *Commission v Servier and Others*, C-176/19 P, EU:C:2024:549 ('*Servier*').

[15] Judgment in *CB v Commission*, C-67/13 P, EU:C:2014:2204.

[16] Judgments in *Toshiba Corporation v Commission*, C-373/14 P, EU:C:2016:26, para. 29, and in *EDP – Energias de Portugal and Others*, C-331/21, EU:C:2023:812, paras 100 to 103.

[17] Judgment in *Servier*, para. 97 and the case law cited.

[18] Judgment in *Intel v Commission*, C-413/14 P, EU:C:2017:632 ('*Intel I*').

A good illustration of this requirement is the recent *Diarra* judgment, that was handed out recently by the Second Chamber of the Court, of which Judge Wahl was a member. The case leading to this judgment involved a former football player who sued the *Fédération internationale de football association* (FIFA) for damages he claimed to have suffered as a result of the implementation of some aspects of the Regulations on the Status and Transfer of Football Players.[19] In its judgment, the Court concluded that these rules have an anti-competitive object, based notably on their substantive impact on cross-border competition between professional football clubs, their geographical scope within the EU, and their permanence. The Court reached this conclusion after a detailed analysis of not only the content of the rules and their objectives, but also the actual context in which they apply. It is this context, in particular, that allowed the Court to determine that these rules are such as to significantly restrain competition between all EU-based professional football clubs in relation to the unilateral recruitment (as opposed to the negotiated transfer) of players. This contextual analysis also led the Court to the conclusion that, although the rules have a different form and mode of operation, they are, in effect, similar to a no-poach agreement directly concluded between football clubs.

Secondly, *Superleague* summarises earlier case law by listing the main examples of types of conduct that "must" be regarded as having an anti-competitive object, while pointing out that other types of conduct "may" be regarded as such. In doing so, the Court points out the existence of a form of hierarchy between cartels and similar practices, which are universally considered particularly harmful to competition and without redeeming virtues (thus, prohibited per se, at least in practice), and other types of horizontal or vertical agreements, which may not be as harmful but may still be regarded as having an anti-competitive object, without prejudice to the possibility of justifying them under Article 101(3) TFEU. This point is essentially repeated in the judgment in *Commission v Servier and Others*.

This hierarchy is not merely an abstract legal classification. It reflects the tangible reality that, in some cases, practices that "may" be regarded as having an anti-competitive object in certain economic and legal contexts "may" also be found *not* to have such an object in other contexts. Instead, they could either have an anti-competitive effect (only), or not be anti-competitive at all. This means that a thorough analysis of their actual or potential effects on competition is required, considering all their relevant market, regulatory, and factual characteristics, as well as the relevant evidence. From this point of view, the case law regarding Article 101 TFEU is consistent with that relating to Article 102 TFEU, as recalled in the *Servizio Elettrico Nazionale* judgment of the Court.[20]

Irrespective of its conclusions regarding the existence of an infringement of competition rules, the recent judgment in the *Super Bock* case,[21] which concerned vertical price-fixing agreements, more specifically retail price maintenance, provides a

[19] Judgment in *FIFA*, C-650/22, EU:C:2024:824 (or '*Diarra*').

[20] Judgment in *Servizio Elettrico Nazionale and Others*, C-377/20, EU:C:2022:379.

[21] Judgment in *Super Bock Bebidas*, C-211/22, EU:C:2023:529.

good illustration of how flexibly and carefully case law operates in relation to whether a given practice is anti-competitive and how it should be assessed. In its judgment, the Court recalled that, to determine whether a vertical agreement fixing minimum resale prices constitutes a "restriction of competition by object", one must ascertain whether the agreement presents a sufficient degree of harm to competition. This may be evaluated by considering the content of its provisions, its objectives, and the economic and legal context in which it operates. This seems like an obvious reminder of the standard case law, but in reality it is a big move from earlier cases, that had treated retail price maintenance as quasi per se violations of competition law, irrespective of their actual context.

Another relevant example is the recent judgment in a Portuguese case concerning an exchange of information between banks. In this judgment, the Court explains in great detail in which circumstances such a practice can, or conversely, cannot, be regarded as anti-competitive by object, while synthesising its previous case law on this matter.[22] It explains that a standalone exchange of information between competitors may constitute a restriction of competition by object if the exchange leads to a form of coordination that, by its nature, is necessarily harmful to the proper functioning of normal competition. In short, this situation may arise if the exchange of information allows operators on the market to remove uncertainty about the future conduct of other participants, especially in relation to strategic aspects of this conduct.

Thirdly, the Court has clarified the scope and application of its previous case law, which states that certain practices that inherently restrict commercial freedom and competition may fall outside the scope of the prohibition laid down in Article 101(1) TFEU, provided certain conditions are met.[23] As implied but necessarily inferred from the wording used by the Court, this case law applies only to practices with an inherent anti-competitive "effect", not those with an anti-competitive object, which are inherently more harmful to the market. In such cases, only Article 101(3) may permit the practice in question if the conditions for its application are met.

It is therefore a clarification[24] of the case law established in previous cases, such as *Meca-Medina*, which allowed certain exclusions from the scope of Article 101(1) but was sometimes unclear as to whether the contested practice was considered a restriction of competition by object or by effect. According to this case law, not every agreement between undertakings or decision of an association of undertakings that restricts the freedom of action of those involved necessarily falls within the prohibition of Article 101(1) TFEU. A close examination of the economic and legal context of such agreements may lead to the conclusion that they are justified by the

---

[22] Judgment in *Banco BPN/BIC Português and Others*, C-298/22, EU:C:2024:638.

[23] Judgments in *Wouters and Others*, C-309/99, EU:C:2002:98 ('*Wouters*'), and in *Meca-Medina and Majcen v Commission*, C-519/04 P, EU:C:2006:492 ('*Meca-Medina*').

[24] For further analysis, see B. Zelger, "Object Restrictions in Sports after the ECJ's Decisions in ISU and Superleague", Journal of European Competition Law & Practice, 2024, Vol. 15, No. 2, pp. 90-101 and S. Weatherill, "The impact of the rulings of 21 December 2023 on the structure of EU sports law", *The International Sports Law Journal*, 2023, 23, pp. 409–415.

pursuit of legitimate objectives in the public interest, that the specific means used to pursue those objectives are necessary, or that, even if those means potentially restrict or distort competition, this restriction does not go beyond what is necessary, especially if it does not eliminate competition entirely.[25]

In *Superleague*, the Court clarified that this case law does not apply to conduct that, by its nature, infringes Article 102 TFEU.[26] The Court added that this case law does not apply either to "situations involving conduct that, far from merely having the inherent 'effect' of restricting competition, at least potentially, by limiting the freedom of action of certain undertakings, reveals a degree of harm to competition that justifies a finding that it has as its very 'object' the prevention, restriction, or distortion of competition. Thus, it is only if, following an examination of the conduct at issue in a given case, that conduct proves not to have as its object the prevention, restriction or distortion of competition, that it must then be determined whether it may come within the scope of that case law".[27]

The same approach was followed in the Court's judgment in *Lietuvos notarų rūmai and Others* on 18 January 2024,[28] concerning rules adopted by a private notaries' association in Lithuania regarding how fees should be calculated. The Court found that such horizontal price-fixing for services was so harmful that it must be regarded as a restriction of competition "by object" under Article 101(1) TFEU. The Court clarified that if the conduct is classified as a restriction by object, regulatory objectives such as safeguarding the principles of equal treatment and proportionality, or protecting notaries against unjustified civil liability by standardising notarial practices and filling a regulatory gap, cannot justify it. Since such restrictions do not benefit from the exemption provided in Article 101(3) TFEU, they must be regarded as constituting a restriction of competition "by object" prohibited by Article 101(1) TFEU.

One week later, on 25 January 2024, the Court issued a similar judgment regarding a Bulgarian professional association of lawyers setting minimum fee amounts.[29] The Court considered this to be horizontal price-fixing and a restriction of competition by object. Such restrictions could not be justified by legitimate regulatory objectives, and only Article 101(3) could potentially justify them. Jude Wahl having acted as Judge Rapporteur in the judgment, which is very convincing in our view, we will not detail it further in the present contribution.

These clarifications have now been firmly established in the case law.

One may conclude, after this brief presentation of the most important findings of the Court in *Superleague* in relation to Article 101 TFEU, that this judgment provides clarification of the notion of anti-competitive object and its consequences for

[25] Judgments in *Wouters*, para. 97; *Meca-Medina*, paras 42–48; and in *Ordem dos Técnicos Oficiais de Contas*, C-1/12, EU:C:2013:127, paras 93, 96 and 97.

[26] Judgment in *Superleague*, para. 185, referring to the judgment in *MOTOE*, C-49/07, EU:C:2008:376, ('*MOTOE*') para. 53.

[27] Judgment in *Superleague*, para. 186.

[28] Judgment in *Lietuvos notarų rūmai and Others*, C-128/21, EU:C:2024:49, paras 93 et seq.

[29] Judgment in *Em akaunt BG*, C-438/22, EU:C:2024:71.

the rest of the reasoning in relation to Article 101 TFEU. The Court notably clarified that the principles based on *Meca-Medina* apply if the conduct does not constitute such anti-competitive object. Hence, as far as restrictions by object are concerned, the only possible exemption is Article 101(3) TFEU.

3 Article 102 TFEU: The Specific Challenges Raised by "Gatekeepers"

As regards Article 102 TFEU, the *Superleague* judgment recalls that the same conduct may give rise to an infringement of both Article 101 and Article 102 TFUE, even though these provisions pursue different objectives and have distinct scopes, insofar as their respective conditions of application are met.[30] Accordingly, both provisions must be interpreted and applied consistently, although in compliance with the specific characteristics of each of them. It is interesting to note that this is the first time that the concurrent application of both provisions is explicitly admitted by the Court in its case law and that the Court emphasises the need to interpret and apply them consistently, in compliance with their specific characteristics.

Moreover, this judgment provides interesting insights into the situation of undertakings in a dominant position that are in a "gatekeeper" position within a given market. First, it establishes the principle that the conduct of such undertakings may constitute an abuse if it has the effect, or a fortiori the very object, of preventing potentially competing undertakings from accessing that market.[31] This reference to both the effect and the object of an abuse of dominant position, which may lead to the classification of abuses "by effect" or "by object"[32] (as already stated, in different words, in the *Intel I* and *Generics* judgments) illustrates the statement of the Court that both Article 101 and Article 102 TFUE must be interpreted consistently. Secondly, the judgment emphasises that the existence of such an abuse may be characterised regardless of whether the undertaking holds its dominant position by virtue of exclusive rights granted by the state, enabling it to control market entry, or through its own autonomous conduct.[33] The judgment adds that, where the undertaking concerned has the power to determine the conditions of access to the market of competing undertakings, that power must, in order not to infringe, by its very

[30] The Court refers to that effect to judgments in *Saeed Flugreisen and Silver Line Reisebüro*, 66/86, EU:C:1989:140, para. 37; *Compagnie maritime belge transports v Commission*, C-395/96 P and C-396/96 P, EU:C:2000:132, para. 33; and *Generics*, para. 146.

[31] Judgment in *Superleague*, para. 131, referring, to that effect, to the judgment in *Generics*, paras 154–157.

[32] This notion of abuse of competition "by object" is notably mentioned by G. Íñiguez, "European Super League Company and the (New) law of European Football", *European Papers*, 2024, vol. 9, n°. 1, pp. 1–15, p. 5.

[33] Judgment in *Superleague*, para. 134, referring, to that effect, to the judgment in MOTOE, para. 53.

existence, Article 102 TFEU, be placed within a framework of transparent, non-discriminatory detailed procedural rules. Such requirements are all the more necessary for undertakings in a dominant position placing themselves, through their own conduct and not by virtue of being granted exclusive or special rights by a Member State, in a situation where they are able to deny potentially competing undertakings access to a given market.[34] These statements apply particularly to undertakings in a dominant position that are "gatekeepers". In this regard, it is important to recall that, while this case concerned entities with "double hatting" in associations regulating the exercise of a given sport at a global or European level, there may be other "gatekeeper" undertakings in other fields, particularly in the digital, internet, and media sectors.[35]

That said, while different markets (and, more broadly, legal and economic contexts) may require different analyses, it is interesting to note that, even if from a purely formal point of view a given company can be regarded as being in a "gatekeeping" position, some of these statements have already been taken over in another context. In particular, in a case concerning one of the so-called "GAFAM" undertakings, namely Google, the Court had the opportunity to reaffirm the legal principles summarised in *Superleague* regarding Article 102 TFEU. On 10 September 2024, it confirmed, based on those principles, the EUR 2.4 billion fine imposed on Google for abusing its dominant position by favoring its own comparison shopping service to the detriment of competing undertakings, which were discriminated against. However, the judgment in the *Google Shopping* case was an appeal, not a preliminary ruling. Therefore, the way in which it addressed a number of legal issues, such as the lawfulness of self-preferencing, as well as the way in which it was drafted, are, to some extent, more cautious, case-specific, and less principled than the statements in the *Superleague* judgment. This does not diminish the precedential value of the *Google Shopping* judgment, but it is apparent that the Court focused specifically on the case before it, without setting up more abstract and interpretative principles. As we know, tech markets are fast-moving, and practices, players and regulatory contexts evolve over time. Thus, the Court's caution is understandable. Ongoing cases, such as *Alphabet*,[36] will probably provide a fuller understanding of the law.

Returning to *Superleague*, the various principles summarised in that judgment have already been recalled in subsequent judgments of both the Court of Justice, such as the recent *Intel II* judgment[37] and the General Court, notably in the *Google*

---

[34] Judgment in *Superleague*, paras 135–137.

[35] See, for instance, Regulation (EU) 2022/1925 of the European Parliament and of the Council of 14 September 2022 on contestable and fair markets in the digital sector and amending Directives (EU) 2019/1937 and (EU) 2020/1828 (Digital Markets Act) (OJ 2022 L 265, p. 1), which affects "gatekeeper" platforms on the Internet.

[36] *Supra*, n. 8.

[37] Judgment in *Intel II*, paras 175 et seq.

AdSense for Search judgment on 18 September 2024.[38] The General Court emphasised that "the purpose of Article 102 TFUE is to prevent competition from being restricted to the detriment of the public interest, individual undertakings and consumers, by sanctioning the conduct of undertakings in a dominant position that has the effect of hindering competition on the merits and is thus likely to cause direct harm to consumers, or which causes them harm indirectly by hindering or distorting that competition". However, "it is not the purpose of Article 102 TFEU to prevent an undertaking from acquiring, on its own merits, a dominant position on a market, or to ensure that competitors less efficient than an undertaking in such a position should remain on the market".[39]

4 The Court's First Contact with One of the "New Frontiers" of Competition Law: Labour Markets

Finally, we would like to mention again, but from a different angle, the recent *Diarra* judgment, in which the Court of Justice was asked by a Belgian Court of Appeal to assess the compatibility of FIFA's rules governing the transfer of players with EU law on the free movement of workers and competition law. As mentioned earlier, the Court found that FIFA's rules had the object of restricting, or even preventing, cross-border competition among all EU clubs by preventing them from unilaterally recruiting players under contract with another club or those whose employment contracts had been allegedly terminated without due cause.[40] The Court emphasised that the ability to compete by recruiting players is essential in professional football and that rules imposing a general restriction on such competition, equivalent to a no-poach agreement, partitioned the market and altered the allocation of workers between employers. The Court also noted that these rules did not appear to be indispensable or necessary.

While *Royal Antwerp*[41] had already established several milestones, this judgment is the first in which the Court clarified how Article 101(1) and Article 102 TFEU apply to the "labour market", specifically regarding the recruitment of workers. As is well known, the Court has long held that competition law does not apply to agreements resulting from collective bargaining between the representatives of the two sides of industry (meaning by that workers trade unions and representatives of the employers) aimed at improving working conditions.[42] This case law has been well

[38] Judgment in *Google and Alphabet v Commission (Google AdSense for Search)*, T-334/19, EU:T:2024:634, paras 103-105. See also pending case T-260/24, *Apple and Apple Distribution International v Commission.*

[39] These two quotes from the *Google and Alphabet v Commission (Google AdSense for Search)* judgment refer to paras 103 and 105 of the *Superleague* judgment.

[40] *Supra*, n. 19.

[41] *Supra*, n. 6.

[42] Judgment of 21 September 1999, *Albany*, C-67/96, EU:C:1999:430.

settled. However, in cases not involving such agreements, competition rules do apply, and companies competing in the labour market must comply with them. This issue is also particularly important in other sectors, not just in professional sports. Moreover, the European Commission and many national competition authorities are interested in these matters. Thus, there may be further cases on this topic in the coming years.

5 Concluding Remarks

As mentioned in the introduction of this contribution, Superleague is not only, and perhaps not primarily, a judgment on sports law, even though its impact on that sector is obviously significant. The findings of the Court, as described and discussed in this contribution, demonstrate that it serves as a "recap" judgment regarding Articles 101 and 102 TFEU. As the readers will know, Judge Wahl seated not only in this judgment, but also in a number of other judgments discussed above, notably the Diarra judgment. Moreover, without of course giving any indication as to what his individual positions may have been in these various judgments, it is fair to say—and, in fact, obvious—that, in each case, the chamber tremendously benefited from Nils' expertise, vision and unwavering independence, to which we want to pay tribute.

A final word. Despite the fact that the aim of this contribution was not to focus on sports law as such, we would like to add a few comments on sport. The judgments discussed in this chapter have been widely commented on by academics from the perspective of their implications for sport.[43] The main "legal message" that, in our view, emerges from this is that, insofar as high-level professional sport is an economic activity, it must comply with competition rules, just as it must respect the freedoms of movement, as established in *Bosman*.[44] This does not imply that the sector lacks specificities or cannot be subject to specific regulation, which is currently ensured by FIFA and UEFA. However, the rules set by these associations must, where they apply to the economic aspects of sport, be compatible with Union economic law.

[43] See notably S. Weatherill, "The impact of the rulings of 21 December 2023 on the structure of EU sports law", *The International Sports Law Journal*, 2023, 23, pp. 409–415; S. Weatherill, "Is this the end of football's transfer system? An immediate reaction to the Court's ruling in Diarra (C-650/22)", available on line on EU Law Analysis Blog; A. Duval, "The international skating union ruling of the CJEU and the future of CAS arbitration in transnational sports governance", *The International Sports Law Journal*, 2023, 23, pp. 467–474; G. Íñiguez, "European Super League Company and the (New) law of European Football", *European Papers*, 2024, vol. 9, n°. 1, pp. 1–15; M. Maduro, "Sports governance after the superleague judgment: going into extra time?", *The International Sports Law Journal*, 2023, 23, pp. 482–490; P. Mavroidis and D. Neven, "Eyes on the Ball. The Super-League Litigation before the CJEU", 2023, available on line on ssrn.com.

[44] Judgment in *Bosman*, C-415/93, EU:C:1995:463.

Other pending cases, such as those concerning FIFA's rules on player agents (Cases C-209/23 *RRC Sports* and C-428/23 *Rogon*), or the one concerning the relationship between FIFA's system of dispute resolution before the Court of Arbitration for Sport (CAS) and the principle of effective judicial protection under EU law (Case C-600/23, *Royal Football Club Seraing*),[45] or also the one dealing with the action taken by the Portuguese football clubs participating in the National Championship during the Covid-19 global shutdown (Case C-133/24, *CD Tondela*), will certainly give the Court the opportunity to reconsider and develop these issues further.

[45] See Opinion of Advocate General Ćapeta in *Royal Football Club Seraing*, C-600/23, EU:C:2025:24.

Thoughtful Competition Law: Power and Reflexivity

Nicolas Petit

1 Introduction: Competition Law as a Power Structure

What does it truly mean for a legal practitioner or scholar to engage in competition law, beyond merely applying existing rules?[1] Outside competition law circles, an argument has been drawing increasing support: competition jurists maintain a socially constructed power structure. Professor Katarina Pistor argues that property, contracts, and trust laws are subverted by attorneys to generate private wealth, entrench a capitalistic system, and promote inequality. She adds that public rules of antitrust or taxation do little to correct the problem:

> The masters of the code of capital, that is, the private attorneys who fashion different assets as capital mostly in private law also tend to have privileged access to regulators and tax authorities and often vet their coding strategies with them before applying them.[2]

[1] The argument in this paper is based on US antitrust law and EU competition law.

[2] K. Pistor, 'Theorizing Beyond "The Code of Capital": A Reply' I n (2020) *Accounting, Economics, and Law: A Convivium* (2020) 11.1, pp. 65–80. In another essay, Pistor suggests that antitrust codes "*the power to transform free contracting and markets into a controlled space that gives a huge advantage to sellers over buyers*" (K. Pistor, 'Rule by data: The end of markets?' (2020) *Law & Contemp. Probs.* p. 83, at 101.

This paper is dedicated to Professor, Judge, and Advocate General Nils Wahl, whose unique Opinions have ushered in a more commonsensical, rational and thoughtful approach to EU competition law. In particular, I want to highlight his paradigm-shifting work in the *Cartes Bancaires*, *Intel*, and *MEO* cases. I want to thank my friend and good colleague Prof. N. M. Rajkovic for helping me wrap my head around the difficult questions addressed in this article.

N. Petit (✉)
European University Institute, Firenze, Italy
e-mail: Nicolas.Petit@eui.eu

L. Prete, L. Rezki (eds.), *Judging & (Re)Thinking European Union Law*,
https://doi.org/10.1007/978-3-032-13473-8_14

Arguments about the social construction of competition law reach beyond the academy. The rise of a neo-Brandeisian school of competition policy in the US is a clear sign of practical impact. With its focus on corporate bigness, neo-Brandeisianism is distinct from Pistor's argument. However, neo-Brandeisianism also advances a power structure narrative. Large firms, their attorneys, lobbyists, and hired academics are said to control not just markets, but also politics.[3]

The argument of competition law as a power structure, while compelling, may however mislead if it were to take the shape of a conspiracy theory, as I think it does here. Practitioners of competition law understand that legal systems are far too complex to function as power structures run by group-based hierarchies to dominate others. That would require implausibly high levels of time consistency, coalition-building efforts, and initial value alignment. However competition law has a rather messy life echoing what Justice Oliver Wendell Holmes Jr. famously said when he observed that "*the life of the law has not been logic: it has been experience*".[4]

Now if engaging in competition law means something other than enforcing a socially constructed power structure, what would that be? That odd-sounding question matters a great deal.[5] Absent a good understanding of what we do as competition jurists, we would not be in a position to account for our social practice. The cost of non-reflexivity in turn exposes the field to criticism from outside which does not reflect the complexities that its practitioners are aware of.[6] And, at any rate, without some self-critical awareness, which Pistor's work invites us to have, it is hard to challenge bad competition law reform proposals (or to promote good competition law reform proposals).

2 Competition Law as an Epistemological Enterprise

I think that a more realistic social theory of competition law can be proposed. This theory would view the legal system as a system for determining the truth about the interests that it purports to protect, what Michel Foucault called a 'site of veridiction,' or a place where truth is established.[7]While private law seeks the truth about

---

[3] Pistor, herself, noted the difference, see above at pp. 116–117.

[4] O. W. Holmes, Jr., *The Common Law,* Mark de Wolf Howe ed, Little Brown and Company 1963 (1st ed 1881) 5.

[5] D. Lefkowitz, 'Systematicity, normativity, and The Nature of International Law' (2021) Revus – Journal for Constitutional Theory and Philosophy of Law/Revija za ustavno teorijo in filozofijo prava, p. 43.

[6] Saying that law is political by nature does not imply that all choices in the development and application of the law will be inherently political, in the sense of motivated by political reasons. And it fails to see the multiple corrections by other political input processes, like the justice system and human rights. The fact that law has a political origin does not mean that the system of law is politically biased.

[7] M. Foucault, *The Birth of Biopolitics: Michel Foucault's Lecture at the Collège de France on Neo-Liberal Governmentality*, edited by T. Lenske, translated by G. Burchell, Palgrave Macmillan,

freedom of contract and autonomy, competition law seeks the truth about restraints of competition. Put differently, as a social practice, the legal system is an epistemological enterprise. It is a system that promotes the value of knowledge.

To seek the truth, a legal system first selects 'legal facts' as can be specified in statutes or case law. I take a legal fact in private law to be "*consent*" for example. A legal fact in competition law can be an "*agreement*". Second, to establish that legal fact, the legal system will accept or reject some 'empirical facts'. In private law, the requirement of a written document can constitute one such empirical fact. In competition law, the empirical facts relevant to an agreement can be a "*concurrence of wills*" or a "*meeting of the minds*".

The choices of relevant legal and empirical facts needed to apply the law can be conceptualized under two headings. First, there are choices about what to include. Some facts are added because they are deemed relevant to apply the law. For example, US antitrust law and to some extent EU competition law include a "consumer welfare standard" ("CWS") filter for the evaluation of business conduct and merger transactions. By adding a CWS filter to the evaluation of exclusionary conduct, competition law seeks to know the difference between conduct or transactions that generate efficient rivalry (which, by convenience, it deems low prices and high output to signal) and those that generate inefficient rivalry (which, by contrast, it deems high prices and low output to signal).

On the other hand, there are choices about what to exclude. Some facts are ignored because they are deemed irrelevant to address in this area of the law. For example, mergers that do not significantly lessen competition in product markets are cleared, even if they give rise to wage cuts or adverse impacts on labor markets, consequences which are left for other areas of the law to address.

Why is this relevant? If competition law is a system which proceeds piecemeal, in the way I described, by inclusion and exclusion, then it is difficult to claim, as has been claimed, that competition law is a socially constructed power structure. The reason is that several inconsistent factors shape the choices of inclusion and exclusion of empirical facts.

3 Factors Shaping Competition Law

The first factor that shapes competition law is the basic legal structure, understood as the fundamental legal sources and institutions. In the European Union ("EU"), the law is very granular, compared to the US antitrust statute. The language of Article 101 of the Treaty on the Functioning of the EU ("TFEU") refers to "*undertakings*", and to "*competition*", and an exception rule exists in the third paragraph. In the US, by contrast, Section 1 of the Sherman Act refers more broadly to any "*person*", and to "*trade*", and there is no exception rule. EU law thus gives

2008, p. 32.

competition lawyers less flexibility with respect to choices of exclusion and inclusion. In the *GSK dual pricing* case, for example, the Court of Justice of the EU ("CJEU") refused to soften the *per se* rule against agreements limiting parallel imports. The defendants were trying to argue that their market division practices were neutral on prices to consumers.[8] The Court rejected the argument on the ground that nothing in Article 101(1) TFEU required proof that agreements deprive consumers of certain advantages in order to have an unlawful anti-competitive object.

The second factor is politics. Competition law is commonly said to be apolitical. In the US and more so in the EU, conventional wisdom has it that competition law enjoys substantial independence from the political influence of the legislative or executive branches. That account is incorrect. Majoritarian politics gives rise to exclusions of facts when competition law is applied. For example, in sectors where legislation imposes a form of economic regulation (such as telecoms, railways, postal services…), the duty to perform a thorough economic investigation of the empirical facts is not as demanding as in standard abuse of dominance cases. Conversely, majoritarian politics requires consideration of additional facts in the enforcement of competition law. For example, competition cases involving intellectual property regimes demand a review of additional legal facts, like whether a "*new product*" would have been invented but for a refusal to deal.[9]

The third factor is science. The law embedded in competition statutes seeks to achieve certain results. Generally, competition laws purport to deliver free, fair or undistorted competition. That "*instrumental*" nature of competition laws, as Judge Easterbrook calls it, requires agencies and courts to construe competition statutes purposively.[10] For example, specific legislation or doctrines have been developed to cover mergers and acquisitions as legal facts worthy of competition law scrutiny. The reasoning behind this is that mergers or acquisitions reduce rivalry, and in turn lead to the same risk of substantial lessening of competition that competition laws concern themselves with. Conversely, the prohibition of exploitative practices under abuse of dominance law is a legal fact that has been *de facto* read out of competition law practice. The reasoning underlying this is that a general prohibition of monopoly pricing risks producing false positives that deter entry, expansion, and innovation, and would thus contradict the objectives underwriting the law.

Both examples show that choices of inclusion and exclusion are inherently consequential. The question is whether adding or subtracting legal or empirical facts will increase or decrease market competition. With that in mind, it is no wonder why empirical disciplines focused on market structures and firm behavior like economics or business and management science inform choices of inclusion and exclusion.

The last factor is culture. US antitrust law evolved from the common law. Common law jurisdictions are more prone than other jurisdictions to place absolute

---

[8] Judgment in *GlaxoSmithKline Services and Others v Commission and Others*, C-501/06 P, C-513/06 P, C-515/06 P and C-519/06 P, EU:C:2009:610.

[9] Judgments in *RTE and ITP v Commission*, C-241/91 P and C-242/91 P, EU:C:1995:98; and in *IMS Health*, C-418/01, EU:C:2004:257.

[10] F. H. Easterbrook, 'The Inevitability of Law and Economics' (1989) 1 Legal Educ. Rev. 3.

faith in competition, and to abhor monopoly. Over the past decades, US antitrust law has leaned towards the exclusion of non-competition facts from the antitrust arena. Even progressive antitrust leaders have resisted calls to address broad public policy issues through antitrust law. In 2023, Chair Khan declared that ESG would not stop the FTC, meaning that facts about sustainability would remain excluded from antitrust consideration.[11]

In the EU, by contrast, competition is more amenable to compromise.[12] Social expediency considerations detached from competition play a role in determining liability. A more open yet limited space has been carved out to credit non-economic benefits as justifications for anticompetitive agreements under Article 101(3) TFEU. In 2023, the European Commission revised its guidelines on horizontal cooperation agreements to relax the conditions for the admission of sustainability defenses.[13]

What are the implications of viewing competition law in the way I propose? A first implication is that competition law is a complex aggregate of many incrementally consolidated epistemic choices.[14] As such, the resulting outcome cannot be solely based on ideology and if ideology does creep in it is likely to do so in a haphazard and inconsistent manner. A study of choices of inclusion and exclusion confirms this. Inconsistencies incompatible with the unified nature of ideology become visible. For example, competition law prohibits territorial market protection that is the result of an agreement between a firm and its retailers. But territorial market protection is not cognizable when organized within a vertically integrated firm. The choice of exclusion of vertical integration as a possible restraint of competition shows that if EU law embeds a pro-market integration ideology, it is not unbounded. In fact, ideology here is limited by a requirement of practice and science, which is that it would be both hard and inefficient to declare decisions internal to a firm unlawful.

Another implication is the following. An epistemic filter suggests that choices of inclusion or exclusion tend to be neutral. Adding or subtracting a legal or empirical fact to the competition inquiry will not correlate with a pro or anti enforcement outcome. Take the legal fact of ‘potential competition’. It can be both the basis for the prohibition of mergers discussed as killer acquisitions or for the exoneration of mergers owing to wider market definitions. There are two sides to every legal or empirical fact. And as I said earlier, competition law does not answer all legal concerns because it does not operate in a vacuum. It operates in an ecosystem of different branches of the law.

---

[11] L. Khan, *ESG won't stop the FTC*, Wall Street Journal, 21 Dec. 2022.

[12] R. Joliet, ‘The rule of reason in antitrust law’, Université de Liège [ULg], Faculté de droit, 1967, 198 p at p. 7.

[13] Guidelines on the applicability of Article 101 of the Treaty on the Functioning of the European Union to horizontal co-operation agreements (OJ 2023 C 259, p. 1).

[14] As the law develops incrementally through discrete choices of inclusion and exclusion shaped by multiple factors and constraints, it is hard to track all the *reasons* behind choices of inclusion or exclusion, in one case and the other.

4 Cycles of Epistemological Reexamination

Challenging competition law as a socially constructed power structure does not eliminate the need for self-reflection. Is all good and well in the current epistemological equilibrium reached by competition law? Put more concretely, is competition law's knowledge of what is a restraint of competition and what is not aligned with the truth?

The issue is dauntingly difficult. We are here at the intersection of 'truth' and 'belief'. Competition laws' knowledge of competition only covers the truth about competition that is believed. The truth about competition that is not believed tends to be ignored by competition laws. Put more simply, competition laws operate in a state of epistemological imperfection, shaped by established beliefs, superstitions, or theories.

At some points in their history, competition rules undergo cycles of epistemological reexamination. A fresh discussion arises over how much legal and empirical facts considered in positive law tell what we ought to know about competition, and its restriction. The discussion aims to remove existing beliefs about competition that are not true, or not likely to be truth, and to include some new truths about competition deemed worthy to be believed.[15]

Two illustrations can help. A first deeply anchored belief is that competition comes from substitutes, not complements. That belief leads to begin every antitrust evaluation with the study of a legal fact known as "market definition", and the examination of an empirical fact known as "demand side substitutability". But is this correct in an age where the emergence of digital 'ecosystems' brings to light a new empirical proposition: namely, that, in platform markets, ecosystem complementors compete with ecosystem leaders?

A second widely held belief of competition lawis that *fixed* cost efficiencies are not as relevant as *variable* cost efficiencies. As a result, in coordinated conduct or merger cases, the elimination of fixed cost redundancies is not deemed a cognizable efficiency gain. But is this exclusion faith-based, that is, is it not based on truth? Lack of consideration of fixed cost efficiencies by competition rules leads to blindspots. When fixed cost economies concern sunk assets, firms will repurpose the saved resources towards new investments.

The history of competition law is punctuated by cycles of epistemological reexamination. The advent of the Chicago school of antitrust in the 1960–1970s is one example. It showed that sanctioning below-cost price cuts without including an examination of likely recoupement would lead to consumer harm. The more economic approach initiated in the 2000s in the EU in relation to vertical restraints is another one. It showed that an analysis of vertical agreements detached from market power is likely to condemn efficient distribution systems.

---

[15] The legal system tries to embed more truth about competition, and to filter out beliefs from the competition truth.

Cycles of epistemological reexaminations provide opportunities to improve the law. The challenge is however to avoid substituting past superstitions with new ones. Let us look at some examples where belief undermines epistemological reexamination. The attack on the CWS as a choice of inclusion dictated by a Chicagoan neoliberal ideology is, I think, a strawman. Research shows that signs of a consumer welfare principle existed in US case-law from the 1920s, long before the Chicago school.[16] And in many cases where harm to competition is hard to observe—like in vertical agreements and mergers—the addition of a harm-to-consumer filter facilitates competition law enforcement.

Similarly, the choice of inclusion of "*innovation competition*" only as a theory of harm in merger review is likely to be fraught with ideology to the extent that it is asymmetrical.[17] If the law considers that a merger harms long term innovation through the suppression of rival research and development (R&D) pipelines, it should equally admit that a merger promotes long term innovation through the efficiency of allowing easier redirection of internal assets towards novel R&D targets.

Up to now, the triggers behind cycles of epistemological reexamination have not been discussed. In competition law, scholarship about policymaking initiatives and judicial cases is the usual source. To that extent, epistemological reexamination is mostly practice-oriented. In parallel, cycles of epistemological reexamination may be fueled by broader socio-economic or political events. The Chicago school revolution of the 1960–1970s was supported by concerns that American industries were losing out to Japan. The neo-Brandeisian movement drew much energy from the financial crisis of 2007, the Cambridge Analytica scandal, and the Trump election. And the ongoing discussions over the reorientation of competition towards competitiveness, dynamism, and innovation were reignited following the Draghi report showing that European productivity was falling behind the US in 2024.

5 Thoughtful Competition Law

In 2005, former diplomat and public international law Professor Martti Koskenniemi wrote a book titled "*From Apology to Utopia*".[18] Koskenniemi's book was mostly an attempt to stimulate a reflection seeking to disentangle the assumptions underpinning the social practice of public international law. Today, competition law is at a similar juncture. Unless we can explain what we, as competition jurists do, we risk being swayed by a description of our practice that reduces it to a more or less conscious agent of a socially constructed power structure.

[16] N. Petit, 'A theory of antitrust limits' (2020) Geo. Mason L. Rev. 28, p. 1399; and L. Radic, N. Petit, 'The Superiority of the Consumer Welfare Standard', available at SSRN (2024).

[17] N. Petit, 'Innovation competition, unilateral effects, and merger policy' (2019) Antitrust Law Journal 82.3, pp. 873-920.

[18] M. Koskenniemi, *From Apology to Utopia*, Cambridge University Press, 2005.

This essay presents a new argument: competition law is the social practice of engaging in discussions about the legal and empirical facts that determine what constitutes competition and its restrictions. As a social practice, competition law progresses through cycles of epistemological reexaminations. Episodes of self-reflexivity allow competition law to overcome dogmatism and correct injustices arising from previous inclusion and exclusion choices. An interest in the truth about competition and skepticism towards belief are necessary to keep competition law a "*thoughtful*" social practice.[19]

[19] We borrow that concept from J. Waldron, *Thoughtfulness and the Rule of Law*, Harvard University Press, 2023. Throughout the book, and especially in the opening chapter as well as chapters 4 and 5, Waldron defends, against Hayek, a view of the rule of law as being compatible with the use of standards like "reasonable". He takes it to be compatible because the rule of law cannot, so to speak, rule out the use by law's addressees of their practical intelligence about what to do in concrete circumstances on the basis that the law is vague. In the context of competition law, the use of standards by officials to judge, for example, whether mergers were *killer* acquisitions or *lawful* acquisitions proceeds, I think, in the same way.

Will European Competition Law Survive the Challenges of the Great Transformation of the World Order and Liberal Democracies?

Giovanni Pitruzzella

1 Introduction

The French geopolitical journal *Grand Continent* qualifies the era in which we live as the '*de l'interrègne*' era, using a term coined by the Italian philosopher Antonio Gramsci to refer to those historical phases in which an old social, economic and political order is in crisis but a new order has not yet emerged.[1] This great transformation cannot fail to affect competition law, given that, since its origin in the US Sherman Act of 1890, it has stood at the crossroads between the market, democracy and freedom.[2]

In the political and economic order established after the Second World War, competition law has found an important place: it has constituted an essential aspect of EU constitutional law; it has gradually become embedded in the legal systems of the Member States, playing an increasingly significant role; and it has been included among the Copenhagen criteria for the admission of new Member States. Competition law has also become a part of the Western geo-economic order, uniting the United States, Europe, and other liberal democracies, albeit with significant technical differences. After the dissolution of the USSR and the transitory establishment of a unipolar world order centred on the United States, the success of globalisation and liberal democracy, as well as the rise of neo-liberalism, fuelled the trend towards the globalisation of competition law, with notions and principles circulating from one legal system to another. The International Competition Network (ICN)

[1] Grand Continent, *Politiques de l'interrégne*, Gallimard, Paris, 2022, p. 7 ff.

[2] T. Wu, *The Curse of Bigness: Antitrust in the New Gilden Age*, Columbia, New York, 2018, p. 10 ff.

G. Pitruzzella (✉)
Corte Costituzionale, Rome, Italy

L. Prete, L. Rezki (eds.), *Judging & (Re)Thinking European Union Law*,
https://doi.org/10.1007/978-3-032-13473-8_15

was created in 2001 to function as a forum for the coordination of antitrust enforcement at the global level, with 132 states participating and representing 120 antitrust jurisdictions.

In this context, competition law has been radically separated from politics and has been entrusted with tasks concerning the functioning of the market. On both sides of the Atlantic, these tasks have been summarised since then into a single goal: 'consumer welfare', albeit with meanings that do not always coincide in the US and Europe.

Today, the liberal-democratic world order is experiencing crises and transformative pressures that cannot fail to affect competition law—an essential component of that order until now.

Proceeding in an extremely concise approach and limiting the focus to Europe, several factors of crisis and change can be identified. Some are endogenous to European competition law, deriving from tensions and conflicts between different principles and requirements that are 'intrinsic' to the European antitrust enforcement system. However, these tensions and conflicts were exacerbated during a period of rapid and widespread change. Others, on the other hand, are exogenous to that system, because they consist of political motivations to modify it, i.e. to relax its rules in order to take account of changes in the economy, technology and politics.

2 The 'More Economics-Based Approach'

In European competition law, a number of different requirements coexist and sometimes clash. On the one hand, there is the need to ensure predictability and legal certainty, and on the other, there is a need to avoid antitrust enforcement leading to contradictory outcomes with respect to economic efficiency.

The second requirement was to be met by the 'more economics-based approach'.[3] However, this approach no longer seems to be at the heart of the 'Brussels consensus'. It is criticised from a variety of perspectives. One concern is that it would not be conducive to legal certainty. When the lawfulness of a practice depends on contextual evaluation, it becomes difficult for stakeholders to anticipate the outcome of administrative action. Moreover, the case-by-case evaluation of the actual or potential effects of a practice is resource-consuming, as gathering the necessary evidence and checking it against the relevant theory of harm inevitably delays intervention. As a result of these factors, the "more economics-based approach" might lead to underenforcement. However, the rapid development of digital markets, with their tendency towards the concentration of economic power and swift evolution, has swung the pendulum of attention away from the risk of underenforcement, and

[3] P. Ibánez Colomo, *The New EU Competition Law*, Hart, Oxford, 2023, p.43 ff.

towards the risk of overenforcement. This places greater emphasis on the timing of administrative activity.[4]

Nevertheless, recent case law from the Court of Justice considers and allows for the 'more economics-based approach'. An example is offered by the judgment in the *Unilever* case.[5] The Italian Competition and Market Authority sanctioned Unilever, a producer and seller of widely consumed packaged ice creams under brands such as Algida and Carte d'Or. These are sold in places such as bars, sports clubs and public swimming pools through a network of around 150 distributors. Unilever has a dominant position in this market and, at the time in question, its distributors included an exclusivity clause in their contracts with vendors, obliging the latter to deal exclusively with Unilever for the supply of industrial ice cream. In return, the vendors obtained discounts and commissions related to the sales of specific Unilever products. According to the Italian Competition Authority, given the characteristics of the specific market—and in particular the limited space in outlets for the display of ice cream—the above conduct would have influenced consumer choice by excluding, or in any case limiting, the possibility for competitors to engage in competition based on the merits of the products.

The case presents several interesting points, including a preliminary question submitted by the judge before whom Unilever had challenged the Authority's measure. Of particular interest is the part of the question in which the judge asked the Court of Justice whether, when examining an abuse of a dominant position committed through the use of exclusivity clauses, Article 102 TFEU must be interpreted as requiring the Competition Authority to verify whether such clauses exclude an equally efficient competitor from the market. This would entail a specific obligation to assess the economic analysis produced by the interested party, particularly concerning the current capacity of the conduct under examination to exclude an equally efficient competitor from the market.

In summary, the Court's answer is that Article 102 TFEU must be interpreted to mean that, in the presence of exclusivity clauses in distribution contracts, the Competition Authority must demonstrate that these clauses are capable of restricting competition, taking into account all the relevant circumstances of the case and the economic analysis produced by the undertaking concerning the ability of the conduct to exclude equally efficient competitors from the market. While, in principle, the use of the '*as efficient competitor test*' is optional, if the results of that test are produced by the undertaking in the course of the administrative procedure, the Authority is obliged to take them into account to verify their probative value.

The Court, in its reasoning, pays formal deference to the judgment of 13 February 1979 in the *Hoffman-La Roche* case, where exclusivity clauses by a dominant undertaking were considered an exploitation of a dominant position, even if not accompanied by rebates. However, in its ruling on the Unilever case, the Court enhances the Intel precedent of 6 September 2017, according to which the

[4] Ibid., p. 63 ff.

[5] Judgment in *Unilever Italia Mkt. Operations*, C-680/20, EU:C:2023:33.

Competition Authority is required to analyse the outcome of the dominant position in the relevant market, the market shares referable to the practice in question, the conditions and agreements necessary to grant the rebates, their duration and amount. The Authority must also verify the possible existence of a strategy aimed at excluding from the market other competitors that are at least as efficient as the dominant undertaking. The Court, in the Unilever case, holds that the balancing of the favourable and unfavourable effects of the practice in question on competition can only be carried out after an analysis of the intrinsic ability of that practice to foreclose competitors that are at least as efficient.

The judgment, therefore, contains a particular enhancement of the '*as efficient competitor test*'. It is true that its use is only optional, but it seems that it is sufficient for the undertaking concerned to put forward an economic analysis based on that test in its defence in order to impose an obligation on the Competition Authority to assess the results of that test in the concrete case. Thus, reaffirming and further reinforcing what was said in the Intel case, it seems that the case law leans in favour of the '*more economics-based approach*'.

In contrast, new paradigms and analytical frameworks are emerging in the academic debate and even in administrative practice: reliance on efficiency and consumer welfare to guide enforcement has been seen as overly reductionist. In the digital markets the 'Brussels consensus' is moving towards the goal of fairness and contestable markets.[6] Suggestions from the Neo- Brandeisian movement also feature in the debate, emphasising the relationship between competition and democracy.[7]

Ultimately, competition law seems to operate on a terrain characterised by ambiguity regarding its aims, methods and limits—an ambiguity that undermines predictability, legitimacy and effectiveness. Without a clear compass, the unpredictability of the case-by-case decision may prevail, while the real usefulness of antitrust enforcement is undermined by the burden of the decision-making timeframe; too many years may pass between the start of an investigation and the Court of Justice's final ruling for it to really have an impact on market dynamics. It is sufficient to cite the timeframe of the Intel case: the investigation was launched in 2003, the decision to sanction Intel was made in 2009, the final act that definitively closed the affair—after two decisions by the Court and one by the Court of Justice—is the Court of Justice's ruling of October 2024.[8]

---

[6] P. Ibánez Colomo, *supra* n. 3, p. 68 ff.

[7] OECD, The Interaction between Competition and Democracy, 2024.

[8] Judgment in *Commission v Intel Corporation*, C-240/22 P, EU:C:2024:915CJEU.

3 Competition Law and Innovation

In public discourse, and even in certain documents about the Union's future, competition law is frequently criticized for discouraging innovation, prompting calls to amend portions of it.

The European economy is characterised by low productivity growth; therefore, it must transform itself into a more efficient economy capable of producing more value per hour of work. An important reason behind the productivity gap with the United States consists, according to the two reports signed by Enrico Letta and Mario Draghi respectively, in the fact that established European firms are not using new technologies or innovating much themselves, while small and innovative firms are often unable to grow.[9]

In his report, Draghi points out the main problem behind European low productivity growth as its stagnant business environment. Europe's largest firms are older than America's business giants, and they have focused on incremental innovation without pressure to embrace radical change. Innovation is also at the heart of Enrico Letta's report, which, after highlighting Europe's backwardness, proposes the creation of a fifth economic freedom to be added to the traditional freedoms of the Treaty: the freedom to innovate.

Europe's competition policy is perceived to hinder innovation. Over recent decades, its enforcement has been tougher than that of the US. It is supposed to be more willing to block mergers and to sanction dominant undertakings for abuse of their dominant position in the market. The goal of competition law is supposed not only to keep prices low, but also to pressure firms to innovate. It has performed the first task well. The European economy is less concentrated and less profitable than that of the US. This sounds good for consumers and social fairness. But European firms are making fewer productive investments than their US counterparts and are investing far less in research and development. In the long run, innovation benefits consumers much more than lower prices.

The relationship between innovation and competition has always been controversial among economists. Some argue that competition drives firms to innovate, while others believe that only the benefit of gaining a transitory monopoly stimulates innovation, especially disruptive innovation. Others argue that the relationship between innovation and competition is U-shaped. When market power becomes too concentrated, the firm has no incentive to innovate because it now feels secure in its position in the market, while other firms lack the strength to challenge the incumbent. Conversely, in the case where there are many firms competing neck-and-neck, they focus on reducing prices by cutting costs and are unable to take risks with innovation, lacking the scale necessary to sustain major investments. This is probably the prevailing situation in Europe to which Draghi's report refers.

---

[9] M. Draghi, The Future of European competitiveness, September 2024; and E. Letta, Much more than a Market, April 2024.

In traditional industries in which the European economy was strong, such as the automotive and mechanical engineering industries, robust antitrust enforcement was able to benefit the consumer, not least because there was incremental innovation rather than radical innovation in these sectors. By contrast, in sectors characterised by disruptive innovation, such as those of the digital economy, Europe remained weak. Its companies relied on the innovation produced by American companies, which then extended it globally.

This situation is no longer sustainable for at least three reasons. The first is that the international economic order has changed. The golden age of globalisation is over and—as will be emphasised in the next section—the economy and technology are central areas of competition between international powers, while more or less substantial barriers are being introduced to the movement of production factors between countries. In the changed order of international economic relations, the demands of security and strategic autonomy dominate. The second reason is that most of the future's growth will be connected to the new digital technologies, in which Europe is still too far behind; and without starting a path of innovation in these sectors, it risks losing the 'existential' challenge of growth. The third reason is that even mature industrial sectors, such as automotive, are now exposed to radical innovations, such as those related to batteries and electric vehicles.

Against this backdrop, both Draghi and Letta seem to be looking at the American economy, where there are large companies whose scale allows them to sustain the gamble of innovation and invest in innovative technologies. Therefore, the first rules to be questioned are those on mergers. Mergers, according to Draghi's proposal, should be allowed even if they lead to higher prices for European consumers, provided the companies themselves commit to investing more in innovation in Europe, or if such mergers are necessary to help them compete in foreign markets. Thus, the drive to create 'European champions', which in the past has seen the convergence of the German and French governments' involvement in the notorious merger between Siemens and Alstom in 2019, which was prevented by the European Commission, is a notable example of this.

A further push to revise competition law, especially merger rules, comes from the renewed focus on industrial policy. The twin transitions—digital and energy—in which the Union is engaged lead to the inclusion of green and digital transition considerations in antitrust practice. Competition Commissioner Teresa Ribera stated that it is important not just to focus on the lowest possible price when evaluating mergers, as this could result in "the lowest possible price for everything - including labour". She added that other factors—such as 'the environmental standards, innovation components, and social engagement'—should be taken into account.[10]

Actually, Draghi and Letta are aware that reforming competition law alone is not enough to foster innovation. Both emphasise the need to create an effective European capital market, to remove barriers to the full deployment of the single market, and

[10] H. Foy, 'How the EU wants to tweak its merger rules to boost growth', Financial Times, 26 February 2025.

to pursue a shrewd trade policy that opens up new markets for European companies. However, while a change in competition law is likely to gain the consensus of Member States, other reforms may face resistance and will take longer to implement. If this were to happen, it could create a competition law and policy tailored to the innovation economy, without creating real innovation, due to the continuing fragmentation of relevant parts of the internal market and the lack of capital. In other words, the risk is that of weakening antitrust enforcement, with the negative aspects of the recent American experience—high prices and limitations on consumer freedom of choice—without having the advantages in terms of investment and innovation.[11]

4 Competition Law and Political Capitalism

Competition law is also threatened by the spread of forms of 'political capitalism', which originated in authoritarian regimes (e.g., China) and is now extending to some liberal democracies, such as the United States, where the wall separating economics from politics has collapsed.

With the unipolar world order—and, with it, the golden age of globalisation—now over, geopolitics and power politics are once again dominating the international scene. The strategic competition between the US and China; the conflict between liberal democracies and autocracies, exemplified by Russia's war of aggression against Ukraine and the alliance between Russia, Iran, North Korea, and China; Turkey's Neo-Ottoman ambitions under Erdogan; and the Global South's push for a rebalancing of world order have all shaped the past decade. This jungle of turmoil is expanding globally, where force prevails over the rule-based order. Even the economy is being instrumentalised for political ends.

In this context, the expression 'political capitalism' has gained traction. The term, originally coined by Max Weber, has experienced renewed popularity today. It is used to summarise several interrelated phenomena: the use of trade, finance and technology for political ends; the designation of industries and strategic enterprises as 'enemies' on account of their geographical or economic connection to a state considered to be a systemic competitor; and competition in international bodies for technical standards. Since economist Branko Milanović identified a structural opposition between liberal meritocratic capitalism—of which Washington was the champion—and Beijing's political capitalism, political and economic realities have changed profoundly. The separation between politics and economics has also been radically challenged in the United States. Even during the Biden presidency, a remarkable consensus had formed around a post- liberal economic order, made up of a certain degree of economic protectionism (e.g., The Inflation Reduction Act

[11] Centre for European Reform, Competition policy must reflect Europe's reality, not its aspirations, by Z. Meyers, 23 October 2024.

and the CHIPS Act), a critique of the excesses of globalisation with a push towards reshoring, as well as renewed public intervention in the economy. But it was Donald Trump's second presidency (January 2025) that marked a radical turnaround, under the banner of the dominance of politics over economics, with the goal of 'Make America First Again'. The result was a trade policy aimed at dismantling multilateral relations and imposing duties on the various states calculated according to the US trade deficit with each of them.

The American presidency has followed trade policies aimed at closing world markets through tariffs, restricting foreign investment and protecting American industry from international competition. Added to this is the development of a special relationship between the presidency and tech companies, exemplified by the presence of Elon Musk in the presidential cabinet.

The EU's rules on Big Tech are a major flashpoint between Brussels and the US. The rules on digital giants have taken centre stage in the increasingly lively confrontation between the US and the EU. On the one hand, under the banner of the protection of freedom of expression as guaranteed by the First Amendment of the US Constitution, European rules on the digital economy have been accused of introducing new forms of censorship in stark contrast to American values. This criticism has fuelled a torrent of statements, among which those of Vice- President Vance stand out. At the Munich Security Conference in February 2025, he linked the permanence of the United States in NATO with overcoming European rules concerning the digital economy.

On the other hand, Donald Trump has compared the EU's fines with 'overseas extortion' and called them a 'form of taxation'. Among the rules most contested by the United States are, of course, competition rules, which—since the famous *Google Shopping* case—have been applied with particular care in digital markets and which have been joined by the *ex ante* obligations introduced by the Digital Market Act. It imposes some twenty-two obligations on digital companies and special duties on so-called 'gatekeepers', and is accompanied by a very strong sanctioning apparatus (penalties of up to 10 per cent of worldwide turnover).

In April 2025, European Commission President Ursula von der Leyen warned that it could hit US services exports, including Big Tech's operations in Europe, in retaliation for US tariffs. From this perspective, the rules on competition in digital markets would also lend themselves to 'political' use—or at least be suspected of being used as a tool to respond to the new US trade policy.

In this context, there were the first fines adopted by the commission under the DMA. The Commission fined Apple and Facebook owner Meta a total of €700 million for breaching the DMA's rules. Apple and Meta were hit with the penalties on 23 April 2025, in what is seen as a test case for the European Commission's new mandate to rein in digital gatekeepers.

The Commission fined Apple €500 million and ordered it to revise its App Store rules within two months, following an investigation into whether Apple's rules prevented app developers from sending consumers to offers outside its platform. The

Commission also imposed a further fine of €200 million on Meta and stated that the tech group must change its "pay or consent" model, which forces users to either consent to data tracking or pay a subscription fee for ad-free experience.

The Commission ruled out heavier sanctions, which would have been possible under the DMA, in an effort to avoid escalating tensions with US President Donald Trump. The EU's competition commissioner said: 'This is a very new regulation, and we are very conscious that these are the very first decisions'.[12]

Nevertheless, Apple said it would appeal and called the Commission's decision 'yet another example of Europe unfairly targeting Apple in a series of decisions that are bad for the privacy and security of users, bad for products and force us to give away our technology for free'. Meta affirmed that the Commission was attempting to 'handicap successful American businesses while allowing Chinese and European companies to operate under different standards'.

The sanctions on Apple and Meta were adopted shortly after the 90-day pause of Trump's so- called reciprocal tariff scheme, as the US and the EU sought to reach a deal to avoid a commercial war. Competition law—and its new incarnation through the DMA—runs the risk of being used, or perceived, as tools in the negotiating confrontation between the two sides of the Atlantic, bending to political logic.

5 Conclusions

At present, it is not possible to predict what impact the above-mentioned trends may have on European competition law—and thus on the relationship between markets, law and politics. One can only warn of the dangers that lie ahead.

The transformational thrusts to which competition law is subject may correspond to real needs for change, but they may also bring with them far-reaching risks. Firstly, there is the risk of a loss of effectiveness: in a confused system lacking shared references and objectives, competition law may end up serving little purpose—or worse, aggravating a situation of uncertainty. Secondly, competition law can be politicised and loaded with the most disparate aims to achieve contingent objectives. Thirdly, there is the marginalisation of antitrust enforcement, either because it is overridden by other public policies, or because it is deemed to conflict with other, overriding policy objectives.

The ultimate consequences may be the disappearance of the level playing field for competing companies, the strong concentration of economic power, distributional consequences to the detriment of the consumer and to the advantage of large companies, and the capture of the democratic political process by groups with great economic power.

[12] B. Moens, 'EU fines Apple and Meta total of euro 700mn for antitrust violations', Financial Times, 23 April 2025.

Being aware of the dangers we face is an indispensable starting point for dealing with them. But in order not to be irrelevant or wishy-washy, we must have the courage to untie some Gordian knots, such as those concerning the objectives and methods of antitrust enforcement, and the kind of relationship that is possible and desirable to maintain with the US in the midst of the great transformation we are going through.

Of Justice and Force: Advocate General Wahl's Opinions on the Commission's Powers of Investigation in Antitrust Proceedings

Luca Prete and Leila Rezki

1 Introduction

The competition rules enshrined in the EU Treaties are amongst the most essential economic rules on which the European Union is founded. The function of those rules is 'to prevent competition from being distorted to the detriment of the public interest, individual undertakings and consumers, thereby ensuring the well-being of the European Union'.[1] The existence of a system which ensures that competition is not distorted is a pre-condition for the correct functioning of the internal market,[2] the establishment of which is one of the Union's main goals.[3] It is for that reason that Article 3(1)(b) TFEU lists 'the establishing of the competition rules necessary for the functioning of the internal market' as one of the areas in which the Union enjoys exclusive competence.

As regards the competition rules applicable to undertakings, Articles 101 and 102 TFEU occupy a central position within the EU Treaties. Those provisions prohibit anticompetitive agreements and abuses of dominant position, respectively. The Treaties do not, however, include any provision concerning the enforcement of those provisions. The main rules on enforcement are currently set out in Regulation

[1] See, to that effect, judgments in *Roquette Frères*, C-94/00, EU:C:2002:603, para. 42, and *TeliaSonera Sverige*, C-52/09, EU:C:2011:83, paras 20–22.

[2] See Protocol No 27 on the internal market and competition, annexed to the Treaty of Lisbon (OJ 2010 C 83, p. 309).

[3] Article 3(3) TEU.

L. Prete · L. Rezki (✉)
Court of Justice of the European Union, Luxembourg, Luxembourg
e-mail: Luca.Prete@curia.europa.eu; Leila.Rezki@curia.europa.eu

L. Prete, L. Rezki (eds.), *Judging & (Re)Thinking European Union Law*,
https://doi.org/10.1007/978-3-032-13473-8_16

No 1/2003[4]—the instrument that replaced Regulation No 17 of 1962,[5] which had been in force for over 40 years.[6]

To enable the Commission to fulfil its task, set out in Article 105(1) TFEU, to ensure the application of the Treaty rules on competition, Regulation No 1/2003 endows it with a number of investigative tools. The powers of investigation provided for in Chapter V of that Regulation are as follows: to carry out investigations into sectors of the economy and into types of agreements (Article 17), to send requests for information (Article 18), to take statements (Article 19) and to conduct inspections (Articles 20 and 21). Altough the burden of proving an infringement of EU competition rules rests on the Commission,[7] undertakings subject to measures of investigation are nonetheless under a duty to cooperate actively with that institution.[8]

According to settled case-law, the Commission enjoys broad discretion in the exercise of its powers of investigation, inter alia as regards the decision to use those powers[9] and, if it does, the appropriate moment to do so[10] and the relevant facts to investigate.[11] However, it does not enjoy *unfettered* discretion in that regard, since the way it uses its powers of investigation is subject to a number of limitations.[12] First, the Commission mustis to apply Articles 17 to 21 of Regulation No 1/2003 in compliance with the general principles of EU law (such as the principle of proportionality), which form part of EU primary law. Second, since *Hoffmann-La Roche*, the Court recognized that 'the right of defence is a fundamental principle of European Union law which must be complied with even if the proceedings in question are administrative'.[13] As made clear by Recital 37 of Regulation No 1/2003, the the Commission must ensure therespect of fundamental rights and the principles recognised, in particular, by the EU Charter of Fundamental Rights ('Charter') in the exercise of its powers. In that regard, it should not be overlooked that, despite the wording of Article 23(5) of Regulation No 1/2003—according to which decisions imposing fines for infringements of competition rules are not of a criminal law

[4] Council Regulation (EC) 1/2003 of 16 December 2002 on the implementation of the rules on competition laid down in Articles 81 [EC] and 82 [EC] (OJ 2003 L 1, p. 1).

[5] Council Regulation (EEC) 17 of 6 February 1962: First Regulation implementing Articles 85 and 86 of the Treaty (OJ, English Special Edition 1959–1962, p. 87).

[6] For some recent contributions on this topic, see W. Wils, *EU Antitrust Enforcement: Law, Economics, History, Policy & Practice*, Concurrences, 2024, pp. 1–21.

[7] Article 2 of Regulation No 1/2003.

[8] See judgment in *Orkem v Commission*, 374/87, EU:C:1989:387, para. 27.

[9] See judgments in *Solvay v Commission*, 27/88, EU:C:1989:388, paras 12–13, and *Orkem v Commission,* 374/87, EU:C:1989:387, paras 15–16.

[10] See, to that effect, judgments in *Automec v Commission*, T-24/90, EU:T:1992:97, para. 77; and *Ufex and Others v Commission*, C-119/97 P, EU:C:1999:116, para. 88.

[11] See, to that effect, judgment in *AM & S Europe v Commission*, 155/79, EU:C:1982:157, para. 17.

[12] See, in particular, Van Bael & Bellis, *Competition Law of the European Union*, 6th ed., Wolters Kluwer 2021, pp. 1034–1056.

[13] See judgment in *Hoffmann-La Roche v. Commission*, 85/76, EU:C:1979:36, para. 9.

nature—, penalties imposed on undertakings for infringements of EU competition rules are generally considered to fall within the realm of criminal law.[14]

If that is the case, the rights provided for in Article 47 (right to an effective remedy and to a fair trial), Article 48 (presumption of innocence and right of defence), Article 49 (principles of legality and proportionality of criminal offences and penalties) and Article 50 (*ne bis in idem*) of the Charter acquire particular significance in respect of the undertakings subject to an investigation. Moreover, given the importance of the matter, it is not surprising that the Court had already affirmed, in its pre-Charter case-law, that the Commission was under a duty to respect fundamental rights, and in particular the right of defence, when investigating possible breaches of Articles 101 and 102 TFEU.[15] Moreover, the Court had also expressly recognised, *inter alia*,[16] the right not to incriminate oneself,[17] the presumption of innocence,[18] as well as the principles of legality[19] and non-retroactivity.[20] More generally, the Court has consistently held that the need to protect individuals against *arbitrary* or *disproportionate* intervention by public authorities into their private activities, including when those authorities are enforcing competition rules, is a general principle of EU law.[21] That principle is also set out in Article 7 of the Charter, under which '[e]veryone has the right to respect for his or her private and family life, home and communications'. A measure of investigation is arbitrary when adopted in the absence of facts capable of justifying the interference with the fundamental rights of an undertaking,[22] and disproportionate when it constitutes an excessive and, thus, intolerable interference with those rights.[23]

[14] See, inter alia, Opinion of AG Sharpston, in *KME Germany and Others v Commission*, C-272/09 P, EU:C:2011:63, points 64–67; and judgment in *Air Canada v Commission*, T-9/11, EU:T:2015:994, para. 33. See also judgment of the EFTA Court in *Posten Norge v ESA*, E-15/10, 2012 EFTA Ct Rep 246, paras 87–88. In legal scholarship, see J. Kokott, H-P Nehl, 'Are there any Limits to Unlimited Jurisdiction?—Judicial Review of Commission Discretion in Setting Fines for Breaches of EU Competition Rules', in D. H. Ginsburg, T. Eicke (eds), *Judicial Review of Competition Cases*, Concurrences, 2023, pp. 113–114; and W. Wils, *op. cit.*, p. 158. Cf also K. Lenaerts, 'Due Process in Competition Cases' (2013) 1 NZKart 5, 175.

[15] See e.g. judgments in *Hoechst v Commission*, 46/87, EU:C:1989:337, paras 13–15; and *Orkem v Commission*, paras 32–33.

[16] For a more complete overview of the procedural rights recognised by the EU Courts in the context of antitrust proceedings, see W. Wils, *op. cit.*, p. 177–178; D. Bailey, L. E. John (eds), *Bellamy & Child - European Union Law of Competition*, 7th ed., OUP, 2018, pp. 1125–1129; and A. Scordamaglia-Tousis, Chapter 11, in E. Rousseva (ed.), *EU Antitrust Procedure*, OUP, 2020, pp. 337–410.

[17] See judgment in *Orkem v Commission*, para. 35.

[18] See judgment in *Hüls v Commission*, C-199/92 P, EU:C:1999:358, para. 149.

[19] See judgment in *Dansk Rørindustri and Others v Commission*, C-189/02 P, EU:C:2005:408, paras 217–218.

[20] Ibid., para. 202.

[21] See judgments in *Hoechst v Commission*, para. 19, and *Roquette Frères*, paras 27, 50 and 52.

[22] See judgments in *Dow Chemical Ibérica and Others v Commission*, 97/87 to 99/87, EU:C:1989:380, para 52; and *Roquette Frères*, para. 55.

[23] See, to that effect, judgment in *Roquette Frères*, paras 76 and 80 and the case law cited.

Some authors suggest that the case law on competition law procedures has been characterized by a progressively greater attention given by the EU Courts to the undertakings' rights of the defence.[24] In many cases, the analysis carried out by the Advocates General in their Opinions has shaped the reasoning of the Court and in particular its interpretation of the provisions of Regulation No 1/2003.[25]

The present contribution aims at briefly illustrating Advocate General ('AG') Wahl's key contribution to the development of the EU case-law in this field, namely in relation to requests for information, power to take statements and powers of inspection.

2 Requests for Information

The Commission's power to request information, set out in Article 18 of Regulation No 1/2003, includes the right to request undertakings and associations of undertakings—by simple request or by decision[26]—to provide 'all necessary information', meaning to provide answers to specific questions and disclose documents in their possession.[27] Notably, the Commission may address a decision, which is an act having binding effect pursuant to Article 288 TFEU, to *any* undertaking (or association thereof) which might hold relevant information, irrespective of its involvement in the suspected infringement. The information requested must be *necessary* for the Commission to give effect to Articles 101 and 102 TFEU. In order to allow the recipients of requests for information to assess the scope of their duty to cooperate and, at the same time, safeguard their rights of defence, the Commission must indicate the *legal basis* and the *purpose* of the request in the decision.[28]

In the *Cement* cases, the Court was given the opportunity to provide further clarifications on the Commission's powers under Article 18 of Regulation No 1/2003.[29] In 2008 and 2009, the Commission carried out a number of inspections at the prem-

[24] See, for example, M. Bernatt, M. Knapp, 'Rights of Defence: An overview of EU and national case law', 15 November 2024, e-Competitions, Art. N° 121144.

[25] G. Pitruzzella, "The EU Competition Procedures from the Perspective of an Advocate General", in K. Dekeyser, C. Gauer, J. Laitenberger, N. Wahl, W. Wils, L. Prete (eds), *Regulation 1/2003 and EU Antitrust Enforcement: A Systematic Guide*, Kluwer, 2023.

[26] In the present paper we shall not deal with the Commission's power to request information 'by simple request'. For detailed and exhaustive reviews of the Commission's powers under Article 18 of Regulation No 1/2003, see A. Geulette, M. Scholz, Comment to Article 18, in K. Dekeyser, C. Gauer, J. Laitenberger, N. Wahl, W. Wils, L. Prete (eds), *op. cit.*. pp. 429–440; and A. Lamadrid, M. Kellerbauer, Chapter 7, in L. Ortiz Blanco (ed.), *EU Competition Procedure*, 4th ed., 2021, pp. 389–412.

[27] See judgments in *Commission* v *SGL Carbon*, C-301/04 P, EU:C:2006:432, para. 41; and *Aalborg Portland and Others* v *Commission*, C-204/00 P etc., EU:C:2004:6, para. 61.

[28] See, generally, judgment in *Roquette Frères*, para. 47 and the case-law cited.

[29] On some of the issues raised in the *Cement* cases before the judgments of the Court, see C. Kerse, N. Khan, *EU Antitrust Procedure*, 6th ed., Sweet&Maxwell, 2012, pp. 112 ff.

ises of several companies active in the cement industry. Those inspections were followed by a number of requests for information and, in December 2010, by the opening of proceedings. Subsequently, in March 2011, the Commission addressed a number of decisions to several companies, requiring them to complete a questionnaire. The Commission also annexed to its request a set of instructions and some templates illustrating the manner in which it expected the information to be provided. The questionnaire was comprised of nearly 100 pages and multiple sets of questions and sub-questions. The questions posed were 'extraordinarily numerous and cover[ed] very diverse types of information', such as the quantity and costs of CO2 emissions of production facilities, the means of transport and distance travelled for shipments of the goods sold, the type of packaging used for the shipments, the transport and insurance costs for those shipments, statistics regarding building permits, customers' VAT numbers, the technology and fuel used in the production facilities, and the costs of repair and maintenance of those facilities.[30] Moreover, some questions 'concerned a particularly significant amount of information over a 10-year period'. In total, the annexes formed 'almost 30 pages of extremely detailed instructions', including several tables that had to be filled in.[31]

A number of those companies challenged the Commission's decisions before the General Court arguing, inter alia, that the requests were disproportionate and the information requested was unnecessary for the purposes of the investigation. Their applications were, however, by and large dismissed at first instance. Some of those companies then filed an appeal before the Court of Justice. In four Opinions, all delivered on the same day, AG Wahl proposed that the Court set aside the judgments under appeal and annul the contested decisions.

First, he took the view that, in the light of the stage of the procedure at which the contested decisions were adopted, the statement of reasons contained therein, which had to indicate the 'purpose' of the inspection, was *unclear and to some extent ambiguous*. In that regard, he considered that it was 'important to enable [the recipients of a request for information] to grasp the reasons for that act without an excessive interpretative effort, so that they can exercise their rights effectively and in good time'. Furthermore, the undertakings in question could not gain any more clarity by looking at the subject-matter of the questions posed: the AG found it 'extremely difficult to identify a connecting thread between many of the questions included in the questionnaire'. Moreover, he added that some of the questions did not seem to be fully in line with what was stated in the earlier decisions to initiate proceedings, which was another source of confusion and uncertainty. Accordingly, he took the view that the statement of reasons in the contested decisions did not, on the one hand, enable the addressees to exercise their rights of defence and assess

[30] See, in particular, Opinion of AG Wahl in *HeidelbergCement v Commission,* C-247/14 P, EU:C:2015:694, point 46.

[31] Ibid, points 46 and 115.

their duty to cooperate with the Commission nor did it, on the other hand, permit the exercise of judicial review by the EU Courts.[32]

Second, AG Wahl was of the opinion that the contested decisions breached the *principle of proportionality* insofar as they created an 'excessively and unreasonably onerous' workload for the appellants. In addition to the significant quantity and diversity of data requested, the AG took issue with the *format* imposed by the Commission for the submissions of the information requested which was quite complex to understand and time-consuming to comply with. He considered that, 'even to an experienced businessman, the format in question would, at first glance, appear to be a brain-racking puzzle'. More importantly, the Commission required the recipient undertakings to format and re-format data (including some that had previously been submitted, and some that were in the public domain) which, in principle, should have been carried out by the Commission. Obviously undertakings cannot submit the requested information in a 'chaotic, unsystematic or fragmented manner'—he argued. On the other hand, however, the Commission cannot—he went on to point out—require the recipients 'to carry out such extensive, complex and time-consuming clerical and administrative tasks when submitting the information requested that the building of a case against [them] appears effectively "outsourced" to the undertaking[s] under investigation'.

For that reason, AG Wahl also took the view that—*third*—the General Court had erred in its interpretation of the concept of 'information' within the meaning of Article 18 of Regulation No 1/2003.[33]

Fourth, AG Wahl also considered that the Commission decisions failed to comply with the 'necessity' criterion set out in Article 18 of the regulation. In that regard, he argued that the term 'necessary' in that provision 18 is to be understood as meaning that a *sufficiently close* correlation must exist between the information requested and the presumed infringement such that the Commission could reasonably suppose, at the time of the request, that the information would help it to carry out its duties in the context of an ongoing investigation. However, he observed that the purpose of a request for information is not to bring to light *any* possible infringement of EU competition rules in a given sector or by a given undertaking. Indeed, Article 18 requires the Commission to be in possession of a number of indicia which lead it to suspect the existence of certain specific infringements. In this context, AG Wahl made clear that the lack of concrete indicia does not mean that the Commission is denied the possibility of making inquiries where it considers that some markets do not function properly. In fact, Article 17 of Regulation No 1/2003 permits the Commission to investigate sectors of the economy or types of agreements across various economic sectors where the trend of trade between Member States, the rigidity of prices or other circumstances suggest that competition may be restricted or distorted within the internal market. However, he pointed out that Article 17

---

[32] Ibid., points 31–55.

[33] Ibid., points 98–123. See also Opinion of AG Wahl in *Buzzi Unicem v Commission*, C-267/14 P, EU:C:2015:696, points 97–117.

differs from Article 18. The latter article—under which the contested decisions had been adopted—does not allow the Commission to request information 'on a speculative basis without having any actual suspicions'. In the cases at hand, the AG took the view that the General Court had embraced an overly lax concept of 'necessity' and that the contested decisions did not permit to verify whether the vast amount of information requested was necessary for the Commission to investigate specific forms of conduct in respect of which it had concrete indicia.[34]

Fifth, AG Wahl also came to the conclusion that the General Court had (i) erred in its assessment of the scope of the right to avoid self-incrimination in EU competition law, and (ii) failed to censure the Commission for the questions which the first instance judges had in fact found to be self-incriminatory. In particular, he rejected the General Court's contention whereby a distinction should be drawn between questions which can be classified as 'purely factual' and those which cannot because the former could never lead to a breach of that right. He argued that the fact that no information of a subjective nature is asked of an undertaking does not exclude the possibility that, in certain circumstances, that undertaking's right to avoid self-incrimination may be breached. In his view, 'what is key is whether an answer from the undertaking to which the question is addressed is in fact *equivalent* to the admission of an infringement'. He came to the conclusion that certain questions posed to the appellants in question did in fact breach their right to avoid self-incrimination.[35]

Sixth and last, AG Wahl found that, as argued by one of the appellants, the Commission had erred in choosing one of the addressees of the request for information. The Commission had, for some unexplained reason, sent its request for information to a company which merely held shares in (and acted as holding company for) the companies suspected of having infringed Article 101 TFEU. Indeed, it would have been easier and faster to obtain the same information from the latter companies, which had previously been in contact with the Commission whichwere, thus, well known to itt. That choice generated extra work and costs for the companies concerned, and increased uncertainty for the appellant.[36]

On 10 March 2016, in four almost identical decisions,[37] the Court annulled the judgments under appeal and the contested decisions. Following the Opinions of AG Wahl, the Court found the statement of reasons in the decisions at issue to be excessively brief, vague, generic and, in some respects, ambiguous. In particular, the decisions did not set out, with the minimum degree of clarity, the subject matter of

[34] See, in particular, Opinion of AG Wahl in *HeidelbergCement v Commission*, points 70–95.

[35] Ibid., points 149–168. See also P. Van Cleynenbreugel, 'The right to avoid self-incrimination: Yet another elephant in the automated competition law enforcement room?' (2024) European Papers, pp. 978-997.

[36] See Opinion of AG Wahl in *Italmobiliare v Commission*, C-268/14 P, EU:C:2015:697, points 27–52.

[37] Judgments in *HeidelbergCement v Commission*, C-247/14 P, EU:C:2016:149; *Schwenk Zement v Commission*, C-248/14 P, EU:C:2016:150; *Buzzi Unicem v Commission*, C-267/14 P, EU:C:2016:151; and *Italmobiliare v Commission*, C-268/14 P, EU:C:2016:152.

the investigation, the alleged infringements, and the suspicions that the Commission intended to investigate. The Court therefore found that the parties had been unable to determine whether the information requested was 'necessary' within the meaning of Article 18 of Regulation No 1/2003. Consequently, such a statement of reasons could not justify requests for information that were sent more than 2 years after the first inspections, several months after the decision to initiate proceedings, and after the Commission had already sent a number of requests for information. FHowever, the Court did not rule on the other grounds of appeal put forward by the appellants, arguably for reasons of judicial economy.

The innovative aspects and the potentially significant impact of those decisions were immediately noted by legal scholars and practitioners,[38] which praised the guidance provided by AG Wahl's 'sensible and balanced contribution'.[39] The Court's findings were also confirmed in subsequent case-law of the EU Courts. An example of this is the *Qualcomm I* case,[40] in which the EU Courts had to review the validity of a request for information sent by the Commission in the course of its investigation concerning possible predatory pricing on the part of Qualcomm. The applicant alleged, inter alia, that the Commission decision lacked an adequate statement of reasons and did not meet the requirements of necessity and proportionality. It should be noted that, at several points in the judgment, the General Court expressly refers to AG Wahl's Opinions in the cement cases.[41] Furthermore, in *Meta Platform/ Facebook*[42] and in *Qualcomm II*,[43] the principles developed in the cement cases (such as the preclusion of 'fishing expeditions') have been taken into account by the EU Courts when assessing the lawfulness of requests for information issued in the

[38] See e.g. F. Carloni, G. Da Costa, 'Judgments in the Cement Case: Requirement for Greater Clarity, Specificity, and Justification of Information Requests from the Commission' (2016) *Journal of European Competition Law & Practice*, pp. 456–457; K. Le Croy, 'Cracks in the Finish: Affirming Fundamental Rights in the Cement Cartel Case', *Competition Policy International*, June 2016; and K. Havu, 'Duty to State Reasons and Competition Investigation Information Request Decisions: the Cement Judgments' (2016) Review of European administrative law, pp. 43–59. See also OECD, Global Forum on Competition, Investigative Poewers in Practice, 'Requests for Information: Limits and Effectivenerss, 2018, pp. 5-6.

[39] See e.g. A. Lamadrid, 'On the Commission's powers to request information (II) - Opinion of AG Wahl in case C-247/14 P, Heidelberg Cement', Chillin' Competition, 23 October 2015. See also P. Citron, 'The EU Advocate General Nils Wahl recommends the avoidance of "fishing expeditions" during dawn-raid (Deutsche Bahn)', 12 February 2015, e-Competitions, Art. N° 71836.

[40] Judgment in *Qualcomm and Qualcomm Europe v Commission*, T-371/17, EU:T:2019:232, paras 37–46, confirmed on appeal in judgment *Qualcomm and Qualcomm Europe v Commission*, C-466/19 P, EU:C:2021:76). See also order in *Qualcomm and Qualcomm Europe v Commission*, T-371/17 R, EU:T:2017:485 (interim measures).

[41] Judgment in *Qualcomm and Qualcomm Europe v Commission*, T-371/17, EU:T:2019:232, paras 46, 138 and 171.

[42] Judgments in *Meta Platforms Ireland v Commission,* T-451/20, EU:T:2023:276 and T-452/20 EU:T:2023:277, currently under appeal (C-496/23 P and C-497/23 P). See also order in *Facebook Ireland v Commission*, T-451/20 R, EU:T:2020:515 (interim measures).

[43] Judgment of 18 September 2024, *Qualcomm v Commission (Qualcomm – Predation)*, T-671/19, EU:T:2024:626, currently under appeal (C-819/24 P).

context of antitrust investigations. In fact, both the judgments of the Court and the Opinions of AG Wahl in the *cement* cases have been expressly referred to in those decisions. Interestingly, a number of references to the AG Wah's Opinions in those cases are also found in judgments of the General Court and in the Opinions of AGs which do not concern requests for information issued under Article 18 of Regulation No 1/2003, but concern other types of investigatory measures adopted by the Commission (or other EU institutions) either in the field of antitrust or in other areas of activity.[44]

3 Power to Take Statements

It is generally acknowledged, in particular in Anglo-American legal systems, that the competent authorities hearings may conduct hearings at different stages of competition law enforcement procedures. However, the procedures beforer the European Commission are primarily carried out in a written form. Therefore, the power to take statements—set out in Article 19 of Regulation No 1/2003—is considered by some to be merely a 'complementary tool' among the different investigatory powers provided for in that regulation.[45] It is thus unsurprising that the relevant legal provisions include little detail on the manner in which that power is to be exercised.

Recital 25 of Regulation No 1/2003 simply states that the Commission should, in particular, be empowered to interview any persons who may be in possession of useful information and to record the statements made. Article 19(1) of that regulation provides: 'In order to carry out the duties assigned to it by this Regulation, the Commission may interview any natural or legal person who consents to be interviewed for the purpose of collecting information relating to the subject-matter of an investigation.' In turn, Article 19(2) specifies: 'Where an interview pursuant to paragraph 1 is conducted in the premises of an undertaking, the Commission shall inform the competition authority of the Member State in whose territory the

[44] See judgments in *České dráhy v Commission*, T-325/16, EU:T:2018:368, para. 40; in *Casino, Guichard-Perrachon and AMC v Commission*, T-249/17, EU:T:2020:458, para 111; and in *Red Bull and Others v Commission*, T-306/23, EU:T:2025:959, para. 43; Opinion of AG Pikamäe in *Consob*, C-481/19, EU:C:2020:861, footnote 55; Opinion of AG Pitruzzella in *Casino, Guichard-Perrachon and AMC v Commission,* C-690/20 P, EU:C:2022:579, footnote14; Opinion of AG Szpunar in *PACCAR and Others*, C-163/21, EU:C:2022:286, paras 97 and 101. See also Opinion of AG Medina in *Ryanair and Airport Marketing Services v Commission*, C-758/21 P, EU:C:2023:274, pars 66–74, who applied the principles devolving form the cement case-law, by analogy, to the procedural rules regarding state aid control; and judgment in *PNB Banka v ECB*, T-275/19, EU:T:2022:781, para. 163, in which the General Court referred to one of the Opinions of AG Wahl in a case which concerned a challenge to the validity of a decision of the ECB ordering a bank to subject to an on-site inspection.

[45] See P. Berbel Fernández, T.P. Maass, Comment to Article 19, in K. Dekeyser, C. Gauer, J. Laitenberger, N. Wahl, W. Wils, L. Prete (eds), *op. cit.*, pp. 441 ff. see also A. Colombani, J. Kloubt, E. Sakkers, Chapter 8, in J. Faull, A. Nikpay (eds), *The EU Law of Competitioni*, 3rd ed., 2014, pp. 1168–1172.

interview takes place. If so requested by the competition authority of that Member State, its officials may assist the officials and other accompanying persons authorised by the Commission to conduct the interview.'

Recital 3 of Regulation (EC) No 773/2004[46] explains that, when the Commission conducts interviews, the persons interviewed ought to be informed of the purpose of the interview and of any record which may be made. Article 3 of that regulation, which supplements Article 19 of Regulation No 1/2003, provides:

1. Where the Commission interviews a person with his consent in accordance with Article 19 of Regulation [No 1/2003], it shall, at the beginning of the interview, state the legal basis and the purpose of the interview, and recall its voluntary nature. It shall also inform the person interviewed of its intention to make a record of the interview.
2. The interview may be conducted by any means including by telephone or electronic means.
3. The Commission may record the statements made by the persons interviewed in any form. A copy of any recording shall be made available to the person interviewed for approval. Where necessary, the Commission shall set a time-limit within which the person interviewed may communicate to it any correction to be made to the statement.

The well-known *Intel I* case[47] was the first dispute, brought before the Court,[48] that raised questions concering the nature and scope of the Commission's power to take statements under Article 19 of Regulation No 1/2003. We must not lose sight of the fact that, although the core aspect of that case concerned the assessment of the loyalty rebates under Article 102 TFEU and the question of a more 'effects-based approach',[49] this case also raised novel and important procedural issues with respect to that investigative power.

---

[46] Regulation (EC) No 773/2004 of 7 April 2004 relating to the conduct of proceedings by the Commission pursuant to Articles 81 and 82 [EC] (OJ 2004 L 123, p. 18).

[47] Judgment in *Intel v Commission*, C-413/14 P, EU:C:2017:632.

[48] Prior to this case, the General Court had the opportunity to provide some indications. In *FMC Foret*, it was clarified that the Commission is not obliged to take statements under Article 19 of Regulation 1/2003. The Commission is required to hear natural or legal persons who have a sufficient interest only in so far as such persons actually apply to be heard. The Commission therefore has a reasonable margin of discretion to decide how expedient it may be to hear persons whose evidence may be relevant to the investigation. The guarantee of the rights of the defence does not require the Commission to hear witnesses put forward by the parties concerned, where it considers that the investigation of the case has been sufficient. The General Court also pointed out that, since the procedure before the Commission is purely an administrative procedure, the Commission is not required to afford the undertaking concerned the opportunity to cross-examine a particular witness and to analyze his statements at the investigation stage. It is sufficient that the statements used by the Commission were provided in the file sent to the applicant, who is able to challenge them before the EU judicature (judgment in *FMC Foret v Commission*, T-191/06, EU:T:2011:277, paras 137 and 139).

[49] As regards AG Wahl's contribution on the substantive issues, see, for example, P. Ibáñez Colomo, 'AG Wahl in Intel, or the value of realism and consistency in the context of Article 102 TFEU',

In May 2009, after almost 10 years of investigation, the Commission adopted a decision in which it found that Intel had abused its dominant position by implementing a strategy aimed at foreclosing a competing company from the market for a specific type of microprocessors, and imposed on Intel the (then) ground-breaking fine of EUR 1.1 billion. One of the Commission's complaints concerned alleged fidelity rebates granted by Intel to Dell and three other companies.

During the administrative procedure which led to the adoption of the contested decision, the Commission held a meeting with a senior executive of Dell without taking minutes or otherwise recording the meeting. When Intel asked about that meeting, the Commission first denied that such a meeting had taken place. It admitted this only after Intel had demonstrated the existence of an indicative list of topics concerning the meeting in question. At that point in time, the Commission continued to deny that a record had been made of it. Some months later, however, the Hearing Officer acknowledged that a note to the file existed but pointed out that the appellant did not have a right of access to that note. Nevertheless, the Commission sent a copy of the non-confidential version of the note to Intel 'as a matter of courtesy'. That copy was heavily redacted.

Only during the proceedings before the General Court—in which it challenged the lawfulness of the Commission's final decision—was Intel finally able to obtain a confidential version of that note, following an order to that effect by the General Court. In those proceedings, Intel argued that its right of access to the file had been infringed and so, as a consequence, had its rights of defence. However, the General Court rejected that claim, in essence endorsing the Commission's view that the meeting in question was only an informal interview, and thus did not need to be recorded in accordance with Article 19 of Regulation No 1/2003. Nevertheless, the General Court did find a breach of the right to good administration although, in its view, that procedural irregularity was cured by the fact that, during the administrative procedure, a non-confidential version of the note to the file was made available to Intel, which was also given the opportunity to submit its observations on that document.[50]

On appeal, Intel alleged a procedural error resulting from an incorrect interpretation of Article 19 of Regulation No 1/2003, read in conjunction with Article 3 of Regulation No 773/2004, concerning the absence of an obligation to record an interview. In essence, Intel argued that the General Court erred in law in concluding that no procedural error had taken place regarding the 2006 meeting with the Dell executive. In that regard, Intel claimed, first, that the General Court erred in holding that the meeting in question was not an interview within the meaning of Article 19 of

Concurrences 2017 n° 1 pp. 17–20; J. Clarke: 'The Opinion of AG Wahl in the Intel Rebates Case: A Triumph of Substance over Form?', *World Competition,* 2017 n° 2 p. 241–269; D. Geradin, 'The opinion of AG Wahl in Intel: bringing coherence and wisdom into the CJEU's pricing abuses case-law', TILEC Discussion Paper No. 2016–034, available at SSRN.COM; and M. Cole, 'No data, no abuse: the lesson from Intel's "more economic approach"' (2023) *European Competition Law Review* pp. 419–428.

[50] Judgment in *Intel v Commission*, T-286/09, EU:T:2014:547, paras 601–664.

Regulation No 1/2003. Second, it contended that the General Court erred in considering that although the Commission ought to have recorded the meeting in question due to its importance, the breach of the principle of good administration that that failure entailed was cured by the fact that Intel had been given access to a non-confidential version of the Commission's note to the file. Third, it argued that the General Court erred in its assessment in the alternative as to whether such a procedural error could lead to the annulment of the contested decision.

In his Opinion,[51] AG Wahl carried out a meticulous analysis of the above issues. He started by observing that the power to take statements is a logical corollary of the Commission's wide investigative powers under Regulation No 1/2003, but that such power is not without limits. First, Article 19(1) of the regulation requires the Commission to obtain consent prior to conducting its interviews and, second, that they are (only) carried out for the purposes of collecting information relating to the subject matter of an investigation. AG Wahl further considered that, under Article 3(1) and (3) of Regulation 773/2004, the Commission is under a legal obligation to record interviews so that it cannot omit to record the substance of that interview. The Commission remains, however, free to choose how to record it (that is, the medium to be employed). He then observed that the General Court had distinguished between 'informal' and 'formal' interviews, but that no such distinction exists in the legislative framework laid down by Regulation No 1/2003. He considered that distinction to be highly problematic. According to him, devising, by way of judicial construction, a new tool with which the Commission could conduct its investigations would amount to circumventing the rules that the legislature had put in place to regulate the powers granted to that institution in the context of investigations relating to infringements of competition rules. Consequently, AG Wahl considered that any meeting with a third party that is specifically arranged in order to collect substantive information for the assessment of a case must fall within the scope of Article 19 of Regulation No 1/2003. That does not imply—he added—that the Commission could never contact third parties informally: where exchanges between the Commission and third parties do not relate to the subject matter of a particular (usually ongoing) investigation, no obligation to record such exchanges exists.

In its judgment, the Court agreed with the interpretation of Article 19 suggested by AG Wahl, thus censuring the General Court's assessment in that regard. In particular, the Court found nothing to support the view that the EU legislature had intended to establish a distinction between two categories of interviews relating to the subject matter of an investigation or to exclude some of those interviews from the scope of that provision. The General Court had therefore erred in considering that a distinction had to be made between *formal* and *informal* interviews. The interview with the Dell executive should, thus, have been recorded. Next, the Court rejected the argument that, by providing Intel with the non-confidential version of

[51] Opinion of Advocate General Wahl in *Intel Corporation v Commission*, C-413/14 P, EU:C:2016:788, paras 226–234.

the internal note concering the meeting during the administrative procedure, the Commission had remedied the omission resulting from the failure to record the interview.[52]

That said, unlike AG Wahl, the Court did not find the General Court's error in law invalidated the contested decision. Despite the General Court's misinterpretation of the legal provision, Intel had not—the Court held—managed to prove that the non-disclosure of the documents in question was able to influence, to its detriment, the course of the procedure and the content of the Commission's decision. The Court observed, first, that during the administrative procedure Intel was provided not only with the non-confidential version of the internal note drawn up by the Commission, but also with a 'follow-up document' containing Dell's written responses to oral questions put to its executive during that interview. In addition, the Court pointed out that, although Intel was able to submit, during the proceedings before the General Court, its observations in the light of the confidential version of that internal note, it had not adduced any evidence to suggest that the Commission had failed to record, during that interview, exculpatory evidence which could have been useful in its defence. Finally, the Court emphasised that Intel had also failed to make use of the possibility of requesting that the Dell executive be summoned before the General Court. Nor had Intel been able to show—the Court added—that it had attempted to contact that executive in order to clarify the type of information discussed during the interview.[53]

The Court's findings in *Intel I* with regard to the Commission's power under Article 19 proved to be consequential, as they have been confirmed and further developed in subsequent case-law. That was so, in particular, in the *French Supermarket* cases. In those cases, the General Court had taken the view that the requirement to record interviews did not apply before the Commission choose to open the investigation. Nevertheless, the General Court added that those interviews could become evidence even if not recorded, from the date on which they took place (and not from the point at which they were reported, as the applicants had argued).[54] On appeal, the Court disagreed with the General Court. The Court observed that the Commission is required to record any interview that it conducts in order to collect information relating to the subject matter of an investigation. The obligation in question thus applies irrespective of whether the interview in question is conducted before the formal opening of an investigation, in order to collect *indicia* of an infringement, or afterwards, for the purpose of collecting evidence of an infringement. In that context, the Court added that the Commission may record the interviews in any form, including oral, thereby ensuring the effectiveness and speed

[52] Judgment in *Intel v Commission,* C-413/14 P, EU:C:2017:632, paras 84–93.

[53] Ibid., paras 94–102. Generally, on the consequences of procedural errors made by the Commission during competition procedures, see Opinion of AG Emiliou in *HSBC Holding v Commission,* C-883/19 P, EU:C:2022:384, points 38-59.

[54] Judgments in *Casino, Guichard-Perrachon and AMC v Commission,* T-249/17, EU:T:2020:458; *Intermarché Casino Achats v* Commission, T-254/17, EU:T:2020:459; and *Les Mousquetaires and ITM Entreprises v Commission,* T-255/17, EU:T:2020:460.

of the investigation. The Court made clear that the question of whether an interview is subject to the Commission's obligation to record is dependent on whether it is aimed at collecting information relating to the subject matter of an investigation, having regard to its content and context.[55]

The judgments of the Court in those cases largely followed the Opinion of AG Pitruzzella, who had broadly endorsed the approach suggested by AG Wahl.[56] Indeed, AG Pitruzzella indicated that 'it is sufficient … for a file to have been opened at the Commission's registry to take the view that such interviews are conducted with the aim of 'collecting information relating to the subject matter of an investigation' within the meaning of that provision. … In other words, as [AG] Wahl stated in his Opinion in *Intel Corporation v Commission*, …'any meeting with a third party which is specifically arranged to collect substantive information to be employed in the assessment of a case must fall within the scope of Article 19 of Regulation No 1/2003'.[57] In fact, AG Wahl's analysis in *Intel* was extensively referred to in the parties' pleadings, both before the General Court and the Court of Justice.

Finally, it may be interesting to note that a number of recent rulings of the EU Courts echoed the case law on the need to record hearings during antitrust investigations, developed under the impetus of AG Wahl. In the *Qualcomm cases,*[58] as well as in the *Google Android*[59] and *Bulgarian Energy*[60] cases, the examination of the pleas alleging an infringement of the relevant provision of Regulation No 1/2003 were largely based on the Court's findings in *Intel.*

[55] Judgments in *Les Mousquetaires and ITM Entreprises v Commission*, C-682/20 P, EU:C:2023:170; *Casino, Guichard-Perrachon and AMC v* Commission, C-690/20 P, EU:C:2023:171; and *Intermarché Casino Achats v* Commission, C-693/20 P, EU:C:2023:172. These rulings, following the *Intel* and *Qualcomm* (T-235/18) cases, constituted the third time that a failure to register declarations has been censured. Since then the Commission's practice has changed.

[56] See Opinion of AG Pitruzzella in *Les Mousquetaires and ITM Entreprises v Commission*, C-682/20 P, EU:C:2022:578, points 156–160.

[57] Ibid, point 186.

[58] Judgments in *Qualcomm v Commission (Exclusivity payments)*, T-235/18, EU:T:2022:358, paras 182–190; and *Qualcomm v Commission (Predation)*, T-671/19, EU:T:2024:626, paras 174–196.

[59] Judgment in *Google and Alphabet v Commission (Google Android)*, T-604/18, EU:T:2022:541, paras 903–960.

[60] Judgment in *Bulgarian Energy Holding and Others v Commission*, T-136/19, EU:T:2023:669, paras 1155–1177 (currently under appeal).

4 Powers of Inspection

The Commission's powers of inspection are set out in Article 20 (in business premises) and in Article 21 (in non-business premises) of Regulation No 1/2003.[61] While inspections are clearly a key tool in the detection of competition infringements, they are also a particularly intrusive prerogative which must, therefore, be exercised with due regard to the rights of the parties involved.

The legality of the Commission's inspection of an undertaking's premises depends on the content of the Commission's decision ordering that undertaking to submit itself to the inspection. Pursuant to Article 20(4) of Regulation No 1/2003, the decision must 'specify the subject matter and purpose of the inspection'. As the Court has held, the Commission is obliged to indicate as precisely as possible the evidence sought and the matters to which the investigation must relate, although it is not required to define precisely the relevant market, to set out the exact legal nature of the presumed infringements, or to indicate the period during which those infringements were allegedly committed.[62] Neither is the Commission required to communicate to the addressee of a decision ordering an investigation all the information at its disposal concerning the presumed infringements, or to make a precise legal analysis of those infringements, provided it clearly indicates the presumed facts which it intends to investigate.[63] That obligation to state specific reasons is a fundamental requirement not only to show that the intervention envisaged with respect to the undertakings concerned is proportionate, but also to enable those undertakings to understand the scope of their duty to cooperate, preserving their rights of defence.[64] Subject to those requirements, the Commission's decision is not, in itself, subject to *ex ante* judicial review. Only where coercive measures are envisaged, and the applicable national law requires a prior judicial authorisation for that purpose, could there be an incidental judicial review of the inspection decision before a national court.[65]

---

[61] The present contribution will only deal with Article 21 of Regulation No 1/2003. For a full overview of Articles 20 and 21 of Regulation No 1/2003, see inter alia N. Jalabert-Doury, C. Hoogter, Chapter 5, in N. Jalabert-Doury (ed.), *Competition Inspections 25 in Jurisdictions – A Practitioner's Guide*, 2nd ed., Concurrences, 2024; R. Sauer, L. Ortiz Blanco, Chapter 8, in Ortiz Blanco (ed.), *op. cit.,* pp. 416–477; and the contributions by A. De Moncuit, M. Jaspers, C. Moriarty (Article 20) and by A. De Moncuit, C. Moriarty (Article 21), in K. Dekeyser, C. Gauer, J. Laitenberger, N. Wahl, W. Wils, L. Prete (eds), *op. cit.*, pp. 451–484 and pp. 491–509, respectively.

[62] See, to that effect, judgments in *Dow Chemical Ibérica and Others v Commission*, para. 46, and *Roquette Frères*, para. 82.

[63] Judgment in *Dow Chemical Ibérica and Others v Commission*, para 45.

[64] See, to that effect, judgment in *Hoechst v Commission*, para. 29.

[65] Opinion of AG Wahl in *Deutsche Bahn and Others v Commission*, C-583/13 P, EU:C:2015:92, point 20. As regards that Opinion, see also Chapter 4 of this volume. On a related issue, in a different context, see the Opinions of AG Medina in *Imagens Médicas Integradas*, C-258/23 to C-260/23, EU:C:2024:537 and EU:C:2025:814.

Under Article 28 of Regulation No 1/2003, any document or information collected in the course of an inspection must, save for the exceptions provided for in that regulation, be used only for the purpose for which it was acquired. As made clear by the Court, that requirement is intended to protect the rights of defence of the undertakings concerned. Those rights would be seriously compromised if the Commission could rely on evidence against undertakings which was obtained during an investigation, but which was not related to the subject-matter or purpose of that particular investigation.[66] However, as the Court held in *Dow Benelux*, the above provision does not prevent the Commission from initiating an inquiry in order to verify or supplement information which it happened to find by chance during another investigation, if such information indicates the possible existence of another infringement of the EU competition rules. Preventing the Commission from doing so would constitute an unnecessary hindrance to its investigative powers, since the undertaking responsible for the potential breach is free to exercise its rights of defence fully in the context of the new investigation.[67] There is, therefore, no bar on the use of information found fortuitously, provided that a new investigation is opened and conducted in accordance with Regulation No 1/2003.[68] Finally, the Court has consistently held that an undertaking that has undergone an inspection ordered by the Commission can contest the decision ordering that inspection before the EU Courts. If the decision is annulled, the Commission may not rely on any documents or other evidence which it obtained in the course of that investigation, and if it does, any decision on the alleged infringement taken on the basis fo that information might be annulled by the EU Courts.[69]

The *Deutsche Bahn* case[70] gave the Court the opportunity to refine that case-law on two important aspects. The first such aspect concerned the lack of *prior* judicial authorisation of the Commission's inspection decisions. In the appellants' view, the absence of any form of *ex ante* control of an inspection decision constituted a violation of their fundamental right to the inviolability of the home provided for in Articles 7 of the Charter and Article 8 of the ECHR, and of the right to an effective judicial protection recognised in Article 47 of the Charter and Article 6(1) of the ECHR. The second issue which arose in the dispute concerned the appellants' allegation that the inspection constituted an impermissible 'fishing expedition'. It was undisputed that, immediately before the inspection took place, the relevant Commission's officials were informed that another complaint against one of the appellants had been received, and was appraised of the subject-matter of that complaint. However, the subject-matter of the second complaint was not covered by

---

[66] See judgment in *Roquette Frères*, para. 48 and the case-law cited.

[67] See judgments in *DowBenelux v Commission*, 85/87, EU:C:1989:379, paras 17–19; and *Limburgse Vinyl Maatschappij and Others v Commission*, C-238/99 P etc., EU:C:2002:582, para 301.

[68] Opinion of AG Wahl in *Deutsche Bahn and Others v Commission* C-583/13 P, EU:C:2015:92, point 22.

[69] See judgment in *Roquette Frères*, para. 49 and the case-law cited.

[70] Judgment in *Deutsche Bahn and Others v Commission*, C-583/13 P, EU:C:2015:404.

the inspection decision. During the raid, the Commission staff found documents concerning the alleged 'new' infringement ('the DUSS documents') and immediately informed their superiors. The next day, while the first raid was still ongoing, the Commission adopted a second inspection decision which was followed, some months later, by a third inspection decision. The latter two decisions also concerned the second alleged infringement. The General Court dismissed the appellant's claims that the inspection costitued, in part, a 'fishing expedition'. The General Court took the view that there were valid reasons for providing the officials with general background information on the new case, altough it did not explain what those reasons actually were.[71] On appeal, the Commission defended the General Court's reasoning, contending that it was helpful for Commission staff to be aware of the context in which the inspection was to be carried out.

In his Opinion, AG Wahl first suggested the Court to dismiss the appellants' claim alleging a breach of Article 7 of the Charter. The AG examined the relevant EU and ECtHR case-law. In particular, AG Wahl noted that, in recent rulings, the Strasbourg Court made clear that, in similar cases, the absence of a prior judicial warrant may be compensated by effective *ex post* judicial review dealing with all issues of law and fact. The AG took the view that that was the case within the EU system. He emphasised that the EU Courts' jurisdiction over inspection decisions, which are acts 'open to challenge' under Article 263 TFEU, covers all aspects of law and fact that may be relevant in order to verify the lawfulness of such decisions. In addition, there is a clear penalty for any law breach: the annulment of an inspection decision by the EU Courts bars the Commission from making use of documents found in the course of that inspection.

By contrast, AG Wahl agreed with the appellants' arguments that the General Court had erred in designating the DUSS documents as 'found by chance' within the meaning of the *Dow Benelux* case-law.[72] First, he stressed the wide investigative powers enjoyed by the Commission under Regulation No 1/2003 which severely interfere with certain fundamental rights of companies and individuals. He went on to add that these powers are exercised 'on the basis of no (or little) *ex ante* judicial control' and without 'the internal checks and balances typically provided for when the Commission is to adopt decisions and other legally binding acts [applying] to their full extent'. Indeed, the power to adopt decisions pursuant to those provisions has been entrusted to the Commissioner responsible for competition policy, who, in turn, has sub-delegated that power to the Director-General of DG Competition. He concluded by stating that the above meant 'that inspection decisions are virtually decided by the staff of DG Competition alone, with other Commission services playing little or no role in the decision-making'. Therefore, 'because those powers are so extensive, the discretion so ample, and the decision-making subject to so few (judicial or administrative) prior controls', he considered it to be of the utmost

[71] Judgment in *Deutsche Bahn and Others v Commission*, T-289/11, T-290/11 and T-521/11, EU:T:2013:404, para 162.

[72] Judgment in *Dow Benelux*, EU:C:1989:379.

importance that the EU Courts carry out meticulous and rigorous verifications as to whether, in exercising those powers, the Commission stays within limit of the law. In his view, the provisions of Regulation No 1/2003 prevents 'the Commission from going on 'fishing expeditions',[73] using as a pretext an ongoing investigation into a possible breach of the competition rules'. The Commission cannot search—he went on to add—for evidence relating to potential breaches of the EU competition rules other than those relating to the subject-matter of the investigation. Against that background, in the light of the facts of the case—which were largely common ground between the parties—he found that the Commission had, deliberately or through negligence, circumvented the rules laid down in Regulation No 1/2003 governing inspections, by using an inspection to look for documents which concerned another, unrelated, matter. Indeed, he dismissed the view that information concerning the second alleged infringement could be regarded as being part of the 'context' of the inspection, or as 'background information' concerning the first infringement. In fact, after examining the arguments put forward by the Commission, he came to the conclusion that the only plausible explanation for that institution's pre-inspection conduct was that 'information on the [second] suspected infringement was given to [its] staff so that they could 'keep their eyes peeled' for evidence related to the second complaint'. In his view, that is 'clearly not the type of conduct which the Court meant to allow under its *Dow Benelux* case-law'. Fundamentally, he saw no difference between a case in which the Commission launches an inspection without a valid decision and one in which the Commission proceeds on the basis of a valid decision, but searches for information relating to another investigation, not covered by that decision. Accordingly, he suggested that the Court set aside the judgment under appeal and annul the second and third Commission decisions, which were adopted after the supposedly fortuitous find of the DUSS documents.

The Court agreed with AG Wahl on both aspects. As regards the appellants' first ground of appeal, the Court upheld the General Court's assessment. The Court referred to the case-law of the ECtHR,[74] according to which the lack of prior judicial authorisation is only one of the factors relevant in determining whether Article 8 of the ECHR has been infringed. Indeed, that element may be counterbalanced by judicial review post inspection, covering all relevant questions of fact and law. The Court noted that, in cases where a violation of Article 8 of the ECHR had been found, there were other factors which contributed to that finding, such as: the far reaching powers held by the national authorities, the particular circumstances in which an interference with the rights took place, or the limited number of safeguards in place in the national legislation. In that respect, the case at hand differed—the Court

[73] In that regard, see also Opinion of AG Kokott in *Nexans and Nexans France v Commission*, C-37/13 P, EU:C:2014:223, point 43.

[74] In particular, judgments of the ECtHR in *Delta Pekárny AS v Czech Republic* (CE:ECHR:2014:1002JUD000009711, §§ 83, 87 and 92); *Bernh Larsen Holding AS and Others v Norway* (CE:ECHR:2013:0314JUD002411708); *Colas Est and Others v France* (CE:ECHR:2002:0416JUD003797197); *Harju v Finland* (CE:ECHR:2011:0215JUD005671609); and *Heino v Finland* (CE:ECHR:2011:0215JUD005672009).

found—from those examined by the ECtHR. As far as effective judicial protection was concerned, the Court emphasised that, unlike the systems censured in some rulings of the ECtHR, the EU system (i) allows undertakings subject to an inspection to challenge, before the EU Courts, the lawfulness of the inspection decision issued by the Commission immediately after being notified of it, without the need to wait until the Commission has adopted a final decision on the suspected infringement, and (ii) the EU Courts have the power to review all aspects of law and fact relating to inspection decisions and to annul them, in whole or in part, on all issues.[75]

With regard to the appellants' complain that the Commission carried out a 'fishing expedition', the Court found—here too in line with AG Wahl's Opinion—that the General Court' had indeed erred in law. It held that the prior information given to the Commission's officials was not merely general background information on the case, but rather pertained to a separate complaint, which was unrelated to the subject-matter of the first inspection decision. The Court concluded that the lack of reference to that complaint in the description of the subject-matter of that inspection decision infringed the obligation to state reasons and the rights of defence of the undertaking concerned. The appeal was, accordingly, successful in part.[76]

The principles flowing from *Deutsche Bahn* have been confirmed and developed in subsequent case-law.[77] In particular, in the *French Supermarket* cases, the EU Courts emphasised that 'the statement of reasons for [an inspection] decision limits the powers conferred on the Commission's agents by Article 20(2) of Regulation No 1/2003' and, consequently, 'the measures taken by the Commission during [an inspection that] are not consistent with the scope of the decisions ordering it' may 'lead to the annulment of [a] new inspection decision'.[78] Interestingly, the Court went further here. Indeed, it found that insofar as the inspection decisions challenged by the appellants were mainly based on indicia gathered during interviews which the Commission had failed to record,[79] they had been invalidly adopted and, therefore should be annulled.[80] As recently stated by former AG Pitruzzella, the *Deutsche Bahn* case provides '[a]nother example of a case, in which the Advocate General's Opinion – in this case ... AG Wahl – has clearly shaped the Court's interpretation of [Regulation No 1/2003]'.[81]

---

[75] Judgment in *Deutsche Bahn and Others v Commission*, C-583/13 P, EU:C:2015:404 paras 44 ff.

[76] Ibid., paras 54 ff.

[77] See e.g., judgments in *České dráhy v Commission*, T-325/16, EU:T:2018:368, para. 41; *Nexans France and Nexans v Commission*, T-449/14, EU:T:2018:456 para. 65; and *Prysmian Cavi e Sistemi v Commission*, T-475/14, EU:T:2018:448 para. 61. For numerous references to the Opinion of AG Wahl in *Deustche Bahn*, see judgment in *Casino, Guichard-Perrachon and AMC v Commission*, T-249/17, EU:T:2020:458, paras 70, 78, 146 and 202.

[78] Judgment in *Intermarché Casino Achats v Commission,* C-693/20 P, EU:C:2023:172, para. 59.

[79] See above, Section III of this paper.

[80] Judgment in *Intermarché Casino Achats v Commission,* C-693/20 P, EU:C:2023:172, para. 142.

[81] G. Pitruzzella, *op. cit.*, p. 851.

5 Conclusive Remarks

It is generally accepted that, because of the importance of EU competition rules within the scheme of the EU Treaties, the Commission should be entitled to enjoy extensive powers to investigate possible infringements thereof.[82] Through the provisions of Regulation No 1/2003, even more than under its predecessor (Regulation no 17 of 1962),[83] the EU legislature has bestowed on the Commission a variety of wide-ranging investigative tools to detect infringements and, where appropriate, to penalise the companies responsible. In addition, the development of forensic digital instruments and techniques—in which all competition authorities, including the Commission, have recently made significant investments—opens new and far reaching possibilities for the investigation environment of companies' digital sphere (and, where appropriate, of their staff), allowing Commisison's staff to locate, protect and copy information that is relevant to the investigation.[84]

Nevertheless, the Commission's powers must be exercised in a way that is compatible with the general principles of EU law (such as proportionality), and which does not constitute an unacceptable interference with the fundamental rights of individuals and undertakings (such as the inviolability of homes, or effective judicial protection). The possibility for an undertaking to exercise its rights of defence in a timely, adequate and effective manner is manifestly crucial in that regard.

Evidently, tension exists between the interest of promoting the swift and effective enforcement of competition rules, and the need to ensure respect for basic rights and values which are accorded the utmost significance in the EU legal order.[85] This explains why striking the correct balance between those competing interests is not always an easy task, for either the EU judiciary or the EU legislature.[86]

The EU Courts' case law confirms the need to balance the Commission's investigative powers with the respect for undertakings' rights of defence. This balancing act is meant to reconcile two types of 'effectiveness' which are crucial in this

---

[82] See, recently, judgment in *Nexans France and Nexans v Commission*, C-606/18 P, EU:C:2020:571, para. 64: "while it is true that it is settled case-law that the Commission's powers of investigation concerning competition law are strictly circumscribed (see, to that effect, judgment of 18 June 2015, *Deutsche Bahn and Others v Commission*, C-583/13 P, EU:C:2015:404, para. 31 and the case-law cited), nonetheless that does not mean … that the provisions conferring the powers of investigation on that institution must be interpreted narrowly, even though, from that point of view, it must be ensured that those powers do not infringe the rights of the undertakings concerned.'

[83] Regulation of 6 February 1962: first regulation implementing Articles [81] and [82 EC] (OJ, English Special Edition 1959–1962, p. 87).

[84] See F. Laina, 'Moving Towards a Digital Competition Enforcement', in in K. Dekeyser, C. Gauer, J. Laitenberger, N. Wahl, W. Wils, L. Prete (eds), *op. cit.*, pp. 484 ff.; and H. Andersen, *Dawn Raids under Challenge - Due Process Aspects of the European Commission's Dawn Raid Practices*, Hart, 2018, 286 p. 252. See also Opinion of AG Kokott in *Nexans France and Nexans v Commission*, C-606/18 P, EU:C:2020:207, points 77–78.

[85] Cf. Opinion of AG Geelhoed, in *Commission v SGL Carbon*, C-301/04 P, EU:C:2006:53, point 67.

[86] On this issue, in general, see H. Andersen, *op. cit.*, pp. 231–262.

context. On one hand, competition law should be enforced effectively so that the EU internal market remains competitive to the benefit of the society as a whole. On the other hand, effective legal protection, as required by Article 19(1) TEU and Article 47 of the Charter, must be duly safeguarded in competition proceedings, as required in a legal system which is based, inter alia, on principles such as the rule of law and the respect for fundamental rights.

As regards the EU legislature, then, it should not be overlooked that Regulation No 1/2003 is currently undergoing a 'fitness check'.[87] It is thus possible that a revision of that regulation may be tabled in the next months. It is obviously too early to say whether, in that case, the powers of investigation set out in Chapter V of the regulation could be amended and, if so, how. In this context, it may be interesting to point out that some of the latest legislative acts in this field (namely, the 'ECN+ Directive' and the 'Digital Market Act'[88]) lay down a slightly different legal frameworks on this matter.

Regardless of the above, it is ultimately for the Court of Justice to ensure that a fair and correct balance between those competing interests is struck in the specific cases that are brought before it. Indeed, the principles and rights discussed above are mostly enshrined in EU primary law. Consequently, any legal provision—as set out currently in Regulation No 1/2003, or in a future 'revised Regulation 1' or a wholly new 'Regulation 2'—would have to be interpreted and applied in accordance with those principles and rights. As observed by philosopher Blaise Pascal, 'justice without force is powerless; force without justice is tyrannical'.[89] The need to reconcile justice and force appears to be the lodestar of the Opinions discussed in the present paper.

The EU Courts' decisions rendered in those seminal cases, as well as in the cases which built and developed on them, show the significant and lasting legacy that AG Wahl left in this area of EU antitrust law, and possibly beyond. Indeed, as indicated above, the EU Courts have also referred to the case-law discussed in this paper also in decisions that did not concern antitrust investigations. It is, after all, reasonable to

[87] See European Commission, Commission publishes findings of evaluation of EU antitrust enforcement framework, 5 September 2024 (IP/24/4550). On 10 July 2025, the Commission published a call for evidence and a public consultation questionnaire, seeking the views of stakeholders on policy options to revise Regulation No 1/2003.

[88] Respectively, Directive (EU) 2019/1 of the European Parliament and of the Council of 11 December 2018 to empower the competition authorities of the Member States to be more effective enforcers and to ensure the proper functioning of the internal market (OJ 2019 L 11, p. 3), especially Articles 6–9, and recitals 28–36 thereof, and Regulation (EU) 2022/1925 of the European Parliament and of the Council of 14 September 2022 on contestable and fair markets in the digital sector (OJ 2022 L 265, p. 1), especially Articles 21–23 and recitals 80–83 thereof.

[89] In the original: '*La justice sans la force est impuissante; la force sans la justice est tyrannique*' (fragment from '*Raisons des effets*') (Blaise Pascal, *Œuvres complètes,* édition de Louis Lafuma, Paris, Seuil, 1963, no 103. In legal scholarship, emphasising the contribution of AG Wahl on this matter: see for example, M. Tricker, C. Angeli, '*Deutsche Bahn*: Advocate General Wahl has made a start on the tricky process of reconciling robust enforcement with the rights of investigated companies' (2015) *Competition Law Insight*.

take the view that similar legal issues may arise from situations in which the Commission makes use of its powers of investigation regardless of the field of law concerned and, to some extent, the wording of the provisions in question. The principles devolving from cases such as *Cement*, *Intel* and *Deutsche Bahn* may thus be applicable, *mutatis mutandis*, in a variety of areas of EU administrative activity.[90]

[90] See Opinion of AG Wahl In *HeidelbergCement*, point 33.

Unlimited Jurisdiction in European Competition Law and the Prohibition of Reformatio in Pejus

Fredrik Schalin

1 Introduction

When the EU Courts examine appeals under Article 263 TFEU against decisions adopted by the Commission on the basis of Articles 101 and 102 TFEU, they are competent to review the legality of these decisions. However, under Article 261 TFEU and Article 31 of Regulation 1/2003[1,2] the General Court and the Court of Justice have unlimited jurisdiction in reviewing the penalties imposed by the decisions in question.

It has been argued that the EU Courts, when exercising their unlimited jurisdiction have the right, or at least should have the right, not only to cancel or reduce the fine but also to increase it—even in the absence of an appeal or an explicit claim or plea to this effect.[3] So to what extent is the unlimited jurisdiction really "unlimited"

The author would like to thank the members of his cabinet for their valuable help in the preparation of this contribution, and the members of his colleagues' cabinets for providing and verifying the content of national laws.

[1] Council Regulation (EC) No 1/2003 of 16 December 2002 on the implementation of the rules on competition laid down in Articles 81 and 82 of the Treaty (OJ 2003 L 1, p. 1).

[2] Article 16 of Council Regulation (EC) No 139/2004 of 20 January 2004 on the control of concentrations between undertakings (the EC Merger Regulation), (OJ 2004 L 24, p. 1), is formulated in a similar manner. For reasons of readability and simplicity, this article will only focus on Regulation 1/2003.

[3] See, for example, L. Bernardeau, J.-P. Christienne, *Les amendes en droit de la concurrence, pratique décisionnelle et contrôle juridictionnel du droit de l'Union*, Larcier, 2013, pp. 823–824; F. Clausen, *Les moyens d'ordre public devant la Cour de justice de l'Union européenne*, Bruylant,

F. Schalin (✉)
Court of Justice of the European Union, Luxembourg, Luxembourg
e-mail: Fredrik.Schalin@curia.europa.eu

L. Prete, L. Rezki (eds.), *Judging & (Re)Thinking European Union Law*,
https://doi.org/10.1007/978-3-032-13473-8_17

or, on the contrary, circumscribed and limited by various rules and conditions? And what is the role, if any, of the principle of reformatio in pejus—which prohibits the modification of a decision or a judgment to the detriment of a party that alone has launched an appeal—when the EU Courts exercise their unlimited jurisdiction?

These are the questions that we are going to touch on in this contribution. In the first part, we are going to examine some of the case law concerning the EU Courts' exercise of their unlimited jurisdiction. It is, of course, a matter that has already been the subject of very rich commentary in the doctrine. We will focus on certain issues that seem relevant for the purpose of the second part of this article—especially the procedural framework but also some of the main features of the unlimited jurisdiction of the EU Courts. In the second part, we are going to shed some light on the prohibition of reformatio in pejus and investigate if it may have an influence on how the EU Courts exercise their unlimited jurisdiction. That, on the other hand, is a question that has been the subject of much more limited interest. Is there, at all, a case for recognizing the prohibition? And is the rhetoric of the EU Courts, according to which they may increase the fine regardless of an appeal, in conformity with their practice? In order to examine this issue in its proper context, it is useful to also consider the application of the prohibition of reformatio in pejus in the Member States.

2 Unlimited Jurisdiction in Competition Law Cases

2.1 Background: The Concept of Unlimited Jurisdiction

The concept of unlimited jurisdiction in European law seems to find its origin in French administrative law.[4] Nevertheless, similar rules, that permit the national courts not only to annul administrative decisions but to reform and replace them, exist in the other Member States. This, however, does not mean that the application of unlimited jurisdiction in Union law follows more or less the same lines as in French law or in any other national law.

The concept has furthermore been evolving over time. In addition, in Union law, the concept of unlimited jurisdiction exists in different areas of law and is applied in different ways in these different areas. So the concept of unlimited jurisdiction

---

2018, pp. 407–413; M. Cournot, "L'interdiction de statuer ultra petita s'applique-t-elle au juge de l'amende?", (2015) *Revue des Affaires Européennes*, N° 1, pp. 123–124. See also G. Gaulard, *La pleine juridiction du juge de l'Union européenne en droit de la concurrence*, Bruylant, 2020, pp. 269–281. For a very recent Opinion discussing the concept of 'unlimited jurisdiction', see the Opinion of Advocate General Emiliou of 12 March 2026 in *Crédit Agricole and Others v. Commission*, C–548/24, points 102–124

[4] L. Bernardeau, J.-P. Christienne, op. cit., pp. 795–796.

exists in intellectual property law[5] as well as in civil service law[6] and in certain other areas.[7] This article will focus on unlimited jurisdiction of the EU Courts as regards the determination of fines in competition law cases that is explicitly authorized by Article 261 TFEU and, in its turn, by Article 31 of Regulation 1/2003.

2.2 *The Legal Basis: Article 261 TFEU*

The legal basis for unlimited jurisdiction is found in Article 261 TFEU, which provides that regulations adopted by the Council and the Parliament or by the Council alone may give "the Court of Justice [...] unlimited jurisdiction with regard to the penalties provided for in such regulations". Certain authors have claimed that an application for unlimited jurisdiction under Article 261 TFEU should be viewed as an autonomous remedy that is independent of an action of annulment under Article 263 TFEU.[8]

This argument was put forward in a case before the General Court where the action was brought after the deadline in Article 263 TFEU.[9] The General Court did not accept this line of reasoning. It found that contrary to the applicant's argument and with reference to the list of actions and remedies mentioned in Article 257, paragraph 1, TFEU, the Treaty did not consider unlimited jurisdiction in Article 261 TFEU as an autonomous remedy. Consequently, the action, that was brought after the expiry of the time-limit laid down in Article 263 TFEU, was dismissed as out of time and inadmissible.[10]

---

[5] Article 72(3) of Regulation (EU) No 2017/1001 of the European Parliament and of the Council of 14 June 2017 on the European Union trade mark (codification) (OJ 2017 L 154, p. 1).

[6] Article 91(1) of the consolidated version of Regulation No 31 (EEC), 11 (EAEC), laying down the Staff Regulations of Officials and the Conditions of Employment of Other Servants of the European Economic Community and the European Atomic Energy Community (OJ 1962 P 45, p. 1385).

[7] See, for example, Article 145(9) of Regulation (EU, Euratom) 2024/2509 of the European Parliament and of the Council of 23 September 2024 on the financial rules applicable to the general budget, (OJ L 2024/2509), replacing Regulation (EU, Euratom) 2018/1046 of the European Parliament and of the Council of 18 July 2018 on the financial rules applicable to the general budget of the Union, amending Regulations (EU) No 1296/2013, (EU) No 1301/2013, (EU) No 1303/2013, (EU) No 1304/2013, (EU) No 1309/2013, (EU) No 1316/2013, (EU) No 223/2014, (EU) No 283/2014, and Decision No 541/2014/EU and repealing Regulation (EU, Euratom) No 966/2012, (OJ 2018 L 193, p. 1). The EU Courts also have unlimited jurisdiction in disputes concerning compensation for damages involving the liability (contractual and non-contractual) of the Union (Articles 268 and 340 TFEU).

[8] See, in particular, S. Van Raepenbusch, "Chapitre 3. - Le recours en annulation" in *Droit institutionnel de l'Union européenne*, Larcier, 2016, p. 721, with further references in footnote 236.

[9] See order in *FNICGV v Commission*, T-252/03, EU:T:2004:326.

[10] Ibid., paras 21–27.

2.3 The Applicable Rule: Article 31 of Regulation 1/2003

The notion of unlimited jurisdiction is to a certain extent misleading. In fact, a literary interpretation of the notion seems to imply that the Court's jurisdiction is free from any formal (or substantial) requirements and limitations. This claim has, nonetheless, been firmly denied.[11] The nature and scope of the review will vary according to the subject matter and the specific legal framework. Perhaps, then is it appropriate to define it in comparison to a simple action for annulment. It is clear that the scope of the review is wider than in an action for an annulment that it is not limited to questions of law and that the reviewing Court has the power to reform the contested decision. In order to examine in more detail the conditions and the scope of the review it is however necessary to look at the specific subject matter. Pursuant to the above-mentioned Article 261 TFEU, Article 31 of Regulation 1/2003 provides that "[t]he Court of Justice shall have unlimited jurisdiction to review decisions whereby the Commission has fixed a fine or a periodic penalty payment". The article, furthermore, specifies that the Court "may cancel, reduce or increase the fine or periodic penalty payment imposed".

In its judgment in the *Galp* case, the Court of Justice clarified the interpretation and scope of Article 261 TFEU and Article 31 of Regulation 1/2003 by making a comparison between the scope of the review of legality in Article 263 TFEU and the unlimited review in Article 261 TFEU and Article 31 of Regulation 1/2003.[12] The Court stated that whereas the review of legality in Article 263 TFEU extended to all elements of the contested decision, in law and in fact, in the light of the pleas raised by the appellants, the EU Courts cannot "substitute their own reasoning for that of [the] author of the contested [decision]".[13] On the other hand, while unlimited jurisdiction empowers the EU Courts, in addition to examine the mere legality of the penalty, to substitute their own assessment of the fine or penalty for that of the Commission, the review is strictly limited to the determination and assessment of the fine "to the exclusion of any alteration of the constituent elements of the infringement lawfully determined by the Commission" in the contested decision.[14]

[11] F. Castillo de la Torre, E. Gippini Fournier, "Scope and Intensity of Judicial Review", *Evidence, Proof and Judicial Review in EU Competition* Law, Edward Elgar, 2017, p. 443, para. 6.146.

[12] See judgment in *Galp Energía España and Others v Commission*, C-603/13 P, paras 72–78.

[13] Ibid., para. 73.

[14] Ibid., para. 77.

2.4 *The Formal Requirements*

2.4.1 How Is the Matter of Unlimited Jurisdiction Raised?

The question is then what is required for the Court, in an action for annulment under Article 263 TFEU, to exercise unlimited jurisdiction in Article 261 TFEU, in combination with Article 31 of Regulation 1/2003. Should the party, normally the applicant, be required to make an explicit and formal submission in the application? Or could a request be considered to be implicit in an action for annulment of the contested decision? Or has the Court even the power to raise the issue on its own motion?

It should be said that the case law of the EU Courts is not crystal clear on these questions.

As regards the first question, concerning the necessity of a formal request, the Court of Justice concluded, in one of its early cases, that a formal request was not necessary when the applicant had asked for the annulment of the decision as a reduction of the fine was not ultra petita—that is to say beyond the scope of the relief requested—but amounted to a partial acceptance of the application.[15] In other words, the principle of major includit minor—or what is more includes what is less—should be applied. This approach has also been followed by the General Court in some of its case-law.[16]

In some cases the EU Courts have exercised their unlimited jurisdiction even if it could be argued that they acted ultra petita. In *Groupe Danone* the applicant pleaded that the General Court had acted ultra petita when it recalculated the amount of the fine. The Court of Justice did not accept this argument in the light of the fact that the applicant had criticized the Commission for deviating from the guidelines and concluded that "the Community judicature is empowered to exercise its unlimited jurisdiction where the question of the amount of the fine is before it".[17]

That seems to be as far as the Court of Justice is prepared to go. It has subsequently pointed out in *KME Germany* that "the exercise of unlimited jurisdiction does not amount to a review of the Court's own motion, and that proceedings before the Courts of the European Union are inter partes".[18]

---

[15] See judgment in *ALMA v High Authority*, 8/56, EU:C:1957:12.

[16] See especially judgment in *AstraZeneca v Commission*, T-321/05, EU:T:2010:266, para. 884, referring to judgment in *Tate & Lyle and Others v Commission*, T-202/98, T-204/98, T-207/98, EU:T:2001:185, paras 22 and 164.

[17] Ibid., paras 57 and 62.

[18] Judgment in *KME Germany and Others v Commission*, C-389/10 P, EU:C:2011:816, para. 131.

2.4.2 Are Formal Pleas Necessary?

Should the party be obliged to formulate pleas or at least put forward arguments? After having concluded in *KME Germany* that unlimited jurisdiction does not amount to a review of its own motion, the Court of Justice stated that, with the exception of pleas involving matters of public policy which the Courts are required to raise of their own motion such as the failure to state reasons, it is for the applicant to raise pleas of law and adduce evidence in support of those pleas.[19]

The Court has been criticized for using the notion of plea of law in connection with the exercise of unlimited jurisdiction, which does not presuppose the existence of a violation of law.[20] Although, the criticism does not appear to be completely unjustified, from a theoretical standpoint, the applicant is, nevertheless, expected to put forward arguments in support of the reduction of the fine, due, for example, to its inappropriate character, even if there is no claim of a violation of law.

2.4.3 The Ordinary Rules of Procedure Are Applicable with a Couple of Exceptions

At what stage of the proceedings should the parties submit their claims, their pleas or other arguments and their evidence? The simple answer is that the usual procedural rules are applicable and that these submissions should be presented immediately in the application, in the cross-appeal or in the defense unless there is some justification.[21]

A question that is more complicated to answer in a simple way is to what extent pleas or arguments and evidence that have not been submitted to the Commission during the administrative procedure can be presented for the first time before the General Court. The case-law of the EU Courts seems to allow for new elements to a greater extent when exercising unlimited jurisdiction than otherwise.

This has been borne out by the Court of Justice in its decision in *Westfälische Drahtindustrie* where it stated that "the EU Courts are entitled to take into account all the factual circumstances which they consider to be relevant, whether they be prior to or subsequent to the contested decision" and that "this applies a fortiori where [...] the exercise of unlimited jurisdiction relates to [...] the ability to pay on the part of the undertaking concerned".[22] The Court concluded that "if the EU Courts were unable to assess that capacity by taking into account the prevailing factual situation at the time at which they give their ruling, they could be required to refuse or to grant a reduction or a cancellation of a fine owed or not owed, in such a

[19] Ibid., para. 131.

[20] L. Bernardeau and J.-P. Christienne, op. cit., para. II. 1585, p. 823, as well as F. Castillo de la Torre and E. Gippini Fournier, op. cit., p. 450, paras 6.163–6.164.

[21] See Articles 76 to 86 of the Rules of Procedure of the General Court.

[22] See order in *Westfälische Drahtindustrie and Others v Commission*, C-523/15 P, EU:C:2016:541, para. 43.

way as to cause a disadvantage or provide an unfair competitive advantage for that undertaking". An illustration of this principle can be found in the judgment in *Romana Tabacchi* where the General Court rejected a claim of inability to pay, presented for the first time before the Court, in the review of legality while taking it into consideration when exercising its unlimited jurisdiction.[23]

It seems important to note that the aforementioned cases all concerned the capacity of the applicant to pay the fine. To what extent new circumstances and new evidence will be taken into consideration in other situations is more uncertain.[24] As regards the capacity to pay the fine, a further question is if an applicant should be allowed to invoke circumstances for the first time before the General Court—if the circumstances existed already during the administrative procedure. To accept such a conduct hardly seems in line with a proper management of the procedure.

2.5 Unlimited Jurisdiction in the Assessment of the Fine

2.5.1 The Review of the Fine Must Not Alter the "Constituent Elements of the Infringement"

In *Galp* the General Court took into consideration new evidence related to the infringement itself in the exercise of unlimited jurisdiction.[25] The judgment was however set aside by the Court of Justice that found that the unlimited jurisdiction only concerned the assessment of the fine to the exclusion of any alteration of the constituent elements of the infringement determined by the Commission in its decision.[26] Although it is clear that the practices which fall under Articles 101 TFEU and 102 TFEU are constituent elements of the infringement, it may be difficult to determine the circumstances that are covered by this notion in the concrete situation.[27] A cautious approach is probably advisable.

[23] See judgment in *Romana Tabacchi v Commission*, T-11/06, EU:T:2011:560, paras 261–263 and 281–283.

[24] See, however, judgments in *Shell and others v Commission*, T-343/06, EU:T:2012:478, paras 102–103 and 120–124; and *Google and Alphabet v Commission (Google Android),* T-604/18, EU:T:2019:743, paras 87–101.

[25] See judgment in *Galp Energía España and Others v Commission*, T-462/07, EU:T:2013:459, paras 605–636.

[26] See judgment in C-603/13 P, *Galp Energía España, supra*, paras 75–79.

[27] H. Expert and C. Poullet, "La compétence de pleine juridiction conférée au juge de l'Union en matière de concurrence: complément ou accessoire du contrôle de légalité?", in Peyronnel, Verdure (eds), *Contentieux du droit de la concurrence de l'Union européenne*, Bruylant, 2017, pp. 558–566.

2.5.2 The Review of the Fine Does Not Presuppose Any Illegality

So what is the relationship between the review of legality in an action for annulment and the review of the fine? Does a review of the fine presuppose an illegality? As we have already touched on in the foregoing, the answer is negative. Although, the position of the EU Courts, especially the General Court, has not been completely stable over the years, it seems to be established today in the case law, that the exercise of unlimited jurisdiction does not presuppose the prior finding of illegality.[28]

Nevertheless, it is not unreasonable to believe that the General Court will exercise its power of unlimited jurisdiction most in situations where there are violations of law that justify the partial annulment of the contested decision. The General Court will use its unlimited jurisdiction in order, *first*, to draw the appropriate conclusions from its findings with respect to the lawfulness of that decision and, *secondly*, to establish whether it is appropriate to substitute its own assessment for that of the Commission so that the amount of the fine is appropriate.[29] These situations may include the proportionality of the fine, the incorrect calculation of the basic amount of a fine as well as a failure to take into account mitigating circumstances.

2.5.3 The EU Courts Are Not Bound by the Commission's Guidelines or Practice

In order to determine the amount of the fine, it is for the EU Courts to assess for themselves the circumstances of the case and the nature of the infringement in question.[30] This assessment involves, in accordance with Article 23, paragraph 3, of Regulation 1/2003, taking into account the seriousness and the duration of the infringement and the principles of adequate reasoning, proportionality, the individualization of penalties and equal treatment.[31] The EU Courts are not bound by the

[28] Even if the Court of Justice had repeatedly stated that the amount of the fine could be modified even in the absence of an annulment (see, for example, judgment in *Limburgse Vinyl Maatschappij and Others v Commission*, C-238/99 P etc., EU:C:2002:582, para. 692), the case law of the General Court seemed to imply that a finding of illegality was a precondition for the exercise of unlimited jurisdiction (see, for example, judgment in *Avebe v Commission*, T-314/01, EU:T:2006:266, paras 27 and 147). Furthermore, in its BASF (*Vitamins*) judgment, the General Court explicitly required a finding of illegality in order to exercise its unlimited jurisdiction (T-15/02, EU:T:2006:74, para. 582). In its more recent case law, especially in the judgment in *Baltic Rail*, the General Court has, however, reduced the fine without finding any illegality (*Lietuvos geležinkeliai v Commission*, EU:T:2020:545, T-814/17, paras 365–388).

[29] See judgment in *Orange Polska v Commission*, T-486/11, EU:T:2015:1002, para. 67, which contains further references to case law of the EU Courts.

[30] See judgment in *Nederlandsche Banden-Industrie-Michelin v Commission*, 322/81, EU:C:1983:313, para. 111.

[31] See C-603/13 P, *Galp Energía España, supra,* 2016, para. 90.

indicative rules defined by the Commission in its guidelines or by the Commission's practice in previous decisions.[32] However, in the absence of any finding of illegality, the EU Courts seem to exercise unlimited jurisdiction with caution. Furthermore, certain authors have observed that the EU Courts have tried to strike a balance between a too frequent use of unlimited jurisdiction that would infringe on the Commission's discretion in setting fines and a very rare use of this faculty that would render this guarantee illusory.[33]

2.6 *Unlimited Jurisdiction on Appeal*

We have seen that the General Court has unlimited jurisdiction in its assessment of the fine determined by the Commission in its decision. So what is the role of the Court of Justice when it reviews the judgment on appeal? The short answer is that the Court of Justice does not have unlimited jurisdiction during the appeal procedure. The Court of Justice has repeatedly pointed out that, in an appeal, the Court cannot substitute, on grounds of fairness, its assessment for that of the General Court giving judgment in the exercise of its unlimited jurisdiction as to the amount of the fines imposed on undertakings by reason of their infringement of Union law.[34] However, the Court may come to the conclusion that the General Court has erred in law and that the appealed judgment should be annulled—completely or partially. Depending on the circumstances, the Court of Justice may then send the case back to the General Court for a new assessment or decide to try the case by itself. In the second situation, the Court of Justice will have unlimited jurisdiction to assess the fine.[35]

---

[32] Ibid., para. 90. See also judgment in *Ziegler v Commission*, C-439/11 P, EU:C:2013:513, para. 134.

[33] F. Castillo de la Torre, E. Gippini Fournier, op. cit., pp. 436–437, para. 6.132.

[34] See, for example, judgments in *Sarrió v Commission*, C-291/98 P, EU:C:2000:631, para. 96; and in *Erste Group Bank and Others v Commission*, C-125/07 P etc., paras 187 and 255. See also A. Arabadjiev, 'Unlimited Jurisdiction: What Does It Mean Today?', in Cardonnel, Rosas, Wahl (eds.), *Essays in Honour of Pernilla Lindh: Constitutionalising the EU Judicial System*, p. 400, and M. Wathelet, with J. Whildemeersch, *Contentieux européen*, Larcier, 2011, N° 238.

[35] See, for a recent example, judgment in *Altice Group Lux v Commission*, C-746/21 P, EU:C:2023:836, paras 235–248. As an older example of a partial annulment of a judgment of the General Court, it seems appropriate to mention the judgment in *Commission v SGL Carbon*, C-301/04 P, EU:C:2006:432, paras 67–70. See, also, judgment in *Baustahlgewebe v Commission*, C-185/95 P, EU:C:1998:608, in which the Court of Justice reduced the fine determined by the Commission and confirmed by the General Court because of the excessive duration of the procedure before the General Court. In subsequent case law, this solution has been reversed. In its judgment in *Groupe Gascogne v Commission*, C-58/12 P, EU:C:2013:770, paras 80–90, the Court of Justice stated that, in such a situation, a claim for damages should be brought before the General

2.7 Concluding Remarks of the First Part

In summary, the EU Courts' exercise of their unlimited jurisdiction is limited and circumscribed by both formal and substantial rules. Furthermore, the EU Courts exercise their unlimited jurisdiction within the same basic procedural framework as in an action for annulment—although the rules are applied in a less strict fashion. This seems especially to be the case as regards the rule non ultra petita. As Advocate General M. Poiares Maduro commented in *Groupe Danone:* "within this area, the *non ultra petita* rule, properly understood as a restriction on the exercise of judicial power, has only a limited role to play".[36]

3 Unlimited Jurisdiction in the Light of the Prohibition of Reformatio in Pejus

3.1 The Background to and Rationale for the Prohibition of Reformatio in Pejus

As we have already seen in the foregoing, Article 31 of Regulation 1/2003 provides that the EU Courts have the power, under unlimited jurisdiction, to "cancel, reduce or increase the fine". We have also seen that the exercise of "unlimited jurisdiction" is not really unlimited or unconditional but subject to formal as well as substantial requirements and conditions. In this second part, we are going to focus on one specific aspect of the exercise of unlimited jurisdiction—the power of the EU Courts to increase the fine fixed by the Commission in the light of the principle of reformatio in pejus, a principle that traces its roots back to roman law[37] and that has found a renewed importance from the early nineteenth century and onwards.[38]

The literary translation of the latin notion of *reformatio in pejus* is "change for the worse".[39] The notion concerns the possibility to change an administrative decision or a judgment to the detriment of a party that has launched an appeal. The

Court. See also Opinion of Advocate General Wahl in *European Union v Kendrion*, C-150/17 P, EU:C:2018:612, para. 127.

[36] Opinion of Advocate General Poiares Maduro in *Groupe Danone v Commission*, C-3/06 P, EU:C:2006:720, para. 49.

[37] C. Herke, D. Tóth, 'Theoretical and Practical Issues of the Prohibition of *Reformatio in Peius in Hungary*' (2011) Issues of Business and Law, Vol. 3, pp. 95–109.

[38] Ibid., pp. 95–96; See also, to this effect, opinion of the French Council of State, 12 November 1806, on whether, in an appeal by the civil party, criminal courts may amend unchallenged provisions of judgments rendered in correctional matters (IV, Bulletin CXXVI, No. 2044).

[39] As opposed to the notion of *reformatio in melius*, which could be translated as "change for the better".

meaning of the legal principle is that a party that appeals a decision of an administrative body or a judgment of a court should not be put in a less advantageous position than that in which he would have found himself if he had not brought that appeal, unless there is an appeal of another party to the proceedings.[40]

The principle is often—in criminal and administrative procedural law—justified by the fundamental right to an effective judicial protection as provided by Article 47 of the Charter of Fundamental Rights of the European Union (the Charter) and Article 6 of the European Convention on Human Rights (ECHR).[41]

The prohibition of reformatio in pejus is, however, also applicable in civil procedural law which is not necessarily governed by the same or, at least, identical objectives as criminal or administrative procedural law. According to Advocate General Bot in *Heemskerk and Schaap* "the principle of the prohibition on reformatio in pe[j]us is closely associated with the principle that it is for the parties to delimit the subject-matter of the proceedings".[42]

It would seem that the prohibition, in a broader sense, is also justified by reasons of legal certainty, legitimate expectations and foreseeability.[43] It follows that the prohibition favors the formal framework and predictability over materially correct solutions.[44] It gives the parties involved in a litigation the possibility to foresee the consequences and risks of their actions and to act in full knowledge of the possible consequences of their actions without being deterred from using the remedies at their disposal.[45]

---

[40] See, for example, Opinion of Advocate General Bot in *Heemskerk and Schaap*, C-455/06, EU:C:2008:258, para. 81.

[41] See, for example, L. Bernardeau, J.-P. Christienne, op. cit., II 1582, p. 820; J.-V. Louis and others, *La Cour de justice: les actes des institutions*, Vol. 10 of *Le droit de la Communauté économique européenne* (Bruxelles, Université de Bruxelles, 1983), p. 95; Prop. 1971:30 Del 2 s. 580; H. Leifman, "Prövningsramens omfattning — Överklagande av. ett grundbeslut jämfört med ett omprövningsbeslut", Examensarbete i offentlig rätt, Juridiska institutionen, Stockholms universitet (2017); U. von Essen, *Processramen i förvaltningsmål* (2016), pp. 149–150; H. Ragnemalm, *Förvaltningsprocessrättens grunder* (2014), p. 169 f.

[42] Opinion of Advocate General Bot in *Heemskerk and Schaap*, *supra*, footnote 21. Although the "principe dispositif" mentioned by Advocate General Bot is applicable in French civil procedural law, the case at hand concerned Article 8:69 of the General Law on Administrative Law (*Algemene wet bestuursrecht*), applicable in the Netherlands. The Civil Service Tribunal, in its order in *Bleser v Court of Justice*, F-25/07, EU:F:2007:98, para. 132, also concluded that the prohibition of reformatio in pejus is closely related to the "principe dispositif"—the right of the parties to dispose freely of the object of their appeal.

[43] See L. Bernardeau, J.-P. Christienne, op. cit., p. 820; and Bot, ibid., footnote 21.

[44] U. von Essen, op. cit., pp. 146–148.

[45] A delicate question that goes beyond the scope of this article is whether, especially in criminal and administrative cases, a modification of a decision or a judgment is a "change for the worse" that infringes the prohibition of reformatio in pejus. In criminal law, for example, one criminal sentence, like a community sentence that is not a fixed prison sentence, may on appeal be exchanged for another one that is similar but not identical. This article is, however, focused on the imposition of fines and other penalty payments in competition law cases that do not normally raise this kind of problems. See, also, on a similar topic, judgment in *TP v Commission*, T-776/22, EU:T:2024:908, in which the applicant argued, inter alia, that the contested decision breached legal certainty by

The purpose of the second part of this contribution is to examine the relationship between the exercise of unlimited jurisdiction in competition law and the prohibition of reformatio in pejus. The first question that should be examined is if the prohibition of reformatio in pejus is explicitly recognized in Union law—and particularly in competition law. The second question to be examined is if the power of the EU Courts to exercise their unlimited jurisdiction, especially the power to increase the fine, is limited or, at least, influenced by the prohibition in question. Before examining the eventual role of the principle in Union law it is however useful to examine briefly the significance of the principle in the national legal systems of the Member States.

3.2 *The Prohibition of Reformatio in Pejus in the Member States*

Although this brief overview does not claim to give an exhaustive or in-depth description of the principle in the Member States, a cursory comparison of their national legal orders shows that it exists in almost all Member States.[46] Furthermore, in the overwhelming majority of Member States, the prohibition of reformatio in pejus seems to be applicable as well in criminal, civil and administrative procedural law. In several legal orders there are certain exceptions to this general prohibition, exceptions that in many cases, however, seem to be well-defined, motivated and justified.

To illustrate the application of the principle on the national level, it can be useful to give a brief overview of the relevant rules in a number of national legal orders.

- In the *Swedish legal order* the prohibition of reformatio in pejus is applied almost without exception by administrative bodies as well as courts in both administrative, criminal and civil procedural law.[47] In competition law cases the competent courts—the Patent and Market Court (Patent- och marknadsdomstolen) and, on appeal, the Superior Patent and Market Court (Patent- och marknadsöverdomstolen)—mostly apply civil procedural law.[48] Both courts are bound by the prohibition of reformatio in pejus.

retroactively upholding an exclusion penalty under Regulation 2018/1046 (on the financial rules applicable to the general budget) which was more severe than a financial penalty (cf. footnote 10). However, this argument was not examined by the General Court, as it annulled the contested decision on the basis of another argument.

[46] The prohibition does not seem to apply in the Irish legal order.

[47] Section 29 of the Swedish Administrative Court Procedure Act (förvaltningsprocesslagen 1971:291); Chapter 51, Section 25 and Chapter 17, Section 3 of the Swedish Code of Judicial Procedure (rättegångsbalken 1942:740).

[48] Chapter 8, Section 2, of the Swedish Competition Act (konkurrenslagen 2008:579). The Patent and Market Court forms part of the District Court of Stockholm (*Stockholms tingsrätt*), and the Superior Patent and Market Court forms part of the Svea Court of Appeal (*Svea hovrätt*).

- In *German law,* the prohibition of reformatio in pejus is known in criminal and civil procedural law. However, the principle is not applicable in the field of administrative offenses where civil fines are imposed and, therefore, in competition law. In case of an appeal against a decision of the Federal Competition Authority (Bundeskartellamt, BKartA), an increase in the fine by the Higher Regional Court (Oberlandesgericht)[49] is generally permissible according to the general rules on administrative offenses (Ordnungswidrigkeitenrecht)[50] that do not make an exception for fines imposed in competition cases.
- In the *Netherlands*, the principle is generally applicable if an explicit derogation is not provided. The prohibition is applicable in both Dutch administrative and civil procedural law but—unlike most other Member States not in criminal procedural law. The prohibition is however applicable in competition law cases where administrative procedural law is applied.[51]
- In *France* the prohibition of reformatio in pejus is applicable in criminal, civil and commercial law as well as in administrative law. In competition law the decisions of the French competition authority can be appealed to the Court of Appeal of Paris (Cour d'appel de Paris) which has unlimited jurisdiction and applies procedural rules in the Commercial Code (Code de commerce).[52] The Court of Appeal is not bound by the principle in the event of a cross-appeal by the Minister in charge of the Economy.[53]
- In *Luxembourgish law* the prohibition of reformatio in pejus is also generally applicable.[54] As regards competition law, the national competition authority can decide to impose fines on economic operators for violations of rules in this field of law.[55] The Administrative Court (Tribunal administratif) has unlimited jurisdiction in its review of the fines imposed[56] but is in principle prohibited from

49 Appeals against decisions of the Bundeskartellamt are examined by the Higher Regional Court of Düsseldorf (*Oberlandesgericht Düsseldorf*).

50 OLG Düsseldorf, 6. Kartellsenat, Urteil v. 17.8.2020 – V-6 Kart 10/19 (OWi)—Kaffee im Drogeriemarkt (Rossmann).

51 Article 7:11 and Article 8:69 of the General Administrative Law Act (*Algemene wet bestuursrecht*).

52 Articles L.464-7 and L.464-8 of the Commercial Code (*Code de commerce*).

53 Judgments of the Court of Appeal of Paris of June 28, 2005, No. 05/02333, and of January 15, 2008, No. 07/02775.

54 In criminal law see, Court of cassation, Cass. Mai 16 (2002) n° 14/2002; in administrative proceedings, the Council of State of the Grand Duchy of Luxembourg recalls that the prohibition of reformatio in pejus must be respected where only the sanctioned person files an appeal, Conseil d'État, *Avis du 26 juin 2012 sur le projet de loi ayant pour objet la discipline dans l'armée, la police grand-ducale et l'inspection générale de la police*, Doc. parl. No 63791, p. 9), see also case law cited in footnote 62.

55 Article 49 of the Luxembourgish Competition Act (*Loi du 30 novembre 2022 relative à la concurrence*).

56 Articles 22, 44–46, 48–50, 58, and 60 of the Luxembourgish Competition Act.

increasing the fine, unless the competition authority makes an explicit claim that is justified by new elements of fact and law.[57]

- In the *Portuguese legal order* there is also a general prohibition of reformatio in pejus in criminal law and in the domain of "contra-ordenações" which is a penalty system halfway between criminal law and administrative law.[58] Nevertheless, both in the field of criminal law and in the domain of "contra-ordenações" the fines can be raised if the economic conditions of the defendant have improved significantly.[59] The general prohibition of reformatio in pejus does not apply in several specific fields of "contra-ordenações", for example in actions against fines imposed by the national competition authority.[60] On appeal the prohibition of reformatio in pejus is however applicable again and the appeal court cannot increase the fine.
- In *Maltese law* the prohibition is explicitly provided for in criminal law[61] and can be inferred from the relevant provisions applicable to civil and administrative law proceedings.[62] As regards the fines in competition law they are not set by the Competition authority but by the courts and the prohibition is applicable.[63]
- In *Hungarian law* the prohibition is mainly applicable in criminal law.[64]
- In the other Member States, with the exception of *Ireland*, the prohibition seems to be applicable, in principle, as well in criminal,[65] administrative[66] and civil

[57] Judgment of the Luxemburg administrative court, Mars 30, (2015), (33903a).

[58] Article 409 of the Portuguese Criminal Procedure Code (*Código de Processo Penal*) and Article 72-A(1) of the *Regime Geral das Contraordenações* (approved by Decree-Law 433/82, of October 27, and modified on several occasions).

[59] The fines referred to are called "multa"—a daily amount applied as a sanction in criminal law and "coima" in the domain of "contra-ordenações".

[60] Article 88 of the Portuguese Competition Law (Law No. 19/2012) stipulates that the Court of First Instance (specialized in competition) has "full jurisdiction" and can reduce or increase the sanction/fine applied by the Portuguese Competition Authority.

[61] Article 502(1), al 2, Criminal Code (Chapter 9 of the *Laws of Malta*), Malta.

[62] Article 238 of the Maltese Code of Organisation and Civil Procedure provides (Chapter 12 of the *laws of Malta*), in sum, that the reversal or variation of a judgment shall operate in favour of the appellant. This article is also applicable to administrative proceedings as Civil courts in Malta have jurisdiction to rule on the validity of any administrative act (see Article 469A of the Code of Organisation and Civil Procedure under 'Judicial Review of Administrative Action').

[63] *Federation of Estate Agents v Director General (Competition) and ors*, Judgment, Case C-87/2013, OCL 167 (MT 2015), 21st April 2015, Malta.

[64] See, in this regard, E. Belovics, M. Tóth, *Büntető eljárásjog*, HVG-ORAC, (Budapest 2006), p. 441.

[65] See, in particular, for Bulgaria, Article 337 of the Criminal Procedure Code (*Наказателно-процесуалния кодекс*); for Poland, Article 434 of the Criminal Procedure Code (*Kodeks postępowania karnego*); for the Czech Republic, Article 259(4) of the Criminal Procedure Code (*zákon č. 141/1961 Sb., trestní řád*); for Romania, Article 418 of the Criminal Procedure Code (*Codul de procedură penală*); for Slovakia, Article 322(4) of the Criminal Procedure Code (*Trestný poriadok*); for Italy, Article 597(3) of the Criminal Procedural Code (*Codice di Procedura Penale*).

[66] See, as an example, for Estonia, para. 2, al. 3 of Chapter 1: Administrative court procedure in Part 1: Principal 99 provisions of the Code of Administrative Court Procedure (*Halduskohtumenetluse*

law[67]—in many cases with a stronger protection in criminal law.

After this brief overview, it is interesting to note that the prohibition is, in many cases, applicable in situations and procedures that are comparable to the procedure in Regulation 1/2003 and it is also notable that the form of the procedure—civil, criminal or administrative—does not seem to be decisive. However, as already mentioned, it also seems clear that the principle is not identically applied and that certain exceptions to the principle exist in several national legal orders.

3.3 *Is the Prohibition of Reformatio in Pejus Explicitly Recognized in the Union's Law?*

After having concluded that the prohibition of reformatio in pejus is, more or less, universally, even if not identically, applicable in the Member States, the question is if it is protected in Union law.

First, it may be of interest to have a look at the fundamental rights in the ECHR that, in the terms of Article 6, paragraph 3, of the TEU, "constitute general principles of the Union's law". Is the prohibition of reformatio in pejus, for example, protected by Article 6 of the ECHR as an element of the rights of defense of accused persons in criminal cases? The answer to this question is negative. The prohibition of reformatio in pejus does not seem to be protected by the ECHR.[68] And although the European Court of Human Rights has not explicitly denied the applicability of the principle, some of its judges have expressed this point of view in their individual opinions in certain judgments.[69] It follows that Article 47 and the other relevant articles of the Charter—which should be given the same meaning and scope as the

seadustik); for the Czech Republic, Article 90(3) of The Administrative Procedure Code (*zákon č. 500/2004 Sb., správní řád*); for Croatia, Article 118 of the Administrative Procedure Code (*Zakon o općem upravnom postupku*); for Slovakia, Article 195 of the Administrative Procedure Code (*Správny súdny poriadok*).

[67] See, as an example, for Poland, Article 384 of the Civil Procedure Code (*Kodeks postępowania cywilnego*); for Romania, Article 481 of the Civil Procedure Code (*Codul de procedură civilă*); for the Czech Republic, judgment of the Supreme Court of the Czech Republic (*Nejvyššího soudu ČR*), file no. 22, Cdo 2258/2021, January 26, 2023; for Slovenia, Article 359 of the Civil Procedure Code (*Zakon o pravdnem postopku*).

[68] The Committee of the Ministers of the Council of Europe has, however, in its Recommendation No. R(92)17 of the Committee of Ministers to Member States, October 19, (1992), stated that "[t]he principle of the prohibition of reformatio in pejus should be taken into account where only the defendant appeals". The "defendant" should probably be understood as the "accused".

[69] Partly concurring and partly dissenting opinion of Judge K. Wojtyczek (ECtHR, *Janowiec and Others v Russia*, CE:ECHR:2013:1021JUD005550807, para. 11); concurring opinion of Judge B. Zupančič (ECtHR, *Ruslan Yakovenko v Ukraine*, CE:ECHR:2015:0604JUD000542511).

corresponding rights of the ECHR—do not protect the prohibition of reformatio in pejus either.[70]

Furthermore, the prohibition is not explicitly protected by the treaties or by any other legal act adopted by the institutions of the Union.[71] This is perhaps not surprising in the light of the fact that even in certain national legal orders the prohibition is not explicitly protected in legal texts but recognized as a general principle that has to be respected by the public authorities and the courts.[72] The question is therefore if the principle is recognized and protected by the EU Courts. It is clear that parties have invoked the prohibition in a number of cases before the EU Courts not only in competition law but also in other fields of law—not least in intellectual property law.[73]

Whether the prohibition of reformatio in pejus should be regarded as a general principle of the Union's law is, of course, a question that has to be decided by the EU Courts—and ultimately by the Court of Justice. In the past, the Court of Justice has not always clearly laid out how it has come to the conclusion that a certain principle is a general principle of law. In certain cases, however, it is clear that the Court has used a comparative method.[74] That is to say that it has compared the national legal orders and concluded that a general principle of law exists where a principle is common to the Member States or, at least, applicable in a majority of the Member States.[75] In the light of the fact that the prohibition of reformatio in pejus, in one form or another, is applicable in almost all Member States, it appears that the prin-

[70] Article 52(3) of the Charter. Nevertheless, this provision does not prevent Union law from providing more extensive protection.

[71] Even if the principle is not protected as such, it may be explicitly protected in certain legal acts in certain areas of law (see, as regards an invalidity pension received by a civil servant, Opinion of Advocate General Lenz in *Suss v Commission*, 265/83, EU:C:1984:333, p. 4052.

[72] See the legal orders of Bulgaria, Cyprus, Greece, Latvia, Luxembourg and The Netherlands. In Swedish civil and administrative law, the principle is not explicitly mentioned but is derived by the national courts from Chapter 17, Section 3 of the Swedish Code of Judicial Procedure (rättegångsbalken 1942:740), and by the administrative courts, from Section 29 of the Swedish Administrative Court Procedure Act (förvaltningsprocesslagen 1971:291).

[73] See orders in *Dimitriadis v Court of Auditors*, C-140/96 P, EU:C:1997:493, paras 48–51; and *Primagran v EUIPO*, T-624/21, EU:T:2022:620, paras 41–42; and judgments in *Les Éditions Albert René v OHIM*, C-16/06 P, EU:C:2008:739C-16/06 P, paras 33–50; *Evets v OHIM*, T-20/08 and T-21/08, EU:T:2009:356, para. 37; and *Stryker v EUIPO*, T-204/21, EU:T:2022:116, paras 23 and 49.

[74] See J. Hettne, I. Otken Eriksson, '*EU-rättslig metod, Teori och genomslag i svensk rättstillämpning*', Norstedts förlag (2011), p. 68 f.

[75] See, for example, judgments in *Kampffmeyer and Others v EEC*, 56/74 to 60/74, EU:C:1976:78, para. 6; and *AM & S Europe v Commission*, 155/79, EU:C:1982:157, paras 18–27. For a more recent example, see the Opinion of Advocate General Léger in *Köbler*, C-224/01, EU:C:2003:207, paras 77–86. Advocate General Léger based his conclusion of the existence of a principle of State liability for breach of Union law partly on a comparison of the legal orders of the Member States and the existence of the principle in these legal orders. The Court of Justice reached the same conclusion as the Advocate General but without referring to a comparison of the national legal orders or to the existence of a general principle of law.

ciple fulfils the requirements that the Court has set up in order to consider a principle to be a general principle of law.

So far, the EU Courts have refrained from taking an explicit position on the issue.[76] The Court of justice has repeatedly avoided responding to arguments founded on the prohibition of reformatio in pejus. It has, however, interestingly, considered that a prohibition of reformatio in pejus in national law could limit the impact and application of Union law. In *Heemskerk and Schaap*, the Court of Justice was asked whether Union law required national courts to examine, of their own motion, pleas in law derived from Union law, where such an examination would result in denial of the prohibition of reformatio in pejus.[77] The Court stated that "[s]uch an obligation would be contrary not only to the principles of respect for the rights of the defense, legal certainty and protection of legitimate expectations, which underlie the prohibition, but would expose an individual who brought an action against an act adversely affecting him to the risk that such an action would place him in a less favourable position than he would have been in, had he not brought that action".[78] Although, this case concerned a prohibition of reformatio in pejus enshrined in national law, in the case at hand Dutch law, the Court emphasized the importance of the prohibition for the judicial protection of the individual.

Like the Court of justice, the General Court has refrained from recognizing the principle of reformatio in pejus. In several Trade Mark cases, the General Court has responded to arguments based on the principle by stating that regardless of whether the prohibition of reformatio in pejus is applicable or not, the contested decision does not contravene the prohibition in question.[79] In one case concerning a civil servant, the Civil Service Tribunal made a similar statement, stating that "even supposing that the prohibition of reformatio in pejus could be invoked in a non-criminal matter, it can not [...] be invoked against either the legislature, when it amends the statutory rules or the administration, when it fixes the grade classification of civil servants".[80]

If the EU Courts, and especially the Court of Justice, have been reluctant to react to arguments founded on the prohibition of reformatio in pejus, certain Advocate Generals have made statements in their opinions implying that they consider that the principle should be respected.[81]

---

[76] See judgments in *Evets Corp. v OHIM*, paras 41 and 42; and *Stryker Corp. v EUIPO*, paras 23 and 49; and the order in *Primagran v EUIPO*, paras 41 and 42 (*supra*, n. 74).

[77] See judgment in *Heemskerk and Schaap*, C-455/06, EU:C:2008:650, paras 44–48.

[78] Ibid., para. 47.

[79] See *supra*, n. 74.

[80] See judgment in *Bleser* (*supra* n. 43), para 132. Translation to English by the author.

[81] See Opinions of Advocate General Ruiz-Jarabo Colomer in *Commission v Greece*, C-387/97, EU:C:1999:455, paras 118–119; of Advocate General Trstenjak in case C-16/06 P, *Les Éditions Albert René v OHIM*, EU:C:2007:728, paras 35 f.; of Advocate General Bot in case C-43/15 P, *BSH v OHIM*, EU:C:2016:129, para 105; and of Advocate General Rantos in *Lietuvos geležinkeliai v Commission*, C-42/21 P, 2022, paras 161 and 162.

In summary, at the present time, the principle has not been explicitly recognized by the Union's legislator or by the EU Courts as a general principle of law—but neither has it been rejected.

3.4 Does the Prohibition of *Reformatio in Pejus* Influence the EU Courts' Exercise of their Unlimited Jurisdiction?

The second question to be examined is if the power of the EU Courts to exercise their unlimited jurisdiction, especially the power to increase the fine, is limited or at least influenced by the prohibition in question. As a reminder, Article 31 of Regulation 1/2003 authorizes the EU Courts, when they are exercising their unlimited jurisdiction, not only to cancel or reduce the fine imposed by the Commission but also to increase it.

According to some commentators, this article authorizes, in reality, an increase of the fine without any consideration to the prohibition of reformatio in pejus (or even to the prohibition of *non ultra petita*).[82] They argue that an applicant that has been fined by the Commission has no interest in asking for an increase of the fine. They also claim that the Commission would not, in most circumstances, even if it could, appeal its own decision. So what does the EU Courts' practical application of its unlimited jurisdiction in Article 31 of Regulation 1/2003 look like? In other words, what are the situations in which the EU Courts consider an increase of the fine justified?

The EU Courts frequently reiterate the wording of Article 31 of Regulation 1/2003, stating that they have the power not only to annul and reduce the fine but also to increase it.[83] The General Court has stated that "there is nothing preventing the Commission from also referring to the EU judicature the question of the amount of the fine and from applying to have that fine increased".[84] Against this background, it is interesting to note that the EU Courts have, in reality, been very reluctant to increase fines imposed by the Commission".[85]

To my knowledge, there is only one case, *BASF and UCB,* in which the overall fine has been increased. It is interesting to note that the Commission had not

[82] See L. Bernardeau and J.-P. Christienne, op. cit., pp. 819–821; F. Clausen, op. cit., p. 407; G. Gaulard, op. cit., p. 273.

[83] See, for example, judgmentgs in *Lietuvos geležinkeliai v Commission*, C-42/21 P, EU:C:2023:12, para. 152; *E.ON Energie v Commission*, C-89/11 P, EU:C:2012:738, para. 124 and the case-law cited; and *Pometon v Commission*, C-440/19 P, EU:C:2021:214, para. 136.

[84] See judgments in *Schunk and Schunk Kohlenstoff-Technik v Commission*, T-69/04, EU:T:2008:415, para. 244; and *Quanta Storage v Commission,* T-772/15, EU:T:2019:519, para. 274.

[85] F. Castillo de la Torre, E. Gippini Fournier, op. cit., pp. 465–470, paras 6.196–6.209.

formally requested an increase and that BASF had only requested the General Court to examine the amount of the fine.[86]

As regards the General Court, only a certain number of examples can be given where an increase has been seriously considered. In the judgment in *Roquette Frères*, the General Court considered an increase after it was revealed, during the Court proceedings, that the applicant had provided misleading information during the administrative procedure.[87] A specific amount was added by the General Court on this ground but the overall fine was reduced for other reasons. In another case, *Tokai Carbon,* the applicant Nippon Carbon was penalized for challenging before the General Court certain facts which the Commission had good reasons to consider that it would no longer call in question. Exercising its unlimited jurisdiction, the General Court increased Nippon Carbon's fine by two percentage points for this reason.[88] The overall fine imposed on Nippon Carbon was however almost halved due to the General Court's different approach concerning the division of the members of the cartel into categories and the fixing of the respective starting amounts of the fines.[89] In a similar fashion, in *Shell,* the General Court stated that when "an undertaking has failed to submit, intentionally or negligently, during the administrative procedure, decisive evidence for the setting of the amount of the fine [...] that factor will be taken into consideration when the Court determines the appropriate amount of the fine".[90] The General Court concluded, however, that the applicants had not failed to fulfil their obligation of sincere cooperation. In *Clariant* the applicants had benefited from a 10% reduction of the fine because of a settlement they had reached with the Commission. During the appeal, the Commission made a counterclaim asking the General Court to increase the fine arguing that the applicants had challenged facts recognized by them during the settlement procedure.[91] The General Court found that the arguments of the Commission were unfounded and rejected the counterclaim.

It has also been argued that there is, in reality, an increase of the fine in situations where the EU Courts find that certain circumstances or considerations in the contested decisions have not been established.[92] In *AEG* the Court of Justice found that

---

[86] See judgment in *BASF and UCB v Commission*, T-101/05 and T-111/05, EU:T:2007:380, paras 24 and 212–223. BASF cooperated with the Commission on the global cartel, but as it was time-barred, the Court recalculated the fine solely on the European cartel, excluding the previously granted reduction.

[87] See judgment in *Roquette Frères v Commission*, T-322/01, EU:T:2006:267, paras 13–24 and 293–316.

[88] See judgment in *Tokai Carbon and Others v Commission*, T-236/01 etc, EU:T:2004:118, esp. para. 112.

[89] Ibid., paras 216–237, especially paras 236 and 237, 254, 290, 319, 457.

[90] See judgment in *Shell Petroleum and Others v Commission*, T-343/06, EU:T:2012:478, paras 116–128.

[91] See judgment in *Clariant and Clariant International v Commission*, T-590/20, EU:T:2023:650 23, paras 220–230.

[92] See F. Clausen, op. cit., pp. 393–394 and 409.

"[t]he fact that the Commission has not succeeded in proving a number of individual cases does not [...] affect the scope of the infringement" and did not justify a reduction of the fine.[93] And in *Volkswagen* the General Court found that the reduction of the fine did not necessarily have to be proportionate to the reduction of the period which the Commission had taken into account.[94]

An interesting question is if there is reformatio in pejus in the aforementioned situations. Is this the case where the fine is increased as regards certain aspects of the infringement but the overall fine is reduced? A similar question is if there is reformatio in pejus if the court does not find that all of the circumstances that constitute the infringement have been proven but still does not reduce the fine, or does not reduce it sufficiently? Certain commentators are of the opinion that at least the second situation constitutes reformatio in pejus.[95] This seems to be a reasonable position. It is however not the only possible one. The prohibition of reformatio in pejus can also be seen as a limit that should be respected and not exceeded but that does not preclude the courts from making different assessments on the subject matter within that framework. Such an interpretation seems to satisfy the interest of previsibility and legal certainty, two of the main reasons behind the prohibition, in the same time as it is less complicated and gives the jurisdictions greater flexibility.[96]

4 Concluding Remarks

We have seen that the EU Courts, in the exercise of their unlimited jurisdiction, have repeatedly stated that they have the power to increase the fine that has been set by the Commission. If the EU Courts have been prepared to increase certain components of the fine in some cases, they have been very reluctant to increase the overall fine. It thus seems that the rhetoric of the EU Courts does not completely match their action. A further observation is that when the EU Courts have increased a component of a fine it has often been due to an action or an inaction on the part of the applicant during the administrative procedure that has been revealed during the court procedure. As it would be illogical for the Commission to appeal its own

[93] See judgment in *AEG-Telefunken v Commission*, 107/82, EU:C:1983:293, paras 136–138.

[94] See judgment in *Volkswagen v Commission*, T-62/98, EU:T:2000:180, paras 346 and 347.

[95] See L. Bernardeau, J.-P. Christienne, op. cit., II 1582, p. 821, and footnote 3669, in which they refer to judgments in *BPB de Eendracht v Commission*, T-311/94, EU:T:1998:93, paras 337–339; *Dansk Rørindustri v Commission*, T-21/99, EU:T:2002:74, paras 62 and 251; and *JCB Service v Commission*, T-67/01, EU:T:2004:3, paras 184 and 185.

[96] It is interesting to note in this regard that, in Swedish criminal law, the appeal court can confirm the sentence of the lower court even where it finds the appellant not guilty on one of the charges for which he or she had been found guilty by the lower instance court (NJA 1998 s. 713). See, also, the commentary by P. Fitger, M. Sörbom, T. Eriksson, P. Hall, R. Palmkvist and C. Renfors, Rättegångsbalken, (Juno 1 October 2024), on Chapter 51, Section 25 of the Swedish Code of Judicial Procedure.

decisions, it seems reasonable to allow it to request, as a counterclaim, an increase of the fine in certain exceptional circumstances. If, for example, the applicant has left misleading information during the administrative procedure that has affected the contested decision, it would be appropriate to permit the Commission to react and eventually demand an increase of the fine.[97] Otherwise, the administrative procedure could be circumvented.

Even though the EU Courts do not recognize the prohibition of reformatio in pejus—at least not explicitly—they seem to hesitate to go against it in their judicial activity, only allowing a derogation when it may be clearly justified. So it seems possible that the prohibition plays a role, indirectly and, maybe, unconsciously in the judicial activity of the EU Courts. This is probably not very surprising in view of the almost universal application of the principle in the Member States. So, what may the future have in store for the EU Courts' exercise of their unlimited jurisdiction and the prohibition of reformatio in pejus? This is of course not easy to foresee. But if the EU Courts felt the need to recognize the prohibition of reformatio in pejus, they may choose to clarify its relationship to the exercise of unlimited jurisdiction. They may, to be more specific, define and justify eventual exceptions to the prohibition. In this regard, the Court of Justice may clarify if there is any reason at all to provide an exception to the prohibition when it exercises unlimited jurisdiction after a partial annulment of a judgment of the General Court. In fact, the need to provide exceptions in this situation does not appear evident as all the parties have the possibility to appeal the judgments of the General Court.

It is difficult to predict the circumstances that may bring the EU Courts to clarify the relationship between the exercise of unlimited jurisdiction and the prohibition of reformatio in pejus. It may be a wish to bring the procedure before the EU Courts more in line with national procedural principles and rules or maybe future developments in the case-law of the European Court of Human Rights concerning Articles 6 or 13 of the ECHR.[98] At this point, this is, however, only pure speculation.

---

[97] See M. Polzin, 'Die Erhöhung von Kartellbußgeldern durch den Unionsrichter' (2011) WuW, No. 5, pp. 454–462.

[98] In a case concerning the procedure followed in competition law cases in Italy, which was similar to the procedure before the Commission and the EU Courts, the European Court of Human Rights considered that the fine imposed on the applicant was a criminal penalty, so the criminal limb of Article 6, para. 1 of the ECHR was applicable. No violation of that article was, however, found by the Court's majority (ECtHR, *Menarini Diagnostics v Italy*, CE:ECHR:2011:0927JUD004350908). On this subject, see also N. Wahl, 'The role of the Court of Justice in ensuring compliance with fundamental rights in competition cases since the Lisbon Treaty', in Derenne, Merola (eds), *The Role of the Court of Justice of the European Union in Competition Law Cases*, pp. 267–276; I. S. Forrester, 'A challenge for Europe's judges: the review of fines in competition cases' (2011) European Law Review, Vol. 36, No. 2, pp. 185–207; and N. Wahl, 'Enjeu et limites actuelles de la jurisprudence relative à la compétence de pleine juridiction conférée au juge de l'Union en matière de concurrence', in *La Cour de justice de l'Union européenne sous la présidence de Vassilios Skouris (2003–2015), Liber amicorum Vassilios Skouris*, Bruylant, 2015, pp. 727–740.

The Quest for Evidence in Private Enforcement of EU Competition Law: An Overview of the Court's Case Law on Disclosure of Evidence

Andreas Scordamaglia-Tousis

1 Introduction

The present contribution aims at presenting an overview of the case law of the Court of Justice on the interpretation of the provisions of Directive 2014/104/EU which governs actions for damages under national law for infringements of competition law[1] (commonly referred to as the "Damages Directive"), with a focus on rules pertaining to facilitate claimant's access to evidence.

Since its adoption, the Court of Justice has been called to interpret the provisions of the Damages Directive in nine cases,[2] three of which concerned the interpretation

[1] OJ 2014 L 349, p. 1.

[2] See, in chronological order, judgments in *Cogeco Communications*, C-637/17, EU:C:2019:263; *Volvo and DAF Trucks*, C-267/20, EU:C:2022:494; *PACCAR and Others*, C-163/21, EU:C:2022:863 ('*Paccar*'); *RegioJet*, C-57/21, EU:C:2023:6 ('*RegioJet*'); *Tráficos Manuel Ferrer*, C-312/21, EU:C:2023:99 ('*Tráficos Manuel Ferrer*); *Repsol Comercial de Productos Petrolíferos*, C-25/21, EU:C:2023:298; *Heureka Group (Online price comparison services)*, C-605/21, EU:C:2024:324; and *ASG 2*, C-253/23, EU:C:2025:40 ('*ASG2*'). It is also worth noting that one request for a preliminary ruling led to the adoption of an Order in *Deutsche Bank (Cartel – Euro interest rate derivatives)*, C-198/22 and C-199/22, EU:C:2023:166. Note that the Court has also referred and interpreted provisions of the Damages Directive in the context of other requests for a preliminary reference, namely, in judgments in *Apple Sales International and Others*, C-595/17, EU:C:2018:854, para. 35; *Skanska Industrial Solutions and Others*, C-724/17, EU:C:2019:204, paras.33 to 35; *Sumal*, C-882/19, EU:C:2021:800, paras. 40–41 ('*Sumal*'); *Booking.com and Booking.com (Deutschland)*, C-264/23, EU:C:2024:764, and *Consiglio nazionale delle Ricerche*, C-439/23, EU:C:2024:773, paras. 52 and 53.

A. Scordamaglia-Tousis (✉)
Court of Justice of the European Union, Luxembourg, Luxembourg
e-mail: Andreas.Scordamaglia-tousis@curia.europa.eu

L. Prete, L. Rezki (eds.), *Judging & (Re)Thinking European Union Law*,
https://doi.org/10.1007/978-3-032-13473-8_18

of its provisions relating to disclosure of evidence, namely *Paccar*, *RegioJet* and *Tráficos Manuel Ferrer*. These cases are closely linked to the honouree of this *liber amicorum*, Nils Wahl, who, in his capacity as reporting judge, held the pen in drafting the respective judgments, thus providing useful guidance to national courts on the potential and use of these provisions.

2 The Importance of Access to Evidence in Private Enforcement

At the outset, it should be recalled that, according to settled case law, the main competition provisions of the Treaty—Articles 101 and 102 TFUE—produce direct effect in relations between individuals, thus creating, for the individuals concerned, both rights and obligations, which national courts must enforce.[3] National courts have therefore an equally essential part in applying competition rules as the Commission and the national competition authorities (NCAs), by protecting subjective rights under EU law, for example, by awarding damages to the victims of infringements.[4] Indeed, the full effectiveness of EU competition and, in particular, the practical effect of the prohibitions set out in these Treaty provisions would be put at risk if it were not open to any individual to claim damages for loss caused to him or her by an infringement of competition law.[5] It follows that any person is entitled to claim compensation for harm suffered where there is a causal link between that harm and such an infringement.[6]

In this context, it is no secret that actions for damages for infringements of EU competition law typically require a complex factual and economic analysis. Moreover, the evidence necessary to prove a claim for damages is often held exclusively by the alleged defender (usually the infringer, particularly in stand-alone claims) or by third parties (such as NCAs, particularly in follow-on claims) and is not sufficiently accessible to claimants. In view of this so-called "information asymmetry", from a legal standard point of view, adopting strict legal requirements for claimants to assert in detail all the facts of their case at the beginning of an action for damages could ultimately impede the effective exercise of the right to compensation guaranteed by the TFEU.[7]

---

[3] See judgments in *BRT and Société belge des auteurs, compositeurs et éditeurs*, 127/73, EU:C:1974:6, para.16, and *ASG 2*, para.60.

[4] See recital 7 of Council Regulation (EC) No 1/2003 of 16 December 2002 on the implementation of the rules on competition laid down in Articles [101] and [102 TFEU] (OJ 2003 L 1, p. 1) ('Regulation 1/2003').

[5] See judgments in *Courage and Crehan*, C-453/99, EU:C:2001:465, para.26; *Sumal*, para.33; and *ASG 2*, para.61.

[6] See *Sumal*, para.34, and *ASG 2*, para.62.

[7] See recital 14 of the Damages Directive.

3 The Key Provisions of the Damages Directive

The EU legislator, acknowledging the importance of evidence in bringing actions for damages for infringement of competition law and the above-described information asymmetry, adopted some rules aiming to ensure that claimants are afforded the right to obtain the disclosure of evidence that is needed for their claim, a sort of "equality of arms".[8] Indeed, Chapter II of the Damages Directive contains specific provisions dedicated to the "disclosure of evidence".

First, Article 5 of the Damages Directive sets out a number of general rules on the disclosure of evidence in proceedings relating to actions for damages for infringements of competition law. These rules reflect a minimal harmonisation approach, as Member States are permitted to maintain or introduce rules leading to wider disclosure of evidence [Article 5(8)]. According to Article 5(1), national courts should be able to order the defendant or a third party to disclose relevant evidence upon request of a claimant, provided that such request contains a "reasoned justification" including "reasonably available facts and evidence sufficient to support the plausibility of its claim for damages". Article 5(2) adds that the evidence disclosed can take the form of "specified items" or "categories of evidence" circumscribed as precisely and as narrowly as possible on the basis of the aforementioned "reasoned justification". Moreover, as per Article 5(3), such disclosure of evidence should be proportionate as to the legitimate interests of all parties and third parties concerned. Finally, special provisions exist for the protection of disclosure of evidence containing confidential or legally privileged information [see, respectively, Article 5(4) and Article 5(6)].

Second, Article 6 of that directive lays down rules that are specific to the disclosure of evidence contained in the file of a competition authority. These rules reflect a balance between the need, on the one hand, to ensure that disclosure does not negatively impact the leniency programmes and settlement procedures, as they contribute significantly to the detection and efficient prosecution of cartels and, ultimately, to bringing follow-on damages actions in cartel cases, and, on the other hand, to ensure that injured parties retain sufficient alternative means by which to obtain access to the evidence needed to prepare their actions.[9]

Evidence therefore is granted a level of protection that differs according to the type of information requested and the need to preserve the effectiveness of public enforcement. Hence, Article 6 distinguishes between three categories of evidence: (i) *evidence on the black list*, i.e., leniency statements and settlement submissions (and verbatim quotations therefrom included in other documents) that are exempted from disclosure [Article 6(6)][10]; (ii) *evidence on the grey list,* i.e., evidence prepared

[8] See recital 15 of the Damages Directive.

[9] See recitals 26 and 27 of the Damages Directive. See also *RegioJet*, paras.41 and 53.

[10] See recital 26 of the Damages Directive, the *ratio legis* being that if self-incriminating statements such as leniency statements and settlement submissions, which are produced for the sole purpose of cooperating with the competition authorities, were to be disclosed, undertakings could be

by a natural or legal person specifically for administrative proceedings initiated by a competition authority, information that that latter authority has drawn up and sent to the parties in the course of those proceedings, and settlement submissions that have been withdrawn, which, national courts may order the disclosure of only after a competition authority has closed its proceedings [Article 6(5)]; and, (iii) *evidence on the white list*, i.e., evidence in the file of a competition authority that does not fall into any of the other two categories [Article 6(9)].[11]

Third, reflected in Article 5(3) and Article 6(4) of the Damages Directive, the latter establishes a specific set of rules that is applicable to requests for the disclosure of evidence, meaning that those requests are not automatically granted but are assessed in terms of the principle of proportionality, taking into account the circumstances and legitimate interests involved. The national court dealing with the matter is therefore called upon to carry out a rigorous review of proportionality, while taking account, as appropriate, of the views which the competition authority concerned may submit to that court, in accordance with Article 6(11) of the Damages Directive.[12]

Fourth, Article 7 contains specific provisions ensuring the practical application of Article 6 and the actual protection of evidence that falls within aforementioned black or grey list, by setting the limits on the use of evidence obtained solely through access to the file of a competition authority.

Fifth, Article 8 provides for the possibility for national courts to impose penalties with regard to specific situations linked to disclosure of evidence, including, the event of a refusal to comply with a disclosure order, the destruction of relevant evidence, or breach of the limits on the use of evidence.

Last but not least, the Court held that these disclosure provisions of the Damages Directive are solely procedural in nature, insofar as they relate to procedural measures applicable before the national courts, conferring on them particular powers in order to establish the facts relied on by the parties. Indeed, they cannot be considered substantive provisions, as they do not relate to the constituent elements of non-contractual civil liability.[13] This qualification was of practical importance for the temporal application of these rules, to the extent that, contrary to substantive provisions, as per Article 22(2) of the Directive, Member States enjoyed a measure of discretion in deciding when such procedural rules would be applicable.[14]

It is in light of these preliminary remarks that I propose to delve into the Court's recent case law.

---

deterred from cooperating with competition authorities under leniency programmes and settlement procedures. Indeed, such disclosure would pose a risk of exposing cooperating undertakings or their managing staff to civil or criminal liability under conditions worse than those of co-infringers not cooperating with the competition authorities.

[11] See *RegioJet*, paras.57–59.

[12] See *Paccar*, para.60.

[13] See *RegioJet*, paras.42–44.

[14] See *RegioJet*, para.45.

4 Overview of the Case Law on "Disclosure of Evidence"

4.1 Paccar: *Disclosure of Evidence Created* de novo *from Pre-Existing Evidence*

In *Paccar*, a Spanish court made a first request for the interpretation of Article 5(1) of the Damages Directive, which, as described above, is the provision intending to give national courts the power to order the defendant or a third party, under certain conditions, to disclose evidence that lies in their control. The request arose in the context of follow-on damages litigation brought in the wake of the adoption of the European Commission's *Trucks* cartel decision (Case AT.39824),[15] which found that 15 truck manufacturers had colluded pricing practices for medium and heavy trucks in the EEA for over 14 years.

The claimants, who had purchased trucks falling within the scope of this decision, sought from the Spanish court access to evidence held by the defendant truck manufacturers, arguing that such evidence was necessary to quantify the artificial price increases resulting from the infringement and, in particular, to carry out a comparison of recommended prices before, during and after the cartel period concerned. The defendants, for their part, opposed the disclosure request arguing that the evidence sought did not pre-exist the request and would require compilation and classification of internal data on an *ad hoc* basis, constituting a disproportionate burden for them, contrary to Article 5(1) of the Directive. Indeed, the wording of the first subparagraph of Article 5(1) and of recital 14 of the Damages Directive, which refers respectively to 'relevant evidence which lies *in their control*' and to 'evidence [...] *held* exclusively by the opposing party', would suggest, according to them, that the requested evidence must have existed prior to the disclosure request and could not be created following that request.[16]

In those circumstances, the Spanish court asked the Court whether the disclosure of relevant evidence, within the meaning of Article 5(1) of the Damages Directive, relates only to documents which already exist or also to documents that the party to whom the request to disclose evidence is addressed must create *ex novo* by compiling or classifying information, knowledge or data in its possession.

The Court's answer was unequivocal. Article 5(1) had to be interpreted as allowing disclosure orders that require the creation of documents *ex novo*, provided such orders conform to the principles of specificity, necessity, and proportionality, and adequately protect the legitimate interests and fundamental rights of the parties involved.[17]

[15] See Commission Decision C(2016) 4673 final relating to a proceeding under Article 101 [TFEU] and Article 53 of the EEA Agreement (Case AT.39824—Trucks), a summary of which was published in the *Official Journal of the European Union* of 6 April 2017 (OJ 2017 C 108, p. 6).

[16] See *Paccar*, para. 21. Emphasis added.

[17] See *Paccar*, para. 69.

The Court's expansive reading of the term "evidence" reflects its underlying aim to interpret the provision in a manner that facilitate claimants, particularly in follow-on actions, in establishing the existence of harm. While the Court acknowledges that the wording of Article 5(1) does suggest that it concerns only 'pre-existing evidence', by referring to the *context* and the *objectives* of the Damages Directive, the Court "elucidated" (in its own terms) the wording of this provision.[18] Indeed, as regards the context, according to the Court the reference to "evidence *in control* of the defendant" merely reflects the finding of a factual situation, which the EU legislature intends to remedy, namely that the defendant (infringer) is normally the sole holder of the relevant evidence, and that there is asymmetry of information between the claimant and the defendant.[19] As to the objectives, the Court sought this opportunity to strengthen the traditionally complementary role attributed to private enforcement in the application of EU competition rules. In the words of the Court "the participation by the private sphere in the *financial penalisation of anticompetitive conduct* and, therefore, *also in its prevention*, is all the more desirable because it is capable not only of providing a remedy for the direct damage alleged to have been suffered by the person in question, *but also for the indirect harm done to the structure and operation of the market*, which was not able to reach full economic efficacy, in particular as regards benefits to the consumers concerned".[20] This finding differs from the traditional (more nuanced) language used by the Court in its previous case law.[21] We can but note that such an "enhanced" role of private enforcement converges with Nils Wahl's perception that private enforcement must have primarily a deterrent rather than a mere compensatory function.[22] It is in light of this "enhanced" role of private enforcement that the Court explained that, on the one hand, from a practical point of view, to provide the claimant only unprocessed, pre-existing and possibly very numerous documents would correspond only imperfectly with its request[23] and deprive the injured parties of an effective tool capably of compensating information asymmetry. On the other hand, excluding at the outset the possibility of requesting disclosure of evidence created *ex novo* could impose obstacles to the overall effectiveness of private enforcement.[24] Besides, disclosure of evidence created *ex novo* will not lead to "information fishing" given the rigorous examination that national courts must conduct, under Article 5(2)

[18] Ibid., para. 49.

[19] Ibid., paras. 42–45.

[20] Ibid., paras.55–56. Emphasis added.

[21] See, for example, *Sumal*, para.35; and *ASG 2*, para.63 where the Court held that "the right for any person to seek compensation for such harm *strengthens the working of the EU competition rules, since it discourages conduct, frequently covert,* which is liable to restrict or distort competition, thereby contributing to the maintenance of effective competition in the European Union".

[22] As noted by N. Wahl, "[i]n my view - and I am aware that this might be provocative - rules on a right to damages under competition law should be used as a deterrent and not primarily as a means of reparation" (in N. Wahl, *Damages for infringement of competition law*, Tort liability and insurance, Scandinavian studies in law, vol.41, 2001, p. 554).

[23] See *Paccar*, para.61.

[24] Ibid., para.62.

and (3), as regard the relevance of the evidence requested, the link between that evidence and the claim of damages submitted, the sufficiency of the degree of precision of that evidence and its proportionality.[25] With regard to the latter, the national court will have to take into account whether the request for evidence created *de novo* imposes a disproportionate burden on the defendant in terms of cost or workload.[26]

4.2 **RegioJet***: Disclosure of Evidence in the Context of an Ongoing Investigation*

In *RegioJet* the Court further clarified the conditions under which national courts may order the disclosure of evidence in the specific context of an ongoing investigation. On the facts, RegioJet, a private Czech rail operator, brought an action for damages before the Czech courts against České dráhy, the national railway carrier, alleging an abuse of a dominant position on a specific regional route and requesting disclosure of evidence which it assumed to be in the possession of České dráhy and available to the Czech competition authority (ÚOHS). The latter had initiated administrative proceedings against České dráhy concerning the same possible abuse of domination position. However, the ÚOHS had stayed its own proceedings due to the European Commission initiating an investigation into the same conduct.

In this context, the Czech Supreme Court submitted five preliminary questions to the Court on the interpretation of Articles 5 and 6 of the Damages Directive, essentially questioning whether it could order such disclosure of evidence.

By its *first question*, the referring court asked, in essence, whether Article 5(1) must be interpreted as precluding a national court from ordering the disclosure of evidence in relation to an alleged infringement of competition law, when administrative proceedings in respect of the same infringement are pending before the Commission, leading the national court to stay the proceedings initiated before it.[27] The Court answered that, in such circumstances, the national court must be allowed to order the disclosure of evidence, but it also has to ensure that such disclosure does not go beyond what is necessary in light of the claim for damages brought before it.[28]

In reaching this interpretation, the Court noted, first, that, under both Regulation 1/2003 and the Damages Directive, national courts, contrary to NCAs, are not required to automatically stay proceedings brought before them concerning actions for damages for infringement of competition law due to the fact that the Commission has initiated proceedings in respect of the same infringement.[29] Indeed, while public and private enforcement must interact in a coherent manner, including in relation to

[25] Ibid., para.64.

[26] Ibid., paras.64 and 68.

[27] See *RegioJet,* para. 52.

[28] Ibid., para.78.

[29] Ibid., paras.63–65.

the arrangements for access to documents held by NCAs, they are "complementary" and may therefore in principle be carried out simultaneously.[30] In fact, Article 6(9) of the Damages Directive provides that the disclosure of evidence on the white list may be ordered "in actions for damages at any time", thus including when proceedings are ongoing before a competition authority.[31]

Second, the Court went on to explain that, in the above scenario, when ordering the disclosure of evidence a national court *is not in principle taking a decision which may conflict with the decision contemplated by the Commission in those proceedings*, within the meaning of Article 16(1) of Regulation No 1/2003 (the so-called "*Masterfoods rule*").[32] However, such disclosure it to be ordered provided the requested evidence is limited to what is strictly relevant, proportionate and necessary, as to not unduly interfere with an ongoing investigation by a competition authority over an infringement of competition law.[33] Hence, particular attention will have to be paid to preventing 'fishing expeditions', namely non-specific or overly broad searches for information that is unlikely to be of relevance for the parties to the proceedings, which could risk unravelling the investigation strategy of a competition authority by revealing which documents are part of the file or negatively affect the way in which undertakings cooperate with the competition authorities.[34] Yet, where national proceedings have been stayed owing to the Commission's initiation of investigation proceedings, a combined reading of the principle of sincere cooperation, laid down in Article 4(3) TEU and the objective of effective and uniform application of EU competition law require national courts to "take account of the proceedings pending before the Commission" and therefore ensure that the disclosure, which must follow a request that is sufficiently circumscribed and substantiated, is necessary and proportionate for the purpose of pursuing an action for damages.[35]

By its *third question*, which the Court saw fit to examine before the second, the referring court asked whether a stay of administrative proceedings before a NCA on the ground that the Commission has opened proceedings may be equated to a closing of these administrative proceedings by that authority, within the meaning of Article 6(5) of the Damages Directive. As a reminder, the latter provides that national courts may order the disclosure of evidence on the grey list "only after a competition authority, *by adopting a decision or otherwise*, has closed its proceedings".[36] The Court answered that it may not.[37] For a start, this would be contrary to the literal

[30] Ibid., para.66.

[31] Ibid., para.67.

[32] Ibid., para.70.

[33] Ibid., para.72. Those courts are therefore called upon to carry out a thorough examination of the request submitted to them as regards the relevance of the evidence requested, the link between that evidence and the claim for damages submitted, whether that evidence is sufficiently precise and as regards its proportionality.

[34] Ibid., para.73.

[35] Ibid., paras.76 and 77.

[36] Ibid., para.79.

[37] Ibid., para.91.

sense of the term "stay" of proceedings, the latter resuming once the reason for the stay is no longer present.[38] Moreover, similarly, a stay of administrative proceedings until the Commission has closed the investigation does not amount to a closing of these proceedings either, in the sense that a final act concerning the infringement in question has been adopted, particularly given that, if the Commission decides to close its proceedings without giving a decision on the infringement, the NCA concerned may, in principle, decide to reopen its proceedings.[39] Finally, as regards the objectives pursued by Article 6(5) of the Damages Directive, read in conjunction with recital 25 of that Directive, the protection applicable to the evidence on the grey list is intended to ensure that a disclosure of documents does not unduly interfere with an ongoing investigation by a NCA. Allowing the disclosure of such evidence after a stay of proceedings ordered by a NCA, but during an ongoing investigation by the Commission, could seriously undermine the effectiveness of that Commission investigation and, therefore, the objectives of that Directive.[40]

By its *second question*, the referring court sought, in essence, to ascertain whether Article 5(8) and Article 6(5)(a) and (9) of Damages Directive precluded the adoption of national legislation that temporarily limits the disclosure of evidence falling within the grey list to not only information 'prepared' specifically for the proceedings of the competition authority, but to all information 'submitted' in the course of such proceedings, including pre-existing information. The Court replied that such legislation broadening the range of information excluded from disclosure was clearly contrary to the Directive provisions.[41] Indeed, the Court explained, based on a literal, systematic and teleological interpretation of these provisions, that evidence falling within the grey list does not concern all information expressly submitted for the purpose of proceedings initiated by that authority, but only information "prepared specifically" for such proceedings,[42] while evidence on white list can include "pre-existing information", i.e., evidence that exists independently of the proceedings of a competition authority, whether or not such information is in the file of a competition authority.[43] Besides, under Article 5(8) of the Damages Directive, Member States can adopt rules leading to wider disclosure of evidence, but cannot qualify the conditions under which evidence is classified as being on the grey, black or white lists. If Member States were able to introduce more restrictive rules in relation to disclosure of evidence than those laid down in Articles 5 and 6, this would not only undermine the harmonisation objective of the Damages Directive but also possibly lead to more limited disclosure.[44] Yet, that does not mean that a national court, when so requested, must automatically order the disclosure of all the

[38] Ibid., para.81.
[39] Ibid., para.86.
[40] Ibid., para.90.
[41] Ibid., para.112.
[42] Ibid., para.101.
[43] Ibid., para.103.
[44] Ibid., paras.107–108.

documents that have not been prepared for administrative proceedings pending before a NCA, as it would still need to verify that such request does not go beyond what is necessary in light of the claim for damages brought before it.[45]

By its *fourth question* addressed to the Court the referring court sought to ascertain whether a national court may order the disclosure of evidence to assess whether that evidence contains information falling within the grey list of evidence.[46] The Court answered in essence that the relevant provisions of the Damages Directive—Article 5(1) read in conjunction with Article 6(5)—do not preclude a national court from ruling on the disclosure of evidence and from ordering that evidence to be placed under sequestration, while postponing the examination of whether that evidence contains information falling within the grey list of evidence, to a time when that court has access to that evidence. The use of such an instrument must, however, comply with the requirements arising from the principle of proportionality, as set out in Article 5(3) and Article 6(4) of the Damages Directive.[47] The Court noted that, while Article 6(7) of the Directive provides for "a prior review mechanism" enabling national courts to access evidence on the black list for the sole purpose of ensuring that its contents correspond to a "leniency statement" or a "settlement submission", no such mechanist exists with regard to evidence on the grey list, given that the protection afforded to such evidence is merely temporary.[48] Yet, this does not preclude a Member State from setting up such a "review mechanism".[49] In fact, rather unusually, the Court went as far as to embrace such a "review mechanism" in so far as it could also serve to prevent excessive recourse to the "grey list" exemption, and thus contribute to the overall effectiveness of private enforcement while maintaining the protection afforded to evidence in the grey list.[50] However, for such a review mechanism to be compliant with the Damages Directive two conditions would need to be met: first, access to the evidence on the grey list should not be granted to claimants or to other third parties before the competition authority has closed its proceedings, as this could unduly interfere with an ongoing investigation and undermine public enforcement,[51] and, second, the mechanism must be applied in conformity with the requirements arising from the principle of proportionality, as to avoid granting non-specific or overly broad searches for information base on "generic" requests.[52]

By its *fifth and last question*, the referring court asked, in essence, whether Article 6(5)(a) of the Damages Directive must be interpreted as meaning that where

45 Ibid., paras.109–110.

46 Ibid., paras.113–114.

47 Ibid., para.128.

48 Ibid., paras.115 and 116.

49 On the facts, the review mechanism consisted in enabling the national court to order the disclosure of evidence that could fall within the grey list, with the sole intention of placing the documents concerned under sequestration, such evidence being disclosed to the claimant only after the court has ascertained whether it did indeed contain evidence falling within that list.

50 See *RegioJet*, paras.123–124.

51 Ibid., paras.119–121.

52 Ibid., paras.125–127.

a national court postpones the examination of whether the evidence whose disclosure has been requested contains information falling within the grey list, that court may, under Article 5(4) of that Directive, refuse access to that evidence to the claimant or to other parties to the proceedings and their representatives. As expected, the Court held that, in such circumstances, national courts have not only the right but also the duty to ensure that another party to the proceedings does not have access, in the course of proceedings initiated by a competition authority, to information prepared by a natural or legal person specifically for those proceedings before it has completed its review, where that evidence falls within the white list, or, where that evidence falls within the grey list, before the competent competition authority has closed its proceedings.[53]

4.3 Tráficos Manuel Ferrer: *Evidence and Judicial Quantification of Harm*

Unlike the previous two cases, which focused on the availability of evidence in order to show the existence of an infringement, the *Tráficos Manuel Ferrer* case concerns evidence used the context of the determination of the quantum of damages, under Article 17 of the Damages Directive. Indeed, the provisions of the Directive concerning disclosure of evidence "interact" with those pertaining to the judicial quantification of harm, since the need to undertake a judicial estimation of harm may depend, in particular, on the result obtained by the claimant following a request for disclosure of evidence.[54]

Similar to *Paccar*, this case originated from follow-on litigation triggered by the Commission's decision in the *Trucks* cartel case.[55] The defendant, Daimler, was

[53] Ibid., paras.130–131.

[54] See *Tráficos Manuel Ferrer,* paras.44 and 56. The Court held that the asymmetry of information existing between the claimant and the defendant in the type of actions covered by that directive, since, according to recital 14 of that directive, 'the evidence necessary to prove a claim for damages is often held exclusively by the opposing party or by third parties, and is not sufficiently known by, or accessible to, the claimant'—required the Member States to lay down measures enabling the claimant to remedy that asymmetry. To that end, the Damages Directive, in the first place, obliges those States to confer on that party the power to ask national courts to require the defendant or a third party, under certain conditions, to disclose relevant evidence in their possession, pursuant to Article 5 of that directive. In the second place, that directive requires the Member States to empower those courts, under certain conditions, where it is practically impossible or excessively difficult to quantify the harm, to estimate it, in accordance with Article 17(1) of that directive, where appropriate, if they so wish, with the assistance of the NCA, as is apparent from Article 17(3) of that directive. In the third place, that directive requires Member States to introduce presumptions, in particular relating to the existence of harm arising from a cartel, as provided for in Article 17(2) of that directive".

[55] See Commission Decision C(2016) 4673 final relating to a proceeding under Article 101 [TFEU] and Article 53 of the EEA Agreement (Case AT.39824—Trucks), a summary of which was published in the *Official Journal of the European Union* of 6 April 2017(OJ 2017 C 108, p. 6).

among the addressees of that decision, while the two claimants, who brought an action for damages against Daimler, claim to have suffered damage consisting in an overcharge on the vehicles purchased owing to the wrongful conduct of the defendant. In order to quantify that overcharge, they produced an expert report concluding that there was an average overcharge of 16.35% on the market affected by that cartel. The defendant disputed the merits of the action, in particular by producing its own expert report. Following a preliminary hearing before the referring court, it was agreed between the parties that the claimant would have access to the data taken into consideration in the expert report submitted by the defendant, with the twofold aim of allowing a more thorough analysis of this data and of leading to a possible reformulation of the expert report produced by those claimants.

The referring court was called upon to rule on the allocation of costs under national civil procedural law, according to which, where the heads of claim are upheld or rejected in part, each party is to bear the costs which it has incurred itself and half of the common costs, unless the costs are to be borne by one party for a vexatious dispute.

Entertaining doubts as to the compatibility of national procedural law with EU law, the Spanish court referred three questions to the Court of Justice for a preliminary ruling.[56]

By its *second and third questions*, which are relevant for "evidence"[57] and which the Court treated together, the referring court asked, in essence, whether Article 17(1) of the Damages Directive[58] allows a judicial estimation of the harm caused by the defendant's anticompetitive conduct in circumstances in which, first, the defendant has given access to the claimant to information on the basis of which it had itself drawn up its expert report in order to rule out the existence of harm in respect

[56] See *Tráficos Manuel Ferrer*, paras.30–33. While the national court did not mention the Damages Directive in these three questions, to the extent these questions referred to concepts contained therein, and to provide the national court with an answer that would be of use to it for adjudicating the case pending before it, the Court decided to reformulate these questions.

[57] By its *first question*, the referring court asked whether the right to full compensation for harm suffered as a result of anticompetitive conduct, as recognised and defined in Article 3(1) and (2) of the Damages Directive and arising from Article 101 TFEU, precludes a national rule of civil procedure under which, in the event that the claim is upheld in part, costs are to be borne by each party and each party bears half of the common costs, except in cases of wrongful conduct. The Court answered in the negative. Indeed, while the right to full compensation for the harm suffered as a result of anticompetitive conduct includes compensation for actual loss (*damnum emergens*), and loss of profit (*lucrum cessans*), plus the payment of interest, this principle does not concern the rules on the allocation of costs in the context of judicial proceedings relating to the implementation of that right, since those rules do not aim to compensate for the harm, but determine, at the level of each Member State, in accordance with its own law, the manner in which the costs incurred in the exercise of such proceedings are to be allocated (see *Tráficos Manuel Ferrer*, paras.34–49).

[58] According to which Member States shall ensure that neither the burden nor the standard of proof required for the quantification of harm renders the exercise of the right to damages practically impossible or excessively difficult and that national courts should be empowered to estimate the amount of harm if it is established that a claimant suffered harm but it is practically impossible or excessively difficult to quantify the harm suffered on the basis of the available evidence.

of which compensation may be claimed and, second, the claim for damages is brought against only one of the addressees of a decision finding an infringement of Article 101 TFEU, which has only marketed part of the goods acquired by the claimant and in relation to which an overcharge is alleged to have been imposed as a result of that infringement.

In this regard, the Court noted at the outset that, like any other action for civil liability, actions for competition damages entail a certain degree of uncertainty when determining the amount of compensation. Indeed, such uncertainties are inherent in such litigation, and arise, from the confrontation of the arguments and expert reports in the exchange of arguments. However, the mere existence of such uncertainties does not correspond to the degree of complexity in the assessment of damages required to trigger the judicial estimation provided for in Article 17(1) of the Directive.[59] Indeed, the very wording of the provision limits the scope of the judicial estimation of the harm to situations in which it is practically "impossible" or "excessively difficult" to quantify the harm, once it has been established that the claimant suffered such harm.[60] The reason behind this is that asymmetry of information is not relevant, to the extent that, even where parties are on an equal footing as regard the information available, difficulties may arise during the specific quantification of the harm.[61] Nevertheless, proper use of disclosure of evidence can be pertinent, to the extent that "practical impossibility of assessing harm", cannot be the result of inaction on the part of the claimant—it is not for the national court to replace the latter or to remedy its shortcomings.[62] *In casu*, the Court considered however that the facts, on the one hand, that the defendant has of itself, after being authorised to do so by the referring court, made available to the claimant the data on which it relied in order to refute that claimant's expert report or, on the other hand, that the claim for damages was directed against only one of the addressees of the decision finding an infringement, which marketed only part of the products acquired by the claimant, were not, in themselves, relevant for the purposes of assessing whether it is permissible for the national court to undertake an estimation of the harm.[63]

5 Conclusion

The existing case law, although recent and still under development, has laid out some key elements in the interpretation of the disclosure provisions of the Damages Directive. While the situations at hand concerns mostly "follow-on" damages, it

---

[59] See *Tráficos Manuel Ferrer*, para. 52.

[60] Ibid., para. 53. For instance, particularly significant difficulties in interpreting the documents disclosed as regards the proportion of the passing on of the overcharge resulting from the cartel on prices of products acquired by the claimant from one of the parties to the cartel.

[61] See *Tráficos Manuel Ferrer*, para. 54.

[62] Ibid., para. 57.

[63] Ibid., paras. 59 and 64.

will be interesting to observe how these provisions will be considered in "stand-alone" claims. One such case, is pending case C-286/24, *Meliá Hotels International*, where the Court has been asked to examine the possibilities of disclosure under Article 5(1) in the context of an action for access to evidence separately, and prior to the bringing of an action for damages within the meaning of Article 2(4) of the Directive.[64]

[64] See, Opinion of Advocate General Szpunar in *Meliá Hotels International* (C-286/24, EU:C:2025:436) and upcoming judgment.

The Right to be Heard Orally in Competition Proceedings Before the European Commission

Wouter P. J. Wils

1 Introduction

Is there a fundamental right to be heard orally in competition proceedings before the European Commission, or is this a right that is merely granted, or not granted, by the secondary legislator?

Does an addressee of a statement of objections have a right to be heard in the absence of other parties to the proceedings, so as to be able to refer to business secrets or other confidential information?

Does an addressee of a statement of objections have a right to choose the timing of its oral hearing?

And what is the appropriate remedy if a party's right to be heard has been breached?

As for so many questions of EU law, and in particular EU competition law, Nils Wahl has left a clear mark on these four questions, through his characteristically insightful, outspoken and principled Opinion in the *SKW* Case.[1]

[1] Opinion of 3 September 2015 in Case C-154/14 P *SKW Stahl-Metallurgie and SKW Stahl-Metallurgie Holding* v *Commission*, EU:C:2015:543.

W. P. J. Wils (✉)
European Commission, Brussels, Belgium

King's College, London, U.K.
e-mail: Wouter.Wils@ec.europa.eu

L. Prete, L. Rezki (eds.), *Judging & (Re)Thinking European Union Law*,
https://doi.org/10.1007/978-3-032-13473-8_19

Before examining the four questions, and the insights provided by Advocate General Wahl's Opinion and by the Judgments of the General Court and the Court of Justice, [2] it is useful to recall the facts of the SKW Case.[3]

On 24 June 2008, the Commission issued a statement of objections in which it accused, in particular, SKW Stahl-Metallurgie ('SKW') of having participated in a price-fixing cartel contrary to Article 81 EC on the market on calcium carbonate and magnesium intended for the steel and gas industries in the European Economic Area (EEA) with the exception of Ireland, Spain, Portugal and the United Kingdom, during the period from 22 April 2004 to 16 January 2007. In addition, due to the fact that Evonik Degussa ('Degussa') and SKW Stahl-Metallurgie Holding ('SKW Holding') had successively held, directly or indirectly, 100% of the capital of SKW, the Commission also stated that it held, first, Degussa, in respect of the period from 22 April 2004 to 30 August 2004, when SKW had been sold to SKW Holding, and, second, SKW Holding, in respect of the period from 30 August 2004 to 16 January 2007, liable for SKW's conduct.

In their written observations of 6 October 2008 addressed to the Commission in response to the statement of objections, SKW and SKW Holding requested the opportunity to develop, at a hearing, their arguments relating in particular to the absence of SKW Holding's actual exercise of decisive influence over SKW during the period of the infringement, given the continuance of Degussa's decisive influence over SKW, even after the latter's acquisition by SKW Holding.

By email of 31 October 2008, SKW and SKW Holding asked the Hearing Officer to allow them to present the arguments concerning the influence allegedly exerted by Degussa SKW *in camera*. In support of that request, they argued that SKW depended, for its economic survival, on Degussa, since it provided SKW with almost all the calcium carbide which it marketed, and that these two companies were in negotiations about a new supply contract. They added that putting forward that argument in the presence of Degussa would seriously jeopardise the business relationship between Degussa and SKW and could lead to retaliation from Degussa.

On 5 November 2008, SKW and SKW Holding sent another email to the Commission, in which they suggested that a 'practical solution' could be to give Degussa access to their submission *in camera* after the end of 2008 or after the conclusion of a supply contract between the two companies. On 6 November 2008, SKW and SKW Holding provided information on the reasons for their request to present part of their arguments, at the hearing, *in camera*, and also on the content of that argument, and they reiterated their proposed alternative.

By letter of 6 November 2008, the Hearing Officer rejected their request. As a preliminary point, she observed that the request was not based, *stricto sensu*, on the protection of business secrets and other confidential information. The Hearing Officer indicated that she would therefore examine it from the point of view of their

[2] Judgment in *SKW Stahl-Metallurgie Holding and SKW Stahl-Metallurgie* v *Commission*, T-384/09, EU:T:2014:27 and Judgment in *SKW Stahl-Metallurgie and SKW Stahl-Metallurgie Holding* v *Commission*, C-154/14 P, EU:C:2016:445.

[3] See Judgment in C-154/14 P, paras 8 to 17.

right to be heard. In that regard she noted that the argument raised by the appellants concerned Degussa's behaviour and, in order that the Commission could take it into account as a mitigating circumstance, its probative value had to be verified by comparing it with a statement to be obtained from Degussa. Furthermore a hearing *in camera* would deprive Degussa of its right to respond orally to the allegations made by the appellants implicating it at least indirectly. The Hearing Officer added, concerning the alternative solution suggested by the appellants, that it was not feasible, since neither the outcome nor the duration of the negotiations between the appellants and Degussa was certain.

An oral hearing took place on 10 and 11 November 2008.

By letter of 28 January 2009, SKW and SKW Holding, indicated that, in the meantime, negotiations between SKW and Degussa had led to the conclusion of a new supply agreement, so that there was no difficulty for them to make oral submissions in the presence of Degussa, on the part of their argument on the latter's role. They therefore asked the Hearing Officer for a fresh hearing to give them the opportunity to present this part of their oral argument, which they had not presented at the hearing on 10 and 11 November 2008.

By letter of 3 February 2009, the Hearing Officer rejected this new request on the grounds that the right to be heard stemmed from the statement of objections and was granted only once. The Hearing Officer, however, permitted the appellants to supplement in writing, within a period which he laid down, their argument relating to Degussa's role.

In Article 1(f) of its final decision of 22 July 2009,[4] the Commission found that SKW Holding had participated in the infringement from 30 August 2004 to 16 January 2007 and SKW had participated in the infringement from 22 April 2004 to 16 January 2007. As regards SKW, according to recital 226 of that decision, the Commission considered that, during the latter period, the employees of that company had been directly involved in the agreements and/or concerted practices of the cartel at issue. As regards SKW Holding, according to recital 245 of that decision, it held 100% of SKW's capital from 30 August 2004 to 16 January 2007, and, for the reasons given in recital 245 to 250 of the same decision, the Commission considered that it was part of the same economic unit as SKW and could therefore be held liable for the latter's infringement of competition rules.

By Article 2(f) of that final decision, the Commission imposed a fine of EUR 13.3 million, on SKW Holding and SKW, due to their participation in the infringement at issue, for the period from 30 August 2004 to 16 January 2007, designating them jointly and severally liable for the payment of the fine. In addition, under Article 2(g) of that decision, it imposed a fine of EUR 1.04 million, for the period from 22 April 2004 to 30 August 2004, on Degussa and SKW, designating them as jointly and severally liable.

[4] Commission Decision C(2009) 5791 final of 22 July 2009 relating to a proceeding under Article 81 EC and Article 53 of the EEA agreement (Case COMP/39.396 — Calcium carbide and magnesium based reagents for the steel and gas industries).

In their application for annulment of the Commission's final decision, SKW Holding and SKW alleged that their right to be heard had been infringed because the Hearing Officer had refused to organise an *in camera* hearing during the administrative procedure and that the Commission's final decision had to be annulled as a result.

The General Court, Advocate General Wahl and the Court of Justice all three concluded that there was no ground for annulling the Commission's decision, but they disagreed on several points, including on whether there had been a breach of the right to be heard orally.

2 The Right to be Heard Is a Fundamental Right But the Right to be Heard Orally Is Not

Article 41(2)(a) of the Charter of Fundamental Rights of the European Union affirms "*the right of every person to be heard, before any individual measure which would affect him or her adversely is taken*".[5]

According to the Explanations to the Charter,[6] this provision restates case-law of the Court of Justice of the EU on general principles of EU law. According to this case-law:

> Observance of the right to be heard is, in all proceedings initiated against a person which are liable to culminate in a measure adversely affecting that person, a fundamental principle of [EU] law which must be guaranteed even in the absence of any rules governing the proceedings in question […]. That principle requires that the addressees of decisions which significantly affect their interests should be placed in a position in which they may effectively make known their views.[7]

If the right to be heard is thus recognised as a fundamental right in EU law, it would not appear, however, that there is a fundamental right to be heard orally, as long as the addressees of decisions can effectively make know their views in writing.[8]

---

[5] OJ 2007 C 303, p. 1.

[6] OJ 2007 C 303, p. 17.

[7] Judgment in *Commission* v *Lisrestal and Others*, C-32/95 P, EU:C:1996:402, para. 21.

[8] See judgments of the European Court of Human Rights ('ECtHR') in *Jussila* v *Finland* (CE:ECHR:2006:1123JUD007305301), §§ 40-49; *Vilho Eskelinen & Ors* v *Finland* (CE:ECHR:2007:0419JUD006323500), §§ 72-75; and *Produkcija Plus storitveno podjetje d.o.o.* v *Slovenia* (CE:ECHR:2018:1023JUD004707215), § 54; and Decision of the ECtHR in *Bouygues Telecom* v *France* (CE:ECHR:2012:0313DEC000232408), §§ 69-71; as well as Orders in *Troszczynski* v *Parliament*, C-462/18 P, EU:C:2019:239, paras 52-55; in *Gollnisch* v *Parliament*, C-330/18 P, EU:C:2019:240, paras 60-61; and judgments in *Syrian Lebanese Commercial Bank v Council*, T-174/12 and T-80/13, EU:T:2014:52, para. 147; in *Lucchini* v *Commission*, T-185/18, EU:T:2019:298, para. 49; in *HeidelbergCement and Schwenk Zement* v *Commission*, T-380/17, EU:T:2020:471, para. 634; and in *Wieland-Werke* v *Commission*, T-251/19, EU:T:2022:296, para. 694. In its judgment in *Limburgse Vinyl Maatschappij and Others* v *Commission*, T-305/94 etc., EU:T:1999:80, para. 248, the General Court wrote: "The right of the undertakings and associations of undertakings con-

In his Opinion in the SKW Case, Advocate General Wahl expressed this clearly by distinguishing between the substance and the form of the right to be heard:[9]

> the right to be heard has a vital substantive aspect: the effective procedural protection of the parties concerned. Indeed, in proceedings in which fines may be imposed, observance of the rights of the defence is a fundamental principle of EU law which must be complied with, even in administrative proceedings. [...]
>
> However, the particularity of this case is that, in reality, it turns on the question of what form the right to be heard before the Commission ought to take, rather than its substance. In that regard, being heard in writing, rather than orally, is not in itself problematic. [...]

If there is no fundamental right to an oral hearing, addressees of a statement of objections in antitrust or merger proceedings before the European Commission do however have a right to an oral hearing, provided they request so in their written submissions, by virtue of Article 12(1) of Commission Regulation 773/2004[10] and Article 14(1) of Commission Regulation 802/2004.[11]

As Advocate General Wahl has also pointed out, the successive Commission regulations on the conduct of antitrust proceedings have not always granted this right in the same way.[12] In a new regulation replacing Regulation 773/2004, the Commission might thus conceivably also take away the right to an oral hearing. It is to be noted in this context that in the more recent implementing regulation of the Digital Markets Act, no right to an oral hearing is provided for.[13]

The fact that the right to an oral hearing is a mere creature of secondary legislation, not a fundamental right, is also reflected in the Judgment of the Court of Justice in the SKW Case. Indeed, after having found a violation of SKW and SKW Holding's right to be heard orally, the Court concluded that this procedural irregularity did not justify the annulment of the Commission's final decision, also because "after the conclusion of a new supply contract between SKW and Degussa, that is

cerned to put their case on the matters to which the Commission has taken objection, at both the written and oral stages of the administrative procedure, is an essential part of the rights of the defence (*Hoechst*, paragraph 52)", but this appears to reflect the secondary legislation providing for a right to an oral hearing rather than a fundamental right to an oral hearing; the judgment in *Hoechst* v *Commission*, 46/87 and 227/88, EU:C:1989:337, to which the General Court refers, does not mention the oral hearing.

[9] Opinion in the *SKW* Case, paras 48 and 49.

[10] Commission Regulation (EC) No 773/2004 of 7 April 2004 relating to the conduct of proceedings by the Commission pursuant to Articles 81 and 82 of the EC Treaty (OJ 2004 L 123, p. 18, last amended by Commission Regulation (EU) 2015/1348 of 3 August 2015, OJ 2015 L 208, p. 3).

[11] Commission Regulation (EC) No 802/2004 of 21 April 2004 implementing Council Regulation (EC) No 139/2004 on the control of undertakings (OJ 2004 L 133, p. 1, last amended by Commission Implementing Regulation (EU) No 1269/2013 of 5 December 2013, OJ 2013 L 336, p. 1).

[12] Opinion in the *SKW* Case, paragraph 45 and footnote 17.

[13] Commission Implementing Regulation (EU) 2023/814 of 14 April 2023 on detailed arrangements for the conduct of certain proceedings by the Commission pursuant to regulation (EU) 2022/1925 of the European Parliament and of the Council (OJ 2023 L 102, p. 6).

to say, when the appellants no longer had any difficulties in submitting their arguments on Degussa's role, they were able to submit written observations to the Commission".[14]

3 The Right to be Heard Orally in the Absence of Other Parties

As to whether an addressee to a statement of objections may have a right to be heard orally in the absence of other parties, Advocate General Wahl took a radical position in the SKW Case, asserting that "there is no right to an *in camera* hearing".[15]

"So, a party whose request for an *in camera* hearing is refused will have to consider carefully whether it still wishes to participate in the joint oral hearing and, if so, what to say. That party is not obliged to divulge confidential information in front of all the participants. Alternatively, that party could instead choose, at an earlier point in time, to submit confidential information in writing to the Commission in its reply to the SO, and request confidential treatment thereof. That might also involve taking a commercial risk but, depending on the circumstances, it might be a better option than requesting an *in camera* hearing. Accordingly, the administrative procedure ensures that parties may decide whether to present information which they deem confidential to the Commission and, if so, whether they ought to do so orally or in writing (even though, admittedly, they do not have the final say on the issue of confidentiality). Hence, the exercise of the right to be heard invariably involves commercial decisions for the parties. The present case shows this: the appellants (understandably) chose to give priority to one commercial goal — economic survival — over another, that is to say, the possibility of lower fines." [16]

Hence, according to Advocate General Wahl, in the SKW Case, "by charging the Commission, at point 39 of the judgment under appeal, with the duty of striking an appropriate balance, case by case, between, on the one hand, the aim of protecting the rights of the defence of undertakings charged with violating the EU competition rules and, on the other, the lawful interest of third parties in the non-disclosure of their business secrets and other confidential information in the course of the investigation, the General Court erred in law".[17]

The Court of Justice did not follow Advocate General Wahl on this point, observing instead, as a preliminary point, that SKW and SKW Holding, in their appeal, "do not dispute that, as the General Court held in paragraph 39 of the judgment

[14] Judgment in the *SKW* Case, para. 76.
[15] Opinion in the *SKW* Case, para. 52.
[16] Opinion in the *SKW* Case, para. 63.
[17] Opinion in the *SKW* Case, para. 66.

under appeal, it is for the Hearing Officer, when he has to assess whether or not to hold a hearing *in camera*, to reconcile the protection of the rights of the defence of the undertaking prosecuted for an alleged breach of the EU competition rules against the legitimate interest of third parties, persons or companies who provided information or documents related to the alleged infringement to have their business secrets and other confidential information protected".[18]

Indeed, the case law of the EU Courts leaves the Commission a choice whether to hear each addressee that has requested to be heard orally in a separate oral hearing or to hear all those addressees in a single oral hearing,[19] subject to two limitations:

First, the rights of the defence must be observed. This means that the Commission cannot use in its final decision information gathered at the hearing of one addressee of the statement of objections against another addressee not present at that hearing without having allowed the latter addressee to examine that information and give its view thereon. It also means that, if at the hearing of one addressee of the statement of objections evidence exculpating another addressee is disclosed, the Commission must, if it wants to maintain its objections against the latter addressee in the final decision, allow the latter addressee to examine that information and give its view.[20]

Secondly, the different addressees' legitimate interests in the protection of their business secrets and other confidential information must be respected.[21] This means that, to the extent that it is necessary for an addressee of the statement of objections, in order effectively to develop its defence arguments, to refer to business secrets or other confidential information, that addressee must be allowed to be heard in the absence of the other parties.[22]

[18] Judgment in the *SKW* Case, para. 61.

[19] Judgments in *Cimenteries CBR and Others* v *Commission*, T-25/95 etc., EU:T:2000:77, para. 697, and in *Ferriere* v *Commission*, T-667/19, EU:T:2022:692, para. 84, and Opinion of Advocate General Darmon in *Ahlström Osakeyhtiö and Others* v *Commission*, C-89/85 etc., EU:C:1988:258, para. 155.

[20] Judgment in *Cimenteries CBR and Others* v *Commission*, T-25/95 etc., EU:T:2000:77, para. 682, and Opinion of Advocate General Darmon in *Ahlström Osakeyhtiö and Others* v *Commission*, C-89/85 etc., EU:C:1988:258, para. 156, and Judgment in *SKW Stahl-Metallurgie* v *Commission*, T-384/09, EU:T:2014:27, paras 38-58. The principles here are the same as those applicable to the written replies of the different addressees of the statement of objections; see Judgment in *Mitsubishi Electric* v *Commission*, T-133/07, EU:T:2011:345, paras 41–47.

[21] See Article 339 TFEU and Article 28(2) of Regulation 1/2003, and judgment in *Bank Austria Creditanstalt* v *Commission*, T-198/03, EU:T:2006:136, para. 71.

[22] See Article 14(6) of Regulation 773/2004 and Article 13 of Decision 2011/695/EU of the President of the European Commission of 13 October 2011 on the function and terms of reference of the Hearing Officer in competition proceedings (OJ 2001 L 275/29; see further my paper 'The Oral Hearing in Competition proceedings before the European Commission', (2012) 35 *World Competition* 397, updated version accessible at ssrn.com, text accompanied by footnotes 73 to 76).

4 Timing of the Oral Hearing

Article 12(1) of Decision 2011/695 provides that "after consulting the Director responsible, the Hearing Officer shall determine the date, the duration and the place of the hearing. Where a postponement is requested, the hearing officer shall decide whether or not to allow it."

Where there are only one or two addressees of the statement of objections, the Hearing Officer may also consult these parties before determining the date of the hearing.[23] In merger proceedings, there may however be little or no choice as to possible hearing dates, given the strict time limits imposed by the Merger Regulation.

Advocate General Wahl put the issue very clearly in *SKW* Case:

> The right to be heard is intended to give undertakings the opportunity of being heard, not necessarily of being heard at the time of their best convenience.[24]

5 Consequences Arising from a Breach of the Right to be Heard Orally

Advocate General Wahl concluded his Opinion in the *SKW* Case with once more quite interesting considerations in the alternative as to the consequences that would arise "in the event that the Court were — unlike me — to hold that the appellants were entitled to an *in camera* hearing".[25]

He first recalled that, "according to case-law, the rights of the defence are infringed where the outcome of the administrative procedure conducted by the Commission might have been different as a result of an error committed by it. An undertaking establishes that there has been an infringement where it adequately demonstrates, not that the Commission's decision would have been different in content, *but rather that the undertaking would have been better able to ensure its defence had there been no error*".[26]

He then argued that this case-law, which has its origin in cases concerning access to the file, should not be simply transposed to cases in which the right to an oral hearing has been breached:

> In my view, there is a difference between considering whether a party might have been able to better defend itself, on the one hand, had it been given access to the entire case file and,

[23] See judgment in *Compagnie générale maritime and Others* v *Commission*, T-86/95, EU:T:2002:50, paras 463 to 466 as to the time to prepare for the oral hearing and as to the issue of certain persons not being able to attend the oral hearing on the determined date.

[24] Opinion in the *SKW* Case, para. 71.

[25] Opinion in the *SKW* Case, para. 74.

[26] Opinion in the *SKW* Case, para. 75.

> on the other hand, had it been granted an *in camera* hearing. While the significance of unlawfully withheld documents can be appraised ex post, that of an *in camera* hearing cannot: it is impossible to be entirely certain of what actually takes place during such meetings. There is also nothing to prevent a party from submitting other relevant confidential information to the Commission during such a meeting that has not been alluded to beforehand. Hence, if there is a right to an *in camera* hearing before the Commission, and if an oral hearing is held only once — as in the case under consideration — then the party who was entitled yet deprived thereof, *cannot be considered to have been heard at all.* In the interest of justice being seen to done, I am thoroughly unconvinced by the idea of validating a pre-emptive reasoning denying an *in camera* hearing because it could not possibly have helped that party.
>
> Moreover, it would be insufficient to give the deprived party, by way of compensation, the opportunity to provide an additional written statement. A written statement cannot replace an *in camera* hearing, if parties have a right thereto.[27]

The Court of Justice did indeed find that SKW and SKW Holding's right to be heard orally had been breached, because "the argument that the appellants wished to put forward *in camera* concerned the role of Degussa for the period following its sale of SKW to SKW Holding. Degussa has not been the subject of Commission proceedings in respect of that period, either at the time the hearing took place or subsequently. Accordingly, it must be held that, in refusing to grant the appellants' request to hold an *in camera* hearing, the Hearing Officer took into account Degussa's rights of defence, even though the latter could not rely on those rights due to the fact that it was a third party to the proceedings in respect of that period".[28]

As to the consequences of this procedural irregularity, the Court of Justice did however stick to it case-law, and found that the outcome of the procedure could not have been different because "the General Court found, in its assessment of the facts, that imputing liability for the infringement in question to SKW Holding could, in any event, be grounded on several factors which were, according to the General Court, by themselves sufficient as a basis for the conclusion that SKW Holding exercised decisive influence over SKW. In the light of that finding, the General Court was entitled to conclude, without erring in law, in particular in paragraphs 48, 49 and 52 of the judgment under appeal, to which it refers in paragraph 53 thereof, that, in order to challenge the attribution of liability, SKW Holding had to demonstrate that it did not itself exercise such influence, so that the question of whether another entity, such as Degussa, exercised decisive influence was not relevant".[29]

In thus concluding, the Court of Justice remained silent on the question whether the arguments concerning the influence of Degussa which SKW and SKW Holding were prevented from making at the oral hearing could, by way of attenuating

---

[27] Opinion in the *SKW* Case, paras 79–80.

[28] Judgment in the *SKW* Case, paras 65–66.

[29] Judgment in the *SKW* Case, para. 72.

circumstance, have had an influence on the amount of the fine imposed on SKW and SKW Holding. Indeed, as the General Court had found, it was with regard to that question that the arguments concerning the influence of Degussa could have benefitted SKW and SKW Holding.[30] The General Court itself did anyway not consider that those arguments justified a reduction of the fine.[31]

[30] Judgment of the General Court in the *SKW* Case, para. 54.

[31] Judgment of the General Court in the *SKW* Case, paras 56 and 214–228.

Judicial Proceedings

La compétence de la Cour de justice de l'Union européenne dans le cadre de la PESC: les progrès et les limites infranchissables (?) d'une *lex imperfecta*

Stefano Boni

1 Introduction

Il est fréquent que les règles de la politique étrangère et de sécurité commune (PESC) soient qualifiées, dans la doctrine,[1] de *lex imperfecta*. L'utilisation, dans ce contexte, d'un tel concept emprunté au droit romain[2] trouve ses origines dans les conclusions[3] que Nils Wahl, en tant qu'avocat général, a présentées dans l'affaire *H*.[4]

Selon l'avocat général, ces règles donnent lieu à une *lex imperfecta* au motif que, d'une part, les traités ne prévoient pas expressément de procédure juridictionnelle d'application et de sanction desdites règles, de sorte qu'il n'existe pratiquement pas de moyen de garantir leur respect par les États membres récalcitrants ou par les institutions de l'Union qui ne s'y conforment pas. D'autre part et, aux fins de la

[1] R. A. Wessel, Lex imperfecta: Law and Integration in European Foreign and Security Policy, *Europen Papers,* 2016, n° 2, pp. 439-468; S. Poli, The Common Foreign Security Policy after Rosneft: Still Imperfect but gradually subject to the rule of law, *CML Rev.*, 2017, n° 6, pp. 1799-1834; L. Prete, The Scope of the Court's Jurisdiction in the CFSP: H v Council and Others, dans G. Butler et R. A. Wessel (dir.), *EU External Relations Law*, Oxford, 2022, pp. 831-839; P. Van Elsuwege, Judicial review and the Common Foreign and Security Policy: Limits to the gap-filling role of the Court of Justice, *CML Rev.*, 2021, n° 6, pp. 1731–1760.

[2] Voir F. Senn, Leges perfectae, minus quam perfectae et imperfectae, Paris, 1902, chapitre II.

[3] Conclusions de l'avocat général Wahl dans l'affaire H/Conseil e.a. (C-455/14 P, ci-après les «conclusions H», EU:C:2016:212).

[4] Arrêt du 19 juillet 2016, H/Conseil e.a. (C-455/14 P, ci-après l'«arrêt H», EU:C:2016:569).

S. Boni (✉)
Court of Justice of the European Union, Luxembourg, Luxembourg
e-mail: Stefano.Boni@curia.europa.eu

L. Prete, L. Rezki (eds.), *Judging & (Re)Thinking European Union Law*,
https://doi.org/10.1007/978-3-032-13473-8_20

présente contribution, surtout, les particuliers dont les droits pourraient être violés par des actes adoptés dans le cadre de la PESC ne disposent que de voies de recours limitées. En effet, l'accès à la Cour de justice de l'Union européenne[5] (ci-après la «CJUE»), que ce soit directement, au moyen de recours directs, ou indirectement, par l'intermédiaire d'un renvoi préjudiciel, est restreint. Et l'avocat général de mettre en exergue que la nature de *lex imperfecta* des règles de la PESC est clairement un reliquat de la nature *sui generis* du «deuxième pilier» créé par le traité de Maastricht: un système hybride qui a assimilé les caractéristiques du droit (alors) communautaire et du droit international public. Tout en reconnaissant que, après l'entrée en vigueur du traité de Lisbonne, la PESC fait désormais partie intégrante de l'ordre juridique de l'Union, l'avocat général a noté que celle-ci conserve certaines caractéristiques particulières, au nombre desquelles figure notamment l'existence de limites, résultant de l'article 24, paragraphe 1, second alinéa, TUE, et de l'article 275 TFUE, au «système complet de voies de recours et de procédures destiné à assurer le contrôle de la légalité des actes de l'Union »[6] établi par les articles 263 et 277 TFUE ainsi que par l'article 267 TFUE. Il a fait remarquer qu'il s'agissait là d'un choix conscient opéré par les auteurs des traités qui, en rédigeant l'article 24, paragraphe 1, TUE et l'article 275 TFUE, avaient décidé de ne pas accorder au juge de l'Union une compétence générale et absolue à l'égard de l'ensemble des traités. Il a donc suggéré à la Cour de ne pas interpréter les règles ainsi posées dans ces traités pour élargir sa compétence au-delà de la lettre de ces règles, lesquelles lui attribuent une compétence limitée. Il a ajouté que, cela étant, la compétence que les traités accordent à la CJUE, bien que limitée, ne devrait pas être ignorée et que la jurisprudence, notamment par l'arrêt *Elitaliana*,[7] avait déjà établi certains principes quant à la portée de cette compétence.[8]

La thèse ainsi exprimée dans ces conclusions n'est pas sans rappeler certaines considérations que la Cour avait formulées dans son avis 2/13,[9] rendu à peu près une année et demi avant lesdites conclusions. À cette occasion, la Cour a constaté que l'état du droit de l'Union était tel que certains actes adoptés dans le cadre de la

[5] Conformément à la terminologie utilisée dans les traités, l'expression «Cour de justice de l'Union européenne» désigne l'institution dans son ensemble, en incluant les deux juridictions qui la composent actuellement, tandis que l'expression «Cour» indique seule la juridiction suprême.

[6] Cette expression résulte d'une jurisprudence constante: voir, notamment, arrêt du 3 octobre 2013, Inuit Tapiriit Kanatami e.a./Parlement et Conseil (C-583/11 P, EU:C:2013:625, point 92 et jurisprudence citée).

[7] Arrêt du 12 novembre 2015, Elitaliana/Eulex Kosovo (C-439/13 P, EU:C:2015:753). Sur cet arrêt, voir R. da Silva Passos, Jurisdiction of the EU Courts in the CFSP when Linked to the EU Budget: Elitaliana, dans G. Butler et R. A. Wessel (dir.), *EU External Relations Law*, précité, pp. 679–688.

[8] Conclusions H, points 35, 36, 38 à 40, 45, 46, 49, 50, 63 et 64.

[9] Avis 2/13 (Adhésion de l'Union à la CEDH), du 18 décembre 2014 (EU:C:2014:2454, points 251 à 253). Voir, à cet égard, notamment, F. Benoit-Rohmer, À propos de l'avis 2/13 de la Cour de Justice, *RTDE*, 2015, n° 3, pp. 593–611, partie IIB; G. Butler, The ultimate stumbling block? The Common Foreign and Security Policy, and accession of the European Union to the European Convention on Human Rights, *Dublin University Law Journal*, 2016, n° 1, pp. 229–244.

PESC échappaient à son contrôle juridictionnel et qu'une telle situation était inhérente à l'aménagement des compétences de la CJUE prévu par les traités.

Surtout, ladite thèse correspond à la *Weltanschauung* juridique de Nils Wahl, telle que j'ai pu la comprendre au cours de la période que j'ai eu l'honneur, et le plaisir, de passer au sein de son cabinet de juge à la Cour. En effet, il me semble que, quelles que soient ses préférences personnelles quant à la réponse à donner, parmi celles envisageables, à une question juridique, il accorde la plus grande importance au libellé des dispositions pertinentes, qui traduit l'intention de leur auteur (souvent le législateur, ayant une légitimité démocratique) de prévoir, ou de ne pas prévoir, quelque chose.

À cet égard, il a été observé en doctrine que les traités ne contiennent aucune disposition énumérant, et ordonnant hiérarchiquement, les méthodes d'interprétation que la Cour peut ou doit suivre. Partant, elle est, en principe, libre de choisir, parmi les méthodes possibles, celles qui sont les plus en accord avec l'ordre juridique de l'Union, tout en devant veiller à maintenir la juste balance entre une protection juridictionnelle effective, d'une part, et le respect des principes d'équilibre institutionnel et de coopération loyale, d'autre part.[10] La jurisprudence de la Cour consacre, en substance, cette liberté, en ce qu'elle ne confère pas de priorité absolue au libellé. En effet, selon la Cour, l'interprétation d'une disposition du droit de l'Union ne saurait, certes, avoir pour résultat de retirer tout effet utile au libellé clair et précis de cette disposition. Cela étant, le juge de l'Union ne se trouve pas privé de la possibilité de recourir dans certaines situations aux méthodes d'interprétation qu'il considère appropriées en vue d'éclairer la portée exacte d'une disposition du droit de l'Union en apparence claire, étant précisé que chaque disposition du droit de l'Union doit être replacée dans son contexte et interprétée à la lumière de l'ensemble des dispositions de ce droit, de ses finalités, et de l'état de son évolution à la date à laquelle l'application de la disposition en cause doit être faite.[11]

Il est bien connu que, dans son arrêt *H* ainsi que dans ses arrêts ultérieurs *Rosneft,*[12] *KF*[13] et *Bank Refah,*[14] la Cour a interprété les limites de sa compétence dans le cadre de la PESC de manière telle que celle-ci est plus étendue que ce que les libellés de l'article 24, paragraphe 1, TUE et de l'article 275 TFUE pourraient laisser présager. Ce faisant, la Cour a privilégié une approche holistique,[15] fondée,

---

[10] K. Lenaerts et J. A. Gutíerez-Fons, *Les méthodes d'interprétation de la Cour de justice de l'Union européenne*, 2020, Bruxelles, pp. 8 et 9.

[11] Arrêt du 3 septembre 2024, Illumina et Grail/Commission (C-611/22 P et C-625/22 P, EU:C:2024:677, points 126 et 127 ainsi que jurisprudence citée). Voir également, en ce sens, arrêt du 2 juillet 2020, Magistrat der Stadt Wien (Grand hamster) (C-477/19, EU:C:2020:517, point 23 et jurisprudence citée).

[12] Arrêt du 28 mars 2017, Rosneft (C-72/15, ci-après l'«arrêt Rosneft», EU:C:2017:236).

[13] Arrêt du 25 juin 2020, CSUE/KF (C-14/19 P, ci-après l'«arrêt KF», EU:C:2020:492).

[14] Arrêt du 6 octobre 2020, Bank Refah Kargaran/Conseil (C-134/19 P, ci-après l'«arrêt Bank Refah», EU:C:2020:793).

[15] P. Van Elsuwege, Judicial review and the Common Foreign and Security Policy: Limits to the gap-filling role of the Court of Justice, précité, pp. 1735, 1740, 1745 et 1750. L'avocat général

en particulier, sur une interprétation systémique et contextuelle de ces dispositions. Cette approche a comme point de départ le constat que lesdites dispositions, en limitant la compétence de la CJUE, introduisent une dérogation à la règle de la compétence générale que l'article 19 TUE confère à cette institution en vue d'assurer le respect du droit dans l'interprétation et l'application des traités. Par conséquent, les dispositions en cause doivent être interprétées restrictivement.[16]

Dans les pages qui suivent, d'abord, seront brièvement rappelés les principaux apports jurisprudentiels découlant des arrêts susmentionnés. Ensuite, seront examinés les éclaircissements quant à la portée de la compétence du juge de l'Union en matière de PESC que la Cour a apportés dans l'arrêt *KS et KD*[17] ainsi que dans l'arrêt *Neves*,[18] rendus récemment en grande chambre, dans le cadre, le premier, de deux pourvois dirigés contre une ordonnance[19] d'incompétence manifeste adoptée par le Tribunal et, le second, d'un renvoi préjudiciel. Enfin, des considérations conclusives seront formulées sur les «imperfections» qui demeurent.

2 Les arrêts H, Rosneft, KF et Bank Refah "in a nutshell"

L'affaire ayant donné lieu à l'arrêt *H* avait pour objet un pourvoi dirigé contre une ordonnance[20] par laquelle le Tribunal s'était déclaré incompétent pour connaître d'un recours formé par une magistrate italienne, détachée auprès de la Mission de police de l'Union européenne (MPUE) en Bosnie-Herzégovine, une entité relevant la PESC. Ce recours tendait à l'annulation de deux décisions du chef du personnel de cette entité portant sur l'affectation de la requérante ainsi qu'à l'octroi de dommages et intérêts.[21] Dans son arrêt, la Cour souligne que le fait que les décisions litigieuses s'inscrivent dans le contexte de la PESC ne conduit pas nécessairement à exclure la compétence du juge de l'Union. En ce qu'elles constituent, par leur essence même, des actes de gestion du personnel, de telles décisions ne sont pas soumises à la limitation dérogatoire à la compétence de la CJUE résultant de l'article 24, paragraphe 1, second alinéa, dernière phrase, TUE et de l'article 275, premier

---

Hogan s'est prononcé en faveur d'une interprétation holistique de ces dispositions dans les conclusions qu'il a présentées dans l'affaire Bank Refah (C-134/19 P, EU:C:2020:396, point 68).

[16] La Cour a procédé à cette lecture conjointe des dispositions en cause dès l'arrêt du 24 juin 2014, Parlement/Conseil (C-658/11, EU:C:2014:2025, points 69 et 70).

[17] Arrêt du 10 septembre 2024, KS et KD/Conseil e.a. et Commission/KS et KD (C-29/22 P et C-44/22 P, ci-après l'«arrêt KS et KD», EU:C:2024:725).

[18] Arrêt du 10 septembre 2024, Neves 77 Solutions (C-351/22, ci-après l'«arrêt Neves», EU:C:2024:723).

[19] Ordonnance du 10 novembre 2021, KS et KD/Conseil e.a. (T-771/20, EU:T:2021:798).

[20] Ordonnance du 10 juillet 2014, H/Conseil e.a. (T-271/10, EU:T:2014:702).

[21] Il résulte de l'arrêt H (point 68) que les décisions litigieuses sont imputables au Conseil de l'Union européenne. Dès lors, la MPUE en Bosnie-Herzégovine, en tout cas à l'époque des faits pertinents, ne semble pas être un organe de l'Union au sens de l'article 263 TFUE.

alinéa, TFUE. En effet, le juge de l'Union étant, en tout état de cause, compétent pour contrôler de tels actes lorsqu'ils concernent des agents détachés auprès d'une entité relevant de la PESC par les institutions de l'Union, il doit l'être également lorsqu'il s'agit d'agents détachés par un État membre.[22]

Par l'arrêt *Rosneft*, la Cour a reconnu sa compétence pour statuer à titre préjudiciel sur la validité d'une décision PESC[23] relative à des mesures restrictives, pour autant que la demande de décision préjudicielle porte soit sur le contrôle du respect de l'article 40 TUE par cette décision, soit sur le contrôle de la légalité de mesures restrictives à l'encontre des personnes physiques ou morales. À cet égard, elle a d'abord rappelé les dispositions relatives au «carve-out» et au «claw-back»[24] que sa compétence connaît s'agissant de la PESC. Ensuite, elle a exposé que les traités ne prévoient aucune modalité particulière pour effectuer le contrôle du respect de cet article 40, de sorte que ce contrôle relève de la compétence générale que lui confère l'article 19 TUE, dont fait partie l'appréciation de la validité d'un acte dans la cadre de renvois préjudiciels. Enfin, et surtout, la Cour a mis en avant que le contrôle de la légalité des actes de l'Union repose sur deux procédures juridictionnelles complémentaires, qui donnent lieu à un système complet. Elle en a tiré la conséquence que cette caractéristique essentielle du système de protection juridictionnelle de l'Union s'étend au contrôle de la légalité des décisions prévoyant l'adoption de mesures restrictives à l'encontre de personnes physiques ou morales dans le cadre de la PESC, non seulement par un recours en annulation, mais également dans le

[22] Arrêt H, en particulier points 42, 43, 44, 54 et 55. Pour une analyse plus approfondie de cet arrêt, voir P. Van Elsuwege, Upholding the rule of law in the Common Foreign and Security Policy: *H* v. *Council*, *CML Rev.*, 2017, n° 2, pp. 841-855. La possibilité de séparer les actes de gestion du personnel des objectifs d'une action opérationnelle d'une mission relevant de la PESC est critiquée par J. Heliskoski, "Made in Luxembourg: The fabrication of the law on jurisdiction of the Court of Justice of the European Union in the field of the Common Foreign and Security Policy", *Europe and the World: A Law Review*, 2018, n° 2, pp. 1–20, en particulier pp. 10 et 19.

[23] Décision 2014/512/PESC, du 31 juillet 2014, concernant des mesures restrictives eu égard aux actions de la Russie déstabilisant la situation en Ukraine (JO 2014, L 229, p. 13).

[24] Depuis les conclusions de l'avocat général Wathelet dans l'affaire Rosneft (C-72/15, EU:C:2016:381, notamment points 41 et 51), il est devenu usuel d'employer les expressions «carve-out» et «claw-back» pour désigner respectivement: i) l'exception à la compétence générale de la Cour résultant de l'article 24, paragraphe 1, second alinéa, dernière phrase, TUE et de l'article 275, premier alinéa, TFUE; ii) les deux «exceptions à cette exception» prévues à cette dernière phrase ainsi qu'à l'article 275, second alinéa, TFUE. Ces exceptions à l'exception établissent explicitement la compétence de la Cour, d'une part, pour contrôler le respect de l'article 40 TUE et, d'autre part, pour se prononcer sur les recours, formés dans les conditions prévues à l'article 263, quatrième alinéa, TFUE, concernant le contrôle de la légalité des décisions du Conseil adoptées sur le fondement des dispositions relatives à la PESC, qui prévoient des mesures restrictives à l'égard de personnes physiques ou morales. Voir également conclusions de l'avocate générale Ćapeta dans les affaires KS et KD (C-29/22 P et C-44/22 P, EU:C:2023:901, notamment points 125 à 127). En doctrine, voir P. Van Elsuwege, Judicial review and the Common Foreign and Security Policy: Limits to the gap-filling role of the Court of Justice, précité, p. 1732; S. Poli, The right to effective judicial protection with respect to acts imposing restrictive measures and its transformative force for the Common Foreign and Security Policy, *CML Rev.*, 2022 n° 4, pp. 1045–1080, en particulier p. 1051.

cadre d'un renvoi préjudiciel. En revanche, la Cour a exclu sa compétence pour apprécier la validité de mesures restrictives qui, ayant une portée générale, ne visent pas des personnes physiques ou morales identifiées.[25]

Dans l'affaire *KF*, il s'agissait, de manière semblable à l'affaire *H*, d'une question concernant un membre du personnel d'un organe[26] relevant de la PESC – le centre satellitaire de l'Union européenne (CSUE) –, qui avait obtenu du Tribunal[27] l'annulation de deux décisions adoptées par son employeur ainsi que des dommages et intérêts. Le règlement du personnel de cet organe prévoyait des voies de recours spécifiques pour les affaires relatives à ses agents, devant une commission de recours dont les décisions n'étaient pas susceptibles de recours. La Cour considère que l'attribution à cette commission d'une compétence exclusive pour interpréter et appliquer ce règlement du personnel se heurte aux principes et dispositions du droit primaire en vertu desquels les juridictions nationales et la CJUE garantissent notamment la protection juridictionnelle effective que les justiciables tirent du droit de l'Union. En effet, la Cour détient une compétence exclusive pour fournir l'interprétation définitive de ce droit. Elle précise également que les dispositions prévoyant le «carve-out» ne s'étendent pas jusqu'à exclure que le juge de l'Union soit compétent pour contrôler la légalité d'actes de gestion du personnel adoptés par un organe relevant de la PESC. Par ailleurs, la Cour relève que la nature contractuelle de la relation de travail liant le requérant au CSUE ne s'oppose pas à ce que celui-ci puisse saisir le juge de l'Union d'un recours en annulation au titre de l'article 263 TFUE et d'un recours en indemnité au titre de l'article 268 TFUE. À cet égard, elle souligne que, le règlement du personnel en cause excluant explicitement la compétence des juges nationaux, si le juge de l'Union renonçait à l'exercice des compétences qui lui sont conférés par ces articles, le requérant ne disposerait pas de remèdes juridictionnels.[28]

Dans l'arrêt *Bank Refah*, la Cour a considéré que la CJUE est compétente pour connaître de recours tendant à obtenir réparation de préjudices prétendument subis

[25] Arrêt Rosneft, en particulier points 62 à 81 et 96 à 98. Pour une analyse plus approfondie de cet arrêt, voir I. Bosse-Platière, Le juge de l'Union, artisan de la cohérence du système de contrôle juridictionnel au sein de l'Union européenne, y compris en matière de PESC, *RTDE*, 2017, n° 3, pp. 555-563; T. Henze et J. Jahn, Die Gemeinsame Außen- und Sicherheitspolitik der EU Unter der Kontrolle des EuGH, *Europäische Zeitschrift für Wirtschaftsrecht*, 2017, pp. 506-511; S. Poli, The Common Foreign Security Policy after Rosneft: Still Imperfect but gradually subject to the rule of law, précité; P. Van Elsuwege, Securing a Coherent System of Judicial Protection in Relation to Restrictive Measures: Rosneft, dans G. Butler et R. A. Wessel (dir.), *EU External Relations Law*, précité, pp. 881–889.

[26] Au vu de la solution retenue par la Cour, il ne fait pas de doute qu'elle considère le CSUE comme étant un organe de l'Union au sens de l'article 263 TFUE.

[27] Arrêt du 25 octobre 2018, KF/CSUE (T-286/15, EU:T:2018:718).

[28] Arrêt KF, en particulier points 58 à 66 et 78 à 85. Pour une analyse plus approfondie de cet arrêt, voir D. Simon, Juridiction de l'Union – Systématique des contentieux, *Europe*, 2020, n°s 8-9, Commentaire 248; S. Poli, The right to effective judicial protection with respect to acts imposing restrictive measures and its transformative force for the Common Foreign and Security Policy, *CML Rev.*, 2022, en particulier pp. 1048-1050.

en raison de l'adoption de mesures restrictives individuelles prévues par des décisions PESC. Après avoir indiqué que l'article 275 TFUE «ne mentionne pas expressément» cette compétence, la Cour a notamment relevé, d'une part, que le recours en indemnité doit être apprécié au regard de l'ensemble du système de protection juridictionnelle des particuliers instauré par les traités et, d'autre part, que le juge de l'Union est compétent pour statuer sur un recours en indemnité en tant qu'il concerne des mesures restrictives prévues par des règlements fondés sur l'article 215 TFUE, qui établit une passerelle entre les objectifs du traité UE en matière de PESC et les actions de l'Union comportant des mesures économiques relevant du traité FUE. Partant, la nécessaire cohérence du système de protection juridictionnelle prévu par le droit de l'Union exige que, en vue d'éviter une lacune dans la protection juridictionnelle des personnes physiques ou morales visées, la CJUE soit également compétente pour statuer sur le préjudice prétendument subi en raison de mesures restrictives prévues par des décisions PESC, lesquelles ne sont pas toutes nécessairement reprises dans ces règlements.[29]

3 La systématisation et les développements résultant de l'arrêt KS et KD

L'arrêt *KS et KD* a été rendu à l'occasion de deux pourvois dirigés contre l'ordonnance par laquelle le Tribunal s'était déclaré manifestement incompétent pour connaître d'un recours en indemnité tendant à obtenir réparation des préjudices censés résulter de divers actes et omissions du Conseil de l'Union européenne, de la Commission européenne et du Service européen pour l'action extérieure (SEAE), dans le cadre de la mission «État de droit» menée par l'Union européenne au Kosovo (EULEX Kosovo). Statuant sur ces pourvois, la Cour a systématisé les principes qui permettent de déterminer la portée de la compétence de la CJUE dans le cadre de la PESC s'agissant des recours directs.

À cet effet, la Cour s'est appuyée sur de nombreuses dispositions du droit primaire, à l'aune desquelles elle a lu celles qui prévoient le «carve-out». Premièrement, elle a relevé que, selon l'article 3, paragraphe 5, TUE, dans ses relations avec le reste du monde, l'Union contribue notamment à la protection des droits de l'homme. Deuxièmement, en vertu de l'article 23 TUE, l'action de l'Union sur la scène internationale, au titre du chapitre 2 du titre V du traité UE, repose sur les principes, poursuit les objectifs et est menée conformément aux dispositions générales visés au chapitre 1 de ce titre. Troisièmement, conformément à l'article 21, paragraphe 1,

---

[29] Arrêt Bank Refah, en particulier points 29 à 40. Pour une analyse plus approfondie de cet arrêt, voir L. Coutron, La consécration de la possibilité de demander réparation du préjudice causé par des mesures restrictives prévues par des décisions PESC: un gain de protection juridictionnelle en trompe-l'oeil?, *RTDE*, 2021, n° 3, pp. 627-636; S. Poli, The right to effective judicial protection with respect to acts imposing restrictive measures and its transformative force for the Common Foreign and Security Policy, précité, en particulier pp. 1050-1057.

premier alinéa, TUE, qui fait partie de ce chapitre 1, l'action de l'Union sur la scène internationale repose sur les principes qui ont présidé à sa création, à son développement et à son élargissement et qu'elle vise à promouvoir dans le reste du monde, notamment l'État de droit. Quatrièmement, l'article 51, paragraphe 1, de la charte des droits fondamentaux de l'Union européenne (ci-après la «Charte») confirme que les droits fondamentaux garantis dans l'ordre juridique de l'Union ont vocation à être appliqués dans toutes les situations régies par le droit de l'Union.[30]

Au vu de ces dispositions, la Cour a constaté que l'inclusion de la PESC dans le cadre constitutionnel de l'Union, consécutive au traité de Lisbonne,[31] implique que les principes fondamentaux de l'ordre juridique de l'Union s'appliquent également dans le cadre de cette politique. Parmi ceux-ci figurent, notamment, le respect de l'État de droit et des droits fondamentaux, valeurs énoncées à l'article 2 TUE et concrétisées par l'article 19 TUE, qui exigent que tant les autorités de l'Union que les autorités des États membres soient soumises à un contrôle juridictionnel.[32]

Toutefois, dans ce contexte, si la Cour n'a pas manqué de se référer également au droit à la protection juridictionnelle effective découlant de l'article 47 de la Charte et des articles 6 et 13 de la convention européenne de sauvegarde des droits de l'homme et des libertés fondamentales, signée à Rome le 4 novembre 1950 (ci-après la «CEDH»), elle a rappelé que l'article 47 de la Charte ne peut pas lui conférer une nouvelle compétence lorsque les traités l'excluent. À cet égard, la Cour précise que la jurisprudence en vertu de laquelle cet article 47 ne saurait modifier les règles relatives à la recevabilité établies à l'article 263, paragraphe 4, TFUE exprime un principe d'interprétation, applicable à l'ensemble des voies de recours prévues par les traités. Ce principe est pertinent également lorsqu'il s'agit de délimiter la portée de la compétence du juge de l'Union.[33]

Par ailleurs, elle a souligné que le principe d'attribution, prévu à l'article 5, paragraphes 1 et 2, TUE, et le principe de l'équilibre institutionnel, consacré à l'article 13, paragraphe 2, TUE, s'appliquent également dans le domaine de la PESC. Ainsi, d'une part, l'Union ne peut agir que dans les limites des compétences que les États membres lui ont attribuées dans les traités pour atteindre les objectifs établis par ces derniers, tandis que toute compétence non attribuée à l'Union dans les traités appartient aux États membres. D'autre part, chacune des institutions exerce ses compétences dans le respect de celles des autres.[34]

---

[30] Arrêt KS et KD, points 62, 63, 66, 67 et 69.

[31] J. Heliskoski (Made in Luxembourg: The fabrication of the law on jurisdiction of the Court of Justice of the European Union in the field of the Common Foreign and Security Policy, précité, en particulier p. 2.) souligne que le traité de Lisbonne a entraîné un « changement de paradigme » en ce qui concerne le contrôle juridictionnel en matière de PESC. A. Wessel(Lex imperfecta: Law and Integration in European Foreign and Security Policy, précité, p. 440) met en avant la «constitutionnalisation» et la «normalisation» de la PESC consécutives à ce traité.

[32] Arrêt KS et KD, point 68.

[33] Arrêt KS et KD, points 70, 71, 93 et 94.

[34] Arrêt KS et KD, point 72.

La mise en balance de tous ces principes et dispositions permet à la Cour d'exclure, contrairement à ce qu'avait proposé, en substance, l'avocate générale Ćapeta[35] dans ses conclusions, que la compétence du juge de l'Union pour connaître d'un recours puisse être établie en raison du seul fait qu'un particulier invoque la violation de ses droits fondamentaux par les actes ou les omissions faisant l'objet de son recours.[36]

Dans ce contexte, la Cour note que, si elle doit veiller à ce que soit assuré un niveau de protection juridictionnelle qui ne méconnaît pas celui garanti par la CEDH, telle qu'interprétée par la Cour européenne des droits de l'homme (ci-après la «Cour EDH»), cette dernière considère notamment qu'il ne lui appartient pas de s'immiscer dans l'équilibre institutionnel entre le pouvoir exécutif et les juridictions nationales. Cet équilibre peut se refléter dans une limitation constitutionnelle des compétences des juridictions d'un État s'agissant d'actes non détachables de la conduite des relations internationales de celui-ci.[37]

La Cour précise également que la détermination de la portée de sa compétence n'est pas tributaire de l'adhésion de l'Union à la CEDH, prévue à l'article 6, paragraphe 2, première phrase, TUE. En effet, en vertu de l'article 2, première phrase, du protocole n° 8,[38] l'accord relatif à cette adhésion doit garantir que celle-ci n'affecte ni les compétences de l'Union ni les attributions de ses institutions. Partant,

---

35 Conclusions KS et KD, en particulier points 83, 84, 89, 118, 124, 154 et 155.

36 Arrêt KS et KD, points 73 et 81. Aux points 74 à 76, la Cour ajoute que le cadre de la PESC est différent de celui du traité instituant le mécanisme européen de stabilité, conclu à Bruxelles le 2 février 2012 (ci-après le «traité MES»), sur lequel elle s'était prononcée dans l'arrêt du 20 septembre 2016, Ledra Advertising e.a./Commission et BCE (C-8/15 P à C-10/15 P, EU:C:2016:701). À cette occasion, elle s'est reconnue compétente pour connaître d'un recours en réparation d'un préjudice prétendument causé, en violation des droits fondamentaux des requérants, par la Commission, alors que celle-ci n'agissait qu'au titre du traité MES, qui ne fait pas partie du droit de l'Union. La Cour précise, en substance, que la Charte s'adresse aux institutions de l'Union même lorsqu'elles agissent en dehors du cadre de l'Union et que le cadre constitué par traité MES, contrairement à celui de la PESC, ne contient pas de dispositions prévoyant un «carve-out». Il convient d'ajouter que, ainsi que l'ont relevé plusieurs commentateurs de l'arrêt Ledra Advertising e.a./Commission et BCE, dans ce dernier, la Cour (point 59) s'est fondée sur le fait que la Commission conserve, dans le cadre du traité MES, son rôle de gardienne des traités, tel qu'il ressort de l'article 17, paragraphe 1, TUE, de sorte qu'elle devrait s'abstenir de signer un protocole d'accord dont elle douterait de la compatibilité avec le droit de l'Union (A. Spagnolo, The Loan of Organs between International Organisations as a "Normative Bridge": Insights from Recent EU practice, *The Italian yearbook of international law*, 2017, n° 1, pp. 171-190, en particulier pp. 179 et 184; A. Poulou, The Liability of the EU in the ESM framework, *Maastricht Journal of European and Comparative Law*, 2017, n° 1, pp. 127-139, en particulier p. 132; R. Repasi, Judicial Protection against Austerity Measures in the Euro Area: Ledra and Mallis, *CML Rev.*, 2017, n° 4, pp. 1123-1156, en particulier pp. 1134, 1151-1153). Or, dans le cadre de la PESC, le contrôle de l'exercice de ce rôle par la Commission doit tenir compte du «carve-out».

37 Arrêt KS et KD, points 77 à 80. À cet égard, la Cour se réfère notamment à l'arrêt de la Cour EDH, 14 septembre 2022, H.F. et autres c. France (CE:ECHR:2022:0914JUD002438419, § 281).

38 Protocole (n°8), relatif à l'article 6, paragraphe 2, [TUE] sur l'adhésion de l'Union à la [CEDH].

cet article 6, paragraphe 2, ne saurait élargir les compétences de la CJUE en matière de PESC.[39]

Par ailleurs, dès lors que les recours pour lesquels le Tribunal s'était déclaré incompétent étaient de nature indemnitaire, la Cour fournit également des précisions importantes quant aux enseignements pouvant être tirés de l'arrêt *Bank Refah*. En particulier, elle souligne que les dispositions sur le «carve-out» et le «claw-back» sont des *leges speciales* au regard des articles 268 et 340 TFUE. Ces derniers ne peuvent donc pas fonder une compétence générale de la CJUE pour connaître des recours en indemnité en matière de PESC. Ce ne sont que les recours concernant la réparation de préjudices censés découler d'actes de nature individuelle qui peuvent être examinés, conformément à ces *leges speciales*.[40]

Après avoir ainsi systématisé les principes et les dispositions qui, dans leur ensemble, permettent de comprendre la portée de la compétence de la CJUE s'agissant de recours relatifs à des situations liées à la PESC, la Cour en vient à définir, en substance, des critères qui, bien que formulés spécifiquement à l'égard des recours en indemnité, semblent se prêter à une application plus générale.

Aussi, pour vérifier si un recours relève de cette compétence, il y a lieu, *dans un premier temps*, de déterminer si la situation en cause tombe dans l'un des cas de figure visés par le «claw-back».[41] Si tel n'est pas le cas, il convient, *dans un second temps*, d'apprécier si cette compétence peut être fondée sur la circonstance que les actes ou les omissions dont il s'agit se rattachent directement aux choix politiques ou stratégiques effectués par les institutions ou par les organes et organismes de l'Union dans le cadre de la PESC. Dans la négative, ladite compétence est établie, alors que, dans l'affirmative, la CJUE doit se déclarer incompétente. Dès lors, la Cour est incompétente pour apprécier la légalité ou pour interpréter des actes ou des omissions se rattachant directement à la conduite, à la définition ou à la mise en œuvre de la PESC, à savoir, en particulier, l'identification des intérêts stratégiques de l'Union ainsi que la définition tant des actions à mener et des positions à prendre par l'Union que des orientations générales de la PESC, au sens des articles 24 à 26, 28, 29, 37, 38, 42 et 43 TUE. Et la Cour de conclure, en substance, que ce résultat: i) est conforme au libellé des dispositions prévoyant le «carve-out», qui, en principe, excluent la compétence de la CJUE en matière de PESC; ii) se trouve corroboré par le contexte dans lequel ces dispositions s'inscrivent, dès lors qu'il permet

---

[39] Arrêt KS et KD, point 82. Dans ses conclusions (points 4, 26 et 145 à 153), l'avocate générale Ćapeta a consacré quelques développements au fait que ces affaires peuvent être vues dans le contexte des progrès que, à la suite de l'avis 2/13, a connu la procédure d'adhésion. En particulier, la seule question restante semble être l'étendue de la compétence des juridictions de l'Union dans le domaine de la PESC.

[40] Arrêt KS et KD, points 85 à 92.

[41] Au vu des principes issus de l'arrêt Bank Refah, il semble acquis que le «claw-back» inclut les recours en indemnité concernant la réparation de préjudices supposés découler de mesures restrictives individuelles contenues dans des décisions PESC.

de préserver leur effet utile, sans toutefois porter indûment atteinte au droit à un recours effectif; iii) correspond à la finalité poursuivie par lesdites dispositions.[42]

La Cour a ainsi défini un «test de compétence» qui peut s'étendre sur deux étapes, dont la seconde est, pour l'essentiel, fondée sur le rattachement direct aux choix politiques ou stratégiques effectués par les institutions ou par les organes et organismes de l'Union dans le cadre de la PESC.

Si, au vu des précisions apportées par la jurisprudence, la première étape du test en cause semble relativement facile à appliquer et si la seconde étape repose a priori sur un critère clair, il n'en reste pas moins que certaines distinctions peuvent être très subtiles. Par exemple, la Cour, lorsqu'elle a examiné les arguments des requérants selon lesquels la mission Eulex Kosovo avait violé certaines dispositions en raison de l'absence d'enquêtes adéquates consécutive à un défaut de ressources nécessaires et de personnel adéquat de cette mission pour exercer son mandat, a retenu une dichotomie qui peut susciter quelques difficultés. En effet, la Cour expose, d'une part, que le prétendu défaut de ressources nécessaires se rattache directement aux choix politiques ou stratégiques effectués dans le cadre de la PESC, sur le fondement de l'article 28, paragraphe 1, premier alinéa, TUE. D'autre part, le prétendu défaut de personnel adéquat de la mission Eulex Kosovo concerne la capacité de celle-ci d'employer du personnel et constitue donc un acte de gestion quotidienne qui s'inscrit dans le cadre de l'exécution du mandat de ladite mission et ne se rattache pas directement aux choix politiques ou stratégiques effectués par la même mission dans le cadre de la PESC. La Cour en déduit qu'il incombe à Eulex Kosovo de veiller, dans le cadre des ressources qui sont mises à sa disposition, à ce que le personnel qu'elle emploie soit adéquat.[43]

Il peut être observé que l'article 28, paragraphe 1, premier alinéa, TUE mentionne non seulement les moyens mis à disposition de l'Union pour des actions opérationnelles, mais aussi, notamment, la mise en œuvre des actions opérationnelles de l'Union. Or, il n'est pas exclu de considérer que la détermination des tâches à attribuer à un personnel limité en nombre puisse relever de cette mise en œuvre.

En dépit des questions que le test établi par la Cour, en particulier sa seconde étape, pourra susciter, les clarifications apportées dans l'arrêt *KS et KD* doivent être saluées. En particulier, le critère du rattachement direct aux choix politiques ou stratégiques effectués par les institutions ou par les organes et organismes de l'Union dans le cadre de la PESC pourrait devenir le «overarching criterion»[44] que la Cour n'avait pas eu besoin de définir dans les arrêts *H* et *KF*. Par ailleurs, l'application de ce critère pourrait s'inspirer des conclusions de l'avocat général Bobek dans l'affaire *KF*. En particulier, celui-ci, après avoir souligné que, lorsque le lien entre un acte de l'Union et une action ou une opération se rapportant à sa politique étrangère ou à sa

---

[42] Arrêt KS et KD, points 115 à 120.

[43] Arrêt KS et KD, points 125 à 128.

[44] L. Prete, The Scope of the Court's Jurisdiction in the CFSP: H v Council and Others, précité, p. 837.

sécurité n'est qu'indirect, il est difficile de justifier l'exclusion de la compétence de la Cour, a conçu un test comprenant les questions suivantes: «l'acte attaqué qui, formellement, est basé sur une disposition relative à la PESC, aurait-il pu être adopté dans un autre contexte, ne relevant pas de la PESC ? Dans l'affirmative, ce contenu et les considérations ayant conduit à son adoption pourraient-ils être similaires, voire identiques, en cas d'adoption dans un contexte ne relevant pas de la PESC ?». Il a proposé de considérer que, si la réponse à ces deux questions est affirmative, il est vraisemblable que l'acte en cause ne renferme pas un véritable contenu relatif à la PESC.[45]

4 La compétence préjudicielle en interprétation à la lumière notamment de l'arrêt Neves

Dans l'arrêt *Rosneft*, la Cour, n'y étant pas tenue, ne s'est pas prononcée sur le point de savoir si elle dispose de la compétence pour répondre à des questions préjudicielles en interprétation en matière de PESC. Dans les conclusions qu'il a présentées à cette occasion, l'avocat général Wathelet avait, en substance, considéré que, puisque «qui peut le plus peut le moins», si les juridictions de l'Union peuvent contrôler, y compris dans le cadre d'un renvoi préjudiciel, la légalité d'une décision prévoyant des mesures à l'encontre de personnes physiques ou morales, elles peuvent sûrement interpréter les termes de ces décisions.[46]

Si la thèse de l'avocat général semble tout à fait raisonnable, elle laisse néanmoins ouverte la question de savoir si la Cour est compétente pour interpréter des dispositions dont elle ne peut pas apprécier la validité, telles des dispositions de portée générale en matière de PESC, ainsi que cela résulte clairement de l'arrêt *Rosneft*.[47]

Certains arrêts postérieurs à ce dernier semblent permettre de considérer que la Cour, dans certains cas, interprète des dispositions relevant de la PESC qui n'ont pas une nature individuelle et ne rentrent donc a priori pas dans le «claw-back», tel que défini dans l'arrêt *Rosneft*. Ainsi, premièrement, dans l'arrêt *A e.a.*,[48] la Cour,

[45] Conclusions KF, points 77 et 82.

[46] Conclusions Rosneft, points 73 à 76. La thèse de l'avocat général Wathelet a été considérée comme convaincante par S. Poli, The common foreign security policy after Rosneft: still Imperfect but gradually subject to the rule of law, précité, notamment p. 1829.

[47] Arrêt Rosneft, points 96 à 98.

[48] Arrêt du 14 mars 2017, A e.a. (C-158/14, EU:C:2017:202, en particulier points 72 à 75 et 97). Dans les conclusions présentées dans cette affaire (EU:C:2016:734, points 89 à 91), l'avocate générale Sharpston relève que les renvois préjudiciels jouent un rôle fondamental pour les personnes susceptibles de subir les conséquences préjudiciables de mesures adoptées dans le cadre de la PESC qui ne leur sont pas adressées individuellement. En effet, ces personnes ne sont en principe pas recevables à attaquer ces mesures devant le juge de l'Union sur la base de l'article 275, second alinéa, TFUE. Sur cet arrêt et ces conclusions, voir P. A. Sáenz de Santa María, Mejorando la lex imperfecta: tutela judicial efectiva y cuestión prejudicial en la PESC (a propósito del asunto

sans se prononcer sur sa compétence, a interprété la notion d'«acte de terrorisme» qui figurait dans une position commune PESC,[49] sans que les noms des requérants au principal, qui faisaient l'objet de mesures restrictives nationales prises sur le fondement de cet acte, soient inscrits sur la liste annexée à ce dernier. Deuxièmement, dans l'arrêt *Eulex Kosovo*,[50] la Cour a répondu à une demande de décision préjudicielle introduite la juridiction belge saisie par des (anciens) membres du personnel de la mission Eulex Kosovo, dans le but de comprendre qui était l'employeur de ceux-ci, et donc d'établir qui devait être qualifié de partie défenderesse dans l'affaire pendante devant cette juridiction.[51] Dans son arrêt, la Cour a interprété une disposition, contenue dans un acte relevant de la PESC,[52] qui attribuait à la mission Eulex

Rosneft), *Revista de Derecho Comunitario Europeo,* 2017, pp. 871-903, en particulier p. 902; M. Wimmer, Counter-terrorism sanctions, non-international armed conflicts and Tamil Tigers, *CML Rev.*, 2018, pp. 1573-1593, en particulier p. 1582; S. Boni et D. Dittert, Le rapport entre le renvoi préjudiciel et les autres voies de recours, dans F. Ferraro et C. Iannone (dir.), *Le renvoi préjudiciel*, 2023, Bruxelles, en particulier pp. 318-321 et 325.

[49] Position commune 2001/931/PESC du Conseil, du 27 décembre 2001, relative à l'application de mesures spécifiques en vue de lutter contre le terrorisme (JO 2001, L 344, p. 93).

[50] Arrêt du 24 février 2022, Eulex Kosovo (C-283/20, EU:C:2022:126, en particulier points 2, 14, 15, 23, 37 et 47). Dans les conclusions présentées dans cette affaire (EU:C:2021:781, points 42 à 50), l'avocat général Tanchev a, en substance, considéré que la compétence de la Cour découlait du fait que l'affaire au principal portait sur des questions de gestion du personnel (conclusion de contrats de travail, non-renouvellement de ceux-ci, reclassification de certaines fonctions), lesquelles, à la lumière de l'arrêt *H*, ne relèvent pas du «carve-out». C. Hillion (The EU External Action as Mandate to Uphold the Rule of Law Outside and Inside the Union, *Columbia Journal of European Law*, 2023, Special Issue, pp. 228-282) observe que, par l'arrêt Eulex Kosovo, la Cour a élargi ce qu'elle avait reconnu dans l'arrêt Rosneft (p. 256).

[51] Une partie du personnel affecté à des entités relevant de la PESC est souvent recrutée sur la base d'un (ou d'une série de) contrat(s) de travail de droit privé. Ces contrats n'indiquent pas toujours quelle est la juridiction compétente pour connaître du contentieux pouvant découler de ceux-ci et/ou ne précisent pas quel est le droit applicable. Par ailleurs, dès lors que ces entités ne disposent pas toujours de la personnalité juridique, peut également se poser la question de savoir qui est l'employeur. Si l'examen de ces questions dépasse l'objectif de la présente contribution, il peut néanmoins être signalé qu'il est souhaitable que les institutions qui ont un rôle dans la création de ces entités et dans la gestion de celles-ci agissent pour garantir une plus grande sécurité juridique au profit de ce personnel. Pour des exemples des «péripéties» qui caractérisent les actions intentées par ce personnel contractuel, voir, notamment, en plus de l'arrêt Eulex Kosovo, arrêts du 5 juillet 2018, Jenkinson/Conseil e.a. (C-43/17 P, EU:C:2018:531); du 18 janvier 2024, Jenkinson/Conseil e.a. (C-46/22 P, EU:C:2024:50); du 13 juillet 2022, JC/EUCAP Somalia (T-165/20, EU:T:2022:453); du 13 juillet 2022, JF/EUCAP Somalia (T-194/20, EU:T:2022:454), et du 26 juillet 2023, Stockdale/Conseil e.a. (T-776/20, EU:T:2023:422). Ce dernier arrêt, rendu par le Tribunal en chambre élargie, n'a pas mis fin à l'instance, mais était limité à l'appréciation de questions de compétence et de recevabilité. À ce jour, il fait l'objet d'un pourvoi pendant devant la Cour, formé par le Royaume d'Espagne (C-728/23 P, Espagne/Conseil e.a.). Sur ces questions, voir J. Heliskoski, Responsability and liability for CSDP operations, dans S. Blockmans et P. Koutrakos (dir.), *Research Handbook on the EU's Common Foreign and Security Policy*, 2018, Cheltenham, pp. 132-153, en particulier pp. 142–144.

[52] Action commune 2008/124/PESC du Conseil, du 4 février 2008, relative à la mission « État de droit » menée par l'Union européenne au Kosovo, Eulex Kosovo (JO 2008, L 42, p. 92), telle que modifiée par la décision 2014/349/PESC du Conseil, du 12 juin 2014 (JO 2014, L 174, p. 42).

Kosovo, à compter d'une certaine date, la responsabilité pour toute plainte et obligation découlant de l'exécution de son mandat.

Dans l'affaire *Neves*, la Cour était appelée à interpréter une disposition d'une décision PESC[53] énonçant, en tant que mesure restrictive de portée générale, l'interdiction de fourniture de services de courtage en rapport avec des activités militaires. Cette mesure, qui servait de fondement à une mesure nationale à l'encontre de la requérante au principal, n'avait pas été mise en œuvre par le Conseil dans un règlement au titre de l'article 215 TFUE.

S'agissant de l'une des deux situations envisagées par le «claw-back», la Cour rappelle que c'est la nature individuelle des actes qui ouvre l'accès au juge de l'Union, alors que la disposition en cause en l'occurrence contient une mesure de portée générale. S'agissant de l'autre situation, la Cour relève que, lorsqu'elle contrôle le respect de l'article 40 TUE, il lui incombe de veiller à ce que la mise en œuvre de la PESC par le Conseil n'affecte pas l'application des procédures et l'étendue respective des attributions des institutions prévues par les traités pour l'exercice des compétences de l'Union au titre du traité FUE. Cela implique, en particulier, de veiller à ce que, en ce qui concerne la mise en œuvre de l'article 215 TFUE, lequel établit une passerelle entre les objectifs du traité UE en matière de PESC et les actions de l'Union comportant des mesures restrictives relevant du traité FUE, le Conseil ne contourne pas la compétence de la Cour, qui n'est aucunement limitée s'agissant d'un règlement au titre de cet article. À cet égard, elle souligne que, en raison des termes utilisés à l'article 215, paragraphe 1, TFUE, le Conseil se trouve dans une situation de compétence liée. Dès lors, la compétence conférée à la Cour par les traités en vue d'assurer la protection juridictionnelle des tiers ne saurait être limitée par la circonstance que le Conseil, tout en étant dans une telle situation, n'a pas pris toutes les mesures nécessaires sur le fondement de l'article 215, paragraphe 1, TFUE. Par conséquent, la possibilité de saisir la Cour à titre préjudiciel doit être ouverte à l'égard de toutes les dispositions qu'il aurait incombé au Conseil d'inclure dans un tel règlement et qui servent de fondement à une mesure nationale de sanction prise à l'égard des tiers.[54]

[53] Voir note en bas de page n° 23 ci-dessus.

[54] Arrêt Neves, en particulier points 37 à 49. À ce dernier point, la Cour cite, par analogie, l'arrêt du 31 mars 1971, Commission/Conseil (22/70, EU:C:1971:32, points 38 à 40), également connu comme l'arrêt «AETR», où elle a reconnu le caractère «attaquable» d'une délibération du Conseil relative à la négociation et à la conclusion, par les États membres, d'un accord international, au motif que celle-ci produit des effets juridiques déterminés. Une analogie semble pouvoir être également faite avec les arrêts du 27 février 2007, Segi e.a./Conseil (C-355/04 P, EU:C:2007:116), et du 27 février 2007, Gestoras Pro Amnistía e.a./Conseil (C-354/04 P, EU:C:2007:115). En effet, aux points 50 à 54 de ces arrêts, la Cour a reconnu la possibilité d'un renvoi préjudiciel également s'agissant de tous les actes de l'ancien «troisième pilier» produisant des effets juridiques à l'égard de tiers, indépendamment du fait que ces actes, selon leur dénomination, relèvent ou non des catégories d'actes pour lesquels ce renvoi était prévu à l'article 35, paragraphe 1, UE. Sur ces arrêts, voir D. Dittert, CJCE, 27 février 2007, Gestoras Pro amnistia e.a./Conseil et Segi e.a./Conseil, *RAE*, 2007-2008, n° 1, pp. 121- 125, et A. I. Santamaría Dacal Las sentencias Segi y Gestoras del TJCE:¿ un sermón sin mayores consécuencias ou un primer toque de atención? *Revista de Derecho Comunitario Europeo*, 2007, pp. 313–322.

La Cour ajoute, en substance, que le fait d'admettre cette possibilité, d'une part, est conforme à l'objectif de l'article 267 TFUE, qui est d'assurer une application uniforme du droit de l'Union par les juridictions nationales, et, d'autre part, permet d'assurer la nécessaire cohérence du système de protection juridictionnelle prévu par le droit de l'Union. À cet égard, la Cour souligne que l'existence d'un contrôle juridictionnel effectif, dont la clé de voûte est la procédure de renvoi préjudiciel, est inhérent à l'existence d'un État de droit, qui est une valeur fondatrice de l'Union et qui s'étend à la PESC.[55]

À la lumière de ces considérations, la Cour conclut que, eu égard aux articles 19, 24 et 40 TUE ainsi qu'à l'article 215, paragraphe 1, TFUE, lus à la lumière des articles 2 et 21 TUE, elle est compétente pour statuer à titre préjudiciel sur l'interprétation d'une mesure de portée générale contenue dans un acte adopté sur le fondement des dispositions relatives à la PESC dans l'hypothèse où il aurait incombé au Conseil de mettre en œuvre cette mesure, qui sert de fondement à des mesures nationales de sanction imposées à une personne physique ou morale, dans un règlement au titre de l'article 215 TFUE.[56]

L'arrêt *Neves* a donc permis à la Cour, réunie en grande chambre, de préciser, pour l'essentiel, que le contrôle qu'elle est compétente à exercer quant au respect de l'article 40 TUE s'étend aux situations dans lesquelles le Conseil aurait manqué à son obligation de mettre en œuvre une disposition relevant de la PESC, à l'égard de laquelle la compétence de la Cour est limitée, dans un règlement, à l'égard duquel cette compétence n'est pas limitée. Dès lors que, dans cet arrêt, la Cour a fondé sa compétence sur les circonstances particulières caractérisées par un tel manquement de la part du Conseil, il semble difficile d'en extrapoler des enseignements généraux quant au rôle que les renvois préjudiciels en interprétation peuvent avoir dans le cadre de la PESC.

5 Remarques finales

Il découle de la jurisprudence qui vient d'être examinée que les règles de la PESC donnent lieu à une *lex* moins *imperfecta* que ce qu'il serait possible d'imaginer à la lecture des seules dispositions relatives au «carve-out» et au «claw-back». Ce résultat a été rendu possible par le fait que, s'il est indéniable que l'existence de limites à la compétence de la CJUE dans le contexte de la PESC est la conséquence d'un choix des auteurs des traités, ce choix doit être appréhendé dans un contexte plus large que les seuls termes retenus lors de la rédaction de ces dispositions. À cet égard, il doit être souligné que ces mêmes auteurs ont également mis fin à la structure en trois piliers qui caractérisait l'Union avant le traité de Lisbonne et renforcé

[55] Arrêt Neves, points 50 à 52. La Cour s'appuie tant sur l'article 2 TUE, figurant dans les dispositions communes du traité UE, que sur l'article 21 TUE, concernant l'action extérieure de l'Union, auquel renvoie l'article 23 TUE, relatif à la PESC.

[56] Arrêt Neves, point 53.

le rôle des valeurs de l'Union, telles que l'État de droit, ainsi que la protection des droits fondamentaux.

Face à ce « puzzle constitutionnel »,[57] la Cour, suivant une approche holistique,[58] a comblé certaines lacunes, par une conception de sa compétence qui, si elle n'était pas la seule possible et si elle n'a pas manqué de susciter de critiques,[59] n'a pas privé de tout effet utile le «carve-out» prévu dans les traités. En effet, le « gap-filling » auquel la Cour procède est soumis à des limites, dès lors qu'il doit demeurer compatible avec le principe d'attribution et l'équilibre institutionnel, consacrés à l'article 13, paragraphe 2, TUE,[60] auquel Nils Wahl s'est référé dans les conclusions qu'il a présentées dans l'affaire *H*[61] et sur lequel la Cour s'est également appuyée dans l'arrêt *KS et KD.*[62] Partant, ainsi que le reconnaît ce dernier arrêt, lorsque le critère du rattachement direct aux choix politiques ou stratégiques effectués par les institutions ou par les organes et organismes de l'Union dans le cadre de la PESC est satisfait, des situations peuvent se présenter dans lesquelles la CJUE est incompétente pour examiner des actes ou des omissions de ces institutions, organes et organismes.

De manière similaire, l'arrêt *Neves* permet de nourrir des doutes quant à la possibilité que la Cour interprète des dispositions de portée générale contenues dans des actes PESC, en dehors des cas où le Conseil aurait oublié de mettre en œuvre ces dispositions dans un règlement fondé sur l'article 215 TFUE.

Une telle situation n'est certes pas idéale, et ce d'autant plus qu'elle risque d'être perçue comme donnant lieu à une tension avec le fait que l'action extérieure de l'Union repose notamment sur l'État de droit, auquel l'existence d'un contrôle juridictionnel effectif est inhérente. Ainsi, le fait que ce contrôle connaisse des limites pourrait nuire à ce que l'Union promeuve et soutienne, de manière crédible, l'État de droit par son action extérieure.[63]

Toutefois, d'une part, l'existence de limites au contrôle juridictionnel dans l'exercice de la politique étrangère n'est pas inconnue à d'autres ordres juridiques

[57] C. Hillion, The EU External Action as Mandate to Uphold the Rule of Law Outside and Inside the Union, précité, p. 252.

[58] Voir note en bas de page n° 15 ci-dessus.

[59] J. Heliskoski, Made in Luxembourg: The fabrication of the law on jurisdiction of the Court of Justice of the European Union in the field of the Common Foreign and Security Policy", précité; P. Koutrakos, Judicial Review in the EU's common foreign and security policy, *International & Comparative Law Quarterly,* 2018, n° 1, pp. 1–35.

[60] P. Van Elsuwege, Judicial review and the Common Foreign and Security Policy: Limits to the gap-filling role of the Court of Justice, précité, en particulier p. 1733. Cet auteur note également, en substance, que la Cour a procédé d'une manière qui n'est pas sans rappeler le «gap-filling» que la Cour a exercé à compter notamment de l'arrêt du 23 avril 1986, Les Verts/Parlement (294/83, EU:C:1986:166), tout en admettant l'existence de limites infranchissables établis par les rédacteurs des traités, que seuls ceux-ci peuvent modifier (arrêt du 25 juillet 2002, Unión de Pequeños Agricultores/Conseil, C-50/00 P, EU:C:2002:462, points 43 à 45)

[61] Conclusions H, précitées, point 49.

[62] Voir note en bas de page n° 34 ci-dessus.

[63] C. Hillion, The EU External Action as Mandate to Uphold the Rule of Law Outside and Inside the Union, précité, p. 253.

que celui de l'Union[64] et semble pouvoir être acceptée par la Cour EDH, dans certaines circonstances.[65] D'autre part, l'article 19 TUE, à son paragraphe 2, attribue un rôle important aux juridictions des États membres en vue d'assurer une protection juridictionnelle effective. Il est vrai que la reconnaissance d'une compétence des juridictions des États membres à l'égard d'actes ou d'omissions pour lesquelles la CJUE n'a pas de compétence est susceptible de nuire à l'application uniforme du droit de l'Union.[66] Cependant, ainsi que l'a relevé Nils Wahl, en cas de doutes, ces juridictions pourraient soumettre à la Cour une demande de décision préjudicielle afin que celle-ci leur apporte une assistance pour juger les affaires pendantes devant elles tout en restant dans les limites imposées par le «carve-out». En particulier, la Cour serait en mesure d'interpréter les dispositions du droit de l'Union ayant une nature horizontale ou les principes généraux de ce droit qui pourraient être également applicables dans la procédure au principal. La Cour pourrait également préciser les limites de l'autonomie procédurale nationale en explicitant les conséquences juridiques découlant de l'obligation pour la juridiction nationale de fournir, conformément à l'article 19, paragraphe 1, TUE, des voies de recours suffisantes pour assurer une protection juridique effective aux particuliers.[67]

---

[64] Conclusions Rosneft, note en bas de page n° 26.

[65] Voir note en bas de page n° 37 ci-dessus.

[66] Sur cette question, voir notamment C. Hillion et R. A. WesseL, 'The Good, the Bad and the Ugly': three levels of judicial control over the CFSP, dans S. Blockmans et P. Koutrakos (dir.), *Research Handbook on the EU's Common Foreign and Security Policy*, précité, en particulier pp. 81–97.

[67] Conclusions H, points 90 et 91.

Le contrôle de légalité des actes administratifs de l'Union – oui, mais de quelle légalité ?

Heikki Kanninen and Sven Frisch

L'article 47, premier alinéa, de la charte des droits fondamentaux de l'Union européenne (ci-après la « Charte ») garantit le droit à un recours effectif devant un tribunal dans le cadre de l'application du droit de l'Union. Fondée sur l'article 13 de la convention européenne des droits de l'homme et des libertés fondamentales (ci-après la « Convention EDH »),[1] cette disposition réaffirme le principe général « inhérent à l'existence d'un État de droit »[2] qu'est la protection juridictionnelle effective et que la Cour déduisait déjà des traditions constitutionnelles communes aux États membres bien avant que la Charte devienne juridiquement contraignante avec l'entrée en vigueur du traité de Lisbonne le 1er décembre 2009.[3]

Conformément à ce principe, les institutions, organes et organismes de l'Union sont soumis au contrôle juridictionnel de la conformité de leurs actes au droit de l'Union.[4] Afin de concrétiser ledit principe, le traité sur le fonctionnement de

[1] Explications afférentes à l'article 47 de la Charte.

[2] Conclusions de l'avocat général Bobek dans l'affaire C-14/19 P, CSUE/KF, EU:C:2020:220, point 68.

[3] Arrêt du 15 mai 1986, Johnston, 222/84, EU:C:1986:206, points 18 et 19. Pour une réaffirmation récente, voir arrêt du 15 juillet 2021, Commission/Pologne (Régime disciplinaire des juges), C-791/19, EU:C:2021:596, point 52 et jurisprudence citée.

[4] Arrêts du 5 novembre 2019, BCE e.a./Trasta Komercbanka e.a., C-663/17 P, C-665/17 P et C-669/17 P, EU:C:2019:923, point 54, ainsi que du 25 juillet 2002, Unión de Pequeños Agricultores/Conseil, C-50/00 P, EU:C:2002:462, point 38.

H. Kanninen
Court of Justice of the European Union, Luxembourg, Luxembourg
e-mail: Heikki.Kanninen@curia.europa.eu

S. Frisch (✉)
Luxembourg, Luxembourg

L. Prete, L. Rezki (eds.), *Judging & (Re)Thinking European Union Law*,
https://doi.org/10.1007/978-3-032-13473-8_21

l'Union européenne (ci-après le « TFUE ») a établi un « système complet de voies de recours et de procédures destiné à assurer le contrôle de la légalité des actes de l'Union, en le confiant au juge de l'Union ».[5] Ce dernier jouit du monopole de l'appréciation la légalité des actes de l'Union.[6] Mais, il n'assure pas seul le contrôle juridictionnel du respect de l'ordre juridique de l'Union. Il partage ce rôle avec les juridictions des Etats membres,[7] auxquels l'article 19, paragraphe 1, second alinéa, du traité sur l'Union européenne (ci-après le « TUE ») impose, dans le respect du principe d'autonomie procédurale,[8] de prévoir un système de voies de recours et de procédures garantissant le droit à une protection juridictionnelle dans les domaines couverts par le droit de l'Union.[9]

Les tâches qui incombent respectivement au juge de l'Union et aux juridictions nationales dans le « système complet de voies de recours et de procédures » du TFUE font l'objet d'une « répartition rationnelle et constitutionnelle ».[10] La clé de cette répartition réside dans les deux procédures juridictionnelles complémentaires du recours en annulation et du renvoi préjudiciel en appréciation de validité.[11]

Le recours en annulation est la « voie procédurale idoine pour contester la légalité d'un acte de l'Union ».[12] Fondé sur l'article 263 TFUE (droit commun), sur différents règlements en matière de propriété intellectuelle (marques, dessins et modèles et obtentions végétales)[13] ou sur les articles 270 TFUE et 91 du statut des

[5] Arrêt du 3 octobre 2013, Inuit Tapiriit Kanatami e.a./Parlement et Conseil, C-583/11 P, EU:C:2013:625, point 92. Voir également arrêts du 25 juillet 2002, Unión de Pequeños Agricultores/ Conseil, C-50/00 P, EU:C:2002:462, point 40, et du 23 avril 1986, Les Verts/Parlement, 294/83, EU:C:1986:166, point 23.

[6] Arrêt du 22 octobre 1987, Foto-Frost, 314/85, EU:C:1987:452, points 17 et 18.

[7] Arrêt du 28 avril 2015, T & L Sugars et Sidul Açúcares/Commission, C-456/13 P, EU:C:2015:284, point 45. Voir également ordonnance du 7 décembre 2022, WhatsApp Ireland/Comité européen de la protection des données, T-709/21, EU:T:2022:783 (sous pourvoi), point 68.

[8] Voir, en ce sens, arrêt du 21 décembre 2021, Randstad Italia, C-497/20, EU:C:2021:1037, point 58.

[9] Le champ d'application de l'article 19, paragraphe 1, TUE est plus étendu que celui de l'article 47 de la Charte dès lors que ce dernier ne s'applique aux Etats membres que lorsqu'ils mettent en œuvre le droit de l'Union (voir arrêt du 27 février 2018, Associação Sindical dos Juízes Portugueses, C-64/16, EU:C:2018:117, points 37 et 40).

[10] Conclusions de l'avocat général Bobek dans l'affaire Nordstream 2/Parlement et Conseil, C-348/20 P, EU:C:2021:831, point 73.

[11] Voir, en ce sens, arrêt du 28 mars 2017, Rosneft, C-72/15, EU:C:2017:236, point 66.

[12] Conclusions de l'avocat général Campos Sánchez-Bordona, Georgsmarienhütte e.a., C-135/16, EU:C:2018:120, point 40. En présence d'actes composites (ou complexes), l'identification de la voie procédurale idoine est plus complexe. Sur cette problématique, voir notamment les arrêts du 19 décembre 2018, Berlusconi et Fininvest, C-219/17, EU:C:2018:1023, et du 3 décembre 1992, Oleificio Borelli/ Commission, C-97/91, EU:C:1992:491.

[13] Règlements (UE) 2017/1001 du Parlement européen et du Conseil du 14 juin 2017 sur la marque de l'Union européenne, article 72 (JO 2017, L 154, p. 1); (CE) n° 2100/94 du Conseil du 27 juillet 1994 instituant un régime de protection communautaire des obtentions végétales (JO 1994, L 277, p. 1), article 62; et (CE) 6/2002 du Conseil du 12 décembre 2001 sur les dessins ou modèles communautaires (JO 2002, L 3, p. 1), article 61.

fonctionnaires (fonction publique),[14] ce recours permet au justiciable de saisir directement le juge de l'Union de la légalité d'un tel acte.[15] En cas d'illégalité, ce dernier ne statue pas à la place de l'administration,[16] mais annule l'acte attaqué *ex tunc*, en tout ou en partie.[17] En matière de propriété intellectuelle, il peut aussi modifier l'acte entaché d'illégalité.[18] Conformément à l'article 277 TFUE, il peut encore, dans le cadre d'un recours en annulation, déclarer inapplicable au cas d'espèce un acte de portée générale dont l'illégalité est excipée et dont la partie requérante n'aurait pas pu directement solliciter l'annulation.[19]

Les recours en annulation et l'exception d'illégalité ne suffisent, cependant, pas à garantir la protection juridictionnelle effective des droits et libertés que le justiciable tire du droit de l'Union. Les conditions de recevabilité propres à ce recours peuvent, en effet, priver le justiciable d'un accès direct au juge de l'Union.

C'est donc dans une « logique correctrice »[20] que l'article 267 TFUE confère au justiciable la possibilité de faire valoir, à titre incident, l'invalidité d'un tel acte devant les juridictions nationales en leur présentant un recours contre les mesures nationales d'application de ce dernier.[21] En leur qualité de juge de droit commun du droit de l'Union,[22] devant lesquelles les règles de droit de l'Union dotées d'effet direct sont directement invocables, ces juridictions sont tenues, de saisir la Cour d'un renvoi préjudiciel lorsqu'elles sont convaincues de l'invalidité de l'acte en question.[23]

---

[14] L'article 91 du statut des fonctionnaires ne s'applique pas à certains agents de l'Union, tels que ceux de la Banque européenne d'investissements ou de la Banque centrale européenne. Ces agents peuvent néanmoins soumettre au Tribunal les litiges qui les opposent à leur employeur, conformément au règlement du personnel qui leur est applicable.

[15] En cas de passivité de l'autorité publique, il n'y a pas d'acte, auquel cas un recours en carence est ouvert au titre de l'article 265 TFUE. Une disposition expresse du droit de l'Union peut néanmoins prévoir que, à l'expiration d'un délai déterminé, cette passivité vaut décision implicite. Ces problématiques se situent toutefois en dehors du champ de la présente contribution.

[16] Les obligations de l'institution dont émane l'acte annulé figurent à l'article 266 TFUE. Ce dernier prévoit que l'institution concernée est tenue de prendre les mesures que comporte l'exécution de l'arrêt d'annulation. Cela étant, l'article 261 TFUE dispose qu'un règlement peut accorder à la Cour la compétence de pleine juridiction en ce qui concerne les sanctions prévues dans ce règlement, auquel cas le juge de l'Union peut être habilité à fixer directement le montant d'une amende.

[17] L'article 264 TFUE prévoit toutefois de la possibilité de maintenir certains effets d'un acte annulé.

[18] Voir les références citées à la note en bas de page 13 ci-dessus.

[19] Arrêt du 6 mars 1979, Simmenthal/Commission, 92/78, EU:C:1979:53, point 39.

[20] Conclusions de l'avocat général Wathelet dans l'affaire Industrias Químicas del Vallés/Commission, C-244/16, EU:C:2017:635, point 68. Voir également conclusions de l'avocat général Bobek dans l'affaire FBF, C-911/19, EU:C:2021:294, point 138.

[21] Arrêt du 25 juillet 2002, Unión de Pequeños Agricultores/Conseil, C-50/00 P, EU:C:2002:462, point 40.

[22] Conclusions de l'avocat général Szpunar dans l'affaire Commission/Belgique (Article 260, paragraphe 3, TFUE – Réseaux à haut débit), C-543/17, EU:C:2019:322, note en bas de page 24.

[23] Arrêt du 3 juillet 2019, Eurobolt, C-644/17, EU:C:2019:555, points 28 et 29. Voir également arrêt du 25 juillet 2002, Unión de Pequeños Agricultores/Conseil, C-50/00 P, EU:C:2002:462,

Ce renvoi constitue ainsi une modalité de contrôle de la légalité des actes de l'Union au même titre que le recours en annulation.[24] Il n'en reste pas moins « compensatoire »[25] ou « subsidiaire par rapport au recours en annulation », qui « offre la pleine protection juridictionnelle aux particuliers ayant qualité pour agir ».[26] La question de la nature et des limites du contrôle qu'exerce le juge de l'Union lorsqu'il est saisi d'un tel recours est donc centrale au bon fonctionnement du « système complet de voies de recours et de procédures » du TFUE et à l'efficacité du principe de protection juridictionnelle effective que ce dernier concrétise.

L'étude de la jurisprudence révèle que la conception classique de l'office du juge européen de l'annulation en tant qu'arbitre du « procès fait à un acte »[27] s'est enrichie d'une prise en compte accrue des impératifs inhérents à une Union de droit. Certes, le contrôle auquel se livre ce juge se conçoit encore et toujours comme la confrontation objective de l'acte attaqué aux normes pertinentes de droit de l'Union (Sect. 1).

Les limites traditionnelles de ce contrôle font néanmoins l'objet d'une amorce d'assouplissement, au fil d'un exercice casuistique de conciliation des limites traditionnelles de l'office du juge de l'annulation avec les impératifs de légalité et de protection juridictionnelle effective. Cet exercice se révèle, au premier chef, dans la répartition des rôles entre le juge de l'annulation et les parties au procès. Si les secondes restent maîtresses du procès, dont elles délimitent toujours le cadre, le premier joue d'office un rôle assumé dans la protection de la légalité (Sect. 2).

En même temps, le souci d'assurer une protection juridictionnelle effective justifie une prudente modulation de la contrainte qu'exercent les contours de l'acte attaqué et de la procédure administrative préalable sur les éléments de fait et de droit au regard desquels le contrôle de légalité est exercé (Sect. 3).

---

point 40.; et ordonnance du 7 décembre 2022, WhatsApp Ireland/Comité européen de la protection des données, T-709/21, EU:T:2022:783 (sous pourvoi), point 68.

[24] Arrêt du 3 octobre 2013, Inuit Tapiriit Kanatami e.a./Parlement et Conseil, C-583/11 P, EU:C:2013:625, point 95.

[25] Conclusions de l'avocat général Wathelet dans l'affaire Industrias Químicas del Vallés/Commission, C-244/16, EU:C:2017:635, point 68.

[26] Conclusions de l'avocat général Campos Sánchez-Bordona, Georgsmarienhütte e.a., C-135/16, EU:C:2018:120, point 40 et note en bas de page 42. Il existe d'ailleurs un degré d'interdépendance entre le recours en annulation et le renvoi préjudiciel en appréciation de validité, le second étant irrecevable si les requérantes au principal sont sans aucun doute recevables à saisir directement le Tribunal. Voir arrêt du 25 juillet 2018, Georgsmarienhütte e.a., C-135/16, EU:C:2018:582, point 43.

[27] E. Lafferrière. *Traité de la juridiction administrative et des recours contentieux*, 2ème éd.1887, t. 2, p. 560. La formule est utilisée s'agissant du recours en annulation dans les conclusions de l'avocat général Mengozzi dans l'affaire Areva e.a./Commission, C-247/11 P et C-253/11 P, EU:C:2013:579, point 53.

1 La confrontation d'un acte aux normes pertinentes du droit de l'Union

Conformément à l'article 263, premier alinéa, TFUE et à l'article 91, paragraphe 1, du statut des fonctionnaires, le contrôle qu'exerce le juge de l'annulation porte sur la seule « légalité » de l'acte attaqué,[28] à l'exclusion de toute considération d'opportunité[29] ou d'équité.[30] L'article 263, deuxième alinéa, TFUE définit indirectement la notion de « légalité » en indiquant que celle-ci est fonction du respect des règles de compétence, des formes substantielles, des traités et de toute règle de droit relative à leur application ainsi que de l'interdiction du détournement de pouvoir.[31]

Aux fins du contrôle de cette légalité, le juge de l'Union confronte l'acte attaqué aux normes pertinentes de droit de l'Union de rang supérieur audit acte et apprécie si l'annulation de ce dernier se justifie au regard de l'un des quatre cas d'ouverture visés à l'article 263, deuxième alinéa, TFUE.[32] Sont en principe pertinentes l'ensemble des normes justiciables de droit de l'Union, qu'elles aient ou non pour vocation de protéger les droits et intérêts du justiciable qui les invoque.[33]

Pour la facilité de l'exposé, ces normes peuvent être regroupées en deux catégories distinctes, en fonction de leur place dans la hiérarchie des normes.

La première catégorie englobe, en substance, le droit primaire. Il s'agit non seulement des traités proprement dits (TUE, TFUE, traité instituant la Communauté européenne de l'énergie atomique[34] et traités d'adhésion[35]) et des protocoles annexés

[28] Voir, en ce sens, arrêts du 19 décembre 2013, Telefónica/Commission, C-274/12 P, EU:C:2013:852, points 56 et 57; du 12 novembre 1996, Royaume-Uni/Conseil, C-84/94, EU:C:1996:431, point 23, et du 31 mars 1971, Commission/Conseil, 22/70, EU:C:1971:32, point 40.

[29] Voir, en ce sens, arrêts du 12 novembre 1996, Royaume-Uni/Conseil, C-84/94, EU:C:1996:431, point 23.

[30] Arrêt du 19 septembre 2019, WI/Commission, T-379/18, EU:T:2019:617, points 64 à 67. Il est, néanmoins, des situations où l'Union est tenue à une exigence juridique et justiciable d'équité dans l'exercice de ses compétences. Voir, par exemple, arrêt du 27 septembre 2006, Jungbunzlauer/Commission, T-43/02, EU:T:2006:270, point 290 et jurisprudence citée. Des considérations d'équité peuvent également entrer en ligne de compte dans le cadre de la procédure de règlement amiable visée à l'article 125 *bis* du règlement de procédure du Tribunal.

[31] Les règlements applicables au contentieux de la propriété intellectuelle visent les mêmes cas d'ouverture, si ce n'est qu'ils ne visent pas « les traités » et « toute règle de droit relative à leur application », mais le « traité sur le fonctionnement de l'Union européenne » ou le « traité », le « présent règlement » et « toute règle de droit relative à leur application ».

[32] Arrêt du 11 septembre 2024, CQ/Cour des comptes, T-386/19, EU:T:2024:613, point 188.

[33] Voir, en ce sens, arrêt du 21 décembre 2011, Air Transport Association of America e.a., C-366/10, EU:C:2011:864, points 107 à 110. Voir, toutefois, arrêt du 4 septembre 2019, Hamas/Conseil, T-308/18, EU:T:2019:557, points 230 et 231.

[34] Arrêt du 29 mars 1990, Grèce/Conseil, C-62/88, EU:C:1990:153, point 8.

[35] En revanche, nous serions réticents à considérer que les accords de retrait conclus au titre de l'article 50, paragraphe 2, TUE relèvent du droit primaire et donc de la catégorie des « traités », au

à ceux-ci,[36] mais aussi tous les autres instruments de même rang, dont notamment la Charte.

La seconde catégorie comprend toute règle de droit de l'Union autre que de droit primaire. Relèvent notamment de cette catégorie les actes de droit dérivé à caractère obligatoire visés à l'article 288 TFUE (règlements, directives et décisions) et les actes dits innomés de nature contraignante, dont les règles de conduite par lesquelles les institutions, organes et organismes de l'Union s'autolimitent dans l'exercice de leur pouvoir d'appréciation.[37]

Relèvent également de ladite catégorie les conventions internationales auxquelles l'Union est formellement partie ou auxquelles elle est tenue au titre de la théorie de la succession fonctionnelle.[38] Il est, en effet, de jurisprudence constante que les stipulations de ces conventions forment partie intégrante de l'ordre juridique de l'Union à compter de leur entrée en vigueur.[39] L'aptitude desdites conventions à être mobilisées aux fins du contrôle de la légalité des actes de l'Union n'est cependant pas automatique. Il faut que leur nature et leur économie l'autorisent et que leurs stipulations apparaissent, du point de vue de leur contenu, inconditionnelles et suffisamment précises.[40] Il en va de même des normes de droit international coutumier auxquelles l'Union est tenue. Celles-ci relèvent, en effet, aussi de l'ordre juridique de l'Union[41] et leur respect devrait, selon nous, être justiciable aux mêmes conditions que celui du droit international conventionnel.[42]

En revanche, conformément au principe de primauté du droit de l'Union, les règles de droit national ne relèvent pas de l'ordre juridique de l'Union et ne font donc pas partie du corps normatif au regard duquel la légalité d'un acte de l'Union

---

sens de l'article 263, deuxième alinéa, TFUE. En effet, à la différence des traités d'adhésion, les accords de retrait sont conclus par l'Union (et non par les Etats membres) et sont insusceptibles de modifier le droit primaire.

[36] Voir, par exemple, arrêt du 1er juillet 2009, T-273/06 et T-297/06, ISD Polska e.a./Commission EU:T:2009:233, points 89 à 104.

[37] Voir, par exemple, arrêts du 28 juin 2005, Dansk Rørindustri e.a./Commission, C-189/02 P, C-202/02 P, C-205/02 P à C-208/02 P et C-213/02 P, EU:C:2005:408, points 209-223, ainsi que du 18 novembre 2004, Ferriere Nord/Commission, T-176/01, EU:T:2004:336, point 134.

[38] Est ici visé le cas dans lequel l'Union n'est pas formellement partie à un accord international conclu par ses États membres, mais se trouve liée par celui-ci parce qu'elle a entretemps assumé les compétences précédemment exercées par ses États membres dans le domaine concerné (voir arrêt du 12 décembre 1972, International Fruit Company e.a., 21/72 à 24/72, EU:C:1972:115, point 18).

[39] Arrêts du 30 avril 1974, Haegeman, 181/73, EU:C:1974:41, point 5, et du 3 juillet 2007, Commune de Champagne e.a./Conseil et Commission, T-212/02, EU:T:2007:194, point 65.

[40] Arrêt du 9 septembre 2008, FIAMM e.a./Conseil et Commission, C-120/06 P et C-121/06 P, EU:C:2008:476, point 110.

[41] Arrêts du 4 octobre 2024, Commission et Conseil/Front Polisario, C-778/21 P et C-798/21 P, EU:C:2024:833, point 205, ainsi que du 16 juin 1998, Racke, C-162/96, EU:C:1998:293, point 46.

[42] Voir, en ce sens, conclusions de l'avocat général Wathelet dans l'affaire C-266/16, Western Sahara Campaign UK, EU:C:2018:1, point 96; et de l'avocate générale Kokott dans l'affaire C-366/10, Air Transport Association of America e.a., EU:C:2011:637, point 110.

s'apprécie.[43] Il s'agit de règles dont l'interprétation et l'application incombent en principe aux seules autorités nationales.[44]

L'interpénétration des ordres juridiques nationaux et de l'Union et le rôle croissant que le droit national est appelé à jouer dans l'action administrative de l'Union commandent, cependant, de nuancer cette conclusion.[45] Schématiquement, il convient de distinguer deux cas de figure.

Le premier cas de figure survient lorsque le droit national relève du cadre factuel du litige. Comme a pu le relever l'avocat général Jääskinen, « [l]'application des dispositions du droit de l'Union relatives aux aides d'État en fournit de nombreux exemples, notamment en ce qui concerne les notions d'avantage et de sélectivité. Dans ce type de situation, l'analyse du droit national est donc requise afin d'établir une situation de fait qui entre en ligne de compte dans le cadre de l'application du droit de l'Union ».[46] À titre d'illustration, l'examen d'une mesure fiscale au titre de l'article 107, paragraphe 1, TFUE suppose d'interpréter le droit national pour délimiter le cadre de référence pertinent, l'existence d'un avantage économique ne pouvant être établie que par rapport à une imposition dite « normale ».[47]

Dans cette hypothèse, le droit national est un fait, dont la preuve incombe aux parties.[48] Sa qualification au regard de l'article 107, paragraphe 1, TFUE est cependant une question de droit et il appartient au Tribunal de la contrôler comme telle.[49]

Le second cas de figure survient lorsque l'instrument de droit de l'Union que l'institution, l'organe ou l'organisme de l'Union concerné est appelé à appliquer fait référence au droit national. La place de ce dernier dans le contrôle de légalité dépend alors du régime procédural auquel il est soumis dans le cadre de la procédure administrative.

D'un côté, si c'est à l'une des parties qu'il appartient de demander l'application du droit national et d'en établir le contenu, le juge de l'annulation exerce un contrôle qui se situe entre celui du droit et du fait. Il s'agit d'un plein contrôle de l'appréciation de l'administration sur les éléments de preuve que la partie concernée a présentés en vue de s'acquitter de la charge qui lui incombe.[50] Ce contrôle, qui

---

43 Ordonnance du 5 septembre 2007, Document Security Services/BCE, T-295/05, EU:T:2007:243, point 62; et arrêt du 6 juillet 2000, AICS/Parlement, T-139/99, EU:T:2000:182, point 40, confirmé par ordonnance du 21 juin 2001, AICS/Parlement, C-330/00 P, EU:C:2001:352. Voir, déjà, sous l'empire du traité CECA, arrêt du 15 juillet 1960, Präsident Ruhrkohlen-Verkaufsgesellschaft e.a./ Haute Autorité, 36/59, EU:C:1960:36, p. 890.

44 Ordonnance du 5 septembre 2007, Document Security Services/BCE, T-295/05, EU:T:2007:243, point 62.

45 À ce sujet, voir, généralement, conclusions de l'avocat général Jääskinen dans les affaires jointes Commission et Espagne/Government of Gibraltar et Royaume-Uni, C-106/09 P et C-107/09 P, EU:C:2011:215, points 40 et 41.

46 *Ibid.*, point 45.

47 Arrêt du 10 septembre 2024, Irlande e.a./Commission, C-465/20 P, EU:C:2024:724, point 77.

48 *Ibid.*, point 174.

49 Voir, en ce sens, *ibid.*, points 175 et 176.

50 Arrêt du 5 juillet 2011, Edwin/OHMI, C-263/09 P, EU:C:2011:45, point 52.

s'apparente à première vue à celui de l'erreur d'appréciation des faits, est toutefois complété par le pouvoir du juge de vérifier, au-delà des documents produits, la teneur, les conditions d'application et la portée des règles invoquées.[51] C'est notamment le cas en matière de contentieux de la propriété intellectuelle, où le droit dérivé prévoit qu'une marque peut être déclarée nulle si son usage peut être interdit en vertu d'un droit antérieur selon la législation nationale qui en régit la protection.[52]

De l'autre côté, il arrive que le droit de l'Union impose à l'administration une obligation d'appliquer le droit national. Cette obligation peut être explicite ou directe, comme en matière de surveillance prudentielle des établissements de crédit, où la BCE est tenue d'appliquer « toutes les dispositions pertinentes du droit de l'Union et, lorsque celui-ci comporte des directives, le droit national transposant ces directives ».[53] Elle peut aussi être implicite ou indirecte, *via* l'utilisation de notions régies par le droit national. C'est notamment le cas dans le domaine du recrutement en matière de fonction publique, où la condition d'admission de détention d'un diplôme universitaire s'interprète au sens du droit de l'État membre concerné.[54]

Dans un cas comme dans l'autre, les dispositions de droit national pertinentes relèvent du corps normatif au regard duquel le Tribunal apprécie la légalité de l'acte attaqué.[55] Leur interprétation est alors une question de droit, dont le contrôle juridictionnel est entier,[56] mais qui s'opère sur base de la jurisprudence nationale idoine,[57] sous la seule réserve de la conformité de cette dernière au droit de l'Union.[58] Ce n'est qu'en l'absence d'une telle jurisprudence que le Tribunal peut se prononcer de manière autonome sur la portée des dispositions de droit national en question.[59]

L'identification des normes de droit de l'Union au regard desquelles l'acte attaqué est contrôlé ne relève, cependant, pas de la libre appréciation du juge de l'annulation. Sous réserve d'une prise en compte limitée de l'impératif de légalité, il ne contrôle cet acte que dans les limites du recours dont il est saisi.

---

[51] Arrêt du 27 mars 2014, OHMI/National Lottery Commission, C-530/12 P, EU:C:2014:186, point 44.

[52] Règlement (UE) 2017/1001 du Parlement européen et du Conseil, du 14 juin 2017, sur la marque de l'Union européenne (JO 2017, L 154, p. 1), article 60.

[53] Règlement (UE) nº 1024/2013 du Conseil, du 15 octobre 2013, confiant à la Banque centrale européenne des missions spécifiques ayant trait aux politiques en matière de surveillance prudentielle des établissements de crédit (JO 2013, L 287, p. 63), article 4, paragraphe, 3.

[54] Arrêt du 7 mars 2019, Commission/Brouillard, C-728/17 P, non publié, EU:C:2019:178, point 33.

[55] Arrêts du 7 février 2024, Hatherly/AUEA, T-40/23, EU:T:2024:64, points 53 à 58, ainsi que du 24 avril 2018, Caisse régionale de crédit agricole mutuel Alpes Provence e.a./BCE, T-133/16 à T-136/16, EU:T:2018:219, point 49.

[56] Voir, explicitement, en matière de fonction publique, arrêt du 5 novembre 2014, Commission/Thomé, T-669/13 P, EU:T:2014:929, point 26.

[57] Arrêt du 28 février 2024, BAWAG PSK/BCE, T-667/21, EU:T:2024:131, points 57 et 58.

[58] *Ibid.*, point 62.

[59] Arrêt du 13 décembre 2017, Crédit mutuel Arkéa/BCE, T-712/15, EU:T:2017:900, point 132.

2 La répartition des rôles entre le juge de l'annulation et les parties au procès

Conformément au « choix de structurer le contentieux de la légalité en droit de l'Union comme un contentieux dépendant de l'introduction d'un recours »,[60] le juge de l'Union n'est pas habilité à contrôler de sa propre initiative la légalité d'un acte de l'Union.[61] Il se prononce seulement « si – et dans la mesure où – il est investi d'un recours introduit par l'un des sujets habilités à le présenter [...] ».[62]

Maîtresses du procès,[63] les parties requérantes ont l'initiative de celui-ci[64] et déterminent et circonscrivent le litige.[65] C'est à elles seules qu'il incombe de prouver l'illégalité de l'acte attaqué, celui-ci jouissant d'une présomption de légalité et produisant des effets juridiques aussi longtemps qu'il n'a pas été retiré, annulé dans le cadre d'un recours en annulation, déclaré invalide à la suite d'un renvoi préjudiciel ou déclaré inapplicable à la suite d'une exception d'illégalité.[66]

Cette répartition des rôles entre les parties au litige et le juge de l'Union se traduit par une interprétation stricte de l'interdiction de statuer *ultra petita* (Sect. 2.1), que contrebalance l'importance de l'exigence de légalité dans l'application du principe dispositif (Sect. 2.2).

2.1 L'interprétation stricte de l'interdiction de statuer ultra petita

C'est aux seules parties requérantes qu'il appartient d'identifier dans leurs conclusions l'acte, ou la partie de celui-ci, qu'elles entendent soumettre au contrôle de légalité[67] et de formuler les chefs de conclusions auxquelles elles demandent qu'il soit fait droit.[68] De son côté, le juge de l'Union doit se prononcer sur tout ce qui lui

[60] Conclusions de l'avocat général Mengozzi dans l'affaire British Airways/Commission, C-122/16 P, EU:C:2017:406, point 86.

[61] *Ibid.*, point 88.

[62] Conclusions de l'avocat général Mengozzi dans l'affaire British Airways/Commission, C-122/16 P, EU:C:2017:406, point 87.

[63] Voir, par analogie, conclusions de l'avocate générale Kokott dans l'affaire Duarte Héros, C-32/12, EU:C:2013:128, point 32.

[64] Arrêt du 14 novembre 2017, British Airways/Commission, C-122/16 P, EU:C:2017:861, point 87.

[65] Arrêt du 10 décembre 2013, Commission/Irlande e.a., C-272/12 P, EU:C:2013:812, point 27.

[66] Voir, en ce sens, arrêts du 6 octobre 2015, Schrems, C-362/14, EU:C:2015:650, point 52; du 13 juillet 2000, Griesel/Conseil, T-157/99, EU:T:2000:192, point 25, et du 19 novembre 1996, Brulant/Parlement, T-272/94, EU:T:1996:167, point 35. Le recours en annulation n'a d'ailleurs pas d'effet suspensif, conformément à l'article 278 TFUE.

[67] Arrêt du 14 novembre 2017, British Airways/Commission, C-122/16 P, EU:C:2017:861, point 87.

[68] Ordonnance du 1er février 2022, Macías Chávez e.a./Parlement et Espagne, C-322/21 P, EU:C:2022:80, point 38.

est demandé (*ne infra petita*), et seulement sur ce qui lui est demandé (*ne ultra petita*).[69]

La règle *ne infra petita* n'interdit pas au juge de l'Union de régler un litige en accordant au demandeur moins que ce qu'il demandait,[70] mais lui impose de statuer sur l'ensemble des chefs de conclusions des parties. Rarement invoquée sous ce nom devant le juge de l'Union, cette règle n'en est pas moins ancrée dans le règlement de procédure du Tribunal. L'article 165, paragraphe 1, de ce règlement permet, en effet, à une partie de saisir le Tribunal par voie de demande pour omission de statuer « soit sur un chef isolé de conclusions, soit sur les dépens ».

Inversement, la règle *ne ultra petita* limite le pouvoir d'annulation du juge de l'Union en lui imposant de trancher le litige dans la limite des conclusions dont il est saisi.[71] Elle lui interdit ainsi d'aller au-delà des conclusions des parties,[72] notamment en prononçant une annulation dont la portée excède celle que sollicite la partie requérante.[73]

Cette règle a des conséquences majeures du point de vue de l'exigence de protection de la légalité. Il résulte, en effet, de ladite règle que le Tribunal n'est pas habilité à prononcer l'annulation intégrale d'un acte dont seule l'annulation partielle est sollicitée, quand bien même cette dernière serait nécessaire pour corriger l'illégalité constatée, fût-elle d'ordre public.[74] Si la partie de l'acte attaqué dont l'annulation est sollicitée est détachable, le Tribunal peut en prononcer l'annulation.[75] En revanche, si cette partie n'est pas détachable, la demande d'annulation est irrecevable et l'acte illégal survit dans son intégralité.[76]

La rigueur de cette interprétation tranche avec celle du principe dispositif, qui laisse une plus grande place à la protection de l'impératif de légalité dans l'appréciation des moyens des parties et des éléments invoqués à leur soutien.

[69] Conclusions de l'avocate générale Kokott dans l'affaire Commission/Alrosa, C-441/07 P, EU:C:2009:555, point 146. Voir également, en ce sens, conclusions de l'avocat général Wahl dans l'affaire Total/Commission, C-597/13 P, EU:C:2015:207, point 58; et, déjà, arrêt du 14 décembre 1962, Meroni/Haute Autorité, 46/59 et 47/59, EU:C:1962:44, p. 801.

[70] Conclusions de l'avocat Dámaso Ruiz-Jarabo Colomer dans l'affaire Commission/Schneider Electric, C-440/07 P, EU:C:2009:48, point 118.

[71] Arrêt du 15 février 2001, Nachi Europe, C-239/99, EU:C:2001:101, point 24.

[72] Conclusions de l'avocat général Mengozzi dans l'affaire British Airways/Commission, C-122/16 P, EU:C:2017:406, points 103 et 104.

[73] Arrêt du 14 novembre 2017, British Airways/Commission, C-122/16 P, EU:C:2017:861, point 81. Voir également arrêt du 14 septembre 1999, Commission/AssiDomän Kraft Products e.a., C-310/97 P, EU:C:1999:407, point 52.

[74] Arrêt du 14 novembre 2017, British Airways/Commission, C-122/16 P, EU:C:2017:861, points 89 à 92.

[75] Voir, en ce sens, arrêt du 16 décembre 2015, British Airways/Commission, T-48/11, EU:T:2015:988, points 92 et 93.

[76] Ordonnance du 1er décembre 2015, Banco Espírito Santo/Commission, T-814/14, EU:T:2015:936, point 24.

2.2 *L'importance de l'exigence de protection de la légalité dans l'application du principe dispositif*

Il résulte du « principe directeur de la procédure »[77] qu'est le principe dispositif que c'est aux parties requérantes qu'il appartient de soulever des moyens contre l'acte attaqué et d'apporter à l'appui de ces derniers des éléments de preuve.[78] De son côté, le juge de l'annulation est « lié par le cadre factuel et par les moyens juridiques invoqués par les parties » à l'appui de leurs conclusions.[79] Il effectue un contrôle entier, en droit et en fait, de l'acte attaqué, mais seulement en réponse aux moyens présentés par les parties,[80] dans les limites de ceux-ci[81] et sur la base des éléments apportés à leur soutien.[82]

Le juge de l'annulation n'est pas pour autant confiné à un rôle purement passif ni relégué à la fonction de « bouche des parties ».[83] D'une part, le Tribunal peut d'office prendre des mesures d'organisation de la procédure[84] ou des mesures d'instruction[85] pour compléter le dossier, dans le respect des règles régissant la répartition de la charge de la preuve entre les parties et des éventuelles interdictions faites à ces dernières de produire certains éléments de preuve.[86] D'autre part, lorsque l'intérêt public – et notamment l'impératif de protection de la légalité – l'exige, il appartient au juge de l'annulation de relever d'office certains moyens ou arguments. Doivent à cet égard être distingués l'obligation de relever d'office les moyens d'ordre public

[77] Conclusions de l'avocat général Wahl dans l'affaire Total/Commission, C-597/13 P, EU:C:2015:207, point 59. Voir également, en ce sens, conclusions de l'avocat général Mengozzi dans l'affaire British Airways/Commission, C-122/16 P, EU:C:2017:406, point 84 « principe directeur du contentieux de la légalité devant le juge de l'Union »); et conclusions de l'avocat général Ruiz-Jarabo Colomer dans l'affaire Vedial/OHMI, C-106/03 P, EU:C:2004:457, point 33 (« principe fondamental du droit procédural »).

[78] Arrêts du 29 février 2024, Methanol Holdings (Trinidad)/Commission, C-688/22 P, EU:C:2024:180, point 35, et du 22 septembre 2016, Pensa Pharma/EUIPO, C-442/15 P, EU:C:2016:720, point 26.

[79] Conclusions de l'avocat général Ruiz-Jarabo Colomer dans l'affaire Vedial/OHMI, C-106/03 P, EU:C:2004:457, point 33. Voir également, en ce sens, arrêt du 8 mars 2023, Assaad/Conseil, T-426/21, EU:T:2023:114, point 142.

[80] Ordonnance du 7 septembre 2016, Lotte/EUIPO, C-586/15 P, EU:C:2016:642, point 29.

[81] Arrêts du 19 mars 2020, ClientEarth/Commission, C-612/18 P, EU:C:2020:223, point 33, et du 9 septembre 2008, MyTravel/Commission, T-212/03, EU:T:2008:315, point 85.

[82] Arrêt du 8 décembre 2011, KME e.a./Commission, C-272/09 P, EU:C:2011:810, point 102. Voir également conclusions de l'avocat général Bot dans l'affaire BSH/EUIPO, C-43/15 P, EU:C:2016:129, point 49.

[83] Conclusions de l'avocat général Léger dans l'affaire Parlement/Gutiérrez de Quijano y Lloréns, C-252/96 P, EU:C:1998:157, point 36. Voir également conclusions de l'avocat général Bot dans l'affaire BSH/OHMI, C-43/15 P, EU:C:2016:129, point 50.

[84] Règlement de procédure du Tribunal, articles 89 et 90.

[85] *Ibid.*, articles 91 à 102.

[86] À ce sujet, voir notamment la sous-section 3.2.2 ci-dessous.

(Sect. 2.2.1) et, dans le strict cadre de l'appréciation des moyens soulevés par les parties, la liberté de déterminer le sens de la loi (Sect. 2.2.2).[87]

2.2.1 L'obligation de relever d'office les moyens d'ordre public

C'est le souci de protection de la légalité dans l'intérêt général qui sous-tend l'obligation incombant au juge de l'annulation de relever d'office les moyens d'ordre public.[88] Dans ses conclusions dans l'affaire *Les Éditions Albert René*, l'avocat général Trstenjak relevait ainsi que la notion d'ordre public était « réservé[e] aux questions qui, en raison de leur importance pour l'intérêt général, ne sont pas à la disposition des parties ni de la juridiction elle-même et doivent être examinées d'office *in limine litis* même lorsqu'elles n'ont pas été soumises à un débat ».[89] Outre les fins de non-recevoir d'ordre public, cette notion ne recouvre en principe que certains moyens de légalité externe,[90] tels que ceux tirés de l'incompétence de l'auteur de l'acte ou de la violation des formes substantielles.

Parmi les rares exceptions à ce principe compte le moyen de légalité interne tiré de la violation du champ d'application de la loi, que le Tribunal et feu le Tribunal de la fonction publique ont à plusieurs reprises qualifié d'ordre public.[91] Le caractère d'ordre public de ce moyen s'explique au regard de l'office même du juge de l'annulation, qui exige de ce dernier qu'il respecte lui-même le droit de l'Union et s'abstienne de trancher un litige en faisant application d'une norme inapplicable au cas d'espèce.[92]

C'est cette même préoccupation qui explique que, dans le strict cadre de l'appréciation des moyens soulevés par les parties, le juge de l'annulation demeure libre de déterminer du sens de la loi compte tenu également d'arguments que ces dernières n'ont pas avancés.

---

[87] Sur cette distinction, voir F. Clausen, *Les moyens d'ordre public devant la Cour de justice de l'Union européenne*, Bruylant (2018), p. 325.

[88] Voir, en ce sens, conclusions de l'avocat général Mengozzi dans l'affaire British Airways/Commission, C-122/16 P, EU:C:2017:406, point 5.

[89] Conclusions de l'avocat général Trstenjak dans l'affaire Les Editions Albert René/OHMI, C-16/06 P, EU:C:2007:728, point 39. Voir également conclusions de l'avocat général Ruiz-Jarabo Colomer dans l'affaire Buzzi Unicem/Commission, C-217/00 P, EU:C:2003:83, point 217.

[90] Voir, en ce sens, arrêt du 2 décembre 2009, Commission/Irlande, C-89/08 P, EU:C:2009:742, point 40.

[91] Arrêts du 15 juillet 1994, T-576/93 à T-582/93, EU:T:1994:93, point 35, et du 21 février 2008, Putterie-De-Beukelaer/Commission, F-31/07, EU:F:2008:23, point 50. Voir également, en ce sens, arrêt du 1er juin 2006, P & O European Ferries (Vizcaya) et Diputación Foral de Vizcaya/ Commission, C-442/03 P et C-471/03 P, EU:C:2006:356, point 45 (caractère d'ordre public du moyen de légalité interne tiré de la violation de l'autorité de la chose jugée).

[92] Conclusions de l'avocat général Pikamäe dans l'affaire EUIPO/Neoperl, C-93/23 P, EU:C:2024:751, point 72; et arrêt du 21 février 2008, Putterie-De-Beukelaer/Commission, F-31/07, EU:F:2008:23, point 51.

2.2.2 La détermination du sens de la loi

Ainsi que le relevait l'avocat général Léger dans l'affaire *Quijano y Lloréns*, le juge de la l'annulation est investi d'une « mission de *juris dictio* », qui « suppose qu'il soit en mesure d'appliquer les règles de droit pertinentes pour la solution du litige aux faits qui lui sont présentés par les parties ».[93] Aussi le juge de l'annulation dispose-t-il de « la possibilité, tout en restant dans le cadre du litige qui lui est soumis, de rechercher la meilleure solution possible de diverses façons »,[94] notamment en développant un argument au soutien d'un moyen invoqué par la partie requérante.[95]

Cette possibilité s'incarne, au premier chef, dans la jurisprudence selon laquelle, « dans le cadre du litige circonscrit par les parties, le juge de l'Union, tout en ne devant statuer que sur la demande des parties, ne saurait être tenu par les seuls arguments invoqués par celles-ci au soutien de leurs prétentions, sauf à se voir contraint, le cas échéant, de fonder sa décision sur des considérations juridiques erronées ».[96] En vertu du principe *iura novit curia*, la détermination du sens de la loi ne relève pas du champ d'application d'un principe de libre disposition du litige entre les mains des parties.[97] C'est au juge qu'il appartient d'appliquer aux faits qui lui sont présentés par les parties les règles de droit pertinentes pour la solution du litige,[98] conformément à l'adage *da mihi factum, dabo tibi jus*.[99]

Il en résulte que, lors de l'examen d'un moyen, le juge de l'annulation ne saurait « se limiter aux seuls arguments invoqués par [la] partie [requérante], mais doit procéder à une analyse complète de celui-ci, en tenant compte de toutes les règles et de tous les principes de droit applicables ».[100] Il est ainsi notamment habilité à faire usage des règles applicables *ratione temporis* quand bien même les parties ne les auraient pas invoquées[101] ou à donner son « interprétation autonome » des règles et

[93] Conclusions de l'avocat général Léger dans l'affaire Parlement/Gutiérrez de Quijano y Lloréns, C-252/96 P, EU:C:1998:157, point 36.

[94] *Ibid.*, point 37.

[95] *Ibid.*, point 38 et 39.

[96] Arrêts du 20 janvier 2021, Commission/Printeos, C-301/19 P, EU:C:2021:39, point 58, ainsi que du 21 septembre 2010, Suède e.a./API et Commission, C-514/07 P, C-528/07 P et C-532/07 P, EU:C:2010:541, point 65. Voir également conclusions de l'avocat général Léger dans l'affaire Parlement/Gutiérrez de Quijano y Lloréns, C-252/96 P, EU:C:1998:157, point 36.

[97] Arrêt du 5 octobre 2009, Commission/Roodhuijzen, T-58/08 P, EU:T:2009:385, point 36.

[98] *Ibid.*

[99] Voir, en ce sens, conclusions de l'avocat général Jacobs dans les affaires jointes van Schijndel et van Veen, C-430/93 et C-431/93, EU:C:1995:185, p. 4718.

[100] Arrêt du 24 septembre 2015, Italie et Espagne/Commission, T-124/13 et T-191/13, EU:T:2015:690, point 37.

[101] Voir, en ce sens, arrêt du 6 septembre 2013, Europäisch-Iranische Handelsbank/Conseil, T-434/11, EU:T:2013:405, point 123.

principes applicables,[102] y compris à la lumière de tout élément de droit pertinent que les parties auraient omis de faire valoir.[103]

Dans un même ordre d'idées, la Cour a reconnu dans un arrêt non publié de 2009 à la charge du juge de l'annulation une obligation de prendre d'office en considération les « données de droit du litige ».[104] Les rares développements jurisprudentiels dont cette obligation prétorienne a depuis lors fait l'objet laissent à penser qu'elle vise, elle aussi, les éléments du droit de l'Union pertinents aux fins de trancher le litige.[105] Le juge de l'annulation pouvant déjà les prendre en compte au titre de la jurisprudence exposée aux paragraphes précédents, il est toutefois permis de s'interroger sur la valeur ajoutée d'une telle obligation.

L'application, par le juge, d'une norme non invoquée par les parties reste un exercice délicat, encadré notamment, d'une part, par l'idée directrice qu'il appartient à la partie requérante de soulever les illégalités dont elle entend se prévaloir et, d'autre part, par l'interdiction au juge de procéder à une substitution des motifs de l'acte attaqué.

3 La cristallisation du litige à la date d'adoption de l'acte attaqué

Si les voies de recours visées à l'article 263 TFUE ainsi qu'aux articles 270 TFUE et 91 du statut des fonctionnaires visaient à établir directement l'existence d'un droit, d'un avantage ou d'une obligation dans le chef d'un justiciable, le juge devrait pouvoir tenir compte de tout élément de fait et de droit pertinent pour trancher le litige. La répartition de la charge de produire de tels éléments et le rôle du juge dans la constitution du dossier dépendraient alors de la nature de l'affaire. L'acte attaqué ne constituerait qu'une prise de position de l'administration, insusceptible de figer le cadre du litige et de limiter ainsi les éléments pouvant être pris en compte dans le cadre de la procédure juridictionnelle.

Il est, cependant, de principe que le recours en annulation ne soumet pas directement au juge de l'Union la question de savoir si la partie requérante doit se voir

[102] Arrêt du 21 mars 2014, Commission/Macchia, T-368/12 P, EU:T:2014:266, point 24.

[103] Arrêts du 16 mars 2016, Xinyi PV Products (Anhui) Holdings/Commission, T-586/14, EU:T:2016:154, point 35 (travaux préparatoires), et du 8 novembre 2012, Commission/Strack, T-268/11 P, EU:T:2012:588, point 29 (autres règles pertinentes de droit de droit dérivé). Se pose la question de savoir si de tels éléments doivent, à l'instar des moyens d'ordre public, être soumis au contradictoire.

[104] Arrêt du 2 avril 2009, Mebrom/Commission, C-373/07 P, non publié, EU:C:2009:218, point 80 (concernant un avis).

[105] F. Clausen, *Les moyens d'ordre public devant la Cour de justice de l'Union européenne*, Bruylant (2018), p. 326 (travaux préparatoires). Voir également arrêts du 15 janvier 2013, Welte-Wenu/OHMI – Commission (EUROPEAN DRIVESHAFT SERVICES), T-413/11, EU:T:2013:12, point 33 (directive), et du 13 décembre 2012, Grèce/Commission, T-588/10, EU:T:2012:688, point 214 (décision).

accorder un droit ou un avantage ou se voir imposer une obligation. Ledit recours ne soumet au juge que la légalité de l'acte attaqué. Ce dernier fait office d'écran entre l'affaire – a priori close – dont a connu l'administration et le juge de l'annulation, qui n'a pas vocation à réexaminer *de novo* les circonstances de l'espèce.

L'acte attaqué intervient lui-même à la suite d'une procédure administrative assortie de garanties procédurales, qui prévoient à la charge de l'administration des obligations, tels que celles d'impartialité et de motivation, et reconnaissent aux intéressés des droits, tels que celui d'être entendu.[106] Dans le cadre de leur participation à cette procédure, les intéressés ont la faculté – voire, selon les cas, l'obligation – de présenter des éléments de droit et de fait, dont l'administration tient compte dans l'édiction de l'acte.

Appelé à contrôler si l'administration a respecté les règles de droit de l'Union pertinente en prenant cet acte, le juge de l'annulation se place à la date d'adoption de ce dernier. C'est à cette date que se cristallise le litige. Selon la conception classique du contentieux de la légalité, il en résulte une double contrainte pour l'office de le juge de l'annulation. D'un côté, le contrôle de ce juge ne s'exerce qu'au regard des éléments de fait et de droit qui sont antérieurs à l'adoption de l'acte attaqué (Sect. 3.1). De l'autre, une exigence de parallélisme entre les procédures administrative et juridictionnelle limite la recevabilité de tels éléments si l'administration n'en avait pas connaissance à la date d'adoption de cet acte (Sect. 3.2).

Néanmoins, comme il sera exposé ci-après, l'interprétation de ces contraintes fait l'objet d'une prudente modulation compte tenu des impératifs de légalité et du principe de protection juridictionnelle effective.

3.1 *L'exigence relative d'antériorité chronologique des éléments de fait et de droit invoqués*

Le principe est établi sous sa forme actuelle depuis un arrêt France/Commission du 7 février 1979: la légalité d'un acte de l'Union s'apprécie en fonction des éléments de fait et de droit existant à la date à laquelle il a été adopté.[107]

L'apparente simplicité de ce principe occulte cependant le phénomène de prudente relativisation dont il a fait l'objet dans la jurisprudence récente. Délimiter ce phénomène suppose de distinguer entre les éléments de droit (i) et de fait (ii) propres à fonder une prétention, et les éléments de preuve (iii), qui visent à établir l'existence des faits allégués lorsqu'ils sont contestés et ne sont pas notoires.

---

[106] Voir notamment l'article 41 de la Charte sur le droit à une bonne administration.

[107] 15/76 et 16/76, EU:C:1979:29, point 7. Voir, plus récemment, arrêt du 3 septembre 2015, Inuit Tapiriit Kanatami e.a./Commission, C-398/13 P, EU:C:2015:535, point 22.

3.1.1 Les éléments de droit

La légalité d'un acte doit être appréciée au regard des dispositions qui régissaient son adoption à la date de celle-ci.[108] Il s'agit des dispositions en vigueur à cette date, conformément aux règles générales régissant l'application de la loi dans le temps et sous réserve de dispositions dérogatoires particulières.[109] Une disposition qui entre en vigueur postérieurement à l'adoption de l'acte attaqué ne peut ainsi, en principe, entrer en ligne de compte aux fins du contrôle de la légalité de ce dernier.[110]

Semble néanmoins pouvoir faire exception le contrôle de certains actes, dont les effets ne sont pas instantanés, mais ont vocation à se déployer au-delà de la date d'adoption desdits actes. C'est ainsi que, dans l'affaire *Schrems*, la Cour a pu tenir compte des dispositions de la Charte aux fins de contrôler la validité d'une décision prise plus de 9 ans avant que la Charte devienne contraignante et même plusieurs mois avant l'adoption de celle-ci.[111]

3.1.2 Les faits

Les faits postérieurs à l'adoption de l'acte attaqué ne sont, en principe, pas plus susceptibles d'affecter sa légalité que les règles de droit qui lui sont ultérieures.[112] Selon la jurisprudence, il en va de la préservation de l'équilibre institutionnel: « si le Tribunal devait examiner les actes attaqués à la lumière d'éléments de fait qui n'existaient pas à la date où l'acte a été pris, il se substituerait à l'institution dont émane l'acte en cause ».[113]

Le principe de protection juridictionnelle effective exige, toutefois, de modérer la rigueur dudit principe en l'assortissant de plusieurs exceptions.

La première exception concerne la matière pénale, au sens de l'article 6 de la Convention EDH. Cette matière relève normalement de la compétence des

---

[108] Arrêt du 16 avril 2015, Parlement/Conseil, C-540/13, EU:C:2015:224, point 35.

[109] Voir, en ce sens, arrêts du 10 septembre 2015, Schniga/OCVV, T-91/14 et T-92/14, EU:T:2015:624, point 75; du 19 juillet 2016, Stips/Commission, F-131/15, EU:F:2016:154, point 39, ainsi que du 31 janvier 2008, Di Bucci/Commission, F-98/05, EU:F:2008:11, point 43.

[110] Voir, par exemple, arrêt du 13 mars 2013, Inglewood e.a./Parlement, T-229/11 et T-276/11, EU:T:2013:127, point 144.

[111] Arrêt du 6 octobre 2015, Schrems, C-362/14, EU:C:2015:650. Voir également, en ce sens, arrêt du 17 mars 2011, AJD Tuna, C-221/09, EU:C:2011:153, point 49 à 51.

[112] Arrêts du 17 octobre 2019, Alcogroup et Alcodis/Commission, C-403/18 P, EU:C:2019:870, point 45, et du 19 octobre 2022, Sogias Ellas/Commission, T-347/20, EU:T:2022:639, point 134. Relevons, cependant, que le droit dérivé peut, dans des situations spécifiques, imposer que le recours juridictionnel national prévoie un examen *ex nunc* d'une décision et donc la prise en compte de faits survenus après l'adoption de celle-ci. Arrêt du 25 juillet 2018, Alheto, C-585/16, EU:C:2018:584, points 110 à 112. Cette problématique est distincte de celle de la disparition de l'objet ou de l'intérêt à agir de la partie requérante du fait de la survenance d'un fait ou acte nouveau, auquel cas un jugement au fond n'est plus nécessaire.

[113] Arrêts du 26 juin 2024, PB/CRU, T-789/22, EU:T:2024:426, point 149.

juridictions. La convention de sauvegarde des droits de l'homme et des libertés fondamentales admet néanmoins que la tâche de poursuivre et de réprimer des infractions pénales puisse être confiée à des autorités administratives, à condition que les décisions de sanction qu'elles prennent puissent subir « le contrôle ultérieur d'un organe judiciaire de pleine juridiction », c'est-à-dire d'un tribunal habilité à « se pencher sur toutes les questions de fait et de droit pertinentes pour le litige dont il se trouve saisi ».[114]

Parmi ces décisions figurent notamment celles par lesquelles la Commission européenne sanctionne des infractions aux règles de concurrence.[115] Conformément à la jurisprudence de la Cour EDH, le juge de l'Union assure un contrôle approfondi desdites décisions, en droit comme en fait.[116] A cette fin, il doit notamment pouvoir prendre en compte « l'ensemble des éléments soumis par ces dernières, que ceux-ci soient antérieurs ou postérieurs à la décision entreprise ».[117]

La seule limite à la prise en compte de ces éléments est leur pertinence « pour le contrôle de la légalité de la décision de la Commission ».[118]

Or, il ne nous semble pas exclu que des faits postérieurs à une telle décision puissent être pertinents aux fins du contrôle de sa légalité. Certes, il est peu vraisemblable que tel soit le cas dans des affaires d'ententes. Dans ces affaires, la question factuelle centrale est, en effet, généralement celle de savoir si les entreprises incriminées ont participé à une concertation illicite qui s'est terminée au plus tard à la date d'adoption de la décision d'infraction.

En revanche, dans des affaires d'abus de position dominante ou de restriction de concurrence « par effet », des éléments postérieurs à une décision d'infraction pourraient se révéler pertinents. Il est ainsi, par exemple, envisageable que des évolutions immédiatement postérieures à une telle décision infirment les appréciations de la Commission quant à la capacité des pratiques incriminées à restreindre la concurrence.

La seconde exception concerne certains domaines dans lesquels l'Union est tenue à une obligation d'adaptation ou de mise à jour de sa réglementation. C'est notamment le cas des « décisions d'adéquation » de la Commission, qui permettent le transfert sans autorisation spécifique de données à caractère personnel vers un pays tiers et ou une organisation internationale qui assure un nouveau de protection

---

[114]Arrêt du 27 septembre 2011, A. Menarini Diagnostis c. Italie, nº 43509/08, CE:ECHR:2011:0927JUD004350908, points 58 et 59.

[115]Arrêt du 16 décembre 2015, Martinair Holland/Commission, T-67/11, EU:T:2015:984, points 29 et 30. Voir également, en ce sens, arrêt du 18 juillet 2013, Schindler Holding e.a./Commission, C-501/11 P, EU:C:2013:522,, point 33.

[116]Arrêt du 21 janvier 2016, Galp Energía España e.a./Commission, C-603/13 P, EU:C:2016:38, point 72.

[117]*Ibid.* La portée de cette jurisprudence semble toutefois se limiter aux décisions d'infraction. Voir, en ce sens, arrêts du 17 octobre 2019, Alcogroup et Alcodis/Commission, C-403/18 P, EU:C:2019:870, point 45 (décision d'inspection), ainsi que du 28 janvier 2021, Qualcomm et Qualcomm Europe/Commission, C-466/19 P, EU:C:2021:76, points 82 et 83 (demande de renseignements par voie de décision).

[118]*Ibid.*

adéquat de protection de ces données. Ces décisions devant faire l'objet d'un réexamen régulier en fonction du contexte factuel et juridique pertinent, l'omission de les modifier à la suite de l'intervention de faits nouveaux revient à confirmer implicitement la validité de l'appréciation initiale.[119]

Le contrôle juridictionnel effectif desdites décisions suppose donc de pouvoir vérifier si cette appréciation demeure valable au regard du contexte factuel et juridique actuel[120] et donc, selon l'arrêt *Schrems* de la Cour, des « circonstances intervenues postérieurement à [leur] adoption [...] ».[121]

Il est, cependant, permis de se demander dans quelle mesure cette solution est transposable à d'autres matières, notamment celles dans lesquelles l'obligation d'adaptation et de mise à jour incombant à la Commission fait l'objet d'une procédure clairement structurée. Il semblerait, en effet, cohérent du point de vue de la systématique des voies de recours que les circonstances intervenues postérieurement à l'adoption de l'acte originel soient prises en compte à l'occasion d'un recours dirigé contre l'acte nouveau pris en vertu de cette obligation[122] ou, à défaut d'acte nouveau, dans le cadre d'un recours en carence dirigé contre l'abstention illicite de l'administration de mettre à jour sa réglementation.[123]

La troisième et dernière exception concerne le cas particulier des actes qui « s'inscri[ven]t dans des processus ou des tendances dont il revient au juge de l'Union de s'assurer de la réalité »,[124] notamment pour permettre aux intéressés de se défendre utilement contre des motifs prétextuels. L'affaire *Manéa* est illustrative. Cette affaire portait sur la décision de ne pas renouveler le contrat d'engagement d'un agent temporaire pour des motifs d'intérêt du service tenant notamment à la mise en œuvre cohérente et conséquente d'une politique de remplacement des agents temporaires par des agents contractuels. Or, pour le Tribunal, apprécier la réalité de cette mise en œuvre pouvait supposer de tenir compte des mesures de réorganisation effectivement prises après l'adoption de la décision attaquée.[125] Ainsi, des éléments de fait existants au moment de la décision attaquée peuvent être éclairés par la survenance d'éléments ultérieurs.[126]

---

[119] Conclusions de l'avocat général Bot dans l'affaire Schrems, C-362/14, EU:C:2015:627, point 137.

[120] *Ibid.*, points 137 et 138.

[121] Arrêt du 6 octobre 2015, Schrems, C-362/14, EU:C:2015:650, point 77. Le renvoi préjudiciel en appréciation de validité, qui n'a pas de limite dans le temps, est en pratique plus propice à la survenance de ce cas de figure que le recours en annulation, dont l'introduction est soumise à un délai de deux mois. Nous ne voyons, cependant, pas de raison de principe d'exclure que ledit cas de figure puisse également survenir dans le cadre d'un recours en annulation.

[122] Voir, en ce sens, arrêt du 6 novembre 2024, Karić/Conseil, T-520/22, EU:T:2024:774, points 140 et 141, ainsi que du 18 mai 2022, Foz/Conseil, T-296/20, EU:T:2022:298, points 133 à 136.

[123] Arrêt du 22 octobre 2002, National Farmers' Union, C-241/01, EU:C:2002:604, point 38.

[124] Arrêt du 12 septembre 2019, Manéa/CdT, T-225/18, EU:T:2019:595, point 99; confirmé sur pourvoi par ordonnance du 14 janvier 2021, Manéa/CdT, C-892/19 P, EU:C:2021:30.

[125] Arrêt du 12 septembre 2019, Manéa/CdT, T-225/18, EU:T:2019:595, points 99 à 102.

[126] *Ibid.*, point 99.

Il nous semble, cependant, que la survenance de tels cas de figure est relativement rare en pratique. Ce cas de figure est, en tout cas, bien plus rare que la celui de l'invocation d'éléments de preuve établis postérieurement à l'adoption de l'acte attaqué.

3.1.3 Les éléments de preuve

La pertinence aux fins du contrôle de la légalité d'un acte d'éléments de preuve qui lui sont postérieurs dépend au premier chef de la date à laquelle sont survenus les faits qu'ils visent à établir. Lorsque ces faits sont eux-mêmes postérieurs à l'acte attaqué, ce n'est en toute logique que s'ils peuvent être pris en compte aux fins de contrôler la légalité de l'acte attaqué que les éléments de preuve visant à les établir peuvent l'être également.

En revanche, lorsque lesdits faits sont antérieurs à la décision attaquée, la jurisprudence est moins restrictive. En dehors de la matière pénale au sens de l'article 6 de la Convention EDH, où les parties requérantes peuvent se prévaloir de tout élément de preuve,[127] deux cas de figure doivent être distingués.

D'un côté, la jurisprudence admet que des pièces établies postérieurement à l'adoption de l'acte attaqué peuvent être prises en compte « dans la mesure où elles tendent à prouver la réalité et la portée des informations dont disposait l'auteur » de cet acte.[128] C'est ainsi que le Tribunal a pu s'appuyer sur des annexes qui développaient des points mentionnés dans le curriculum vitae sur la base duquel le Parlement avait décidé de nommer un fonctionnaire à un poste de direction.[129]

De l'autre côté, la jurisprudence reconnaît aux parties requérantes la faculté de produire, dans l'exercice de leurs droits de la défense, des pièces établies postérieurement à l'adoption de l'acte attaqué, mais fondées sur des éléments de fait préexistants. Il est ainsi loisible au destinataire d'une décision d'interdiction d'une concentration de présenter devant le Tribunal des rapports d'analyse économique destinés à contester cette décision, à condition qu'ils se fondent sur de tels éléments de fait.[130]

---

[127] Arrêt du 21 janvier 2016, Galp Energía España e.a./Commission, C-603/13 P, EU:C:2016:38, point 72. Pour une application, voir arrêt du 11 juillet 2019, Silver Plastics et Johannes Reifenhäuser/Commission, T-582/15, EU:T:2019:497, points 38 et 39.

[128] Voir arrêt du 4 mai 2010, Petrilli/Commission, F-100/08, EU:F:2010:35, point 34 et jurisprudence citée. Voir également arrêt du 5 juin 2003, O'Hannrachain/Parlement, C-121/01 P, EU:C:2003:323, point 24.

[129] Arrêt du 16 janvier 2001, Chamier et O'Hannrachain/Parlement, EU:T:2001:8, point 58. Voir également, en ce sens, du 28 février 2002, Atlantic Container Line e.a./Commission, T-395/94, EU:T:2002:49, point 254.

[130] Arrêt du 20 décembre 2023, enercity/Commission, T-65/21, EU:T:2023:844, point 141.

3.2 L'exigence à géométrie variable de parallélisme entre les procédures administratives et judiciaires

De la lecture des seules dispositions du règlement de procédure du Tribunal, il se dégage l'impression d'une grande latitude laissée aux parties s'agissant de la présentation des moyens et arguments (juridiques ou factuels) et de la production des preuves. L'article 76 de ce règlement prévoit simplement que la requête doit contenir les moyens et arguments invoqués et, s'il y lieu, les preuves et offres de preuve. L'article 81 du même règlement prévoit des exigences analogues pour le mémoire en défense. Il ne prévoit d'ailleurs aucune obligation à la charge de la partie défenderesse de communiquer au Tribunal le dossier de la procédure administrative, laissant ainsi les parties libres de sélectionner les documents de la phase administrative qu'elles soumettent au Tribunal.

La seule limite que pose le règlement de procédure à la présentation des moyens, preuves et offres de preuves figure à ses articles 84 et 85. Le premier interdit ainsi la production de moyens nouveaux en cours d'instance, à moins que ceux-ci ne se fondent sur des éléments de droit et de fait qui se sont révélés pendant la procédure. Le second prévoit que les preuves et les offres de preuve sont présentées dans le cadre du premier échange de mémoires, leur production à un stade ultérieur de la procédure supposant « que le retard soit justifié », sous réserve toutefois de la preuve contraire et de l'ampliation des offres de preuve.[131] En revanche, le règlement de procédure n'interdit pas explicitement la production d'arguments nouveaux en cours d'instance, à moins qu'ils visent, en réalité, à contourner les restrictions concernant la production de moyens ou preuves nouveaux.[132]

Le règlement de procédure ne conditionne pas non plus la recevabilité des arguments – ni d'ailleurs celle des moyens, preuves ou offres de preuve – à leur invocation lors de la procédure administrative préalable. Le Tribunal a, cependant, jugé que « l'examen de la légalité d'une décision doit, en principe, se faire sur la base des éléments de fait et de droit mentionnés par les parties au cours de la procédure administrative et/ou repris dans cette décision ».[133] « Dans le cas contraire », le Tribunal a-t-il expliqué, « le parallélisme entre la procédure – antérieure – administrative et la procédure de contrôle – subséquente – judiciaire, reposant sur une identité des éléments de fait et de droit, serait remis en question ».[134]

Un examen approfondi de la jurisprudence révèle cependant qu'il s'agit là d'une exigence à géométrie variable. Elle varie, au premier chef, selon que les éléments de fait ou de droit dont il n'a pas été fait état pendant la procédure administrative sont

---

[131] Règlement de procédure du Tribunal, article 92.

[132] Arrêt du 2 février 2022, LU/BEI, T-536/20, EU:T:2022:40, point 53. Voir, toutefois, arrêts du 19 juin 2024, PV/Commission, T-78/21, non publié, EU:T:2024:403, point 97, ainsi que du 22 novembre 2017, von Blumenthal e.a./BEI, T-558/16, EU:T:2017:827, points 48 à 50.

[133] Arrêt du 27 septembre 2006, Roquette Frères/Commission, T-322/01, EU:T:2006:267, point 325.

[134] *Ibid.*

invoqués au stade de la procédure juridictionnelle pour contester l'acte attaqué ou pour le défendre.

3.2.1 Les éléments nouveaux invoqués pour défendre l'acte attaqué

Lorsque de tels éléments sont invoqués pour défendre l'acte attaqué, le principe est que le Tribunal doit se limiter à un contrôle de la légalité de celui-ci sur la base des motifs qu'il contient.[135] Le Tribunal n'est donc pas habilité à substituer ou à ajouter sa propre motivation à celle de l'administration,[136] ni à tenir compte de motifs nouveaux que cette dernière aurait fait valoir au cours de la procédure juridictionnelle.[137]

Le Tribunal n'en demeure pas moins habilité à examiner les éléments de preuve et arguments invoqués pendant la procédure administrative de manière plus approfondie ou intensive que l'auteur de l'acte attaqué,[138] à faire sienne une lecture alternative de ce dernier[139] ou à en opérer une analyse globale, par exemple en puisant des motifs dans une section pour contrôler le bien-fondé d'une autre.[140]

Le Tribunal dispose aussi, en principe, de la faculté d'appuyer son contrôle sur des éléments de preuve dont l'auteur de l'acte ne disposait pas pendant la procédure administrative, mais qui tendent à prouver la réalité et la portée des informations dont il disposait.[141] L'étendue de cette faculté est, toutefois, sujette à caution, notamment dans le contentieux des mesures restrictives. En la matière, le contrôle de légalité s'opère non seulement à l'aune des éléments figurant dans les exposés des motifs des actes litigieux, mais également de ceux que le Conseil fournit, en cas de contestation, au Tribunal pour établir le bien-fondé des faits allégués dans ces

---

[135] Voir arrêt du 9 septembre 2015, Philips/Commission, T-92/13, non publié, EU:T:2015:605, point 43 et jurisprudence citée.

[136] Arrêts du 25 juillet 2018, Orange Polska/Commission, C-123/16 P, EU:C:2018:590, point 105, et du 10 novembre 2021, Google et Alphabet/Commission (Google Shopping), T-612/17, EU:T:2021:763, point 135.

[137] Arrêt du 16 septembre 2013, Wabco Europe e.a./Commission, T-380/10, EU:T:2013:449, points 107 à 110.

[138] Voir, en ce sens, conclusions de l'avocat général Mengozzi dans l'affaire Areva e.a./Commission, C-247/11 P et C-253/11 P, EU:C:2013:579, point 53; et de l'avocate générale Kokott dans l'affaire Frucona Košice/Commission, C-73/11 P, EU:C:2012:535, point 94.

[139] Arrêt du 16 septembre 2013, Wabco Europe e.a./Commission, T-380/10, EU:T:2013:449, point 142.

[140] Voir, en ce sens, arrêt du 25 juillet 2018, Commission/Espagne, C-128/16 P, EU:C:2018:591, points 93 à 101; conclusions de l'avocat général Rantos dans les affaires Air Canada e.a./ Commission, C-367/22 e.a., EU:C:2024:702, points 69 et 70; et conclusions de l'avocat général Fennelly dans l'affaire Italie et Sardegna Lines/Commission, C-15/98 et C-105/99, EU:C:2000:203, point 68.

[141] Voir, en ce sens, arrêts du 15 juillet 2004, Valenzuela Marzo/Commission, T-384/02, EU:T:2004:239, point 98, et du 4 mai 2010, Petrilli/Commission, F-100/08, EU:F:2010:35, point 36.

exposés.[142] Selon certains arrêts, il suffit que ces éléments de preuve soient produits pour confirmer le bien-fondé des faits contestés et que ces éléments soient antérieurs à l'adoption de l'acte attaqué.[143] Il ressort de certains autres arrêts que ces éléments doivent avoir été versés au dossier du Conseil à la date d'adoption dudit acte.[144]

La jurisprudence relative à la matière pénale, au sens de l'article 6 de la Convention EDH, est, encore une fois, plus restrictive. Le juge de l'Union a ainsi itérativement retenu que la participation d'une entreprise à une infraction aux règles de concurrence doit être appréciée en fonction des seuls éléments de preuve réunis par la Commission dans l'acte attaqué.[145] Ce n'est que pour corroborer les appréciations figurant dans cette décision et spécifiquement en réponse à des éléments de preuve n'ayant pas été invoqués au stade de la procédure administrative ou pour réfuter ceux-ci que la Commission peut elle-même se prévaloir d'éléments de preuve dont elle ne s'est pas prévalue dans l'acte attaqué.[146]

3.2.2 Les éléments nouveaux invoqués pour contester l'acte attaqué

La jurisprudence est plus complexe lorsque c'est pour contester l'acte attaqué que sont invoqués pour la première fois devant le Tribunal des éléments de droit ou de fait. La question de savoir si le contrôle de légalité peut s'effectuer au regard de ces éléments doit s'envisager sur un continuum, où les solutions peuvent varier en fonction des matières, des situations procédurales et de la répartition de la charge de la preuve dans le cadre de la procédure administrative.

À une extrémité du spectre se situent à nouveau les procédures qui relèvent de la matière pénale, au sens de l'article 6 de la Convention EDH. Comme indiqué dans la section 3.1.2 ci-dessus, il s'agit notamment des procédures tendant à la répression des infractions aux règles de concurrence. Si les décisions d'infraction qu'adopte la Commission représentent l'aboutissement d'une procédure administrative contradictoire assortie d'une panoplie de garanties procédurales, le respect des

---

142 Arrêt du 22 avril 2021, Conseil/PKK, C-46/19 P, EU:C:2021:316, point 64.

143 Arrêt du 11 septembre 2024, NSD/Conseil, T-494/22, EU:T:2024:607 (sous pourvoi), point 75. Voir également, en ce sens, arrêts du 15 février 2023, Belaeronavigatsia/Conseil, T-536/21, EU:T:2023:66, point 47, et du 28 février 2019, Souruh/Conseil, T-440/16, non publié, EU:T:2019:115, point 93.

144 Voir, en ce sens, arrêts du 1er juin 2022, Prigozhin/Conseil, T-723/20, EU:T:2022:317, points 55 et 56; du 15 juin 2017, Kiselev/Conseil, T-262/15, EU:T:2017:392, points 102 et 103, ainsi que du 6 septembre 2013, Bateni/Conseil, T-42/12 et T-181/12, EU:T:2013:409, point 53. Voir également, en ce sens, arrêt du 14 avril 2021, Al-Tarazi/Conseil, T-260/19, EU:T:2021:187, point 69.

145 Arrêts du 19 juillet 2012, Alliance One International et Standard Commercial Tobacco/Commission, C-628/10 P et C-14/11 P, EU:C:2012:479, point 79, ainsi que du 30 mars 2022, Latam Airlines et Lan Cargo/Commission, T-344/17, EU:T:2022:185 (sous pourvoi), point 484.

146 Pour une analyse approfondie de cette question, voir F. Castillo de la Torre et E. Gippini Fournier, *Evidence, Proof and Judicial Review in EU Competition Law*, Edward Elgar (2024), p. 385 à 388. Voir également arrêt du 24 octobre 2024, Commission/Intel, C-240/22 P, EU:C:2024:915, points 138, 158 et 162 à 166.

droits de la défense et du droit à un recours effectif face à des accusation de nature pénale exige que les entreprises incriminées puissent faire valoir devant le Tribunal tout élément de fait ou de droit pertinent, qu'il ait ou non été soulevé au cours de la procédure administrative.[147] La conséquence en est que de telles décisions peuvent être annulées sur la base d'éléments dont la Commission n'a pas eu connaissance pendant la procédure administrative et dont il ne peut lui être reproché de ne pas avoir cherché à les recueillir.

À l'autre extrémité du spectre se trouvent les matières non-pénales, au sens de l'article 6 de la Convention EDH, dans lesquelles la recevabilité du recours juridictionnel est conditionnée à l'épuisement d'une procédure précontentieuse, qui fige le cadre juridique ou factuel dans lequel le Tribunal exerce son contrôle.

L'exemple classique en est le contentieux de la fonction publique. Ce contentieux est soumis à la règle prétorienne de concordance, qui interdit au fonctionnaire de faire valoir devant le Tribunal des chefs de contestation reposant sur une cause différente de celle sur laquelle reposent les chefs de contestation invoqués dans la réclamation administrative.[148] La finalité de cette règle est de préserver l'effectivité de la procédure précontentieuse et la probabilité d'un règlement extra-judiciaire qu'elle vise à favoriser, en encourageant l'intéressé à communiquer à l'administration avec une précision suffisante ses griefs ou desiderata.[149]

La jurisprudence est encore plus restrictive lorsque la procédure précontentieuse prend la forme d'un recours administratif devant un organe quasi-juridictionnel.[150] Dans ce cas de figure, c'est non seulement l'invocation de moyens nouveaux qui est proscrite, mais encore celle de faits ou d'éléments de preuve qui n'ont pas été présentés devant ledit organe.

Le cas du contentieux de la propriété intellectuelle est illustratif. Le contrôle juridictionnel des décisions des chambres de recours de l'EUIPO[151] et de l'Office

[147] Voir, en ce sens, arrêts du 21 janvier 2016, Galp Energía España e.a./Commission, C-603/13 P, EU:C:2016:38, point 72 du 1er juillet 2010, Knauf Gips/Commission, C-407/08 P, EU:C:2010:389, points 87 à 92. Seuls pourraient éventuellement faire exception les moyens de défense dont la charge de la preuve incombe à ces entreprises.

[148] Arrêt du 25 octobre 2013, Commission/Moschonaki, T-476/11 P, EU:T:2013:557, point 73. Voir également, s'agissant des agents de l'Union auxquels le statut des fonctionnaires ne s'applique pas, arrêt du 5 octobre 2022, SV/BEI, T-311/21, EU:T:2022:600, point 70.

[149] Arrêt du 21 mai 2014, Mocová/Commission, T-347/12 P, EU:T:2014:268, point 39.

[150] Dans ce cas de figure, le Tribunal joue en principe le rôle de première et dernière instance juridictionnelle. Conformément à l'article 58 *bis* du statut de la Cour de justice de l'Union européenne, l'examen des pourvois dirigé contre les décisions du Tribunal portant notamment sur la décision d'une chambre de recours indépendante de l'EUIPO, de l'OCVV, de l'ECHA et de l'AESA est subordonné à leur admission préalable.

[151] Voir, notamment, en contentieux des marques, arrêts du 24 avril 2024, Tsakiris/EUIPO – Coca-Cola 3E Ellados (Le Petit Déjeuner TSAKIRIS FAMILY), T-303/23, EU:T:2024:269, point 25, ainsi que du 8 mars 2023, Sympatex Technologies / EUIPO – Liwe Española (Sympathy Inside), T-372/21, EU:T:2023:111, point 142 et jurisprudence citée. Voir également, en contentieux des dessins et modèles, arrêt du 21 juin 2023, Rauch Furnace Technology/EUIPO – Musto et Bureau (Creuset), T-347/22, EU:T:2023:344, point 24; et, en contentieux des obtentions végétales, arrêt du

communautaire des variétés végétales[152] ne peut ainsi aller au-delà du cadre juridique et factuel tel qu'il a été porté devant elles et le Tribunal ne peut examiner des moyens nouveaux ni réexaminer les circonstances de fait à la lumière des éléments de preuve présentés pour la première fois devant lui. La légalité de ces décisions doit être appréciée en fonction des éléments d'information dont lesdites chambres pouvaient disposer au moment où elles les ont arrêtées.[153]

La jurisprudence tend à fonder cette conception restrictive de l'office du juge sur la nature du recours visés aux articles 72 du règlement n° 2017/1001 (marques), 61 du règlement n° 6/2002 (dessins et modèles) et 73 du règlement n° 2100/94 (obtentions végétales), qui vise au contrôle de la légalité des décisions des chambres de recours concernées.

La nature du recours en annulation en matière de propriété intellectuelle ne suffit, cependant, pas à expliquer le caractère restrictif de ladite conception. L'office du juge est, en effet, moins étroitement encadré dans le cadre des recours en annulation formés dans les autres matières du droit de l'Union. Or, comme le recours en matière de propriété intellectuelle, ces recours tendent au contrôle de la légalité des actes contre lesquels ils sont dirigés. C'est peut-être pourquoi il arrive au juge de l'annulation de fonder également le caractère restrictif de son contrôle en contentieux de la propriété intellectuelle sur une règle de procédure propre à ce contentieux. Il s'agit de l'article 188 du règlement de procédure du Tribunal, qui prévoit que les mémoires des parties ne peuvent pas modifier l'objet du litige devant la chambre de recours.[154]

Cette explication n'est cependant pas plus satisfaisante que la première. En effet, l'office du juge de l'annulation se conçoit de manière aussi étroite qu'en contentieux de la propriété intellectuelle dans le contentieux des décisions d'autres organes quasi-juridictionnels de recours (par exemple l'Agence pour la coopération des régulateurs de l'énergie[155] et l'Agence européenne des produits chimiques[156]). Or, ce contentieux ne connaît pas de règle analogue à l'article 188 du règlement de procédure du Tribunal.

L'explication réside donc plus vraisemblablement, comme en matière de fonction publique, dans le souci de préserver l'efficacité de la procédure précontentieuse, les garanties qu'offre le caractère quasi-juridictionnel de l'organe de recours justifiant peut-être une approche encore plus restrictive de l'exigence de parallélisme entre les procédures administrative et juridictionnelle.

---

13 septembre 2010, Schniga/OCVV – Elaris et Brookfield New Zealand (Gala Schnitzer), T-135/08, EU:T:2010:397, point 34.

[152] Arrêt du 13 septembre 2010, Schniga/OCVV – Elaris et Brookfield New Zealand (Gala Schnitzer), T-135/08, EU:T:2010:397, point 34.

[153] Ordonnance du 3 mars 2016, AgriCapital/OHMI, C-440/15 P, EU:C:2016:144, point 23.

[154] Voir, par exemple, arrêt du 6 mars 2003, DaimlerChrysler/OHMI (Calandre), T-128/01, EU:T:2003:62, point 18.

[155] Arrêt du 16 mars 2022, MEKH et FGSZ/ACER, T-684/19 et T-704/19, EU:T:2022:138, point 48.

[156] Voir, en ce sens, arrêt du 22 novembre 2023, Symrise/ECHA, T-656/20, EU:T:2023:737, point 106.

Entre les deux extrémités du spectre, les solutions divergent en fonction de la matière. Cela étant, trois balises se dégagent.

Premièrement, conformément au principe de protection juridictionnelle effective, le juge de l'annulation est habilité à tenir compte d'arguments ou d'éléments de preuve invoqués pour la première fois devant lui pour contester des éléments de fait ou de droit retenus dans l'acte attaqué au sujet desquels le justiciable n'a pas pu prendre position au cours de la procédure administrative.[157] Deuxièmement, le juge de l'annulation peut exercer son contrôle au regard d'éléments de preuve qui n'ont pas été présentés pendant la procédure administrative, mais qui sont constitués spécifiquement en vue de contester ledit acte (par exemple des rapports d'expertise).[158] Troisièmement, le pouvoir du juge de l'annulation de prendre en compte des éléments nouveaux est fonction du rôle reconnu aux intéressés dans le cadre de la procédure administrative préalable. Plus leur coopération est importante à cette procédure, plus elle doit être encouragée et moins la jurisprudence est encline à accepter la présentation d'éléments de fait ou de droit pour la première fois au stade de la procédure juridictionnelle.

La jurisprudence s'avère ainsi particulièrement restrictive lorsque la partie requérante sollicite un droit, un avantage ou une faveur et qu'il lui appartient d'apporter seule tous les éléments au soutien de sa demande. L'affaire *OY*[159] est illustrative. Dans cette affaire de recrutement en matière de fonction publique, la Commission avait, faute de preuve suffisante, refusé de tenir compte d'une expérience professionnelle de la partie requérante aux fins de déterminer son classement en grade. Devant le Tribunal, la partie requérante avait apporté une preuve de cette expérience qu'elle n'avait pas présentée lors de la procédure administrative, à savoir son contrat de travail. Le Tribunal avait toutefois déclaré ce contrat irrecevable au motif que la partie requérante aurait pu le soumettre à la Commission avant la fin de ladite procédure.[160]

La jurisprudence est sensiblement plus permissive lorsque la partie requérante sollicite un droit, un avantage ou une faveur, mais que l'administration peut ou doit recueillir des informations en complément de celles que lui a fournies l'intéressé. Dans ce cas de figure, le Tribunal apprécie la légalité de l'acte attaqué au regard des éléments dont l'administration pouvait avoir connaissance dans le cadre de la procédure administrative, plutôt que ceux qui se trouvaient matériellement en sa possession.[161]

---

[157] Voir, en ce sens, arrêt du 17 juillet 2024, Bytedance/Commission, T-1077/23, EU:T:2024:478 (sous pourvoi), point 234.

[158] Voir arrêts du 20 décembre 2023, enercity/Commission, T-65/21, EU:T:2023:844, points 138 à 141; du 16 octobre 2018, OY/Commission, T-605/16, non publié, EU:T:2018:687, point 58 et jurisprudence citée, ainsi que du 21 septembre 2005, EDP/Commission, T-87/05, EU:T:2005:333, point 158.

[159] Arrêt du 16 octobre 2018, OY/Commission, T-605/16, EU:T:2018:687; confirmé sur pourvoi par ordonnance du 12 juin 2019, OY/Commission, C-816/18 P, EU:C:2019:486.

[160] Arrêt du 16 octobre 2018, OY/Commission, T-605/16, EU:T:2018:687, points 24 et 25.

[161] Arrêt du 5 novembre 2014, Commission/Thomé, T-669/13 P, EU:T:2014:929, point 64.

L'approche du juge de l'Union est comparable en matière d'aides d'Etat, où la Commission supporte certes la charge de la preuve,[162] mais dépend de la coopération de l'Etat membre concerné et des parties intéressées. Afin de protéger les incitations de ceux-ci à participer à la procédure administrative et à coopérer pleinement lors de celle-ci, la jurisprudence retient que la légalité des décisions de la Commission est appréciée en fonction des éléments d'information dont la Commission « pouvait disposer » au moment où elle l'a arrêtée.[163] Une fois que la Commission a mis les intéressés en mesure de présenter utilement leurs observations, il ne peut lui être reproché d'avoir ignoré d'éventuels éléments de fait qui auraient pu lui être présentés pendant la procédure administrative, mais qui ne l'ont pas été.[164] Quand bien même elle n'aurait pas participé à la procédure administrative, une partie requérante est donc irrecevable à se prévaloir au stade de la procédure juridictionnelle d'arguments factuels inconnus de la Commission, seuls des moyens juridiques nouveaux pouvant être invoqués.[165]

L'état du droit est similaire dans d'autres matières, telles que le contrôle des concentrations[166] ou les mesures de défense commerciale,[167] où la Commission supporte également la charge de la preuve tout en dépendant de la coopération de tiers.

En revanche, dans d'autres matières, où la coopération des intéressés est moins centrale à la procédure, le juge de l'annulation fait face à des contraintes moindres. C'est notamment le cas dans le domaine des mesures restrictives. Outil de la politique étrangère et sécurité commune de l'Union, ces mesures peuvent revêtir un caractère individuel et prendre la forme de restrictions à l'admission de personnes physiques dans les États membres ou d'un gel de fonds ou de ressources financières situés sur le territoire de l'Union. Sans relever de la matière pénale,[168] ces mesures restreignent sensiblement les droits fondamentaux des personnes visées.

Conformément à l'article 41 de la Charte, les droits de la défense de ces personnes doivent être garantis. En tant qu'auteur des mesures qui visent lesdites personnes, le Conseil devrait en principe leur communiquer les motifs et les éléments retenus à leur charge et leur permette de faire connaître utilement leur point de vue à cet égard. La jurisprudence admet, néanmoins, que l'efficacité des décisions d'inscription sur la liste des personnes, entités et organismes faisant l'objet de

---

[162] Arrêt du 12 mai 2021, Luxembourg/Commission, T-816/17 et T-318/18, EU:T:2021:252, points 125 et 126.

[163] Arrêt du 26 septembre 1996, France/Commission, C-241/94, EU:C:1996:353, point 33. Les informations dont la Commission « pouvait disposer » incluent celles dont elle aurait pu, sur sa demande, obtenir la production au cours de la procédure administrative. Arrêt du 20 septembre 2017, Commission/Frucona Košice, C-300/16 P, EU:C:2017:706 P, point 71.

[164] Arrêt du 6 avril 2006, Schmitz-Gotha Fahrzeugwerke/Commission, T-17/03, EU:T:2006:109, point 54.

[165] Arrêts du 19 octobre 2022, Sogias Ellas/Commission, T-347/20, EU:T:2022:639, point 67.

[166] Arrêt du 27 janvier 2021, KPN/Commission, T-691/18, EU:T:2021:43, point 141.

[167] Arrêt du 20 mars 2019, Foshan Lihua Ceramic/Commission, T-310/16, EU:T:2019:170, point 129.

[168] Arrêt du 9 décembre 2014, Sport-pari/Conseil, T-439/11, EU:T:2014:1043, points 89 et 90.

mesures restrictives suppose qu'elles puissent bénéficier d'un effet de surprise et donc s'appliquer immédiatement, sans préalablement entendre l'intéressé.[169]

Dans ce cas de figure, l'intéressé ne saurait évidemment être tenu à une quelconque exigence de parallélisme entre les procédures administrative et juridictionnelle. La garantie d'une protection juridictionnelle effective et des droits de la défense requiert que le juge de l'annulation puisse exercer son contrôle au regard de tout élément de fait ou de droit pertinent.

L'exigence de parallélisme ne s'applique pas non plus au contentieux des décisions de maintien du nom de l'intéressé sur la liste des personnes, entités et organismes faisant l'objet de mesures restrictives.[170] La raison en est vraisemblablement la faible importance accordée à la coopération de l'intéressé, qui dispose d'une simple faculté de présenter des observations ou de nouveaux éléments de preuve pendant la procédure de réexamen. C'est le Conseil qui supporte la charge de la preuve et qui détermine, au terme d'une évaluation propre et sur la base d'un dossier qu'il lui revient de constituer, les personnes ou entités devant faire l'objet de mesures restrictives.[171]

4 Conclusion

Le contrôle de légalité consiste encore et toujours en la confrontation objective d'un acte aux normes de droit de l'Union de rang supérieur à lui, dans l'esprit du « procès fait à un acte ». Mais, l'office du juge de l'annulation n'est plus simplement celui d'un arbitre de ce procès. Il œuvre activement à la protection de l'impératif de légalité, non seulement en relevant d'office les traditionnels moyens d'ordre public de légalité externe, mais encore en reconnaissant un moyen d'ordre public tiré de la violation du champ d'application de la loi et en déterminant d'office le sens de cette dernière dans les interstices du principe dispositif.

L'office du juge de l'annulation tend également à s'imprégner de l'impératif de protection juridictionnelle effective. Si ce juge se place toujours à la date de l'adoption de l'acte attaqué, il s'efforce de moduler la contrainte qu'exercent les contours de l'acte attaqué et de la procédure administrative préalable sur les éléments de fait et de droit au regard desquels il exerce son office. Cette contrainte est désormais appréciée en fonction d'une multitude de facteurs que les juridictions de l'Union ont jusqu'ici dégagées selon une approche casuistique. Ces facteurs comprennent notamment le but dans lequel les éléments nouveaux sont invoqués

---

[169] Arrêt du 12 mai 2022, Boshab/Conseil, C-242/21 P, EU:C:2022:375, point 59 et jurisprudence citée.

[170] Voir arrêt du 26 octobre 2022, Ovsyannikov/Conseil, T-714/20, EU:T:2022:674, point 73 et jurisprudence citée. Voir, toutefois, arrêt du 14 juillet 2021, Benavides Torres/Conseil, T-35/19, EU:T:2021:466, points 60 à 64.

[171] Arrêt du 18 juillet 2013, Commission e.a./Kadi, C-584/10 P, C-593/10 P et C-595/10 P, EU:C:2013:518, point 121.

(défendre ou contester l'acte attaqué), la nature (pénale au sens de l'article 6 de la Convention EDH ou non) et les modalités (recours précontentieux ou non) de la procédure administrative ou encore le rôle des intéressés dans celle-ci.

Gageons que ces questions feront l'objet de réflexions et d'efforts de systématisation supplémentaires, dans l'intérêt de la sécurité juridique et de la prévisibilité de la justice.

The Registry of the Court: Between Positivism and Pragmatism

Maria Krausenboeck

1 Introduction

When it came to procedural decisions, Nils Wahl, to me, always seemed to be quite the positivist. If an exception was not foreseen in the rules of procedure (for example, the postponement of a hearing because of an ill lawyer or agent, or the extension of a deadline during the vacation period), he would recommend to the President not to grant one. In this, it must be said, he was not always in line with the general decisional practice of the Court. Overall, the Court tends to take rather nuanced and, more often than not, generous procedural decisions. Does this mean that the Court does not base its decisions on the enacted procedural legal framework? Not at all. Things are, as so often, more complex.

Unlike national courts and, up until recently,[1] unlike the General Court, the Court of Justice does not only deal with classic inter-party proceedings, but hears a wide range of cases, where it encounters a wide range of litigants and their representatives. For all these different types of proceedings, the Court must base its decisions on one and the same procedural legal framework. A procedural framework that, by necessity, contains rather abstract and general provisions as it is subject to a burdensome amendment process and as it needs to serve many different needs.

[1] Since 1 October 2024, the General Court now also has the competence to hear preliminary references in six specific areas of EU law (see Article 50b of the Statute of the Court of Justice—hereafter "the Statute").

M. Krausenboeck (✉)
Court of Justice of the European Union, Luxembourg, Luxembourg
e-mail: Maria.Krausenboeck@curia.europa.eu

L. Prete, L. Rezki (eds.), *Judging & (Re)Thinking European Union Law*,
https://doi.org/10.1007/978-3-032-13473-8_22

In order to meet the specific needs of a case, provisions might be interpreted differently in different situations or gaps in the rules might need to be filled by decisional practice. It is the Registry's task, among others, to ensure that procedural decisions nevertheless do not violate the general principles of EU law, in particular legal certainty and equal treatment of the parties in judicial proceedings. At the same time, the Registry seeks to promote procedural decisions that favour general and procedural economy and that best meet the needs of the Court as a judicator.

That is why at times the Courts procedural decisions might seem (unduly) positivist, while at other times decisions seem more pragmatic. This contribution seeks to show that, in any case, the decision-makers seek to take their decisions, to the greatest extent possible, in service of the European people and the adjudicated.

In the following, I will briefly describe the different types of proceedings heard by the Court (Sect. 2) and the procedural legal framework applicable (Sect. 3), before describing the various responsibilities of the Registry as well as its approach in fulfilling them (Sect. 4). Finally, I will provide a short conclusion (Sect. 5).

2 The Different Types of Proceedings Before the Court of Justice

In 2024, the Court received a total of 920 new cases, the grand majority of which were preliminary references,[2] followed by appeals (on points of law)[3] and direct actions.[4] The remaining cases concerned either appeals concerning interim measures or interventions, or special types of procedure[5] (such as requests for legal aid, requests for taxation of costs or requests for a Court Opinion pursuant to Article 218(11) TFEU).

These statistics show one thing: the Court of Justice is not a court of fact. In the vast majority of cases, the Court is merely concerned with the interpretation of EU law, but not with the nitty gritty facts of the individual case. In preliminary references, and the appeals that are referred back to the General Court, the Court does not render the ultimate decision. The parties thus have another opportunity to argue their case and take position on the interpretation provided by the Court before final judgment is given.

A look behind the statistics and at individual cases shows another thing: not only does the Court deal with many different types of procedure; it also deals with many different actors within those proceedings. In requests for preliminary rulings pursuant to Article 267 TFEU, the Court provides an interpretation of EU law for

[2] Namely, 62.3%. See Annual Report 2024, Statistics concerning the judicial activity of the Court of Justice, p. 5 (www.curia.europa.eu > The Institution > Annual Report).

[3] Appeals made up 28.8% of all cases (*idem*).

[4] 5.8% of cases were direct actions (*idem*).

[5] *Idem*.

questions referred to it by the national courts of any of the Member States of the European Union. Cases are referred by all levels of jurisdiction and in matters ranging from inheritance issues and consumer protection, to intellectual property disputes and big scale competition law proceedings. In some of these proceedings, parties may represent themselves,[6] in others, a small firm lawyer working by himself/herself and without any experience before the EU courts will represent a private party in a dispute against big business, and yet in other cases, hotshot lawyers will battle each other by taking recourse to the full arsenal of procedural weapons available to them.

When it comes to appeals, the litigants are usually companies or EU civil servants on the one side and EU institutions on the other.[7] The former are in most cases represented by lawyers specialised in EU law who regularly plead before the EU courts. The EU institutions, just like the Member States that bring direct actions before the Court or who are taken to court by the Commission, are usually represented by their own agents whose principal task is to appear in Luxembourg. They know the Court's procedural provisions and decisions well and, in many instances, even have been involved in the legislative process leading to the adoption of the Court's procedural framework. The appeals heard by the Court often concern big money (competition decisions, State aids), whereas direct actions deal with emotionally charged and/or sensitive political issues (such as the introduction of motorway tolls in Germany that were targeted only at non-residents[8] or the introduction of a law inhibiting the work of NGOs[9]).

From time to time,[10] the Court also is seised by a Member State or an EU institution with a request for a Court Opinion pursuant to Article 218(11) TFEU. This procedure can only be introduced by a Member State or an EU institution, interventions by parties other than those actors being precluded. Here the Court is asked to provide an interpretation of laws not yet adopted or not yet entered into force.

[6] See Article 47(2) of the Rules of Procedure of the Court of Justice—hereafter "the Rules of Procedure".

[7] In recent years there has also been an increasing number of cases brought by persons subject to sanctions decided by the United Nations. However, this is a rather temporary phenomenon as the adopted restrictive measures are always linked to specific political events (e.g. Decision 2014/145/CFSP concerning restrictive measures in respect of actions undermining or threatening the territorial integrity, sovereignty and independence of Ukraine or Council Decision 2013/255/CFSP of 31 May 2013 concerning restrictive measures against Syria). The Court has power to review the legality of decisions providing for restrictive measures against natural or legal persons adopted by the Council on the basis of Chapter 2 of Title V of the Treaty on European Union in accordance with Article 275, second alinéa, TFEU.

[8] See judgment in *Austria v Germany*, C-591/17, EU:C:2019:504.

[9] See judgment in *Commission v Hungary (Transparency of associations)*, C-78/18, EU:C:2020:476.

[10] On average, once per year.

3 The Legal Framework Guiding the Court's Procedural Decisions

For all these different types of proceedings, involving all these different types of actors, the Court has one and the same procedural legal framework. This legal framework, principally, consists of the Treaty provisions concerning the Court of Justice, the Statute and the Rules of Procedure. These main procedural documents are supplemented by other documents,[11] of which the *Practice directions to parties concerning cases brought before the Court*[12] are most relevant in practice.

The applicable Treaty provisions lay down the Court's competences and establish the different types of proceedings that are brought before the Court. For very rare proceedings, they may even be the only guidance the Court has for dealing with certain procedural questions. For instance, in the case of an action on grounds of infringement of the principle of subsidiarity by a legislative act, notified by a Member State in accordance with its legal order on behalf of its national Parliament,[13] no clear provision exists for determining by whom the application for such an action must be signed. Should the application be signed by the legal representative of the Member State concerned, the Parliament's members that initiated the action or the lawyer representing the national Parliament in question? When the first application of that type was lodged, the Court had to find the answer to that question mostly based on the interpretation of the expression "notified by them" mentioned in the relevant Treaty provision.[14]

The Statute of the Court, in turn, is laid down in Protocol (No 3) on the Statute of the Court of Justice of the European Union, annexed to the Treaties, and may only be amended by the European Parliament and the Council, acting in accordance with the ordinary legislative procedure, on proposal either of the Court of Justice or the Commission.[15] The Statute provisions concern the Court of Justice as an institution, rather than the judicial body. As such it governs organisation and procedure of

[11] These are the Decision of the Court of Justice of 23 October 2012 concerning the judicial functions of the Vice-President of the Court (OJ 2012 L 300, p. 47), the Decision (EU) 2016/2386 of the Court of Justice of 20 September 2016 concerning the security rules applicable to information or material produced before the General Court in accordance with Article 105 of its Rules of Procedure (OJ 2016 L 355, p. 5), the Decision of the Court of Justice of 4 September 2024 on the lodging and service of procedural documents by means of e-Curia (OJ L 2024/2490), and the Conditions of Use of e-Curia (www.curia.europa.eu > Court of Justice > Procedure).

[12] OJ L 2024/2173 ('the Practice Directions to the Parties').

[13] See Article 8, first alinéa, of Protocol (No 2) on the application of the principles of subsidiarity and proportionality, annexed to the Treaties ('Protocol (No 2)').

[14] Article 8, first alinéa, Protocol (No 2): 'The Court of Justice of the European Union shall have jurisdiction in actions on grounds of infringement of the principle of subsidiarity by a legislative act, brought in accordance with the rules laid down in Article 263 of the Treaty on the Functioning of the European Union by Member States, or *notified by them* in accordance with their legal order on behalf of their national Parliament or a chamber thereof' (emphasis added)—See Case C-553/24, *Assemblée nationale / Parliament and Council*, pending.

[15] See Article 281 TFEU.

both the Court and the General Court (as well as any specialised court(s) that may exist). Title III of the Statute lays down the "Procedure before the Court of Justice". Here, general provisions are laid down concerning, among others, representation,[16] the various stages of the procedure,[17] the content of applications initiating proceedings[18] and the very foundational rules of adjudication by the Court, such as the fact that hearings are public[19] and the secrecy of the judges' deliberations.[20]

The Statute is supplemented by the Rules of Procedure which are established by the Court but require the approval of the Council.[21] The Rules of Procedure contain more detailed rules than the Statute and answers to the more practical questions of Court proceedings (such as methods of service of procedural documents[22] or the calculation of time limits[23]). That is why there are individual Rules of Procedure for the Court, on the one hand, and the General Court, on the other. The Court's Rules of Procedure are, apart from the first two titles on Organisation of the Court and the Common Procedural Provisions and the final title, dedicated to the specific types of procedure.[24] While they seek to be complete, in certain instances, the Rules of Procedure present *lacunae* or require extensive interpretation due to abstract wording or cross-referencing, which makes them accessible only to those "in the know".

For instance, the chapter on interim measures[25] provides very little guidance on the exact procedure to be followed. Thus, while Article 160(5), Rules of Procedure, makes clear that submissions are to be made within a short time limit, everything else seems to be decided by the Vice-President[26] *ad hoc*. It is, however, rather established practice that, save for very exceptional circumstances, the application for interim measures will be notified to the opposite party/parties right away and a time limit of three to four weeks is set for written observations. The possibility for the Vice-President to immediately set a date for oral submissions while foregoing the written part of the procedure seems to be of little relevance in practice as, in accordance with Article 160(7), Rules of Procedure, an application may be granted even before the observations of the opposite party have been submitted.[27]

[16] Article 19, Statute.

[17] Article 20, Statute.

[18] Article 21, Statute.

[19] Article 31, Statute.

[20] Article 35, Statute.

[21] Article 253, sixth alinéa, TFEU.

[22] Article 48, Rules of Procedure.

[23] Article 49, Rules of Procedure.

[24] Title III "References for a preliminary ruling"; Title IV "Direct actions"; Title V "Appeals against decisions of the General Court"; Title VI "Review of decisions of the General Court"; Title VII "Requests for Opinions"; Title VIII "Particular forms of procedure".

[25] Chapter 10 "Suspension of operation or enforcement and other interim measures".

[26] See Decision of the Court of Justice of 23 October 2012 concerning the judicial functions of the Vice-President of the Court (OJ 2012 L 300, p. 47), Article 1.

[27] Sometimes in as little as two days: see Order of the Vice-President of the Court of 27 July 2017, *Commission v Poland (Białowieża Forest)*, C-441/17 R, EU:C:2017:622. See also Orders of the

The lack of guidance by the procedural rules is even greater when it comes to summary proceedings in the context of an appeal brought against a decision on interim measures taken by the General Court. By dint of Article 190, Rules of Procedure, the provisions on interim measures also apply to the procedure for appeals against such decisions taken by the General Court. However, no other provision is made for the specific procedural aspects of summary appeal proceedings. If, for instance, a cross-appeal is lodged in such a summary appeal proceeding, the only guidance in the procedural texts are the provisions applicable to cross-appeals within ordinary appeal proceedings. Here, Article 179 expressly prescribes a time limit of two months for the reply to a cross-appeal. Certainly, this provision cannot be applied in a literal manner where the time limit to respond to the appeal against a decision on interim measures itself is only three to four weeks. In that instance, Article 160(5), Rules of Procedure, as *lex specialis* takes precedence over Article 179 and the Vice-President will set a short time limit for the response to the cross-appeal.[28]

Similarly, it might not be clear whether or not the parties have the right to request a hearing within the context of summary proceedings.[29] While Article 76 of the Rules of Procedure, which provides for such requests, is in Title II on the "Common Procedural Provisions", parties to summary proceedings are not explicitly invited to submit such a request when notified of the close of the written part of the procedure—unlike in the other types of proceedings. This lack of invitation is of course motivated by the aim to keep the procedure as short as possible and thereby to give due regard to the summary character of the proceedings. As the Rules of Procedure do not provide for an exception to the common provision concerning the right to request a hearing, the Court will nevertheless always accept such a request and register it in the case file, even in summary proceedings.[30] However, the parties cannot

---

Vice-President of the Court of 8 July 2024, *Vivendi v Commission*, C-470/24 P(R)-R, EU:C:2024:592; of 22 July 2022, *Telefónica de España v Commission*, C-478/22 P(R)-R, EU:C:2022:598; and of 4 October 2017, *Wall Street Systems UK v ECB*, C-576/17 P(R)-R, EU:C:2017:735.

[28] See Orders of the Vice-President of the Court of 21 October 2024, *Lagardère v Commission*, C-569/24 P(R), EU:C:2024:945, and of 22 June 2022, *Puigdemont i Casamajó e.a. v Parliament*, C-81/22 P(R), EU:C:2022:594.

[29] While in English the word "hearing" is used also in this context, in French there is a distinction between "*audience de plaidoiries*" for normal proceedings and "*audition*" for summary proceedings.

[30] In practice, such a request is often denied though on the basis of Article 76(2), Rules of Procedure (see Case C-632/24 P(R), *Commission v Courtois e.a.*, pending; Orders of the Vice-President of the Court of 24 May 2022, *Puigdemont i Casamajó e.a. v Parliament and Spain*, C-629/21 P(R), EU:C:2022:413; and of 20 September 2021, *Czech Republic v Poland*, C-121/21 R, EU:C:2021:752, para. 13). However, see also Orders of the Vice-President of the Court of 20 July 2018, *ECB v Latvia*, C-238/18 R, EU:C:2018:581, para. 27; of 2 July 2018, *Comune di Milano v Council*, C-182/18 R, EU:C:2018:524, paras 11–13; and of 20 November 2017, *Commission v Poland*, C-441/17 R, EU:C:2017:877, para. 7.

compel the Court to hold a hearing even if they have not submitted any written observations, as Article 76(3) only applies to the preliminary reference procedure.[31]

When it comes to summary proceedings, it is fairly obvious why the relevant provisions of the Rules of Procedure must be succinct and thus give broad discretion to the Vice-President in handling these cases. The approach followed is always an exercise in balancing the right to be heard with the right to effective judicial protection by way of a swift decision. Depending on the urgency of the matter before him, the Vice-President can make the balance tilt in favour of one or the other right.

In other instances, the not always so straightforward wording of the procedural provisions on which the Court bases its decisions might be due to the drafting history or process. The adoption of new Rules of Procedure usually happens in the context of broader reforms that also require the amendment of the Court's Statute. The Court thus will submit a proposal for Statute amendments to Council and Parliament and the proposal for the amended Rules of Procedure to the Council only. The comments on those proposals might then require further changes to be made to one or both instruments. As negotiations on amendments are often burdensome and lengthy,[32] once provisions have been agreed upon by all the relevant actors, the Court seeks to avoid further changes simply for "cosmetic" reasons, in order to drive the process forward.

This pragmatic approach at times might even lead to apparent inconsistencies between the Statute and the Rules of Procedure. Article 19, 3rd and 4th *alinéas*, of the Statute and Article 97(3) of the Rules of Procedure may serve as an example here. While the Statute requires a party's representative to be "a lawyer authorised to practise before a court of a Member State or of another State which is a party to the Agreement on the European Economic Area", the Rules of Procedure in the relevant provision applicable to requests for preliminary ruling, require the Court to "take account of the rules of procedure in force before the referring court or tribunal". As the case may be, the national rules of procedure may impose greater or lesser restrictions. In some Member States, only specially qualified lawyers may plead before the highest courts. Does this mean that only those lawyers may represent parties before the Court of Justice in cases referred by the highest courts? The short answer is "no". Here the Statute takes precedence over the Rules of Procedure

[31] Article 76(3) provides that the Court may not dispose of the need to hold a hearing even if it considers that it has sufficient information to give a ruling on the basis of the written observations, "where a request for a hearing, stating reasons, has been submitted by an *interested person referred to in Article 23 of the Statute* who did not participate in the written part of the procedure" (emphasis added). Article 23 of the Statute deals only with cases governed by Article 267 TFEU.

[32] The legislative process for the latest reform of Statute and Rules of Procedure took almost two years (the process was initiated on 30 November 2022 and the amendment finally published in the Official Journal on 12 August 2024; see Interinstitutional File 2022/0906 (COD) (available at on the Council's website) and Regulation (EU, Euratom) 2024/2019 of the European Parliament and of the Council of 11 April 2024 amending Protocol No 3 on the Statute of the Court of Justice of the European Union, OJ L, 2024/2019). For details, see: Gaudissart, M.-A., Genèse et négociation de la réforme de l'architecture juridictionnelle de l'Union européenne, Revista de Derecho Comunitario Europeo, 79, 27–48.

and the solution retained in practice is that any lawyer authorised to practise before a court of a Member State or another EEA State may represent the parties. Article 97(3) of the Rules of Procedure thus only becomes relevant where national rules are more lenient.

In order to make its procedural framework more accessible also to those who do not regularly plead before the EU courts, the Court publishes the Practice Directions to the Parties which are, save for some minor additions such as the prescribed length for procedural documents, in fact akin to explanatory notes to the Rules of Procedure. Here parties get a more practical overview of the procedural rules and detailed explanations on how to lodge certain requests and other documents.[33] As these Practice Directions are established and adopted by the Court itself, they can be amended more easily and thus are able to address developments in a swifter manner.

In addition, the Registry of the Court, among other tasks, provides information on Court procedure to representatives and national judges, but also ensures that procedural decisions—despite the occasional need for extensive interpretation—nevertheless do not violate the general principles of EU law, such as legal certainty and equal treatment of the parties in judicial proceedings. At the same time, the Registry seeks to promote procedural decisions that favour general and procedural economy and that best meet the needs of the Court as an adjudicator.

In the following, I will first describe the responsibilities of the Registry as laid down in the Statute and Rules of Procedure before providing some insight into how these responsibilities translate to the role it assumes within the proceedings before the Court.

4 The Registry of the Court

The Treaties and the Statute, actually, make no mention of the Registry but only of the Registrar.[34] The Registrar takes an oath like the Members of the Court, whose privileges and formal obligations he shares.[35] He is the Court's Head of Administration, under the authority of the President of the Court.[36] While some of the Registrar's responsibilities can be inferred from the Statute,[37] his main responsibilities are laid down in the Rules of Procedure and notably Article 20 thereof. Pursuant to that provision, the Registrar is (1) responsible, under the authority of the President of the Court, for the acceptance, transmission and custody of all

[33] The most important and most often referred to provisions in this respect being points 48 to 54 on 'The form and structure of procedural documents' (Practice Directions to the Parties, pp. 11 and 12).

[34] See Article 253 TFUE and, notably, Articles 10 to 12 of the Statute.

[35] Article 3, 4th paragraph and Article 14 of the Statute.

[36] See Articles 10 and 12 of the Statute.

[37] See, e.g., Article 23 on the notification of requests for preliminary ruling, Article 33 concerning the minutes of the hearing, Article 37 on the signature of judgements.

documents and for effecting service; (2) must assist the Members of the Court in all their official functions; (3) has the custody of the seals and is responsible for the records, as well as the publications of the Court and, in particular, the European Court Reports; and (4) the Registrar directs the services of the institution under the authority of the President of the Court. As such, he is responsible for the management of the staff and the administration, and for the preparation and implementation of the budget.

The Rules of Procedure thus make the Registrar responsible for the management and administration of the Court as an institution, but also for the administrative tasks linked to the Court's judicial activity. However, the list provided there is but an incomplete picture of the Registrar's tasks. In fact, the Registrar (or the Registry) are mentioned over 100 times throughout the Rules of Procedure. Looking at those provisions as a whole will give a more complete depiction of the Registrar's role within Court life.[38] In practice, the Registrar fulfils the responsibilities pertaining to the management of the institution and the representative functions of the post, while the other responsibilities have been delegated to the Deputy Registrar of the Court and the Registrar of the General Court who lead the day-to-day business of the two registries. With an institution of over 2300 staff dealing with nearly 3000 pending cases that are taken care of by 81 Judges,[39] it is not surprising that the responsibilities have been split between different roles.[40]

The Registry of the Court consists of a team of about 50 persons, of which 13 are administrators with university degrees in law. The team is divided into two units with several language sections and one specialised unit responsible for feeding procedural information into the Court's databases. The team of the Registry acts in the Registrar's name and takes on his responsibilities pertaining to the judicial proceedings as mentioned in the Statute and Rules of Procedure. These responsibilities are spread over the entire procedure before the Court. New cases are lodged with the Registry;[41] it keeps the case file;[42] it receives all procedural documents from national courts, the parties and interested persons;[43] and it serves all outgoing documents on national courts, the parties and interested persons, including the final decision of the

[38] See, e.g., Article 39 "Responsibilities of the Registrar concerning language arrangements", Article 48 "Methods of service", Article 52 "Setting and extension of time limits", Article 74 "Minutes of inquiry hearings", Article 84 "Minutes of hearings", Article 88 "Delivery and service of the judgment", Article 90 "Signature and service of the order", Article 119 "Obligation to be represented", Article 154 "Rectification".

[39] See the Annual Report 2023 – The Year in Review, pp. 16 and 17 (available at curia.europa.eu > The Institution > Annual Report).

[40] This understanding of shared responsibilities is actually acknowledged in recent amendments to the Rules of Procedure. In Articles 80a (Broadcasting of hearings) and 93a (Preliminary analysis of requests for a preliminary ruling) of the Rules of Procedure, responsibilities have directly been allocated to the Registry.

[41] Article 57 "Lodging of procedural documents", Article 167 "Lodging of the appeal", Rules of Procedure.

[42] Cf. Article 21 "Keeping of the Register", Rules of Procedure.

[43] Article 48 "Methods of service", Rules of Procedure.

Court.[44] The Registry thus stays with the case throughout the proceedings and serves as an interface between those inside the Court and those outside.[45] That is why the Registry also coordinates the workflow of a case within the institution: it requests translations for procedural documents; calculates internal deadlines for the chambers of the Judge-Rapporteur and Advocate General; prepares the hearings in collaboration with the Directorate of Interpretation, the Court's building maintenance unit, the service of the court ushers and the Multimedia team; organises the delivery of judgments and Advocates' Generals Opinions; prepares the authentic original of judgments and orders; and gives the final "green light" for the publication of Court decisions and procedural documents. The Registry therefore is singularly placed when it comes to knowing where a case stands within the procedure as it is involved, in one way or another, at every step of the procedure (save for the deliberations).

As cases may have any of the 24 languages mentioned in Article 36 of the Rules of Procedure as language of procedure,[46] and procedural documents therefore are lodged in those languages, the Registry manages cases based on language of procedure. When a case is lodged, an assistant and administrator are allocated to it and they usually stay with the case throughout the proceedings. Ideally both of them master the language of the case, but at least one of them will do so. Therefore hiring at the Registry is done based on, inter alia, language skills. The 13 administrators of the Registry are lawyers versed in the languages that most often are used in the proceedings before the Court. This is necessary, on the one hand, so that the Registry can communicate with the national courts and parties in their own language and, on the other hand, so that there is no delay in analysing procedural documents before they are translated into the working language of the Court.

Simply in order to gather all the information necessary to register a case, it is sometimes necessary to have a deeper understanding of the legal procedure within which a preliminary reference came about.[47] In addition, requests for preliminary ruling accompanied by a request for expedited or urgent procedure are immediately forwarded to the President's chambers, the translation services and the Research and Documentation Directorate with a short summary of the legal issues at hand and the factual background, as well as a recommendation concerning the application of a special procedure. This is done in the interest of procedural economy and to avoid an unduly lengthy duration of proceedings. These aims have gained increasing importance over the last years as the Court's caseload has come to a rather stable

[44] Cf. Article 88 "Delivery and service of the judgment" and Article 90 "Signature and service of the order", Rules of Procedure.

[45] Judges of the Court of Justice, in fact, do not have any direct contact with the national courts or the parties in the context of a proceeding (apart from the hearings), nor may they directly receive any documents pertaining to a case.

[46] "The language of a case shall be Bulgarian, Croatian, Czech, Danish, Dutch, English, Estonian, Finnish, French, German, Greek, Hungarian, Irish, Italian, Latvian, Lithuanian, Maltese, Polish, Portuguese, Romanian, Slovak, Slovenian, Spanish or Swedish."

[47] For instance, to discern all the parties to administrative or criminal proceedings.

800 to 900 cases per year since 2018,[48] while it seeks to keep the average duration of proceedings nevertheless at a similar level.[49] Procedural economy[50] and duration of proceedings therefore are recurring themes in the Registry's work.

As soon as a case is lodged, the Registry's administrators undertake a *prima facie* analysis thereof in order to "weed out" potentially inadmissible or manifestly unfounded cases that may be dealt with by way of order,[51] but also cases that could be stayed until an earlier case dealing with the same questions has been decided.[52] In that case, usually translation of the application initiating proceedings is requested only into French, the working language of the Court, and the case is not notified. Such an approach saves valuable resources in the translation services but also the chambers of the Court, as no written pleadings need to be processed. The reduction in duration of proceedings is striking: while preliminary references decided by way of judgement after an exchange of written pleadings and, as the case may be, oral submissions, in 2024 took an average of 18.6 months to be decided, preliminary references decided by way of order took only 8.5 months.[53] For appeals the difference is even more striking: 26 months (on average), compared to 5.4 months (on average).[54] It must be noted though that the written part of the procedure for appeals is rather lengthy with often two rounds of written pleadings which alone lasts almost seven months on average.

[48] 2019: 966 new cases; 2020: 737 new cases (outlier due to the Covid-19 health crisis where many national courts remained closed over months); 2021: 838 new cases; 2022: 806 new cases; 2023: 821 new cases; 2024: 920.

[49] Cf. the Court's Annual Reports 2012 to 2023 (available at curia.europa.eu > The Institution > History > Annual Reports).

[50] For the sake of procedural economy, the principle of subsidiarity also seems to be applied to procedural decisions: in the context of preliminary references, the Court only tackles those aspects of the procedure that cannot be taken care of by the national court having submitted the request for a preliminary ruling. For instance, no interim measures are taken by the Court in preliminary reference procedures and no urgent or expedited procedure is granted if the national court could address the urgency of the required decision by means of adopting interim measures itself (Fact sheet "Urgent preliminary ruling procedure and expedited procedure", pp. 26–28; www.curia.europa.eu > Judicial Network of the EU > Fact sheets). Also, while the Court may provide legal aid to parties who are wholly or in part unable to meet the costs of the proceedings before the Court, this is only done where costs for the proceedings before the Court cannot be covered by national legal aid (see Article 115, paragraphs 1 and 3, of the Rules of Procedure).

[51] See Articles 53(2) and 181 of the Rules of Procedure. In certain instances, this approach has been systematised when it comes to the treatment of cases by the Court. Requests for preliminary ruling and certain types of appeal (at the moment, appeals concerning access to documents, public procurement or civil service cases) are not only subject to a *prima facie* analysis of the Registry, but are also analysed more thoroughly by the Research and Documentation Directorate prior to notification. The resulting note will provide a recommendation as to whether a case may be dealt with by way of order or may be stayed until a "pilot type case" has been decided.

[52] See Article 55, Rules of Procedure.

[53] This excludes non-judicial orders such as orders deleting a case from the Register. See Annual Report 2024 – Statistics of judicial activity (available at curia.europa.eu > The Institution > Annual Report).

[54] Idem.

In contrast, the written part of the procedure for preliminary references takes only about four months on average. In recent years, the Registry has undertaken to reduce this number further by adopting a rather practical solution. It now actively requests lawyers representing parties in such proceedings to open an e-Curia account[55] so that procedural documents can be exchanged electronically and thus instantaneously. As cases are notified all over the European Union, it may take up to two weeks for recipients to receive a postal notification, even longer during vacation times when law firms might not be staffed and mail thus not be recuperated at the postal office. An errant postal notification may delay proceedings even for up to three months as it takes time to return the non-delivered item. The "e-Curia rate" obtained based on those efforts reached 91% in 2024. As a result, there were no procedural delays caused by errant postal notifications. As an unexpected side effect, this approach has also helped reduce the number of procedural errors committed by the parties' lawyers. Since the latter are contacted by the Registry's administrator in charge of their case before it is even notified, they have a point of contact in case of procedural questions and also know better what to expect, even if they do not have any prior experience with the Court. In addition, with the request to open an e-Curia account lawyers receive information about the Practice Directions to the Parties and are alerted to the formal requirements of written pleadings before the Court. While seemingly simplistic, these measures have contributed to keeping the duration of proceedings reasonable while not affecting the quality of judicial decision-making.

In addition, when registering documents, apart from the usual verifications concerning time-limits, representation and overall compliance with the Rules of Procedure, the Registry nowadays also makes sure that the recommended length of applications lodging a case and of written submissions is respected,[56] unless otherwise justified by the particular circumstances of a case.[57] Length of procedural documents has significant impact on the duration of the proceedings. Not only will the studying of a case by the Judges and Advocate General take longer, but translation time will increase as the deadlines for lawyer linguists at the Court are based on a set formula of pages per day. As all procedural documents have to be translated into

[55] e-Curia is an application of the Court of Justice that enables the representatives of parties in cases brought before the Court of Justice and the General Court, as well as national courts and tribunals in the context of a reference to the Court of Justice for a preliminary ruling, to exchange procedural documents with the Registries by exclusively electronic means. For more information see the page 'e-curia', on the Court's website. As the exchange of procedural documents via e-Curia was made obligatory before the General Court a few years ago, this is not an issue in appeal proceedings as all lawyers usually already dispose of an e-Curia account. The issue also does not exist for direct actions, as all the Member States and Institutions operate with e-Curia.

[56] 30 pages for direct actions, 25 pages for appeals and 20 pages for written observations in preliminary references (see, respectively, points 18, 26 and 15 of the Practice Directions to the Parties).

[57] These special circumstances might be number of questions referred for a preliminary ruling, number of pages of the General Court's judgment subject to appeal, complexity of the case. Ideally, parties will provide the justification for exceeding the recommended number of pages in a letter accompanying the lodged document.

the working language of the Court, the duration of the proceedings is already substantially impacted (translation adds between one and two months at every step of the procedure). In case of an overly long request for preliminary ruling, the effect of the delay created even has repercussions on many other cases, as the requests are translated into 21 languages and therefore "block" 21 lawyer linguists at the same time.

When raising a procedural issue to the President (who will hear the Judge-Rapporteur and the Advocate General before taking a decision),[58] the Registry will take a stricter, more positivist, stance *vis-à-vis* the Rules of Procedure where the issue has a negative effect on procedural economy or duration of proceedings. It is one of the reasons why the Court renders very strict decisions when it comes to documents that are not foreseen in the Rules of Procedure. Often lawyers, who are either used to several rounds of written submissions in their national law or who simply do not want to leave any stone unturned when fighting their case, submit replies to the submissions made in the course of preliminary references or to the Opinion of the Advocate General. The Registry will always raise this as an issue and recommend to the President to not enter the document into the case file. Nevertheless, where parties present a document after the closure of the written part of the procedure in direct actions or appeals and that document could have the effect of making a revision to the judgment necessary,[59] the Registry takes a more pragmatic approach and recommends to accept the document in order to avoid unnecessary proceedings.[60]

In trainings with national court staff in Ireland a participant once expressed surprise that the Registry of the Court would make recommendations for procedural decisions to the Members of the Court and even more so that the Members would actually follow them. From a national perspective, it might indeed seem strange that one of the Registry's main tasks is to advise the Members on procedural matters and raise any procedural issues relating to a case with the President, especially so in a Member State where judicial office is open only to the most senior members of the legal community. In fact, the role of the Registry in this regard has changed over the years and has become more prominent recently. As so often when it comes to the European Union, the cause for this is the enlargement and the subsequent increase in Judges and Advocates General as well as the ever-growing resulting caseload.

More judges require more chambers to which the judges can be assigned. At present, the Court's judges are assigned to five Chambers of Five Judges and five Chambers of Three Judges, which accordingly are headed by ten different Presidents

[58] Cf. Article 53(2), Articles 54 to Article 56 and Article 80a, Rules of Procedure.

[59] Cf. Article 159, Rules of Procedure.

[60] This is often the case where a Member States provides information on recent developments concerning the transposition of EU law and where the Commission consequently amends its head of claim. See, e.g., judgments in *Commission v Ireland (European Electronic Communications Code)*, C-439/22, EU:C:2024:229, paras. 15 et seqq.; and in *Commission v United Kingdom (Fiscal marking of gas oil)*, C-692/20, EU:C:2023:707, para. 27.

of Chamber who are susceptible to take procedural decisions,[61] in addition to the President and the Vice President. This can lead to important divergences in procedural decisions. To take a simple example, requests by the parties to postpone a hearing may be treated in a very different manner in different cases. While the President as the head of the Grand Chamber will almost always deny such a request, the Presidents of Chamber might not be that strict. The starkest contrasts in this respect could be seen during the Covid-19 health crisis. Once the Court resumed its activity in May 2020, no hearings of the Grand Chamber were postponed, not even when a party's representative fell sick him- or herself and could not attend the hearing. On the other hand, hearings organised by smaller chambers were more frequently postponed, once even because a Commission agent did not want to expose his pregnant wife to the risk of catching Covid due to his journey to Luxembourg.

While at first glance this might seem unfair, the divergence in decisions can be explained by objectively different circumstances. For a hearing before the Grand Chamber, 15 judges need to be available and, as it tends to hear the more complex cases,[62] they usually involve participation of numerous parties and Member States. As Member States may use their own language for the oral submissions before the Court,[63] interpreters need to be present at the hearing. While the Court has some interpreters among its own staff, they cannot always cover all languages required for a hearing, especially when a hearing is set to last many hours. In that case, freelance interpreters or interpreters from other institutions need to be booked. Once this is done, the Court needs to pay for their travel to Luxembourg and the work contracted, unless the booking is cancelled at least 21 days before the hearing. To postpone a hearing of the Grand Chamber thus will have much more dire consequences for the duration of the proceedings (as it is often difficult to find a new date) and the budget of the Court than a hearing organised by a Chamber of Three Judges. In order to ensure that like cases are treated alike, the Registry provides recommendations as well as additional information relevant for the procedural decision to be taken[64] when presenting a request for postponement of a hearing.

The recommendations are based first and foremost on the procedural legal framework of the Court. However, they are adapted over time and oriented according to the decisional practice. In order to ensure a harmonised approach to procedural decisions, the Deputy Registrar organises bi-weekly meetings of the Registry's administrators where (unusual) procedural decisions are discussed as well as difficult cases analysed before procedural recommendations are proposed. Due to the

[61] As a general rule, the President of the Court is in charge of procedural decisions until a case is assigned to the chamber that will render the final decision. Once the case is assigned, it is the President of chamber who takes all procedural decisions related to a case.

[62] Save for assignments to the Grand Chamber due to Article 16, 3rd alinéa, of the Statute "The Court shall sit in a Grand Chamber when a Member State or an institution of the Union that is party to the proceedings so requests."

[63] Article 38(4), Rules of Procedure.

[64] Such as the fact that bookings for interpreters cannot be cancelled anymore or the number of parties who have announced their presence at the hearing

ever-growing caseload, Judges and Advocates General are more and more appreciative of the Registry's recommendations and consequently follow them. In recent years, they do not only need to handle a much more important portfolio of cases in volume, but also in complexity.[65] Often judges spend three mornings per week in hearings and at least three afternoons in deliberations. Consequently, not much time remains in order to study all the case files and draft texts. In a rather pragmatic manner, this has led to an increased "outsourcing" of procedural expertise to the Registry, under the authority of the President, as the Rules of Procedure so aptly proscribe.[66]

5 Conclusion

I hope that the examples presented show that, while the Court at times acts more positivist and at times more pragmatic, it never acts arbitrarily. Procedural decisions aim to not unduly burden the parties while ensuring equal treatment and legal certainty. At the same time, they take procedural economy and duration of proceedings into account in order to best serve the European people in adjudicating the cases brought before the Court. The Registry seeks to serve both the external and internal actors implicated in those cases as best as it can, while first and foremost guarding the Rules of Procedure.

[65] See Report submitted pursuant to Article 3(2) of Regulation (EU, Euratom) 2015/2422 of the European Parliament and of the Council amending Protocol No 3 on the Statute of the Court of Justice of the European Union, p. 1 (available at curia.europa.eu > Court of Justice > Procedure > Other useful information).

[66] Cf. Article 20, Rules of Procedure.

De la représentation devant la Cour de justice et le Tribunal. À propos de quelques décisions récentes

Marie Meister

1 Introduction

Les conditions relatives à la représentation des personnes physiques et morales dans le cadre des recours directs devant la Cour de justice et le Tribunal, c'est-à-dire des recours par lesquels ces personnes peuvent saisir directement ces juridictions, font, de prime abord, figure de parent pauvre du contentieux. Ces conditions, qui ont trait à la recevabilité de tels recours, ont, semble-t-il, suscité moins de difficultés et donné lieu à moins d'arrêts que d'autres conditions de recevabilité des recours directs introduits par les personnes physiques et morales. Ainsi, pour ne citer qu'un exemple, les conditions figurant à l'article 263, quatrième, alinéa, du Traité sur le fonctionnement de l'Union européenne (TFUE) en ce qui concerne le recours en annulation, ont fait l'objet d'une jurisprudence pléthorique et de très nombreuses réflexions doctrinales. Les conditions relatives à la représentation des personnes physiques et morales dans le cadre des recours directs devant la Cour de justice et le Tribunal n'en sont, pourtant, pas moins importantes dès lors qu'elles peuvent affecter l'effectivité de l'accès au juge et, également, la qualité du débat devant la Cour et le Tribunal.

Pour rappel, l'article 19 du statut de la Cour de justice de l'Union européenne (ci-après le « statut de la Cour »), applicable au Tribunal conformément à l'article 53, premier alinéa, de ce statut, prévoit, d'une part, que les parties autres que les États membres, les institutions de l'Union, les États parties à l'accord sur l'Espace économique européen ainsi que l'Autorité de surveillance AELE doivent être représentées par un avocat et, d'autre part, que seul un avocat habilité à exercer devant une juridiction d'un État membre ou d'un autre État partie à l'accord sur

M. Meister (✉)
Court of Justice of the European Union, Luxembourg, Luxembourg
e-mail: Marie.Meister@curia.europa.eu

L. Prete, L. Rezki (eds.), *Judging & (Re)Thinking European Union Law*,
https://doi.org/10.1007/978-3-032-13473-8_23

l'Espace économique européen peut représenter ou assister une partie devant la Cour.

À ces dispositions du statut de la Cour, il faut, pour comprendre les conditions auxquelles est soumise la représentation des personnes physiques et morales dans le cadre des recours directs, ajouter celles des règlements de procédure. Il découle de l'article 119 du règlement de procédure de la Cour, relatif à la représentation des parties dans le cadre des recours directs, que les personnes physiques et morales ne peuvent être représentées que par leur avocat, que ceux-ci sont tenus de déposer au greffe un mandat délivré par la partie qu'ils représentent et que tout avocat est tenu de déposer au greffe un document de légitimation certifiant qu'il est habilité à exercer devant une juridiction d'un État membre ou d'un autre État partie à l'accord EEE. Les dispositions de l'article 51 du règlement de procédure du Tribunal sont, en substance, identiques à celles du règlement de procédure de la Cour.

De prime abord, ces dispositions semblent plutôt élémentaires de sorte que leur interprétation ne soulèverait pas de difficulté. En effet, on pourrait en déduire que les personnes physiques et morales doivent être représentées par un avocat et que, dans ce contexte, sont considérés comme des avocats, les personnes habilitées par les États membres et définies uniquement par le droit des États membres. De la même manière, on pourrait inférer de ces dispositions que la seule production d'un mandat, quel qu'il soit, suffit pour satisfaire aux exigences procédurales des règlements de procédure.

Et pourtant, tout observateur attentif de la jurisprudence récente de la Cour de justice, même sans être un « aficionado » de la procédure propre aux juridictions de l'Union européenne,[1] n'aura pas manqué de relever que la Cour a récemment rendu plusieurs décisions abordant la question, plutôt technique, de la représentation des personnes physiques et morales dans le cadre des recours directs devant la Cour et le Tribunal. Sans prétendre à l'exhaustivité, on peut se référer à cet égard à des décisions de la Grande chambre de la Cour,[2] de chambres composées de cinq juges,[3] de

[1] Pour reprendre les termes de l'avocat général Bobek dans ses conclusions dans les affaires jointes Uniwersytet Wrocławski et Pologne/REA (C-515/17 P et C-561/17 P, EU:C:2019:774, point 2).

[2] Arrêts du 5 novembre 2019, BCE e.a./Trasta Komercbanka e.a. (C-663/17 P, C-665/17 P et C-669/17 P, EU:C:2019:923, ci-après l'« arrêt Trasta »), ainsi que du 4 février 2020, Uniwersytet Wrocławski et Pologne/REA (C-515/17 P et C-561/17 P, EU:C:2020:73, ci-après l'« arrêt Uniwersytet Wrocławski »). On peut également se référer à d'autres arrêts plus anciens tels que l'arrêt du 18 janvier 2007, PKK et KNK/Conseil (C-229/05 P, EU:C:2007:32).

[3] Arrêts du 24 mars 2022, PJ et PC/EUIPO (C-529/18 P et C-531/18 P, EU:C:2022:218, ci-après l'« arrêt PJ et PC ») ; du 14 juillet 2022, Universität Bremen/REA (C-110/21 P, EU:C:2022:555) ; du 21 septembre 2023, China Chamber of Commerce for Import and Export of Machinery and Electronic Products e.a./Commission (C-478/21 P, EU:C:2023:685) ; du 8 février 2024, Pilatus Bank/BCE (C-750/21 P, EU:C:2024:124), et du 8 février 2024, Pilatus Bank/BCE (C-256/22 P, EU:C:2024:125), ainsi que l'ordonnance du 15 février 2023, Fundacja Instytut na rzecz Kultury Prawnej Ordo Iuris/Parlement (C-546/21 P, non publiée, EU:C:2023:123).

chambres composées de trois juges,[4] de la chambre d'admission des pourvois,[5] mais également à des décisions du Tribunal.[6]

Il ne faut toutefois pas se méprendre, ce n'est pas tant le nombre de décisions rendues qui interpelle, mais leur apport important à la jurisprudence. Il ressort de la lecture de ces décisions de la Cour et du Tribunal qu'elles portent principalement sur deux questions. D'une part, certaines desdites décisions concernent la question de savoir ce qu'est un « avocat habilité à exercer devant une juridiction d'un État membre », au sens de l'article 19 du statut de la Cour. D'autre part, certaines décisions portent sur la représentation à l'instance et la régularité des mandats ad litem.

Afin d'appréhender la portée de la jurisprudence récente s'agissant de ces deux questions ainsi que les raisons pour lesquelles une clarification ou une évolution de la jurisprudence par la Cour se sont avérées nécessaires, ces deux questions seront successivement abordées.

2 La notion d'« avocat habilité à exercer devant une juridiction d'un État membre » au sens de l'article 19 du statut de la Cour

La Cour et le Tribunal ont de longue date interprété la notion d'« avocat habilité à exercer devant une juridiction d'un État membre », au sens de l'article 19 du statut de la Cour. Cette interprétation a récemment été « revisitée » par l'arrêt Uniwersytet Wrocławski. Des décisions rendues postérieurement sont, en outre, venues, d'une part, apporter des précisions supplémentaires quant aux contours de cette notion et, d'autre part, indiquer les éventuelles conséquences de l'absence d'indépendance d'un avocat quant à la recevabilité du recours.

[4] Arrêts du 15 septembre 2022, PNB Banka/BCE (C-326/21 P, non publié, EU:C:2022:693), et du 30 janvier 2024, bonnanwalt/EUIPO (C-580/22 P, non publié, EU:C:2024:101), ainsi que les ordonnances du 21 avril 2023, Kirimova/EUIPO (C-306/22 P, non publiée, EU:C:2023:338) et du 3 juin 2024, Trasta Komercbanka/BCE (C-103/23 P, non publiée, EU:C:2024:483).

[5] Ordonnances du 30 janvier 2023, bonnanwalt/EUIPO (C-580/22 P, EU:C:2023:126) et du 8 mai 2023, Studio Legale Ughi e Nunziante/EUIPO (C-776/22 P, EU:C:2023:441).

[6] On pourrait citer de très nombreux arrêts à cet égard. Ainsi, une recherche sur le site Curia montre que sur les cinq dernières années, près de 38 arrêts et ordonnances font mention de l'article 19 du statut de la Cour.

2.1 Les précisions apportées par l'arrêt Uniwersytet Wrocławski

Cet arrêt, rendu en formation de grande chambre sur demande de la Pologne,[7] a constitué une occasion parfaite, pour la Cour, de se pencher, comme l'y invitait l'avocat général Bobek, sur la jurisprudence antérieure relative à l'article 19, troisième alinéa du statut de la Cour, et, en particulier, à la notion d'« avocat » au sens de cette disposition.

Pour mémoire, la Cour était saisie de pourvois de l'Uniwersytet Wrocławski et la République de République de Pologne contre l'ordonnance du Tribunal de l'Union européenne du 13 juin 2017, Uniwersytet Wrocławski/REA (T-137/16, non publiée, EU:T:2017:407), par laquelle celui-ci avait jugé irrecevable, pour défaut d'indépendance du représentant de l'université de Wroclaw, un recours de cette université tendant, d'une part, à l'annulation de décisions de l'Agence exécutive pour la recherche et, d'autre part, à la restitution par cette agence de certaines sommes. Ce représentant avait la qualité d'avocat au sens du droit polonais et il exerçait dans un cabinet. Toutefois, il donnait également des cours à l'université de Wrocław, en tant qu'enseignant extérieur et avait conclu, dans ce cadre, un contrat de droit civil avec cette université. Le Tribunal avait estimé que, en raison de ce contrat, le représentant de l'université de Wrocław n'était pas indépendant et ne satisfaisait pas à l'exigence d'indépendance découlant de notion d'« avocat » au sens du statut de la Cour.

Au regard du libellé l'article 19, troisième alinéa, du statut de la Cour et de l'absence de référence quelconque à l'indépendance de l'avocat représentant une personne physique ou morale, une telle appréciation ne manque pas de surprendre. Elle s'inscrit pourtant dans la continuité de la jurisprudence de la Cour. En effet, ainsi que l'a mis en évidence l'avocat général Bobek dans ses conclusions, si la Cour avait considéré que la notion d'« avocat » au sens de l'article 19, troisième alinéa, du statut de la Cour est une notion autonome du droit de l'Union, elle avait interprété cette notion en se fondant sur sa jurisprudence relative au *legal privilege* en droit de la concurrence. C'est ainsi que l'indépendance est devenue le trait caractéristique et principal de l'avocat au sens de cette disposition.

Alors que l'avocat général avait mis en exergue tous les écueils engendrés par l'exigence d'indépendance découlant de la notion d'« avocat » au sens du statut de la Cour et l'avait invitée à changer de critère d'interprétation de ladite disposition, celle-ci a, plus modestement, précisé, dans l'arrêt Uniwersytet Wrocławski, comment apprécier si un représentant en justice remplit le devoir d'indépendance. Ainsi, après avoir rappelé que la notion d'indépendance de l'avocat, dans le contexte spécifique de l'article 19 du statut de la Cour, se définit non seulement de manière négative, c'est-à-dire par l'absence d'un rapport d'emploi, mais également de

[7] Voir, à cet égard, le quatrième chef de conclusions de la Pologne. Pour rappel, l'article 16, troisième alinéa du statut de la Cour prévoit que la Cour siège en grande chambre lorsqu'un État membre ou une institution de l'Union qui est partie à l'instance le demande.

manière positive, à savoir par une référence à la discipline professionnelle, la Cour a indiqué que « le devoir d'indépendance incombant à l'avocat s'entend comme l'absence non pas de tout lien quelconque avec son client, mais de liens qui portent manifestement atteinte à sa capacité à assurer sa mission de défense en servant au mieux les intérêts de son client ».[8]

Une telle interprétation qui s'inscrit dans le prolongement de la jurisprudence antérieure permet de préserver la continuité de la jurisprudence et assure, par conséquent, une certaine stabilité. Toutefois, l'exigence d'indépendance découlant de la notion d'« avocat » ainsi interprétée implique une certaine casuistique. En effet, le manque manifeste d'indépendance doit être vérifié au cas par cas en fonction des configurations factuelles et juridiques de la relation entre la représenté et la représentant. Si une telle méthode garantit indéniablement l'individualisation de l'appréciation, elle génère nécessairement une certaine imprévisibilité dans l'application de la règle et, partant, une certaine insécurité juridique qui peut être critiquée.[9] Enfin, la jurisprudence postérieure à l'arrêt Uniwersytet Wrocławski semble confirmer que, depuis cet arrêt, l'indépendance des avocats est, en quelque sorte, présumée, mais que, en cas de manque manifeste d'indépendance, une telle présomption peut être renversée.

2.2 *Les clarifications apportées par la jurisprudence postérieure à l'arrêt Uniwersytet Wrocławski*

Comme souligné en introduction, la jurisprudence récente relative aux conditions de représentation des personnes physiques et morales dans le cadre des recours directs devant la Cour de justice et le Tribunal frappe par son contenu et la quantité de décisions rendues. Ainsi, l'arrêt Uniwersytet Wrocławski n'est pas isolé et, dans la foulée de cet arrêt, la Cour a apporté d'autres clarifications quant à l'appréciation de l'indépendance au sens de de l'article 19 du statut de la Cour.

Ainsi, en faisant application des critères précisés dans ledit arrêt, la Cour a jugé que l'avocat représentant un demandeur ne peut pas être membre du cabinet d'avocats dans lequel ce demandeur est coassocié et dont il est membre fondateur. Une telle appréciation est intervenue aux termes d'un raisonnement particulièrement dense dans lequel la Cour a explicité la raison d'être de la jurisprudence au regard de l'objectif de la mission de représentation par un avocat et a clairement indiqué que les hypothèses d'irrecevabilité en raison d'une défaillance dans la mission de représentation doivent être limitées. Ainsi, selon la Cour, de telles hypothèses sont celles « où il apparaît manifestement que l'avocat n'est pas en mesure d'assurer

[8] Arrêt Uniwersytet Wrocławski, point 64.

[9] À cet égard, l'arrêt de la Cour peut faire l'objet des mêmes critiques que celles formulées à l'encontre de la jurisprudence antérieure par l'avocat général Bobek au point 63 des conclusions.

sa mission de défense en servant au mieux les intérêts de son client, de sorte qu'il doit être écarté dans l'intérêt de ce dernier ».[10]

S'agissant de la situation d'espèce, la Cour a estimé qu'un avocat collaborateur dans un cabinet est présumé satisfaire aux exigences d'indépendance au sens de l'article 19 du statut de la Cour, et ce même s'il exerce ses fonctions dans le cadre d'un contrat de travail ou dans le cadre d'une autre relation subordonnée. Toutefois, elle a ajouté que, pour apprécier l'indépendance, il convient d'opérer une distinction « en fonction de la situation du client représenté ».[11] Or, si la personne représentée est coassociée et membre fondateur du cabinet d'avocats et peut, de ce fait, exercer un contrôle effectif sur le collaborateur, alors les liens existant entre l'avocat collaborateur et l'associé représenté sont tels qu'ils portent manifestement atteinte à l'indépendance de l'avocat.

De façon plus spécifique, la Cour a, dans la lignée des arrêts précédents, décidé qu'un professeur d'université lié à une université par une relation statutaire de droit public, en dehors de tout lien de subordination, est indépendant et est autorisé à représenter cette université devant les juridictions de l'Union.[12]

La jurisprudence postérieure à l'arrêt Uniwersytet Wrocławski a également adressé les critiques formulées par l'avocat général Bobek dans ses conclusions dans cet arrêt, et réitérées quelque temps plus tard par l'avocat général Emiliou dans ses conclusions dans l'affaire Universität Bremen/REA (C-110/21 P, EU:C:2022:133), s'agissant de l'impossibilité de procéder à la régularisation d'un recours en cas de non-respect des exigences relatives à l'indépendance du représentant au sens de l'article 19, troisième alinéa, du statut de la Cour.

Les règlements de procédure de la Cour ou du Tribunal prévoient diverses possibilités de régulariser certains vices affectant les requêtes ou les mémoires des parties. En particulier, l'article 51, paragraphe 4, du règlement de procédure du Tribunal prévoit que « si le document visé au paragraphe 2 [document certifiant que l'avocat est habilité à exercer devant une juridiction d'un État membre ou d'un autre État partie à l'accord EEE] ou celui visé au paragraphe 3 [mandat délivré par la personne morale de droit privé représentée] n'est pas déposé, le greffier fixe à la partie concernée un délai raisonnable pour les produire. À défaut de cette production dans le délai imparti, le Tribunal décide si l'inobservation de la formalité en cause entraîne l'irrecevabilité formelle de la requête ou du mémoire ou si elle conduit à considérer que l'avocat ne représente pas ou n'assiste pas la partie concernée ». Il convient, toutefois, de relever que le non-respect de l'obligation de représentation par un avocat habilité à exercer devant une juridiction d'un État membre ou d'un autre État partie à l'accord sur l'Espace économique européen ne figure pas expressément parmi les exigences susceptibles de faire l'objet d'une régularisation de sorte que le Tribunal considérait qu'il s'agissait d'un vice qui ne pouvait être régularisé et qui entraînait le rejet du recours pour irrecevabilité.

---

[10] Arrêt PJ et PC, point 74.

[11] Arrêt PJ et PC, point 80.

[12] Arrêt du 14 juillet 2022, Universität Bremen/REA (C-110/21 P, EU:C:2022:555).

En dépit des vives critiques de l'avocat général Bobek,[13] dans l'arrêt PJ et PC, la Cour a, à nouveau,[14] validé cette approche du Tribunal et rappelé que le non-respect de l'obligation de représentation par un avocat habilité à exercer devant une juridiction d'un État membre ou d'un autre État partie à l'accord sur l'Espace économique européen ne figure pas au nombre des exigences susceptibles de faire l'objet d'une régularisation après l'expiration du délai de recours. Elle a ajouté qu'aucune disposition du règlement de procédure du Tribunal ou du statut de la Cour n'oblige le Tribunal ou la Cour à avertir l'auteur d'un recours ni de le mettre en mesure de procéder à la désignation d'un nouveau représentant en cours de procédure.

Il faut convenir que les critiques des avocats généraux concernant l'impossibilité de régularisation du recours en cas de non-respect des exigences relatives à l'indépendance du représentant au sens de l'article 19, troisième alinéa, du statut de la Cour ne manquaient pas d'assise. En particulier, dès lors que ces exigences ne sont pas explicitement établies dans ce statut, il peut sembler disproportionné de ne pas en permettre la régularisation et d'en sanctionner automatiquement le manquement par l'irrecevabilité du recours. Dans ce contexte, la conciliation entre l'absence de possibilité de régulariser et l'exigence de l'article 47, premier alinéa, de la Charte, n'était pas évidente. Force est toutefois de constater que la position réitérée par la Cour trouvait un appui solide dans le texte du règlement de procédure du Tribunal de sorte qu'il est difficile de reprocher à la Cour d'avoir fait preuve en la matière d'un formalisme excessif alors qu'elle appliquait à la lettre certaines dispositions de ce règlement de procédure. Dans ces conditions, seule la modification dudit règlement de procédure semblait pouvoir permettre, après la réflexion qu'une telle démarche implique, que soit prévue et autorisée la régularisation en cas de non-respect des exigences relatives à l'indépendance du représentant au sens de l'article 19, troisième alinéa, du statut de la Cour.

On pouvait raisonnablement penser, au regard de ces arrêts et de deux ordonnances de la Cour,[15] que la jurisprudence quant à la notion d'« avocat » au sens de l'article 19, troisième alinéa, du statut de la Cour était, pour ainsi dire, « stabilisée ». En effet, ces deux ordonnances étaient fondées sur l'article 182 du règlement de procédure de la Cour. Or, selon cette disposition, la Cour ne peut déclarer un pourvoi manifestement fondé que si elle a déjà statué sur une ou plusieurs questions de droit identiques à celles soulevées par les moyens du pourvoi, principal ou incident. Ainsi, en ayant recours à une telle base juridique, la Cour indiquait avoir déjà statué

[13] L'arrêt PJ et PC a été rendu le 14 mars 2022 alors que les conclusions de l'avocat général Emiliou dans l'affaire Universität Bremen/REA (C-110/21 P, EU:C:2022:133) ont été lues le 24 février 2022.

[14] Il convient de rappeler sur ce point que, dans l'ordonnance du 5 septembre 2013, ClientEarth/Conseil (C-573/11 P, non publiée, EU:C:2013:564), la Cour avait souligné le caractère exhaustif des conditions énumérées à l'article 44, paragraphes 3 à 5, du règlement de procédure du Tribunal du 2 mai 1991 applicable dans cette affaire, qui peuvent faire l'objet d'une régularisation en vertu du paragraphe 6 du même article, parmi lesquelles ne figurait pas la désignation d'un nouvel avocat.

[15] Ordonnances du 15 février 2023, Fundacja Instytut na rzecz Kultury Prawnej Ordo Iuris/Parlement (C-546/21 P, non publiée, EU:C:2023:123), et du 21 avril 2023, Kirimova/EUIPO (C-306/22 P, non publiée, EU:C:2023:338).

sur l'interprétation de la notion d'« avocat » au sens de l'article 19, troisième alinéa, du statut de la Cour et semblait donner un signal clair quant à la portée de cette interprétation.

Toutefois, par la suite, la Cour a partiellement admis un pourvoi dans lequel étaient soulevées, d'une part, une mauvaise application de la jurisprudence de la Cour relative à l'application de l'article 19, troisième alinéa, du statut de la Cour et, d'autre part, la violation des articles 47 et 52 de la Charte ainsi que la violation de l'article 51, paragraphe 4, et de l'article 55, paragraphe 1, du règlement de procédure du Tribunal, en ce que celui-ci n'aurait pas permis la régularisation du recours.[16]

Certes, on sait, depuis l'ordonnance du 30 janvier 2023, bonnanwalt/EUIPO (C-580/22 P, EU:C:2023:126), que de telles questions juridiques sont importantes pour l'unité, la cohérence et le développement du droit de l'Union au sens de l'article 58 bis, troisième alinéa, de ce statut de la Cour et qu'elles peuvent, par conséquent, justifier l'admission d'un pourvoi sans pour autant donner lieu à des évolutions jurisprudentielles majeures.[17] Toutefois, l'affaire Studio Legale Ughi e Nunziante/EUIPO (C-776/22 P) a été attribuée à la Grande chambre et la Cour a apporté d'importantes précisions. Ainsi, elle a jugé que le Tribunal avait commis une erreur de droit en rejetant comme manifestement irrecevable, pour incompatibilité avec les exigences d'indépendance de l'article 19 du statut de la Cour, le recours d'un cabinet d'avocats représenté par trois avocats exerçant, en qualité d'associés, leur activité au sein de ce cabinet. En outre, selon la Cour, avant de déclarer le recours irrecevable, le Tribunal aurait dû, d'une part, vérifier l'existence d'un rapport d'emploi ou d'éléments concrets portant manifestement atteinte à la capacité de ces trois avocats à assurer leur mission et, d'autre part, inviter ce cabinet d'avocats à présenter ses observations. Enfin, la Cour a estimé que ni le statut de la Cour ni les dispositions du règlement de procédure du Tribunal ne s'opposaient, en l'espèce, à la régularisation du recours de sorte que, compte tenu de la gravité et du caractère irrémédiable de la déclaration d'irrecevabilité de son recours, la cabinet d'avocats requérant devait être en mesure de régulariser son recours et de désigner un nouvel avocat.[18]

S'agissant de la seconde problématique relative à la représentation des personnes de droit privé devant la Cour et le Tribunal, à savoir la représentation à l'instance et la régularité des mandats ad litem, la jurisprudence récente a apporté de nombreuses et importantes précisions, sans pour autant avoir épuisé la question.

[16] Ordonnance du 8 mai 2023, Studio Legale Ughi e Nunziante/EUIPO (C-776/22 P, EU:C:2023:441).

[17] Voir l'arrêt du 30 janvier 2024, bonnanwalt/EUIPO (C-580/22 P, non publié, EU:C:2024:101).

[18] Arrêt du 4 septembre 2025, Studio Legale Ughi e Nunziante/EUIPO (C-776/22 P, EU:C:2025:644).

3 La représentation à l'instance et la régularité des mandats ad litem

S'agissant de la représentation devant les juridictions de l'Union et de la question de la régularité des mandats ad litem, deux évolutions distinctes, mais intrinsèquement liées, ont marqué la jurisprudence récente. Il s'agit, d'une part, des conditions auxquelles est soumise la vérification de la régularité du mandat ad litem par la Cour et le Tribunal et, d'autre part, de la possibilité d'écarter les règles nationales désignant la personne habilitée à délivrer un mandat pour la représentation ad litem d'une personne morale de droit privé en vue de permettre à cette dernière d'introduire un recours devant la Cour ou le Tribunal.

3.1 Les conditions auxquelles la vérification de la régularité des mandats ad litem est soumise

Dès lors que les personnes morales de droit privé ne sont pas en mesure d'accomplir elles-mêmes les actes de procédure afférents à toute procédure contentieuse, elles doivent être représentées. À cet égard, les règlements de procédure de la Cour puis du Tribunal ont connu une évolution notable. Ainsi, à l'occasion de la réforme du règlement de procédure de la Cour en 2012, l'obligation pour les avocats de fournir la preuve de la régularité du mandat ad litem en vertu duquel ils représentent les personnes morales de droit privé a été supprimée. Concrètement l'article 44, paragraphe 1, sous b), et l'article 119, paragraphe 2, du règlement de procédure de la Cour exigent uniquement des avocats, lorsque la partie qu'ils représentent est une personne morale de droit privé, qu'ils déposent au greffe un mandat délivré par cette dernière.[19] Le règlement de procédure du Tribunal a évolué de la même manière à l'occasion de la réforme d'ampleur de 2015.

Il est aisé de comprendre que la vérification de chaque mandat des personnes morales de droit privé était une tâche chronophage, fastidieuse et coûteuse tant pour les parties que pour les greffes. En effet, dès lors qu'il n'y a pas, en droit de l'Union, de dispositions régissant la représentation des personnes morales, il est fait application de la lex incorporationis c'est-à-dire de la loi de l'État dans lequel une société est constituée, pour déterminer la personne ou l'organe autorisé à décider de la représentation d'une personne morale.[20] Par conséquent, la vérification de la régularité d'un mandat ad litem suppose, d'une part, de déterminer la personne ou l'organe qui, selon le droit applicable à une personne morale, est compétent pour

[19] Alors que l'article 38, paragraphe 5, sous b), du Règlement de procédure du 19 juin 1991 faisait obligation aux personnes morales de droit privé de joindre à leur requête « la preuve que le mandat donné à l'avocat a été régulièrement établi par un représentant qualifié à cet effet. »

[20] Arrêt Trasta point 58.

délivrer un mandat de représentation et, d'autre part, d'examiner dans chaque cas si ces règles nationales ont été respectées.

La circonstance que les règlements de procédure de la Cour et du Tribunal n'exigent plus que soit fournie la preuve que le mandat donné à l'avocat représentant une personne morale de droit privé a été régulièrement établi par un représentant qualifié à cet effet signifie-t-elle que la régularité d'un tel mandat ne fait l'objet d'aucun contrôle et qu'elle ne peut plus être contestée en cours d'instance ?

À cet égard, la jurisprudence a, dans un premier temps, été plutôt fluctuante.

Dans certaines affaires, le Tribunal a examiné et rejeté les arguments avancés aux fins de démontrer l'absence de régularité du mandat[21] tout en soulignant que l'article 51, paragraphe 3, de son règlement de procédure, à la différence de l'article 44, paragraphe 5, sous b), du règlement de procédure du Tribunal du 2 mai 1991, n'exige plus la preuve que le mandat donné à l'avocat ait été établi par un représentant qualifié à cet effet. En particulier, dans l'arrêt du 24 novembre 2021, LTTE/Conseil (T-160/19, non publié, EU:T:2021:817), le Tribunal a vérifié minutieusement la régularité du mandat afin de rejeter les arguments du Conseil selon lesquels, en substance, le signataire du mandat ne représentait pas et n'avait jamais représenté la partie requérante. Cela étant, le Tribunal avait tout d'abord rappelé que son règlement de procédure devait être interprété en ce sens qu'il n'exigeait plus la preuve que le mandat donné à l'avocat a été régulièrement établi par un représentant qualifié à cet effet.

Toutefois, on peut comprendre à la lecture d'autres décisions du Tribunal que, du fait des modifications apportées à son règlement de procédure, la régularité des mandats ad litem ne peut plus être contestée ni contrôlée. Dans ce cas, le Tribunal fait observer que son règlement de procédure n'exige plus la preuve que le mandat donné à l'avocat ait été régulièrement établi par un représentant qualifié à cet effet, mais exige simplement qu'un mandat soit fourni.[22]

Enfin, le Tribunal a pu adopter une autre position en permettant à une partie de régulariser un mandat qui n'avait pas été établi par une personne compétente à cet effet.[23]

La jurisprudence du Tribunal pose deux problèmes majeurs.

---

[21] Arrêts du 28 septembre 2016, European Food/EUIPO – Société des produits Nestlé (FITNESS) (T-476/15, EU:T:2016:568, points 16 à 20), ainsi que du 17 février 2017, Batmore Capital/EUIPO – Univers Poche (POCKETBOOK) (T-596/15, EU:T:2017:103, points 18 à 22).

[22] Arrêt du 19 décembre 2019, Amigüitos pets & life/EUIPO – Société des produits Nestlé (THE ONLY ONE by alphaspirit wild and perfect) (T-40/19, non publié, EU:T:2019:890, point 14), ainsi que du 19 mai 2021, China Chamber of Commerce for Import and Export of Machinery and Electronic Products e.a./Commission (T-254/18, EU:T:2021:278, points 133 à 136). Dans les arrêts du 7 décembre 2022, PNB Banka/BCE (T-275/19, EU:T:2022:781, points 59 à 63) ; du 7 décembre 2022, PNB Banka/BCE (T-301/19, EU:T:2022:774, points 47 à 51), ainsi que du 7 décembre 2022, PNB Banka/BCE (T-330/19, EU:T:2022:775, points 62 à 66), le Tribunal a d'office vérifié l'existence du mandat de l'avocat et son absence de révocation par l'administrateur judiciaire de la société requérante sans pour autant en vérifier la régularité.

[23] Arrêt du 13 décembre 2017, Crédit mutuel Arkéa/BCE (T-52/16, EU:T:2017:902).

En raison des divergences soulignées, la jurisprudence est imprévisible et porte atteinte au principe de sécurité juridique ainsi qu'au principe d'égalité de traitement. Surtout, et plus fondamentalement, l'absence de contrôle de la régularité du mandat ne permet pas que soit correctement établie la volonté de la personne morale d'introduire un recours et d'être représentée. Or, ainsi que la Cour l'a indiqué, « pour qu'un tel recours soit recevable, il est nécessaire de démontrer que la personne concernée a réellement pris la décision d'introduire le recours et que les avocats qui prétendent la représenter ont effectivement été mandatés à cette fin » et c'est pour cette raison que la production d'un mandat est obligatoire.[24] Comme l'avocate générale Kokott l'a souligné avec force au regard d'un pourvoi, mais le constat est le même pour tout autre recours direct, « un pourvoi introduit sans avoir de mandat est frappé d'un vice autrement plus grave que celui du simple défaut de qualité pour agir ».[25]

En ce qui concerne les personnes morales de droit privé, la question de savoir si une telle personne a réellement pris la décision d'introduire un recours et si l'avocat qui prétend la représenter a effectivement été mandaté à cette fin suppose de déterminer non seulement si un mandat ad litem a été joint à la requête, mais également si un tel mandat a été régulièrement établi et, plus précisément, s'il a été établi par une personne ou un organe de la personne morale compétent à cet effet. Dans ces conditions, on peut inférer de l'obligation faite aux avocats, à l'article 119, paragraphe 2, du règlement de procédure de la Cour et à l'article 51, paragraphe 3, du règlement de procédure du Tribunal, de déposer un mandat de la partie qu'ils représentent que la question de savoir si la personne concernée a réellement pris la décision d'introduire le recours ne peut être éludée.

Pour le dire autrement, la suppression de l'exigence de fournir la preuve de la régularité du mandat ne signifie pas que ce dernier ne doit pas être régulier. Si le mandat doit avoir été régulièrement établi alors il peut être nécessaire, dans certains cas, de vérifier que tel est le cas. Ainsi que l'a souligné l'avocate générale Medina dans ses conclusions dans l'affaire China Chamber of Commerce for Import and Export of Machinery and Electronic Products e.a./Commission (C-478/21 P, EU:C:2023:117), « l'assouplissement des règles de procédure au stade de l'*introduction* d'un recours en annulation est sans incidence sur l'exigence *matérielle* susmentionnée relative à la représentation des requérants par leurs avocats prévue à l'article 19 du statut de la Cour de justice de l'Union européenne, qui est une norme de rang supérieur à ce règlement de procédure ».[26]

Au regard de ces éléments, il n'est pas étonnant, et il est même salutaire, que la Cour ait réaffirmé l'obligation de procéder à une telle vérification soit à la demande d'une partie soit d'office.

---

[24] Arrêt Trasta point 57.

[25] Conclusions de l'avocate générale Kokott dans l'affaire Commune de Millau et SEMEA/Commission (C-531/12 P, EU:C:2014:1946, point 39).

[26] Conclusions de l'avocate générale Medina dans l'affaire China Chamber of Commerce for Import and Export of Machinery and Electronic Products e.a./Commission (C-478/21 P, EU:C:2023:117, point 119).

Ainsi, dans un premier temps, la Cour a jugé que le fait que le règlement de procédure du Tribunal n'exigeait pas la preuve que le mandat donné à un avocat ait été établi par un représentant qualifié à cet effet « ne dispense cependant pas le Tribunal de vérifier la régularité du mandat concerné en cas de contestation » puisqu'une telle circonstance « n'affecte pas l'obligation, pour cette partie, d'avoir régulièrement mandaté son avocat afin de pouvoir agir en justice ». Par conséquent, si la régularité du mandat conféré par une partie à son avocat est contestée alors cette partie doit démontrer la régularité de ce mandat.[27]

Dans un second temps, la Cour a étendu cette obligation et a jugé que, lorsqu'un tel mandat est « manifestement irrégulier ou en présence d'éléments susceptibles de mettre sérieusement en doute la régularité d'un tel mandat »,[28] il doit être procédé d'office à la vérification de la régularité du mandat. Au nombre de tels éléments susceptibles de mettre sérieusement en doute la régularité d'un mandat de représentation figure l'argumentation de la partie représentée selon laquelle sa représentation n'est pas effective faute pour son représentant de pouvoir accéder à ses locaux ou à ses ressources, notamment financières.

Comme cela a déjà été indiqué, dès lors qu'il n'y a pas, en droit de l'Union, de dispositions désignant les organes d'une personne morale habilités à mandater un avocat, il convient, afin de déterminer la personne ou l'organe autorisé à donner un mandat à un avocat pour représenter une personne morale, de faire application du droit de l'État régissant cette personne morale. Toutefois, afin de permettre à certaines personnes morales de contester des décisions de l'Union, la Cour a jugé que ces règles nationales devaient, dans certaines circonstances, être écartées.

3.2 *La mise à l'écart des règles nationales relatives à la représentation au nom de la garantie de la protection juridictionnelle effective*

Devant les juridictions de l'Union, la représentation des personnes morales est régie par la lex incorporationis. Toutefois, dans l'arrêt Trasta, la Cour a jugé que ces règles nationales peuvent, dans certaines hypothèses, être écartées.

Trasta Komercbanka, un établissement de crédit de droit letton, avait introduit un recours devant le Tribunal afin de contester la décision de le BCE de retirer son agrément pour l'accès à cette activité. Du fait de cette décision de retrait d'agrément, une procédure de liquidation de Trasta Komercbanka avait été ouverte et un liquidateur avait été désigné sans que soient maintenus les pouvoirs de

[27] Arrêt du 21 septembre 2023, China Chamber of Commerce for Import and Export of Machinery and Electronic Products e.a./Commission (C-478/21 P, EU:C:2023:685, points 88 à 99).

[28] Arrêts du 8 février 2024, Pilatus Bank/BCE (C-750/21 P, EU:C:2024:124, point 37), et du 8 février 2024, Pilatus Bank/BCE (C-256/22 P, EU:C:2024:125, point 39).

représentation de l'organe de direction de Trasta Komercbanka aux fins l'introduction d'un recours contre la décision de retrait d'agrément. Le Tribunal avait considéré que les avocats mandatés par l'ancien organe de direction ne disposaient pas d'un mandat valable dès lors qu'ils avaient été mandatés par un organe qui n'avait plus de pouvoir de représentation. Selon le Tribunal, le liquidateur qui disposait du pouvoir de représentation en vertu du droit national pouvait révoquer les mandats ad litem de sorte qu'il n'y avait pas lieu de statuer sur le recours de Trasta Komercbanka.

En pourvoi, la Cour a jugé qu'une juridiction de l'Union a l'obligation de ne pas tenir compte de la révocation du mandat conféré au représentant d'une partie, lorsque cette révocation viole le droit de cette partie à une protection juridictionnelle effective. Selon la Cour, il y avait, dans cette affaire, une atteinte au droit à une protection juridictionnelle effective dans la mesure où le liquidateur, nommé à la suite du retrait de l'agrément de Trasta Komercbanka et qui avait procédé à la révocation du mandat donné par la direction de celle-ci, était en situation de conflit d'intérêts.

Il résulte de cet arrêt que même si, en l'absence de règles de l'Union relatives à la représentation d'une personne morale telle qu'une banque, cette question est, en principe, régie par le droit national, cette autonomie des États membres à cet égard trouve cependant sa limite dans l'obligation de garantir le respect du droit à un recours effectif, consacré par l'article 47 de la Charte.

Ainsi, dans certaines circonstances, les règles du droit des États membres relatives à la représentation des parties peuvent être laisser inappliquées par la Cour et le Tribunal. Toutefois, cela ne signifie pas que la représentation d'une personne morale de droit privé soit alors régie par le droit de l'Union. En effet, d'une part, la Cour a explicitement indiqué, au point 63 dudit arrêt, que le mandat produit par l'avocat ayant introduit le recours devant le Tribunal au nom de Trasta Komercbanka avait été délivré par une personne qui, à la date de délivrance du mandat, était habilitée à cette fin. D'autre part, elle a jugé recevable le recours introduit par cette personne morale ainsi représentée. Par conséquent, dans une situation telle que celle ayant mené à cet arrêt, la Cour écarte certaines règles nationales, celles relatives au pouvoir de représentation du liquidateur, pour appliquer les règles nationales qui auraient été applicables à la représentation de la personne morale en l'absence de procédure de liquidation.

S'agissant des conditions dans lesquelles la solution retenue par la Grande chambre dans l'arrêt Trasta peut trouver à s'appliquer, une double mise en perspective de cet arrêt s'impose.

Premièrement, la solution retenue par la Cour s'agissant du recours de Trasta Komercbanka doit être appréhendée à l'aune de la solution de la Cour en ce qui concerne le recours des actionnaires de cet établissement de crédit.

À cet égard, le Tribunal avait estimé que, dès lors que les actionnaires de Trasta Komercbanka étaient, du fait de la liquidation, concrètement empêchés d'exercer leurs droits d'associés, il y avait lieu, à titre exceptionnel, de reconnaître que les actionnaires étaient recevables à demander l'annulation de la décision de la BCE de retrait d'agrément.

La Cour a considéré que, ce faisant, le Tribunal avait commis une erreur de droit et, après avoir évoqué le litige, elle a jugé, en application de la jurisprudence relative aux actionnaires, que les actionnaires de Trasta Komercbanka n'étaient pas directement concernés par la décision de retrait d'agrément de sorte que leur recours était irrecevable.

Dans ces conditions, dès lors que les actionnaires n'avaient pas qualité pour agir contre la décision de retrait d'agrément, la seule possibilité de soumettre la décision de retrait d'agrément de Trasta Komercbanka au contrôle du juge de l'Union était de juger recevable le recours formé par cet établissement de crédit lui-même.

Deuxièmement, dans l'arrêt Trasta, la Cour s'est référée à la jurisprudence de la Cour européenne des droits de l'Homme qui corrobore la solution retenue à l'égard de Trasta Komercbanka.[29] Toutefois, les organes de la Convention européenne des droits de l'Homme ne mettent que très exceptionnellement à l'écart les règles nationales relatives à la représentation. Il ressort in fine de leur jurisprudence que tel est le cas si les liquidateurs ou les administrateurs chargés de gérer les intérêts d'une entreprise ont failli à leur mission ou s'ils se trouvent en situation de conflit d'intérêts.[30]

Au regard de ces éléments, on peut considérer que l'arrêt Trasta a, dans des circonstances très particulières, introduit un tempérament à un principe établi de longue date, mais sans le remettre en cause. En outre, la portée de cet arrêt devrait être limitée à des hypothèses assez exceptionnelles. En effet, sauf à favoriser l'émergence d'un phénomène de double représentation des personnes morales de droit privé, seules des circonstances qui aboutissent in fine à priver une personne morale de toute possibilité de défendre ses intérêts permettent de justifier que les règles nationales relatives à la représentation ne soient pas appliquées. Concrètement, d'une part, cela suppose de limiter l'application de cet arrêt aux seuls cas de conflits d'intérêts avérés. D'autre part, cela implique que le tempérament introduit par ledit arrêt s'applique exclusivement lorsque, en raison de ce conflit d'intérêts, la personne morale n'a aucune autre possibilité de contester la décision qu'elle entend contester.

Il semblerait que la jurisprudence rendue postérieurement à l'arrêt Trasta prenne une telle orientation.

Ainsi, dans deux arrêts,[31] la Cour a considéré que le conseil d'administration d'une banque à l'égard de laquelle une « personne compétente » avait été nommée par les autorités nationales afin, notamment, d'en assurer la représentation légale et judiciaire, n'était plus habilité à donner mandat à un avocat au nom de cette banque

[29] Points 62 et 76 de l'arrêt Trasta.

[30] Arrêts de la Cour EDH du 24 octobre 1995, Agrotexim e.a c/ Grèce (CE:ECHR:1992:0212DEC001480789, §§ 66 et 68); du 21 octobre 2003, Crédit industriel c. République tchèque (CE:ECHR:2003:1021JUD002901095, §§71 à 73); du 9 septembre 2004, Capital Bank AD c. Bulgarie (CE:ECHR:2004:0909DEC004942999) ainsi que du24 novembre 2005, Capital Bank AD c. Bulgarie (CE:ECHR:2005:1124JUD004942999, §§91, 117 et 118).

[31] Arrêts du 8 février 2024, Pilatus Bank/BCE (C-750/21 P, EU:C:2024:124, points 60 à 65), ainsi que du 8 février 2024, Pilatus Bank/BCE (C-256/22 P, EU:C:2024:125, points 61 à 66).

dès lors que cette « personne compétente » n'était pas en situation de conflit d'intérêts.

Cela étant, dans un autre arrêt,[32] alors même qu'une situation de conflits d'intérêts semblait exister et que la Cour s'est référée à l'arrêt Trasta, elle a privilégié un autre motif afin de justifier la mise à l'écart des règles nationales relatives à la représentation. Il s'agissait d'un recours introduit par un établissement de crédit de droit letton déclaré insolvable et dont les pouvoirs du conseil d'administration avaient été transférés à un administrateur judiciaire. Ce recours visait à contester le refus de la BCE d'enjoindre à l'administrateur judiciaire d'octroyer à l'avocat mandaté par le conseil d'administration de cet établissement de crédit l'accès à ses locaux, aux informations qu'il détient ainsi qu'à son personnel et à ses ressources. En effet, la Cour, sans mentionner un quelconque conflit d'intérêts de l'administrateur judiciaire ni une quelconque atteinte concrète à la protection dont cet établissement devait bénéficier, a justifié le fait que, dans le cadre de ce recours, la partie requérante était cet établissement représenté par son conseil d'administration en s'appuyant sur la circonstance que le conseil d'administration dudit établissement était le destinataire de l'acte contesté de la BCE. Cette justification peut laisser quelque peu perplexe dès lors que, d'une part, la qualité de destinataire d'un acte est une circonstance à prendre en compte pour apprécier la qualité pour agir en annulation et que, d'autre part, le fait qu'un conseil d'administration d'un établissement de crédit soit destinataire d'un acte ne signifie pas nécessairement qu'il soit habilité à prendre la décision d'introduire un recours devant une juridiction de l'Union au nom de cet établissement de crédit et qu'il soit compétent pour mandater un avocat à cet effet.

Cet arrêt soulève quelques doutes quant aux conséquences de l'arrêt Trasta auxquels s'ajoutent des questions qui n'ont pas encore été tranchées par la Cour. Ainsi, dans la configuration factuelle ayant mené à cet arrêt Trasta, le liquidateur était en situation de conflit d'intérêts et avait, au cours de la procédure devant le Tribunal, révoqué le mandat des avocats mandatés par l'ancien organe de direction. Toutefois, en irait-il autrement si le liquidateur avait introduit un recours au nom de Trasta Komercbanka ?

Dans l'affaire Trasta, à la suite de l'arrêt de rendu par la Grande chambre, le Tribunal a rendu l'arrêt du 30 novembre 2022, Trasta Komercbanka e.a./BCE (T-698/16, non publié, EU:T:2022:737) rejetant le recours de cet établissement de crédit contre la décision de la BCE retirant son agrément. Or, cette décision a fait l'objet d'un pourvoi introduit au nom de Trasta Komercbanka par le liquidateur et d'un pourvoi introduit par l'avocat mandaté par l'ancien organe de direction.[33] Certes le premier pourvoi a été rejeté au motif que le liquidateur, qui a signé le pourvoi en tant que représentant de cette personne morale, a remplacé la direction de cette société de sorte que la Cour a considéré que le pourvoi n'avait pas été introduit par Trasta Komercbanka représentée par un avocat, au sens de l'article 19

[32] Arrêt du 15 septembre 2022, PNB Banka/BCE (C-326/21 P, non publié, EU:C:2022:693).

[33] Arrêt du 22 mai 2025, Trasta Komercbanka/BCE (C-90/23 P, EU:C:2025:369).

du statut de la Cour.[34] Cela étant la question de la possibilité pour le liquidateur de décider de l'introduction d'un recours au nom de Trasta Komercbanka demeure, tout comme celle de savoir si une décision du Tribunal peut faire l'objet de deux pourvois distincts introduits par la même partie, puisque, dans une telle configuration, il est difficile d'identifier la volonté de la personne morale d'introduire un recours.

4 Conclusions

Les décisions récemment rendues par la Cour et le Tribunal en matière de représentation ont plusieurs origines. Les modifications apportées aux règlements de procédure ainsi que l'apparition et le développement de nouveaux contentieux ont, pour partie, renouvelé la problématique de la représentation devant les juridictions de l'Union et notamment celle de la régularité des mandats ad litem. Ainsi, par exemple, en matière de mesures restrictives, il est apparu que les dispositions du statut de la Cour et celles des règlements de procédure de la Cour et du Tribunal « n'ont pas été conçues en vue de l'introduction de recours par des organisations n'ayant pas de personnalité juridique »[35] telles que le PKK ou les LTTE alors même que de telles organisations sont visées par des mesures restrictives de l'Union. Par ailleurs, le contentieux en matière de surveillance des établissements de crédit a également donné naissance à de nouvelles interrogations compte tenu des conséquences des décisions de retrait d'agrément selon le droit de certains États membres.[36]

En toile de fond, l'appréhension de la question de la représentation des personnes physiques et morales devant la Cour et le Tribunal est naturellement influencée par la nécessité de garantir l'effectivité de la protection juridictionnelle dont ces personnes doivent bénéficier lorsqu'elles remettent en cause des actes de l'Union. À cet égard, la jurisprudence est à la recherche constante d'un équilibre

[34] Ordonnance du 3 juin 2024, Trasta Komercbanka/BCE (C-103/23 P, non publiée, EU:C:2024:483).

[35] Arrêt du 18 janvier 2007, PKK et KNK/Conseil (C-229/05 P, EU:C:2007:32, point 114), ainsi que arrêts du 24 novembre 2021, LTTE/Conseil (T-160/19, non publié, EU:T:2021:817, point 57), et du 29 septembre 2021, Front Polisario/Conseil (T-279/19, EU:T:2021:639, point 120).

[36] Le lien entre le retrait d'agrément et la liquidation des établissements de crédit n'est pas inhabituel ainsi qu'en témoigne l'article 12 de la directive 2001/24/CE du Parlement européen et du Conseil, du 4 avril 2001, concernant l'assainissement et la liquidation des établissements de crédit (JO 2001, L 125, p. 15). D'autres décisions comme des mesures d'intervention précoce qui peuvent être adoptées sur le fondement des articles 27 et suivants de la directive 2014/59/UE du Parlement européen et du Conseil, du 15 mai 2014, établissant un cadre pour le redressement et la résolution des établissements de crédit et des entreprises d'investissement et modifiant la directive 82/891/CEE du Conseil ainsi que les directives du Parlement européen et du Conseil 2001/24/CE, 2002/47/CE, 2004/25/CE, 2005/56/CE, 2007/36/CE, 2011/35/UE, 2012/30/UE et 2013/36/UE et les règlements du Parlement européen et du Conseil (UE) n° 1093/2010 et (UE) n° 648/2012 (JO 2014, L 173, p. 190) pourraient donner lieu à des difficultés en matière de représentation.

entre le formalisme et l'adaptation des règles relatives à la représentation. Dans ce contexte, ces règles ont pu, dans certaines situations marginales, être assouplies pour éviter un « formalisme excessif » et garantir l'accès au juge de l'Union. Dans des situations marginales, un tel assouplissement se comprend sans difficultés. Au-delà de ces situations marginales, il ne faut pas oublier, comme le dédicataire de ces lignes n'a jamais manqué de le rappeler, que le formalisme est l'ultime, et nécessaire, rempart contre l'arbitraire.

Économie de moyens et efficacité de la justice

Savvas S. Papasavvas

1 Introduction

Parce qu'il en va de sa crédibilité autant que de sa légitimité, le juge de l'Union européenne doit avoir à cœur de tout mettre en œuvre pour rechercher l'efficacité de la justice dans le cadre des compétences qui lui ont été dévolues. Ne nous y trompons pas : on touche ici à la condition de l'existence même de la justice, une justice inefficace ne pouvant s'entendre que comme une absence de justice.

De manière concrète, pour pouvoir prétendre à l'efficacité, la justice doit satisfaire à plusieurs critères et faire ainsi preuve de qualité, d'efficience, dans le sens où elle doit atteindre ses objectifs en optimisant les moyens mis à sa disposition,[1] mais également de célérité.

Ces exigences ne sont pas toujours simples à concilier et il appartient au juge de l'Union de garantir en permanence un équilibre entre chacune d'entre elles. Ainsi, le souci apporté à la qualité de la justice conforte la confiance des justiciables dans les mécanismes juridictionnels. Mais la seule recherche de la qualité ne saurait pallier l'importance pour le juge de se prononcer avec une certaine célérité. Car il est important de garder à l'esprit que le respect du délai raisonnable, garanti par l'article

L'auteur tient à remercier Mme Dominique Adja pour son aide à la préparation de cet article.

[1] Discours de Jean-Marc Sauvé lors de la Conférence nationale des présidents de la juridiction administrative le 29 juin 2012.

S. S. Papasavvas (✉)
Court of Justice of the European Union, Luxembourg, Luxembourg
e-mail: Savvas.Papasavvas@curia.europa.eu

L. Prete, L. Rezki (eds.), *Judging & (Re)Thinking European Union Law*,
https://doi.org/10.1007/978-3-032-13473-8_24

47, deuxième alinéa, de la Charte des droits fondamentaux de l'Union européenne,[2] est une condition sine qua non pour que le justiciable bénéficie d'une protection juridictionnelle effective.[3]

Pour répondre à tous les impératifs induits par le souci permanent de rendre la justice efficacement, le juge de l'Union a développé nombre de techniques contentieuses lui permettant d'allier célérité et efficience tout en ne cédant rien à l'impératif de qualité.

Au nombre de ces techniques, figure celle de l'économie de moyens, qui est une pratique permettant au juge de se dispenser, dans certains cas, de répondre aux moyens recevables, opérants, voire fondés, soulevés par les parties : il s'agit d'une économie de motivation[4] à laquelle se livre le juge lorsqu'il rédige sa décision. Ainsi, alors que le cadre du litige est déterminé par les conclusions formulées par les parties, le juge de l'Union s'octroie une certaine liberté, au regard des limites ainsi fixées, pour la rédaction de sa décision.

Issue du droit administratif français et parfois qualifiée de principe,[5] l'économie de moyens est davantage une pratique fondée sur le pragmatisme en ce sens qu'elle permet de se limiter à faire état, dans la décision mettant fin à l'instance, d'un motif justifiant le dispositif et de passer sous silence le sort réservé aux autres moyens ou aux fins de non-recevoir soulevés respectivement par la partie requérante ou par la partie défenderesse.

On parle principalement d'économie de moyens dans deux situations distinctes. La première, qui est la plus courante, est celle où le juge annule l'acte attaqué en se fondant sur un seul moyen, ne se livrant donc pas, dans la décision mettant fin à l'instance, à l'examen des autres moyens soulevés par la partie requérante. La seconde est celle, plus rare, où le juge rejette un recours sur le fond sans se prononcer, au préalable, sur les questions de recevabilité soulevées par la partie défenderesse.

Dans le contexte des juridictions qui composent la Cour de justice de l'Union européenne où chaque décision est soumise, entre autres impondérables, à des équilibres de traditions juridiques, des contraintes de cohérence jurisprudentielle et des impératifs de traduction, une telle pratique trouve tout son sens tant elle permet d'optimiser la durée des procédures et de rationnaliser la longueur des arrêts. Elle contribue ainsi à assurer que les décisions juridictionnelles sont rendues dans le respect du principe du délai raisonnable tout en garantissant leur lisibilité.[6]

---

[2] « Toute personne a droit à ce que sa cause soit entendue équitablement, publiquement et dans un délai raisonnable par un tribunal indépendant et impartial établi préalablement par la loi ».

[3] Arrêt du 16 juillet 2009, Der Grüne Punkt – Duales System Deutschland/Commission, C-385/07 P, EU:C:2009:456, point 179 et jurisprudence citée.

[4] C. Meurant, *L'"édénisation" de l'office du juge de l'excès de pouvoir*, Note sous CE, Sect. 21 déc. 2018, Soc.Eden, req. n° 409678, au Lebon, Revue général du droit *on line*, 2019, numéro 48863.

[5] Conclusions de l'avocat général Misho, 25 octobre 2001, Degussa/Commission, C-250/99 P, EU:C:2001:570, point 99.

[6] Arrêt du 13 décembre 2018, Union européenne/Kendrion, C-150/17 P, EU:C:2018:1014, points 72 et 73.

L'économie de moyens est donc non seulement une façon pour la justice de l'Union, en particulier dans le contentieux de l'annulation, d'être plus efficiente, en permettant, en substance, au juge d'aller à l'essentiel, mais elle est aussi un facteur participant de la bonification des décisions de justice en tant qu'elle contribue à leur intelligibilité. Pour autant, le tableau ainsi dépeint nécessite d'être nuancé à plusieurs égards.

Première nuance : en tant qu'elle permet de limiter la longueur des motifs de la décision de justice, il est possible de se demander si cette technique pourrait être perçue comme amoindrissant les exigences de motivation, lesquelles sont pourtant considérées comme contribuant à la qualité d'une décision de justice et constituent un droit du justiciable.

Deuxième nuance : il pourrait être soutenu que l'économie de moyens ne donnerait pas une réponse exhaustive aux demandes de la partie requérante dans la mesure où elle ne permettrait pas que soit mise au jour la totalité des illégalités entachant l'acte attaqué.

Troisième nuance : l'économie de moyens pourrait également interroger par les effets qu'elle peut avoir sur l'exécution des décisions de justice dans la mesure où, quand il pratique l'économie de moyens et qu'il s'abstient de répondre à plusieurs moyens potentiellement fondés pour annuler l'acte attaqué, le juge ne donne aucun indice sur le sort qui aurait été réservé à ces autres moyens s'ils avaient été examinés.[7]

Ainsi, si l'économie de moyens est un outil aux multiples facettes participant indéniablement à rendre la justice plus efficace, il n'est pour autant pas exempt de critiques, lesquelles pourraient conduire le juge de l'Union à envisager certaines améliorations pour accroître davantage son efficience et son acceptabilité.

2 L'économie de moyens, un outil protéiforme et performant au service de l'efficacité de la justice

2.1 Un outil protéiforme

Le contentieux de l'Union offre plusieurs possibilités au juge pour procéder à une économie de moyens. Si son usage dans les décisions mettant fin à l'instance est généralement discret, il peut néanmoins être détecté par l'emploi de la traditionnelle formule « *sans qu'il soit besoin de se prononcer / statuer sur les autres moyens de la requête* ».[8,9]

---

[7] À noter que, si le moyen d'annulation retenu est tiré de l'insuffisance voire de l'absence de motivation de l'acte attaqué, il serait, en tout état de cause, très difficile voire impossible de traiter les moyens au fond.

[8] Voir, par exemple, arrêts du 11 juillet 2006, Caviar Anzali/OHMI – Novomarket (Asetra), T-252/04, EU:T:2006:199, point 47, et du 13 décembre 2016, Guiral Broto/EUIPO – Gastro & Soul (CAFE DEL SOL), T-549/15, non publié, EU:T:2016:719, point 46.

[9] On retrouve également d'autres formules comme « sans qu'il soit besoin de répondre aux fins de non-recevoir ». Voir, par exemple, arrêt du 9 septembre 2010, CSL Behring/Commission et EMA, T-264/07, EU:T:2010:371, point 23.

Outre les deux formes traditionnelles recensées plus haut, il est également possible, dans une vision certes extensive de cette technique, de lui rattacher plusieurs cas de figure dans lesquels le juge de l'Union choisit de ne pas s'étendre sur toutes les questions soulevées par le litige lorsque cela ne s'avère pas absolument nécessaire pour le trancher.

Une telle possibilité existe lorsque le juge de l'Union rejette le recours comme irrecevable sur le fondement d'une exception d'irrecevabilité ou d'une fin de non-recevoir soulevée par la partie défenderesse ou relevée d'office par lui-même. Dans ce cas, il sera fait l'économie de l'examen non seulement des autres fins de non-recevoir qui sont éventuellement soulevées par la partie défenderesse mais également de tous les moyens de fond soulevés par la partie requérante, un recours irrecevable ne pouvant, en principe, faire l'objet d'un examen au fond.

Il est également des cas où le juge, lorsqu'il se prononce sur le sort à réserver à un moyen qu'il convient de rejeter, choisit d'examiner directement le bien-fondé dudit moyen sans s'attarder sur sa recevabilité ou sur son opérance alors qu'il est d'usage de commencer le traitement d'un moyen par l'examen de ces deux questions si elles soulèvent des difficultés.

On peut aussi signaler que le juge de l'Union s'abstient le plus souvent, dans un souci de bonne administration de la justice, de soulever d'office un moyen pour le rejeter par la suite. En effet, il est des cas où, bien que non soulevée par les parties, la recevabilité d'une requête interroge et où le juge examine, pendant son instruction de l'affaire, si telle question qui en relève ne pourrait pas conduire au rejet du recours comme irrecevable. Dans le cas où, à l'issue de son examen, il parvient à la conclusion que tel n'est pas le cas, il est d'usage qu'il n'en fasse pas mention dans la décision mettant fin à l'instance, quand bien même cette question aurait été longuement débattue au sein de la formation de jugement pendant la procédure.

Sans être résiduelles et bien que jouant un rôle non négligeable dans la limitation de la longueur des décisions mettant fin à l'instance, ces situations ne sont généralement pas celles qui viennent immédiatement à l'esprit lorsqu'est évoquée la pratique de l'économie de moyens. L'attention est plutôt portée sur les deux cas de figure suivants.

Ainsi, lorsqu'il décide de statuer sur le fond d'une affaire, afin de rejeter un recours, sans en apprécier préalablement la recevabilité, inversant ainsi l'ordre logique de traitement des questions juridiques, le juge de l'Union focalise son examen sur les aspects strictement nécessaires à la résolution du litige. Cette pratique, consacrée par l'arrêt Conseil/Boehringer,[10] se justifie dans un souci de bonne administration de la justice. Il n'est, en effet, pas indispensable de s'interroger sur la recevabilité du recours lorsque l'examen des moyens de fond conduit, en tout état de cause, à son rejet. Consacrée initialement pour les recours dans le cadre desquels

[10] Arrêt du 26 février 2002, Conseil/Boehringer, C-23/00 P, EU:C:2002:118, point 52.

une exception d'irrecevabilité avait été soulevée par acte séparé, cette possibilité a, par la suite, été appliquée en l'absence d'une telle exception.[11]

Mais le cas le plus caractéristique lorsque l'on évoque l'économie de moyens est celui dans lequel le juge de l'Union annule l'acte attaqué en se fondant sur un seul moyen et passe sous silence tous les autres moyens soulevés par la partie requérante. Dans ce cas, le juge est libre de retenir le moyen de son choix, qu'il relève de la légalité externe ou interne, pour annuler l'acte attaqué quand bien même un autre moyen aurait également été de nature à fonder sa décision.

La particularité de l'économie de moyens, quelle que soit d'ailleurs sa forme, est que le silence du juge sur les moyens qui ne sont pas traités dans sa décision ne peut être interprété dans un sens ou dans un autre. Ces moyens tombent alors dans les « ténèbres extérieures »[12] et ne trouveront aucune réponse dans l'instance en cours. Pour autant, le juge aura normalement[13] examiné toutes les questions posées par le litige et tous les moyens soulevés par les parties durant la procédure. Il choisit simplement de ne pas les faire figurer dans la décision mettant fin à l'instance étant donné qu'ils ne sont pas absolument nécessaires pour trancher le litige. Car en cela réside la raison d'être de la pratique de l'économie de moyens : ne laisser perdurer dans la décision mettant fin à l'instance que les éléments qui sont indispensables pour trancher le litige et qui permettent au juge de s'acquitter de sa charge. En pratiquant l'économie de moyens, le juge de l'Union ne saurait donc être perçu comme faisant également l'économie de sa propre compétence,[14] étant entendu que le fait de ne pas se prononcer sur certains moyens ne saurait nullement être interprété comme une intention de s'exonérer de son obligation de statuer sur les demandes des parties.

Si l'économie de moyens est un outil aux multiples facettes dans les mains du juge, celui-ci n'a aucune obligation de l'utiliser. En effet, il est des cas où, dans un souci de purger tous les aspects du litige, de faciliter l'exécution de sa décision ou de mettre toutes les chances de son coté en cas de pourvoi,[15] le juge préfèrera se prononcer sur plusieurs moyens quand bien même l'un d'entre eux aurait été de nature, à lui seul, à justifier l'annulation de l'acte attaqué.[16]

---

[11] Voir, par exemple, arrêt du 14 septembre 2015, Brouillard/Cour de justice, T-420/13, EU:T:2015:633, point 18.

[12] R. Chapus, *Droit du contentieux administratif*, LGDJ Précis Domat, 12ème édition, p. 942.

[13] Il est des hypothèses cependant où le moyen d'annulation s'impose au juge dès le début de l'instruction de l'affaire. Dans ce cas, seul ce moyen sera examiné tout au long de la procédure.

[14] F. Dieu, *La règle de l'économie de moyens doit-elle paralyser le pouvoir d'injonction du juge administratif ?*, AJDA 2009, p. 1082.

[15] En effet, en cas de pourvoi, l'arrêt attaqué ne sera pas annulé si au moins l'un des moyens retenus par le Tribunal dans sa décision est de nature à justifier le dispositif de cette dernière. Il peut donc être prudent, pour le Tribunal, d'examiner plusieurs moyens dans sa décision même quand il annule l'acte attaqué.

[16] Voir, par exemple, arrêt du 26 juin 2024, Paraskevaidis/Conseil et Commission, T-698/21, EU:T:2024:425.

Cet outil s'inscrit d'ailleurs dans une pratique plus large du juge consistant à se concentrer sur l'essentiel et l'amenant à trancher certaines questions en passant sous silence des aspects du litige pour des raisons de bonne administration de la justice.

Il en est ainsi notamment du fait de ne pas analyser, dans un souci de pragmatisme, la qualité pour agir de tous les requérants en cas de recours collectif. Cette possibilité, issue de la jurisprudence et fondée également sur des raisons d'économie de procédure,[17] autorise le juge, si une même décision est contestée par plusieurs requérants dans le cadre d'une requête collective et qu'il est établi que l'un d'eux au moins dispose de la qualité pour agir, à ne pas examiner la qualité pour agir des autres requérants. À l'instar de l'économie de moyens, cette option est une possibilité[18] pour le juge et non une obligation.[19]

D'une manière plus générale, la Cour considère que l'obligation de motivation n'impose pas au Tribunal de fournir un exposé qui suivrait, de manière exhaustive et un par un, tous les raisonnements articulés par les parties au litige, de telle sorte que la motivation peut être implicite à condition qu'elle permette aux intéressés de connaître les raisons pour lesquelles le Tribunal n'a pas fait droit à leurs arguments et à la Cour de disposer des éléments suffisants pour exercer son contrôle.[20]

On le voit, l'économie de moyens est un outil protéiforme qui confère au juge une certaine liberté dans la rédaction de sa décision. C'est également un moyen particulièrement performant pour qui est soucieux de rendre la justice de manière plus efficace.

2.2 *Un outil performant*

Les avantages de l'économie de moyens pour accroître l'efficacité de la justice sont nombreux et expliquent qu'elle soit un instrument utilisé de longue date par le juge de l'Union.

En premier lieu, l'économie de moyens offre au juge un gain de temps non négligeable dans les discussions autour de la solution à adopter voire de la rédaction de la décision mettant fin à l'instance. En effet, si, au cours de la procédure, il est, le plus souvent, procédé à l'analyse de l'ensemble des moyens par le juge rapporteur

---

[17] Ordonnance du président de la Cour du 24 mars 2009, Cheminova e.a./Commission, C-60/08 P(R), non publiée, EU:C:2009:181, point 34.

[18] Ordonnance du président de la Cour du 24 mars 2009, Cheminova e.a./Commission, C-60/08 P(R), non publiée, EU:C:2009:181, point 32.

[19] Elle est d'ailleurs parfois impossible à mettre en œuvre : lorsque, à la suite d'un recours collectif, l'acte attaqué est annulé, il revient au juge de l'Union de se prononcer sur la qualité pour agir de chacun des requérants car un requérant qui ne présente pas de qualité pour agir, d'une part, ne saurait obtenir gain de cause sur le fond et, d'autre part, ne pourrait obtenir la condamnation de la partie adverse aux dépens (voir, par exemple, arrêt du 29 janvier 2020, Aquino e.a./Parlement, T-402/18, EU:T:2020:13).

[20] Voir ordonnance du 31 octobre 2019, Hochmann Marketing/Conseil, C-408/19 P, non publiée, EU:C:2019:946, point 23 et jurisprudence citée.

et par la formation de jugement,[21] il convient de ne pas négliger le temps qui peut être économisé lorsque, au plus tard au moment du délibéré, la formation de jugement décide de focaliser son attention sur un seul moyen pour annuler l'acte attaqué. Lorsque plusieurs moyens sont susceptibles d'entraîner l'annulation de la décision attaquée, le moyen choisit sera, le plus souvent, celui qui aura été considéré comme le plus convaincant et le plus pertinent et, dans la mesure du possible, qui aura fait l'objet d'un consensus entre les membres de la formation de jugement, permettant ainsi d'éviter de longues discussions sur des moyens autrement plus délicats.[22] Le temps de la rédaction s'en trouvera également écourté pour le juge rapporteur. Cet avantage est loin d'être négligeable dans un système où les deux juridictions composant la Cour de justice de l'Union européenne sont constamment invitées à se prononcer dans des délais toujours plus courts.

En deuxième lieu, l'économie de moyens permet de raccourcir la décision mettant fin à l'instance en tant que telle. Or, dans le contexte international et multilingue dans lequel s'inscrit le juge de l'Union, le raccourcissement des décisions de justice est également un gage d'efficacité en ce sens qu'il permet d'éviter des dépenses indues en terme de lecture et de correction[23] des décisions mettant fin à l'instance ou encore de traduction. Car la Cour de justice de l'Union européenne, dont les ressources ne sont pas illimitées, ne saurait s'affranchir des contraintes, notamment budgétaires, qui pèsent sur elle comme sur les autres institutions de l'Union. En cela, la technique de l'économie de moyens permet également une économie de moyens humains et financiers.

En troisième lieu, l'économie de moyens est, dans bien des cas, l'assurance d'une meilleure qualité de la décision mettant fin à l'instance. En effet, la longueur d'une décision est rarement un gage de qualité. Au contraire, une longue décision est parfois traversée par des tensions internes qui peuvent être facilement évitées en faisant abstraction de certaines questions. Car si le rôle du juge est de trancher les litiges, il se doit également de convaincre, d'abord les parties, puis le public, afin d'accroître la légitimité de ses décisions. Or, le fait de choisir le moyen le plus pertinent et le plus solide pour annuler un acte est parfois plus convaincant qu'une analyse plus approfondie qui n'est pas absolument nécessaire.

En dernier lieu, bien que le choix du moyen d'annulation repose dans les mains du juge, force est de constater que, lorsque cela s'avèrera possible, en présence de plusieurs moyens de nature à justifier l'annulation de l'acte attaqué devant lui, il choisira celui qui est le plus à même, in fine, de procurer au requérant ce qu'il souhaite. À titre d'exemple, à une annulation sur le fondement d'un moyen de légalité

[21] Voir cependant note de bas de page n° 14.

[22] Il y a néanmoins des hypothèses où la solution du litige s'impose avec évidence et où le gain de temps, au moins lors du délibéré, est moins substantiel.

[23] La lecture et la correction des décisions mettant fin à l'instance sont effectuées, au sein de la Cour de justice, par les cellules des lecteurs d'arrêts lesquelles sont des entités au service de l'ensemble des cabinets des juridictions. La mission première de la cellule des lecteurs d'arrêts est de lire et/ou de corriger les projets d'arrêts ou d'ordonnances avant et/ou après les délibérations et avant l'envoi à la traduction.

externe portant sur le non-respect d'impératifs procéduraux, le juge de l'Union préfèrera, dans toute la mesure du possible, une annulation sur le fondement d'un moyen de légalité interne. En effet, alors que la première a toutes les chances de conduire à la prise d'une nouvelle décision respectant les formes sans pour autant donner lieu à une décision faisant droit aux prétentions du requérant, la seconde, parce qu'elle éclaire l'auteur de l'acte sur l'erreur commise sur le fond, a davantage de chance de procurer au requérant ce qu'il demande, de surcroît, dans un laps de temps plus court, dans la mesure où l'hypothèse d'un nouveau litige sera éloignée.

Les avantages de l'économie de moyens sont donc difficilement contestables et peuvent expliquer l'appétence du juge de l'Union pour cette pratique d'autant que, selon la jurisprudence, l'autorité de la chose jugée s'étend seulement aux motifs de l'arrêt qui constituent le soutien nécessaire de son dispositif et sont, de ce fait, indissociables de ce dernier. C'est pourquoi, lorsqu'une juridiction de l'Union européenne annule une décision, les motifs par lesquels cette juridiction a rejeté certains arguments évoqués par les parties ne sont pas revêtus de l'autorité de la chose jugée.[24] L'économie de moyens se justifie donc pleinement d'un point de vue purement contentieux. Pour autant, on ne saurait ignorer les critiques, parfois légitimes, dont elle fait l'objet.

3 L'économie de moyens, une technique critiquée pouvant être améliorée

3.1 *Une technique critiquée*

En droit administratif français, la critique de l'économie de moyens est habituelle et ancienne, peut-être autant que la pratique elle-même.[25] Ces critiques se retrouvent également, mutatis mutandis, dans la mise en œuvre de cette pratique par le juge de l'Union.

On le sait, le juge de l'Union est tenu à la motivation de ses arrêts.[26] Il doit expliquer, pour la légitimer, la solution qu'il donne au litige. Or, le fait de pratiquer l'économie de moyens est parfois considéré comme une façon de s'émanciper, au moins en partie, de l'obligation de motivation et, ce faisant, de priver la partie requérante de la possibilité d'être informée de l'ensemble des illégalités dont elle a été victime alors même qu'elle s'est prévalue de ces illégalités dans ses écritures. Une telle situation laisse apparaître un déséquilibre entre les parties et le juge. En effet, les règlements de procédure des juridictions qui composent la Cour de justice de l'Union européenne font obligation à ces parties de développer largement et

[24] Voir arrêt du 15 mai 2019, CJ/ECDC, C-170/18 P, non publié, EU:C:2019:410, points 49 et 50 et jurisprudence citée.

[25] A. Meynaud-Zeroual, *La motivation en droit du procès administratif*, RDA, décembre 2019, p. 65.

[26] Article 36 du statut de la Cour de justice de l'Union européenne.

clairement leur argumentation[27] sous peine de voir rejeter les moyens soulevés voire le recours tout entier comme irrecevables. Au contraire, la technique de l'économie de moyens permet au juge de prendre ses distances vis-à-vis du respect strict de l'obligation de motivation quelle que soit, par ailleurs, la qualité des écritures des parties. Ceci peut faire naître une certaine frustration dans le chef de ces dernières qui pourraient avoir la sensation de ne pas avoir été totalement entendues, leurs arguments n'ayant pas été complètement pris en compte. D'aucuns[28] posent d'ailleurs la question de la compatibilité de l'économie de moyens avec l'office du juge dans l'hypothèse où celui-ci ne se résumerait pas à répondre aux conclusions mais tendrait aussi à apporter une réponse argumentée à chacun des moyens soulevés devant lui.

L'économie de moyens ne permet donc pas à une partie de savoir si les autres moyens qu'elle a soulevés, ou la totalité desdits moyens dans l'hypothèse où le juge relève d'office le moyen d'annulation,[29] auraient pu, eux-aussi, conduire à l'annulation de l'acte attaqué. On l'a dit, le silence du juge ne donne ici aucune piste et ne saurait être interprété ni comme un accueil ni comme un rejet desdits moyens. Comme il a pu être relevé,[30] « il existe donc trois sorts possibles au moyen : son accueil, son rejet, son économie ». Le litige est bien tranché mais il n'est pas pour autant vidé de sa substance. Or, il est loisible de se demander si faire apparaître dans les arrêts un bilan aussi complet que possible des vices entachant les décisions annulées ne concourrait pas plus sûrement à une bonne administration de la justice voire, plus généralement, à la satisfaction de l'intérêt général.[31]

Le fait de ne pas relever toutes les illégalités dont est entaché un acte peut, en outre, entraîner certaines difficultés dans l'exécution de la décision mettant fin à l'instance. En effet, l'article 266 TFUE[32] oblige l'auteur de l'acte annulé à prendre toutes les mesures que comporte l'exécution de l'arrêt de la Cour de justice ou du Tribunal. Ainsi, pour faire application de cet article, l'institution, l'organe ou l'organisme dont émane l'acte annulé prendra appui sur les motifs de la décision ayant annulé l'acte en cause afin de ne pas reproduire l'illégalité qui aura été sanctionnée. Lorsque le juge fait application de l'économie de moyens, il ne se prononce pas sur toutes les illégalités susceptibles d'entacher l'acte en cause de telle sorte que son auteur n'est pas en mesure de connaître avec précision tous les écueils qu'il lui appartient d'éviter. Par suite, il ne saurait être exclu que, prenant une nouvelle décision, il réitère certaines illégalités alors même que celles-ci avaient été pointées du

[27] Une telle exigence a pour objectif de permettre au juge de pouvoir utilement se prononcer.

[28] P.-Y. Sagnier, *Le juge administratif et l'économie des moyens*. E. Cartier (dir.), thèse de doctorat, droit public, Université de Lille, 2019, p. 40.

[29] F. Clausen, *Les moyens d'ordre public devant la Cour de justice de l'Union européenne*, F. Picot (dir.), thèse de doctorat, droit de l'Union européenne, 2018, p. 431–433.

[30] P.-Y. Sagnier, *op.cit.*, p. 580.

[31] R. Chapus, *op.cit.*, p. 942.

[32] « L'institution, l'organe ou l'organisme dont émane l'acte annulé, ou dont l'abstention a été déclarée contraire aux traités, est tenu de prendre les mesures que comporte l'exécution de l'arrêt de la Cour de justice de l'Union européenne ».

doigt par les parties requérantes dans leurs écritures. L'objectif d'une bonne administration de la justice n'est, en pareille hypothèse, pas totalement atteint puisque risque de naître un nouveau contentieux dont le juge de l'Union sera à nouveau saisi. Ceci est particulièrement notable dans les litiges en matière de fonction publique où il pourrait être intéressant pour l'institution qui a la charge d'exécuter la décision de justice de disposer du maximum d'informations sur les illégalités entachant son acte. Néanmoins, en matière de concurrence, cette critique apparaît moins pertinente dans la mesure où, lorsque le juge de l'Union annule l'acte attaqué et/ou recalcule l'amende, la Commission dispose de l'essentiel des éléments dont elle a besoin pour procéder à l'exécution de la décision de justice. On note pour autant que, d'une manière générale, le juge de l'Union donne, dans ces décisions, le maximum de précisions pour assurer une exécution optimale de ces dernières.

Par ailleurs, l'économie de moyens n'est pas toujours la technique la plus efficace pour assurer une bonne administration de la justice. En effet, dans certaines hypothèses, l'efficacité commande non de retenir un moyen afin de procéder à l'annulation de l'acte attaqué mais de prendre en considération tous les motifs dudit acte pour, in fine, rejeter le recours. Il s'agit d'une application du concept de la « neutralisation de motifs » qui a pour objectif d'éviter des annulations de pure forme, lesquelles ne sauraient être considérées comme relevant d'une bonne administration de la justice. Ainsi, lorsqu'une décision est fondée sur plusieurs motifs et que, malgré l'illégalité d'un ou plusieurs d'entre eux, l'un des motifs suffit à justifier la décision, le juge de l'Union renonce à annuler ladite décision.[33] La solution est la même s'agissant des décisions du Tribunal. Ainsi, si certains motifs d'un arrêt du Tribunal révèlent une violation du droit de l'Union, mais que le dispositif apparaît fondé sur d'autres motifs de droit, la Cour en pourvoi juge qu'une telle violation n'est pas de nature à entraîner l'annulation de cet arrêt.[34]

De même, lorsque le juge de l'Union constate que l'acte attaqué est entaché d'un ou de plusieurs vices de procédure, il considère que de tels vices ne peuvent entraîner l'annulation de la décision attaquée que s'il est établi que, en l'absence de ces vices, cette décision aurait pu avoir un contenu différent.[35]

Si les critiques existent, elles ne doivent cependant pas faire oublier que certaines requêtes soumises au juge sont particulièrement longues et fourmillent d'arguments et de moyens de qualité très inégale. Dans ce cas, si le juge de l'Union n'est pas en mesure d'imposer aux parties de raccourcir leurs écritures, il peut, grâce à l'économie de moyens, se concentrer sur le moyen pertinent et fondé et laisser de côté les autres arguments lesquels n'étant pas, de façon évidente, en capacité de pouvoir mener à l'annulation de l'acte attaqué. D'ailleurs, la Cour considère qu'il n'incombe pas au Tribunal de répondre aux arguments invoqués par une partie qui ne sont pas suffisamment clairs et précis, dans la mesure où ils ne font l'objet d'aucun autre

[33] Voir, par exemple, arrêt du 12 juillet 2023, Eurecna/Commission, T-377/21, EU:T:2023:398, point 25.

[34] Arrêt du 31 octobre 2019, Repower/EUIPO, C-281/18 P, EU:C:2019:916, point 37.

[35] Arrêt du 7 septembre 2023, Versobank/BCE, C-803/21 P, non publié, EU:C:2023:630, point 48.

développement particulier et ne sont pas accompagnés d'une argumentation spécifique les étayant.[36]

Il n'est donc pas possible de dénier à l'économie de moyens l'intérêt qu'elle présente pour parvenir à une justice efficace. Pour autant, certaines pistes d'amélioration pourraient être envisagées.

3.2 *Une technique pouvant être améliorée*

On l'a dit, l'économie de moyens appliquée par le juge de l'Union a pour origine une pratique développée en droit administratif français. Cette pratique très ancienne n'est pas remise en cause dans son existence mais a fait l'objet de plusieurs limitations tant législatives que jurisprudentielles dont il est loisible de se demander si certaines pourraient inspirer le juge de l'Union.

Le législateur français a, tout d'abord, interdit l'économie de moyens dans le contentieux de l'urbanisme.[37]

La jurisprudence, ensuite, a semblé vouloir mettre fin à une telle pratique avec l'instauration de la possibilité pour le juge administratif de moduler dans le temps les effets des annulations pour excès de pouvoir.[38] En effet, selon le Conseil d'État, une telle modulation ne peut être mise en œuvre par le juge qu'après avoir recueilli les observations des parties et examiné l'ensemble des moyens, d'ordre public ou invoqués devant lui, pouvant affecter la légalité de l'acte en cause. Cette option offerte au juge administratif paraissait donc difficilement conciliable avec l'économie de moyens qui, elle, supposait de n'examiner, dans la décision mettant fin à l'instance, qu'un seul moyen.

Mais c'est véritablement avec l'arrêt *Société Eden*[39] que le Conseil d'État a introduit un changement majeur dans l'office du juge de l'excès de pouvoir en remettant en cause la liberté dudit juge face aux moyens soulevés dans l'hypothèse où le requérant choisit soit de présenter, outre ses conclusions d'annulation, des conclusions tendant à ce que le juge enjoigne à l'autorité administrative de prendre une décision dans un sens déterminé, soit de hiérarchiser ses prétentions, avant l'expiration du délai de recours contentieux, en fonction de la cause juridique sur laquelle elles reposent. En pareil cas, le juge administratif français est désormais tenu de respecter la préférence exprimée par le requérant, en examinant en priorité les moyens qui seraient de nature, s'ils étaient fondés, à justifier le prononcé de l'injonction demandée ou à satisfaire sa demande principale.[40] Cette solution

[36] Voir arrêt du 18 juillet 2013, FIFA/Commission, C-205/11 P, EU:C:2013:478, point 89 et jurisprudence citée.

[37] Article L. 600-4-1 du code de l'urbanisme (France).

[38] CE, Ass, 11 mai 2004, Association AC !, n° 255886.

[39] CE, Sect, 21 décembre 2018, société Eden, n° 409678.

[40] Conclusions Iljic sous CE, 5 avril 2019, n° 420608.

s'explique par la nécessité de donner son plein effet aux conclusions aux fins d'injonction présentées par les requérants, le juge administratif étant désormais dans l'obligation de choisir le moyen d'annulation qui permettra de prononcer l'injonction demandée par ceux-ci. D'aucuns ont alors parlé d'une « édénisation de l'office du juge de l'excès de pouvoir ».

De telles considérations ne sauraient cependant jouer pour le juge de l'Union étant donné que, d'une part, celui-ci n'est pas compétent pour prononcer des injonctions aux institutions et, d'autre part, le second alinéa de l'article 264 TFUE[41] n'impose pas un examen exhaustif de l'ensemble des moyens.

Une évolution dans le sens d'un plus grand encadrement de la pratique de l'économie de moyens par le juge de l'Union pourrait être envisagée.

Un changement envisageable consisterait à imposer au juge de l'Union, lorsqu'il constate que plusieurs moyens sont susceptibles de conduire à l'annulation de l'acte attaqué, de se prononcer sur chacun d'entre eux. Une telle évolution permettrait de mettre fin aux critiques portant sur les problèmes d'exécution causés par le fait de ne pas mettre en exergue toutes les illégalités dont est entaché l'acte attaqué. Elle aurait également le mérite de ne pas changer de manière drastique la pratique actuelle des juges de l'Union et de ne pas allonger de manière substantielle les procédures. Une telle évolution permettrait de concilier l'accroissement de la qualité au sens large sans revenir sur les gains non négligeables en termes de célérité.

Cependant, un tel changement aurait pour inconvénient notable de remettre en cause l'un des avantages principaux de la pratique en cause, à savoir celui de raccourcir de manière substantielle les décisions mettant fin à l'instance. En outre, le fait de mentionner l'ensemble des moyens soulevés par la partie requérante susceptibles d'entraîner l'annulation de l'acte attaqué ne signifierait pas pour autant que l'ensemble des illégalités dont serait entaché l'acte en cause seraient mises au jour car, exception faite des moyens d'ordre public et comme c'est le cas dans de nombreuses juridictions nationales, le juge de l'Union est tenu par les moyens soulevés par les parties. Ainsi, il ne saurait être exclu que ces moyens ne visent pas la totalité des illégalités entachant l'acte attaqué.

On le voit, limiter, voire renoncer, à l'économie de moyens ne se ferait pas sans dommages. Car on ne saurait ignorer que le choix de répondre de manière exhaustive à l'ensemble des questions de recevabilité et à la totalité des moyens soulevés aurait un impact non négligeable sur les procédures devant le juge de l'Union. Cela alourdirait mécaniquement la durée du délibéré, les membres de la formation de jugement étant contraints de s'accorder sur la rédaction d'un arrêt beaucoup plus long, et aurait également un impact sur les délais de traduction.

La satisfaction des justiciables en serait peut-être accrue mais les gains en termes d'efficacité de la justice ne seraient pas pour autant garantis.

Toutefois, il serait possible, à moindre coût pour l'objectif qui nous occupe, d'envisager, lorsque les circonstances de l'espèce ne s'y opposent pas, d'apporter

[41] « [...], la Cour indique, si elle l'estime nécessaire, ceux des effets de l'acte annulé qui doivent être considérés comme définitifs ».

une motivation succincte des raisons justifiant le recours à l'économie de moyens. Il pourrait ainsi être expliqué pourquoi le juge choisit de se concentrer sur un seul moyen tout en écartant les autres. Ceci pourrait être perçu comme un pas effectué en direction des justiciables et serait l'occasion de mettre en lumière les avantages de cette pratique en termes d'économie de procédure et de bonne administration de la justice tout en ne renonçant à aucun de ses avantages.

L'économie de moyens est donc un outil précieux dans la perpétuelle quête d'efficacité par le juge de l'Union. Développée dans un souci de pragmatisme, elle permet de substantielles économies en termes de motivation notamment.

Néanmoins, la justice est tributaire de l'époque dans laquelle elle s'inscrit et l'époque actuelle semble être à la recherche de davantage de transparence et de pédagogie.

La Cour européenne des droits de l'Homme est sensible à ce souci de transparence et met fréquemment l'accent sur la nécessaire motivation des décisions de justice en tant que composante du droit à un procès équitable au sens de l'article 6 de la convention européenne des droits de l'homme et des libertés fondamentales.[42] Dans cette logique, elle exige notamment que les revirements de jurisprudence soient motivés.[43]

En outre, une plus large motivation des arrêts de la part du Tribunal peut parfois conduire, in fine, à des économies procédurales. Ainsi, en cas d'accueil du pourvoi, le degré d'instruction de l'affaire par le Tribunal, en première instance, ainsi que l'étendue de la motivation figurant dans l'arrêt attaqué peuvent parfois amener la Cour à constater que l'affaire est en état d'être jugée, évitant ainsi un allongement de la procédure inhérent à un renvoi devant le Tribunal.[44]

On le voit bien, l'économie de moyens est une illustration des contraintes pesant sur le juge de l'Union, lequel se trouve sans cesse invité à concilier des impératifs contradictoires.

Dans cet exercice d'équilibriste, qui fait totalement partie de son office, le juge de l'Union a toutefois à cœur de toujours placer le justiciable au centre de ses préoccupations. Et là est bien l'essentiel.

---

[42] CEDH, European Air Transport Leipzig c. Belgique, 11 juillet 2023, CE:ECHR:2023:0711JUD000126913, § 54.

[43] CEDH, Atanasovski et une autre affaire c. « l'ex-République yougoslave de Macédoine », 14 janvier 2010, CE:ECHR:2010:0114JUD003681503.

[44] Arrêt du 8 septembre 2020, Commission et Conseil/Carreras Sequeros e.a., C-119/19 P et C-126/19 P, EU:C:2020:676.

On the Evolving Role of the (First) Advocate General Over the Years

Maciej Szpunar

1 Introduction

From the very beginning of its activity, the Court of Justice of the European Union (the 'Court', 'Court of Justice' or 'ECJ') has included—alongside the judges, of course—the Advocates General.[1] The institution of the Advocate General was modelled on the French Commissaire du Gouvernement[2] at the Conseil d'État (Council of State), including at the lower administrative courts. One of the first two Advocates General was the French lawyer Maurice Lagrange, who previously fulfilled the function of Commissaire du Gouvernement and was also part of the French delegation that negotiated the Treaty establishing the European Coal and Steel Community.

A Commissaire du Gouvernement (now Rapporteur public) prepares independent expert opinions, which contain a legal analysis and a proposed judgment in the respective case. This opinion is prepared on the basis of a previously prepared draft judgment, and the parties to the proceedings can comment on it during the proceedings. The Commissaire du Gouvernement has the right to participate in the judges'

[1] See also Article 19(2) TEU and Article 252 TFEU.

[2] K. Borgsmidt, 'The Advocate General at the European Court of Justice: A Comparative Study' (1988) European Law Review, vol. 13, no. 2, p. 110; D. Ruiz-Jarabo Colomer, M. López Escudero, 'L'institution de l'avocat général à la Cour de justice des Communautés européennes', in *Mélanges en hommage à Fernand Schockweiler*, Baden-Baden 1999, p. 540; and A. Arena, 'The Community System of Judicial Protection: a tale of Two Legal Revolutions', forthcoming in (2025) Yearbook of European Law, Section II. Functions close in character to the Commissaire du Gouvernement existed and continue to exist in Belgium and the Netherlands. On the subject of other institutions fulfilling similar functions, see K. Borgsmidt, op. cit., pp. 109–118.

M. Szpunar (✉)
Court of Justice of the European Union, Luxembourg, Luxembourg
e-mail: Maciej.Szpunar@curia.europa.eu

L. Prete, L. Rezki (eds.), *Judging & (Re)Thinking European Union Law*,
https://doi.org/10.1007/978-3-032-13473-8_25

deliberations. Despite the obvious fact that the office of the Advocate General at the Court of Justice is modelled on the French institution of the Commissaire du Gouvernement, there are substantial differences between these two functions.[3]

In the legal systems of the majority of Member States, we do not find an institution comparable to that of the Advocate General of the Court of Justice. This has led to certain translation difficulties in the designation of this function in some official EU languages. For instance, the Polish translation has turned out to be rather unfortunate and leads to—sometimes quite entertaining[4]—misunderstandings.[5]

This contribution will focus primarily on explaining the changes of an institutional nature that have taken place in recent years with respect to the function of Advocates General Moreover, I will present some thoughts on the role played by the Advocates General's Opinion in the Court's judicial activity. It is for me inevitable that these thoughts are to a large extent informed by my own experience of working at the Court over the last twelve years. Over eleven of these twelve years I had the joy and privilege of working closely with the person at the centre of this *Festschrift*, Nils Wahl. He has lived three 'lives' at the Court of Justice of the European Union: a term as Judge at the General Court, a term as Advocate General and a term as Judge at the Court of Justice. It is in particular the five years during which we both served as Advocate General that our cooperation was the closest. In particular, when I arrived at the Court in 2013, I was very fortunate to count on the invaluable advice of Nils as a more senior colleague. And the best thing about his advice was that it was frank, unapologetic and cut straight through to the subject matters. Very much like his Opinions as Advocate General which I very much enjoyed reading.

2 Number of Advocates General

Article 19(2) of the Treaty on European Union (hereinafter: TEU) states that the Court of Justice shall consist of one judge per Member State. This means that the number of judges corresponds to the number of Member States. Article 252 of the Treaty on the Functioning of the European Union (hereinafter: TFEU), in turn, states that the Court of Justice shall be assisted by eight Advocates General,[6]

[3] This difference is pointed out by D. Ruiz-Jarabo Colomer, M. López Escudero, op. cit., p. 541.

[4] It happens that journalists approach me with a request to comment on some of the Court's judgments.

[5] The term "rzecznik" [Engl. "spokesperson"] may indicate that we are dealing with a body that defends the interests of the State or a particular group of citizens. Especially in countries of Central-Eastern Europe, this may evoke associations with a role similar to that of the public prosecutor in civil proceedings, for example. See M. Bobek, 'A Fourth in the Court: Why Are There Advocates General in the Court of Justice', in The Cambridge Yearbook of European Legal Studies" Vol. 14, 2011-2012, Oxford 2012, p. 546.

[6] On the subject of the development of the number of Advocates General, see: M. Nowacki, Instytucja rzecznika generalnego w ETS [Eng: Institution of the Advocate General at the ECJ], "Europejski Przegląd Sądowy", March 2008, pp. 27 and 28.

although the Council may, at the request of the Court, unanimously increase the number of Advocates General.[7]

Pursuant to Council decision of 25 June 2013, the number of Advocates General was increased to eleven.[8] This was done in such a way that as of October 2013 the number of Advocates General was increased to nine, and as of October 2015, i.e. at the next periodic partial renewal of the Court,[9] by another two.

The system of distribution of the Advocates General among the Member States is quite complicated. At the time of Poland's accession to the EU (1 May 2004), there were eight Advocates General at the Court. Among these eight Advocates General, five of them performed their duties as so-called "permanent Advocates General". Indeed, based on previous agreements,[10] some of the Member States have the right to appoint an Advocate General each time. Until 2013, these were France, Italy, Germany, the United Kingdom and Spain. The three other Advocates General, on the other hand, were so-called "rotating Advocates General", provided by the other Member States on a rotating basis. This means that these latter Member States had the right to appoint an Advocate General for one six-year term only. The successor to this Advocate General then came from another Member State, determined according to the alphabetical order of the names of the Member States participating in the rotation.

In the course of the negotiations leading to the conclusion of the Lisbon Treaty, Poland—which is of a size comparable to that of Spain—requested that it also be granted the right to a "permanent Advocate General".[11] Since increasing the number of "permanent Advocates General" to six would mean that only two Advocates General would remain in the rotation system (and because the Court's workload continued to rise), the Member States decided that the granting of a "permanent Advocate General" to Poland would have to be linked to an increase in the number of "rotating Advocates General".

The negotiators of the Lisbon Treaty did not decide to make this change directly in the Treaty, but decided to make use of the mechanism provided for in the second sentence of the first subparagraph of Article 252 TFEU, i.e. to increase the number of Advocates General by way of a unanimous Council decision. To this end, a declaration was annexed to the Treaty of Lisbon, which provided that—if the Court of

[7] See also Declaration No 38 to the Treaty of Lisbon on Article 252 TFEU.

[8] Council Decision 2013/336/EU of 25 June 2013 increasing the number of Advocates-General of the Court of Justice of the European Union (OJ 2013 L 179, p. 92).

[9] The term of office of Members of the Court (Judges and Advocates General) is six years. This implies in practice that every three years there is a partial renewal of Members.

[10] Joint Declaration (95/1/EC, Euratom, ECSC) on Article 31 of the Decision adapting the documents concerning the accession of new Member States to the European Union (OJ 1995 L 1, p. 221).

[11] The problematic nature of Polish efforts to create the post of "permanent Advocate General" is discussed in detail by J. Barcz, 'Increasing the Number of Advocates General at the European Court of Justice in the Context of the Implementation of the Lisbon Treaty', in *Law of International Organisations in the Light of the Modern World. Anniversary Edition in Honour of Professor Genowefa Grabowska*, Bydgoszcz-Katowice 2014, p. 153 ff.

Justice so requested—the Member States would agree to increase the number of Advocates General to eleven.[12] In this case, one of the three additional Advocates General would be assigned to Poland as a "permanent Advocate General" and the remaining two posts of Advocate General would become part of the rotation system.[13]

As a result, the entry into force of the Lisbon Treaty on 1 December 2009 did not lead to an increase in the number of Advocates General. This was in fact dependent on the submission of a request to this effect by the Court of Justice, which was initially very reluctant to increase the number of Advocates General in accordance with the principles stemming from the joint declaration.[14] A change in the Court's position only occurred in 2013,[15] as a result of which the Council adopted the above-mentioned decision on 25 June 2013.

A further recent development occurred in 2020. At the eve of the departure of the United Kingdom from the European Union, on 29 January 2020, Member States issued a Declaration 'on the consequences of the withdrawal of the United Kingdom for the Advocates General of the Court of Justice of the European Union', in which they clarified that the mandates, inter alia, of members of institutions appointed in relation to the United Kingdom's membership of the Union will automatically end as soon as the Treaties cease to apply to the United Kingdom and that the 'permanent post of Advocate General which was assigned to the United Kingdom' would be integrated in the rotation system.[16] As a consequence, the Advocate General nominated by the government of the United Kingdom left the Court.[17] She was replaced by an Advocate General from Greece with effect from 7 September 2020.[18] This last appointment was challenged by the Advocate General from the United Kingdom before the General Court and, subsequently on appeal

[12] See Declaration (No 38) on article 252 of the Treaty on the Functioning of the European Union regarding the number of Advocates-General in the Court of Justice.

[13] On the subject of the same declaration, see M. Nowacki, op. cit., p. 30.

[14] It seems that the content of the declaration could interfere with the Court's autonomy,since the Member States that negotiated the Lisbon Treaty indirectly persuaded the Court to make a specific claim. This can also be understood in the way that the Member States—since they had not chosen to increase the number of Advocates General by amending the Treaty provisions, which they had the full right to do and which they could have done with simplicity—left the question of increasing the number of Advocates General to the decision of the Court.

[15] A request to this effect was addressed to the Council on 16 January 2013.

[16] See 'Declaration by the Conference of the Representatives of the Governments of the Member States on the consequences of the withdrawal of the United Kingdom from the European Union for the Advocates-General of the Court of Justice of the European Union', Brussels, 29 January 2020, XT 21018/20.

[17] Between 1 February and 7 October 2020, she stayed on, based on Article 5(3) of Protocol (No 3) on the Statute of the Court of Justice of the European Union, as a consequence of which an Advocate-General shall continue to hold office until his successor takes up his duties.

[18] See Article 4 of Decision (EU) 2020/1251 of the Representatives of the Governments of the Member States of 2 September 2020 appointing three Judges and an Advocate-General to the Court of Justice (OJ 2020 L 292, p. 1).

before the Court of Justice. On 16 June 2021, the Court of Justice handed down its definite decision on the matter when it ruled that it upheld the General Court's judgment on appeal, the main reason being that acts adopted by representatives of the governments of the Member States, acting not in their capacity as members of the Council of the European Union or of the European Council but as representatives of their governments, and thus collectively exercising the powers of the Member States, are not subject to judicial review by the EU Courts under Article 263 TFEU.[19]

There are thus currently eleven Advocates General at the Court, five of whom are "permanent Advocates General" appointed by the largest Member States, while the remaining six Advocates General function on a rotating system involving the remaining Member States. Ergo, for the first time in EU history there are more rotating than permanent Advocates General.

3 Advocates General and Judges

Advocates General fulfil a different role at the Court than judges. The involvement of Advocates General in the proceedings before the Court ends, in principle, with the delivery of the Opinion. Advocates General do not participate in the deliberations on judgments and thus do not decide cases directly. Notwithstanding this, the status of the Advocates General is identical to that of the judges. Such equality manifests itself on several levels.

First, Advocates General are appointed according to the same procedure as judges. According to Article 19(2) TEU and the first subparagraph of Article 253 TFEU, judges and Advocates General are chosen from persons whose independence is beyond doubt, who possess[20] the qualifications required for appointment to the highest judicial offices in their respective countries or who are jurisconsults of recognised competence. Advocates General and judges are appointed by common accord of the governments of the Member States for a term of six years. They are eligible for reappointment. As set out above, the possibility of reappointment in practice refers only to the "permanent Advocates General" or, as in the case of Nils, after the term as Advocate General has been served, the subsequent appointment to judge.

The Treaties do not specify precisely how candidates for judges and Advocates General are selected within the Member States. Not all States provide for an internal selection procedure.[21] In the case of judges, insofar as the Treaty itself

[19] See Order of the Court in *Sharpston v Council and Representatives of the Governments of the Member States*, C-685/20 P,EU:C:2021:485, para. 51.

[20] On the issue of the independence of the Advocate General, see K. Borgsmidt, op. cit., p. 107.

[21] In Poland, the selection procedure is governed by Regulation No. 10 of the Minister of Foreign Affairs of 20 May 2013 on the appointment of a committee for the selection of candidates for the posts of Judge and Advocate General of the Court of Justice and Judge of the General Court of the European Union.

requires that they come from each Member State (Article 19(2), first subparagraph, TEU—"one judge from each Member State"), the Treaty does not directly preclude an Advocate General from coming from a Member State other than the State proposing him. However, this is at best a theoretical eventuality. In any case, both judges and Advocates General must receive a positive opinion on their suitability from the committee foreseen in Article 255 TFEU before their appointment. So far, it has only happened twice that this committee has given a negative opinion with regard to a proposal of a Member State for the office of Advocate General.[22]

Secondly, both judges and Advocates General participate in the same way in the General Meeting of the Court (fr. *réunion générale*).[23] This meeting is typically held on a weekly basis, brings together all Members of the Court[24] as well as the Registrar[25] and is chaired by the President.[26] Its principal task is to take decisions concerning administrative issues and procedural matters in each case[27] through the adoption of the so-called "preliminary reports" (fr. *rapport préalable*).[28] This document is drawn up by the judge rapporteur and the Advocate General responsible for the case in question. It contains the proposals for the further procedural issues of the case. Any Member of the Court, be it a judge or an Advocate General, can prepare a note if they disagree with the proposals contained in the "preliminary report". In such a situation, the note is subject to discussion at the General Meeting. If the Members of the Court do not reach an agreement, it may—as *ultima ratio*—come to a vote in which the votes of the judges and those of the Advocates General carry equal weight.

Thirdly, the equality of status of judges and Advocates General is confirmed by the Protocol Rules of the Court. The seniority of Judges and Advocates General is thus determined without distinction according to the date on which they took up their duties.[29]

Fourthly and finally, the equality of status of Judges and Advocates General is evidenced by the fact that it happens that former Advocates General occupy the posts of judges[30] or former judges occupy the posts of Advocates General.[31] In this

[22] After the issuance of the negative evaluation, these candidates renounced of their own accord. The Committee also already issued negative evaluations to candidates for a post of judge at the Court or the General Court. On each occasion, such applications were withdrawn by the Member States.

[23] See Article 25 of the Rules of Procedure of the Court of Justice.

[24] By 'Members' of the Court, one understands Judges and Advocates General.

[25] See Article 25 of the Rules of Procedure.

[26] See Article 9(2) of the Rules of Procedure.

[27] Namely, the proposals contained in preliminary reports, see Articles 25 and 59 of the Rules of Procedure.

[28] On the preliminary report, see, in particular, Article 59 of the Rules of Procedure.

[29] See Article 7(1) of the Rules of Procedure.

[30] G.F. Mancini and Sir Gordon Slynn 1988, C. Gulmann 1994, A. Tizzano 2006, J. L. da Cruz Vilaça 2012, N. Jääskinen 2019 and N. Wahl 2019.

[31] A. Trabucchi 1973, F. Capotorti 1976, A. La Pergola 1995 and M. Wathelet 2012.

case, the Court's Rules of Protocol take into account the length of service achieved in the course of fulfilling the previous function. At this point, it is worth emphasising that there have been a number of occasions of the appointment of a person to the post of Judge or Advocate General at the Court of Justice who has previously performed the function of Judge at the General Court of the European Union. However, it has only occurred once that an Advocate General has taken the place of a judge at the General Court of the European Union, which is a court of 'first' instance in relation to the Court of Justice.[32]

Regardless of the equal status of Judges and Advocates General, both categories of Members of the Court retain their autonomy. In this context, it is worth mentioning one issue that raised certain doubts at the time, namely the election of the President of the Court of Justice. According to Article 253, third subparagraph, TFEU, the judges elect the President of the Court. There is no mention of Advocates General. Yet, the President of the Court of Justice is the President of the entire Court of Justice, which includes judges and Advocates General, as well as President 'Court of Justice of the European Union'—in the sense of the entire institution under Article 19(1), first subparagraph, first sentence, TEU, which includes the Court of Justice and the General Court.

Proposals have cropped up from time to time to amend Article 253, third subparagraph, TFEU in such a way that Advocates General are also admitted to the election of the President of the Court. It seems that regardless of the infinitesimal chance of such an amendment, there are many arguments in favour of retaining the existing system. In my opinion, the non-participation of the Advocates General in the election of the President of the Court constitutes an element of their independence. They are, in fact, persons who—unlike judges, who take their decisions collegially in chambers—act independently. They neither agree nor discuss the legal arguments and views expressed in the Opinions with other Members of the Court, not even with other Advocates General.

Moreover, it seems that the question of the participation of Advocates General in the election of the President of the Court has become less important after changes were made concerning the office of the First Advocate General. Here, before 2015, further to Article 14(1) of the Rules of Procedure of the Court, the First Advocate General was appointed, by the Court, for a period of one year, after consultation of the Advocates General. It was common practice that the First Advocate General was appointed on the basis of the principle of rotation in such a way that this function was conferred for a period of one year on the most senior Advocate General who had not yet exercised this function. In this way, among the eight Advocates General at the time, each of them—in practice—fulfilled this function at least once in the course of his term of office (in the case of the "permanent Advocates General" whose mandate could be renewed, the possibility of fulfilling the function of First Advocate General did not have to concern each of his mandates). In view of the

[32] I am referring here to the situation of J. L. da Cruz Vilaça who went from Advocate General to becoming President of the newly-created Court of First Instance (and, later, judge at the Court of Justice).

increase in the number of Advocates General to eleven, the previous system—at least as far as the "rotating Advocates General" are concerned—this could no longer be ensured and changes were made.

The first change occurred in October 2015 when, as a result of informal agreements, the Advocates General elected among themselves the First Advocate General for a period of three years, aligning the term of office of the First Advocate General with that of the President of the Court and of the President of Chambers of five judges. The change in practice was not accompanied by any amendment to Article 14 of the Rules of Procedure of the Court and constituted a gentleman's agreement, under which General Meeting of the Court would extend the one-year term of office of the First Advocate General, once elected, twice. It was also decided that the First Advocate General would, for the purposes of protocol, be placed on an equal footing with the judges who—on the basis of the election made by the judges—exercise the function of Presidents of the Chambers of five judges. This regime determined the election of the First Advocate General in 2015 and 2018.

The second change occurred in November 2019 and entailed a change to the Court's Rules of Procedure: Article 14 of these Rules of Procedure was substantially overhauled so as to formalise the election of the First Advocate General. In essence, this change codified a practice that had already been in place since 2015 when Advocate General Melchior Wathelet was elected as First Advocate General for the term 2015–2018.[33] Article 14 of the Rules of Procedure now stipulates that the Advocates General elect one of their number as First Advocate General for a term of three years, by secret ballot. Moreover, the name of the First Advocate General is now published in the EU's Official Journal.

To conclude this part of the considerations, it should be recalled that Article 19(1), first subparagraph, TEU decides on another important question. It states that the Advocates General shall assist the Court of Justice.[34] This means that not only Opinions, but also any procedural acts undertaken by the Advocates General should be carried out with a view to assisting the Court or otherwise facilitating its work.[35] This must not, of course, affect the principle of independence and the need for the Advocates General to perform their duties conscientiously.

4 The Role of First Advocate General

Given the autonomy of Advocates General within the EU judicial architecture and their relative lack of involvement within the Court's hierarchy, the term and function of a 'First' Advocate General might, at first sight, amount to an oxymoron. Yet such an understanding would be too intuitive and, in fact, misplaced. Whereas judges

[33] I have held this position since October 2018.

[34] My emphasis.

[35] For more details on the subject: K. Borgsmidt, op. cit., p. 108.

have their interests represented by the President, the Vice-President and, to a certain extent, in particular when it comes to structural matters regarding procedure, by the Presidents of Chambers, there is a case to be made that also the Advocates General should benefit from a person coordinating matters proper to the Advocates General and representing their collective interests within the institution. This is why they designate, among themselves a *Klassensprecher*, in the form of the First Advocate General.

The cardinal responsibility of the First Advocate General is to assign cases to his colleagues, as is stipulated in Article 16(1) of the Court's Rules of Procedure.[36] In addition to this, the First Advocate General has important advisory functions: he is thus systematically heard by the President before the latter takes a decision on procedural matters in cases which have not yet been assigned to a judge and an Advocate General. Moreover, he is heard, together with the Vice-President, by the President before a request for a preliminary ruling is transferred to the General Court. Finally, the First Advocate General plays a crucial role in the review procedure.

I shall come back to all of these aspects below.

5 The Involvement of Advocates General in Judicial Procedures Before the Court of Justice

It is well known that Advocates General draft and deliver Opinions. What is less well known is their involvement in the course of judicial proceedings before the publication of their Opinions. This part shall attempt to shed light on this issue.

Each case received by the Court is assigned to an Advocate General and a Judge Rapporteur. In respect of the Advocates General, this assignment is made by the First Advocate General, and in respect of the judges, by the President of the Court. The assignment of cases is in principle at the discretion of the President of the Court and the First Advocate General. Of course, they take into account the current workload of each of the members of the Court, but also whether the individual cases have parallels. In the case of requests for a preliminary ruling, Judges and Advocates General are not assigned cases filed by the courts of the states from which they originate. Similarly, in the case of direct actions, the Judge Rapporteur and the Advocate General may not come from the State that is a direct party to such proceedings. In principle, the same case will also not be assigned to a Judge and an Advocate General who come from the same State.[37]

My impression is that—to the extent that a certain tendency towards specialisation can be observed in the area of the assignment of cases to judges—in the case of

[36] As a matter of fact, traditionally the First Advocate General's role was confined to this.

[37] It seems to me that only twice, and probably through an oversight, I was assigned cases in which the rapporteur was the Polish judge Prof. Marek Safjan. I am referring to the cases C-375/13, *Kolassa*, and C-310/13, *Novo Nordisk Pharma*.

the Advocates General, the assignment of a specific type of case to the same Advocate General tends to be avoided. This practice is of course the exclusive result of the decisions taken by the President of the Court and First Advocate General. They may be subject to change, together with changes in the persons exercising these functions. It seems, however, that the tendency towards a certain specialisation among judges may be justified by practical reasons connected with procedural economy. In the case of Advocates General, a pursuit of excessive specialisation would not be advisable. Unlike judges, whose judgments are made collegially in chambers, Advocates General prepare their Opinions entirely independently. It can thus be assumed that in cases relating to matters in the same field, the Advocate General will be more likely to follow the reasoning and approach to legal problems presented in previous Opinions concerning similar issues. Put simply, consistency matters more for the Court's case-law than for the Opinions of its Advocates General. In this respect, the role of the Advocate General is different from that of the judge. Indeed, the Advocate General will focus to a lesser extent than the judges on the stability of the case law and the continuation of the same line of judgments. Sometimes it is worthwhile for another Advocate General to look at similar legal issues with a different approach, especially in cases that are characterised by a high degree of sensitivity. Thus, a First Advocate General is, in my view, well advised to follow the practice of allowing different perspectives on similar legal problems and thus avoiding the "monopolisation" of specific areas of EU law by individual Advocates General. After all, the requirement of consistency of case-law ought to be a concern more for judges than for Advocates General.

After the appointment of the Rapporteur and the Advocate General for the respective case, and after the conclusion of the written procedure, the preparation for the "preliminary report" begins. Its aim is to decide on the basic procedural questions. Firstly, it is a matter of determining the composition of the respective case (Chamber of three Judges, Chamber of five Judges, Grand Chamber, Full Court).

Secondly—and this is the most important aspect from the Advocate General's point of view—it has to be decided whether the respective case requires an Opinion. It should be noted that in contrast to the previous legal situation, in which the Advocate General prepared an Opinion on each case, today Article 20, fifth subparagraph, of the Statute of the Court of Justice provides for an exception in this respect. Thus, according to this provision, if the Court considers that a case does not raise a new point of law, it may decide, after hearing the Advocate General, that the case shall be decided without an Opinion of the Advocate General.

Of course, determining whether a case does not raise a new question of law is not a simple task. It happens that—even if such a determination can be made—other points may speak in favour of the need to prepare Opinions, such as the degree of complexity of the facts underlying the case. It seems that this is also how the duty of the Advocates General to assist the Court is implemented.[38]

---

[38] Article 19 para. 1 first paragraph TEU.

It happens that there are differences of opinion between the Judge Rapporteur and the Advocate General as to whether an Opinion should be drafted in a particular case. It seems that this type of doubt should rather be decided in the way that Opinions are to be drafted by the Advocate General. However, if no agreement can be found on this issue at the stage of agreeing the "preliminary report", the case is submitted to the General Meeting, which then takes a decision. In the practice of the functioning of the General Meeting, an unwritten rule has developed, called Cunha Rodrigues[39] rule, according to which, in a case where the Advocate General sees the existence of a new question of law—even in contradiction to the position of the Rapporteur—an Opinion should always be prepared.

In any case where the "preliminary report" recommends that the Advocate General refrain from preparing an Opinion, the motives for such a position should be adequately explained. In this case, the Judge Rapporteur should explain in the "preliminary report" why no substantial questions of law arise in the case and, at the same time, make a preliminary proposal for the judgment in the case, at least as far as the general direction of that judgment is concerned.[40] Moreover, before agreeing that a case should not benefit from an Opinion, an Advocate General should subscribe to the content of the preliminary report, that is to say—without obviously prejudging an ensuing judgment—the Advocate General should subscribe to the point of view as to how the case should be treated on substance, as expressed in the preliminary report.

The remaining points that should be included in a "preliminary report" mainly concern the following questions: should a hearing be held; is there a need to contact the parties to the proceedings or, in the case of questions referred for a preliminary ruling, the referring court, in order to obtain additional information; should a possible hearing be limited to certain aspects of the proceedings; should the Court's Directorate of Research and Documentation be consulted in order to analyse certain points of law? The "preliminary report" may also contain suggestions concerning the application of one of the simplified procedures provided for in the Rules of Procedure of the Court of Justice. This concerns in particular Article 53(2), pursuant to which "[w]here it is clear that the Court has no jurisdiction to hear and determine a case or where a request or an application is manifestly inadmissible, the Court may, after hearing the Advocate General, at any time decide to give a decision by reasoned order without taking further steps in the proceedings". In addition, a special procedure—concerning to questions referred for a preliminary ruling—is provided for in Article 99 of the Rules of Procedure. According to this provision, it is possible to give the decision in the form of an order "[w]here a question referred to the Court for a preliminary ruling is identical to a question on which the Court has already ruled, where the reply to such a question may be clearly deduced from existing case-law or where the answer to the question referred for a preliminary ruling

[39] From the name of a former Portuguese judge.

[40] However, this does not follow from a rule defined in the Court's documents, but from the practice established by the Court's General Meeting.

admits of no reasonable doubt". Moreover, with regard to appeals against judgments of the General Court, Article 181 of the Rules of Procedure states that "[w]here the appeal or cross-appeal is, in whole or in part, manifestly inadmissible or manifestly unfounded, the Court may at any time, acting on a proposal from the Judge-Rapporteur and after hearing the Advocate General, decide by reasoned order to dismiss that appeal or cross-appeal in whole or in part".

It should be added that the appeals procedure before the Court of Justice has recently undergone substantial changes. An appeal brought against a decision of the General Court concerning a decision of an independent board of appeal shall not proceed unless the Court of Justice first decides that it should be allowed to do so. This applies since 1 May 2019 for the European Union Intellectual Property Office, the Community Plant Variety Office, the European Chemicals Agency and the European Union Aviation Safety Agency[41] and since 1 September 2024 for the European Union Agency for the Cooperation of Energy Regulators, the Single Resolution Board, the European Banking Authority, the European Securities and Markets Authority, the European Insurance and Occupational Pensions Authority and the European Union Agency for Railways.[42] Moreover, this procedure applies also to appeals brought against decisions of the General Court concerning a decision of an independent board of appeal, set up after 1 May 2019 within any other body, office or agency of the Union, which has to be seized before an action can be brought before the General Court and decisions of the General Court relating to the performance of a contract containing an arbitration clause, within the meaning of Article 272 TFEU. Such appeals are, in other words, subject to a prior determination, by that Court, that they are admissible. Here, the decision on that request is taken, on a proposal from the Judge Rapporteur and after hearing the Advocate General, by a Chamber specially established for that purpose, presided over by the Vice-President of the Court and including also the Judge-Rapporteur and the President of the Chamber of three Judges to which the Judge-Rapporteur is attached on the date on which the request is made.

As I mentioned above, a member of the Court who disagrees with the proposals contained in the "preliminary report" may submit a memorandum to the General Meeting. The General Meeting then takes the final decision after a discussion. It should also be emphasised that this ensures that each judge and each Advocate General can—at least indirectly—exert an influence on the proceedings conducted before the Court. This system is quite positive, since the Court of Justice, as the highest instance, has a special responsibility for the application of EU law. Put simply, one can therefore assert that all its members, both judges and Advocates General, stand behind the decisions taken by the Court.

---

[41] See Article 58a of the Statute of the Court of Justice, as amended by Article 1 of Regulation (EU, Euratom) 2019/629 of the European Parliament and of the Council of 17 April 2019 amending Protocol No 3 on the Statute of the Court of Justice of the European Union (OJ 2019 L 111, p. 1).

[42] See Article 58a of the Statute of the Court of Justice, as amended by Article 1 of Regulation (EU, Euratom) 2024/2019 of the European Parliament and of the Council of 11 April 2024 amending Protocol No 3 on the Statute of the Court of Justice of the European Union (OJ 2024/2019 L).

In this context, it should be recalled that both "preliminary report" and the memoranda prepared in relation to it by the Judges and Advocates General and discussed at the General Meeting of the Court do not constitute public documents.

To conclude this part of this contribution, it should be noted that the Rules of Procedure of the Court of Justice provide for the participation of the Advocate General in many other procedural measures taken by the Court.[43] Most often, this is based on the hearing of the Advocate General assigned to the particular case. These include, inter alia, the following measures: concerning the joinder of cases;[44] concerning the submission of new evidence after the closure of the written phase of the proceedings;[45] concerning the admission of a language other than the language of the proceedings;[46] concerning the stay of proceedings;[47] concerning the reopening of the oral phase of the proceedings;[48] concerning the application of the urgent preliminary ruling procedure;[49] concerning the disposal of proceedings;[50] and also concerning other formal and individual questions.[51]

As regards the requirement that the parties must have the opportunity to acquaint themselves with the Advocate General's Opinion, it is worth pointing to Article 83 of the Rules of Procedure of the Court. This states that "[t]he Court may at any time, after hearing the Advocate General, order the opening or reopening of the oral part of the procedure, in particular if it considers that it lacks sufficient information or where a party has, after the close that part of the procedure, submitted a new fact which is of such a nature as to be a decisive factor for the decision of the Court, or where the case must be decided on the basis of an argument which has not been debated between the parties or the interested persons referred to in Article 23 of the Statute". This provision thus constitutes the basis for being able, in exceptional situations, to reopen the oral procedure, which would also involve the preparation of new Opinions by the Advocate General.[52]

It is also worth mentioning the practice of the Court of Justice, which may not yet be widely known. Thus, in October 2016, a modified procedure began to be

[43] See more on the subject: M. T. D'Alessio, V. Kronenberger, 'Quelques réflexions sur le nouveau règlement de procédure de la Cour de justice et son impact sur les fonctions de l'avocat général', in *De Rome à Lisbonne : les juridictions de l'Union européenne à la croisée des chemins*, Brussels, 2013, p. 313 ff.

[44] Article 54 para. 2.

[45] Article 128 para. 2.

[46] Article 37 para. 1 lit. c) and Article 37 para. 3.

[47] Article 55 para. 1.

[48] Article 83.

[49] Article 108 para. 1.

[50] Article 149.

[51] Article 151 para. 5.

[52] In the case of proceedings in which I was given the opportunity to present a new Opinion, such a situation has occurred twice. See Order of the Court of 12 October 2017 in Case, *Louboutin*, C-163/16, EU:C:2017:765 and Order of the Court of 23 March 2023 in Case C-470/21, La Quadrature du Net.

applied in the Court of Justice with regard to appeals against judgments of the General Court of the European Union which—on the basis of the above-mentioned Article 181 of the Rules of Procedure before the Court of Justice—may be considered manifestly inadmissible or manifestly unfounded. Now the reasoning that this provision applies has been transferred to the Advocates General. If the Judge-Rapporteur and the Advocate General are positive about the possibility of applying this rule (usually such a recommendation includes a preliminary analysis of the case carried out by the Court's Directorate of Research and Documentation) and this is accepted by the General Meeting, the statement of reasons for the decision is prepared by the Advocate General. This reasoning is then fully incorporated into the decision issued by the competent Chamber of the Court. This chamber then simply states that "for the reasons stated by the Advocate General, the appeal must be dismissed". Currently, this practice is limited to three areas of EU law, namely civil service law, public procurement law and access to documents.

6 The 2024 Reform

The 2024 reform of the Court marks a certain shift in the EU's judicial architecture.[53] Regulation (EU, Euratom) 2024/2019 introduces a number of changes to the competences and procedures of both the Court of Justice and the General Court. At the heart of these changes lies an expanded role for the General Court in preliminary ruling procedures, as well as modifications to the system of appeals before the Court of Justice.

The process leading to the 2024 reform began on November 30, 2022, when the Court of Justice submitted a request to the European Parliament and the Council of the European Union to modify its Statute. Following a favourable opinion from the Commission in March 2023, Parliament and Council, via the ordinary legislative procedure, adopted of Regulation (EU, Euratom) 2024/2019 on April 11, 2024.

This regulation introduced two major changes: First, it conferred on the General Court the competence to hear and determine questions referred for a preliminary ruling by courts of the Member States under Article 267 TFEU in specific areas.[54] However, the Court of Justice retains exclusive competence for preliminary questions that "raise independent questions relating to the interpretation of primary law, public international law, general principles of Union law or the Charter of Fundamental Rights of the European Union" (Article 50b, second paragraph, of the Statute).

---

[53] See in detail M.-A. Gaudissart, 'Genèse et négotiation de la réforme de l'architecture juridictionnelle de l'Union européenne' (2024) Rivista de Derecho Comunitario Europeao, 79, pp. 27–48.

[54] The regulation grants the General Court competence to answer preliminary questions in six specific areas: the common system of value added tax, excise duties, the Customs Code, the tariff classification of goods in the Combined Nomenclature, compensation and assistance to passengers in the event of denied boarding or of cancellation or long delay of flights and the greenhouse gas emission allowance trading system.

In practice, the system established by the Court consists of a "single entry point" (fr. 'guichet unique') system, whereby all preliminary references are initially filed with the Court of Justice. The Court then verifies whether the conditions for transferring the case to the General Court are met.

Secondly, it extended the scope of application of the prior admission mechanism for appeals lodged before the Court of Justice.

These changes aim to enable the Court of Justice to "continue to fulfil its mission of safeguarding and strengthening the unity and consistency of Union law" and to ensure that its decisions "are of the highest quality" (Recital 2 of Regulation 2024/2019).

First, when the Court, via the newly-established single entry point, verifies whether or not to transfer a request for a preliminary ruling to the General Court, the First Advocate General is heard. This new procedure, governed by Article 93a of the Rules of Procedure now looks as follows: a request for a preliminary ruling is immediately transmitted, by the Registry, to the President, the Vice-President and the First Advocate General. The latter two are then heard, before the President takes a decision. If the President considers that the request comes exclusively within one or more of the specific areas referred to in the first paragraph of Article 50b of the Statute, he shall so inform the Registry, which shall transmit the request to the Registry of the General Court. The proceedings then continue before the General Court in accordance with the provisions of its Rules of Procedure.

If, however, the President considers that although the request for a preliminary ruling comes within one or more of the specific areas referred to in the first paragraph of Article 50b of the Statute, it also concerns other areas or raises independent questions relating to the interpretation of primary law, public international law, general principles of Union law or the Charter of Fundamental Rights of the European Union, within the meaning of the second paragraph of Article 50b of the Statute, he shall immediately refer the request to the Court of Justice. This means, in practice, that the matter is submitted to the General Meeting of the Court. After, in practice, a discussion of the case, the Court, in the formation of the General Meeting, takes a decision. If it considers that the request comes exclusively within one or more of the specific areas referred to in the first paragraph of Article 50b of the Statute, the Registry of the Court of Justice transmits that request to the Registry of the General Court and the proceedings continue before the General Court in accordance with the provisions of its Rules of Procedure. Otherwise, the proceedings continue before the Court of Justice in accordance with the provisions of these Rules.[55]

This new task adds considerably to the workload of the First Advocate General. To give an idea of numbers: in 2025 around 75 cases were submitted to this procedure. The overwhelming majority is transferred to the General Court. This does not mean, however, that every single case is not carefully scrutinised.

[55] As per Article 256(3) TFEU, the General Court, during the course of the proceedings, considers that the case requires a decision of principle likely to affect the unity or consistency of Union law, it *may* refer the case to the Court of Justice for a ruling. In such a situation, the procedure is then governed by Article 114b of the Rules of Procedure.

Secondly, the First Advocate General plays a key role in the 'revived'[56] review procedure.[57] As is well known, a dedicated Chamber of five Judges (the Reviewing Chamber) is designated for a period of one year for the purpose of deciding whether a decision of the General Court is to be reviewed in accordance with Article 62 of the Statute.[58] Here, it is for the First Advocate General, if he considers that a review should be carried out, to propose this to the Court.[59] Subsequently, the Reviewing Chamber, acting on a proposal from the Judge-Rapporteur, shall decide whether the decision of the General Court is to be reviewed.[60] The First Advocate's General proposal must be made within one month of delivery of the decision by the General Court. Within one month of receiving the proposal made by the First Advocate General, the Court of Justice shall decide whether or not the decision should be reviewed.[61] All this implies that it is for the First Advocate General to examine each decision of the General Court, made in the context of the preliminary reference procedure. While, at the time of writing, this has mainly consisted in reviewing decisions of removal from the register, further to a withdrawal of a case by the referring court, this will, in future, also considerably bind (human) resources at the disposal of the First Advocate General.

7 Conclusion

The institution of the Advocate General has become very much rooted in the legal system of the European Union. Today, one can hardly imagine a debate on any legal issue without taking into account the Opinion of the Advocates General. One hardly encounters voices proposing a reform of the Court that disregards the role of the Advocates General. The fact that some of their Opinions are criticised in no way diminishes the fundamental role of the Advocates General in shaping the jurisprudence of the Court, and also the jurisprudence of the national courts. As regards more specifically the role of the First Advocate General, it can safely be stated that this has evolved from a role primarily of representation and case-allocation to one which is more embedded in the internal architecture of the Court and where, in particular with the 2024 reform, the advisory function of the First Advocate General has considerably been strengthened.

---

[56] I use this term advisedly, since that procedure had been de-facto dormant, if not buried, following the integration of the Civil Service Tribunal into the General Court.

[57] The review procedure, which is governed by Title VI of the Rules of Procedure, is a special judicial mechanism that allows for the review of decisions made by the General Court under certain conditions, specifically in cases where the decision might seriously affect the unity or consistency of EU law, see Article 256(3) TFEU and Article 62 et seq. of the Court's Statute.

[58] See Article 191 of the Rules of Procedure.

[59] See Article 194(1) of the Rules of Procedure.

[60] See Article 194(5) of the Rules of Procedure.

[61] See Article 62 of the Statute.

Réflexions sur le transfert de certains renvois préjudiciels au Tribunal et sur les nouvelles procédures annexes à la réforme de la Cour de justice de l'Union européenne

Melchior Wathelet

C'est un plaisir et un honneur pour moi de participer au liber amicorum de mon ami, Nils Wahl, dont la carrière à la Cour de justice de l'Union européenne (juge au Tribunal de l'Union européenne, puis avocat général près la Cour de justice et enfin juge à la Cour de justice) a pris fin au mois d'octobre 2024.

Il va pouvoir retrouver en Suède sa famille, sa ferme, ses passions autres que le droit européen (dont le goût que nous partageons pour les belles voitures). Avec de très bons souvenirs, spécialement lorsque nous étions l'un et l'autre avocats généraux entre 2012 et 2018, de nos relations amicales et professionnelles, je lui dédie ces quelques réflexions sur la réforme du statut de la Cour de justice de l'Union européenne (ci-après le « statut de la Cour ») contenue dans le règlement 2024/2019 du 11 avril 2024 publié au *Journal officiel de l'Union européenne* le 12 août 2024 et entré en vigueur le 1er septembre 2024,[1] transférant partiellement au Tribunal de l'Union européenne à partir du 1er octobre 2024 la compétence préjudicielle et étendant, dès le 1er septembre 2024, le mécanisme d'admission préalable des pourvois.[2]

[1] Règlement (UE, Euratom) 2024/2019 du Parlement européen et du Conseil du 11 avril 2024 modifiant le protocole n° 3 sur le statut de la Cour de justice de l'Union européenne (JO 2024/2019).

[2] Les références qui seront faites dans cet article au président de la Cour de justice K. Lenaerts et au juge S. Gervasoni visent les exposés que l'un et l'autre ont présentés lors de la matinée d'étude consacrée à « La compétence préjudicielle au sein de la Cour de justice de l'Union européenne – réorganisation et perspectives » organisée le 31 mai 2024 par P. Dermine, professeur de droit de l'Union européenne à l'Université libre de Bruxelles, et J. Wildemeersch, professeur de droit de l'Union européenne à l'Université de Liège et référendaire à la Cour de justice de l'Union européenne.

M. Wathelet (✉)
Leuven University, Leuven, Belgium

L. Prete, L. Rezki (eds.), *Judging & (Re)Thinking European Union Law*,
https://doi.org/10.1007/978-3-032-13473-8_26

1 Un peu d'histoire : la longue lutte contre l'arriéré judiciaire

Depuis très longtemps et même après la création du Tribunal de première instance des Communautés européennes en 1989, la Cour de justice vit, à juste titre, avec l'obsession de ne pas créer un arriéré judiciaire en gardant en permanence pour chaque type de recours un œil sur le compteur des mois qui séparent l'introduction d'un dossier et l'arrêt ou l'ordonnance qui le clôture. Cette gestion des délais a, en premier lieu, amené la Cour à modifier ses règles de procédure et, en second lieu, inspiré des modifications de l'architecture juridictionnelle de l'Union européenne, par des modifications du Traité et du statut de la Cour.

1.1 Des modifications de procédure

À ce sujet, j'aime raconter une anecdote datant de mes premiers mois à la Cour. À l'époque, une audience était systématiquement organisée pour chaque affaire, les plaideurs pouvant demander (et donc obtenir) trente minutes de temps de parole. Lors d'une réunion générale, ayant constaté l'inutilité de certaines audiences pourtant très longues, où les plaideurs se contentaient de répéter ce qu'ils avaient écrit dans leurs observations et où les juges ne posaient aucune question, j'avais proposé de modifier la règle en vigueur qui voulait « pour toute affaire une audience ». Cela m'avait valu la réflexion de notre collègue grec, doyen de l'assemblée M. K. Kakouris, qui au nouveau et (relativement) jeune collègue que j'étais m'avait lancé : « vous avez le discours de quelqu'un qui n'a jamais connu la dictature. Sachez qu'une audience est toujours utile même lorsqu'elle est inutile ».

En 1995, le nombre d'affaires introduites à la Cour fut de 408, comprenant à la fois les recours directs, les pourvois et les renvois préjudiciels. L'idée d'une réforme a cependant fait son chemin : après plusieurs modifications qui marquèrent une évolution progressive, dont la première fut d'exiger une demande motivée d'audience de plaidoiries présentée par les parties, l'actuel article 76, paragraphe 2, du règlement de procédure de la Cour de justice prévoit que, même dans ce cas, « la Cour peut décider de ne pas tenir d'audience de plaidoirie si elle estime, à la lecture des mémoires ou observations déposées au cours de la phase écrite de la procédure, être suffisamment informée pour statuer ».

Progressivement également, la Cour s'est montrée de plus en plus exigeante sur la motivation des demandes d'audience et a réduit le temps maximum de plaidoirie. Dans les procédures préjudicielles, la Cour de justice a pris contact avec le juge de renvoi pour lui demander si, compte tenu de la jurisprudence existante, ce juge maintenait sa ou ses question(s). L'article 99 du règlement de procédure de la Cour a permis à cette dernière dans certaines hypothèses, à savoir lorsqu'une question posée à titre préjudiciel était identique à une autre question sur laquelle la Cour avait déjà statué ou lorsque la réponse à une telle question pouvait être clairement déduite de la jurisprudence ou encore lorsque la réponse ne laissait place à aucun doute raisonnable, de décider sur proposition du juge rapporteur, l'avocat général entendu, de statuer par voie d'ordonnance motivée.

Au début des années 2000 (au moment où le seuil des 500 affaires introduites à la Cour de justice fut dépassé), l'article 20 du statut de la Cour fut modifié pour prévoir que, lorsque la Cour « estime que l'affaire ne soulève aucune question de droit nouvelle, » elle « peut décider, l'avocat général entendu, que l'affaire sera jugée sans conclusions de l'avocat général », ce qui permet encore de réduire globalement la durée moyenne des procédures devant la Cour.

Si d'autres propositions procédurales ont été avancées, comme par exemple l'exclusion des cours nationales de première instance du mécanisme de renvoi préjudiciel, elles ne furent jamais envisagées par la Cour de justice qui n'a jamais voulu toucher aux caractéristiques essentielles de coopération et de dialogue de ce mécanisme.

1.2 Des modifications de l'architecture juridictionnelle de l'Union européenne

L'augmentation du nombre d'affaires introduites à la Cour de justice avait déjà motivé la création du Tribunal de l'Union européenne devenu opérationnel en 1989 sous l'appellation de « Tribunal de première instance des Communautés européennes ». Il était chargé des recours introduits par les particuliers (personnes physiques et morales), y compris les recours formés en matière de fonction publique.

Le Tribunal a très vite atteint un rythme annuel moyen de 400 affaires, qui n'étaient dès lors plus traitées par la Cour, celle-ci devenant toutefois compétente pour traiter les pourvois introduits contre les arrêts du Tribunal.

C'est alors qu'intervint le Traité de Nice, adopté en l'an 2000 et entré en vigueur en 2003, qui modifia ou permit la modification fondamentale de l'architecture juridictionnelle de l'Union européenne et plus spécifiquement la répartition des tâches entre la Cour de justice et le Tribunal.

Le Traité de Nice a prévu en son article 245 que le statut de la Cour pouvait être modifié à l'exception de son titre I, par une décision du Conseil, statuant à l'unanimité sur demande de la Cour de justice et après consultation du Parlement européen et de la Commission ou sur demande de la Commission et après consultation du Parlement européen et de la Cour de justice.

Par son article 225, le Traité de Nice a aussi renversé le principe d'attribution à la Cour et au Tribunal des principaux types de recours. Alors que jusque-là, ils étaient tous de la compétence de la Cour sauf ceux que le statut de la Cour attribuait au Tribunal, cet article 225 prévoit que le Tribunal sera compétent pour connaître en première instance de tous les recours en annulation, carence, responsabilité « à l'exception de ceux qui sont attribués à une chambre juridictionnelle et de ceux que le statut réserve à la Cour de justice ».

Le Traité de Nice fera l'objet d'une première application à ce sujet dans la décision du Conseil du 26 avril 2004, qui a modifié, sur base de la nouvelle procédure prévue par l'article 245 CE, les articles 51 et 54 du statut de la Cour pour rendre le Tribunal compétent pour les recours introduits par les États membres contre des actes ou des abstentions de statuer de la Commission (sauf en matière de coopération renforcée) ou contre le Conseil (en matière d'aides d'État, d'anti-dumping, ou lorsque le Conseil s'est réservé des compétences d'exécution). Le Tribunal n'était donc plus seulement compétent pour les recours introduits par des particuliers, personnes physiques ou morales.

À partir de cette date, le nombre de recours directs introduits à la Cour a fortement diminué puisque cette catégorie ne concernait plus que les recours en manquement et les recours en annulation ou en carence introduits par une institution de l'Union.

Le Traité de Nice a encore prévu deux autres voies possibles pour réformer le partage des tâches entre les deux juridictions. La première possibilité consiste pour le Parlement européen et le Conseil, soit sur proposition de la Commission après consultation de la Cour de justice, soit sur demande de la Cour de justice après consultation de la Commission, à créer des tribunaux spécialisés (appelés alors chambres juridictionnelles) adjoints au Tribunal et chargés de connaître en première instance de certaines catégories de recours formés dans des matières spécifiques (article 257 TFUE qui a quelque peu modifié l'ancien article 225a du TCE).

Outre la proposition de la Commission en 2003 de créer un tribunal spécialisé en droit des brevets (proposition qui n'a même jamais été discutée), un seul tribunal spécialisé a été créé en 2005 : le Tribunal de la Fonction publique pour la résolution des contentieux survenant entre l'Union européenne et ses collaborateurs, fonctionnaires ou contractuels. Ce Tribunal était composé de 7 juges (un des rares cas dans lesquels les États membres n'ont pas exigé d'avoir chacun un de leurs nationaux siégeant dans une institution !). Ce Tribunal a très bien fonctionné mais sa vie a été de courte durée puisqu'il a réintégré le Tribunal de l'Union européenne en 2016.

Il devenait en effet impératif de réduire la charge de travail accumulée au niveau du Tribunal de l'Union européenne et de raccourcir la durée des procédures qui y étaient introduites particulièrement dans les affaires de droit de la concurrence, le délai de traitement de ces dernières pouvant atteindre près de 50 mois.

Face à cette situation, la Cour de justice avait proposé la nomination de juges supplémentaires au Tribunal, dans un premier temps, douze, puis neuf juges ; les contraintes budgétaires conduisirent le Conseil à rejeter ces propositions. Ce fut dès lors une grande surprise que le Conseil accepte plus tard une augmentation de 28 juges au sein du Tribunal de l'Union européenne de façon … à ce que chaque État membre puisse nommer un second juge !

Cette décision fut mise en œuvre en trois étapes successives : douze nouveaux juges en 2015, réintégration en 2016 des sept juges venant du Tribunal de la Fonction publique et enfin en 2019, neuf autres juges. Le Tribunal de l'Union européenne (nouvelle appellation adoptée par le Traité de Lisbonne en 2009) était ainsi composé de cinquante-six juges, nombre réduit à 54 après le Brexit.

Il n'a pas été facile pour certains États membres de désigner ce deuxième juge car les candidats devaient franchir l'épreuve d'admission prévue par l'article 255 TFUE, si bien que ce n'est qu'en 2022 que la composition du Tribunal de l'Union européenne a été complète. Bien évidemment, du fait de cette réforme, il n'y eut plus de retard au Tribunal de l'Union européenne d'autant plus que le nombre d'affaires relevant du droit de la concurrence avait substantiellement décru, les entreprises préférant souvent un accord avec la Commission plutôt que de longs recours judiciaires. Mais c'est au niveau de la Cour de justice elle-même que le risque de création d'un arriéré judiciaire apparaissait à nouveau. Les chiffres étaient impressionnants :

- Le nombre total de dossiers introduits à la Cour de justice est passé de 502 en 2000, à 624 en 2010, à 950 en 2019 et, après la pandémie de Covid, 838 en 2021, 806 en 2022, 821 en 2023 ;
- Quant aux questions préjudicielles, il y en eut 224 en 2000, 385 en 2010, 641 en 2019, 567 en 2021, 546 en 2022 et 518 en 2023 (soit 63,1 % des affaires introduites à la Cour).

Les procédures préjudicielles représentent donc presque deux tiers des dossiers soumis à la Cour, quelque vingt-six autres pour cent étant constitués par les pourvois, les recours directs ne comptant plus que pour sept pour cent des dossiers introduits à la Cour.

La Cour a alors décidé qu'il était temps d'activer la seconde possibilité prévue par le Traité de modifier la répartition des tâches entre la Cour de justice et le Tribunal de l'Union européenne, à savoir le transfert de certaines questions préjudicielles au Tribunal lorsqu'elles étaient soumises « dans des matières spécifiques déterminées par le statut » (article 256, paragraphe, 3, TFUE, ex-article 225 TCE). Elle a ajouté à sa proposition l'extension du mécanisme d'admission préalable des pourvois.

Toujours dans la crainte d'être submergée de pourvois, la Cour de justice avait demandé que les pourvois formés contre les décisions du Tribunal de l'Union européenne portant sur une décision d'une chambre de recours indépendante, d'un office ou d'une agence de l'Union soient subordonnés à une procédure d'admission préalable à la procédure ordinaire de pourvoi. L'idée était que la décision en cause avait déjà fait l'objet avant la procédure devant le Tribunal, d'une procédure contradictoire de type judiciaire.

Cette demande de la Cour de justice fut acceptée par le Parlement et le Conseil dans un règlement du 17 avril 2019[3] qui a introduit un article 58 bis dans le statut de la Cour. Ce règlement visait dix offices ou agences de l'Union européenne.

Le filtrage s'est révélé plutôt efficace, puisque, sur 216 dossiers introduits depuis l'entrée en vigueur du mécanisme en 2019, seuls sept ont été admis à la procédure de pourvoi. Ce système s'appliquera désormais à toute décision du tribunal portant sur une décision d'une chambre de recours indépendante instituée après le 1er mai

[3] JO 2019 L 111.

2019 au sein de tout organe ou organisme de l'Union et qui doit être saisie avant qu'un recours puisse être porté devant le Tribunal. Le système s'applique aussi depuis 2019 à toute décision du Tribunal relative à l'exécution d'un contrat comportant une clause compromissoire au sens de l'article 272 TFUE.

Pour terminer cette petite fresque historique, j'ajoute que la Cour a aussi examiné la possibilité de transférer au Tribunal les procédures en manquement ou certaines d'entre elles, ce qui n'aurait pas grandement amélioré les statistiques, puisque le nombre de manquements introduits à la Cour de justice a fortement diminué passant de plus de 150 il y a de nombreuses années à quelques dizaines aujourd'hui (18 en 2020, 22 en 2021, 35 en 2022, 52 en 2023). La statistique n'était évidemment pas le seul argument de la décision de la Cour.

2 La demande législative formulée par la Cour le 30 novembre 2022

Cette demande de transfert partiel de la compétence préjudicielle au Tribunal n'a pas été faite par la Cour de gaieté de cœur. Elle apparaissait après toutes les autres réformes de la procédure ou de l'architecture juridictionnelle de l'Union européenne et plus particulièrement le doublement du nombre des juges du Tribunal, comme la solution de dernier recours pour faire face au danger que représentait la hausse continue du contentieux, composé essentiellement à la Cour de justice de questions préjudicielles et de pourvois.

Comme le dit le Président Lenaerts, cette demande « vise, dans ce contexte, à garantir dans l'intérêt général d'une justice de qualité rendue dans des délais raisonnables, un meilleur équilibre de la charge de travail entre la Cour et le Tribunal ».

Il n'a évidemment jamais été question d'augmenter le nombre de juges de la Cour. La demande de la Cour est basée sur l'article 281 TFUE qui permet au Parlement européen et au Conseil, statuant conformément à la procédure législative ordinaire, de modifier les dispositions du statut de la Cour à l'exception de son titre I et de son article 64. Ces deux institutions peuvent statuer, soit sur demande de la Cour de justice et après consultation de la Commission, soit sur proposition de la Commission et après consultation de la Cour de justice. Ce texte a modifié l'article 245 TCE (Traité de Nice) qui prévoyait la compétence du seul Conseil et à l'unanimité.

La Cour a proposé le transfert au Tribunal des questions préjudicielles portant sur les six matières « spécifiques » suivantes (nouvel article 50 ter du statut de la Cour) : (a) la TVA ; (b) les droits d'accises ; (c) le code des douanes ; (d) le classement tarifaire de marchandises dans la nomenclature combinée ; (e) l'indemnisation et l'assistance des passagers en cas de refus d'embarquement ou de retard ou d'annulation de services de transport ; et (f) le système d'échange de quotas d'émission de gaz à effet de serre.

Pour choisir ces domaines et respecter l'exigence de « spécificité » exigée par l'article 256, paragraphe 3, TFUE, la Cour a pris en considération quatre paramètres, que je vais analyser essentiellement du point de vue de la TVA :

i] Le domaine doit pouvoir être clairement identifié à la lecture de la question préjudicielle et être aisément séparé des autres domaines du droit européen, ce qui à l'évidence est le cas de la TVA ;
ii] Dans ces domaines spécifiques, doit exister un nombre substantiel d'arrêts de la Cour de justice permettant de guider le Tribunal de l'Union européenne dans sa jurisprudence, ce qui est aussi le cas pour la TVA ;
iii] Le transfert des questions préjudicielles relevant de ces domaines spécifiques doit avoir un impact substantiel sur le nombre d'affaires en attente devant la Cour de justice. C'est clairement le cas pour les affaires relevant des six domaines spécifiques visés par la demande, puisqu'en 2021 par exemple elles ont représenté 25 % des questions préjudicielles envoyées à la Cour par les juges nationaux, les deux catégories les plus importantes étant la TVA et l'indemnisation des passagers de services de transport. La Cour a donc pu conclure que le transfert des questions préjudicielles dans ces six domaines impliquerait une réduction substantielle de la charge de travail de la Cour de justice ;
iv] Le dernier paramètre à prendre en considération tient à ce que ces « domaines spécifiques » ne devaient soulever que très peu de grandes questions de principe de droit européen. Pour prendre encore l'exemple de la TVA, sur les 286 affaires arrivées à la Cour entre 2017 et 2022 (30/09) visées par la demande de la Cour, seules deux d'entre elles ont été jugées par la Grande chambre de la Cour de justice, compétente pour les problèmes nouveaux, dans lesquels il pourrait y avoir une nouvelle jurisprudence ou encore des dossiers très importants ou très sensibles. 113 d'entre elles ont été examinées par des chambres à cinq juges, 139 par des chambres à trois juges et seulement 113 de ces 286 dossiers ont donné lieu à des conclusions d'avocat général.

D'après le Président Lenaerts, au moment où la demande a été faite, la Cour est partie de l'hypothèse qu'elle viserait environ 100 affaires préjudicielles par an. Des statistiques plus récentes montreraient qu'il s'agirait plutôt de 80 affaires par an. Les raisons données par le Président sont les suivantes :

i] Il y a moins d'affaires de transport aérien comme la jurisprudence est déjà très abondante ;
ii] La demande de la Cour a été amendée pendant la procédure législative pour maintenir à la Cour certaines affaires qui relèvent d'une des six matières spécifiques mais qui soulèvent « des questions indépendantes d'interprétation du droit primaire, du droit international public, des principes généraux du droit de l'Union ou de la Charte des droits fondamentaux de l'Union européenne » (article 50 ter, deuxième alinéa, du statut de la Cour).

Parmi les quelques critiques qui ont été émises sur la demande de la Cour, j'épinglerai celle de Peter Wattel,[4] avocat général près le Hoge Raad des Pays-Bas. M. Wattel s'étonne que la Cour n'ait pas expliqué dans sa demande pourquoi d'autres domaines spécifiques que ceux choisis ne l'avaient pas été, pensant particulièrement à la propriété intellectuelle, aux marques, aux marchés publics, à la coopération judiciaire en matière civile, etc. Il continue par un véritable procès d'intention puisque, selon lui, cela reflète simplement le désir de la Cour de se débarrasser des dossiers de fiscalité indirecte et d'indemnisation des passagers aériens.

La Cour a bien examiné d'autres domaines que ceux choisis mais a estimé qu'ils étaient liés de trop près aux conventions internationales, impliquaient très souvent des notions de droit primaire ou faisaient partie intégrante de l'espace de liberté sécurité et justice. De plus, la plupart des domaines cités par M. Wattel n'auraient pu en termes de nombre de dossiers remplacer par exemple la fiscalité indirecte et l'indemnisation des passagers aériens.

M. Wattel remet aussi fondamentalement en cause le contenu de la proposition estimant que certains juges nationaux ne se sentiraient pas particulièrement honorés de devoir recourir aux services du Tribunal de l'Union européenne. Je ne vois vraiment pas pourquoi et ce n'est en tout cas pas le cas des juristes dirigeants de *l'International VAT Association* qui ont pu rencontrer le Président de la Cour et le Président du Tribunal au début de cette année 2024.

3 Comment fonctionnera le nouveau système ?

La Cour de justice ne s'est pas contentée d'un simple transfert de certains dossiers au Tribunal, comme cela avait pu être fait dans le passé car il était très simple de transférer purement et simplement au Tribunal certains recours en annulation ou en carence qui autrefois étaient de la compétence de la Cour.

Le système préjudiciel impliquait de prendre certaines précautions et garanties et c'est la raison pour laquelle la Cour et le Tribunal se sont associés pour concevoir le nouveau système. Les deux juridictions ont également voulu que tout soit prêt dès le premier jour : alors que le règlement du Parlement et du Conseil modifiant le protocole n° 3 sur le statut de la Cour de justice de l'Union européenne est adopté le 11 avril 2024, il ne sera publié au Journal officiel que le 12 août de la même année, à un moment où les règlements de procédure auront pu être modifiés en vue d'une entrée en vigueur le 1er octobre 2024. Le règlement prévoit que toutes les questions préjudicielles envoyées par les juges nationaux jusqu'à ce 1er octobre seront jugées par la Cour de justice.

Une fois le nouveau système en vigueur, cinq points doivent être soulignés :

[4] P. Wattel, "The transfer of preliminary ruling jurisdiction of the General Court of the EU", in G. Kofler et AL (eds.), CJEU – *Recent developments in value added tax 2023* (*Vienna : Linde*, 2024).

1] Le Tribunal de l'Union européenne appliquera exactement et intégralement les mêmes règles de procédure que celles suivies aujourd'hui par la Cour de justice dans les procédures préjudicielles qui lui sont soumises : la procédure écrite et orale, avec une possibilité de procédure accélérée, le tout donnant lieu soit à un arrêt soit à une ordonnance. L'article 267 TFUE sera pleinement applicable, y compris l'obligation pour les cours suprêmes nationales de saisir la Cour de justice.

2] Le Tribunal de l'Union européenne verra dans le nouveau système deux chambres de six juges affectés exclusivement aux questions préjudicielles. Un des six juges de chacune de ces chambres jouera le rôle d'avocat général dans l'autre chambre de six juges, comme cela est rendu possible par le nouvel article 49 bis du statut de la Cour. L'article 50 du statut de la Cour tel que modifié prévoit que le Tribunal peut également siéger en grande chambre, en chambre de taille intermédiaire entre les chambres à cinq juges et la grande chambre ou en formation à juge unique. Cette disposition prévoit également, à son quatrième alinéa, que, lorsqu'il est saisi d'une question préjudicielle, le Tribunal siège en taille intermédiaire (neuf juges) lorsqu'un État membre ou une institution de l'Union qui est partie à l'instance le demande.

Se dessine donc une spécialisation dans les domaines spécifiques précités au Tribunal de l'Union européenne et c'est évidemment sur base de candidatures que les juges des deux chambres spécialisées seront désignés. Comme le dit le juge Gervasoni, devenu aujourd'hui juge à la Cour de justice, la réforme entre en vigueur à un moment qui n'est pas idéal pour le Tribunal, à savoir un an avant le renouvellement triennal, dans un contexte marqué par le départ de plusieurs membres du Tribunal à la Cour à la suite du récent renouvellement triennal de la Cour de justice. Cela a nécessité la création d'une chambre ad hoc, la chambre préjudicielle composée d'une dizaine de membres y siégeant dans des formations de jugement à cinq par rotation présidées par le Vice-Président du Tribunal. Ces juges auront vocation à intégrer par la suite les deux chambres préjudicielles en octobre 2025.

3] Lorsqu'un juge national soumettra une question préjudicielle dans l'une des six catégories « spécifiques », il ou elle continuera de la soumettre à la Cour de justice : c'est le principe dit du « guichet unique ». C'est la Cour de justice qui vérifiera si le dossier concerne exclusivement une des six matières, le seul critère fixé par l'article 256, paragraphe 3, TFUE étant constitué des mots « matières spécifiques », ce qui exclut de l'analyse par la Cour de justice en vue du renvoi devant le Tribunal tout autre critère comme le type de juge national qui a envoyé la question préjudicielle ou l'importance légale et l'intérêt des questions soumises (article 50 ter, troisième alinéa, du statut de la Cour).

La Cour retiendra donc une affaire si elle soulève également une question relevant d'une matière non spécifique. Le Président Lenaerts donne l'exemple d'une demande de décision préjudicielle concernant à la fois les droits des passagers aériens en vertu du règlement 261/2004[5] et la détermination de la juridiction compétente en application du règlement Bruxelles I (arrêt du 26 mars 2020, *Primera Air Scandinavia,* C-215/18, EU:C:2020:235).

Durant la procédure législative, a aussi été intégrée, à l'article 50 ter, deuxième alinéa, du statut de la Cour, la règle selon laquelle la Cour retiendra également l'affaire si elle considère que celle-ci soulève « des questions indépendantes d'interprétation du droit primaire, du droit international public, des principes généraux du droit de l'Union ou de la Charte des droits fondamentaux de l'Union européenne ». Cette règle est motivée par la nature horizontale d'une telle question qui dépasse donc la matière spécifique.

Le Président Lenaerts donne sur ces sujets trois autres exemples :

i] L'arrêt du 26 février 2013, Åkerberg Fransson (C-617/10, EU:C:2013:105), mettant en question le principe « ne bis in idem » dans le contexte de la TVA. Il ne suffit cependant pas, précise le Président, que la juridiction de renvoi se réfère à la Charte – il faut que la question relative à la Charte soit une question indépendante et il appartiendra à la Cour de déterminer si la question d'interprétation est indépendante de la question relative à la matière spécifique.

ii] L'arrêt du 28 février 2023, Fenix International (C-695/20, EU:C:2023:127), qui porte sur l'interprétation du droit primaire : TVA et actes d'exécution (article 291 TFUE).

iii] L'arrêt du 10 janvier 2006, IATA & ELFAA (C-344/04, EU:C:2006:10), qui porte sur une question de validité du règlement 261/2004 relatif aux droits des passagers à la lumière de la Convention de Montréal.[6]

4] Lorsque la demande préjudicielle arrive à la Cour et concerne un des six domaines spécifiques, il y aura deux possibilités : (a) Comme la règle générale est le transfert au Tribunal de l'Union européenne, la décision de transfert sera prise par le Président de la Cour après consultation du Vice-Président et du Premier Avocat Général. En cas de doute, il saisira la réunion générale qui prendra la décision ; (b) Comme l'exception est de garder la question à la Cour de justice, pareille décision ne sera prise que par la réunion générale de la Cour de justice sur proposition du Président. Selon le Président, cette décision devrait être prise dans un délai aussi bref que possible.

Une fois l'affaire transférée au Tribunal de l'Union européenne, elle sera nécessairement attribuée à l'une des deux chambres spécialisées de six juges ; un juge rapporteur ainsi qu'un avocat général seront désignés. N'oublions pas que, même

---

[5] Règlement du Parlement européen et du Conseil, du 11 février 2004, établissant des règles communes en matière d'indemnisation et d'assistance des passagers en cas de refus d'embarquement et d'annulation ou de retard important d'un vol, et abrogeant le règlement (CEE) n° 295/91 (JO 2004, L 46, p. 1).

[6] Convention pour l'unification de certaines règles relatives au transport aérien international a été approuvée par décision du Conseil, du 5 avril 2001 (JO L 194, p. 3).

s'il n'y a pas, dans l'affaire en cause, de conclusions d'un avocat général, il y aura toujours un avocat général désigné comme c'est le cas devant la Cour de justice, car cet avocat général désigné suivra l'affaire dès le début, sera consulté sur les questions posées, arrêtera avec ses collègues les décisions relatives à la tenue éventuelle d'une audience, de questions éventuelles à soumettre aux parties en vue de cette audience et de la formation qui décidera de l'affaire.

Comme prévu par l'article 20 du statut de la Cour, article qui s'appliquera au Tribunal de l'Union européenne pour les questions préjudicielles dans l'hypothèse de l'application de l'article 49 de ce statut, « quand l'affaire ne soulève pas de questions de droit nouvelles, la Cour peut décider, après avoir entendu l'avocat général, que l'affaire sera jugée sans conclusions de l'avocat général ».

De nouveau, contrairement à M. Wattel, je ne trouve pas inconcevable qu'un membre du Tribunal de l'Union européenne agisse simultanément comme avocat général attaché à une chambre traitant des questions préjudicielles et comme un juge « ordinaire » dans une autre chambre du Tribunal. Les dossiers seront très différents des questions préjudicielles d'un côté qui auront la priorité et des recours directs de l'autre. De plus, il aurait été vraiment très difficile de s'écarter de la logique de l'article 49 du statut de la Cour. Il était en effet évidemment impossible de nommer des avocats généraux permanents en addition aux 54 juges du Tribunal de l'Union européenne !

Doit également être mentionné l'article 256, paragraphe 3, deuxième alinéa, TFUE, selon lequel « lorsque le Tribunal estime que l'affaire appelle une décision de principe susceptible d'affecter l'unité ou la concurrence du droit de l'Union, il peut renvoyer l'affaire devant la Cour de justice afin qu'elle statue ».

5] L'article 256, paragraphe 3, troisième alinéa, TFUE prévoit que des décisions rendues par le Tribunal de l'Union européenne sur les questions préjudicielles pourront exceptionnellement faire l'objet d'un réexamen par la Cour de justice, dans les conditions et limites prévues par le statut de la Cour, et seulement en cas de risque sérieux d'unité ou de cohérence pouvant affecter le droit de l'Union.

À ce sujet, trois éléments doivent être soulignés : (i) les mots sont importants : ce n'est pas un appel ni un pourvoi, c'est un réexamen ; (ii) il sera exceptionnel ; et (iii) il ne peut intervenir que lorsqu'il y a un risque sérieux d'atteinte à l'unité ou à la cohérence du droit de l'Union européenne. En plus de ces trois éléments, cette procédure qui est également prévue à l'encontre des jugements du Tribunal de l'Union européenne statuant en pourvoi d'un jugement d'un Tribunal spécialisé (mais il n'y a plus de Tribunal spécialisé à l'heure actuelle) est très particulière comme le prévoit l'article 62 du statut de la Cour :

- C'est le Premier Avocat Général de la Cour de justice seul (et non les parties ou les institutions de l'Union européenne ou les États membres) qui a le pouvoir de déclencher le mécanisme de « réexamen » prévu par l'article 256, paragraphe 3, troisième alinéa, TFUE, lorsqu'il considère que le risque sérieux en question est présent dans une décision préjudicielle rendue par le Tribunal de l'Union européenne. Dans ce cas, il proposera à la Cour de justice de « réexaminer » le jugement préjudiciel du Tribunal de l'Union européenne. Le Premier Avocat Général de la Cour devra faire cette proposition dans le mois du prononcé du jugement du Tribunal de l'Union européenne.

- Dans le mois de la proposition faite par le Premier Avocat Général, la Cour de justice devra décider de réexaminer ou non le jugement du Tribunal de l'Union européenne.
- Si la Cour de justice décide de réexaminer ce jugement, elle se prononcera à l'issue d'une procédure urgente prévue par l'article 62 bis du statut de la Cour. L'objectif est évidemment que le juge national n'ait pas à attendre plus longtemps qu'aujourd'hui une réponse de la juridiction européenne à sa question préjudicielle, à savoir en moyenne de quinze à seize mois.

Pour bien indiquer combien cette procédure doit être exceptionnelle, je voudrais terminer par une comparaison avec la période pendant laquelle cette procédure a existé, à savoir du temps du Tribunal de la Fonction publique entre 2005 et 2016. Conformément au Traité, les arrêts du Tribunal de la Fonction publique pouvaient faire l'objet d'un pourvoi devant le Tribunal de l'Union européenne. Les arrêts du Tribunal de l'Union européenne rendus sur pourvoi contre les arrêts du Tribunal de la Fonction publique pouvaient à leur tour faire l'objet d'un réexamen par la Cour de justice sur base de la procédure prévue à l'article 62 du statut de la Cour.

Sur 320 jugements rendus sur pourvoi par le Tribunal de l'Union européenne, six seulement ont fait l'objet d'un réexamen par la Cour de justice. Pendant les quatre années au cours desquelles j'ai œuvré en tant que Premier Avocat Général, je n'ai mis en œuvre cette procédure qu'à trois reprises, la Cour n'ayant admis de procéder à ce réexamen que dans deux de ces affaires.

Ceci ne veut évidemment pas dire qu'il en sera de même pour les affaires relevant des six domaines spécifiques dans lesquels les questions préjudicielles seront transférées au Tribunal de l'Union européenne, mais il est certain que les auteurs du Traité ainsi que du statut de la Cour ont clairement voulu que cette procédure soit et demeure exceptionnelle.

4 Quelques considérations finales

Il faut remarquer que toute la procédure prévue par l'article 281 TFUE (consultation de la Commission, décision commune du Parlement européen et du Conseil suite à une procédure législative ordinaire) a été menée et clôturée dans un délai plutôt bref. En effet, la demande législative de la Cour est du 30 novembre 2022 et le règlement 2024/2019 du Parlement et du Conseil date du 11 avril 2024, un peu plus de 16 mois après la demande. La décision a certes été facilitée par la pression exercée par la perspective des élections du Parlement européen toutes proches. Comme je l'ai indiqué plus haut, la publication n'a eu lieu qu'au mois d'août parce que, ce qui relevait de la bonne gestion, la Cour a voulu que les modifications des règlements de procédure de la Cour et du Tribunal soient adoptées avant l'entrée en vigueur du nouveau système.

Cette brièveté du délai indique qu'il y a très vite eu entre la Cour, d'une part, et les autres institutions, d'autre part, un accord global sur la philosophie du nouveau système, même si, comme je l'ai déjà mentionné, certaines modifications ont été apportées à la demande législative pendant les négociations interinstitutionnelles et si le Parlement européen, avec qui les négociations furent les plus difficiles, en profita, comme à son habitude, pour introduire dans la réforme des points qui n'y étaient pas directement ou du tout liés.

Quelques ajouts à la demande législative de la Cour vont paradoxalement accroitre sa charge de travail.

Tout d'abord, les deux amendements proposés par le Parlement européen et qui n'étaient pas liés à la réforme proposée de transfert partiel de la compétence préjudicielle au Tribunal. Ils touchent tous deux à l'article 23 du statut de la Cour.

Dans sa version antérieure, cet article 23 prévoyait que la Cour de justice notifiait une demande de décision préjudicielle aux parties au litige au principal, aux États membres, à la Commission et à l'institution, l'organe ou l'organisme de l'Union qui avait adopté l'acte dont la validité ou l'interprétation était contestée ou demandée. Les mêmes avaient le droit de déposer devant la Cour des mémoires ou des observations écrites.

Le Règlement 2024/2019 a modifié cette partie de l'article 23 du statut de la Cour en donnant au Parlement européen, au Conseil et à la Banque centrale européenne le droit de recevoir notification de la demande de décision préjudicielle et surtout le droit de déposer des mémoires ou des observations écrites devant la Cour de justice lorsqu'ils estiment avoir un intérêt particulier dans les questions soulevées par la demande de décision préjudicielle. L'évolution est importante, même si le Président Lenaerts a souligné que la disposition précédente qui permettait à une institution d'intervenir dans une procédure préjudicielle si elle était l'auteur de l'acte dont la validité ou l'interprétation était contestée ou demandée n'avait pas toujours été appliquée « à la lettre », le Président citant les affaires ayant donné lieu aux arrêts du 27 novembre 2012, Pringle (C-370/12, EU:C:2012:756) et du 16 juin 2015, Gauweiler e.a. (C-62/14, EU:C:2015:400), dans lesquels le Parlement européen avait été admis à intervenir.

Une deuxième modification a été apportée à l'article 23 du statut de la Cour par un nouvel alinéa qui prévoit que « les mémoires ou observations écrites déposées par un intéressé […] sont publiés sur le site Internet de la Cour de justice de l'Union européenne dans un délai raisonnable après la clôture de l'affaire, à moins que cet intéressé ne s'oppose à la publication de son mémoire ou de ses observations écrites ». C'est la disposition qui était la plus difficile à admettre par le Conseil, d'où la possibilité donnée à chaque intéressé de s'opposer à cette publication.

Le règlement 2024/2019 comprend encore quelques ajouts à la demande législative de la Cour de justice qui permettront d'évaluer dans le futur la mise en œuvre de la réforme du statut de la Cour introduite par ce règlement. L'article 62 quinquies du statut de la Cour prévoit désormais qu'avant de recourir à l'article 281 TFUE pour proposer une demande de modification de ce statut, la Cour de justice ou la Commission devront procéder à de larges consultations.

Par ailleurs, l'article 3 du règlement 2024/2019 impose à la Cour de justice de publier au plus tard le 2 septembre 2025 et d'actualiser périodiquement une liste d'exemples d'applications de l'article 50 ter du statut de la Cour. Le paragraphe 2 de cet article 3 lui impose également de présenter au plus tard le 2 septembre 2028 au Parlement européen, au Conseil et à la Commission un rapport sur la mise en œuvre de la réforme indiquant notamment le nombre de demandes préjudicielles qui auront été transférées au Tribunal dans chacune des matières spécifiques, le nombre d'affaires renvoyées par le Tribunal à la Cour ainsi que le nombre de décisions du Tribunal ayant fait l'objet d'une procédure de réexamen, le nombre et la nature des affaires qui n'ont pas été transmises au Tribunal, la durée moyenne du traitement des demandes préjudicielles par la Cour et le Tribunal au titre de l'article 50 ter du statut de la Cour ....

Comme si les auteurs du règlement s'attendaient à pareille évolution, le dernier alinéa de l'article 3 prévoit que « le rapport de la Cour de justice est accompagné d'une demande d'acte législatif visant à modifier le statut, notamment en vue de modifier la liste des matières spécifiques prévue à l'article 50 ter, premier alinéa, du statut ».

Les institutions ont donc déjà pensé à une modification dans le futur des « domaines spécifiques » visés par la réforme. Elles ont bien parlé de modification et pas nécessairement d'augmentation ...

European Union Constitutional and Administrative Law

EU Rulemaking in Response to Crisis: The Dynamic Use of Article 114 TFEU

Carl Fredrik Bergström

1 Introduction

Historically, crises have had a healthy influence on the EU. They have forced the member states closer and triggered processes that have led to better preconditions for cooperation. Exactly this was the most central expectation manifested by the original Paris Treaty (1952). In its Preamble, the heads of state and government stated their resolve to create "a broad and independent community among peoples long divided by bloody conflicts and to lay the bases of institutions capable of giving direction to their future common destiny."

Empirically, crises have also been a regular feature of the evolution of the modern EU. An early example is the Vietnam War, which gave the member states reasons to agree on the form of a common commercial policy; not only against the US but towards the World. Another example is the Oil Shock that followed when OPEC decided to halt their exports to countries supporting Israel. This exposed the paralyzing effects of decision-making by unanimity and paved the way for the first major reform of the EU (1987). Most important was the introduction of treaty provisions relating to the concept of an internal market that should comprise an area without internal frontiers. The centerpiece was Article 114 TFEU (originally Article 100a TEEC). It entrusted the EU—then EC—with a broadly framed competence to adopt 'measures for approximation' of national law which have as their object the establishment and functioning of 'the internal market' and tied that to a procedure that enabled decision-making in the council by qualified majority. Therefore, political initiatives that had previously been blocked by one or a few governments were now possible to realise. Since then, Article 114 TFEU has been more significant for

C. F. Bergström (✉)
Uppsala University, Uppsala, Sweden
e-mail: carl.fredrik.bergstrom@jur.uu.se

L. Prete, L. Rezki (eds.), *Judging & (Re)Thinking European Union Law*,
https://doi.org/10.1007/978-3-032-13473-8_27

rulemaking in the EU than other provisions. Because the procedure is relatively easy to complete and the substance leaves much room for interpretation.

The original model for internal market rulemaking was based on the existing institutional framework and supported by changes to the treaties: new powers for the EU legislature but also better preconditions for delegation of powers to the European Commission.[1] The continuous significance of the treaties was clearly manifested by the so called internal market programme, which included a package of proposals for legal acts to be adopted by the EU legislature over an intense period expiring 1993.[2] Most of these legal acts were to have the form of directives; addressed to the member states and required to leave their authorities the 'choice of form and methods' (Article 288 TFEU). The effectiveness—the transposition of directives into national law—was to be guaranteed by the Commission, in accordance with the treaties' procedure for infringement actions against member states represented by their governments (Article 258 TFEU).

The internal market programme became a political success and cemented the concept of 'harmonisation' based on the use of directives. This, in turn, influenced the nature of union law, typically focusing on legal principles and procedures that should ensure directives' effectiveness in member states. Since then, the original internal market model has been reinforced by subsequent revisions of the treaties. Significant examples are amendments relating to rulemaking and legal acts; strengthening the identity of the EU legislature, clarifying the role of the Commission, and stressing the member states' duty to adopt all necessary measures of national law, but also amendments relating to enforcement; simplifying the procedure for infringement actions against member states and introducing fines. The changes of the treaties have been matched by a variety of initiatives intended to support the internal market model, such as the better lawmaking agenda and the recent single market programme.[3] Typically, these initiatives have focused on the commission and its efforts to enhance member states' transposition of directives.

Also the reform introduced by the Lisbon Treaty (2009) was strongly influenced by crises. Perhaps most strikingly the international upheaval that followed upon the '9/11 Attacks' and the 'War on Terror' but also the growing awareness within the EU that it had made itself dependent on natural gas and other fossil fuels from Russia.

---

[1] See Article 100a TEEC and the amendment to Article 145 TEEC stating that the Council should 'confer on the Commission, in the acts which the Council adopts, powers for the implementation of the rules which the Council lays down', and that the Council was entitled to impose 'certain requirements' in respect of the exercise of these powers.

[2] See Completing the Internal Market: White Paper from the Commission to the European Council (Milan, 28–29 June 1985), COM (1985) 310 final.

[3] See Interinstitutional Agreement between the European Parliament, the Council of the European Union and the European Commission of 13 April 2016 on Better Lawmaking, OJ 2016 L 123/1 and Regulation (EU) 2021/690 of the European Parliament and of the Council of 28 April 2021 establishing a programme for the internal market, competitiveness of enterprises, and statistics (Single Market Programme), OJ 2021 L 153/1.

The latter was something that Russia had started to remind Europe about, capriciously throttling the flow of gas in its largest pipeline, running through Ukraine.[4]

Less than two years before the entry into force of the Lisbon Treaty, the heads of state and government were convinced that it should provide 'a stable and lasting institutional framework' that would allow the EU to fully concentrate on globalisation and some other challenges ahead.[5] Not long thereafter, the global financial system went into meltdown. The conclusions to be drawn confirmed that there was a universal need for repair in all major jurisdictions but stressed that the EU suffered from a specific problem:[6]

The present regulatory framework in Europe lacks cohesiveness. The main cause of this situation stems from the options provided to EU members in the enforcement of common directives. These options lead to a wide diversity of national transpositions related to local traditions, legislations and practices.

Therefore, the EU should equip itself with a uniform set of rules supported by competent supervision. The ensuing reform of the financial market was not introduced through any changes to the treaties, but through a dynamic—unprecedented—use of Article 114 TFEU by the EU legislature.

2 Financial Market Reform

For a long time, the process for integration of the financial market had been consistent with that of the internal market in general. But after the crisis, the development in the financial market took a different direction. The most striking feature of the development is that the traditional use of directives was shifted to use of 'directly applicable' regulations that are binding in their entirety (Article 288 TFEU). This, in turn, made it possible for the EU legislature to bring about a reorganisation of the financial market that should strengthen resilience against a similar crisis in the future. It can be illustrated by the regulations that establish the European Securities Market Authority (ESMA) and some other EU agencies. These agencies were designed to coordinate national authorities' interpretation and application of union law and to investigate potential infringements. They were also empowered to adopt decisions that are binding within member states; on national authorities but also firms and

[4] See C. F. Bergström, 'EU Rulemaking in Response to Crisis: The Emergence of the Principle of Energy Solidarity and Its Use' (2023) Nordic Journal of European Law, Special Issue 2, p. 100, and S. Andoura, 'Energy Solidarity in Europe: From Independence to Interdependence', Studies & Reports No 70, Notre Europe 2013, pp. 30 and 34.

[5] See Presidency Conclusions from the meeting of the European Council in Brussels on 14 February 2008, 16616/1/07 REV 1, point 6 and Annex with EU Declaration on Globalisation.

[6] See Report of the High-Level Group on Financial Supervision in the EU, Brussels 25 February 2009 (De Larosière Report), in particular points 99, 102 and 144.

other private actors.[7] A central idea was that the new EU agencies and their national counterparts should be independent from the political authorities, most obviously the Commission and the national governments (but fully accountable to them).[8]

It is submitted that the changes of the internal market model in the context of the financial crisis constitute a structural shift: from the original—reactive—model based on enforcement of legal acts that give member states much room for interpretation to a modern—proactive—model based on coordination of national authorities and uniform application of legal acts across all member states.

The modern model is not always easy to reconcile with the institutional framework in the treaties or, indeed, the system of legal acts or the procedure for infringement actions against member states. An obvious example is the extensive reliance on binding and non-binding legal acts adopted by EU agencies. This still lacks direct support in the treaties.[9]

The legal acts of ESMA and the other agencies in the financial market, serve to complete some tasks that either national authorities or the European commission used to have a responsibility for. But they also serve to complete some tasks that are genuinely new or, at least, more consciously designed than before. Typically, the tasks relate to the collective involvement of national authorities in the process for integration of the financial market. The consequences of EU agencies assuming responsibility are manifold and subject of extensive study. But while we deepen our understanding of the forms of legal acts that seemed most important, other forms of legal acts are becoming more characteristic, and new forms are being invented.[10]

3 Constitutional Tension

Throughout its history the EU Court of Justice has consistently held that the EU legal and political system is characterised by the constitutional idea of balance of powers: between the EU and its member states but also within the EU itself; between its different institutions. In modern case law these two dimensions of power as the principle of conferral of competence and the principle of institutional balance.[11]

[7] See C. F. Bergström, 'EU Rulemaking in the Internal Market after the Financial Crisis', in C. F. Bergström, M. Strand (eds), *Legal Accountability in EU Markets for Financial Instruments: The Dual Role of Investment Firms*, Oxford University Press, 2021, pp. 15–17.

[8] See De Larosière Report, p. 47 including its note 10.

[9] See C. F. Bergström, 'Shaping the New System for Delegation of Powers to EU Agencies: United Kingdom v European Parliament and Council (Short selling)' (2015) 52 CML Rev 219, at pp. 235–236.

[10] C. F. Bergström, 'EU Resilience within the Internal Market after the Financial Crisis: Political Resolution and Legal Responsiveness', in B. Engelbrekt et al. (eds), *Routes to a Resilient European Union*, Palgrave MacMillan 2022.

[11] See e.g. judgment in *KS and others v Council and others*, Joined Cases C-29/22 P and C-44/22 P, EU:C:2024:725, para 72.

Today the prior finds explicit support in the treaties and most notably Article 5 TEU. The latter rests on Article 13(2) TEU and the submission that the sum of powers entrusted to the institutions constitutes a closed system in which each of them represents a particular aspect of the wider interest. The principle of institutional balance has been central for answers to questions concerning interest representation and ultimately democracy and rule of law. In the words of the Court, the way in which powers are distributed among the institutions amounts to 'a fundamental guarantee' which must be upheld and protected.[12] This, the Court has said, does not only mean that 'each of the institutions must exercise its powers with due regard for the powers of the other institutions' but that the Court itself has 'a duty to ensure that the provisions of the treaties concerning the institutional balance are fully applied'.[13]

From this point of view, it was reasonable to expect that the changes of the internal market model in the context of the financial crisis had been brought about through a formal revision of the institutional framework in the treaties. The process for changes affecting the balance of powers follows from the treaties themselves and reflects the claim that they 'constitute the basic constitutional charter' of the EU.[14]

For many years the EU found itself in a semi-permanent Treaty revision process.[15] The process was intended to strengthen the ability of the EU to deal with internal and external challenges and the changes were often focused on the institutional framework and the system of legal acts. But parallel to this process the number of member states rocketed. The fact that there are now 27 member states has not only made the process slow but politically perilous. This, indeed, was demonstrated during the decade leading up to the Lisbon Treaty.

Unsurprisingly, therefore, the changes of the internal market model in the context of the financial crisis have not been premised on any treaty revision.[16] Instead, they have been manifested in ordinary legal acts adopted by the EU legislature. Typically, these legal acts have had a legal basis in Article 114 TFEU and a dynamic use of that competence has led to 'a significant adaptation of the principle of institutional balance to the new realities of European governance.' [NEW FOOTNOTE: See B. De Witte, 'Actors and Roles in EU Law – Legal Methods for the Study of EU Institutional Practice' (2022) EuConst 637, at pp. 645–650, quoting M. Everson,

[12] See judgment in *Meroni v High Authority*, 9/56, EU:C:1958:77, p. 152.

[13] See judgment in *Parliament v Council*, C-70/88, EU:C:1990:21717, paras 21–25. For a recent example see judgment in *Commission v Council*, C-551/21, EU:C:2024:281, para 62.

[14] See judgment in *Wightman and Others*, C-621/18, EU:C:2018:999, para 44.

[15] See B. De Witte, 'The Closest Thing to a Constitutional Conversation in Europe: The Semi-Permanent Treaty Revision Process', in Beaumont et al. (eds), *Convergence and Divergence in European Public Law*, Hart, 2002.

[16] But see Declaration (39) on Article 290 TFEU: here, the Intergovernmental Conference that concluded the Lisbon Treaty 'takes note of the Commission's intention to continue to consult experts appointed by the member states in the preparation of draft delegated acts in the financial services area, in accordance with its established practice'.

E. Vos, 'European Agencies: What About the Institutional Balance?' in A. Lazowski, S. Blockmans (eds), *Research Handbook on EU Institutional Law*, Edward Elgar, 2016.

4 Judicial Responsiveness

The dynamic use by the EU legislature of Article 114 TFEU in the context of the financial crisis has sometimes been challenged before the Court of Justice, typically by one or a few governments that failed to block voting in the EU council. In the past, this was often the UK. The outcome of such occasions has been crucial for the development, because the Court has demonstrated a striking indulgence with the EU legislature; granting it a wide discretion to interpret the confines of existing competences through 'intelligent drafting' and limiting the judicial review to 'manifest' errors of assessment.[17] This in turn has enabled a broad understanding of the concept of an internal market and institutional innovations. Examples of crucial rulings can be taken from some of the cases that relate to the gradual empowerment of ESMA.

For a long time, the competence in Article 114 TFEU was not considered sufficient for the EU legislature to adopt 'measures for approximation' that gave agencies powers to issue their own legal acts. But a few years before the financial crisis the Court of Justice had approved the use of Article 114 TFEU as a legal basis for the adoption of the regulation establishing the European Network and Information Security Agency (ENISA), in a different sector of the internal market.[18] The judgment became instrumental for the adoption of the regulation establishing ESMA. The significance of the judgment was explicitly confirmed in the preamble and built upon in the underlying proposal to reach the conclusion that it was now in line with the case law of the court to use Article 114 TFEU for the empowerment of ESMA (further below). The reference to the judgment was combined with a reminder that the tasks to be conferred on ESMA were 'closely linked to the measures put in place as a response to the financial crisis' and intended to improve the conditions for the functioning of the internal market.[19]

---

[17] See S. Weatherill, 'The Limits of Legislative Harmonization Ten Years After Tobacco Advertising: How the Court's Case law has Become a Drafting Guide' (2011) 12 German Law Journal 827, at p. 843; and judgment in *United Kingdom v Parliament and Council*, C-270/12, EU:C:2014:18, para. 40.

[18] See judgment in *United Kingdom v Parliament and Council*, C-217/04, EU:C:2006:279.

[19] See Regulation (EU) 2010/1095 of the European Parliament and of the Council of 24 November 2010 establishing a European Securities and Markets Authority (OJ 2010 L 331, p. 84), Recital 17 of the Preamble, and Proposal for a Regulation of the European Parliament and of the Council establishing a European Securities and Markets Authority, COM(2009) 503 final, Part 4 of the Explanatory Memorandum.

In the judgment, the Court of Justice had repeated its finding that the EU legislature had a discretion as regards the choice of harmonisation technique and added that nothing in the wording of Article 114 TFEU implies that the addressees of the measures adopted by the EU legislature can only be member states. Therefore—if the EU legislature would 'deem it necessary'—it was also possible to use Article 114 TFEU for the establishment of 'a body responsible for contributing to the implementation of a process of harmonisation in situations where... the adoption of *non-binding* supporting and framework measures seems appropriate' (emphasis added).[20]

Even if the judgment had made it clear that Article 114 TFEU could, indeed, be used for the establishment of agencies, it did not lend support for an arrangement where agencies—like ESMA—were entrusted with tasks that required them to issue, not only non-binding, but also binding legal acts. Unsurprisingly, therefore, it did not take long before the legality of such an arrangement was challenged before the EU court of justice.

The central case concerned the question if Article 114 TFEU allows the EU legislature to delegate so called intervention powers to ESMA that enable it to issue (general) decisions that are binding within member states; on national authorities and also natural and legal persons. Basing itself on the previous case law, the Court of Justice affirmed that the EU legislature may delegate powers 'for the implementation of the harmonisation sought' to agencies.[21] Then, the court focused its assessment on the manner in which the EU legislature had exercised its discretion under Article 114 TFEU. Essentially, this led the court to the finding that the EU legislature had intended to provide 'an appropriate mechanism' for situations of crisis and also deemed it necessary to use a legal act in the form of a regulation—not a directive—to confer the relevant powers on ESMA.[22]

The overall result was that the Court of Justice allowed the EU legislature to take a new step in its gradual empowerment of ESMA. In its assessment, the Court stressed that the contested provision adopted by the EU legislature should not be considered in isolation but as forming part of 'a series of regulatory instruments' adopted by the EU legislature for the achievement of a specific objective. This was a central reason for the Court to conclude that the contested provision should not be regarded as undermining the institutional framework in the treaties and the balance of powers.[23] In effect, therefore, the institutional framework in the treaties could be amended by the EU legislature.[24] But reaching that result, the court also stressed how important it was that the powers granted to ESMA were 'precisely delineated'

[20] See judgment in *United Kingdom v European Parliament and Council*, C-217/04, *supra*, para. 44.

[21] See judgment in *United Kingdom v Parliament and Council*, C-270/12, EU:C:2014:18, para 105.

[22] Ibid., paras 108–110.

[23] See ibid, paras 84–86.

[24] See C. F. Bergström, above n. 10, at pp. 236–237.

by conditions and criteria and that the exercise of those powers was amenable to judicial review.[25]

Since then, the EU legislature has continued to exploit the competence in Article 114 TFEU in legal acts relating to the financial market. A recent example is the regulation establishing the Authority for Anti-Money Laundering (AMLA) and another the regulation on digital operational resilience for the financial sector.[26] The Court of Justice, in turn, has continued to confirm its responsiveness to the development but also to refine the legal preconditions.

5 Instrument for Resilience

Much time has passed since the global financial crisis. But exogenous—and sometimes endogenous—shocks have continued to shape the EU. The British governments' protests against the reform of the financial market were soon consumed by an unmanaged referendum that led the United Kingdom to Brexit. Since then, the political barbarism that marked the process towards British withdrawal has become normalised in all remaining member states. At the same time, domestic threats against its democracies have reminded Europe of the idea of Rule of Law. This has increased the awareness of courts, brought them together and made them stronger. All this while Europe is learning—again—how to face the fear for indiscriminatory pandemics and borderless wars. Today, the dream of globalisation feels not only naïve but antique. It has been replaced by an acute need to fill storehouses and find strategic partnerships.

For the EU, Article 114 TFEU continues to function as an instrument for resilience against crises. Therefore, it is interesting to note that the rulemaking pattern that characterised the reform of the financial market is repeating itself—with more or less precision—in many sectors of the internal market. This can be seen, most clearly, in an increased use of legal acts in the form of directly applicable regulations instead of directives. During the first five-year-period after the introduction of Article 114 TEFU, it provided a legal basis for 108 directives and 25 regulations (1988–1992). Little more than ten years later this was 83 directives and 22 regulations (2001–2005). Since then, the balance has shifted radically. The first five-year -period after the start of financial crisis it was 44 directives and 52 regulations (2010–2014). During the last five-year-period (2021–2025) Article 114 TFEU provided a legal basis for 30 directives and 92 regulations.

---

[25] See judgment in *United Kingdom v Parliament and Council*, C-270/12, EU:C:2014:18, paras 44, 46 and 53.

[26] See respectively Regulation (EU) 2024/1620 of the European Parliament and of the Council establishing the Authority for Anti-Money Laundering and Countering the Financing of Terrorism (OJ 2024 L 1620) and Regulation (EU) 2022/2554 of the European Parliament and of the Council of 14 December 2022 on digital operational resilience for the financial sector (DORA) (OJ 2022 L 333, p. 1).

The usefulness of Article 114 TFEU in the context of current and coming crises has been emphasised in a series of recent regulations. None of them offer a better illustration than the so-called Internal Market Emergency and Resilience Act.[27] According to its preamble:

Events linked to the COVID-19 crisis have highlighted the need for the Union to take a coordinated approach and be better prepared for possible future crises, especially considering the continuing effects of climate change which result in natural disasters, as well as global economic and geopolitical instabilities. Other crises which might require a quicker response to prevent barriers to free movement in the internal market and to avoid severe disruptions to supply chains that are indispensable in the maintenance of activities in the internal market include, for example, forest fires, earthquakes or large-scale cyberattacks. The fact that such crises constitute exceptional and sudden events of extraordinary nature and scale implies that such events are reasonably unexpected. As it is not known what kind of crises could arise next and have a severe impact on the internal market and its supply chains in the future, it is necessary to provide for an instrument that would apply in the event of a wide range of crises having an impact on the internal market.

Overall, the Internal Market Emergency and Resilience Act sets up a general system that is intended to enable the EU to anticipate, prepare for and respond to a wide range of crises. The central tasks are allocated to a new EU agency: the Internal Market Emergency and Resilience Board. Importantly, the Internal Market Emergency and Resilience Act does not apply to some sectors of the internal market where the EU legislature has already established coherent frameworks relating to emergencies, such as financial services and medicinal products. For some other sectors, it is complemented by more specific legal acts. None of them is more interesting than the so called Critical Raw Materials Act.

The Critical Raw Materials Act is one of the most recent regulations with a legal basis in Article 114 TFEU.[28] It seeks to ensure that the EU has access to a secure and sustainable supply of critical raw materials, and that way safeguard its economic resilience and strategic autonomy. The relevant materials are considered to be critical due to their significance for the modern society; for energy, communication and defence but also due to their exposure to supply risk. So, for example, does the EU secure 97% of its magnesium from China and 63% of all cobalt is extracted in Congo (and processed in China). The demand for critical raw materials will inevitably increase exponentially in the coming decades and, at the same time, 'the risk of supply disruptions is increasing against the background of rising geopolitical tensions and resource competition.'[29]

---

[27] See Regulation (EU) 2024/2747 of the European Parliament and of the Council of 9 October 2024 establishing a framework of measures related to an internal market emergency and to the resilience of the internal market (Internal Market Emergency and Resilience Act) (OJ 2024 L 2747).

[28] See Regulation (EU) 2024/1252 of the European Parliament and of the Council of 11 April 2024 establishing a framework for ensuring a secure and sustainable supply of critical raw materials (OJ 2024 L 1252).

[29] See Regulation (EU) 2024/1252, Preamble recital 1.

Essentially, the Critical Raw Materials Act seeks to mobilise the Member States to explore their geological resources and enable mining companies to apply to the European commission for recognition of 'strategic projects' for critical raw materials. The projects that are granted will receive financial support and priority status that guarantees rapid treatment by national authorities. Sweden is among the member states with richest geological resources. That explains why the state-owned mining giant LKAB has decided to slow the pace of its high-profile investment in 'green steel' (fossil-free sponge iron) and to focus on rare minerals. Currently, LKAB has applications pending for three strategic projects.[30] The procedure introduced by the Critical Raw Materials Act will make the assessment of applications quicker than before. But at the same time, the assessment will be subject to strict legal criteria. These require, for example, that projects are sustainable and based on 'socially responsible practices including respect for human rights, indigenous peoples and labour rights' (Article 6).

In addition to provisions on the strategic projects, the Critical Raw Materials Act includes provisions on circularity, which obliges the member states to adopt national programmes that shall moderate consumption of critical raw materials and increase recycling of products containing critical raw materials (Article 26). It is also noteworthy that the Critical Raw Materials Act introduces a new EU agency, the European Critical Raw Materials Board (ECRMB), which shall coordinate and monitor national authorities (Article 36), and constitute a forum for discussion what 'strategic partnerships' that ought to be concluded with third countries in order to improve security of supply of critical raw materials (Article 37). The ECRMB shall also cooperate closely with IMERA (above) and other crisis-relevant EU agencies and bodies.[31]

Some other recent regulations with a legal basis in Article 114 TFEU that should be mentioned in the same context are the Chips Act, the Net Zero Industry Act, and the Battery Regulation.[32]

Together with the Critical Raw Materials Act, these regulations constitute the core of a new set of rules intended to strengthen resilience against an imminent crisis. Like the regulations adopted in the context of the financial crisis, also these regulations are intended to safeguard the functioning of the internal market. They repeat the essence of the pattern that characterised the reform of the financial market; the choice of regulations to 'ensure that the requirements are implemented in a

[30] See LBAK website (accessed 17 January 2025).

[31] See Regulation (EU) 2024/1252, Preamble recital 47 and Regulation (EU) 2024/2747, Article 5(4).

[32] See respectively Regulation (EU) 2024/1735 of the European Parliament and of the Council of 13 June 2024 on establishing a framework of measures for strengthening Europe's net-zero technology manufacturing ecosystem (OJ 2024 L 1735); Regulation (EU) 2023/1781 of the European Parliament and of the Council of 13 September 2023 establishing a framework of measures for strengthening Europe's semiconductor ecosystem (Chips Act) (OJ 2023 L 229, p. 1); and Regulation (EU) 2023/1542 of the European Parliament and of the Council of 12 July 2023 concerning batteries and waste batteries (OJ 2023 L 191, p. 1).

timely and harmonised way, leading to greater legal certainty' and institutional innovations that affect interaction, interest representation and legal acts.[33] The central functions of the EU agencies established by the new regulations are similar to those of ESMA and the other agencies in the financial market. Most obviously to secure the collective involvement of national authorities responsible for interpretation and application of union law. But their formal powers are less developed. Something that is likely to change over the next few years. The new regulations distinguish themselves, instead, by the extent to which their substance addresses an external and geopolitical dimension that stretches far beyond the internal market, as we have known it this far.

6 Conclusion

This chapter has stressed that the internal market model for rulemaking is subject to a structural shift: from the original—reactive—model based on enforcement of legal acts that give member states much room for interpretation to a modern—proactive—model based on coordination of national authorities and uniform application of legal acts across all member states. This shift challenges the constitutional idea of balance of powers: between the EU and its member states and within the EU itself; between its different institutions. But importantly, it contributes also to the emergence of modern forms of interaction, interest representation and legal acts.

The changes underlying this shift have been brought about without any formal revision of the founding treaties. It has been possible because the EU legislature has agreed to make a dynamic use of Article 114 TFEU. But such political resolve has not been sufficient. The changes have also required responsiveness from the Court of Justice. Through interaction between politics and law, Article 114 TFEU has come to function as an instrument for resilience against crises.

The dynamic use of Article 114 TFEU and other provisions has often been discussed in terms of 'competence creep' and criticised for obscuring the principle of conferral of competence.[34] Clearly, a flexible approach to EU competence can be problematic. But today the political circumstances inside and outside the EU are such that it is irresponsible to insist on any formal revision of the treaties; to extend competence or to shift institutional balance . For a foreseeable future, therefore, there will be a continuous need for a dynamic use of Article 114 TFEU supervised by the Court. The most compelling task for the Court will be to observe and contain institutional innovations and new rulemaking structures. This includes the need for an updated concept of harmonisation that can accommodate the modern use of regu-

[33] Quote from Proposal for a Regulation of the European Parliament and of the Council establishing a framework for ensuring a secure and sustainable supply of critical raw materials, COM (2023) 160 final, Part 2 of the Explanatory Memorandum.

[34] See S. Weatherill, 'Competence Creep and Competence Control' (2004) 23 Yearbook of European Law 1.

lations instead of directives and for clarification of legal preconditions for political choices of legal instruments. Perhaps one further principle relating to the idea of balance of powers could be recognised, to operationalise the statement in the treaties that the EU shall have 'an institutional framework which shall aim to promote its values, advance its objectives, serve its interests, those of its citizens and those of the member states, and ensure the consistency, effectiveness and continuity of its policies and actions' (Article 13(1) TEU)?

Should EU Law Protect Us from Eating Bugs? A Microstudy in Judicial Creativity

Michal Bobek

1 Introduction

Being a sharp, independent legal mind with a great sense of humour, I suspect that a possible reaction on the part of Nils when finding out that there is a collection of essays in his honour—and that I contributed to it—might be along the lines of "*Michal, you really have nothing to do these days, do you*?" In the spirit of our tradition of mutual tease and banter, often exchanged at the margins of a meeting, a hearing, or following a chance encounter in the corridors of the Court, I would strive to come up quick with at least a vaguely witty reply. Would I point out that the booming genre of *Festschriften*, *Libri Amicori* or *mélanges* is not confined only to graveyards, but also to gardens,[1] where the most unexpected flowers of legal schol-

[1] M. Taggart, 'Gardens or Graveyards of Scholarship? *Festschriften* in the Literature of the Common Law' (2002) 22 *Oxford Journal of Legal Studies* 227, who himself borrowed the term of "graveyard" from earlier writings. However, the "graveyard" parallel was not concerned with the quality of the scholarship contained in *Festschriften*, but the non-traceability of the often extremely varied individual contributions in *Festschriften*. For bibliographical purposes, without individual indexing, those contributions were (before the advent of the internet) effectively buried (hence graveyard). On the whole, however, the cited article is a fascinating case study in copying across legal cultures, where the boom of *Festschriften* in the English-speaking legal world since the 1970s can be traced back to the desire of the common law academics, traditionally rather under-rated and under-paid, to acquire a bit of the social gravitas of a German law professor, thus essentially mimicking the predominantly German and Continental tradition of *Festschriften/mélanges*, previously unknown in the common law world, where the *honorationes* are judges, not academics. "*Have we*

M. Bobek (✉)
Supreme Administrative Court of the Czech Republic, Brno, Czech Republic
e-mail: Michal.Bobek@alumni.eui.eu

L. Prete, L. Rezki (eds.), *Judging & (Re)Thinking European Union Law*,
https://doi.org/10.1007/978-3-032-13473-8_28

arship bloom?[2] Or perhaps I would muse that even in a graveyard, spring brings forth beautiful flora? I do not know. What I do know, however, is that I miss those exchanges.

Other contributions in this volume discuss in depth the numerous contributions Nils has made to EU law over the years, be it in his capacity as Judge at the General Court, Advocate General at the Court of Justice, and then Judge there as well. Simply listing the three distinguished roles side by side creates an impressive triptych in its own right. A long list of remarkable cases in competition law, as well as in other areas of EU economic and regulatory law, intellectual property, consumer protection or EU constitutional and procedural law, will undoubtedly be compiled, underlining the lasting contribution made by the *Festschrift* honorand.

By contrast, this short reflection shall focus only on a single case, which, in the broader range of matters regularly dealt with by the Court, was admittedly of little significance: *Entoma*.[3] On its face, the case concerned a rather technical issue: are insects, namely dried mealworms, locust, and crickets, to be consumed whole in the form of chips—considered "novel foods" within the meaning of Article 1(2)(e) of Regulation No 258/97 of 27 January 1997 on novel foods and novel food ingredients?[4] Despite the intellectually highly nutritious nature of the question posed, the case was an unlikely candidate for joining the ranks of the *grands ârrets* of the Court and making its way onto the reading lists of EU law courses at leading universities across Europe. So why choose this particular case?[5]

First, there is the personal dimension. This was one of the few cases in which I had the privilege of encountering Nils not as an esteemed colleague in the college of Advocates General, but as the reporting judge in a case where I delivered the Opinion for the Court.[6] Surprising as it might sound, an Advocate General is likely to have a better knowledge of the judicial thinking and juristic qualities of judges

finally caught up with the Germans?" (at p. 245) as the closing question of the article is quite telling in this regard.

[2] It is both a weakness and a strength that in most *Festschriften*, the authors are free to engage with whatever issue tickle's their fancy at that moment, assuming that they are able to plausibly explain (understood in the most generous sense) how their piece relates to the professional achievements or the personality of the honorand. The dangers of such generosity are obvious, potentially bringing about a collection that shares only the cover. However, that might also be the strength of a *Festschrift*: as a distinct and unconstrained genre, *Festschriften* generate treasure troves not to be found in academic law journals, both in topic and style, but also as to their authorship.

[3] Judgment in *Entoma,* C-526/19, EU:C:2020:769 ('judgment in *Entoma*').

[4] Regulation of the European Parliament and of the Council of 27 January 1997 concerning novel foods and novel food ingredients (OJ 1997 L 43, p. 1).

[5] That is beyond its inherently intriguing subject matter, judging at least from the uncommonly high amount of silly puns that the Advocate General who delivered the Opinion in that case was able to weave into the text or tuck away in footnotes, surpassing even the already above-the-average silliness median of that particular AG. For further exploration of that theme, see M. Bobek, 'La Cour casse mais ne rit pas: Law and Laughter in the Opinions of Advocates General', in C. Barnard, A. Łazowski, D. Sarmiento (eds.), *Pursuit of Legal Harmony in a Challenging World: Essays in Honour of Eleanor Sharpston*, Hart, 2024, p. 325.

[6] Opinion in *Entoma,* C-526/19, EU:C:2020:552 ('Opinion in *Entoma*').

than of his or her fellow AGs. That is not because an AG does not read, at least occasionally, the Opinions written by his or her colleagues. It is rather because Advocates General study daily the reasoning of (reporting) judges through preliminary reports for cases and subsequent judgments. Especially within the first category of documents, the thinking of an individual reporting judge (and his/her legal team) is not yet diluted by input from the other members of the formation deciding the case. The reporting judge and the Advocate General both ponder on exactly the same legal questions, working from an identical case file. In this way, therefore, such a situation comes remarkably close to a laboratory experiment in legal thinking, where one can compare different approaches that lead to different outcomes.

Second, beneath or beyond the technical and definitional issues raised in *Entoma*, which, admittedly, are likely to interest only food law *aficionados*, lies a general question concerning the proper role of judges in further developing (read: completing, supplementing or even expanding) the law (in face of technological developments, but not just there). The referring court in that case, the French *Conseil d'État*, posed just one question, which allows for the broader, systemic legal issue to be neatly separated from[7] the technical context of the case. Such a focused and manageable scope provides for a good discussion as to where proper limits to judicial further development of the law should lie, certainly in contrast to the often rather abstract musings on that issue detached from concrete cases. It is difficult to discuss, in the abstract, whether a court went "too far", without analysing a specific case in detail, pinpointing exactly where the reasoning may have gone astray, and why. Moreover, if suggesting that a given outcome is "wrong", it would be helpful (and intellectually honest) to also suggest which outcome would have been "right" and how one could plausibly arrive there.[8]

Third, *Entoma* is worth discussing precisely because it was a relatively unimportant case. Debates about proper judicial interpretation of the law and its limits tend to focus on grand constitutional and/or deeply ethical issues. That is, to some extent, understandable: after all, which notable constitutional scholar—eager to (finally!) expose the irreconcilable tensions in the decision-making of courts as political and politicised actors, while unmasking the post-(whatever) biases of traditional legal scholarship in assessing this court or that area of law—would find it appealing to write about bugs? Yet, it is not only true that hard cases make bad law; they are also poor subjects for evaluating the use of "proper" methods or reasoning. Focusing on them, or even just them, skews the average and the overall perception of what normal reasoning of a judicial institution is. Taking only big cases as the starting point for discussion about the proper limits of judicial interpretation of the law is bound to generate a different overall picture (and a very different median)

[7] Or even "isolated from" (with regard to the subject matter of the case discussed here, pun intended).

[8] Thinking especially of the category of hard cases, where every outcome and reasoning are simply wrong and prone to doctrinal challenges, and the "best" solution would be if the case was never brought.

than if one were to include also the daily bread and butter of any court—the average cases.

2 Entoma: Are Insects "Novel Food"?

Entoma SAS was a French undertaking marketing products consisting of mealworms, locusts, and crickets intended for human consumption in the form of whole insects. In January 2016, the Paris Prefect of Police ordered Entoma to withdraw those products from the market until that undertaking obtained an authorisation, pursuant to Regulation No 258/97, attesting that those products represent no danger for the consumer.

The case became one of definitions. Are insects eaten as whole novel food or novel food ingredients pursuant to Article 1(2)(e) of Regulation 258/97? At the material time, that provision stated: "*This Regulation shall apply to the placing on the market within the Community of foods and food ingredients which have not hitherto been used for human consumption to a significant degree within the Community and which fall under the following categories: ... (e) foods and food ingredients consisting of or isolated from plants and food ingredients isolated from animals, except for foods and food ingredients obtained by traditional propagating or breeding practices and having a history of safe food use*".

The referring court did not enquire about the first part of the definition, namely whether such insects were *foods and food ingredients which have not hitherto* [i.e. before 15 May 1997[9]] *been used for human consumption to a significant degree within the Community.* It would appear that all the parties to the proceedings before the national court, as well as subsequent interveners before the Court (France, Italy, and the European Commission), agreed that insects for human consumptions were indeed a novel phenomenon, not widely spread in Europe in the mid-1990s.

What became contentious was the second condition of the just outlined legislative definition, namely whether (whole) insects can be subsumed under "*foods and food ingredients consisting of or isolated from plants and food ingredients isolated from animals*". Were whole insects to be eaten as chips "*foods and food ingredients isolated from animals*"?

The answer of the Court was "no". In interpreting the concepts of "food ingredients" and "isolated from", the Court started by noting that neither of those terms was defined in Regulation No 258/97. The natural, ordinary meaning of those concepts would preclude them encompassing also whole animals to be consumed as such. That interpretation was further supported by systemic arguments, both based on internal analogy (comparing the terms used in Article 1(2)(e) with similar ones used elsewhere within the same regulation), and also by drawing broader

[9] Article 15 of Regulation 258/97.

terminological parallels within the field of food law.[10] Thus, *literal* as well as *systemic* arguments led the Court to the intermediary conclusion that Article 1(2)(e) of Regulation No 258/97 did not cover "whole animals", thereby excluding equally whole insects.[11]

The Court further emphasised that the literal (and systemic) interpretation of the provision aligns with both the context and objectives of Regulation No 258/97. Regarding the historical context (the intention of the historical legislator), the EU legislature in the 1990s had no intention of regulating the consumption of insects under "novel foods". As to the (contemporary) objective of the Regulation No 258/97, the Court acknowledged that the high level of protection of human health is one of the two aims of the regulation. That aim admittedly applies equally to the consumption of insect parts and whole insects. Still, it cannot override the clear and precise meaning of the provision at issue. Expanding the scope of a legal provision of EU law beyond its clear meaning would not only go *contra legem*, i.e. a limit to (conform) interpretation repetitively recognised in EU law, but would also encroach upon the regulatory space left to the Member States. In the absence of EU legislation governing the consumption of whole insects, it falls to the Member States to provide for any such safety assessment in their national legislation, should they considered such diets to present a danger for public health.[12]

The Court's judgment shared the assessment previously made by the Advocate General. According to some academic analysis, it did so even to an unhealthy degree.[13] The approach and logic of the Opinion was indeed the same as the one of the judgment. The Opinion nonetheless explored in greater detail the limits of judicial further development of the law, particularly in technically complex areas.[14] The reason for including those general meditations was because the arguments advanced by the interveners in the *Entoma* case, namely France and Italy, had equally merit and were not alien to the approach of the Court itself in the past in other cases.[15]

According to that other line of possible reasoning, drawing too sharp a distinction between "food" and "food ingredients" could prove impractical, as certain ingredients can also serve as food, and vice versa. Moreover, the insistence on treating whole animals as fundamentally distinct from parts of animals for the purposes of safety assessment is not entirely logical. After all, animals that form the backbone of human diet in Europe over the past decades are rarely eaten as whole. Thus, placing excessive weight on a *literal* interpretation of rather transitive notions in the

---

[10] Notably by reference to Regulation (EU) No 1169/2011 of the European Parliament and of the Council of 25 October 2011 on the provision of food information to consumers (OJ 2011 L 304, p. 18).

[11] Judgment in *Entoma*, paras 27–36.

[12] Judgment in *Entoma*, paras 37–44.

[13] V. Paganizza, 'Are Insects Novel Foods?' (2020) 15 (6) *European Food and Feed Law Review* 579, at p. 582, reproaching the Court the "*blind adherence*" to the Opinion of Advocate General, while "*actually omitting some of the most juridically problematic passages of the Opinion*".

[14] Opinion in *Entoma*, points 56–84.

[15] As admitted in point 62 of the Opinion.

specific (and indeed in this sense rather peculiar) case of whole insects is perhaps not the strongest interpretative start.

Next, as far as logic and internal system of the Regulation No 258/97 were concerned, what practical sense would it make to subject parts of insects, or other elements isolated therefrom, to the assessment and authorisation regime for novel foods (since they are likely to be considered foods or ingredients *isolated from* animals), but not the whole animals? If parts of animals may pose risks to public health that warrant control, then *a fortiori*, whole animals would as well. Taken *ad absurdum*, this reasoning would lead to the conclusion that grilled cricket legs, if served as a tasty and nutritious sprinkle on one's green salad, fall under "*food ingredients isolated from animals*", while whole dried crickets served as chips would not. What sense does such a legislative framework make?

That connects to the key purposive argument, rooted in recital 1 of Regulation No 258/97 (the functioning of the internal market and establishing the same level playing field for all undertakings) and, above all, recital 2 (protection of public health by ensuring that novel foods are subject to a single safety assessment throughout the Union). A high level of public health protection will logically only be achieved if any potentially questionable alimentary novelty is subjected to a thorough assessment, and not if the larger problem (in the literal meaning of the word—the whole animal), will not be inspected and assessed, while its parts will.[16] Moreover, if greater emphasis were placed on the imperative of ensuring effective protection of public health against all potential risks presented by novel foods,[17] potentially also adding the precautionary principle into the mix, then "*in dubio pro libertate*" might quickly turn into "*in dubio pro inspectione*". Finally, how much of the same level playing field and harmonization in the internal market will be achieved if Member States remain competent to regulate trade in whole insects? By definition, there would be no "single safety assessment" within the Union for the same type of goods.

On the whole, therefore, one cannot but admit that a more sensible legislative design for novel foods would require subjecting both whole insects and parts thereof—whether mechanically severed or extracted through any other process—to the same assessment procedure. Is a legislative framework that is outdated, making limited practical sense, and arguably failing to protect the consumer, not in indeed of an update? If the legislature for whatever reason failed to do so, is it not the role of the Court to ensure effective protection of public health?

---

[16] The same argument could effectively be put as such an interpretation establishing a discriminatory treatment between different kind of producers, i.e. those marketing whole insects, on the one hand, and those marketing products with food or food ingredients isolated from animals, on the other. That is, however, perhaps not the strongest argument to be advanced, starting already with the fact that undertakings producing different products simply can have no legitimate expectations of being treated the same.

[17] Previously see in particular judgment in *Davitas*, C-448/14, EU:C:2016:839, para. 33. That case concerned the interpretation of letter (c) within the same Article 1(2) of Regulation No 258/97 with regard to clinoptilolite, a mineral substance of volcanic origin, and its potential classification as "*a food or food ingredient with a new molecular structure*".

At this stage, judicial decision-making reaches a (value-driven) crossroads. Which path should be taken next? Both of the argumentative approaches outlined above could plausibly be adopted and defended. Above all, however, both solutions could be reasoned in a judgment, using the standard set of interpretative methods outlined above. The first approach puts greater emphasis on the text and its historical context, while the second highlights the importance of purpose and the need for effective protection of public health and consumers. In such moments, the decisive factor and the guiding principle becomes the individual perception of the judicial function: what is the role of a high judge? Is that role the same in a (European) Court of Justice, as it might be in an apex national court?

The key lies in the question posed. The title of this contribution is intentionally suggestive and misleading: to the question as to whether "*EU law should protect us from eating bugs*", the likely answer from all quarters would be a resounding "yes, of course!". However, that is the wrong question, a least for a judge in some, perhaps more self-restrained legal systems. Such a question is one that only a legislature could validly pose. For a judge, the proper question is far narrower: "*what does the law say at present on the matter of the human consumption of whole insects*"?

Therein lies the fundamental difference of judicial self-perception, for which *Entoma* serves as a small yet compelling illustration. In retrospect, I can gladly give credit to the arguments advances by France and Italy in that case as to what the EU law sensibly *ought to be* on that matter. If one were at the stage of legislative drafting, I would even agree with them. However, as I equally sought to explain in detail in the closing part of my Opinion in that case, to rewrite a (relatively) clear text of the law as it stands should not be the role of judges, EU judges included, even if their role were to be understood, for systemic reasons, in a slightly more creative way than that of their national counterparts. Four reasons were singled out in the closing part of my Opinion.

First, text itself sets the limit. An interpreter may explore the vagueness of a provision to the degree that it remains reconcilable with the text, but must not override it under the guise of interpretation. Incidentally, the Court itself increasingly recognised this line as a general limit to conform interpretation: *no contra legem* results. "Be A" cannot, by the fiat of interpretation, be transformed into "be non-A" *Second*, the closer the interpretative outcome comes to imposing or sanctioning obligations on individuals, the narrower the room for interpretative manoeuvres. *Third*, there is the separation of powers argument, not primarily in the horizontal dimension (between the EU institutions), but in its vertical dimension (the principle of conferral). Taking this principle seriously provides a strong rebuttal to the frequent calls for effective protection of whatever public interests (in the present case public health) at the EU level, coupled with the subliminal threat of lack of protection if EU rules are not recognised or judicially created. If a genuine gap exists in protecting such interests, Member States remain free to act on matters not explicitly delegated to the EU level. If taken dogmatically to the fullest, in contrast to national levels, there are no gaps in EU law in the areas of shared competence. *Fourth*, special caution against judicial interventionism is perhaps called for in areas governed by highly technical secondary legislation, where, in spite of all the collective wisdom assembled, courts possess little technical expertise. In such circumstances, the judicial role may be better confined to policing the procedural dimensions to manage risks and address scientific uncertainty within the framework of the specific secondary law instrument. Substantive judicial intervention should be reserved for exceptional instances of legislative inertia.[18]

3 Gaps in Law in Need of Filling? (Don't Use the "A." Word)

No general conclusions can be drawn from a single case with the exception, perhaps, that the Advocate General in *Entoma* was a rather conservative fellow (or certainly had a self-restrained judicial breakfast), as was the reporting judge, and that the majority of the remaining judges in the third chamber of the Court at that time were ready to go along with what the reporting judge and Advocate General proposed. Nevertheless, the same case can serve as a springboard for broader reflections on the judicial further development of the law, its academic framing, and the limits thereof.

First, except in cases of straightforward mechanical subsumption, the outcome of a case is rarely determined by interpretative methods that dictate, ex ante, the conclusion every interpreter must reach. Both reasoning paths just outlined, which could have been plausibly taken in *Entoma*, relied on what may be considered standard forms of legal interpretation in Europe today: text, context, and purpose of the law.[19] Neither of the two outcomes could be labelled a departure from methods of legal interpretation in the European legal space, or the pursuance of any specific interpretative methods unknown to other similar systems.[20] It is thus not "the method", but rather the stress on or the balancing of the various interests within

---

[18] Opinion in *Entoma*, points 69–84.

[19] For a comparative evaluation, see e.g. D.N. MacCormick, R.S. Summers (eds.), *Interpreting Statutes: A Comparative Study*, Dartmouth, 1991; or S. Vogenauer, *Die Auslegung von Gesetzen in England und auf dem Kontinent: Eine vergleichende Untersuchung der Rechtsprechung und ihrer historischen Grundlagen*, Mohr Siebeck 2001. For the account of the practice of the Court, see K. Lenaerts, J. A. Gutiérrez-Fons, *Les méthodes d'interprétation de la Cour de justice de l'Union européenne*, Bruylant, 2020, pp. 13–73.

[20] Contrast the general statement concerning the methods of legal interpretation employed by the Court of Justice made by the German Federal Constitutional Court in BVferG, Judgment of 5 May 2020, 2 BvR 859/15, 1651/15, 2006/15, 980/16, point 112. In that judgement, the BVerfG repetitively underlined that the interpretation of the Treaties carried out by the Court in its previous Judgment of 11 December 2018 (*Weiss and Others*, C-493/17, EU:C:2018:1000) was incomprehensible and must thus be considered arbitrary from an objective perspective, being *profoundly methodologically flawed* (e.g. paras 116, 118, 133, 153 of the judgment). The BVerfG was of the view that if the Court of Justice followed proper/correct methods of legal interpretation, it could not have validly arrived at the interpretation it reached in *Weiss*. While this in not the place for a discussion of that case, what is in general striking is the level of *methodological positivism* displayed by the BVerfG: if the Court followed the "proper" methods of legal interpretation, it would have arrived at a "proper" conclusion.

those interpretative methods that eventually decides. As such, two individuals running the same seemingly mathematical *Lösung-schema*—the kind diligently learned for their *Klausuren*—can legitimately reach different substantive outcomes, even if both of them looked at the same text, logic, system, historical intent, as well as current aim and purpose of the law.

Second, there certainly exist, beyond or above the hardly quantifiable approaches and personalities of individual judges, systemic or cultural understandings of what ought to be the role of a judge in a given legal system. Some of those systems, notably the Germanic ones, even claim to be able to trace a clear line between the mere "interpretation of the law" (*Rechtsauslegung*) and the judicial "further development of the law" (*Rechtsfortbildung*), with further nuances on either side of this divide.[21] One cannot help but envy the dogmatic clarity with which the world can be ordered. However, the ensuing problem is that the same (national dogmatic and culturally dependent) yardsticks are difficult to carry over to the European level with regard to the European Courts (be it the Court of Justice, but also the European Court of Human Rights).

To provide just one example: would it perhaps matter that when Hjalte Rasmussen first looked at the reasoning of the Court of Justice in the 1980s and was appalled by what he saw,[22] he did so through the lens of a Danish jurist? Danish—or more broadly perhaps, Nordic courts—have not traditionally been known for their expansionist judiciary and assertive constitutional review, to put it mildly.[23] By contrast, consider a Central and Eastern European lawyer in the early 2000s looking at the same set of cases, whose perspective would be shaped by the experience of a system in constant flux, where newly established constitutional courts engaged in highly assertive judicial review, contributing to a fully-fledged societal overhaul, with a rate of annulments and declarations of unconstitutionality rarely seen before.[24] For the first person, the Court of Justice might be "running wild" and engaging in "revolting judicial behaviour".[25] For the second person, the same court might seem

[21] With that distinction going back already to F.C. von Savigny, *System des heutigen Römischen Rechts*, 2. Neudruck der Ausgabe Berlin 1840, Scientia Verlag 1981, § 35 (at 222 ff), if not earlier. For a more contemporary account, see e.g. K. Larenz and C.W. Canaris, *Methodenlehre der Rechtswissenschaft*, 3rd edn, Springer 1995, 133–262; or C.W. Canaris, *Die Feststellung von Lücken im Gesetz*, 2nd edn, Duncker & Humblot, 1983. For the discussion of the further development of the law by a judge when faced with a gap, see e.g. A. Meier-Hayoz, *Der Richter als Gesetzgeber*, Juris-Verlag, 1951.

[22] *On Law and Policy in the European Court of* Justice, Martinus Nijhoff 1986, with a "postscript" published as 'Between Self-Restraint and Activism: A Judicial Policy for the European Court' (1988) 13 *EL Rev* 28.

[23] Cf e.g. J. Elo Rytter, M. Wind, 'In need of juristocracy? The silence of Denmark in the development of European legal norms' (2011) 9 *International Journal of Constitutional Law* 470.

[24] Comparatively see e.g. R. Procházka, *Mission Accomplished: on Founding Constitutional Adjudication in Central Europe*, CEU Press, 2002; W Sadurski (ed.), *Constitutional Justice, East and West*, Kluwer, 2002; O. Luchterhandt et al. (eds), *Verfassungsgerichtsbarkeit in Mittel- und Osteuropa: Teilband I*, Nomos, 2007.

[25] M. Cappelletti, 'Is the European Court of Justice 'Running Wild'?' (1987) 12 *EL Rev* 4.

moderate, even conservative, its decisions resembling a mild constitutional children's matinée, hardly enough to stir more than a bored yawn from a CEE observers.[26]

Therein lies the problem of any meaningful discussion about the proper role of a court in the European legal space: the absence of a common yardstick. Discussion about the proper "European" quickly turns into essentially sub-conscious or even conscious self-projection of one or the other legal culture and its expectations at the European level. The Court is found wanting because it does not do things *like us*, or because it did not even reach the outcome we would reach in a given case. Such critique is often framed using the terminology of the critic's own legal system, or dressed up in references to "common constitutional traditions" or "European methods". However, upon closer inspection, the "European methods" miraculously happen to be exactly the same as those of the critic's own national system.[27]

Third, the cultural relativisation just outlined should not be taken so far as to imply that there are no boundaries to judicial creativity at the European level, or that the Court never makes mistakes in individual cases. Of course it does. The point, rather, is that the precise boundary between "still interpreting the law" and "impermissible judicial legislating" is often shaped heavily by cultural and temporal factors,[28] as well as simple personal preferences. Which case and which judicial reasoning is already "over the line" depends logically on where the line is drawn. In comparative terms, there are quite different lines within Europe, certainly as far as their dogmatic portrayal in national scholarship is concerned.

But what of predictability then? Can a legal system, which is unable to offer a reasonably consistent *ex ante* prediction of the outcome of the cases put through it, still be called *a system*, i.e. a set of principles or procedures according to which something is organised? That is the vexing question, especially if examining strings of cases in one and the same area, or even concerning the same legal issue, and wondering about their varied outcomes.

---

[26] Even leading to suggestions that following the CEE countries accession to the EU in 2004 and the regulatory dislocation from national capitals to Brussels, the intensity of (constitutional) review and access to justice for individuals dropped in consequence—see e.g. A. Albi, 'Ironies in human rights protection in the EU: pre-accession conditionality and post-accession conundrums' (2009) 15 *ELJ* 46, or A. Albi, 'An essay on how the discourse on sovereignty and the co-operativeness of national courts has diverted attention from the erosion of classic constitutional rights in the EU', in M. Claes et al. (eds.), *Constitutional Conversations in Europe: Actors, Topics and Procedures*, Intersentia, 2012.

[27] An additional issue, this time on credibility, is when courts, in particular constitutional courts, who in their own past or even present were not shy in expanding national constitutionalism, fundamental rights protection, and thereby their own competence into any and all areas of law via not particularly constrained interpretation, start accusing the Court of "too much judicial creativity". For a critical view, see e.g. M. Jestaedt, O. Lepsius, C. Möllers, C. Schönberg, *Das entgrentzte Gericht: Eine kritische Bilanz nach sechzig Jahren Bundesverfassungsgericht*, Suhrkamp Verlag, 2011.

[28] The social median for a judicial function is not only formed by space, but also by a given time and epoch within the same geographical space. Legal (dis)continuity and stability of a given system naturally plays a considerable role. In detail, see M. Bobek, *Comparative Reasoning in European Supreme Courts*, Oxford University Press, 2013, p. 205–212.

In retrospect, and with sufficient distance (and knowledge), it is always possible to construct a narrative explaining why certain choices were made. But what about the predictions? When will the dice fall, in a given case, on the side of "necessary" further development of the law, driven by the imperative of effective legal protection, leading to the alteration of the (text of the) rule? And when, by contrast, will it be "the text is the text and I am but a humble judge who cannot touch it"? Why, for instance, in *Davitas*,[29] when interpreting another letter of the same provision of Regulation No 258/97, did the Court appear more protective of public health, whereas in *Entoma*, it was more self-restrained? Why in *Mangold*,[30] did the Court suddenly rewrite the legislative choices of both the EU and the German legislature, while in later cases on general principles of EU law—arguably culminating in *Audiolux*[31]—it took the position that it was not its place to legislate in the form of general principles of law? Why in *Sturgeon*,[32] did the Court ultimately do what the Advocate General in that case had stated was beyond the bounds of judicial power?[33]

A number of other cases could be added to the list of suspects, sitting at the borderline between "necessary closing of gaps" and "impermissible judicial expansionism" or even "judicial activism". The practical (not to say practitioners') question of predictability nonetheless remains. The task of bringing more doctrinal predictability into judicial decision-making at the European level is indeed a Sisyphean one, *inter alia* perhaps for the following reasons.

First, most cases referred to Luxembourg under Article 267 TFEU are not sent there because they are easy, or because the standard methods of judicial interpretation, which by the way were in all likelihood already explored by the national judges who made the reference, were leading to a clear-cut result. The majority of cases referred are complex, often necessitating a subjective (value) choice between two or more interpretative avenues and outcomes, which can all be plausibly defended and reasoned.

Moreover, the docket of preliminary ruling cases before the Court is immensely varied, particularly when compared with the docket of a supreme court at the national level in Continental apex courts, often even with specialised chambers. Thus, at the Court, in terms of their facts, only of a handful of cases are similar.[34] However, it is precisely this similarity of cases that really allows for the evaluation of adherence to past approaches and the formation of reliable predictions about whether such approaches will continue or diverge. In a national supreme court, for

---

[29] Judgment in *Davitas*, C-448/14, EU:C:2016:839.

[30] Judgment in *Mangold*, C-144/04, EU:C:2005:709.

[31] Judgment in *Audiolux and Others*, C-101/08EU:C:2009:626.

[32] Judgment in *Sturgeon and Others*, C-402/07 and C-432/07, EU:C:2009:716.

[33] Opinion of AG Sharpston in *Sturgeon and Others*, C-402/07 and C-432/07, EU:C:2009:416, point 94.

[34] That proposition is naturally dependent on the level of abstraction at which a certain court or a certain judge operate. What is meant here is factual and legal similarity that would allow, as is in fact the practice in a number of Civilian courts, *to copy entire parts* of judicial reasoning from one judgment to another without any or little alteration of the text.

example, in a specialised chamber handling VAT cases, one might encounter a series of cases concerning denied VAT input deductions for overpriced advertising services linked to tax fraud, often involving the same taxable persons within the transaction chain. By the 15th case of this kind, one should be able to predict the outcome with a high degree of certainty. But how far can that dream of predictability be transposed to the earlier stage, where unclear rules must be interpreted, and thereby potentially completed, in the first place?

Second, courts are a "they", not an "it". As banal as that statement sounds, the academic study of judicial institutions and the assessment of their performance still labours, for practical as well as ideological reasons, under the fiction of one faceless "court". Starting with the *ideological* reason, the roots of modern positivistic rationality lie in its de-personification. In this indeed Cartesian vision, there is one correct method of reasoning that leads to the same result, *irrespective of who* decides.[35] This underpins the modern conception of official authority, including judicial authority, which is knowledge- and process-based, not personality-based.[36] As to the *pragmatic* reason, it is rather impossible to account for the degree of personal variety within the study of courts and explanation of their decision-making. Not only would the sheer number of variables become unbearable, but also an academic observer, reading the judicial outcome in the form of a depersonalised decision by "the Court",[37] has no chance of knowing such personal idiosyncrasies of individual judges.[38]

However, the current institutional design of the Court, like that of any other apex Continental jurisdiction, essentially means that, unless the Court sits in the plenary, there is no single "Court", but essentially 12 different courts: five chambers of 3 judges, five chambers of 5 judges, one grand chamber, but of quite varying inner composition,[39] and the plenary court itself. Certainly, in decision-making at the Court, broad consensus is always sought. But where exactly will that consensus be

---

[35] R. Descartes, *Discours de la méthode*, Flammarion, 2000, pp. 124–125: *'It is better never to think of searching for the truth about anything than to do so without a method [...] by method, I understand clear and definite rules thanks to which everybody following them exactly will never allow the false for the true and [...] will arrive at the true knowledge of all the things their mind is capable of.'*

[36] Leading to the Weberian formalistic, impersonal rationality as the basis for modern officialdom and its legitimacy—M. Weber, *Wirtschaft und Gesellschaft: Grundriss der verstehenden Soziologie*, 5th edn, Mohr Siebeck 1980, pp. 496 ff.; 551 ff.

[37] Because to the outside world, in the Continental tradition, a court wishes to remain a faceless court, diluting the individuality of its members in favour of the collegiality of the bench—in detail M. Bobek, 'Judicial Biographies and Judicial Decision-Making: A Fish Reflects on the Work of Marine Biologists', in D. Gallo et al (eds), *The Italian Influence on European Law: Judges and Advocates General (1952-2000)*, Hart, 2024, p. 267.

[38] To make the matters even more complicated, personal world views of judges often are, similarly to those of other humans, equally *internally varied*, i.e. may differ depending on the subject matters. Thus, one and the same person can have quite a different personal "activism median" in, say, tax matters on the one hand, and international protection or environmental cases, on the other.

[39] In detail M. Bobek, 'What Are Grand Chambers for?' (2021) 23 *Cambridge Yearbook of European Legal Studies*, 1.

found in a given case depends on who sits in the given formation, and where the opinion median lied in that formation. Finally, even though judges and Advocates General from the "larger" Member States is renewable mandates, the average tenure at the Court is about nine to ten years. This ensures a regular turn-over.

All of this means that, despite the high degree of collegiality, consensus, and partial rotation between the individual smaller (three and five judges chambers) every 3 years following partial renewal of the Court and election of chamber presidents, the next case addressing a similar legal issue, brought before the Court a couple of months or even years later, is likely to be decided by a differently composed chamber. It is also likely to be guided by the advice of a different Advocate General. When comparing that institutional set-up to some national judicial systems, characterised by a high degree of specialisation and personal continuity over the years,[40] I would even suggest that the decision-making of the Court is characterised by a remarkable degree of continuity and *stability, in spite of* the institutional and procedural factors within which it is carried out.

Third and finally, the Court's abstract and indeed deductive reasoning style should not be mistaken for a lack of awareness within the decision-making formation regarding the context of individual cases, be it legal or factual, furnished by the referring court, or otherwise evident due to the subject matter of the case. The challenge in understanding certain choices arises when those contextual elements are absent from the reasoning. This may happen because such elements are not deemed appropriate as legal arguments of justification in a highly formalised legal text[41] or because of the, in this sense indeed, peculiar nature of the preliminary rulings procedure, which is supposed to be concerned with law and not with facts. Nevertheless, even when interpreting abstract legal rules, the factual context within which the question was posed will be, consciously or not, of major importance in shaping the articulation of the rule.

Coming back to *Entoma*: would it have mattered, perhaps at a more subliminal level in interpreting the scope of the proposition "*foods and food ingredients isolated from animals*", that the Member State in that case concerned about the public health risks of consuming whole insects had not acted on the matter itself, even though it could have? Instead, it chose to advance an expansionist interpretation of EU law that the undertaking(s) were unlikely to expect, thus coming rather close to the nationally popular game of "blaming Brussels".

Similarly, could it have mattered that the definitional issue posed by *Entoma* was, even at the time the case was being decided, of only historical relevance, because

---

[40] With tongue in cheek, it is hardly a great achievement if, say, a specialised chamber of an apex national court composed of the same people for decades always keeps saying the same thing. In the practice of some too specialised national jurisdictions in Europe, that is rather likely to gradually turn into a problem of its own.

[41] See generally e.g.: C. Engel, 'The Psychological Case for Obliging Judges to Write Reasons', in C. Engel, F. Strack (eds), *The Impact of Court Procedure on the Psychology of Judicial Decision Making*, Nomos, 2007, pp. 73–109, or J. Wróblewski, 'Motivation de la decision judiciaire', in C. Perelman, P. Foriers (eds), *La motivation des décisions de justice*, Bruylant 1978, pp. 113ff.

the new EU regulation on novel food from 2015,[42] but not yet applicable *ratione temporis* to the *Entoma* case, already explicitly included whole insects into its scope? Thus, why bother filling, perceived or real, gaps in old legislation, if the problem is already solved for the future?

Next, even if not called to collect or to assess any evidence, members of the Court do not live in a social vacuum, oblivious to broader trends and discussions. Insects were indeed not part of regular (at least not intentionally) diet of the average European in 1997. However, in other parts of the world, where insects appear *à la carte*, it does not seem that the population in those countries would suddenly start dying on the streets because of their dietary choices. Rather to the contrary: insects consumption is being advertised, more recently even in Europe, as an environmentally friendly, sustainable, and protein-rich food source for the future. Within such an (indeed judicially undocumented) context, how much credibility would one, advisedly or subconsciously, give to the arguments about the danger to public health caused by the human consumption of insects?

Would any of these factual or legal details have mattered? Put together, they create a rather unique context for a case within which judicial decision-making takes place. Judges, being human and shaped by their individual sensitivities, may find one specific contextual detail influential, while others might regard it as insignificant. Most crucially, however, when examining the factual and legal context at such a level of abstraction, it becomes clear that it is rare for even two cases concerning the interpretation of the same provision of EU law coming before the Court (not to speak of different provisions within the same or successive legal instruments) to be identical, or even too similar. Seen in this light, for example, *Davitas* and *Entoma* were different cases, with *Entoma* thus hardly a departure from *Davitas*.[43] On the other hand, if one focuses on a higher level of abstraction, framing the issue as a choice between pro-public health and pro-free trade, other conclusions are certainly possible.

That brings the discussion on (im)permissible judicial further development of the law back to the peculiar nature of the preliminary ruling procedure itself and the appropriate level of facts relevant therein,[44] which is itself proxy for a deeper constitutional debate. In the traditional division of powers within national legal systems, it is for the legislature to enact *ex ante abstract* rules, and for judicial power to apply *ex post* those rules to *concrete* facts in individual cases. Thus, the correct and full ascertainment of all relevant facts is a key legitimising element of any judicial decision, including one rendered on extraordinary appeal/cassation before a national apex court, where only questions of law are admitted.

---

[42] Regulation No 2015/2283 of the European Parliament and of the Council of 25 November 2015 on novel foods (OJ 2015 L 327, p. 1).

[43] As suggested in Paganizza, *supra* n. 13, p. 586.

[44] Critically, see my Opinion in *Van Ameyde España*, C-923/19, EU:C:2021:125, then translating into a structural vision for the preliminary rulings procedure in the Opinion in *Consorzio Italian Management*, C-561/19, EU:C:2021:291.

Those lines become admittedly somewhat blurred in national systems when a (constitutional) court is requested to carry out a constitutional review of legislation *in abstracto*, i.e. detached from individual cases. In similar vein, the role of the preliminary rulings procedure may be seen as clarifying or setting the rule for the future: either the immediate future (the disposition of the individual case before the national court that made the reference), or more broadly, for the further future (establishing a precedent for national courts in similar cases). However, when understood as "*requests for preliminary legislation*", should or even can such traditional national limits on the judicial function still apply?

4 Conclusion

Those grand constitutional issues far exceed the scope of this modest contribution. The aim of the present reflection was to pay homage to a fellow judicial mind, whose rather circumspect, not to say conservative, views on the limits of judicial further development of the law[45] certainly shaped the decision of the Court in *Entoma*.

Beyond that, this contribution offered a case study on the limits to judicial further development of the law by the fiat of judicial interpretation. Not many general propositions can be made from just one sample. There certainly are other cases where the Court was more "liberal" with the text of a provision, perhaps more frequently with regard to provisions of the Treaties than secondary law. Equally, this contribution is far from suggesting that if only the reader understood the inner functioning of the Court and/or read a judgment carefully, all would have come together in perfect harmony. Every court and every judge has their off days, occasionally producing poorly reasoned judgment or outright bad decisions.

What has been suggested here, however, is threefold. First, broad generalisations about how things are "always"[46] done in Luxembourg are perhaps best avoided. To such sweeping propositions, just one contrary example about eating dry bugs suffice to rebut the "always".[47] The Court does not always expand the scope of EU law or always decide in favour of the EU. Second, as regards the interpretative methodological arsenal of the Court, the present case study demonstrated that there would hardly be any special, secretive methods of reasoning employed by the select few

---

[45] I must admit, I am ignorant as to where Nils stands on eating bugs. I have just noted it down as a conversation topic for our next encounter.

[46] Or, indeed for the reasons of caution, tuned down to just clear "tendencies", but stating essentially the same.

[47] Or its "never" companion—the judicial review of the EU legislature exercised by the Court is deficient, because it (as good as) never annuls an act of EU law. My impression is that there too, the reality of the last decade or two has changed considerably. However, the normative evaluation of such data would again be heavily depending on the comparator and annulment median chosen—how many acts annulled per year are "enough"?

illuminati and their acolytes in Luxembourg, unknown to national systems. More importantly perhaps, given the type of cases normally referred on a preliminary ruling to Luxembourg, it is hardly ever "the method" that would determine the outcome, but the balancing and value preferences exercised within that standard interpretative methods, for which there is no mathematical blueprint. Third and finally, when evaluating or commenting on the overall tendencies in the reasoning of a court, one should avoid focusing solely on a select few grand constitutional cases, let alone those hard cases where any and every outcome is likely to provoke contestation. One must look at the average cases. How else could one validly claim what is *typically* done if omitting the *average* cases?

Qu'est-ce que l'obligatoriété ? Divertissement sur la dimension déontique de la *soft law*

Jean-Philippe Christienne

1 Introduction

C'est sans enthousiasme, et, pour tout dire, avec méfiance, que le juge de l'Union a accepté de voir prendre place en son monde cet objet juridique non clairement identifié qu'est la *soft law*. Ces derniers termes, dont on attribue la paternité à Lord Arnold McNair,[1] ont, depuis 1930, connu un essor certain, en même temps qu'ils recouvraient une réalité de plus en plus hétérogène.

Les mots « *soft law* » sont apparus, s'agissant de la Cour de Luxembourg, dans des conclusions, sous la plume de l'avocat général Cosmas, en 2000, à propos des engagements internationaux pris par ce qui n'était encore que la Communauté. Il écrivait: « au stade actuel de développement du droit communautaire, la nécessité d'une harmonisation pratique, d'une part, du respect de la répartition des compétences à l'intérieur de la Communauté entre autorités communautaires et autorités nationales et, d'autre part, d'une approche correcte, efficace et solidaire des engagements internationaux de la Communauté doit nécessairement s'appuyer sur des procédures et des obligations s'inscrivant dans un cadre juridique alternatif, souvent marqué par une absence de rigueur (soft law) »,[2] avant de préciser que, « [l]oin

[1] *In* « The Functions and Differing Legal Character of Treaties », *British Yearbook of International Law*, 1930: Voir M. Briard, *Recherche sur la détermination du droit de l'Union européenne par le droit international: l'exemple de la* soft law, Thèse de doctorat Université Aix-Marseille, 2017, p. 13, note en bas de page 1.

[2] Conclusions du 11 juillet 2000 dans les affaires C-300/98 et C-392/98, Dior e.a., EU:C:2000:378, point 76.

J.-P. Christienne (✉)
Référendaire, General Court of the European Union, Luxembourg, Luxembourg
e-mail: Jean-philippe.Christienne@curia.europa.eu

L. Prete, L. Rezki (eds.), *Judging & (Re)Thinking European Union Law*,
https://doi.org/10.1007/978-3-032-13473-8_29

d'être étrange ou contradictoire, cette situation se justifi[ait] par la géométrie variable et par l'institutionnalisation encore incomplète de la coexistence entre ordres juridiques national, communautaire et international. »[3] Sur le plan théorique, il avançait l'hypothèse, séduisante, que, « [d]ans le cadre de cette institutionnalisation, le droit et la politique s'échangent leurs caractéristiques respectives: le premier impose au deuxième sa rigueur et son caractère contraignant tandis que cette dernière apporte à l'autre sa relativité et sa souplesse. »[4]

La *soft law*, ici présente dans son terreau originel, le droit international, sera, par la suite, analysée par de nombreux autres avocats généraux[5] à propos de certains actes qu'adoptent les institutions, organes ou organismes de l'Union dans d'autres domaines, en particulier le droit de la concurrence et le droit bancaire.

À ce jour, toutefois, ni la Cour de justice ni le Tribunal n'ont mentionné les termes « *soft law* » dans leurs décisions autrement que dans le rappel des arguments des parties ou des questions posées par une juridiction nationale.

Cela ne signifie pas, loin s'en faut, qu'à défaut d'employer ces termes, le juge de l'Union ignore la réalité qu'ils tendent à recouvrir, mais illustre plutôt une démarche empirique, visant à analyser les actes que l'on propose de soumettre à son contrôle juridictionnel au cas par cas et non à l'aune d'un classement catégoriel. Ainsi, dans l'arrêt du 31 mars 1971, Commission/Conseil, dit « AETR »,[6] la Cour, après avoir rappelé que le recours en annulation tendait à assurer « le respect du droit dans l'interprétation et l'application du traité »,[7] a indiqué « qu'il serait contraire à cet objectif d'interpréter restrictivement les conditions de recevabilité du recours en

[3] *Eod. loc.*

[4] *Eod. loc.*

[5] Voir notamment conclusions de l'avocat général Jacobs, du 18 septembre 2003, dans l'affaire C-91/01, Italie/Commission, EU:C:2003:476, point 38, à propos des encadrements et « autres types de 'soft law' » en matière d'aides d'État; conclusions de l'avocat général Ruiz-Jarabo Colomer, du 27 novembre 2008, dans l'affaire C-415/07, Lodato Genaro & C., EU:C:2008:658, points 3 et 34 à 36, dans le même domaine; conclusions de l'avocate générale Kokott, du 6 septembre 2012, dans l'affaire C-226/11, Expedia, EU:C:2012:544, point 35, à propos d'ententes, indiquant que « [l]es publications telles que la communication de minimis ont en effet un caractère de 'soft law' dont il convient de ne pas sous-estimer l'importance dans les procédures en matière d'ententes, que ce soit au niveau européen ou au niveau national »; conclusions de l'avocat général Wahl, du 18 février 2016, dans l'affaire C-526/14, Kotnik e.a., EU:C:2016:102 (ci-après les « conclusions Wahl de 2016 »), points 25, 38 et 83, en matière bancaire, desquelles il ressort que les actes de « soft law », « bien qu'ils ne soient pas contraignants pour les particuliers, peuvent néanmoins produire d'autres types d'effets juridiques » (point 25); conclusions de l'avocat général Bobek, du 12 décembre 2017, dans l'affaire C-16/16 P, Belgique/Commission, EU:C:2017:959, à propos d'une recommandation de la Commission relative à la protection des consommateurs et des joueurs de jeux d'argent et de hasard en ligne et de la prévention de ces jeux chez les mineurs (ci-après les « conclusions Bobek de 2017 »); conclusions de l'avocat général Bobek, du 15 avril 2021, dans l'affaire C-911/19, FBF, EU:C:2021:294, rendues en matière bancaire (ci-après les « conclusions Bobek de 2021 »).

[6] 22/70, EU:C:1971:32.

[7] Arrêt AETR, point 40.

limitant sa portée aux seules catégories d'actes visées »[8] par l'article du traité régissant ce recours, avant de juger que ledit recours devait « donc être ouvert à l'égard de toutes dispositions prises par les institutions, quelles qu'en soient la nature ou la forme, *qui visent à produire des effets de droit* ».[9]

Cette énonciation de principe, faisant écho à celle figurant au point 39 de l'arrêt AETR, selon laquelle l'article en question[10] « envisage comme actes susceptibles de recours toutes dispositions prises par les institutions et *visant à produire un effet juridique* »,[11] est éclairée par les conclusions de l'avocat général Dutheillet de Lamothe aux termes desquelles ledit article « ne peut avoir pour effet d'étendre [la] compétence [du juge de l'Union] à la connaissance de manifestations de volonté dont la substance et les effets ne permettraient pas de les considérer ou de les assimiler à des règlements, à des directives ou des décisions »,[12] étant précisé, en revanche, que « c'est la substance même, l'objet, le contenu et les effets de la manifestation de volonté contestée qui lui donnent son véritable caractère et non la forme choisie par ses auteurs. »[13]

Le libellé actuel de l'article 263 TFUE mentionne, lui aussi, les actes, autres que les recommandations et les avis, « destinés à produire des effets juridiques » et précise que ces derniers sont appréciés « à l'égard des tiers ».

D'où vient, alors, l'évolution terminologique qui a conduit à ce que la jurisprudence fasse mention, comme cela a été relevé dans les conclusions Bobek de 2017,[14] de « toutes dispositions adoptées par les institutions de l'Union, quelle qu'en soit la forme, *qui visent à produire des effets de droit obligatoires* »[15] ? L'avocat général, tout en s'interrogeant sur la portée de cette évolution, n'en a pas daté l'origine. Or, les circonstances ayant conduit à l'ajout de l'adjectif « obligatoires » sont fort éclairantes et inclinent à considérer, afin de mieux contrôler la *soft law* en ce qu'elle peut

[8] Arrêt AETR, point 41.

[9] Arrêt AETR, point 42. Italique ajouté.

[10] Alors l'article 173 CEE, aujourd'hui l'article 263 TFUE.

[11] Italique ajouté.

[12] Rec. p. 288.

[13] *Eod. loc.*

[14] « *1) Effets de droit, effet obligatoire ou effets de droit obligatoires ?* », points 69 à 75 des conclusions Bobek de 2017.

[15] Voir, par exemple, arrêts du 13 février 2014, Hongrie/Commission, C-31/13 P, EU:C:2014:70, point 54, et du 25 février 2021, VodafoneZiggo Group/Commission, C-689/19 P, EU:C:2021:142, point 98. Italique ajouté.

avoir, nonobstant certaines de ses définitions,[16] de normatif et d'imposé,[17,18] que le juge de l'Union devrait revenir à sa formulation originelle.

De prime abord, la notion d'« effets de droit obligatoires » paraît constituer un pléonasme, tant le droit est classiquement défini par son caractère obligatoire, par opposition, notamment, à ce qui résulterait de considérations d'ordre moral[19], ludique,[20] social[21] ou plus largement matériel, même si « [n]ous déplorons [...] notre incapacité à comprendre intuitivement comment la norme parvient à évoquer si 'spécifiquement' l'obligatoriété ».[22] Si d'aucuns font valoir, néanmoins, « [l]es faiblesses d'une conception déontique »,[23] en raison, notamment, du fait que l'obligation se rapporterait nécessairement à un comportement, tandis que nombre

---

[16] Comme l'a pertinemment souligné Linda Senden, selon certains auteurs, "the use of the term soft law is a *contradictio in terminis*; soft law without legal effects is not law and soft law with legal effects is hard law" (*Soft law in European Community Law*, Hart Publishers, Oxford, 2004, p. 3). Voir aussi, à cet égard, l'affirmation de l'avocat général Bot dans ses conclusions dans l'affaire Allemagne e.a./Kronofrance (C-75/05 P et C-80/05 P, EU:C:2008:140, point 141) concernant l'absence « de valeur normative » des lignes directrices adoptées par la Commission européenne.

[17] P. Weil écrivait ainsi, dans un article dont la notoriété n'est plus à souligner, « Vers une normativité relative en droit international ? », *RGDIP* 1982, pp. 5–47, « Le fait qu'une règle soit *soft* ou *hard* n'affecte certes en rien son caractère normatif: une règle conventionnelle ou coutumière peut être peu contraignante, *soft*: elle ne cessera pas, pour autant [...] d'être une norme juridique; à l'inverse, une disposition non normative aura beau avoir un contenu déterminé [...], elle n'en deviendra pas, pour autant une norme juridique (p. 8). Il précisait (en note en bas de page 6 de cet article): « Le terme de *soft law* n'est pas utilisé seulement pour exprimer le caractère peu contraignant d'une norme juridique, il l'est aussi parfois pour évoquer la valeur pré-juridique de certains actes non normatifs [...]. Mieux vaut, semble-t-il, réserver l'appellation de *soft law* aux règles peu contraignantes, car les obligations pré-juridiques ne sont ni de la *soft law* ni de la *hard law*: elles ne sont tout simplement pas *law* du tout. »

[18] Voir aussi L. Senden, *op. cit.*.: si l'autrice définit de manière générale la *soft law* en droit de l'Union comme portant sur des « Community legal instruments that have not been attributed legally binding force » (1.7.1, p. 23), elle affine néanmoins cette analyse pour énoncer qu'il s'agit de « rules of conduct that are laid down in instruments *which have not been attributed legally binding force as such*, but nevertheless may have *certain (indirect) legal effects*, and that are aimed at and may produce practical effects » (p. 3 et section 4.3, italique ajouté).

[19] Que l'on songe, par exemple, à l'impératif catégorique kantien.

[20] Le manquement aux règles du jeu n'est pas sans conséquence quant à l'enjeu, ni sur les joueurs, mais l'accord intersubjectif de ces derniers concernant le fait de s'y conformer et de s'en remettre à un ou à des tiers afin de déterminer si elles ont été enfreintes n'est, selon nous, pas de même nature que la rencontre largement involontaire de l'individu et de la règle juridique. Celle-ci, depuis le cri primal jusqu'au dernier soupir de celui-là, va régir son état, définir les conséquences de son comportement à l'égard de lui-même comme d'autrui, réglementer le sort de ses biens, *etc.* Et s'il est exact que, faisant usage de sa liberté, quelles qu'aient été les déterminations l'ayant façonné, cet individu pourra, le cas échéant, choisir de se soumettre à un autre droit (*electio juris*) ou, du fait de sa participation, directe ou par la voie de ses représentants, modifier celui auquel il est *soumis*, ce nouveau droit ou ce droit modifié n'en possédera pas moins la même caractéristique, celle d'être *objectivement obligatoire* à son égard.

[21] *E. g.* les règles de courtoisie.

[22] D. Alland, « La règle, 'K' du juriste ? », *Droits* 2016, n° 63, p. 129.

[23] A. Jeammaud, « La règle de droit comme modèle », *RIEJ* 1990, n° 25, p. 132.

de règles juridiques n'auraient pas un tel objet, ils semblent omettre que, en tant qu'elles visent, par exemple, un état ou un bien, elles enjoignent *ipso jure* aux personnes auxquelles la règle de droit s'applique de traiter d'une certaine manière la personne comme le bien concerné (par exemple en tirant les conséquences de la majorité de cette personne, ou bien en présumant que celle-ci, en possession d'un bien meuble, en est la légitime propriétaire). La circonstance que la règle de droit prévoit elle-même, parfois, la possibilité d'y déroger n'affecte en rien sa nature: elle est obligatoire y compris dans la possibilité de s'en abstraire.

Le juge de l'Union semble s'être trouvé en quelque sorte contraint à la redondance lorsqu'il lui est revenu de clarifier le contentieux des actes préparatoires, ainsi que cela résulte de l'arrêt du 11 novembre 1981, IBM/Commission,[24] qui avait trait à la possibilité de contester directement une communication des griefs. Pour mieux mettre en évidence le fait que ce type d'acte, nonobstant ses effets juridiques incontestables,[25] n'affectait pas les intérêts de son destinataire, il a donc jugé que « constituent des actes ou décisions susceptibles de faire l'objet d'un recours en annulation [...] les mesures produisant des *effets juridiques obligatoires* de nature à affecter les intérêts du requérant, en modifiant de façon caractérisée la situation juridique de celui-ci »,[26] « la forme dans laquelle des actes ou décisions sont pris [étant], en principe, indifférente en ce qui concerne la possibilité de les attaquer par un recours en annulation ».[27] Cette volonté d'opposer les mesures fixant définitivement la position de l'institution à celles de nature purement préparatoire se trouve, par conséquent, à l'origine de la présence, dans la jurisprudence, d'un adjectif, « obligatoires », qui, selon nous, s'avère être un filtre factice lorsque le juge de l'Union doit déterminer si, et à quelles conditions, des actes de *soft law* peuvent être contestés devant lui, puisque tout acte juridique comporte en lui cette obligatoriété, de façon plus ou moins marquée.[28]

Si certains critères jurisprudentiels paraissent donc devoir être adaptés pour que le juge de l'Union soit mieux à même de contrôler certains actes de *soft law*, un tel ajustement semble d'autant plus nécessaire que les voies de recours définies par le traité FUE accentuent cette possible inadéquation.

---

[24] 60/81, EU:C:1981:264, points 9 à 12, ci-après l'« arrêt IBM ».

[25] Indépendamment du fait qu'elle invite le destinataire de cette communication à y répondre, ce qui peut permettre à celui-ci d'éviter que la procédure administrative n'aboutisse à l'infliction d'une sanction (amende ou astreinte), la Commission ne saurait, par exemple, retenir dans sa décision d'infliger une amende un grief qui n'aurait pas été exposé dans ladite communication. L'ajout d'un grief au soutien de la décision de la Commission implique, en effet, au préalable, l'envoi d'une nouvelle communication des griefs.

[26] 60/81, EU:C:1981:264, point 9.

[27] *Eod. loc.*

[28] L'on aura relevé (note infrapaginale 17) que P. Weil définissait la *soft law* par son caractère *peu* contraignant.

2 Une possible inadéquation des voies de recours et des critères jurisprudentiels à l'égard de certains actes de *soft law*

De façon tout à la fois pertinente et impertinente, les conclusions Bobek de 2021 commencent ainsi:

« À l'instar d'une réplique de *Game of Thrones*, 'ce qui est mort ne meurt jamais'. Par conséquent, à l'exception peut-être des Marcheurs blancs, ce qui est mort ne peut pas non plus être tué. Toutefois, quelque chose qui n'a jamais été en vie (ou plutôt qui n'a jamais vu le jour en tant qu'acte contraignant du droit de l'Union) peut-il être annulé (ou plutôt être déclaré invalide) par la Cour sur renvoi préjudiciel ? Alternativement, la Cour peut-elle donner une interprétation (contraignante) d'une mesure non contraignante de l'Union ? »[29]

Si une partie de la doctrine a répondu par la négative à ces deux interrogations,[30] la Cour de Luxembourg en a jugé différemment, et, sans aller jusqu'à énoncer, tel Herbert Hart, que « [p]arler de règles constitue un mythe qui masque la réalité, à savoir que le droit consiste simplement dans les décisions des tribunaux et la prédiction qu'on peut en faire »,[31] il s'agit, bien évidemment, de rendre compte de ce qu'il est convenu d'appeler le droit positif.

2.1 *La finalité propre à chaque voie de recours révèle le statut contradictoire de la soft law en droit de l'Union*

Trois voies de recours ont permis au juge de l'Union d'aborder la question du statut de la *soft law*. Ce sont le recours en annulation, le renvoi préjudiciel et l'exception d'illégalité, respectivement régis par les articles 263, 267 et 277 TFUE. Tandis que le premier, tel qu'interprété par le juge de l'Union, paraît exclure la possibilité pour ce dernier de juger recevable et, le cas échéant, d'accueillir un recours tendant à l'annulation d'un acte de *soft law*, les deux suivants lui ont permis non seulement d'interpréter, mais également d'examiner la légalité de certains actes de *soft law*.

---

[29] Conclusions Bobek de 2021, point 1.

[30] « Tout l'intérêt de la soft law, de la recommandation, du conseil, de l'incitation réside d'ailleurs dans le fait qu'ils n'interdisent précisément pas, qu'ils ne produisent pas d'obligation ou de prohibition inconditionnelle et que, pour cette raison, ils ne donnent lieu à aucune possibilité d'évaluation en termes de légalité ou d'illégalité », D. de Béchillon, *Qu'est-ce qu'une règle de Droit ?*, Éditions Odile Jacob, 1997, p. 194.

[31] H. L. A. Hart,, *Le concept de droit*, Facultés universitaires Saint-Louis, 1976, p. 169.

2.1.1 Une certaine superposition d'état: les articles 267 et 277 TFUE

Tirant argument du libellé général de l'article 267 TFUE, qui lui donne compétence pour statuer, à titre préjudiciel, « sur la validité et l'interprétation des *actes* pris par les institutions, organes ou organismes de l'Union »,[32] la Cour a jugé, d'abord implicitement, à partir de l'arrêt du 15 juin 1976, Frecassetti,[33] puis explicitement, à partir de l'arrêt du 3 décembre 1989, Grimaldi,[34] que des recommandations émises par les institutions, qui sont expressément exclues du champ de l'article 263 TFUE, pouvaient, toutefois, faire l'objet d'une interprétation dans le cadre de l'article 267 TFUE, ce dernier visant « l'interprétation des actes pris par les institutions [...], sans exception aucune ».[35]

La Cour a précisé, dans l'arrêt Grimaldi, « que les actes en question ne peuvent être considérés [...] comme dépourvus de tout effet juridique »,[36] les juges nationaux étant « tenus de prendre les recommandations en considération en vue de la solution des litiges qui leur sont soumis, notamment lorsque celles-ci éclairent l'interprétation de dispositions nationales prises dans le but d'assurer leur mise en œuvre, ou encore lorsqu'elles ont pour objet de compléter des dispositions [de droit de l'Union] ayant un caractère contraignant ».[37]

L'avocate générale Kokott, dans ses conclusions dans l'affaire Expedia, prolongeait cette analyse à propos de la communication de minimis,[38] en mettant en avant le fait que, bien que celle-ci « ne produise pas d'effets juridiques contraignants, il serait incorrect *de lui dénier toute portée juridique* dans les procédures en matière d'ententes »,[39] les publications telles que cette communication ayant « en effet un caractère de 'soft law' dont il convient de ne pas sous-estimer l'importance dans les procédures en matière d'ententes, que ce soit au niveau européen ou au niveau national ».[40]

Dans l'arrêt du 2 avril 2009, Lodato Gennaro,[41] la Cour a fait application de la jurisprudence issue de l'arrêt Grimaldi à des lignes directrices de la Commission,

---

[32] Italique ajouté.

[33] 113/75, EU:C:1976:89, points 4 à 9.

[34] C-322/88, EU:C:1989:646 (ci-après l'« arrêt Grimaldi »), points 8 et 9.

[35] Même arrêt, point 8.

[36] Même arrêt, point 18.

[37] *Eod. loc.* Pour une confirmation du fait que les recommandations peuvent faire l'objet d'une interprétation de la Cour dans le cadre de l'article 267 TFUE, voir arrêt du 21 janvier 1993, Deutsche Shell, C-188/91, EU:C:1993:24, point 18.

[38] Communication de la Commission concernant les accords d'importance mineure qui ne restreignent pas sensiblement le jeu de la concurrence au sens de l'article 81, paragraphe 1, du traité instituant la Communauté européenne (de minimis) (JOCE 2001, C 368, p. 13).

[39] Conclusions de l'avocate générale Kokott, du 6 septembre 2012, dans l'affaire C-226/11, Expedia, EU:C:2012:544, point 35, italique ajouté.

[40] *Eod. loc.*

[41] C-415/07, EU:C:2009:220.

concernant les aides à l'emploi[42] et les aides d'État à finalité régionale,[43] en en faisant mention sous le titre « Le droit communautaire » du cadre juridique et en les interprétant comme elle l'eût fait s'agissant d'un règlement ou d'une directive.[44]

Pour autant, la formulation de l'arrêt Grimaldi semble ambiguë: comment « compléter » des dispositions contraignantes de manière non contraignante ? L'on voit mal que la greffe puisse être de nature autre que le corps incomplet qu'elle vise à restaurer, même si l'origine de la première et du second n'est pas la même. D'ailleurs, la Cour admet indirectement un *certain* caractère contraignant des recommandations, en abordant la finalité de celles-ci, que les institutions adoptent « lorsqu'elles ne détiennent pas, en vertu du traité, le pouvoir d'adopter des actes obligatoires ou lorsqu'elles estiment qu'il n'y a pas lieu d'édicter des règles *plus* contraignantes ».[45]

S'il était exact que les actes de *soft law* fussent dépourvus de tout effet contraignant, comment serait-il même possible de les interpréter au regard des effets de droit qui s'attachent à l'interprétation dans le cadre de l'article 267 TFUE ?

Bien plus, dans l'arrêt du 25 mars 2021, Balgarska Narodna Banka,[46] la Cour a procédé à une appréciation de la validité d'une recommandation, à la suite de laquelle elle a déclaré partiellement invalide cette dernière, qui avait été adoptée par l'Autorité bancaire européenne (ABE). Tout en réaffirmant que « les recommandations ne visent pas à produire des effets juridiques contraignants »,[47] la Cour a donc déclaré invalide un acte juridique non contraignant. Or, comme cela était énoncé avec netteté dans les conclusions Bobek de 2021, « il est de jurisprudence constante que le renvoi préjudiciel en appréciation de validité constitue, au même titre qu'un recours en annulation, une modalité de *contrôle de la légalité* des actes de l'Union »[48] et que si, « en cas de constat d'incompatibilité d'une mesure de l'Union avec le droit de l'Union de rang supérieur, leurs issues sont légèrement différentes formellement [...], ils partagent les mêmes effets erga omnes et, généralement, ex tunc; l'acte de l'Union en cause *doit être considéré comme nul* et ne plus être appliqué ».[49]

Dans le cadre de l'article 277 TFUE, le juge de l'Union a également examiné au fond des exceptions d'illégalité portant sur des actes de *soft law*, inaugurant un tel contrôle par celui des lignes directrices pour le calcul des amendes infligées en application de l'article 15, paragraphe 2, du règlement n° 17 et de l'article 65, paragraphe 5, du traité CECA.[50] Tandis que le Tribunal avait semblé hésitant quant à l'incorporation de ces lignes directrices dans ce qu'il est convenu d'appeler le «

---

[42] JOCE 1995, C 334, p. 4.

[43] JOCE 1998, C 74, p. 9.

[44] Voir points 23 à 32 de l'arrêt ainsi que son dispositif.

[45] Arrêt Grimaldi, point 13, italique ajouté.

[46] C-501/18, EU:C:2021:249 (ci-après l'« arrêt BNB »); points 82 à 101.

[47] Arrêt BNB, point 80.

[48] Point 143 des conclusions et jurisprudence s'y rapportant. Italique ajouté.

[49] *Idem.*

[50] JOCE 1998, C 9, p. 3.

cadre juridique »,[51] mais avait néanmoins considéré que l'exception d'illégalité dont elles faisaient l'objet était recevable, la Cour a jugé avec netteté que lesdites lignes directrices faisaient partie de ce cadre, qu'elles étaient « des règles de conduite visant à produire des effets externes », en tant qu'elles étaient adressées aux opérateurs économiques[52] et qu'il ne pouvait « être exclu que, sous certaines conditions et en fonction de leur contenu, de telles règles de conduite ayant une portée générale puissent déployer *des effets juridiques* »,[53] étant donné que, en adoptant ces dernières et en annonçant par leur publication qu'elle les appliquera dorénavant aux cas concernés par celles-ci, l'institution en question s'autolimite dans l'exercice de son pouvoir d'appréciation et ne saurait se départir de ces règles sous peine de se voir sanctionner, le cas échéant, au titre d'une violation de principes généraux du droit, tels que l'égalité de traitement ou la protection de la confiance légitime.[54] Elle a également souligné que, « eu égard notamment *à leurs effets juridiques et à leur portée générale* »,[55] les mêmes règles relevaient, « en principe, de la notion de 'droit' au sens de l'article 7, paragraphe 1, de la CEDH ».[56]

Le juge de l'Union semble donc, lorsqu'il intervient en application des articles 267 et 277 TFUE, avoir une approche de la *soft law* caractérisée par ce que la physique quantique qualifie de « superposition d'état ». À l'instar du chat imaginé par Erwin Schrödinger, qui peut être, à un moment donné *m*, vivant ou mort, la *soft law* peut, simultanément, être et n'être pas: le plus souvent, elle est en effet décrite dans la jurisprudence comme n'ayant « pas d'effet contraignant »,[57] ce qui ne fait pourtant obstacle ni à son interprétation ni à son appréciation de validité, alors que

---

[51] Voir arrêt du 30 septembre 2003, Michelin/Commission (T-203/01, EU:T:2003:250), aux termes duquel le cadre juridique est « uniquement défini dans le règlement n° 17 et dans les lignes directrices » (points 254, 292 et 298, italique ajouté), tandis que l'arrêt du 20 mars 2002, LR AF 1998/ Commission (T-23/99, EU:T:2002:75), indique, d'une part, que ce cadre est « uniquement, défini dans le règlement n° 17 » (point 234) et fait référence, d'autre part, au « cadre juridique s'appliquant au cas d'espèce, en particulier l'application des nouvelles lignes directrices ou, encore, de la communication sur la coopération » (point 390).

[52] Arrêt du 28 juin 2005, Dansk Rørindustri e.a./Commission (C-189/02 P, C-202/02 P, C-205/02 P à C-208/02 P et C-213/02 P, EU:C:2005:250), points 208 à 210.

[53] Même arrêt, point 211, italique ajouté.

[54] *Eod. loc.*

[55] Même arrêt, point 223, italique ajouté.

[56] *Eod. loc.*

[57] Arrêt du 19 juillet 2016, Kotnik e.a. (C-526/14, EU:C:2016:570), point 45, à propos de la communication de la Commission concernant l'application, à partir du 1er août 2013, des règles en matière d'aides d'État aux aides accordées aux banques dans le contexte de la crise financière (« Communication concernant le secteur bancaire ») (JOUE 2013, C 216, p. 1); voir aussi conclusions Wahl de 2016, aux termes desquelles, « [b]ien que la Cour ait jugé que les dispositions de tels actes de soft law doivent, en vertu de l'obligation de coopération loyale inscrite à l'article 4, paragraphe 3, TUE, être dûment prises en compte par les autorités des États membres, cette obligation ne peut pas être comprise comme rendant ces règles contraignantes – pas même de facto – sous peine de contourner la procédure législative exposée dans le TFUE » (C-526/14, EU:C:2016:102, point 38); voir, en outre, points 37, 39 et 40 de ces conclusions ainsi que *supra*, note en bas de page 39.

celles-ci présupposent, logiquement, une modification minimale de l'ordonnancement juridique et, donc, un tel effet.

La Cour de Luxembourg n'est pas la seule à manier ce genre de paradoxe. À titre d'illustration, le Conseil constitutionnel français a jugé contraire à la Constitution une disposition législative au motif qu'elle était « manifestement dépourvue de toute portée normative » tandis que, « sous réserve de dispositions particulières prévues par la Constitution », « la loi a pour vocation d'énoncer des règles et doit par suite être revêtue d'une portée normative ».[58] Or, comme l'a fait judicieusement observer la doctrine, « comment concevoir l'annulation ou l'inconstitutionnalité d'un énoncé qui n'est pas une norme ? »[59] Une telle contradiction est absente de la jurisprudence du juge de l'Union rendue dans le cadre de l'article 263 TFUE, à tout le moins en l'état, qui exclut tout contrôle de la *soft law* lorsqu'elle (n') est (que) *soft law*.

2.1.2 Une exclusion certaine en l'état: l'article 263 TFUE

Le juge de l'Union a naturellement pris appui sur le libellé de l'article 263 TFUE, excluant les recommandations du champ de cette disposition. En dépit d'une approche privilégiant la teneur même des actes de *soft law*, par-delà leur dénomination, il a seulement jugé recevables les recours en annulation dirigés contre des actes qui n'avaient de la *soft law* que l'apparence.

a) Les recommandations

L'article 263 TFUE visant « les actes, autres que les recommandations et les avis », le juge de l'Union ne pouvait que se conformer à cette exclusion prévue par les auteurs du traité FUE, pour autant, toutefois, qu'il s'agisse bien de recommandations, ce qu'il apprécie au cas par cas. Témoigne de cette approche classique en matière de recours en annulation l'arrêt du 20 février 2018, Belgique/Commission,[60] dans lequel la Cour, après avoir rappelé que, « [e]n instituant les recommandations comme catégorie particulière d'actes de l'Union et en prévoyant expressément qu'elles 'ne lient pas', l'article 288 TFUE a entendu investir les institutions habilitées à les adopter d'un pouvoir d'incitation et de persuasion, distinct du pouvoir d'adopter des actes dotés d'une force obligatoire »,[61] a cependant précisé que, « à titre exceptionnel, l'impossibilité de former un recours en annulation contre une recommandation ne vaut pas si l'acte attaqué, par son contenu, ne constitue pas une véritable recommandation ».[62]

---

[58] Déc. n° 2005-512 DC, 21 avril 2005, JORF 24 avril 2005, p. 7173.

[59] V. Champeil-Desplats, « N'est pas normatif qui peut. L'exigence de normativité dans la jurisprudence du Conseil constitutionnel », *CCC* 2007, n° 21, pp. 93–101.

[60] C-16/16 P, EU:C:2018:79.

[61] Point 26 de l'arrêt.

[62] Point 29 de l'arrêt.

Afin de vérifier que la recommandation en cause correspondait bien à sa dénomination, la Cour a ainsi procédé à l'examen de sa teneur et souligné que, comme l'avait relevé le Tribunal, cette recommandation était libellée, *pour l'essentiel*, en des termes non impératifs et que, si certaines versions linguistiques de ladite recommandation comportaient partiellement des termes *plus impératifs*, elles étaient néanmoins rédigées de manière *essentiellement* non contraignante.[63] Elle a également insisté sur le fait que la même recommandation n'était aucunement destinée à produire des effets juridiques contraignants et que la Commission n'avait nullement eu l'intention de lui conférer de tels effets. Elle a donc conclu, à la suite du Tribunal, que la recommandation en cause n'était pas un acte attaquable au sens de l'article 263 TFUE.

Cela étant, les termes mis en italique ci-dessus semblent révéler les difficultés de prise en considération d'un phénomène juridique, la *soft law*, qui ne saurait s'accommoder, dans bien des cas, d'un raisonnement binaire fondé sur le caractère obligatoire ou non de ses effets de droit.[64]

Néanmoins, ce type de raisonnement a également prévalu, dans le prolongement de l'arrêt AETR, tel qu'infléchi par l'arrêt IBM, pour les autres actes de *soft law*.

b) Les autres actes de *soft law*

La jurisprudence et les motifs de sa constance découlent implicitement des conclusions Wahl de 2016: c'est l'absence de base légale prévoyant l'édiction d'actes ayant un caractère hybride (autrement dit, d'actes plus contraignants qu'un avis et moins contraignants qu'une décision) qui constitue, en réalité, le fondement de la présomption selon laquelle les textes de *soft law* ne peuvent faire l'objet d'un recours en annulation. L'avocat général avait ainsi indiqué, à propos de la Commission, qu'elle n'avait « pas le pouvoir de poser des règles contraignantes générales et abstraites régissant, par exemple, les situations dans lesquelles une aide pourrait être considérée comme étant compatible parce qu'elle vise à remédier à une perturbation grave de l'économie d'un État membre en vertu de l'article 107, paragraphe 3, sous b), TFUE ».[65] Il ajoutait qu'un « tel ensemble de règles contraignantes serait nul et non avenu ».[66]

En effet, la Cour a annulé, par exemple, un code de conduite relatif à la mise en œuvre d'un règlement, relevant, après avoir vérifié s'il établissait « des modalités d'application impliquant des obligations spécifiques »,[67] que tel était le cas, certaines exigences quant à la communication de données ne pouvant « être considérées comme étant déjà inhérentes à l'obligation d'information »[68] prévue par ce règlement, et l'obligation de confidentialité des échanges d'informations entre les

[63] Point 34 de l'arrêt. Italique ajouté.

[64] Voir notes en bas de page nos 28 et 45; voir en outre conclusions Bobek de 2017, points 125 à 142.

[65] Conclusions Wahl de 2016, point 37.

[66] *Eod. loc.*

[67] Arrêt du 13 novembre 1991, Commission/France, C-303/90, EU:C:1991:424, point 15.

[68] Même arrêt, point 21.

États membres et la Commission, résultant de ce code de conduite, étant absente dudit règlement.[69] Elle a, par conséquent, jugé que ledit code de conduite constituait « un acte destiné à produire des effets juridiques propres »[70] et qu'il était, « dès lors, [...] susceptible de faire l'objet d'un recours en annulation ».[71] Au terme de l'examen des différentes bases légales envisageables pour l'imposition de telles obligations, la Cour a conclu qu'aucune d'entre elles ne pouvait être retenue et a, par conséquent, jugé que la mesure attaquée constituait un acte pris par une autorité incompétente.[72]

Inversement, lorsqu'une base légale existe pour adopter des actes tels que des lignes directrices, et que le caractère obligatoire des éléments qui y figurent est reconnu, la même présomption conduit à considérer qu'il ne s'agit plus de *soft law*: « [l]es lignes directrices ont été adoptées, non en tant qu'acte de 'soft law', mais [...] en tant que décision de la Commission et donc sous la forme d'un acte produisant des effets de droit. »[73]

L'on pourrait objecter, quant à cette dernière formulation, que l'adoption sous la forme d'une décision ne devrait pas préjuger de la teneur effective de la mesure en cause et que, par ailleurs, même les actes de *soft law*, selon la jurisprudence,[74] produisent certains effets de droit.

L'idée selon laquelle, lorsque le juge de l'Union est saisi d'un acte hors nomenclature, autrement dit qui ne figure pas à l'article 288 TFUE, il n'est, *a priori*, plus question de *hard law*, mais de *soft law*, et qui constitue le socle de la remarque extraite des conclusions Wahl de 2015, aurait d'ailleurs dû être écartée s'agissant des orientations émises par l'Autorité bancaire européenne (ABE), ont fait valoir certains auteurs.[75] En effet, la lecture conjuguée des articles 12.1 et 14.3 du

---

[69] Même arrêt, point 23: la disposition pertinente du même règlement « ne fait aucune référence à une quelconque obligation, pour [les États membres], de garantir la confidentialité des informations reçues dans le cadre de l'échange d'informations ».

[70] Même arrêt, point 25. L'on retrouve ici le critère de l'intention de l'auteur de l'acte (« destiné à »). De manière surprenante au regard de la jurisprudence consécutive à l'arrêt IBM, il est seulement fait état des « effets juridiques » (à juste titre selon nous). Cela étant mentionné, il est juste d'indiquer que ce retour à la terminologie de l'arrêt AETR n'est qu'apparent, puisque les motifs précédents de l'arrêt portaient sur l'existence d'*obligations* non prévues par le règlement en cause.

[71] *Eod. loc.*

[72] Même arrêt, points 27 à 35.

[73] Conclusions de l'avocat général Wahl, du 5 février 2015, dans l'affaire C-148/14, Nordzucker, EU:C:2015:64 (ci-après les « conclusions Wahl de 2015 »), note en bas de page n° 9. Il s'agissait de la décision 2004/156/CE de la Commission, du 29 janvier 2004, concernant l'adoption de lignes directrices pour la surveillance et la déclaration des émissions de gaz à effet de serre, conformément à la directive 2003/87/CE du Parlement européen et du Conseil (JOCE 2004, L 59, p. 1).

[74] *E.g.* arrêt Grimaldi, point 18; arrêt du 28 juin 2005, Dansk Rørindustri e.a./Commission, point 211.

[75] Voir, en particulier, C. A. Vassilopoulos, "Review of Non-Binding Legal Acts (EBA Guidelines): Paradoxes in Legal Reasoning – Comments on Case C-911/19 Fédération Bancaire Française – (FBF), Judgment of the Court of Justice of the European Union of 15 July 2021, *European Business Law Review* 2023, Volume 34, Issue 3, pp. 391–414, à propos de l'arrêt du 15 juillet 2021, FBF (C-911/19, EU:C:2021:599, ci-après l'« arrêt FBF »).

protocole (n° 4) sur les statuts du Système européen de banques centrales et de la Banque centrale européenne[76] permettrait, au regard du libellé de ces articles, d'assimiler les orientations, dans le cadre de l'Union économique et monétaire (UEM), aux directives en dehors de celle-ci, piste de réflexion que la Cour aurait décidé de ne pas explorer[77] et qui aurait conduit à un résultat tout différent concernant la possibilité de demander l'annulation de telles orientations au titre de l'article 263 TFUE.

Il est donc incontestable que le juge de l'Union traite de manière asymétrique les actes de *soft law*, en fonction de la voie de recours au titre de laquelle ils sont portés devant lui, puisqu'il énonce avec force que « tout acte de l'Union ne produisant pas d'effets juridiques obligatoires échappe au contrôle juridictionnel prévu à l'article 263 TFUE »,[78] ce qui n'est pas le cas dans le cadre de l'article 267 TFUE. Certes, la rédaction respective des articles 263 et 267 TFUE favorise cette asymétrie. Il n'est cependant pas certain que le critère de l'obligatoriété, qui n'est présent que dans la jurisprudence relative à l'article 263 TFUE,[79] soit à même de répondre à ce qui apparaît nécessaire au regard de la généralisation du recours à la *soft law*, à savoir une approche graduée de cette dernière.

2.2 L'obligatoriété, critère d'un seul type de recours, prohibe une approche graduée de la soft law en droit de l'Union

La Cour rappelle régulièrement l'impératif de sécurité juridique tenant au respect des compétences d'attribution des institutions, organes et organismes de l'Union, duquel il découle que « tout acte visant à créer des *effets juridiques* emprunte *sa force obligatoire* à une disposition du droit [de l'Union] qui doit expressément être indiquée comme base légale et qui prescrit la forme juridique dont l'acte doit être revêtu. »[80]

S'agissant du droit de l'Union, la *soft law* prend appui sur des dispositions de droit primaire ou de droit dérivé, qu'elle identifie et contribue à mettre en œuvre. La question de savoir si, et dans quelle mesure, elle est « destinée à produire des effets juridiques à l'égard des tiers » appelle, semble-t-il, une réponse plus nuancée que celle résultant de la jurisprudence actuelle, raison pour laquelle il paraîtrait utile,

[76] JOUE 2016, C 202, p. 230.

[77] C. A. Vassilopoulos, *op. cit.*, pp. 394–395.

[78] Arrêt FBF, point 37; voir également, en ce sens, jurisprudence y citée.

[79] Il convient, en effet, de rappeler à nouveau que l'article 263, premier alinéa, TFUE ne fait état que des actes, autres que les recommandations et les avis, « destinés à produire des effets juridiques à l'égard des tiers ». L'adjectif « obligatoire » n'y est ainsi pas mentionné, même si la notion d'« effets juridiques » ainsi que l'exclusion des recommandations et avis font implicitement référence à l'exigence de la nature contraignante de l'acte en cause.

[80] Arrêt du 1er octobre 2009, Commission/Conseil, C-370/07, EU:C:2009:590, point 39 et jurisprudence y citée.

d'une part, de revenir à la rédaction issue de l'arrêt AETR et, d'autre part, de retenir un critère lié à l'apport normatif de l'acte de *soft law*, en recourant à ce que le Conseil d'État français a qualifié d'« échelle de 'normativité graduée' ».[81]

2.2.1 Un contenu suffisamment impératif: produire des effets de droit

La jurisprudence témoigne déjà d'une reconnaissance de certains effets juridiques de la *soft law*, à travers les notions de « prise en compte » et d'« autolimitation ». L'examen attentif de celles-ci montrent qu'elles répondent souvent à l'exigence figurant à l'article 263, paragraphe 1, TFUE de produire « des effets juridiques à l'égard des tiers » et que l'expression « effets juridiques obligatoires » est non seulement tautologique, mais source de confusion.[82]

a) La prise en compte par les tiers résulte d'effets de droit

Dans l'arrêt Grimaldi, la Cour a jugé que les recommandations n'étaient pas dépourvues de tout effet juridique, « les juges nationaux étant tenus de [les] prendre [...] en considération en vue de la solution des litiges qui leur sont soumis ».[83] Réitérée depuis lors,[84] cette considération amène au constat que "EU soft law indeed applies in both the EU and national legal order and may produce different effects depending on the perception of the authority in charge of implementing it".[85]

Cela était particulièrement net dans le cas de la recommandation en cause dans l'affaire Belgique/Commission,[86] ainsi qu'il ressort du point 107 des conclusions Bobek de 2017: « Il semblerait donc que la Cour a clairement prévu qu'une recommandation puisse produire des effets de droit au niveau national. Après tout, elle est censée être prise en considération dans les États membres, peu importe ce que cela signifie exactement. »[87]

---

[81] *Le droit souple - étude annuelle 2013*, n° 64, 2013, Les rapports du Conseil d'État, point 1.3.4, « Le droit souple s'inscrit dans une échelle de 'normativité graduée' », pp. 65–71.

[82] Voir G. Gentile, "Ensuring effective judicial review of EU soft law via the action for annulment before the EU courts: a plea for a liberal-constitutional approach", *European Constitutional Law Review*, vol. 16, n° 3, 2020, p. 486: "The case law suggests that legal effects and legally binding effects are two distinct categories. Yet, questions may arise as to whether this distinction is sound and practical".

[83] Arrêt Grimaldi, point 18.

[84] Arrêt BNB, point 80.

[85] G. Gentile, *op. cit.*, p. 487.

[86] C-16/16 P, EU:C:2017:959, voir *supra* note en bas de page n° 5.

[87] Voir aussi points 125 à 142 des conclusions Bobek de 2017 et, en particulier, point 133: « [...] la recommandation est destinée à inciter les États membres à adopter une certaine législation et, par l'intermédiaire de cette législation, à avoir une incidence sur les sociétés et les joueurs de jeux d'argent et de hasard qui en sont les destinataires indirects. Il peut ainsi évidemment être soutenu que, formellement et en elle-même, ce n'est pas la recommandation qui aura une incidence sur les droits des tiers, mais l'éventuelle législation nationale. Il est toutefois difficile de nier que c'est la recommandation qui est la véritable source de la législation nationale. »

Ces effets de droit sont, au demeurant, attestés par le fait que, dans l'arrêt BNB, la Cour a partiellement invalidé une recommandation, ce qui, en réalité, traduit la reconnaissance de la modification de l'ordonnancement juridique opérée par l'adoption de cette recommandation et, partant, l'effet contraignant de celle-ci à l'égard des tiers.

Il en va de même des orientations, lignes directrices et autres codes, dont le juge de l'Union a reconnu la conformité au droit de l'Union sur le fondement de l'autolimitation, par les auteurs de ces actes de *soft law*, de la marge d'appréciation dont ils disposent dans l'exercice de leurs compétences.

b) L'autolimitation produit des effets de droit à l'égard des tiers

En dépit du fait que, de manière récurrente, la jurisprudence rappelle que de tels actes de *soft law* n'ont d'effet contraignant qu'à l'égard de leurs auteurs,[88] il n'en demeure pas moins que non seulement les États membres, mais l'ensemble des opérateurs économiques visés par ces actes se verront appliquer les éléments qu'ils contiennent, ce que la doctrine n'a pas manqué de souligner.[89]

Le juge de l'Union a lui-même utilisé des termes traduisant l'existence de tels effets. Ainsi, dans l'arrêt Deufil, du 24 février 1987, la Cour a pris soin de rappeler que le code des aides n'avait pas dérogé aux règles du traité relatives aux aides d'État et ne pouvait le faire, mais a jugé que ce code constituait « des règles indicatives définissant les lignes de conduite que la Commission entend[ait] suivre et *qu'elle demand[ait] aux États membres de respecter* dans le domaine d'aides [concerné]. »[90] Certes, la Commission ne pourrait s'appuyer sur un tel code pour faire sanctionner un manquement de la part d'un État membre; toutefois, en pratique, l'on voit mal les États membres ne pas respecter un acte de *soft law* comme ledit code, la Commission étant en mesure d'opposer une décision défavorable à ces derniers qui trouverait son origine, explicite ou implicite, dans le non-respect du même code. De plus, lorsqu'une institution demande aux États membres de se conformer à un texte qu'elle a édicté, il paraît assez peu douteux qu'elle a l'intention de voir ce texte produire des effets de droit, de telle sorte que le critère de l'intentionnalité semble être rempli.

Nombreux sont les exemples qui attestent de ce que, derrière le paravent du loisible se dissimule souvent l'obligatoire. Ainsi, dans l'arrêt du 5 novembre 1997,

---

[88] Voir, par exemple, s'agissant de la communication de la Commission intitulée « Lignes directrices concernant les aides d'État à la protection de l'environnement et à l'énergie pour la période 2014-2020 » (JO 2014, C 200, p. 1), arrêt du 12 octobre 2023, Est Wind Power, C-11/22, EU:C:2023:765, points 31 à 33.

[89] Comme l'a très pertinemment énoncé G. Gentile, "In this regard, by finding that the EU soft law binds its authors, the Court of Justice seems to overlook the effects of such acts on individuals. The author should, in fact, respect the EU soft law measure *during its interactions with individuals*. As a result, third parties are (indirectly) subject to the consequences of EU soft law"; et d'insister: "It is thus not clear, however, how the bindingness of an EU soft law act on the issuing authority *may not also produce legal effects towards third parties*. De facto, effects may also occur incidentally for individuals", in *op. cit.*, pp. 486 et 482 (italique ajouté).

[90] 310/85, EU:C:1987:96, point 22.

Ducros/Commission,[91] le Tribunal, après avoir rappelé que des lignes directrices concernant les aides d'État au sauvetage et à la restructuration des entreprises en difficulté étaient opposables à la Commission sur le fondement de l'autolimitation par celle-ci de son pouvoir d'appréciation, a relevé que ces lignes directrices « *exigent* que les aides à la restructuration soient encadrées par un plan »,[92] soumis « à trois conditions matérielles »,[93] à savoir le retour de l'entreprise à la viabilité, la prévention des distorsions de concurrence indues et la proportionnalité des aides aux coûts et avantages de la restructuration. Imagine-t-on seulement un État membre, désireux de sauver une ou des entreprises en difficulté, qui ne présenterait pas de plan, ou dont le plan ne respecterait que les deux dernières conditions susmentionnées, au motif, par exemple, que, si la prévention des distorsions de concurrence et le principe de proportionnalité trouvent une base légale dans le droit primaire et dérivé, le retour de l'entreprise à la viabilité ne constitue qu'un objectif fixé par la Commission, compte tenu du type d'aide en cause, et non une obligation juridique *per se* ?

Dans les conclusions Bobek de 2021, il était justement souligné que, même si l'habillage terminologique des orientations en cause n'était pas impératif, leurs véritables destinataires, « à savoir les établissements financiers, n'[avaie]nt guère, voire pas du tout, le choix de décider de s'y conformer ou non »,[94] étant donné qu'il n'en résultait pas clairement que, à supposer qu'elle fût prise, « la décision formelle des autorités compétentes de ne pas s['y] conformer dispense en réalité les établissements financiers du devoir de 'tout mettre en œuvre pour respecter ces orientations' ».[95]

Afin de faire évoluer la jurisprudence pour tenir compte du fait, tangible,[96] qu'un acte de *soft law* peut être contraignant, même si c'est à un degré moindre ou de manière moins évidente que la *hard law*, il semble donc nécessaire de revenir à la formulation retenue dans l'arrêt AETR, afin de permettre au justiciable de contester « toutes dispositions prises par les institutions, quelles qu'en soient la nature ou la forme, qui visent à produire des effets de droit ».[97] Un retour en arrière pour un progrès, puisque pourraient ainsi être examinés par le juge de l'annulation des actes dont le contenu normatif est fréquemment avéré.

[91] T-149/95, EU:T:1997:165.

[92] Point 62 de l'arrêt. Italique ajouté.

[93] *Eod. loc.*

[94] Conclusions Bobek de 2021, point 48.

[95] Conclusions Bobek de 2021, point 49. Voir aussi C. A. Vassilopoulos, *op. cit.*, p. 396: "a simple reading of these specific guidelines lead to the conclusion that there are significant signs of many mandatory rules", de nombreux exemples étant fournis à l'appui de cette assertion (pp. 396 et 397), ce qui n'a rien de surprenant au regard de l'hypothèse émise par cet auteur, selon laquelle une orientation émise dans le cadre de l'UEM équivaut à une directive hors UEM, nonobstant le caractère incomplet à cet égard de l'article 288 TFUE.

[96] Voir note en bas de page n° 63.

[97] Arrêt AETR, point 42.

2.2.2 Un contenu suffisamment normatif: l'exposé de règles et l'apport de méthodes

Dans son étude annuelle de 2013 sur le droit souple,[98] le Conseil d'État français rappelle que, « [d]e manière générale, quels que soient les domaines d'action concernés, l'Union européenne fait une place intégrante au droit souple dans *sa politique normative* ».[99] Il distingue, dans l'« échelle de « normativité graduée' »[100] qu'il suggère, trois degrés « entre droit souple et droit dur, en fonction de l'intensité de l'obligation imposée par l'instrument: obligation pour le destinataire de l'instrument de se justifier lorsqu'il s'en écarte; obligation de prouver sa conformité au droit dur lorsque le destinataire s'écarte de la prescription; obligation de compatibilité avec l'instrument ».[101] Néanmoins, toute révérence gardée, cette thèse encourt deux critiques. D'abord, elle postule que la *soft law* cesse d'être telle lorsqu'émerge, peu ou prou, l'obligatoriété. Nous pensons qu'il n'en est rien[102] et que la *soft law* demeure ce qu'elle est jusqu'à solidification, autrement dit incorporation dans la, ou transformation en, *hard law*, d'où la nécessité de permettre son contrôle avant qu'elle corresponde à cette dernière. Ensuite, l'« échelle de 'normativité graduée' » proposée est, en réalité, une « échelle d''obligatoriété graduée' ». Or, même un acte de *soft law* peu contraignant nous paraît pouvoir revêtir un caractère normatif, dès lors qu'il expose des règles nouvelles au regard du droit positif et qu'il apporte des méthodes destinées à mettre en œuvre ce dernier.

a) L'exposé de règles

Il semble peu douteux que les orientations ou recommandations adoptées par la BCE ou l'ABE,[103] de même, par exemple, que certaines communications de la Commission portant code,[104] orientations,[105] lignes directrices,[106] *etc.* énoncent un certain nombre de règles, procédurales ou de fond, qui étaient absentes du droit dérivé et vont souvent au-delà d'une simple compilation d'exemples ou d'une systématisation de la jurisprudence.

---

[98] Voir note en bas de page n° 81.

[99] *Op. cit.*, p. 32 *in limine*. Italique ajouté.

[100] Voir arrêts Grimaldi, point 13, et du 28 juin 2005, Dansk Rørindustri e.a./Commission (C-189/02 P, C-202/02 P, C-205/02 P à C-208/02 P et C-213/02 P, EU:C:2005:250), points 208 sq.

[101] *Op. cit.*, p. 65.

[102] Voir note en bas de page n° 81.

[103] Voir *supra* notes en bas de page nos 87, 90, 94 et 95.

[104] Voir par exemple, sous l'empire du traité CECA, les codes successifs des aides à la sidérurgie.

[105] *E.g.* « Orientations communautaires sur les aides d'État au transport maritime » (JOCE 2004, C 13, p. 3) ou encore « Orientations sur les priorités retenues par la Commission pour l'application de l'article 82 du traité CE aux pratiques d'éviction abusives des entreprises dominantes » (JOCE 2009, C 45, p. 7).

[106] *E.g.* « Lignes directrices pour le calcul des amendes infligées en application de l'article 23, paragraphe 2, sous a), du règlement (CE) n° 1/2003 » (JOCE 2006, C 210, p. 2), ci-après les « lignes directrices de 2006 ».

Si le juge de l'Union n'accepte pas, jusqu'à présent, d'en examiner la légalité, en tant qu'actes de *soft law*, dans le cadre de l'article 263 TFUE, il en reconnaît la teneur normative, que, parfois, il sanctionne comme contraire à une règle de droit dérivé que la *soft law* tend à interpréter, expliciter ou appliquer.[107]

Le caractère parfois très général du droit dérivé[108] rend utile et praticable ce recours à la *soft law*, d'ailleurs, en certains cas, appelé de ses vœux par le juge de l'Union lui-même.[109] La cohérence d'ensemble des voies de recours devant le juge de l'Union voudrait qu'il fût possible d'en opérer le contrôle sans passer par le truchement hypothétique d'une exception d'illégalité ou d'un renvoi préjudiciel (voir, *infra*, 3.1.1 et 3.1.2).

b) L'apport de méthodes

L'aspect normatif de la *soft law* consiste également, pour les institutions, organes ou organismes qui en sont les auteurs, à fournir des méthodes, de calcul ou d'évaluation. L'un des exemples les plus connus est sans doute fourni par les lignes directrices de 2006, mais l'on peut également songer, parmi de nombreuses illustrations, à la communication de la Commission intitulée « Mise en œuvre de l'article 260, paragraphe 3, TFUE ».[110]

Considérer que de telles méthodes, au regard du degré de détail qui est le leur et des conséquences, économiques et financières, qu'elles comportent pour les opérateurs économiques ou les États membres à qui elles sont appliquées, ne visent pas à produire des effets de droit à l'égard des tiers, mais seulement envers leur auteur, paraît correspondre à une vision passéiste et éloignée du réel. Il semble donc nécessaire de ne pas se réfugier sous l' "Umbrella concept of legal effects"[111] et de faciliter le contrôle juridictionnel de certains actes de *soft law*.

[107] Voir arrêt BNB, points 99 à 101: la Cour y a jugé invalide la recommandation en cause, en ce que l'ABE y avait assimilé la décision de la BNB de placer une banque sous surveillance spéciale et de suspendre ses obligations à un constat d'indisponibilité des dépôts, au sens du droit dérivé applicable, alors que ce dernier requiert qu'un tel constat intervienne par un acte explicite.

[108] Que l'on songe, par exemple, aux seuls critères de gravité et de durée figurant à l'article 23, paragraphe 3, du règlement (CE) n° 1/2003 du Conseil, du 16 décembre 2002, relatif à la mise en œuvre des règles de concurrence prévues aux articles [101 TFUE] et [102 TFUE] (JOCE 2003 L 1, p. 1). « pour déterminer le montant de l'amende ».

[109] Voir arrêt du Tribunal du 6 avril 1995, Tréfilunion/Commission, T-148/99, EU:T:1995:68, point 142: « [...] bien qu'il soit souhaitable que les entreprises – afin de pouvoir arrêter leur position en toute connaissance de cause – puissent connaître en détail, *selon tout système que la Commission jugerait opportun*, le mode de calcul de l'amende qui leur a été infligée, sans être obligées, pour ce faire, d'introduire un recours juridictionnel contre la décision de la Commission – ce qui serait contraire au principe de bonne administration – [...] » (italique ajouté).

[110] Communication 2011/C 12/01, JOUE 2011, C 12, p. 1.

[111] L. Senden, *op. cit.*, p. 23.

3 Une nécessaire facilitation du contrôle juridictionnel de certains actes de *soft law*

Si l'on peut, assurément, comprendre la jurisprudence actuelle relative au traitement des actes de *soft law* dans le cadre de l'article 263 TFUE, qui repose sur une différence de libellé entre les articles 263 et 267 TFUE ainsi que sur une conception stricte de l'obligatoriété, qui ne fait pas place à ce qui est, à certains égards, ou *de facto*, contraignant, il semble cependant que l'augmentation très significative du recours à la *soft law*, en particulier dans des domaines techniques, nécessite de faciliter le contrôle juridictionnel de certains actes relevant de celle-ci.

La première raison est d'assurer une cohérence de la réponse juridictionnelle, quelle que soit la voie de recours. Comme l'a justement souligné Giulia Gentile:

"EU Courts have adopted a 'formalistic' understanding of the notion of legally binding effects when it comes to EU soft law. In this context, they have focused on the intention and the powers of the issuing authority, or the form of the act, without considering the implications of the EU soft law acts in relation to third parties. In turn, by excluding direct judicial review of EU soft law, this jurisprudence creates a gap in the EU judicial protection system in relation to such acts."[112]

La seconde raison vise à permettre la surveillance de cette activité normative qui ne dit pas son nom, tant de la part des juridictions de l'Union que des autres institutions de cette dernière, en particulier celles qui représentent les citoyens européens (le Parlement européen) et les États membres (le Conseil de l'Union européenne).

3.1 Une nécessité fondée sur la cohérence de la réponse juridictionnelle, quelle que soit la voie de recours

Ce souci de cohérence vaut tant s'agissant des procédures relevant du contentieux de l'annulation qu'entre le recours en annulation et le renvoi préjudiciel.

3.1.1 La cohérence entre le recours en annulation et l'exception d'illégalité

Le rapprochement de la jurisprudence rendue dans le cadre de l'application de l'article 263 TFUE et de celle de l'article 277 TFUE met en évidence une profonde discordance. D'une part, il en ressort que « tout acte de l'Union ne produisant pas d'effets juridiques obligatoires échappe au contrôle juridictionnel prévu à l'article

[112] G. Gentile, op. cit., p. 483.

263 TFUE »,[113] étant précisé qu'un acte de *soft law* proprement dit[114] est, jusqu'à présent, toujours considéré comme ne produisant pas de tels effets; d'autre part, le juge de l'Union, à plusieurs reprises, a déclaré recevable une exception d'illégalité portant sur un tel acte, et s'est prononcé sur la légalité de celui-ci au regard, notamment, du droit dérivé, au motif qu'il était susceptible de déployer ses effets juridiques à l'égard des opérateurs économiques,[115] ce qui paraît tout à fait exact et correspond au critère figurant au point 37 de l'arrêt FBF, sauf à considérer que, lorsque la Cour a mentionné, dans le cadre de l'examen de l'exception d'illégalité d'un acte de *soft law*, les effets juridiques de celui-ci à l'égard des tiers, elle ne visait pas les effets juridiques obligatoires au sens de l'arrêt IBM.

Cette dernière interprétation ne saurait convaincre au regard de la rédaction de l'arrêt du 28 juin 2005, Dansk Rørindustri e.a./Commission[116] comme des considérations d'ordre logique tenant au fait qu'une certaine obligatoriété est consubstantielle à la règle de droit, développées ci-dessus.[117]

Par conséquent, de deux choses l'une: ou bien l'acte de *soft law* apparaît suffisamment contraignant pour que sa densité juridique emporte modification de l'état du droit, ce qui permet alors de contester sa légalité, que ce soit par voie d'action ou par voie d'exception, cette branche de l'alternative étant, à notre avis, la seule compatible avec la réalité vécue par les destinataires de certains actes de *soft law*; ou bien l'on extrapole le raisonnement retenu par la Cour dans l'arrêt FBF aux exceptions d'irrecevabilité, et il ne doit pas être possible d'examiner la légalité d'un acte de *soft law* qui, en tout état de cause, n'a pu servir de fondement légal à une décision individuelle, faute d'avoir produit des effets de droit obligatoires.

3.1.2 La cohérence entre le recours en annulation et le renvoi préjudiciel

Le grand écart entre la jurisprudence de la Cour relative au statut des actes de *soft law* dans le cadre de l'article 263 TFUE et celle, de même objet, rendue dans le cadre de l'article 267 TFUE a été abondamment mis en lumière dans les conclusions Bobek de 2017 et de 2021. À la question liminaire reproduite ci-dessus,[118] il proposait la réponse suivante: « Tout ce que la Cour peut faire est d'affirmer avec autorité que cet animal[119] n'est jamais né puisque la physionomie de la mère exclut

---

[113] Arrêt FBF, point 37; voir également, en ce sens, jurisprudence y citée.

[114] Voir, *supra*, 2.1.2, b), pour le cas de figure dans lequel la Cour a jugé se trouver en présence de tels effets obligatoires, mais a annulé le code de conduite édicté par la Commission comme émanant d'une autorité incompétente.

[115] Voir *supra* notes en bas de page nos 52 à 56.

[116] Arrêt Dansk Rørindustri e.a./Commission (C-189/02 P, C-202/02 P, C-205/02 P à C-208/02 P et C-213/02 P, EU:C:2005:250), points 208 à 210.

[117] Voir *supra,* Introduction.

[118] Voir *supra* 2, *in limine*.

[119] Une recommandation présentant un caractère contraignant.

la possibilité de jamais donner naissance à cette créature ».[120] L'on ne saurait se satisfaire de cette pirouette intellectuelle.

Tout d'abord, cette assertion fait litière du constat selon lequel un acte de *soft law* peut être contraignant à un certain degré, comme cela ressort de l'arrêt Grimaldi lui-même, puisqu'il y est indiqué que de tels actes sont adoptés, notamment, lorsque les institutions « estiment qu'il n'y a pas lieu d'édicter des règles plus contraignantes »,[121] ce qui implique que lesdits actes le soient au moins un peu et qu'ils ont, en particulier, vocation à « compléter des dispositions [de droit de l'Union] ayant un caractère contraignant »,[122] ce qui suppose, *nolens volens*, une nature homogène.[123] La Cour n'a pas utilisé le verbe « interpréter » ou « expliciter », mais « compléter ».

Ensuite, il serait extrêmement déplaisant de devoir amoindrir, par exigence de concordance intellectuelle entre le champ du contrôle du juge de l'Union dans le cadre des articles 263 et 267 TFUE, la protection juridictionnelle existante. Ainsi que cela figure avec netteté dans les conclusions Bobek de 2021, « restreindre la portée de l'arrêt Grimaldi signifierait en quelque sorte qu'une certaine cohérence entre l'article 263 et l'article 267 TFUE serait certes réintroduite »,[124] mais elle « se ferait en fait sur le plus petit dénominateur commun et au détriment de toute protection juridique effective offerte par le droit de l'Union ».[125] Cela reviendrait à dire que, « étant donné qu'aucun accès effectif à un contrôle juridictionnel de mesures de droit souple ne serait ouvert en vertu de l'article 263 TFUE, il serait préférable qu'il n'y en ait aussi aucun en vertu de l'article 267 TFUE ».[126]

Enfin, la doctrine commence à s'émouvoir de ce résultat insatisfaisant, tant sur le plan théorique que pratique: "in principle, EU soft law may be found to have 'legal effects' or 'legally binding effects' (or none) depending on the action brought, and against whom the effects of EU soft law are tested".[127]

Or, indépendamment du fait que le recours en annulation, soumis à un délai de deux mois à compter de la publication ou de la notification de l'acte qui en fait l'objet, ou, à défaut, à compter de la connaissance acquise par la partie requérante de cet acte, conformément à l'article 263, sixième alinéa, TFUE, offre plus de garanties au regard du principe de sécurité juridique, il permet également un contrôle de légalité plus ample que dans le cadre de l'article 267 TFUE où, d'une part, les questions posées au juge de l'Union peuvent ne porter que sur l'*interprétation* de

---

[120] Conclusions Bobek de 2021, point 100.

[121] Arrêt Grimaldi, point 13 et *supra*, 2.1.1.

[122] Arrêt Grimaldi, point 18 et *supra*, 2.1.1.

[123] *Supra*, 2.1.1.

[124] Conclusions Bobek de 2021, point 108.

[125] *Eod. loc.*

[126] *Eod. loc.*

[127] G. Gentile, *op. cit.*, p. 486.

la *soft law* et, d'autre part, la Cour est tributaire, dans une large mesure,[128] s'il lui revient de se prononcer sur la *validité* de la *soft law*, des questions qui lui sont posées.

Bien plus, c'est au juge national et à lui seul qu'il revient de déterminer si une question tenant à la validité d'un acte de *soft law* émanant d'une institution, d'un organe ou d'un organisme de l'Union se pose dans le litige dont il est saisi, ce qui limite significativement la possibilité effective de contester la légalité d'un tel acte devant le juge de l'Union.

3.2 Une nécessité fondée sur la surveillance de l'action normative institutionnelle, quel qu'en soit le mode

P. Amselek définit la norme en fonction de son « outilité »,[129] car lui « est impartie la vocation instrumentale de donner la mesure du possible, d'indiquer la marge ou degré de possibilité de l'avoir lieu de certaines choses en fonction de certaines circonstances ».[130] L'importance croissante de l'emploi d'instruments de *soft law*, soit en raison de la complexité technique ou de la difficulté politique ou pratique[131] du recours aux normes classiques, énumérées à l'article 288 TFUE, atteste de manière éclatante de leur outilité. Cela n'en rend que plus indispensable une évolution permettant, d'une part, un meilleur contrôle juridictionnel et, d'autre part, un meilleur contrôle interinstitutionnel de certains actes de *soft law*.

3.2.1 L'importance d'un meilleur contrôle juridictionnel

Il importe de préciser que, parmi les nombreux instruments de *soft law*, certains se bornent à recenser des exemples, des commentaires ou à présenter des pistes de réflexion quant à ce que devrait être l'évolution du droit de l'Union dans tel ou tel domaine. Notre propos n'est pas de suggérer que de tels actes puissent faire l'objet d'un contrôle juridictionnel, étant donné que leur densité juridique est nulle ou quasi nulle.

---

[128] Il résulte en effet d'une jurisprudence constante que la Cour peut fournir à la juridiction de renvoi « tous les éléments d'interprétation relevant du droit de l'Union qui peuvent être utiles au jugement de l'affaire » (arrêt du 4 mars 2021, Frenetikexito, C-581/19, EU:C:2021:167, point 36 et jurisprudence y citée).

[129] P. Amselek, *in Itinéraire I*, partie I, notamment pp. 85, 139, 173 et s. ainsi que *in* « Les fonctions normatives ou catégories modales », *Philosophiques*, vol. 33, n° 2, 2006, p. 392. Il précise que « les règles sont des outils mentaux qui appartiennent au monde de l'intelligible et non du sensible: ce à quoi est assignée une finalité instrumentale, c'est du sens, et notamment du sens véhiculé par des énonciations écrites ou orales » (*op. cit.*, pp. 391 et 392).

[130] *Op. cit.*, p. 392.

[131] Voir, concernant l'utilisation massive de la *soft law* durant la pandémie de COVID-19, O. Stefan, "COVID-19 Soft Law: Voluminous, Effective, Legitimate? A Research Agenda", *European Papers, European Forum*, 3 June 2020, p. 1.

Il ne nous paraît pas non plus opportun d'inviter à rendre plus difficile le contrôle de certains actes de *soft law* dans le cadre des articles 267[132] et 277 TFUE. C'est donc, nous semble-t-il, sur le seul recours en annulation que doit porter l'analyse, que ce recours ait pour objet une demande d'annulation de ces actes ou une demande d'annulation du refus d'en abroger tout ou partie.

a) En cas de recours ayant pour objet une demande d'annulation de certains actes de *soft law*

Trois arguments principaux sont généralement avancés pour justifier le refus du juge de l'Union de considérer comme recevable un recours en annulation d'un acte de *soft law*. Deux d'entre eux sont d'ordre juridique, le troisième est d'ordre pratique. Aucun n'est décisif.

Le premier argument est tiré de ce qu'un acte de *soft law* ne produit pas d'effets de droit obligatoires. Étant donné que la *soft law* ne saurait être approchée, comme cela a été souligné, sous l'angle d'une dichotomie obligatoire-non obligatoire, mais doit être dépeinte à l'aide d'une palette allant du non-contraignant au contraignant en passant par de nombreuses nuances, il importe de privilégier un contrôle juridictionnel portant sur les actes de *soft law* comportant des dispositions qui produisent, au moins dans une certaine mesure, des effets de droit à l'égard des tiers.[133] Typiquement, des instruments tels que des orientations ou des lignes directrices devraient, en fonction de leur teneur souvent normative, pouvoir faire l'objet d'un recours en annulation au titre de l'article 263 TFUE. Les juridictions de certains États membres, comme la France, jugent parfois recevables des recours en annulation ayant pour objet des actes de *soft law*.[134]

Le deuxième argument est propre aux recommandations et repose sur le libellé explicite de cet article, les excluant du champ d'application de ce dernier. Naturellement, cette disposition de droit primaire ne peut être méconnue. Toutefois, la Cour a précisé, dans l'arrêt du 20 février 2018, Belgique/Commission,[135] qu'un recours en annulation était possible, à titre exceptionnel, si, au regard du contenu de l'acte en cause, il ne s'agissait pas d'une véritable recommandation.[136] Il pourrait

[132] *Supra*, 3.1.2.

[133] Voir *supra*, 2.2.

[134] Voir, en particulier, arrêt du Conseil d'État du 21 juin 2019, Association française de l'industrie pharmaceutique pour une automédication responsable, n° 419996, à propos des recommandations prises par l'Agence nationale de sécurité du médicament et des produits de santé, et arrêt du 12 juin 2020, GISTI, n° 418142, à propos d'une note d'actualité de la division de l'expertise en fraude documentaire et à l'identité de la direction centrale de la police aux frontières. Ce dernier arrêt énonce que « les documents de portée générale émanant d'autorités publiques, matérialisés ou non, tels que les circulaires, instructions, recommandations, notes, présentations ou interprétations du droit positif peuvent être déférés au juge de l'excès de pouvoir lorsqu'ils sont susceptibles d'avoir des effets notables sur les droits ou la situation d'autres personnes que les agents chargés, le cas échéant, de les mettre en œuvre. Ont notamment de tels effets ceux de ces documents qui ont un caractère impératif ou présentent le caractère de lignes directrices. »

[135] C-16/16 P, EU:C:2018:79.

[136] Point 29 de l'arrêt.

être concevable d'avancer sur ce terrain également dans le cas où certains éléments de la recommandation paraîtraient présenter un caractère suffisamment contraignant. Il semblerait en ce cas envisageable de raisonner sur le terrain de l'acte détachable, de telle sorte que la recommandation dans son ensemble ne serait pas affectée et le texte comme l'esprit de l'article 263 TFUE seraient respectés.

Le troisième argument consiste à faire valoir le risque d'envolée du nombre de recours devant le juge de l'Union en cas d'assouplissement des conditions de recevabilité portant sur certains actes de *soft law*. Cela n'est guère réaliste. Il suffit de rappeler, à cet égard, qu'un recours tendant à l'annulation d'un acte de portée générale pris sous la forme d'une décision est soumis à un *locus standi* exigeant, tenant à ce que la partie requérante soit directement et individuellement concernée par l'acte en cause.[137]

Une autre possibilité, non exclusive de la première, consisterait à juger recevable un recours lorsqu'il tend à l'annulation d'un refus d'abrogation d'un acte de *soft law* ou de certains des éléments qu'il contient.

b) En cas de recours ayant pour objet une demande d'annulation d'un refus d'abrogation de certains actes de *soft law*

L'avantage évident de ce qui s'apparente à un recours administratif préalable[138] est de permettre à l'auteur de l'acte de *soft law* d'être informé, premièrement, des éléments de cet acte dont un tiers considère qu'ils produisent des effets de droit à son égard, deuxièmement de ce en quoi ces éléments affectent sa situation juridique et, troisièmement, des raisons pour lesquelles il estime qu'ils contreviennent à une norme de droit primaire ou de droit dérivé. En conséquence, le travail juridictionnel s'en trouverait facilité, notamment en ce qui concerne l'appréciation de la recevabilité du recours, puisque les aspects plus ou moins contraignants et possiblement illégaux dudit acte seraient déjà identifiés et réfutés par cet auteur. Un tel mécanisme est appliqué en droit administratif français.[139]

Il n'est pas non plus exclu qu'une telle démarche porte ses fruits dès la saisine de l'institution, l'organe ou l'organisme concerné, en fonction de la qualité des arguments présentés à son appui, et l'amène à abroger ou modifier les aspects problématiques de l'instrument de *soft law* en question.

---

[137] Il semble, en effet, très difficile de raisonner à partir de l'hypothèse d'un acte réglementaire ne comportant pas de mesures d'exécution (article 263, quatrième alinéa, TFUE), s'agissant d'actes hors nomenclature dont l'obligatoriété est variable et la normativité relative.

[138] Il importe de préciser, néanmoins, qu'un recours portant directement sur un acte de *soft law* jugé suffisamment contraignant aurait, en cas d'annulation, un effet *ex tunc*, tandis qu'un recours portant sur un refus d'abrogation aurait, par définition, en cas d'annulation, un effet *ex nunc*, l'abrogation, objet de la demande initiale, ne valant que pour l'avenir.

[139] Arrêt du Conseil d'État du 4 décembre 2019, Fédération des entreprises de la beauté, n° 416798, à propos d'une recommandation de l'Agence nationale de sécurité du médicament et des produits de santé. Le juge administratif français ne contrôle, en cas de refus d'abrogation, que la compétence de l'auteur de l'acte contesté, la légalité du contenu de cet acte et l'existence éventuelle d'un détournement de pouvoir.

3.3 L'importance d'un meilleur contrôle interinstitutionnel

Un meilleur contrôle interinstitutionnel est souhaitable afin de préserver l'équilibre du processus décisionnel voulu par les auteurs des traités; il l'est également afin que la *soft law* conserve, à certains égards, une dimension horizontale caractérisant le milieu dans lequel elle a vu le jour.

a) En vue d'une préservation de l'équilibre du processus décisionnel

Le processus décisionnel de l'Union européenne a été pensé dans une logique d'efficacité et d'équilibre, en donnant d'emblée une place importante au Conseil et, progressivement, une place similaire au Parlement, en particulier par l'accroissement du recours à la procédure de codécision et par le rôle dévolu à cette dernière institution lors du vote du budget, afin de renforcer le caractère démocratique des règles de droit de l'Union. La fonction de la Commission, en tant que force de proposition, d'exécution ainsi qu'en qualité de gardienne des traités, vient contrebalancer les pouvoirs des deux premières institutions.

Or, l'utilisation parfois massive de la *soft law* par certaines institutions, au premier rang desquelles la Commission, vient perturber cet équilibre institutionnel en accroissant significativement le poids décisionnel ou quasi décisionnel de cette dernière. Un contrôle du juge de l'Union, par le biais du recours en annulation, de certains actes de *soft law*, à savoir ceux dont il est incontestable qu'ils produisent des effets juridiques à l'égard des tiers, même si ces effets sont innomés et, pour des raisons d'architecture institutionnelle, doivent demeurer tels, serait de nature à prévenir un dévoiement du processus décisionnel voulu par les auteurs du traité.

Pour reprendre les mots de Claudia Gentile, "[b]y subjecting EU soft law to effective judicial review via the action for annulment, the Court of Justice would safeguard effective judicial review and institutional balance in a coherent EU legal order. The direct review of EU soft law would offer the opportunity for the Court of Justice to mould the 'limits' of the EU constitutional order, both from a vertical perspective (EU–member states) as well as horizontal (among EU institutions)".[140]

Cette citation nous rappelle que la dimension horizontale est essentielle dans la compréhension de ce qu'est la *soft law*.

b) En vue d'une restauration de la dimension horizontale de la *soft law*

La simple possibilité, pour d'autres institutions, de pouvoir brandir la menace d'un recours en annulation, en cas d'un usage jugé illégal de la *soft law* par une institution dans tel ou tel domaine, serait de nature à restaurer une logique de rapports *inter pares* qui caractérise, notamment, le droit international,[141] milieu dans lequel est né la *soft law*.[142] Cette horizontalité permettrait également de faire valoir

[140] G. Gentile, *op. cit.*, pp. 468 et 469.

[141] Voir J. Combacau, « Le droit international: bric-à-brac ou système ? », *Archives de philosophie du droit*, 1986, p. 85.

[142] Voir notes en bas de page nos 1 et 17.

des considérations d'opportunité, tenant, par exemple à la sensibilité politique ou aux enjeux éthiques d'une intervention quasi normative sur un sujet donné, lesquels mériteraient, non pas une crypto-réglementation, mais une discussion interétatique et parlementaire en bonne et due forme, tel que prévue par le traité FUE.

Cette possibilité de penser le droit de l'Union autrement qu'en termes de verticalité présuppose que la perspective d'un tel recours soit crédible et puisse aboutir, le cas échéant, à une annulation, ce qui implique une inflexion de la manière dont le juge de l'Union interprète l'article 263 TFUE à propos d'actes de *soft law* qui ne soient que de *soft law*. Cette évolution nous semble possible. Elle est, en tout cas, souhaitable. Elle implique de ne pas accorder trop d'importance à des facteurs parfois peu pertinents, comme la terminologie employée. Le plus souvent, l'auteur de la *soft law* va précisément veiller à proscrire l'emploi de termes impératifs qui, à l'inverse, fleurissent dans des publications dont l'obligatoriété est des plus douteuses. L'horoscope en est plein.

La possibilité de contester devant le juge de l'Union certains actes de droit souple dépend donc, avant tout, d'une question d'interprétation de l'article 263 TFUE. Cela ne doit pas nous étonner, pas plus que ne doit surprendre le fait que l'appréhension d'un phénomène pour ainsi dire inconnu des auteurs des traités déconcerte encore les juridictions chargées de mettre en œuvre cette disposition. Comme le résumait brillamment Denis Alland, « [s]i personne ne nie que des questions d'interprétation se posent nécessairement dans la vie du droit, rares sont ceux qui voient que c'est la question du droit tout entière qui s'y absorbe ».[143]

[143] D. Alland, « À la recherche de la primauté du droit communautaire », *Droits* 2007, n° 45, p. 121.

The Enforcement System Put in Place by Articles 82 and 83 of the GDPR in Light of the Court's Case-law

Niilo Jääskinen and Elina Paunio

1 Introduction

Plus ça change, plus c'est la même chose. This famous sentence of the French writer and journalist *Alphonse Karr* (1808–90)[1] describes well the impact of the EU General Data Protection Regulation ('GDPR')[2] that entered into force in May 2016 and became applicable two years later. This regulation built much on existing legislation, especially the Data Protection Directive 95/46/EC,[3] and the case-law of the Court of Justice of the European Union ('CJEU' or 'Court') relating to it. In many cases, the interpretation of the GDPR coincides with that of the directive.[4] This said, the GDPR represents, both quantitatively and qualitatively, a major development in EU data protection law. It constitutes a directly applicable, comprehensive and up-to-date legislative framework for the protection of the fundamental rights of indi-

[1] This often-quoted sentence was an ironical description of the development of French politics after the February revolution in 1848. According to Karr, Frenchmen continued to drink the same sour wine despite changes to the label, price or cork.

[2] Regulation (EU) 2016/679 of the European Parliament and of the Council of 27 April 2016 on the protection of natural persons with regard to the processing of personal data and on the free movement of such data, and repealing Directive 95/46/EC (General Data Protection Regulation), *OJ 2016 L 119, p. 1.*

[3] Directive 95/46/EC of the European Parliament and of the Council of 24 October 1995 on the protection of individuals with regard to the processing of personal data and on the free movement of such data, OJ 1995 L 281, p. 31 ('Data Protection Directive').

[4] See, e.g. judgment in Vyriausioji tarnybinės etikos komisija, C-184/20, EU:C:2022:601, para. 58.

N. Jääskinen · E. Paunio (✉)
Court of Justice of the European Union, Luxembourg, Luxembourg
e-mail: Niilo.Jaaskinen@curia.europa.eu; Elina.Paunio@curia.europa.eu

L. Prete, L. Rezki (eds.), *Judging & (Re)Thinking European Union Law*,
https://doi.org/10.1007/978-3-032-13473-8_30

viduals to privacy and data protection as set out, respectively, in Articles 7 (right to private and family life) and 8 (right to the protection of personal data) the Charter of Fundamental Rights of the European Union ('Charter'), in a field undergoing constant and unforeseeable developments.

As to its enforcement, the GDPR contains the same building blocks as the Data Protection Directive. However, whereas the directive devoted only a handful of provisions on enforcement,[5] the GDPR contains eight articles in Chapter VIII under the heading "Remedies, liability, penalties" and, depending on the definition, at least two dozen articles relating to external and internal supervision structures.

In this paper, the focus is on Articles 82 (entitled 'Right to compensation and liability') and 83 (entitled 'General conditions for imposing administrative fines') of the GDPR. Those provisions constitute the core of *private* and *public enforcement* of that regulation. Those provisions introduce significant material precisions and/or additions to their predecessors in the Data Protection Directive. Moreover, the shift from a directive to a directly applicable regulation entails a major legal development that deepens and enforces the normative weight of EU law in the field. However, that shift simultaneously creates new problems as to the interaction between that legal order and the national legal systems of the Member States.

2 Private Enforcement Based on Article 82 GDPR

2.1 Compensation for Non-material Damage in EU Law

In his Opinion in the *Petillo and Petillo* case, Advocate General Wahl observed that it was an almost universally recognised principle that the damage in respect of which a person may seek compensation could include non-material damage.[6] In his view, 'non-material damage' referred generally speaking to 'losses which do not relate to a person's assets, wealth or income and, as such, cannot be quantified in an objective manner by reference to a market price or value'.

Even though EU law does not encompass any generally applicable, coherent tort law regime, or for that matter, a single overarching definition of non-material damage, that observation arguably holds true also with regard to EU law in general and data protection in particular. Indeed, where the conditions laid down by CJEU case-law[7] or specific EU secondary legislation are met, a person may seek, as a matter of EU law, compensation for losses that are not material.

[5] Those were: remedies (Article 22), liability (Article 22), sanctions (Article 24) and supervision (Article 28).

[6] Opinion of Advocate General Wahl in Petillo, C-371/12, EU:C:2013:652, paras 38–39.

[7] See on extra-contractual liability of EU institutions, judgment in Kočner v Europol, C-755/21 P, EU:C:2024:202, paras 117 and 140.

EU secondary legislation that specifically refers to non-material damage now includes the GDPR, which provides in Article 82 thereof that anyone who has 'suffered material or non-material damage as a result of an infringement of this Regulation' shall have the right to compensation. Other examples of secondary legislation include Directive 2004/48 on the enforcement of intellectual property rights, which mentions 'moral prejudice' as a category of harm that may be compensated and Directive 2016/943 on trade secrets, which uses similar terminology. According to recital 34 of Directive 2015/2302 on package travel, compensation should also cover non-material damage, such as loss of enjoyment of the trip or holiday.

The Court's understanding of what may constitute damage is a broad one. To that understanding attests the case-law that accepts as falling under the umbrella of 'non-material damage' things such as a person's fear that his or her personal data have been disclosed to third parties or will be misused,[8] the loss of time,[9] the loss of enjoyment of a holiday,[10] or indeed harm caused by the loss of luggage.[11] The Court has moreover emphasised that non-material damage should be no less important than, for example, physical injury.[12]

As is the case with the precise scope of the concept of non-material damage itself, no general EU law approach exists with regard to issues such as the conditions to receive compensation for non-material damage, or the amount of compensation due. Indeed, in many cases, especially where compensation is sought before a national court on the basis of EU secondary legislation, those questions are resolved on the basis of national procedural rules which, in accordance with the principle of procedural autonomy, fill the gaps left by the regulatory framework set up by EU legislation.

Given that the principle of full compensation underpins EU damages liability law, some have suggested that from that principle follows that non-material damage should be recoverable alongside material damage where no clear signs indicating otherwise exist.[13] Nevertheless, it seems difficult to infer from that principle a general rule according to which all non-material damage, regardless of how serious it is and irrespective of the field of EU law concerned, is eligible for compensation.[14] For example, the Court has accepted the compatibility with EU legislation of national law, which, for the purposes of calculating compensation, differentiates between

---

[8] Judgment in Scalable Capital, C-182/22 and C-189/22, EU:C:2024:531, para. 58.

[9] Judgment in *Sturgeon and Others*, C-402/07 and C-432/07, EU:C:2009:716, para. 52.

[10] Judgment in *Leitner*, C-168/00, EU:C:2002:163, para. 22.

[11] Judgment in *Walz*, C-63/09, EU:C:2010:251, para. 39.

[12] Judgment in Scalable Capital, *supra*, para. 39.

[13] K. Havu, 'Damages Liability for Non-material Harm in EU Case Law' (2019) EL Rev, pp. 492–514.

[14] See Opinion of Advocate General Campos Sánchez-Bordona in *Österreichische Post (Non-material damage in connection with the processing of personal data)*, C-300/21, EU:C:2022:756, para. 105.

non-material damage linked to physical injury caused by an accident depending on the origin of that accident.[15]

In another one of his Opinions in the *Kendrion and Gascogne Sack* cases, Advocate General Wahl returned to discuss non-material damage, this time addressing, in particular, the difficulties related to quantifying such damage. As he notes, non-material damage is difficult to quantify in particular because pecuniary compensation cannot re-establish the status quo ante. It is therefore unavoidable that, to determine the existence of such damage, to identify the best means to adequately compensate it and, where appropriate, to calculate the sum to be awarded, courts enjoy significant leeway. In particular, the court having jurisdiction in affording pecuniary compensation of non-material damage must estimate an amount that adequately reflects the injury suffered by the victim, without unduly punishing the author of the unlawful conduct. In the absence of obvious or generally-accepted economic benchmarks, courts may only find guidance in general principles such as, for instance, fairness, justice and proportionality on the one hand, and predictability, legal certainty and equal treatment on the other.[16]

That said, while quantifying non-material damage in an exact manner may indeed prove impossible, the medical, psychological and social consequences of an unlawful act such as suffering, anxiety, fear, shame or distress can generally be shown to exist, typically by recourse to observable evidentiary facts relating, inter alia, to the victim's emotional status, behaviour and life situation. Moreover, the difference between material and non-material damage is sometimes a slim one. Indeed, courts may encounter difficulties in quantifying material damage too. This is so, for example, where the harm for which compensation is sought pertains to the loss of earning capacity due to physical injury resulting from a traffic accident, or to the loss of value of a damaged work of art. Just as is the case with quantifying non-material damage, the court having jurisdiction in affording pecuniary compensation will need to determine the correct amount of compensation and may have to rely on general principles such as proportionality and reasonableness in doing so.

2.2 Development of an EU Law Regime for Compensation of Damages Caused by Breaches of Data Protection Rules

Article 23 of the Data Protection Directive—the predecessor of Article 82 GDPR—constituted a concise civil liability regime. On the one hand, in accordance with Paragraph 1 thereof, Member States were to ensure that any person who had suffered damage due to an unlawful processing operation or any act incompatible with the national provisions adopted pursuant to that directive was entitled to

[15] Judgment in Petillo, C-371/12, EU:C:2014:26, para. 46.

[16] Opinion of Advocate General Wahl in European Union v Kendrion, C-150/17 P, EU:C:2018:612, paras 107–109.

compensation from the controller for the damage suffered. On the other hand, Paragraph 2 stated that the controller may be exempted from liability, in whole or in part, if he proved that he was not responsible for the event having given rise to the damage.

Article 23 of the Data Protection Directive, read together with recital 55 thereof,[17] included many of the normative elements that were later set out in Article 82 (1) to (3) GDPR, with a few important exceptions. First, the right to compensation for non-material damages was not explicitly mentioned.[18] Second, Article 23 was silent on the liability of data processors and on issues pertaining to joint and/or shared responsibility between the controllers and/or the processors.[19]

Interestingly, the provision corresponding to Article 23 of the Data Protection Directive in the Commission proposal for what later became the GDPR did not spell out a right to compensation for non-material damage resulting from an infringement of the regulation by data controllers or data processors.[20] This element was included only later on during the negotiations to clarify the state of the law, in particular in Member States that were reluctant to allow the award of non-material damages without an explicit statutory provision.[21]

The Court never interpreted the liability scheme established by Article 23 of the Data Protection Directive.[22] Thus, until the entry into force of the GDPR, the Court's case-law provided no guidance on the concept of 'non-material damage'.

[17] In that regard, recital 55 of the directive explained, first, that if the controller fails to respect the rights of data subjects, national legislation must provide for a judicial remedy; second, that any damage which a person may suffer as a result of unlawful processing must be compensated for by the controller; and third, that the controller may be exempted from liability in particular in cases where he establishes fault on the part of the data subject or in case of force majeure.

[18] Given the reference in recital 55 to 'any damage', that category of damage was probably also covered. Indeed, later case-law of the Court has confirmed that the notion of damage must be interpreted in the context of provisions protecting individuals or groups of individuals and that this notion also covers non-material damages even if they are not separately mentioned in the legislative provision. Opinion of Advocate General Campos Sánchez-Bordona in, para. 104 and case-law cited.

[19] These issues were discussed in detail by the co-legislators during the preparation of what became Article 82 GDPR. See Opinion of Advocate General Campos Sánchez-Bordona in *Österreichische Post, supra,* footnote 28.

[20] See, Article 77 in COM (2012) 11 [Proposal for a Regulation of the European Parliament and of the Council on the protection of individuals with regard to the processing of personal data and on the free movement of such data (General Data Protection Regulation)].

[21] See Opinion of Advocate General Campos Sánchez-Bordona in *Österreichische Post, supra,* footnotes 27 and 72. According to the Advocate General, the negotiations prior to the adoption of the GDPR centered on dispelling the doubts surrounding the inclusion of non-material damage.

[22] Hence, the reference in Recital 146 of the GDPR the Court's case-law must be understood as referring to the notion of damage in general, as interpreted by the Court.

2.3 The Court's Case-law on Article 82 GDPR

Since its date of application on 25 May 2018, Article 82 GDPR has given rise to a significant number of references for a preliminary ruling. Those references relate, explicitly or implicitly, to non-material damages and stem, for the most part, from courts belonging to the German legal tradition. This trend may reflect difficulties in accommodating the new EU provision in the traditional doctrinal and jurisprudential conceptions which prevail in that legal culture in relation to compensation of non-material damages.[23]

In the cases dealt with by the Court at the time of writing, the main proceedings before the referring courts have concerned a claim for damages against a data controller and not against a data processor. Therefore, in what follows, data processors will not be discussed separately. Moreover, apart from two exceptions,[24] those cases have concerned ordinary civil actions for damages before general judicial courts.

Before the referring courts, data subjects have invoked a variety of non-material damage: emotional distress and shame resulting from a wrongful assignment of a political affiliation to a far-right party;[25] fear of misuse of personal data, in particular of identity theft or fraud, resulting from intrusion to a data system;[26] feeling of loss of control of personal data that has been displayed illicitly in public,[27] disclosed without the data-subject's consent[28] or processed despite the data subject's objections,[29] and non-material damage resulting from illegal processing of and access to health data[30] or from erroneous transmission of personal data to a third person.[31]

In a relatively short period, CJEU has forged a case-law that can be synthetized as follows.

[23] The CJEU has so far issued the following judgments interpreting Article 82 GDPR: judgments in *Österreichische Post (Non-material damage in connection with the processing of personal data)*, C-300/21, EU:C:2023:370; *Natsionalna agentsia za prihodite*, C-340/21, EU:C:2023:986; *Gemeinde Ummendorf*, C-456/22, EU:C:2023:988; *Krankenversicherung Nordrhein*, C-667/21, EU:C:2023:1022; *MediaMarktSaturn*, C-687/21, EU:C:2024:72; *juris*, C-741/21, EU:C:2024:288; Scalable Capital, *supra*; PS (Incorrect address), C-590/22, EU:C:2024:536; *Agentsia po vpisvaniyata*, C-200/23, EU:C:2024:827; and *Patērētāju tiesību aizsardzības centrs*, C-507/23, EU:C:2024:854.

[24] Judgment in *Natsionalna agentsia za prihodite, supra*, a case brought before an administrative court against a public authority acting as data controller; and judgment in *Krankenversicherung Nordrhein, supra*, a case brought before a labour court against a public law employer.

[25] Judgment in *Österreichische Post, supra*.

[26] Judgments in *Natsionalna agentsia za prihodite*, and Scalable Capital, *supra*.

[27] Judgment in *Gemeinde Ummendorf, supra*.

[28] Judgments in PS (Incorrect address), and *Patērētāju tiesību aizsardzības centrs, supra*.

[29] Judgments in *juris*, and *Agentsia po vpisvaniyata, supra*.

[30] Judgment in *Krankenversicherung Nordrhein, supra*.

[31] Judgment in *MediaMarktSaturn, supra*.

First, the function of the right to reparation of non-material damages pursuant to Article 82 GDPR serves a purely reparatory or compensatory function. It aims, as is clear from recital 85, at full and effective compensation of the concrete damage suffered by an individual because of a violation of the GDPR be that damage material on non-material.

The Court has now clarified that in contrast with Articles 83 and 84 GDPR, which govern the imposition of administrative fines and other penalties, the civil liability regime established by Article 82 does not serve a punitive or dissuasive function. Thus, no punitive or repressive damages exceeding the scope or value of the damage actually suffered by the data subject can be based on this provision. In other words, any financial compensation awarded pursuant to that provision must compensate the damage actually suffered resulting from the infringement in full, but should not constitute a sanction for unlawful behaviour.[32]

That exclusively compensatory function does not however mean that the right to compensation would not also act as a deterrent against violations of the GDPR. Indeed, Article 82 GDPR is complementary to Articles 83 and 84 thereof. While all these provisions seek to ensure compliance with the GDPR, they do so by different means. As regards Article 82, by allowing private individuals to seek compensation for damages, it arguably reinforces the effectiveness of the protection afforded to data subjects and is thus likely to discourage the reoccurrence of unlawful conduct.[33]

Second, and as a logical consequence of its purely reparatory function, a mere violation of the GDPR does not suffice to give rise to a right to compensation under Article 82 GDPR. This is so irrespective of the degree of seriousness of the damage suffered by the person concerned.[34] As the Court held in *Österreichische Post*, a data subject, as defined in Article 4(1) GDPR, has a right to compensation only where three cumulative conditions are met: there is damage, an infringement of the GDPR and a causal link between that damage and that infringement.[35]

As regards the concept of 'damage', it also includes non-material damage, which must be dealt with in the same way as material damage.[36] Article 82(1) GDPR thus precludes a national rule or practice, which makes compensation for non-material damage within the meaning of that provision subject to the condition that the damage suffered by the data subject has reached a certain degree of seriousness.[37]

As regards the requirement of a causal link, the fact of being a victim of an illegal or illicit act does not as such constitute 'non-material damage' within the meaning of Article 82 GDPR. The victim, usually the data subject, is required to show that

---

[32] Judgments in *Österreichische Post*, *supra*, paras 57 and 58, and *juris*, *supra*, para. 61.

[33] Judgments in *Krankenversicherung Nordrhein*, *supra*, para. 85; *MediaMarktSaturn*, *supra*, para. 85; and Scalable Capital, *supra*, para. 22.

[34] Judgments in *Krankenversicherung Nordrhein*, *supra*, para. 103; and *MediaMarktSaturn*, *supra*, para. 52.

[35] Judgment in *Österreichische Post*, para. 32.

[36] Ibid., paras 31, 32 and 45.

[37] Ibid. See also judgment in *Gemeinde Ummendorf*, *supra*, paras 16 and 19.

the consequences of the infringement that he or she claims to have suffered constitute damage, which is different from the infringement of the GDPR.[38] Therefore, the person seeking compensation is required to establish not only the infringement of provisions of the GDPR, but also a causal link between that infringement and the damage allegedly suffered, be that damage material or non-material.[39]

Third, the concept of 'damage' under the GDPR is an autonomous EU law concept.[40] The national laws of the Member States may not impose additional or supplementary conditions that may limit the right to compensation laid down in Article 82 GDPR. Hence, Member States cannot, for example, impose *de minimis* thresholds for the severity of recoverable non-material damage or any similar supplementary condition not specifically referred to in Article 82.[41]

Thus, the three cumulative conditions are both necessary and sufficient conditions for the right to compensation to arise. Indeed, the legal interest protected by Article 82 GDPR is the fundamental right to data protection enshrined in Article 8 of the Charter.[42] Consequently, any infringement of the GDPR can trigger a right to compensation, without there being a need to identify another protected value or interest.

Fourth, as the Court clarified in *Krankenversicherung Nordrhein* and *MediamarktSaturn*, Article 82 GDPR provides for fault-based liability in which the burden of proof rests with the controller.[43] The liability of a data controller under Article 82 GDPR is thus neither purely objective nor what would traditionally be understood as civil liability based on fault, where intention or negligence constitute a necessary condition for liability for damages. In fact, liability under Article 82 GDPR constitutes fault-based responsibility with a presumption of fault (intention or negligence) on the part of the data controller regarding the infringement of the GDPR that has caused the alleged damage. In other words, the fault of the data controller is not a positive condition for the right to compensation under Article 82, but its absence may count as a factor exonerating that controller from liability.

The threshold for rebutting the presumption of liability is nevertheless high. The Court held in *Krankenversicherung Nordrhein* and *Natsionalna agentsia za prihodite* that the existence of fault on the part of the controller is presumed, unless the controller proves that the event, which gave rise to the damage is *in no way attributable to it.*[44]

---

[38] Judgment in *MediaMarktSaturn*, *supra*, para. 60 and the case-law cited.

[39] Judgments in *Österreichische Post*, *supra*, paras 42 and 50; and *juris*, *supra*, para. 35.

[40] Judgment in *Österreichische Post*, *supra*, para. 30.

[41] Judgments in *Gemeinde Ummendorf*, *supra*,paras 17 and 19; and *Patērētāju tiesību aizsardzības centrs*, paras 25–27.

[42] Judgment in *Patērētāju tiesību aizsardzības centrs*, *supra*, para. 28.

[43] Judgments in *Krankenversicherung Nordrhein*, *supra*, para. 103; and *MediaMarktSaturn*, *supra*, para. 52.

[44] Judgments in *Krankenversicherung Nordrhein*, *supra*, paras 94–95; and *Natsionalna agentsia za prihodite*, *supra*, para. 70.

That said, under the liability regime established by the GDPR, a controller may be able to rely on a wider range of circumstances to exonerate itself from liability than what was the case under the Data Protection Directive.[45] In addition to fault on the part of the data subject or *force majeure*, exoneration may be possible where the data controller is able to show that a third person, who is not acting under the authority of the data controller and whose action is not attributable to it, has caused the damage.[46] The fact that the controller has followed a legally non-binding opinion of the supervisory authority, issued on the basis of Article 58(3)(b) of the GDPR, does not, however, demonstrate that the damage is not attributable to that controller and does not suffice to exempt that controller from liability under Article 82(3) of the GDPR.[47]

It should also be borne in mind that, in this context, the data controller is responsible for its staff[48] and jointly responsible with other data controllers participating in the same processing.[49] A diligent data controller does not however need to attain an absolute level of security in the course of data processing. As the Court held in *Nazionalna agentsia za prihodite*, the security measures should be 'appropriate' in the sense of what can reasonably be expected with respect to risks and the nature of the personal data and processing at issue. Indeed, an intrusion by a third person to the data controller's system does not itself prove that the security measures were not appropriate. Nevertheless, it is for the data controller to show that it has taken all the appropriate measures to prevent the harmful event from occurring, or that the damage was a consequence of an event or action that it could not reasonable foresee or prevent.[50] This renders the responsibility of the data controller 'quasi-objective', yet leaving to the data subjects the risk to suffer the consequences of what in data technology are referred to as 'zero day vulnerabilities'. These unknown system vulnerabilities are exploited by malicious actors before the data service providers and their clients become aware of them.

Fifth, the concept of 'non-material damage' should be interpreted broadly in the context of the GDPR, provided however that there is 'something more' to it than a mere infringement of the GDPR and the feeling of discomfort generally felt by victims of an unlawful act.

Recital 85 of the GDPR mentions examples of damage that can result from an infringement of the GDPR. These include the data subject's loss of control over their personal data, limitation of their rights, discrimination, identity theft or fraud, financial loss, unauthorized reversal of pseudonymisation, damage to reputation, loss of confidentiality of personal data protected by professional secrecy or any

[45] See Recital 55 of the directive.

[46] Judgment in *Agentsia po vpisvaniyata, supra*, paras 163–166.

[47] Ibid., paras 174–176.

[48] Judgments in *MediaMarktSaturn, supra* paras 41, 44 and 45; and *Natsionalna agentsia za prihodite, supra*, para. 66.

[49] See Article 82(4), GDPR.

[50] Judgment in *Natsionalna agentsia za prihodite, supra*, paras 30–38.

other significant economic or social disadvantage to the natural person concerned. While the examples provided constitute a somewhat confusing mix of norm violations and their material and non-material consequences, the variety of situations envisaged supports the view that a wide range of harmful of consequences for the victim may count as non-material damages.

In that regard, the Court has ruled, for example, that non-material damage may include harm resulting from the fear experienced by a data subject with regard to a possible misuse of his or her personal data by third parties. Fear can constitute recoverable damage if there has been or can be abuse of such data. Thus, a person's fear that his or her personal data have been disclosed to third parties as a result of an infringement of the GDPR, without it being possible to establish that that was in fact the case, is sufficient to give rise to a right to compensation, provided that that fear, with its negative consequences, is duly proven.[51]

However, no right to compensation arises where no concrete damage has occurred. Thus, a mere allegation of fear, with no proven negative consequences, cannot give rise to compensation under Article 82 GDPR.[52] Similarly, where a document containing personal data has been forwarded to an un-authorized third party and it has been established that that third person did not become aware of those personal data, 'non-material damage', within the meaning of that provision, does not exist. Indeed, the fact that a data subject fears that a dissemination or abuse of their personal data may occur in the future following an unlawful communication of a document containing their personal data—which has been subsequently recovered—does not constitute recoverable non-material damage.[53]

What is more, in order to be classified as 'identity theft', and to give rise to compensation under Article 82, the identity of the person affected must have been misused by a third party. However, compensation for non-material damage caused by the theft of personal data, is not, according to the Court in *Scalable Capital*, limited to situations of identity theft or fraud.[54]

Sixth, the quantification of the recoverable damages is not regulated by the GDPR. The question is thus a matter of national law, in accordance with the principle of national procedural autonomy, provided though that the principles of equivalence and effectiveness are observed.[55] Thus, to the extent that national law ensures full and effective reparation for the harm suffered by the victim, Member States must provide compensation similar to that applicable in a comparable national situation. By contrast, awarding nominal or symbolic compensation where there is an infringement but where the victim has not been able to prove having suffered any

---

[51] Judgments in *Natsionalna agentsia za prihodite*, *supra*, para. 85; and PS (Incorrect address), *supra*, para. 32 and the case-law cited.

[52] Judgment in PS (Incorrect address), *supra*, paras 35–36.

[53] Judgment in *MediaMarktSaturn*, *supra*, para. 69.

[54] Judgment in Scalable Capital, *supra*, para. 58.

[55] Ibid., para. 43.

damage resulting from that infringement is not compatible with Article 82 GDPR.[56] In situations where the damage suffered is minimal, the compensation afforded may reflect the scope of damage and thus be very small.[57] Moreover, in so far as the solution is accepted as a matter of national law, Article 82 GDPR does not exclude the use of public excuses as a remedy for non-material damage, provided however that form of compensation must serve to compensate in full the non-material damage that has actually been suffered as a result of the infringement of that regulation. This is for the national court before which the case has been brought to ascertain, taking account of the circumstances of each individual case.[58]

The scope of national autonomy regarding the determination of the amount of compensation is further limited by the following four conditions. First, the guidelines for determining the administrative fines in Article 83 (2) GDPR may not be applied in this context.[59] Second, the degree of guilt or negligence by the person liable for paying the damages does not have an effect on the amount of the compensation that should only depend of the damage suffered.[60] Third, it is not necessary to take account of simultaneous infringements of national provisions, which relate to the protection of personal data but which do not specify the rules of the GDPR.[61] Fourth, when determining the amount of damages due in respect of the right to compensation for non-material damage, it is appropriate to consider that such damage caused by a personal data breach is not, by its nature, less significant than physical injury.[62]

3 Public Enforcement Based on Article 83 GDPR

3.1 Overview of the Powers of Supervisory Authorities Under the GDPR

In comparison with the Data Protection Directive, the GDPR provides a more detailed regulatory framework for supervisory authorities to monitor compliance with the relevant data protection rules. This is explained by several factors. First, as was mentioned above, the GDPR is, unlike its predecessor, a directly applicable regulation. Second, an entire Chapter—Chapter VI—of the GDPR is devoted to

---

[56] See Opinion of Advocate General Campos Sánchez-Bordona in *Österreichische Post*, *supra*, paras 90–92.

[57] Judgment in Scalable Capital, *supra*, paras 45–46.

[58] Judgment in *Patērētāju tiesību aizsardzības centrs*, *supra*, paras 36–37.

[59] Judgments in *juris*, *supra*, para. 57; and PS (Incorrect address), *supra*, paras 43 and 44.

[60] Judgments *Krankenversicherung Nordrhein*, *supra*, para. 103; and *MediaMarktSaturn*, *supra*, para. 52.

[61] Judgment in PS (Incorrect address), *supra*, paras 48 and 50.

[62] Judgment in Scalable Capital, *supra*, paras 38 and 39.

regulating the role, tasks, powers and status of supervisory authorities. Third, and perhaps most importantly from the perspective of this article, Article 58 of that regulation, which lays down the powers of supervisory authorities, does so in an elaborate manner.

Article 28(3) of the Data Protection Directive left it to the Member States to regulate in more detail the powers of supervisory authorities. As regards corrective powers, the directive simply stated that those authorities must have the power to block, erase or destruction data, to impose a temporary or definitive ban on processing, to warn or admonish the controller, or to refer the matter to national parliaments or other political institutions. By contrast, Article 58(2) GDPR now explicitly lays down a catalogue of the wide-ranging powers[63] that those authorities are to enjoy in monitoring compliance with that regulation. Those powers expand on the few mentioned in the directive, but now include a variety of other powers such as the right to impose administrative fines, as set out in Article 58(2)(i) GDPR.

However, in accordance with Article 58(2)(i) thereof, those authorities enjoy leeway in choosing the most appropriate measure in a given case to ensure that the GDPR is complied with. Specifically, they may impose administrative fines pursuant to Article 83 of that regulation, 'in addition to, or instead of', the other corrective measures listed in Article 58(2) of the GDPR, such as warnings, reprimands or orders. They may do so, at their discretion, 'depending on the circumstances of each individual case'. Indeed, as recital 148 of that regulation states, in case of a minor infringement or if the administrative fine likely to be imposed would constitute a disproportionate burden to a natural person, supervisory authorities may refrain from imposing an administrative fine and instead issue a reprimand. Undoubtedly, the possibility to impose such a fine constitutes an important tool for those authorities to ensure that data controllers and data processors comply with their obligations under the GDPR. Without the possibility of imposing such fines, supervisory authorities arguably would lack a crucial tool to ensure compliance with the GDPR.

Article 58 GDPR goes beyond laying down the corrective powers of supervisory authorities. It also regulates in a detailed manner the investigative powers (Article 58(1)) and authorisation and advisory powers (Article 58(3)) that those authorities are to have. Here too, the GDPR is far more detailed than its predecessor, the Data Protection Directive. Under the general heading of 'Powers of intervention', the directive simply referred to powers of access to data to collect all the information necessary for the performance of its duties and the power to deliver opinions. By dint of Article 58(2) and (3) GDPR, supervisory authorities now explicitly enjoy, to

[63] Supervisory authorities can: (a) issue warnings, (b) issue reprimands, (c) order the controller or the processor to comply with the data subject's requests to exercise his or her rights pursuant to the GDPR, (d) order the controller or processor to bring processing operations into compliance with the GDPR, (e) order the controller to communicate a personal data breach to the data subject, (f) order the rectification or erasure of personal data or restriction of processing and the notification of such actions to recipients, (g) impose a temporary or definitive limitation on processing, (h) withdraw a certification or to order the certification body to withdraw a certification to order the certification body not to issue certification, (i) impose an administrative fine and (j) order the suspension of data flows to a recipient in a third country or to an international organisation.

name a few, the power to carry out investigations, to obtain access to any premises of the controller and the processor, to authorise processing, to accredit certification bodies and to approve binding corporate rules.

How the corrective powers, in particular the power to impose administrative fines, laid down in Article 58(2) GDPR are to be employed by supervisory authorities and what kind of limits, if any, Member States may place on those powers will be discussed in the following section in the light of the Court's case-law.

3.2 *The Court's Case-law on Article 83 GDPR*

Article 83 of the GDPR lays down the conditions under which supervisory authorities may impose fines on data controllers on the basis of the corrective powers granted to them by dint of Article 58(2) of that regulation. At the time of writing, the Court has interpreted Article 83 in less than a handful of cases of which *Deutsche Wohnen*[64] and *Nacionalinis,*[65] handed down by the Grand Chamber in late 2023, are by far the most important ones. The central issues clarified by the Court in those cases may be summarised as follows.

First, an administrative fine within the meaning of Article 83 GDPR requires that a controller has breached that regulation in a faulty manner.

Although Article 83(1) GDPR provides that those fines must be effective, proportionate and dissuasive, none of the paragraphs of that article expressly state that only infringements committed intentionally or negligently may be penalised by a fine. Some intervening governments and the Council of the European Union inferred from this open language in the *Deutsche Wohnen* case that the EU legislature intended to leave discretion to the Member States in implementing that provision. They argued, in particular, that that provision allowed them to impose administrative fines, where deemed appropriate, without it being necessary to establish that the infringement was committed intentionally or negligently.[66]

The Court rejected that view. Referring to, in particular, the overall scheme of Article 83 of the GDPR, and the objectives of the regulation, the Court held that an administrative fine can be imposed pursuant to that provision only where it is established that the controller has intentionally or negligently committed an infringement referred to in paragraphs 4 to 6 of that article.[67] Unlike civil liability under Article 82 GDPR, Article 83 GDPR does not operate with a presumption of fault. In addition to establishing an objective breach of the GDPR, the data

[64] Judgement in Deutsche Wohnen, C-807/21, EU:C:2023:950.

[65] Judgment in *Nacionalinis visuomenės sveikatos centras, supra.*

[66] Judgement in *Deutsche Wohnen, supra*, para. 63.

[67] Ibid., paras 72–78. See also judgment in *Nacionalinis visuomenės sveikatos centras, supra*, paras 77–80 and 86.

protection authority must prove at least a minimum level of negligence or intent on the behalf of the controller in order to impose a fine.

Although the Court did not explicitly rule on whether administrative fines provided for by the GDPR constitute criminal sanctions,[68] a fault-based approach to the application of Article 83 of the GDPR is arguably in line with such an understanding of their nature. To the criminal nature of the fines points, in particular, the severity of the sanctions envisaged by the EU legislature. Depending on the type of infringement, it may lead to the imposition of fines of, on the one hand, up to EUR 10000000 or, in the case of an undertaking, up to 2% of the total worldwide annual turnover of the preceding financial year, whichever is higher (Article 83(4) GDPR). On the other hand, in the event of more serious infringements fines up to EUR 20,000,000 or, in the case of an undertaking, up to 4% of the total worldwide annual turnover of the preceding financial year may be imposed (Article 83(5) and (6) GDPR).

Having said that, the threshold for what might constitute a negligent infringement of the GDPR is probably very low, making it difficult to envisage situations where it will be impossible to impose a fine for the mere reason that that element is not satisfied.[69] By applying its case-law in the field of competition law,[70] the Court held that a controller can be penalised for conduct falling within the scope of the GDPR where it could not be unaware of the infringing nature of its conduct, whether or not it is aware that it is infringing the provisions of the GDPR being irrelevant.[71] Crucially, where the controller is a legal person, action by or knowledge on the part of the management body of that legal person is not necessary.[72]

Indeed, it is likely that the failure to take any action in a situation where the controller or processor is unsure about the legality of the processing undertaken might, as some have suggested, constitute deliberate acceptance of potentially infringing the GDPR and, thus, gross negligence.[73] Furthermore, a negligent infringement may equate an 'unintentional' infringement, since such an infringement can exist where there was no obvious intention to cause the infringement but where the controller or

---

[68] See Opinion of Advocate General Campos Sánchez-Bordona in *Deutsche Wohnen*, C-807/21, EU:C:2023:360, paras 73–81; and Opinion of Advocate General Emiliou in *Nacionalinis visuomenės sveikatos centras*, C-683/21, EU:C:2023:376, paras 74–75. From the criminal character of administrative fines would follow that Article 49 of the Charter and pursuant to Article 52(3) thereof Article 7 of the European Convention on Human Rights are applicable in the context of imposing those fines.

[69] Opinion of Advocate General Emiliou in *Nacionalinis visuomenės sveikatos centras*, *supra*, para. 80.

[70] Judgments in *Schenker & Co. and Others*, C-681/11, EU:C:2013:404, para. 37 and case-law cited; *Lundbeck v Commission*, C-591/16 P, EU:C:2021:243, para. 156; and *Arrow Group and Arrow Generics v Commission*, C-601/16 P, EU:C:2021:244, para. 97.

[71] Judgement in *Deutsche Wohnen*, *supra*, para. 76.

[72] Ibid., para. 77 and case-law cited.

[73] P. Nemitz, 'Fines under the GDPR', in R. Leenes et al. (eds), *Data Protection and Privacy: The Internet of Bodies*, Hart Publishing, 2019, p. 241.

processor merely has breached its duty of care. In particular, even plain and simple 'human error' may be indicative of negligence.[74]

Second, the Court has stated that EU law alone governs the substantive conditions pertaining to the imposing of an administrative fine. Member States have thus no discretion with regard to the substantive conditions laid down in Article 83(2) GDPR.[75]

Arguably, leaving discretion to the Member States in defining any substantive conditions pertaining to the imposition of fines would be liable to distort competition between economic operators within the European Union. It would also be contrary to the aim of ensuring consistent application of the GDPR by data protection authorities and the imposition of equivalent sanctions.[76] Indeed, the GDPR not only aims to protect data subjects, but also, as is evident in particular from recital 9 thereof, to ensure a level playing field for economic operators through regulatory harmonisation.

Third, as a logical consequence of the fact that the GDPR sets the substantive conditions for imposing administrative fines, the addressee of an administrative fine (controller or processor) is determined solely on the basis of EU law.

Article 4(7) GDPR defines the concept of 'controller' broadly and expressly includes legal persons. Where a legal person acts as a controller within the meaning of that provision, it is responsible for any infringement referred to in Article 83(4) to (6) GDPR committed by that person or on its behalf.[77] From this follows that Member States cannot impose any further conditions on imposing an administrative fine on a controller that is a legal person. In the *Deutsche Wohnen* case, the Court explicitly held that the German attribution model for corporate sanctions was contrary to the GDPR, given the requirement that in order for a legal person to be fined for an unlawful act that act must have previously been attributed to an identified natural person belonging to the management of that legal person.[78]

Fourth, the concept of an 'undertaking', within the meaning of Articles 101 and 102 TFEU, has no bearing on whether and under what conditions an administrative fine may be imposed on a controller who is a legal person. This is because Article 58(2) and Article 83(1) to (6) of that regulation exhaustively regulates that issue.[79]

According to recital 150 of the GDPR, where 'administrative fines are imposed on an undertaking, an undertaking should be understood to be an undertaking in accordance with Articles 101 and 102 TFEU for those purposes.' However, it now

[74] See 'Guidelines on the application and setting of administrative fines for the purposes of the [GDPR]' of the Article 29 Data Protection Working Party, adopted on 3 October 2017; and Opinion of Advocate General Emiliou in *Nacionalinis visuomenės sveikatos centras*, *supra*, para. 81.

[75] Judgements in *Deutsche Wohnen*, *supra*, para. 65; and *Nacionalinis visuomenės sveikatos centras*, *supra*, para. 67.

[76] To that end, see in particular recitals 11 and 129 of the GDPR, which emphasise the role of supervisory authorities.

[77] Judgement in *Deutsche Wohnen*, paras 42 and 43.

[78] Ibid., para. 60.

[79] Ibid., para. 53. See also Opinion of Advocate General Medina in *ILVA*, C-383/23, EU:C:2024:752.

follows from the Court's case-law that that concept is relevant only for the purpose of determining the amount of the administrative fine imposed under Article 83(4) to (6) GDPR on a controller. Accordingly, where the addressee of the administrative fine is or forms part of an undertaking, within the meaning of Articles 101 and 102 TFEU, the maximum amount of the administrative fine is calculated on the basis of a percentage of the total worldwide annual turnover in the preceding business year of the undertaking concerned. By contrast, the competition law concept of undertaking has no relevance in the context of determining which entity should be regarded as the relevant data controller in relation to a specific data processing operation. That question is resolved on the basis of the definition of 'controller' contained in Article 4(7) GDPR.[80]

Fifth, the case-law sets limits to the circumstances in which an administrative fine may be imposed on a data controller for data processing operations carried out by a processor.[81]

As a matter of principle, a controller is responsible and liable not only for any processing of personal data which it itself carries out, but also for any processing carried out on its behalf. Therefore, an administrative fine may also be imposed on a controller for unlawful processing, which was carried out by a processor, rather than the controller itself.[82] However, the controller's liability for the unlawful conduct of processors does not extend to the following situations: where the processor has processed personal data for its own purposes or processed such data on behalf of the controller contrary to the controller's guidelines, or where the controller reasonably cannot have consented to such processing.[83] This follows from Article 28(10) GDPR, according to which a processor is to be regarded as a controller in respect of such processing.

[80] For the purposes of applying EU competition rules, the concept of 'undertaking' covers any entity engaged in an economic activity, irrespective of the legal status of that entity and the way in which it is financed. The concept of an undertaking therefore defines an economic unit even if in law that economic unit consists of several persons, natural or legal. That economic unit consists of a unitary organisation of personal, tangible and intangible elements which pursues a specific economic aim on a long-term basis (judgment in *Sumal*, C-882/19, EU:C:2021:800, para. 41 and the case-law cited).

[81] According to the definition contained in Article 4(8) of that regulation, a processor is 'a natural or legal person, public authority, agency or other body which processes personal data on behalf of the controller'.

[82] Judgment in *Nacionalinis visuomenės sveikatos centras*, paras 36 and 84.

[83] Ibid., para. 85.

4 Concluding Remarks: Is the Enforcement of EU Data Protection Rules a Mirror Image of EU Competition Law Enforcement?

As the above shows, the enforcement system put in place by Articles 82 and 83 GDPR bears, in many respects, unmistakable resemblance to how EU competition law—Nils Wahl's area of predilection—is enforced. Both fields rely on a combination of private and public enforcement.

On the one hand, public enforcement is in both systems carried out by authorities who enjoy wide-ranging investigatory powers. Administrative fines imposed by those authorities constitute the cornerstone of public enforcement in both systems, not least because of their high degree of severity. Because of their severity and punitive nature there is good reason to argue that they are criminal in nature and thus fall within the scope of Article 49 of the Charter.[84] Moreover, the fining system put in place by Article 83 GDPR mimics Article 23(1) of Regulation No 1/2003 that governs the imposition of fines for competition law infringements in so far as Article 83 GDPR only applies if intention or negligence is established. It is, indeed, clear from recital 150 of the GDPR and other similarities between the two fining systems (such as the fact that the amount of the fines can in both systems, as far as undertakings are concerned, be based on their turnover) that Article 83 GDPR was inspired by the corresponding system in the field of competition law. The influence of competition law on public enforcement of data protection law has its limits though. In particular, the determining of which entity should be regarded as the relevant data controller in relation to a specific data processing operation is not made by reference to conceptual calques from competition law, but on the basis of the definition of 'controller' in Article 4(7) GDPR.

Private enforcement, on the other hand, relies in both contexts on the activeness of private litigants. In our view though, it is in the sphere of private enforcement that the perhaps most obvious differences between the two enforcement systems can be observed.

First, the enforcement of EU competition law is based on close complementarity between public and private enforcement. This is because follow-on damages claims by private litigants regularly come to complement and reinforce public enforcement by competition authorities. By contrast, public and private enforcement of EU data protection rules seem to inhabit different realms. Although not excluded by the GDPR, to our knowledge, there is no similar tendency of follow-on claims in data protection law. That may be explained by the obvious difference in the status of the victims: victims of unlawful processing of personal data are private individuals who

[84] This is so despite the fact that Article 23(5) of Council Regulation No 1/2003 of 16 December 2002 on the implementation of the rules on competition laid down in Articles 81 and 82 of the Treaty (OJ 2003 L 1, p. 1) states that decisions taken pursuant to paragraphs 1 and 2 of Article 23 shall not be of a criminal law nature.

do not enjoy the same legal and financial means to bring damages actions as companies—be they competitors or customers—in the context of antitrust damages do.

Second, a breach of competition rules will inevitably result in competitive harm, which will spread across the relevant market ultimately harming the consumer. As a rule however, a breach of data protection rules only causes harm to the data subject(s) concerned, without that breach having any broader (market or other) implications. In that regard, unlike competition law which is in principle value-free, data protection law and the system put in place by Article 82 GDPR is closely rooted in the ethical values underpinning Articles 7 and 8 of the Charter, and seeks to protect the data subjects themselves and not the market.

Third, it follows from the Court's case-law in the field of competition damages that EU law precludes national rules that require a direct causal link to be established between the breach of competition rules and the damage suffered.[85] To what extent national courts may rely on national concepts of causation in the context Article 82 GDPR remains to be clarified. Nevertheless, drawing an analogy between the principles of causation applicable in the two fields might prove strenuous. This is so, in particular, because Article 82 seeks to protect data subjects and not the proper functioning of the market, because restrictions of competition inflict harm on competition which ultimately harm consumers, and perhaps most importantly, because the case-law on Article 82 now explicitly requires a causal link to be established between the damage and the infringement of the GDPR.

Fourth and finally, an important difference pertains to the procedural position of victims in the two fields. Directive 2014/104[86] on competition damages contains not only provisions lowering the evidentiary burden of victims, even in relation to the establishment of indirect damages, but also provisions that establish presumptions favouring the victim. No such element to specifically facilitate damages claims can be found in the GDPR or the case-law. As illustrated above, the Court's case-law on Article 82 GDPR requires that the victim demonstrates the existence of the violation of the relevant data protection rule and the reality of the damage. The victim's burden of proof is only somewhat eased by the fact that the fault of the data controller is presumed. That crucial difference might be a consequence of the fact that the fight against restrictions on competition constitutes a central EU policy objective. By contrast, data protection is not an objective in and of itself. It constitutes a necessary safeguard and restraint on a particular activity, i.e. the processing of personal data, which as such is an unavoidable and useful activity in modern societies.

[85] On 'umbrella-pricing', see judgment in Kone and Others, C-557/12, EU:C:2014:1317, paras 31–34.

[86] Directive of the European Parliament and of the Council of 26 November 2014 on certain rules governing actions for damages under national law for infringements of the competition law provisions of the Member States and of the European Union (OJ 2014 L 349, p. 1).

The Contribution of the Court of Justice to a 'Fairer' Internal Market in the Areas of Social Law and Tax Law

Koen Lenaerts and Stanislas Adam

Pursuant to EU primary law, the establishment of the internal market must be combined with the objective of the sustainable development of Europe based in particular on 'a highly competitive social market economy, aiming at full employment and social progress'.[1] As the Court has held, the EU has not only an economic purpose, but also a social objective.[2] Legal scholarship has devoted considerable attention to the interactions between the economic and social dimensions of the EU constitutional framework. From a methodological standpoint, a free and competitive internal market is often portrayed as being inherently in tension with the achievement of the EU social market economy.[3] In this conflict, the argument goes, social rights are on the losing side because the Court favours the free market over social progress in

[1] Art. 3(3), first subparagraph, TEU.

[2] Judgments in *AGET Iraklis,* C-201/15, EU:C:2016:972, paras 76–77, and *Lithuania and Others v Parliament and Council (Mobility package)*, C-541/20 to C-555/20, EU:C:2024:818, para. 263.

[3] See *inter alia*: F. W. Scharpf, "The asymmetry of European integration, or why the EU cannot be a 'social market economy'" (2010) *Socio-Economic Review* 8(2), pp. 211–250; J. Mulder, "Responsive adjudication and the 'social legitimacy' of the internal market" (2016) *European Law Journal* 22(5), pp. 597–620; S. Garben, "The Constitutional (Im)balance between 'the Market' and 'the Social' in the European Union" (2017) *European Constitutional Law Review* 13(1), pp. 23–61.

K. Lenaerts · S. Adam (✉)
Court of Justice of the European Union, Luxembourg, Luxembourg
e-mail: Koen.Lenaerts@curia.europa.eu; Stanislas.Adam@curia.europa.eu

L. Prete, L. Rezki (eds.), *Judging & (Re)Thinking European Union Law*,
https://doi.org/10.1007/978-3-032-13473-8_31

its interpretation of economic freedoms[4] and Union citizenship rights.[5] This article calls these assumptions into question in the light of case law in the areas of social security and tax law.

The EU social market economy covers a series of individual social rights, most of which are now guaranteed in the Charter of Fundamental Rights of the EU. Those rights range from access to healthcare to the entitlement to social security and social assistance benefits when persons face unexpected circumstances making them more vulnerable. This conception of the internal market is consistent with the value of solidarity reflected in Article 2 TEU, which characterises the society in which the EU develops. Creating sustainable solidarity through social security and social assistance requires not only an appropriate legal framework and public infrastructure, but also adequate financing, either through social security contributions or through taxation. It is therefore essential that EU law, including the fundamental freedoms of the internal market, does not undermine such financing and, by extension, the protective functions of the welfare state. On the contrary, the EU should stimulate them, within the limits of the competences conferred upon it by the Treaties. That is in line with the EU's objectives enshrined in the Treaties, which include social progress, the combat against social exclusion, the promotion of social justice and protection, solidarity between generations,[6] 'economic, social and territorial cohesion, [as well as] solidarity among Member States'.[7]

This article, which pays tribute to Nils Wahl's exceptional legacy in EU economic law, concentrates on the threat that abusive, fraudulent, or other 'unfair' practices by economic operators create for those protective functions. More specifically, the article highlights the significant role that the Court of Justice has played in enhancing fairness in the internal market through its fight against such practices in the areas of tax law (Sect. 1) and social law (Sect. 2).[8] The overarching argument can be summarised as follows. If certain market operators can artificially and at

[4] See *inter alia*: K. Tuori, *European Constitutionalism*, Cambridge University Press2015, pp. 234–243; D. Schiek, "Towards More Resilience for a Social EU – the Constitutionally Conditioned Internal Market" (2017) *European Constitutional Law Review* 13(4), pp. 611–640, at pp. 622–623; M. L. Zaccaria, "Old problems and new solutions? Some current questions of labour and social rights regarding the European pillar of social rights and the actual case law of the Court of Justice of the European Union" (2020) *Lex et Scientia International Journal* 27(1), pp. 85–100.

[5] See for example A. Aranguiz, M. Quené, "Is There a Way Where There's a Will? The Tensions between the Court's Case Law and the Pillar in Delimiting Transnational Solidarity" (2019) *European Journal of Migration and Law* 21(4), 509–539.

[6] Art. 3(3), second subparagraph, TEU.

[7] Art. 3(3), third subparagraph, TEU.

[8] The purpose of this chapter is to highlight how fair *competition* in the internal market, in the broad sense of that term, helps preserve the Member States' capacity to finance their welfare policies. It therefore does not cover the detrimental effects on that capacity of abuse or fraud committed by individuals, for example EU citizens or their family members, making use of their free movement rights, for example in the context of Directive 2004/38/EC of the European Parliament and of the Council of 29 April 2004 on the right of citizens of the Union and their family members to move and reside freely within the territory of the Member States (OJ 2004 L 158, p. 77) (see e.g. the judgment in *McCarthy and Others,* C-202/13, EU:C:2014:2450, para. 47), or the coordination of

limited cost create conditions allowing them to benefit from advantages under EU law in those areas, this may result in an erosion of tax revenues or of social contributions. The aggregate effects of such practices, which tend to proliferate in the absence of appropriate responses from the public authorities, not only create competitive distortions but also inevitably affect the ability of certain Member States to finance their public expenditure in general and the provision of high levels of social protection to the citizens in particular. Avoiding such an outcome is essential to preserve the trust placed by citizens in the ability of the Union to bring about social progress. The Court's role is, however, also to uphold the constitutional framework of the Union, which has occasionally led it to clarify the conditions under which both the Union and the Member States are entitled to address 'unfair' practices of undertakings in the areas of tax and social law (Sect. 3).

1 Tackling Fraudulent, Abusive or Other 'Unfair' Practices in the Field of Social Law

1.1 'Free-riding' and 'Forum Shopping' in the Context of the Coordination of Member States' Social Security Systems

Social law is characterised by a high degree of normative fragmentation in the EU. That is due, in particular, to the fact that EU law merely establishes a system for the coordination of the social security legislation among Member States, without harmonizing their social security schemes. Regulation 883/2004 (hereinafter 'the basic Regulation')[9] relates to the determination of the social security legislation applicable to nationals of the Member States.[10] It aims to guarantee the effective exercise of their right to free movement, thereby contributing to the improvement of the standard of living and conditions of employment of those who move within the

the social security systems of the Member States (see e.g. judgment in *Paletta*, C-206/94, EU:C:1996:182, paras 24 and 27).

[9] Regulation (EC) No 883/2004 of the European Parliament and of the Council of 29 April 2004 on the coordination of social security systems (*O.J.* 2004, L 166, p. 1). The basic Regulation, which must be read together with Regulation (EC) No 987/2009 of the European Parliament and of the Council of 16 September 2009 laying down the procedure for implementing Regulation (EC) No 883/2004 on the coordination of social security systems (*O.J.* L 284, p. 1, hereafter the 'Implementing Regulation'), repealed Regulation (EC) No 1408/71 of 14 June 1971 on the application of social security schemes to employed persons, to self-employed persons and to members of their families moving within the Community (*O.J.* 1997 L 28, p. 1), which nevertheless remains in force in a number of areas.

[10] Other persons are also covered by that coordination. See Art. 2 of the basic Regulation, and Art. 2 of Regulation (EC) No 1408/71.

EU.[11] The standard rule is that a person should only be subject to the social security regime of one Member State.[12] Moreover, subject to a number of derogations, an individual pursuing an activity as an employed or self-employed person in a Member State is in principle subject to the legislation of that Member State (*lex loci laboris*).[13]

It is inherent in such a system of coordination that differences remain among the social security schemes of the Member States, not least with regard to the level of social security contributions.[14] Those differences lead to substantial variations in wage costs for employers, depending on which social security legislation applies. This leads to significant variations in the competitive conditions in which undertakings operate in the internal market, especially in labour-intensive services sectors such as construction or transport.[15] In that context, undertakings should not be able to circumvent the relevant EU coordination rules in order to reduce artificially their social security contributions. As the Court explained:

> … the objective of [the EU system for the coordination of the social security legislation of the Member States] might be undermined if […] employers [were] able to resort to purely artificial arrangements in order to exploit the EU legislation with the sole aim of obtaining an advantage from the differences that exist between the national rules. In particular, such exploitation of that legislation would be likely to have a 'race to the bottom' effect on the social security systems of the Member States and perhaps, ultimately, reduce the level of protection offered by those systems.[16]

In other words, the normative fragmentation of social security law should not result in social 'dumping' by undertakings. That would create significant distortions of competition and, in the long term, threaten the financial equilibrium of schemes offering the highest levels of social protection. It would undermine the conception of the internal market as a social market economy conducive to social progress.

The *posting of workers* is the area where the risk of 'manipulating' EU rules on the coordination of social security appears most clearly. In the event that an employer normally carrying out his activities in a Member State posts a worker to another Member State, a specific coordination rule applies. The worker 'shall continue to be subject to the legislation of the first Member State, provided that the anticipated duration of such work does not exceed twenty-four months and that he is not sent to

[11] Judgment in *Szoja*, C-89/16, EU:C:2017:538, para. 34. That objective is also pursued by Regulation (EC) No 1408/71. See, to that effect, judgment in *VI*, C-33/18, EU:C:2019:470, para. 41.

[12] See Art. 11(1) of the basic Regulation and Art. 13(1) of Regulation (EC) No 1408/71.

[13] See Art. 11(3)(a) of the basic Regulation, and Art. 13(2)(a) of Regulation (EC) No 1408/71.

[14] Judgments in *Pinna*, 41/84, EU:C:1986:1, para. 20; *Piatkowski*, C-493/04, EU:C:2006:167, para. 20; *AFMB*, C-610/18, EU:C:2020:565, para. 68; and *TEAM POWER EUROPE*, C-784/19, EU:C:2021:427, para. 63.

[15] D. Carrascosa Bermejo, J. Molina Millán, "The binding nature of posting PDA 1 issued under EU social security Coordination Regulations and the possible role of national courts", 24 *ERA Forum* (2023), 69, at 70.

[16] Judgment in *AFMB*, para. 69. See also judgment in *TEAM POWER EUROPE*, para. 64.

replace another person.'[17] This is a temporary derogation to the *lex loci laboris*, aimed at promoting the posting undertaking's freedom to provide services.[18] The EU legislature takes the view that, when certain conditions are satisfied, the posting of workers constitutes in principle a legitimate exercise of the freedom to provide (or receive) services. In such cases, the social security legislation of the Member State from which the workers concerned are posted applies to them. This avoids unnecessary complications which would result from subjecting posted workers to the social security legislation of a Member State where they are sent to perform work of short duration.[19]

However, the EU legislature has long been conscious of the risks of social dumping associated with this derogation from the *lex loci laboris* rule. Substantial differences in the levels of social security contributions may create an incentive for undertakings active in Member States with high social protection to reduce their labour costs by making use of posted workers. They may, for example, outsource a significant part of their activities to employers established in Member States with lower social protection, or hire a workforce employed by a temporary employment undertaking or placement agency operating in the territory of such a Member State.[20] One of aforementioned risks thus relates to the potentially *fictitious nature* of an entity employing posted workers in a Member State with low social protection and significantly lower social security contributions in comparison to other Member States. That is why the expression 'which normally carries out its activities there' in the basic Regulation must be interpreted as referring to 'an employer that ordinarily performs substantial activities, other than purely internal management activities, in the territory of the Member State in which it is established, taking account of all criteria characterising the activities carried out by the undertaking in question'.[21] Only undertakings that ordinarily perform *substantial activities* in the territory of the Member State in which they are established can thus benefit from the derogation.[22]

---

[17] Art. 12 of the basic Regulation and art. 14 of the Implementing Regulation. Under the coordination regime of Regulation (EC) No 1408/71, the social security legislation of the Member State of origin remained applicable, in principle, for a posting of up to twelve months. See Art.13(a) of that Regulation.

[18] Judgment in *FTS*, C-202/97, EU:C:2000:75, para. 28.

[19] Judgment in *Walltopia*, C-451/17, EU:C:2018:861, para. 39.

[20] The different forms of posting recognized by EU law are enumerated in Article 1(3) of Directive 96/71/EC of the European Parliament and of the Council of 16 December 1996 concerning the posting of workers in the framework of the provision of services (*O.J.* 1996 L 18, p. 1).

[21] Art. 14(2) of the Implementing Regulation. That provision states, in addition, that '[t]he relevant criteria must be suited to the specific characteristics of each employer and the real nature of the activities carried out'.

[22] Decision A2 of 12 June 2009 of the Administrative Commission for the Coordination of Social Security Systems, concerning the interpretation of Article 12 of Regulation (EC) No 883/2004 of the European Parliament and of the Council on the legislation applicable to posted workers and self-employed workers temporarily working outside the competent State (*O.J.* 2010 C 106, p. 5), at recital 5 and para. 1. The Administrative Commission insisted on the necessity 'to carry out,

The interpretation of that condition in *Team Power Europe* clearly contributed to reducing the risks of social dumping.[23] The central issue raised by the referring court in that case concerned the circumstances in which a temporary-work agency carries out 'substantial activities, other than purely internal management activities' in the Member State where it is established. A Bulgarian temporary-work agency employing a Bulgarian national sought to assign the latter to an undertaking in Germany. The competent authority in Bulgaria refused to issue an A1 certificate establishing that the Bulgarian legislation was applicable to that worker during the period of assignment, on the ground in particular that Team Power Europe did not carry out any substantial activity in Bulgaria. Whilst it was not in dispute that that agency employed administrative and managerial staff in Bulgaria, it did not employ workers in that Member State and its entire turnover was derived from the activities undertaken by temporary agency workers assigned to Germany. According to the Court, selecting, recruiting and assigning temporary workers to user undertakings does not qualify as 'performing substantial activities' in the Member State where the temporary-work agency is established in so far as it assigns temporary workers only to user undertakings established in other Member States. The Court admitted that, in such circumstances, the activities of the agency cannot be regarded as 'purely internal management activities'.[24] It nevertheless took account of the fact that the sole purpose of the selection and recruitment activities of a temporary-work agency was 'the subsequent assignment [of] workers to user undertakings' and that it was only that assignment which actually generated the turnover of such agencies.[25] Consequently, a temporary-work agency performs 'substantial activities' in the Member State in which it is established 'only if it also carries out there, to a significant extent, the activities of assigning those workers for the benefit of user undertakings established and performing their activities in the same Member State'.[26]

That judgment illustrates how the Court simultaneously promotes high levels of social protection within the EU and fairer competition between undertakings. The strict interpretation of the 'substantial activities' condition is indeed justified by the objective of the basic Regulation to 'improv[e] the standard of living and conditions of employment of persons who move within the European Union'.[27] This interpreta-

throughout the period of posting, all the checks, in particular with regard to the payment of contributions and the maintenance of the direct relationship, required to prevent wrongful use of the abovementioned provisions, and to ensure that administrative bodies, employers and workers are suitably informed' (para. 8).

[23] See footnote 14.

[24] *Ibid.*, para. 46. The Court explained that '[t]hat concept covers only activities of an exclusively managerial nature which are intended to ensure the effective internal functioning of the undertaking'.

[25] *Ibid.*, paras 48 and 49.

[26] *Ibid.*, para. 50. Conversely, it does not fulfil that condition if it does not, or only 'to a negligible extent', assign workers to user undertakings in that Member State (para. 53).

[27] Recital 1 of the basic Regulation.

tion was necessary to deter temporary-work agencies from 'choos[ing] the Member State in which they wish establish themselves on the basis of the latter's social security legislation with the sole aim of benefiting from the legislation which is most favourable to them in that field, and thus to allow "forum shopping".'[28] The Court identified the risk of a 'race to the bottom' that such forum shopping would create, ultimately forcing some Member States to reduce their levels of social protection. A different interpretation would create moreover competitive distortions between the various modes of employment in favour of temporary agency work as opposed to undertakings directly recruiting their workers and therefore having to affiliate them to the social security system of the Member State in which they work.[29]

Another issue concerns the circumstances in which the presumptive validity of certificates of affiliation of a posted worker to a given national social security scheme can be rebutted. Facilitating the exercise of fundamental freedoms in the context of posting is only effective if, as a rule, the certificates issued by the competent authority of a Member State are accepted by the institutions of the other Member States as long as they have not been withdrawn or declared invalid in the former Member State.[30]

However, in *Altun*,[31] the question arose whether that rules out any calling into question of the validity of certificates on the part of the competent authorities of the Member State in which the workers are posted in case of serious suspicion of fraud or abuse. The 'E 101/A 1 certificate' delivered by the Member State of origin aims to establish that a posted worker is properly registered with the social security scheme of the Member State in which the undertaking employing him or her is established. Subject to holding that certificate, the posted worker is allowed to work in the host Member State without having to be registered with that State's social security system.[32] A Belgian company active in the construction sector outsourced all its work to companies established in Bulgaria, who posted workers to Belgium. A judicial investigation conducted in Bulgaria found that the Bulgarian companies did not have any significant activities there, although E 101 (now A 1) certificates had been issued by the Bulgarian authorities. Accordingly, the Belgian Social Security Inspectorate requested the Bulgarian authorities to reconsider or withdraw those certificates. Since the competent institution in Bulgaria did not take the results of the investigation into consideration in its reply, the Belgian authorities initiated legal proceedings against the employers for failing to register the workers with the Belgian social security system. The doubts of the Belgian Court of Cassation resulted from previous case law in which the Court considered that E 101/A 1 cer-

[28] Judgment in *TEAM POWER EUROPE*, para. 62.

[29] *Ibid.*, para. 65.

[30] Art. 5(1) of Regulation No 987/2009 creates a presumption that the worker concerned is properly affiliated to the social security scheme of the Member State whose competent institution has issued those certificates.

[31] Judgment in *Altun and Others*, C-359/16, EU:C:2018:63.

[32] See art. 19(2) of the Implementing Regulation. In the main proceedings, it was the corresponding provision in the former implementing regulation which applied.

tificates, which are based on mutual trust between the competent institutions of the Member States concerned, are 'binding on the competent institution of the Member State in which that person actually works'.[33] The central question raised by the referring court was whether the authorities in the host Member State may nonetheless disregard such certificates in specific circumstances.

The Court stressed first that each Member State must carry out a diligent examination of the application of its own social security system.[34] If the institution of the Member State in which the employee concerned actually works expresses doubts as to the validity of the certificate, the issuing institution should therefore reconsider the grounds for delivering it.[35] If the disagreement subsists, it is open to the competent institutions to refer the matter to one of the administrative commissions established in accordance with the regulations on the coordination of social security between the Member States.[36] If an administrative commission fails to reconcile the points of view of the competent institutions within six months,[37] the Member State in which the person concerned actually works may bring infringement proceedings under Article 259 TFEU, during which the issue of which legislation applies to the workers concerned and whether the particulars contained in the certificate are accurate can be addressed.[38]

However, in *Altun*, the Court has taken a further step, combining the EU secondary law scheme at issue with the general principle of EU law that fraud and abuse of rights are prohibited (*fraus omnia corrumpit*). If, upon request by the institution of the host Member State, the issuing institution fails to review the challenged certificates in the light of the concrete evidence available to it, such evidence may be relied on by judicial authorities of the latter Member State to disregard the certificates. By referring to this general principle, the Court thus nuanced existing case

[33] See judgments in *A-Rosa Flussschiff*, C-620/15, EU:C:2017:309, point 39, and *Alpenrind and Others*, C 527/16, EU:C:2018:669, para. 47.

[34] Judgment in *Altun*, para 42. Decision A1 of 12 June 2009 of the Administrative Commission for the Coordination of social security systems, concerning the establishment of a dialogue and conciliation procedure concerning the validity of documents, the determination of the applicable legislation and the provision of benefits under Regulation No 883/2004 (*O.J.* 2004 C 106, p. 1), offers guidance to the social security institutions responsible for applying EU law in that sphere. It is however not a legislative act and is therefore not binding for the Member States. See judgment in *Commission v Belgium*, C-356/15, EU:C:2018:555, paras 110 and 111.

[35] By contrast, there is no mutual trust issue in relation to the probative value of an E 101/A 1 certificate when the *issuing* institution wishes to withdraw it of its own motion because of the inaccuracy of the particulars contained therein. In such circumstances, the issuing authority does not have to initiate the dialogue and conciliation procedure with the competent institutions of the host Member State(s). It must only communicate to the competent authority in the host Member State and the person concerned all the information and data necessary for establishing and determining that person's rights. See judgment in *Zakład Ubezpieczeń Społecznych Oddział w Toruniu*, C-422/22, EU:C:2023:869.

[36] See art. 80 of Regulation (EC) No 1408/71 and Art. 71 of the basic Regulation.

[37] Art. 5(4) of the implementing Regulation.

[38] Judgment in *Altun*, para. 92.

law in order to address growing concerns about widespread fraud in the posting of workers in the European Union.

In the *Commission v. Belgium* judgment,[39] delivered a few months after *Altun*, the Court explained that the basic Regulation precludes national legislation which entitles the competent authorities in the host Member State to make a worker who holds an E 101/A 1 certificate subject to its legislation on social security matters unilaterally.[40] Courts of the host Member State may only disregard such a certificate if two conditions are fulfilled. Firstly, the reconciliation procedure is promptly initiated, enabling the competent institution of the issuing Member State to review the certificates in the light of concrete evidence submitted by the competent institution of the host Member State indicating that those certificates were fraudulently obtained or relied, and secondly, the competent institution of the issuing Member State fails to undertake such a review and to make a decision on this evidence within a reasonable time.[41]

Whilst confirming those conditions, the judgment in *Bouygues travaux publics*[42] contains another important nuance. The French authorities argued that the fact that the workers subject to inspection held E 101/A 1 certificates did not preclude a requirement under French law to declare the names of employees, including posted workers, prior to their engagement. The Court considered that, if the sole purpose of such a declaration is to verify whether a worker is affiliated to one or other branch of the social security scheme and thus to ensure the payment of social security contributions in France, that declaration is incompatible with the value conferred upon those certificates by EU law. There is no incompatibility with EU law, however, if that declaration's purpose is, even in part, to protect the *effectiveness of checks* aimed to ensure compliance with conditions of employment and working conditions imposed by (in this case French) employment law. That indeed does not amount to affiliating the workers concerned to one or other branch of the social security system.[43] That interpretation of the scope of the EU system for the coordination of social security schemes indisputably preserves each Member State's capacity to detect and sanction violations of its employment laws. For that reason, the *Bouygues travaux publics* judgment further illustrates the role played by the Court in enhancing social and competitive fairness in the internal market.

---

[39] See footnote 34.

[40] That is so even where it is quite obvious that the conditions for delivery of an A 1 certificate were not satisfied.

[41] See judgments in *CRPNPAC and Vueling Airlines*, C-370/17 and C-37/18, EU:C:2020:260, para. 80, and *DRV Intertrans and Verbraeken J. en Zonen*, C-410/21 and C-661/21, EU:C:2023:138, para. 61.

[42] Judgment in *Bouygues travaux publics and Others*, C-17/19, EU:C:2020:379.

[43] *Ibid.*, para. 53.

1.2 Promoting Social and Competitive Fairness Beyond Fraudulent or Abusive Practices

The role of the Court in enhancing 'fairness' within the internal market in the context of social law is not limited to the sphere of abusive or fraudulent practices. As the *Team Power Europe* judgment demonstrates, the interpretation of concepts and conditions in the relevant EU secondary acts may be sufficient in that regard. The interpretation given by the Court to the special rules on social security legislation applicable to persons employed in the transport sector and carrying out their work in two or more Member States provides additional illustrations.[44]

For example, in *DRV Intertrans*, the Court interpreted the concept of 'registered office or place of business' of a road transport company.[45] That concept can, in some circumstances, be decisive for determining the legislation applicable to road transporters who normally pursue an activity in two or more Member States. The Court held in this respect that the registered office or place of business is where the 'essential decisions of the undertaking are adopted and where the functions of its central administration are carried out'.[46] Consequently, the relevant criterion for determining the applicable social security legislation is the place from which an undertaking is in fact managed and organised, which may not always correspond to the place where it has an effective and stable establishment.[47] That interpretation reduced the possibility for road transport companies to artificially 'connect' their business to a Member State with the sole purpose of reducing social security contributions paid for their road transporters.

The same conclusion can be drawn from the *AFMB* judgment.[48] AFMB, an undertaking established in Cyprus, had entered into fleet management agreements with transport undertakings established in the Netherlands. Under these contracts, AFMB was to manage, on behalf of and at the risk of those undertakings, the heavy goods vehicles operated by them as part of their businesses. For that purpose, it entered into employment contracts with a number of long-distance lorry drivers. Whilst those contracts specified that Cypriot law was applicable to those employment relationships, the lorry-drivers continued to live in the Netherlands and worked, on behalf of the transport undertakings, in two or more Member States and sometimes also in one or more EFTA States. Those elements led the competent authority in the Netherlands to consider that these workers should be affiliated with the Dutch social security system. AFMB and some of the lorry-drivers concerned challenged that decision. It was quite clear that the fleet contracts were concluded with a view to applying conditions of employment under Cypriot law and Cypriot social security legislation, despite the fact that neither the workers concerned nor

---

[44] Art. 13 of the basic Regulation and Art. 14(2)(a) of Regulation (EC) No 1408/71.

[45] See art. 13(1)(b)(1) of the basic Regulation.

[46] Judgment in *DRV Intertrans*, para. 75.

[47] *Ibid.*, para. 79.

[48] See footnote 14.

the transport activities they carried out presented any clear connection to that Member State. The Court held, in essence, that the determination of the employer depends exclusively on who exercises *effective authority* over the worker, taking into account all relevant circumstances of the employment relationship.[49] This means that the competent authorities and courts are not necessarily bound by contractual terms when determining which undertaking actually exercises authority over the worker, bears the actual wage costs, and has the actual power to dismiss that worker.[50] The objective of the Union's coordination system to establish criteria of attachment, taking into account the objective situation of a worker, would be undermined if the applicable legislation were determined on the basis of formal considerations. Allowing employers to 'resort to purely artificial arrangements in order to exploit the EU legislation with the sole aim of obtaining an advantage from the differences that exist between the national rules' would entail the risk, ultimately, of a reduction of the level of protection offered by the social security systems of the Member States.[51]

The methodology reflected in *AFMB* is thus multifactorial, as it focuses on who effectively exercises authority over the worker concerned based on his or her objective situation. In that sense, that judgment was in line with the Court's interpretation of the concept of 'habitual place of performance of work' for the purposes of ascertaining a court's jurisdiction to settle a dispute arising from an employment contract in accordance with the Brussels I Regulation.[52] The latter contains a derogation to the rule that defendants must in principle be sued in the Member State where they reside or are established, taking into account the usually-weaker position of employed persons. An employer can indeed be sued before the courts of another Member State, 'where the employee habitually carries out his work'.[53]

The Court interpreted that concept of 'habitual place of performance of work' in *Nogueira*.[54] The case concerned an airline's cabin crew, employed under contracts concluded directly with the airline or seconded in the airline by another company. The contracts stipulated that their activities were to be regarded as carried out in Ireland because their duties were performed on board aircrafts registered in that Member State and belonging to that airline. An airport in Belgium was designated as the 'home base' and required that the workers concerned live within an hour's journey of that base.[55] The workers initiated judicial proceedings before Belgian

[49] Judgment in *AFMB*, paras 53–55.

[50] *Ibid.*, para. 61.

[51] *Ibid.*, para. 69.

[52] Council Regulation (EC) No 44/2001 of 22 December 2000 on jurisdiction and the recognition and enforcement of judgments in civil and commercial matters (*O.J.* 2001 L 12, p. 1).

[53] Art. 19(2) of the Brussels I Regulation.

[54] Judgment in *Nogueira and Others*, C-168/16 and C-169/16, EU:C:2017:688.

[55] The 'home base' is used in the basic Regulation for determining the social security legislation applicable to flight crew or cabin crew members performing air passenger or freight services [see Art. 11(5) of the basic Regulation, which replaced Article 14(2)(a)(i) of Regulation (EC) No 1408/71]. It is the location nominated by the operator to the crew member from where the crew

courts, claiming financial compensation from the airline as employment conditions under Belgian law should apply, instead of Irish law. A Belgian court had doubts about its jurisdiction to decide on the merits of the workers' actions. In its judgment, the Court of Justice rejected, in particular, the argument of the defendants that the concept of 'habitual place of performance of work' in the context of air transport should be determined by reference to the Member State where the aircraft is registered. The correct approach, instead, is a 'circumstantial method' identifying the habitual place of performance of work on the basis of a set of *indicia* specifically related to the activities of the worker.[56] Although the 'home base' is a distinct concept, it constitutes a 'significant indicium' for the purposes of determining that 'habitual place'.[57] Interestingly, the Court justified the circumstantial method, in particular, by the need to prevent that concept from being exploited or contributing to the *circumvention strategies* of employers aiming to deprive workers from the right of access to courts in the place where they actually carry out their activities for disputes with their employer.[58] Once more, such reasoning serves simultaneously to enhance social rights and thus social progress and the protection of competitive fairness between undertakings.

That convergence can also be reflected in the margin of discretion left to the EU legislature when the Court exercises judicial review of EU internal market measures. In the cases *Hungary v. Parliament and Council*[59] and *Poland v. Parliament and Council*,[60] the Court examined the validity of a directive[61] amending the 1996 Directive concerning the posting of workers in the framework of the provision of services.[62] That amendment aimed in essence to ensure that the terms and conditions of employment of posted workers were as close as possible to those of workers employed by undertakings established in the host Member State.[63] As a result, posted workers would, in particular, no longer be subject to the 'minimum rates of

member normally starts and ends a duty period, or a series of duty periods, and where, under normal conditions, the operator is not responsible for the accommodation of the crew member concerned (see recital 18b of the basic Regulation).

[56] Judgment in *Nogueira and Others*, paras 61–63. The place where the employee returns after his tasks, receives instructions concerning his tasks and organises his work is amongst the relevant criteria.

[57] In the light of circumstances of the cases as described by the referring court, it could be reasonably considered that the habitual place of performance of work was the Belgian airport and, moreover, that Belgian social security legislation applied considering that that airport constituted the workers' 'home base'.

[58] Judgment in *Nogueira and Others*, para. 62.

[59] Judgment in *Hungary v Parliament and Council*, C-620/18, EU:C:2020:1001.

[60] Judgment in *Poland v Parliament and Council*, C-626/18, EU:C:2020:1000.

[61] Directive (EU) 2018/957 of the European Parliament and of the Council of 28 June 2018 amending Directive 96/71/EC concerning the posting of workers in the framework of the provision of services (*O.J.* 2018 L 173, p. 16).

[62] See footnote 20.

[63] That amendment and by extension the cases therefore did not concern the distinct issue of determination of the applicable social security legislation.

pay' fixed by the legislation of the host Member State, but to the 'remuneration' provided for by that legislation, on an equal footing with 'local' workers. The preamble of the Directive on the posting of workers already recognized that 'promotion of the transnational provision of services (through the posting of workers) requires a climate of fair competition and measures guaranteeing respect for the rights of workers'.[64] However, twenty years after the adoption of that Directive, the EU legislature considered that greater account should be taken of the protection of posted workers, while also ensuring that the freedom to provide services in the host Member State can be exercised fairly.[65]

The plea raised by the applicant Member States, to the effect that the amending Directive disregarded the freedom to provide services guaranteed in Article 56 TFEU, deserves close examination. In their opinion, substitution of the concept of 'remuneration' for that of 'minimum rates of pay' constituted a discriminatory restriction on that freedom, since it imposes an additional financial and administrative burden on a service provider employing posted workers. The EU legislature ignored the fact that such service providers are in a more difficult position than service providers established in the host Member State as they have to comply with the rules of their Member State of origin and of the host Member State. Moreover, the amending Directive nullified the lawful competitive advantage of certain easily identifiable Member States in which the level of pay is lower.

The Court rejected those arguments. Referring to the EU legislature's broad discretion in areas in which its action involves, in particular, political, economic and social choices, it considered that the decision to increase the protection of workers reflected in the amending Directive fell within that discretion.[66] The EU legislature could legitimately decide that a re-balancing was necessary between the objective of facilitating the exercise of freedom to provide services and the enhancement of fair competition between undertakings, through the reduction of excessive differences in the terms and conditions of employment to which the undertakings of various Member States are subject within one and the same Member State. Such a re-balancing did not remove any competitive advantages based on costs which the service providers in some Member States may have enjoyed, for example productivity or efficiency of the workers, and therefore did not create any distortion of competition.[67] The Court expressly accepted the legislature's choice, expressed in the amending Directive, not only to create a 'truly integrated and competitive internal market' but also to bring about 'genuine social convergence'.[68] This conception of the EU legislature's margin of discretion in harmonizing internal market rules

---

[64] Recital 7 of Directive 96/71.

[65] Judgments in *Hungary v Parliament and Council*, para. 53, and *Poland v Parliament and Council*, para. 58.

[66] Judgments in *Hungary v Parliament and Council*, para. 124, and *Poland v Parliament and Council*, para. 108.

[67] Judgment *Hungary v Parliament and Council*, para. 128.

[68] Judgments *Hungary v Parliament and Council*, para. 129, and *Poland v Parliament and Council*, para. 107.

plainly promotes the Union's general objective of enhancing 'social progress', set out in Article 3(3) TEU.

Methodologically, this case law paved the way for the judgment in the *Mobility Package* cases, delivered on 4 October 2024.[69] In that judgment, the Court broadly confirmed the validity of the challenged EU acts, which aimed to enhance competitive fairness and social protection of road transport workers essentially by combatting social dumping and the phenomenon of 'letterbox' companies in that sector.[70]

2 Combating Fraudulent, Abusive or Other 'Unfair' Practices of Economic Operators in the Area of Tax Law

The Court has consistently held that the pursuit by a taxpayer, including a company, of the tax regime most favourable to it cannot, as such, lead to a general presumption of fraud or abuse depriving the taxpayer of the enjoyment of free movement rights or other advantages resulting from EU law.[71] However, taxpayers cannot enjoy such rights or advantages arising from EU law in situations where they are unable to put forward any valid commercial reasons justifying a given transaction.[72] That is so when that transaction is disconnected from any economic reality and has as its sole purpose reduction of the tax burden.

2.1 Abusive or Fraudulent Practices in the Field of VAT

Those principles were initially applied in VAT cases. Preventing possible tax evasion through abuse or fraud is an objective recognised and encouraged by the Sixth Directive.[73] As a result, the general principle that abusive practices are prohibited

[69] See footnote 2.

[70] See, for example, judgment in *Lithuania and Others v Parliament and Council (Mobility package)*, paras 854, 1071, 1154, 1155, 1223 and 1224.

[71] Judgments in *Cadbury Schweppes and Cadbury Schweppes Overseas*, C-196/04, EU:C:2006:544, para. 50; *National Grid Indus*, C-371/10, EU:C:2011:785, para. 84; *SECIL*, C-464/14, EU:C:2016:896, para. 60; *N Luxembourg 1 and Others*, C-115/16, C-118/16, C-119/16 and C-299/16, EU:C:2019:134, para. 109; and *X (Intérêts relatifs à un emprunt intragroupe)*, C-585/22, EU:C:2024:822, para. 59.

[72] Judgments in *Centros*, C-212/97, EU:C:1999:126, para. 24 and the case-law cited; *Halifax and Others*, C-255/02, EU:C:2006:121, para. 68; *Cadbury Schweppes and Cadbury Schweppes Overseas*, para. 35; and *Cussens and Others*, C-251/16, EU:C:2017:881, para. 27.

[73] Sixth Council Directive 77/388/EEC of 17 May 1977 on the harmonisation of the laws of the Member States relating to turnover taxes — Common system of value added tax_ uniform basis of assessment (*O.J.* 1977 L 145, p. 1). That Directive was replaced by Council Directive 2006/112/EC of 28 November 2006 on the common system of value added tax (*O.J.* 2006 L 347, p. 1) (hereafter the 'VAT Directive'). See judgments in *Halifax and Others*, para. 71; *Kittel and Recolta*

must be relied on to refuse an advantage on the basis of EU provisions governing VAT in a situation where the taxpayer has artificially created the conditions for it to apply.

It was not yet entirely clear from the wording used in the initial judgments whether the interpretation of EU law merely created a possibility or an obligation for national administrations and courts. That uncertainty was resolved in the *Schoenimport 'Italmoda'* judgment, where the Court held that it is, in principle, 'the responsibility of the national authorities and courts to refuse the benefit of the rights laid down by the Sixth Directive when they are claimed fraudulently or abusively'.[74] Since the absence of fraud or abuse is one of the conditions for obtaining an advantage under the Sixth Directive, it was logical to consider that when such fraud or abuse is established, the advantage in question *must* be refused.[75] Those principles remain unchanged in the regime established by the VAT Directive, which replaced the Sixth Directive.[76]

Thus, national authorities and courts must refuse the benefit of advantages provided for in the field of VAT when an operator indulges in abusive practices intended to benefit from such advantages, *even in the absence of specific national provisions to that effect*. This concerns in particular the general rights to VAT deduction, exemption or refund.[77] Refusal of such advantages does not require a specific legal basis in national law, because it does not amount to imposing an obligation on the individual concerned under the Sixth Directive or the VAT Directive.[78] It rather concerns the impossibility for the taxable person to claim a right under EU law, when the *objective criteria* for the granting of that advantage have not been satisfied because of an abusive practice affecting the transaction carried out by the taxable person itself.[79] The Court has consistently held that a taxable person who has created the conditions for obtaining a right only by participating in fraudulent or abusive transactions is clearly not justified in invoking the principles of protection of legitimate expectations or legal certainty in order to oppose the refusal to grant the right in question.[80]

Recycling, C-439/04 and C-440/04, EU:C:2006:446, para. 54; and *Mahagében and Dávid*, C-80/11 and C-142/11, EU:C:2012:373, para. 41.

[74] Judgment in *Schoenimport 'Italmoda' Mariano Previti and Others*, C-131/13, C-163/13 and C-164/13, EU:C:2014:2455, para. 49.

[75] *Ibid.*, para. 57.

[76] See, to that effect, judgment in *UP CAFFE*, C-171/23, EU:C:2024:840, para. 43.

[77] Judgments in *Schoenimport 'Italmoda' Mariano Previti*, para. 62, and *Cussens and Others*, C-251/16, EU:C:2017:881, para. 33.

[78] Judgments in *Schoenimport 'Italmoda' Mariano Previti*, para. 57, *Cussens and Others*, para. 32, and *UP CAFFE*, para. 37.

[79] See judgments in *Halifax*, paras 68 and 69, and *Collée*, C-146/05, EU:C:2007:549, para. 38.

[80] See, to that effect, judgments of 8 June 2000, *Breitsohl* (C-400/98, EU:C:2000:304), para. 38, and *Schoenimport 'Italmoda' Mariano Previti*, para. 60. The Court has considered that such outcome is justified even with regard to transactions carried out prior to its judgment in *Halifax and Others* on abusive or fraudulent practices in connection with VAT (see judgment in *Cussens and Others*, paras 40 to 42).

The range of situations where fraudulent or abusive behaviour that is incompatible with the objectives pursued by EU law must lead national authorities to refuse to grant the rights of deduction of, exemption from or refund of VAT have been defined broadly, which testifies to the importance attached by the Court to the integrity of the VAT system. Thus, such rights must be refused not only where tax evasion has been carried out by a taxable person itself, but also where that taxable person knew, or should have known, that it was participating in a transaction involving evasion of VAT carried out by the supplier or by another trader acting upstream or downstream in the supply chain.[81] Therefore, the fraudulent nature of a chain of transactions as a whole justifies refusing the advantage at any level of that chain, at least in so far as the taxable person concerned can be reasonably held to know that it is participating in such a chain. Moreover, in the recent judgment in *UP CAFFE*, the Court confirmed that the principles stemming from *Schoenimport 'Italmoda'* and *Cussens* on the compulsory refusal of advantages in the field of VAT in cases of fraud or abuse also apply in a situation where a given exemption scheme is purely optional for the Member States.[82]

Of course, refusing the benefit of a right or advantage granted by EU law in a tax case is a radical measure—one might even call it a sanction—which cannot be applied 'lightly' by tax authorities or national courts. The prohibition of abusive practices is therefore not relevant where the economic activity being carried on does not have as its sole aim to secure tax advantages.[83] In particular, an abusive practice in the field of VAT exists only if, first, the transaction concerned, notwithstanding the fact that the conditions laid down by the relevant provisions of the VAT Directive and the national legislation transposing that directive formally apply, results in a tax advantage that is at odds with the purpose of those provisions and, second, objective factors indicate that the transaction's *essential* aim is to obtain that tax advantage.[84]

Another important issue is whether EU law requires a certain level of 'proactivity' from national tax authorities in detecting such fraudulent or abusive practices.

---

[81] See judgment in *Kittel and Recolta Recycling*, paras 45, 46, 56 and 60, and judgments of 6 December 2012, *Bonik* (C-285/11, EU:C:2012:774), paras 38 to 40, and of 18 May 2017, *Litdana* (C-624/15, EU:C:2017:389), para. 33.

[82] Judgment in *UP CAFFE*, para. 24. That case concerned Article 287 of the VAT Directive, which allows the Member States to exempt taxable persons with a limited annual turnover and is intended to relieve small undertakings and tax authorities from the administrative burdens of VAT liability where the tax amounts involved are small. In its judgment of 5 July 2007, *Kofoed* (C-321/05, EU:C:2007:408) (esp. paras 38 and 48), the Court seems to have nuanced the requirements of combatting fraud and abusive practices based on the principle that a directive cannot of itself impose *obligations* on an individual and cannot therefore be relied on as such, by a Member State, against that individual. In *Cussens* and *UP CAFFE*, however, the Court explained that that reasoning only concerned the specific provision of the directive at issue in *Kofoed* and was therefore 'not applicable to the general principle of the prohibition of abusive practices' (see judgment in *UP CAFFE*, para. 39 and case-law cited).

[83] See, by analogy, judgment in *Halifax and Others*, paras 74 and 75.

[84] *Ibid.* See also judgment in *UP CAFFE*, para. 23.

VAT constitutes an important part of the EU's own resources.[85] This means that a direct link exists between the collection of VAT revenue in compliance with EU law and the availability of the corresponding VAT resources to the EU budget, since any lacuna in the collection of the first inevitably causes a reduction in the second.[86] Consequently, the obligation for the Member States, pursuant to Article 325 TFEU, to counter fraud and any other illegal activities affecting the financial interests of the EU is applicable. Accordingly, the Court has interpreted the VAT Directive, in conjunction with Article 4(3) TEU, to the effect that 'Member States are not only under a general obligation to take all legislative and administrative measures appropriate for ensuring collection of all the VAT due on their territory, but must also fight against tax evasion'.[87] It is reasonable to consider that the Member States are under an EU law obligation to ensure that the national tax administrations have the necessary human and material resources to investigate cases of suspected fraud or abuse in the field of VAT effectively. That is essential to the protection of the Union's financial interests and budget, which gives practical effect to the solidarity between the Member States.[88]

2.2 *Fraudulent and Abusive Practices in Taxation on Income and Profits*

In the field of income tax, more limited harmonization at EU level would appear to reduce the capacity of the Court of Justice to enhance tax fairness.[89] Several judgments delivered in the past few years nevertheless demonstrate that the Court is involved in the fight against tax evasion here too, within the limits of its judicial function. It promotes tax fairness and thus protects the Member States' capacity to finance their public policies, including social assistance and social security.

---

[85] Article 2(1)(b) of Council Decision 2007/436/EC, Euratom of 7 June 2007 on the system of the European Communities' own resources (*O.J.* 2007 L 163, p. 17)

[86] Judgment in *Åkerberg* Fransson, C-617/10, EU:C:2013:105, para. 26.

[87] See judgment in *Taricco and Others*, C-105/14, EU:C:2015:555, para. 36.

[88] See, to that effect, judgments in *Hungary v Parliament and Council*, C-156/21, EU:C:2022:97, para. 129, and *Poland v Parliament and Council*, C-157/21, EU:C:2022:98, para. 147. See, on the contribution of those judgments to defining the legal implications of that principle, K. Lenaerts, S. Adam, 'Sink or Swim Together: Solidarity between the Member States as a Foundational Principle of the European Union', *in* C. Barnard, A. Łazowski, D. Sarmiento (Eds), *Pursuit of Legal Harmony in a Turbulent Europe. Essays in Honour of Eleanor Sharpston*, Hart Publishing, 2024, pp. 52–53.

[89] See also the third section.

The *N Luxembourg*[90] and *T Danmark*[91] judgments, delivered in 2019, are a first illustration of that point. The cases concerned, respectively, the "Interest and Royalty Payment Directive"[92] (*N Luxembourg*), and the Dividends Directive,[93] which was replaced by the Parent-Subsidiary Directive[94] (*T Danmark*).[95] The underlying objective of both directives is to avoid the double-taxation of such payments in the cross-border transactions which they regulate. In principle, payments covered by the Directives benefit from an exemption from all taxation in the Member State of origin in respect of the Interest and Royalty Payment Directive or from the payment of a withholding tax in the case of the Dividends Directive. In the case of the Interest and Royalty Payment Directive, this goal is achieved by allowing taxation only in the receiving Member State, thus eliminating possible taxation in the Member State of origin. In *N Luxembourg*, however, the companies receiving the interest and dividends from their Danish subsidiaries paid almost all of them to their own parent companies under complex arrangements, sometimes involving several successive payments of virtually identical amounts within the same group. The amounts were subsequently transferred to tax havens such as the Cayman Islands and Bermuda. The result of this scheme was that, ultimately, taxation of the payments within the EU was avoided altogether. The referring courts had doubts whether such a situation could arise from the proper application of EU law.

The Court of Justice decided in the first place that the concept of 'beneficial owner of the interest', within the meaning of the Interest and Royalty Payment Directive, must be interpreted narrowly as designating only an entity which *actually benefits* from the interest that is paid to it. According to the Court, this can only be the case if the entity receives those payments for its own benefit and not as an intermediary, such as an agent, trustee or authorised signatory, for some other person. Mere "letter-box entities" certainly do not fulfil this criterion. Even more importantly, Member State authorities do not only have the *possibility*, but a legal *obligation* to refuse to grant a right or an advantage arising under EU law, irrespective of whether national (tax) law formally contains an anti-abuse provision, where the provisions of EU law are relied upon not with a view to achieving the objectives of those provisions but in order to benefit from that right or advantage even though the

[90] Judgment in *N Luxembourg 1 and Others*, C-115/16, C-118/16, C-119/16 and C-299/16, EU:C:2019:134.

[91] Judgment in *T Danmark and Y Denmark*, C-116/16 and C-117/16, EU:C:2019:135.

[92] Council Directive 2003/49/EC of 3 June 2003 on a common system of taxation applicable to interest and royalty payments made between associated companies of different Member States (*O.J.* 2003 L 157, p. 49).

[93] Council Directive 90/435/EEC of 23 July 1990 on the common system of taxation applicable in the case of parent companies and subsidiaries of different Member States (*O.J.* 1990 L 255, p. 6).

[94] Council Directive 2011/96/EU of 30 November 2011 on the common system of taxation applicable in the case of parent companies and subsidiaries of different Member States (*O.J.* 2011 L 345, p. 8).

[95] See already, on those judgments, K. Lenaerts, "Le juge de l'Union, promoteur de la lutte contre l'abus de droit en matière fiscale", *Revue Générale du Contentieux Fiscal*, 6/2019, pp. 433–449.

conditions for benefiting from it are fulfilled only formally.[96] This obligation reflects the general EU law principle of sincere cooperation between Member States and the EU, which—just like in the *Altun* case—is essential to prevent EU law from being deflected from its real objectives.

In its more recent *Viva Telecom Bulgaria* judgment, the Court has confirmed the interpretation of the concept of 'beneficial owner' under the Interest and Royalty Payment Directive that it had given in *N Luxembourg*.[97] It has also confirmed in the *X BV* judgment that the effective fight against abuses or fraud in the field of direct taxation may constitute a legitimate ground for the Member States to justify limitations of fundamental freedoms.[98]

Of significant importance also is the Anti-Tax Avoidance Directive (ATAD 1), an EU law act which is for its part specifically aimed at tackling unfair tax practices.[99] The ATAD 1 followed the 15-Point Action Plan of the OECD and the G20 against base erosion and profit shifting (BEPS).[100] It lays down rules aimed at 'strengthen[ing] the average level of protection against aggressive tax planning in the internal market', by limiting the erosion of tax bases in the internal market and the shifting of profits out of the internal market. One of its most emblematic provisions is the general anti-abuse rule contained in Article 6 ATAD 1, which requires Member States, for the purposes of calculating corporate tax liability, to 'ignore an arrangement or a series of arrangements which, having been put into place for the main purpose or one of the main purposes of obtaining a tax advantage that defeats the object or purpose of the applicable tax law, are not genuine having regard to all relevant facts and circumstances'.[101] The Court will undoubtedly have the opportunity in the future to clarify the scope of that provision and of other anti-tax avoidance measures covered by the Directive. It should be emphasised however that the ATAD 1 explicitly confirms the principle, resulting from well-established case-law, that taxpayers must have the right to choose the most tax efficient structure for their business activities.[102]

---

[96] Judgment in *T Danmark and Y Denmark*, para. 72.

[97] See judgment in *Viva Telecom Bulgaria*, C-257/20, EU:C:2022:125, paras 51–53.

[98] Judgment in *X (Intérêts relatifs à un emprunt intragroupe)*, C-585/22, EU:C:2024:822. Thus, '[w]hilst the pursuit by a taxpayer of the tax regime most favourable for him or her cannot, as such, set up a general presumption of fraud or abuse, the fact remains that such a taxpayer cannot enjoy a right or advantage arising from EU law where the transaction at issue is purely artificial economically and is designed to circumvent the application of the legislation of the Member State concerned' (para. 59 and case-law cited).

[99] Council Directive (EU) 2016/1164 of 12 July 2016 laying down rules against tax avoidance practices that directly affect the functioning of the internal market (*O.J.* 2016 L 193, p. 1).

[100] See in this respect E. C.C.M. Kemmeren, "Editorial. Where is EU Law in the OECD BEPS Discussion?", *EC Tax Review*, 2014-4, pp. 190–193.

[101] See, for a comparative analysis between that clause and the case-law of the Court of Justice on abuse of EU law, L. De Broe, D. Beckers, "The general anti-abuse rule of the Anti-Tax Avoidance Directive: an analysis against the wider perspective of the European Court of Justice's case law on abuse of EU law", 2017-3, *EC Tax Review*, Vol. 26, pp. 133–144.

[102] Recital 11.

2.3 Cooperation Mechanisms Between the Tax Administrations of the Member States

The Court's concern to protect the *effet utile* of cooperation mechanisms between national tax administrations is another example of how the Court contributes to tackling tax avoidance and evasion strategies in the internal market. A smooth and effective cooperation is essential to maintain fair competition within the internal market and to avoid tax base erosion detrimental to the Member States' capacity to conduct their public policies effectively.

Thus, in the recent *Belgian Association of Tax Lawyers* judgment,[103] the Court upheld the validity of various provisions of the Tax Cooperation Directive.[104] That Directive, which does not apply to VAT,[105] established a system of cooperation between the Member States' tax administrations in order to address increasing difficulties encountered by them in assessing properly the taxes due as a result of the huge rise in the mobility of taxpayers and the number of cross-border transactions, as well as the internationalisation of financial instruments.[106] In proceedings before the Belgian Constitutional Court, organisations representing lawyers and tax consultants, and various bar associations, argued that several provisions of the Tax Cooperation Directive violated the Charter and certain general principles of EU law. The *Belgian Association of Tax Lawyers* case concerned, in particular, the obligation created by the Directive for all intermediaries and, in their absence, the taxpayer involved in potentially aggressive cross-border tax arrangements[107] that may lead to tax avoidance and evasion, to report them to the competent tax authorities.[108]

Firstly, the Court rejected the argument that the Tax Cooperation Directive infringed the principles of equal treatment and non-discrimination laid down in Articles 20 and 21 of the Charter in so far as it did not limit the reporting obligation to corporate tax. In the light of the general objective of combating aggressive tax planning and preventing the risk of tax avoidance and evasion, corporate tax and other taxes such as income tax applicable to natural persons can be regarded as comparable. The reporting obligation's broad scope was not therefore manifestly

[103] Judgment in *Belgian Association of Tax Lawyers and Others*, C-623/22, EU:C:2024:639.

[104] Council Directive 2011/16/EU of 15 February 2011 on administrative cooperation in the field of taxation (*O.J.* 2011 L 64, hereafter, the 'Tax Cooperation Directive'). The Court examined the version of that directive as amended by Council Directive (EU) 2018/822 of 25 May 2018 (*O.J.* 2018 L 139, p. 1).

[105] Art. 2(2).

[106] Recitals 1 and 2.

[107] Those arrangements are primarily defined by reference to the 'main benefit test', which requires determining whether 'the main benefit or one of the main benefits which, having regard to all relevant facts and circumstances, a person may reasonably expect to derive from an arrangement is the obtaining of a tax advantage' (see Annex IV of the Tax Cooperation Directive).

[108] Art. 8ab of the Tax Cooperation Directive. The arrangements reported to a tax administration of a Member State give rise to an automatic exchange of information to the competent authorities of all other Member States. See Art. 8ab(13) of the Tax Cooperation Directive.

inappropriate.[109] A parallel can be drawn between that latter aspect of the reasoning and the reference made to the EU legislature's wide discretion to enhance fairness in the functioning of the internal market in the *Hungary v. Parliament and Council* and *Poland v. Parliament and Council* judgments examined in the first section.

Secondly, the Court considered that a number of concepts used in the Tax Cooperation Directive to define the scope of the reporting obligation, in particular the criteria for identifying aggressive tax planning arrangements subject to them, were sufficiently clear and precise to satisfy the general principles of legal certainty and legality in criminal matters. In particular, an intermediary or the taxpayer should be in a position to assess without much difficulty whether the main benefit or one of the main benefits that can reasonably be expected of the arrangement they design and/or use is fiscal in nature.[110] The Court held furthermore that the reporting obligation defined sufficiently clearly the information which it covers and that, therefore, the limitation which it entails in respect of the private life of the intermediary and the relevant taxpayer is defined in a sufficiently precise manner.[111]

Thirdly, the Court shed light on the limits of its reasoning in the *Orde van Vlaamse Balies and Others* judgment.[112] In that judgment, the Court had declared invalid the obligation to notify set out in Article 8ab(5) of the Tax Cooperation Directive, in so far as it applies to lawyers. According to that provision:

> Each Member State may take the necessary measures to give intermediaries the right to a waiver from filing information on a reportable cross-border arrangement where the reporting obligation would breach the legal professional privilege under the national law of that Member State. In such circumstances, each Member State shall take the necessary measures to require intermediaries to notify, without delay, any other intermediary or, if there is no such intermediary, the relevant taxpayer of their reporting obligations under paragraph 6. [...]

The Court considered that that notification requirement violated the legal professional privilege of the lawyer protected by Article 7 of the Charter.[113] It interfered with the secrecy of legal consultation in so far as it required the lawyer-intermediary to notify other intermediaries who are not his or her clients about their reporting obligations. That notification indeed meant that third-party intermediaries would

---

[109] Judgment in *Belgian Association of Tax Lawyers and Others*, para. 33.

[110] *Ibid.*, para. 74.

[111] *Ibid.*, para. 89.

[112] Judgment in *Orde van Vlaamse Balies and Others,* C-694/20, EU:C:2022:963. See also the third section.

[113] Drawing inspiration from the case-law of the European Court of Human Rights on Article 8(1) ECHR, the Court held that that Article 7 of the Charter 'guarantees the secrecy of th[e] legal consultation, both with regard to its content and to its existence' and that individuals who consult a lawyer can therefore 'reasonably expect that their communication is private and confidential' [*ibid.*, para. 27, citing the judgment of the ECtHR in *Altay v. Turkey (No 2)*, CE:ECHR:2019:0409JUD001123609, § 49]. The legal professional privilege guaranteed in EU law for communication between lawyer and his or her client applies 'whatever the area of law to which [the legal advice] relates', including for example company law. See judgment in *Ordre des avocats du Barreau de Luxembourg*, C-432/23, EU:C:2024:791, para. 51.

'become aware of the identity of the notifying lawyer-intermediary, of his or her assessment that the arrangement at issue is reportable and of his or her having been consulted in connection with the arrangement'.[114] A further breach of Article 7 of the Charter arose from the fact that third-party intermediaries were, in turn, required to disclose this information to the tax authorities, given that the identification of other intermediaries forms part of the reporting obligation under Article 8ab(1) of the Directive.[115] The Court accepted that the legal professional privilege granted by the Charter is not absolute and that combating aggressive tax planning and preventing the risk of tax avoidance and evasion constitute objectives of general interest recognised by the EU, which can justify limiting it. However, the notification requirement at issue failed to pass the proportionality test, considering the fact, in particular, that the waiver from the reporting obligation for the lawyer-intermediary is without prejudice to the same obligation bearing on other intermediaries and to the requirement for that lawyer-intermediary to notify without delay his or her client of his or her reporting obligations, and that disclosing the identity of the lawyer-intermediary and of his or her having been consulted is not such as to assist tax authorities because information covered by legal professional privilege cannot be communicated to them without the client's consent.

In the *Belgian Association of Tax Lawyers* judgment, the Court explained that those findings were justified by the very specific protection that the relationship between a lawyer[116] and his or her clients warrants. That requirement is therefore valid, on the other hand, in so far as it applies to *other professionals* who may be authorised to ensure legal representation such as tax advisers, notaries, auditors, accountants or bankers. In the Court's view, exempting all those other intermediaries from the notification requirement would risk undermining the effectiveness of the reporting mechanism.[117] The referring court also observed that the reporting obligation may concern cross-border arrangements that are lawful, genuine, non-abusive and the main advantage of which is not fiscal in nature. It had doubts whether the interference that that obligation entails with the right of taxpayers and intermediaries to a private life[118] was valid from that perspective. The Court confirmed that the reporting obligation did indeed constitute such an interference. However, it enables tax administrations to 'remedy promptly the regulatory disparities and loopholes on which the cross-border arrangements are based', which is 'such as to reduce the interest for taxpayers in having recourse to tax arrangements the effective duration of which is likely to be correspondingly shortened.' Consequently, that obligation was such as to deter both those taxpayers and their

[114] Judgment in *Orde van Vlaamse Balies and Others*, para. 29.

[115] *Ibid.*, paras 31 and 32.

[116] Within the meaning of Directive 98/5/EC of the European Parliament and of the Council, of 16 February 1998, to facilitate practice of the profession of lawyer on a permanent basis in a Member State other than that in which the qualification was obtained (*O.J.* 1998 L 77, p. 36).

[117] Judgment in *Belgian Association of Tax Lawyers and Others*, para. 99.

[118] In a nutshell, 'revealing to the administration the result of tax design and engineering work' (*ibid.*, para. 129).

advisers from designing and implementing cross-border, tax-planning mechanisms which, while lawful, are based on disparities between the various applicable national rules and entail erosion of tax revenues.[119] That interference with the right to private life at issue was moreover proportionate. The reporting obligation 'is [indeed] a particularly effective means of combating aggressive tax planning and preventing the risks of tax avoidance and evasion'. Transmitting to the tax administration, at a very early stage, information on the cross-border tax planning arrangements containing one of the relevant hallmarks 'allows the Member States to react with precision and speed, if necessary in a coordinated manner, to aggressive tax-planning mechanisms, which the examination and monitoring of tax behaviour a posteriori does not allow quite as much'.

3 The Court as Guarantor of the Union's Constitutional Framework

The previous sections demonstrate that the Court has played a pivotal role in the promotion of social and fiscal fairness in the Union and its Member States. Yet, this solidarity-oriented approach has to be reconciled with the broader EU constitutional framework. That framework covers in particular the principle of conferral, respect of fundamental rights and the fundamental freedoms of the internal market.

3.1 Enhancing Tax Fairness Whilst Respecting Fiscal Autonomy in the Context of State Aid

A first illustration relates to respect for the Member States' fiscal autonomy. State aid law also protects fair competition, which can be undermined *inter alia* by the granting of selective advantages to certain undertakings through tax measures.[120] In this respect, the Court has developed a three-step test, offering guidance not only to the Commission but also to national administrations and courts.[121] A recurring question in that context is whether the general prohibition of State aid in Article 107 TFEU is an appropriate instrument for achieving 'tax fairness' despite the absence of EU harmonising measures on a given aspect of direct taxation.

[119] *Ibid.*, paras 130 and 131.

[120] In its judgment in *Italy v Commission*, 173/73, EU:C:1974:71, the Court considered that 'the [...] fiscal nature [...] of the measure in issue cannot suffice to shield it from the application of [what is now] Article 107 [TFEU].'.

[121] See judgments in *Fiat Chrysler Finance Europe v Commission*, C-885/19 P and C-898/19 P, EU:C:2022:859, para. 68; *Luxembourg and Others v Commission*, C-451/21 P and C-454/21 P, EU:C:2023:948, para. 107; and *United Kingdom and Others v Commission (Taxation of SEC Benefits),* C-555/22 P, C-556/22 P and C-564/22 P, EU:C:2024:763, para. 93.

A sequence of landmark judgments of the Court offers a nuanced answer. The *Commission v. Poland* and *Commission v. Hungary*[122] judgments concerned, respectively, a Polish tax on turnover in the retail sector and a Hungarian tax on turnover linked to advertisements. Both tax regimes had two common characteristics: (a) they were based on turnover rather than profit and (b) they applied progressive rates. In its examination of selectivity, the Commission considered that the progressive structure of those taxes did not form part of the 'reference system'. It argued that progressive rates would favour undertakings with a low turnover by unjustifiably reducing the average tax rate applied to them compared with that borne by other undertakings subject to the higher levels of the scale of progressive rates. That advantage thus derogated from a reference system deemed to consist of a fictive flat-rate turnover tax. Both the General Court and the Court of Justice in the appeal proceedings disagreed with that assessment. The determination of the characteristics constituting each tax remains within the discretion of the Member States, as it falls within their fiscal autonomy when no EU harmonising measures have been adopted. Therefore, they should be able to apply progressive rates to a turnover tax. The progressive structure of the tax regimes at issue thus formed part of the reference system and could not be regarded as giving rise to a selective advantage.

That approach paved the way to the judgment in *Fiat Chrysler*,[123] where the Court essentially held that, in the absence of harmonising measures at EU level, it is for the Member States alone to apply and to give substance to the "arm's length principle". The origin of the case was a tax ruling by the Luxembourg authorities addressed to Fiat Chrysler Finance Europe (FFT) concerning the calculation of a 'fictive' remuneration ('transfer pricing') for treasury services and financing provided by that company to the companies of the Fiat Chrysler group established in Europe. The objective of such transfer pricing is to ensure that intra-group transactions do not artificially benefit from a reduction of the tax burden compared to transactions between independent companies. The tax ruling at issue had been granted on the basis of a provision of the Luxembourg Tax Code and a ministerial circular. However, the Commission considered that those elements of national law, focusing on intra-group transactions, did not constitute the correct reference system. In its opinion, the correctly defined system was the general Luxembourg corporate income tax system, the objective of which was to tax the profits of all companies resident in Luxembourg. Against that background, it argued that the tax ruling at issue granted a selective advantage to FFT. The methodology applied for calculating transfer pricing departed from the 'state-of-the-art' methodology recommended by the Organisation for Economic Co-operation and Development (OECD). According to the Commission, this departure resulted in an unfair reduc-

---

[122] Judgments in *Commission v Hungary*, C-596/19 P, EU:C:2021:202, and *Commission v Poland*, C-562/19 P, EU:C:2021:201. See already, on those judgments, K. Lenaerts, "The broadening of EU competences through the case law of the Court of Justice: myth or reality?", (2023) *ERA Forum* 24(4), p. 597.

[123] Judgment in *Fiat Chrysler Finance Europe v Commission*, C-885/19 P and C-898/19 P, EU:C:2022:859.

tion in the tax liability of FFT compared to an independent company delivering the same type of services. Unlike the General Court, the Court of Justice held that the Commission failed to conduct an objective examination of the 'content, interaction and concrete effects' of the Luxembourg rules when defining the reference system.[124] In the absence of EU harmonising measures, the detailed rules for the application of the arm's length principle must be determined exclusively by reference to national law. By relying on the OECD guidelines, the Commission disregarded both the principle of legality of taxation and the provisions of the TFEU relating to the adoption by the European Union of measures for the approximation of Member State legislation relating to direct taxation.[125]

The respect due to the Member States' fiscal autonomy in the context of State aid was also centre-stage in the Court's judgment in *Engie*, which again concerned tax rulings granted by the Luxembourg authorities.[126] The tax rulings at issue concerned complex corporate and financial arrangements within the Engie group whereby income from participations in subsidiaries established in Luxembourg was exempted from tax. According to the Commission, those rulings had enabled that group to avoid taxation on almost all of the profit made by those subsidiaries. In order to define the reference system, the Commission interpreted Luxembourg law as making the possibility of a tax exemption for parent companies conditional upon the prior taxation of distributed income at the level of their subsidiaries, which had not been the case here.[127] It also considered that the selectivity of the advantage granted through the tax rulings resulted from the fact that the Luxembourg authorities omitted to apply a provision of Luxembourg tax law on abuse of law in taxation. Luxembourg argued that the relevant provisions of its tax law did not expressly make the exemption of income from participations at the level of a parent company dependent on the taxation of distributed profit at the level of its subsidiary. However, the Commission departed from that interpretation, finding that it was incompatible with the general objective of taxing all resident companies.[128] The Court held that approach to be incompatible with the scope of the Commission's powers in the field of State aid. In light of the principles of fiscal autonomy and legality in taxation, that institution is in principle bound by the interpretation of national law made by the Member State concerned.[129] Consequently, the Commission was entitled to depart from this interpretation only by providing 'reliable and consistent evidence' demonstrating that another interpretation prevailed in national case law or administrative practice. Since the Commission had failed to do so, the Court rejected its analysis based on a reference system requiring a link between the tax advantage granted to

[124] *Ibid.*, para. 92.

[125] *Ibid.*, paras 93–97.

[126] Judgment in *Luxembourg and Others v Commission,* C-451/21 P and C-454/21 P, EU:C:2023:948.

[127] *Ibid.*, para. 127.

[128] There was no indication that the situation at issue fell within the scope of application of the Interest and Royalty Payment Directive and the Dividend Directive examined by the Court in the *T Denmark* and *N Luxembourg* judgments.

[129] Judgment in *Luxembourg and Others v Commission*, paras. 118–120.

the parent company and the tax burden borne by its subsidiaries.[130] As a result of that erroneous definition of the reference system, the Commission's subsidiary line of reasoning on selectivity based on an omission to apply a national anti-abuse provision was necessarily flawed too.[131]

The *Fiat Chrysler* and *Engie* judgments clearly indicate that the Member States' fiscal autonomy—given the division of competences between the Union and the Member States and in accordance with the Union's constitutional principle of conferral—limits the Commission's margin to tackle what it regards as 'unfair' tax treatments through Article 107(1) TFEU.

As the recent judgment in *Apple* demonstrates,[132] however, this does not mean that State aid law provides no useful basis for addressing unfair tax treatment. It can indeed fulfil that function provided that the Commission correctly identifies the reference system on the sole basis of national law. The case concerned two tax rulings granted by Irish tax authorities in favour of two non-resident Irish companies belonging to the Apple Group ('ASI' and 'AOE'). The Irish tax authorities excluded the profits generated by the intellectual property licences held by ASI and AOE from the tax base, on the ground that those companies' head offices were located outside of Ireland, and that the management of those licences depended on decisions taken by the Apple Group in the United States. The Commission, by contrast, based its analysis on an interpretation of a provision of Irish law concerning calculation of the tax base of non-resident companies, and considered that the IP licences and related profits had to be allocated to the Irish branches of ASI and AOE. The Court upheld the appeal against the judgment of the General Court annulling the Commission's decision. It confirmed, in particular, that, under the relevant provision of Irish law relating to the calculation of tax payable by non-resident companies, the activities of the branches of ASI and AOE in Ireland had to be compared not to activities of other Apple Group companies, for example a parent company in the United States, but to those of other entities within those companies, particularly their head offices situated outside Ireland. Against that background, the Commission was able to consider, under its primary line of reasoning on selectivity, that the lack of active or critical functions performed by the head offices in relation to the IP licences and the multiplicity and centrality of the functions performed and risks assumed by the Irish branches should have led the Irish authorities to attribute the profits generated by those licences to those branches.

[130] *Ibid.*, paras. 121 and 127–128.

[131] *Ibid.*, para. 173.

[132] Judgment in *Commission v Ireland and Apple Sales International*, C-465/20 P, EU:C:2024:724.

3.2 Respect for Fundamental Rights

As the judgment in *Orde van Vlaamse Balies and Others* examined above already illustrates, the efforts made to reinforce fairness in the functioning of the internal market are only legitimate if they respect fundamental rights, especially those guaranteed by the Charter.

An example is the right to an effective judicial remedy in the context of investigation measures aimed at detecting and sanctioning fraudulent or abusive practices. A key condition for achieving the objectives of the Tax Cooperation Directive in this respect is the effective and timely execution of requests for information addressed by a tax administration of a Member State to that of another Member State, which may require the latter to adopt 'information orders' when it does not yet possess the requested information.[133] The Tax Cooperation Directive therefore requires the Member States to take all necessary measures to ensure the smooth operation of the administrative cooperation arrangements which it provides for. The *Berlioz Investment Fund* case concerned the remedies that should be available to the addressee of an information order issued within the scope of that Directive, in the context of a penalty imposed for failure to comply with it.[134] That Directive does not specify the 'necessary measures' which Member States must adopt for ensuring the smooth operation of the administrative cooperation arrangements. The Court explained that they must include arrangements, such as pecuniary penalties, which ensure that there is sufficient incentive for the relevant person to respond to tax authorities' requests, and thereby enable the requested authority to fulfil its obligations towards the requesting authority.[135] As a Member State 'implements' EU law when adopting such a sanction, however, the person to which it is addressed is entitled to the right to an effective judicial remedy, as guaranteed by Article 47 of the Charter. The Court considered that that person must be able to challenge *indirectly* the validity of the information order when it contests the penalty imposed on him.[136]

In the *État luxembourgeois (Right to bring an action against a request for information in tax matters)* judgment,[137] the Court went a step further and considered that Article 47 of the Charter additionally requires that a person who is subject to an information order without being the taxpayer under investigation may bring a *direct* action against that information order. Indeed, the essence of the right to an effective

---

[133] Article 5. That aspect of the Tax Cooperation Directive must be distinguished from the reporting obligations set out in article 8ab of the Tax Cooperation Directive, examined in Sect. 2 above.

[134] Judgment in *Berlioz Investment Fund*, C-682/15, EU:C:2017:373.

[135] *Ibid.*, paras 36 and 38.

[136] *Ibid.*, paras 55 and 56. That challenge may for example concern the 'foreseeably relevant' nature of the information requested for the administration and application of the tax legislation of the requesting Member State [art. 1(1) of the Directive].

[137] Judgment in *État luxembourgeois (Right to bring an action against a request for information in tax matters)*, C-245/19 and C-246/19, EU:C:2020:795.

remedy guaranteed by that provision is not respected if a person first has to infringe an information order and thus be subject to the penalty attached to non-compliance with it before it can challenge the validity of that order.[138] By contrast, the Court considered that the fact that the taxpayer concerned by the investigation and third parties with whom that taxpayer had legal, banking, financial or economic relations were unable to bring a direct action against the information order addressed to the information holder did not violate their right to an effective remedy. That exclusion contributed to the speed and efficiency of cooperation between tax authorities[139] and was suitable for combating international tax fraud and tax evasion more effectively.[140] The Court concluded that the limitation on the right to an effective remedy was not disproportionate. A decision such as that at issue in the main proceedings did not place the taxpayer concerned under any legal obligation or at any risk of a penalty, and could be challenged by that taxpayer indirectly, in the context of an action against a subsequent correction or adjustment decision.[141] In the light of that reasoning, it seems that the taxpayer itself should also be entitled to challenge an information order directly before courts when that order is addressed to him or her.[142]

That judgment was followed by the *État luxembourgeois (Information on a group of taxpayers)* case.[143] The Court's ruling in that case again illustrates the importance of 'balancing' the legitimate objective of combating international tax fraud and tax evasion with respect for fundamental rights. In the main proceedings, the information holder, being unable to directly challenge the information order due to the aforementioned exclusion rule, had brought an action against the administrative fine imposed by the Luxembourg tax authority. The legality of the information order was then confirmed in the course of that action. This raised the question whether, in these circumstances, the taxpayer was entitled to a 'period of grace' to provide the information without being fined or whether, on the contrary, the admin-

[138] *Ibid.*, paras 68–69.

[139] The Court referred in particular to Article 7 of the Directive, which states that 'the [requested] information [...] must be provided as quickly as possible and, except in certain special cases, within two months or six months depending on whether the requested authority is or is not already in possession of the requested information'.

[140] Judgment in *État luxembourgeois (Right to bring an action against a request for information in tax matters)*, paras 86–91, 103 and 104.

[141] The Court emphasized in that respect that a decision ordering information to be provided is adopted during the preliminary stage of the investigation concerning the taxpayer in question, whilst only the last stage of that investigation, which begins with the sending of a proposal for correction or adjustment to the taxpayer concerned, should be regarded as contentious for that taxpayer during which the latter is able to exercise his or her right to be heard (see *ibid.*, para. 81 and case-law cited).

[142] See, in that sense, A. Antoniou, "Judicial protection in exchange for tax information procedures: why ex post protection is not 'effective' protection", in M. Malmgrén, M. Serrat Romaní, J. Korving, M. Eliantonio (eds), *Exchange of information in the EU. Taxpayers' rights, Transparency and Effectiveness*, Elgar, Cheltenham, 2024, p. 105.

[143] Judgment in *État luxembourgeois (Information on a group of taxpayers)*, C-437/19, EU:C:2021:953.

istrative penalty operated *ex tunc*.[144] After recalling its previous case law, the Court considered that a new time limit was necessary in order to safeguard effectively the essence of the right enshrined in Article 47(1) of the Charter. That new time limit 'compensated' for the fact that the exclusion of a right to challenge the information order directly did not respect the essence of the right to an effective remedy as guaranteed by Article 47 of the Charter.[145]

3.3 Fundamental Freedoms of the Internal Market

As we have seen in the first section, it is settled case law that the general principle of EU law that fraud and abuse of rights are prohibited deprives legal or natural persons from the enjoyment of, inter alia, fundamental freedoms of the internal market based on fraudulent or abusive practices. However, that does not mean that Member States may justify any restriction to those freedoms by the objective of preserving social and fiscal fairness in the internal market. The judgment in *Commission v Belgium* on 'bogus self-employment' illustrates that point.[146] The Commission argued that, by imposing a prior declaration requirement on self-employed service providers established in other Member States, Belgium had violated Article 56 TFEU. The Court first considered that the formalities implied by the declaration requirement at issue, which concerned in particular the starting date and duration of the 'posting' in Belgium, constituted an obstacle to the freedom to provide services.[147] That Member State argued that the declaration was necessary to prevent the abusive use of the self-employed status with the aim of circumventing the minimum standards of social protection for workers in Belgium. The Court recognised the prevention of social security fraud and the detection of 'bogus self-employed persons' are overriding reasons in the public interest.[148] Those objectives contribute to the financial balance of social security systems, as well as the maintenance of fair competition and the protection of workers. The Court also excluded the existence of a discrimination, since self-employed service providers established in Member States other than Belgium were in a position objectively different from the Belgian ones regarding the risk of fraud.[149] However, the provision failed the test of proportionality. Firstly, the declaration obligation was not restricted to cases where there was cause to ascertain that tax and social security obligations under Belgian law were met.[150] Secondly, Belgium failed to demonstrate that the very

[144] *Ibid.*, para. 86.

[145] *Ibid.*, paras 89–95, 97 and 98.

[146] Judgment in *Commission v Belgium* (C-577/10, EU:C:2012:814).

[147] *Ibid.*, paras 39–42.

[148] *Ibid.*, para. 45.

[149] *Ibid.*, paras 46–48.

[150] *Ibid.*, paras 53 and 54.

detailed information covered by the declaration obligation was suitable or strictly necessary to achieve those objectives.[151]

The Court's judgment in *Čepelnik* is based on largely similar reasoning.[152] In that judgment, the Court held that the freedom to provide services precludes national measures which enable the competent authorities of a Member State to order a commissioning party established in that Member State to suspend payments to his or her contractor established in another Member State, or to pay a security, in order to guarantee payment of the fine which might be imposed on that contractor in the event of a proven infringement of the labour law of the first Member State. Admittedly, such measures contribute to the effectiveness of penalties that might be imposed on the service provider in the event of fraudulent or abusive use of posting of workers. However, various aspects of the scheme at issue in the main proceedings led the Court to consider that it was not proportionate. That included, in particular, the fact that the service provider against whom a reasonable suspicion of fraud or abuse existed did not have the possibility to put forward his or her observations before the adoption of the measures.

4 Concluding Remarks

Legal fragmentation across the EU in the areas of social (security) law and tax law may constitute fertile ground for distortions of competition in the internal market. Such fragmentation places economic operators on an unequal footing, depending, for example, on the Member State(s) in which they are established, whether they form part of a group of affiliated companies, or the nature of the products or services that they put on the market. In principle, nothing precludes economic operators from benefitting from those disparities when exercising their free movement rights. The rationale underpinning the internal market indeed implies that choices concerning whether and how to exercise, in particular, the freedom of establishment and the freedom to provide services, may legitimately be guided by the search for the most economically advantageous outcome, taking account of differences in the regimes applicable in various Member States.[153] In more general terms, given the disparities existing between the relevant legislation of the Member States, the exercise of those fundamental freedoms may or may not be to an undertaking's advantage in terms of tax or social security contributions, depending on the circumstances.[154]

---

[151] *Ibid.*, paras 55 and 56.

[152] Judgment in *Čepelnik*, C-33/17, EU:C:2018:896. See also the Opinion of Advocate General Wahl in the same case (EU:C:2018:311).

[153] In particular, as we explained in Sect. 2, EU law in principle does not preclude a taxpayer from searching the most favourable tax treatment, for example by choosing the most tax efficient structure for his or her business activities.

[154] See, e.g., judgments in *National Grid Indus*, C-371/10, EU:C:2011:785, para. 62; *X*, C-686/13, EU:C:2015:375, para. 33; and *VP CAPITAL*, C-414/21, EU:C:2022:871, para. 19. Although these

The case law examined in this article nevertheless shows how the Court of Justice contributes to reducing some of the harmful impacts that such fragmentation has on fair competition in the internal market. That concerns situations where the exercise of free movement rights can no longer be regarded as legitimate, as it amounts instead to unjustifiable 'dumping', diverting fundamental freedoms from their purpose, as intended by the authors of the Treaties, and undermining competition based on the merits. In the first place, the Court has used the general principle of EU law that fraud and abuse of rights are prohibited to tackle 'free-riding' opportunities that persist in the internal market in the absence of (full) legal harmonisation in social and tax matters. The case law indicates that national courts and administrations are required to apply that general principle directly, irrespective of the existence of relevant provisions in national law, which clearly reinforces its impact in practice. Furthermore, the Court strongly supports EU legislative action against certain forms of intra-EU social and fiscal dumping. The EU legislature has indeed taken numerous initiatives over the past three decades to fight what it perceived as unfair practices by economic operators in those areas, even going beyond situations of outright fraud and abuse. In the context both of references for a preliminary ruling and of infringement proceedings, the Court regularly monitors whether those EU secondary law measures are being properly implemented in the Member States.

The analysis reveals that several forms of solidarity are required from the Member States in that endeavour of reinforcing fair competition within the internal market. Solidarity is not confined to abstention from certain practices, such as the granting of tax advantages to undertakings on a discriminatory basis. Positive obligations also bear on the Member States, such as investing sufficient administrative resources to detect abuses or fraud in the areas of social security or tax involving a cross-border dimension, initiating or accepting cooperation with the competent authorities of other Member States when so required by EU law, and ensuring that that cooperation is conducted in good faith and with a reasonable degree of care. Reinforced social and fiscal fairness in the functioning of the internal market would be illusory if certain Member States failed to comply with those requirements, as this would inevitably create or maintain 'loopholes'. Any such failure would increase opportunities for economic operators to divert free movement rights from their intended purpose by engaging in illegitimate cross-border 'dumping' in the areas of social (security) law and tax law. In that sense, the case law examined in this article highlights the role that the Court plays in reducing the risk of 'races-to-the-bottom' and forum shopping in those areas and the harmful consequences that they have for both fair competition and social progress. This is crucial to preserve

cases concerned tax treatment in the context of freedom of establishment, the principle that they reflect equally applies to consequences which exercise of that freedom may have on the level of social security contributions that a given economic operator may be entitled to. See, by analogy, judgments in *Hervein and Others*, C-393/99 and C-394/99, EU:C:2002:182, para. 51; and *Pöpperl*, C-187/15, EU:C:2016:550, para. 24 (which concerned the impact of the exercise by a worker of his right to free movement in terms of social protection).

the Member States' capacity to finance their welfare policies, in particular those offering the highest levels of social protection to citizens.

That case law also calls into question the existence of a natural tension between the free and competitive internal market, on the one hand, and the EU social pillar, on the other. It suggests rather that the 'purely' economic and social dimensions of the internal market are both indispensable to achieving the highly competitive social market economy envisaged in Article 3(3) TEU. Social and fiscal fairness are not collateral interests to be taken into account, but instead constitute essential 'ingredients' for ensuring that the internal market effectively contributes to the well-being of the Union's peoples and thus serves the overall objectives which Article 3 TEU assigns to the Union. That fairness is, in that sense, an essential condition for the trust which citizens place in the Union.

The Court's role in promoting a 'fairer' internal market is not unlimited. The challenges arising in relation to taxation, social security, fiscal transfers, and multi-level fiscal and social governance within the EU must be addressed by taking due account of structural and substantive principles governing its action, including the distribution of competences, subsidiarity, proportionality, institutional balance and fundamental rights guaranteed by the Charter. The various illustrations examined in the third section reflect the Court's key responsibility in reconciling the pivotal objective of enhancing fairness in the internal market, and thus fostering the value of solidarity laid down in Article 2 TEU, within the Union's wider constitutional framework.

For the Sake of Appearances: Rethinking the Principle of Impartiality

William Lindsay-Poulsen

1 Introduction

Many will remember the light comedy series "*Keeping Up Appearances*", which aired on the BBC in the early 1990s. The series revolved around a very British phenomenon: class distinction. Many—myself included—were at the same time bemused and in slight disbelief the first time we saw and heard the show's reluctant protagonist, Hyacinth Bucket, and the way in which she introduced herself, insisting on pronouncing her surname as "Bouquet" (BOO-KAY), and also how she vehemently attempted to keep herself at a good distance from her relatives out of fear of being associated with them and their social station.[1]

Hyacinth attempted to paint a prettier picture than the reality of her social and family status might have warranted. In what follows, I wish to focus on the reverse situation, namely where a given set of circumstances does not paint a pretty picture but rather a dire one. However, as the saying goes, appearances are deceiving, and books should not be judged by their cover.

I am grateful to P. Pohjankoski and M-L. Lindsay-Poulsen for taking time to provide valuable feedback.

[1] The series also aired in Denmark, where it was given the title "*Fint skal det være*", which apparently comes from the saying, "*Fint skal det være, men skidt og forbandet er det*" ("It ought to be classy, but actually it's rubbish and bothersome").

W. Lindsay-Poulsen (✉)
Copenhagen City Court, Copenhagen, Denmark
e-mail: WLP@domstol.dk

L. Prete, L. Rezki (eds.), *Judging & (Re)Thinking European Union Law*,
https://doi.org/10.1007/978-3-032-13473-8_32

The focus of my contribution to this *Liber Amicorum* is a State aid case which, although not the subject of much comment,[2] is rather interesting—to me at least! The case in point, *Danske Slagtermestre*,[3] was dealt with by the General Court in a chamber of three judges and turned, in its most interesting part, on a point of administrative law of general importance to the proper functioning of the rule of law.[4] In that case, the General Court considered that a European commissioner, who shall remain anonymous (henceforth called "Commissioner X"), ought to have recused herself when dealing with a State aid case hailing from her Member State of origin, Denmark—which also happens to be my home Member State.

Another reason why I find that judgment interesting is that even if it concerns the actions of an administrative decision-making body—namely the European Commission—the principle of impartiality is evidently also of great importance to the European judiciary. The judgment, therefore, has triggered certain personal reflections on the duty of impartiality as a judge. Before sharing them, I shall provide an outline of the duty of impartiality, before moving on to the case which caught my attention.

2 On the Principle of Impartiality

The principle of impartiality is clearly not the result of new legal thinking—in that respect, it is no surprise that the recipient of this *Liber Amicorum* has also had the opportunity to provide certain reflections on that principle.[5] It is claimed that the principle of impartiality can trace its roots back to the ancient Latin maxim, *nemo iudex in causa sua*, that is to say, no one should act as a judge in a case in which they have a personal (vested) interest. In EU administrative law, that principle is now enshrined in Article 41(1) of the Charter of Fundamental Rights ('Charter'), which provides that "[e]very person has the right to have his or her affairs handled *impartially*, fairly and within a reasonable time by the institutions, bodies, offices and agencies of the Union" (emphasis added).

It is commonly said that the principle of impartiality has a two-fold purpose: *first*, it ensures that decisions adopted are legally sound. *Second*, it helps the public at large retain confidence in the decisions taken by the courts and administrations.

---

[2] See, however, S. Thomas, 'Taking the principle of impartiality seriously in State aid procedures (Case T-486/18 RENV, *Danske Slagtermestre v Commission*)', EU Law Live, 19 April 2024.

[3] Judgment in *Danske Slagtermestre v Commission*, T-486/18 RENV, EU:T:2024:217.

[4] It is also not without interest to note that among the judges hearing the case was a former President of the European Court of Human Rights ('ECtHR') (currently Advocate General at the Court of Justice).

[5] See the Opinion of Advocate General Wahl in *Torresi and Torresi*, C-58/13 and C-59/13, EU:C:2014:265.

In particular, the ECtHR has, when interpreting Article 6(1) of the European Convention on Human Rights ('ECHR') as applicable to judicial proceedings and the judges presiding over them, stated that the principle of impartiality encompasses, on the one hand, a *subjective test*, where regard must be had to the personal conviction and behaviour of a particular judge, that is, whether the judge held any personal prejudice or bias in a given case. Moreover, it also gives rise to an *objective test*, that is to say by ascertaining whether the tribunal itself and, among other aspects, its composition, offered sufficient guarantees to exclude any legitimate doubt in respect of its impartiality. It is, in particular, when dealing with the objective test that the ECtHR has (in-)famously stated that "*justice must not only be done, it must also be seen to be done*".[6]

Given the scope of Article 6(1) of the ECHR, according to which "*[i]n the determination of his civil rights and obligations or of any criminal charge against him, everyone is entitled to a fair and public hearing within a reasonable time by an independent and* impartial *tribunal established by law*" (emphasis added), focus has mainly been on whether a "tribunal" was sufficiently independent and impartial, rather than an administrative decision-making body. However, if an administrative decision-making body, which determines rights and obligations under the Convention, is shown to be biased, the ordinary courts (to whom Article 6(1) applies directly) must have the powers sufficient to "cure" the procedural irregularity and thus provide an effective remedy.[7]

In EU Law, the principle of impartiality is also well-known, although more likely originally an off shoot from principles of EU administrative law such as the duty of care (or diligence)[8] rather than developed from a pure human rights approach. The seminal judgment, C-269/90, *Technische Universität München*, thus stated that, "*where the Community institutions have ... a power of appraisal, respect for the rights guaranteed by the Community legal order in administrative procedures is of even more fundamental importance. Those guarantees include, in particular, the duty of the competent institution to examine carefully and* impartially *all the relevant aspects of the individual case, the right of the person concerned to make his views known and to have an adequately reasoned decision.*"[9]

In its later case-law, the Court of Justice, for its part, has followed closely in the footsteps of the ECtHR. In Case C-680/16 P, *August Wolff and Remedia v Commission*, it reasoned as follows:

> ...the need for impartiality, required of institutions and bodies in carrying out their missions, is intended to guarantee equality of treatment, which is at the heart of the European

---

[6] See, among many others, judgment in *Micallef v Malta*, CE:ECHR:2009:1015JUD001705606, §98.

[7] Cf. judgments in *Kingsley v United Kingdom*, CE:ECHR:2002:0528JUD003560597, and *Tsfayo v United Kingdom*, CE:ECHR:2006:1114JUD006086000.

[8] On that principle, see, e.g., P. Craig, *EU Administrative Law*, 2nd ed., Oxford University Press, 2012, pp. 333–334.

[9] Judgment in *Technische Universität München*, C-269/90, EU:C:1991:438, para. 14 (emphasis added). This judgment is also mentioned in the official explanations relating to Article 41(1) of the Charter (OJ 2007 C 303, p. 28).

> Union. That requirement is intended, inter alia, to avoid a situation where there could be a conflict of interest on the part of officials or agents acting on behalf of those institutions and bodies. Having regard to the fundamental importance of ensuring the independence and probity of EU institutions and bodies as regards both their internal functioning and external reputation, the requirement of impartiality covers all circumstances in which an official or agent who is called upon to decide on an issue must reasonably consider that issue as being of such a nature as to be viewed by third parties as a possible source of impairment of his or her independence in that matter …
>
> Thus, it is incumbent upon those institutions and bodies to comply with both components of the requirement of impartiality, which are, on the one hand, subjective impartiality, by virtue of which no member of the institution concerned may show bias or personal prejudice and, on the other, objective impartiality, under which there must be sufficient guarantees to exclude any legitimate doubt as to possible bias on the part of the institution concerned …
>
> As regards, more particularly, the second component of the principle of impartiality, it should be made clear that, where a number of EU institutions or bodies are given separate responsibilities of their own in the context of a procedure that is liable to result in a decision adversely affecting a party, each of those institutions and bodies is required, in respect of its own activities, to comply with the requirement of objective impartiality. Consequently, even where only one of them has breached that requirement, such a breach is liable to render the decision adopted by the other at the end of the procedure at issue unlawful.[10]

Still, it is not devoid of interest to note, however, that according to the Court of Justice, not every legitimate doubt as to the impartiality of a particular official gives rise to a breach of the principle of impartiality. That finding requires quite readily an individual analysis and assessment. Thus, in Case C-615/19 P, *Dalli v Commission*, the Court of Justice held:

> In view of the role assigned to the [OLAF] Supervisory Committee, the fact that one of its members has been directly involved in carrying out an OLAF investigative activity is admittedly of such a nature as to give rise to legitimate doubt as to the existence of any prejudice, positive or negative, on his part, in the exercise of his supervisory functions within the committee, as to the conditions under which the investigative activity in question was carried out.
>
> Nevertheless, although the objective impartiality of a member of the [OLAF] Supervisory Committee could thus be called into question in the exercise of the supervisory functions that he or she exercises in that capacity, the fact that that person may subsequently be called upon to exercise such supervision cannot, however, give rise to a legitimate doubt as to his or her impartiality when participating in an investigative activity.
>
> Therefore, although the lack of objective impartiality raised by Mr Dalli could, where appropriate, be invoked with regard to the [OLAF] Supervisory Committee's opinion on the OLAF investigation, it is not capable of calling into question compliance with the principle of impartiality in the context of that investigation and, in particular, during the hearing in which a member of that committee took part.[11]

Obviously, the principle of impartiality is a multi-faceted concept which merits further exploration—such as whether the duties of independence and impartiality apply in the same fashion to both the judiciary and to administrative

---

[10] Judgment in *August Wolff and Remedia v Commission*, C-680/16 P, EU:C:2019:257, paras 26–28.

[11] Judgment in *Dalli v Commission*, C-615/19 P, EU:C:2021:133, paras 121–123.

decision-making bodies.[12] Moreover, it is clear that EU law has its own distinct voice in this matter, with the right to unbiased administration being set out directly in Article 41(1) of the Charter, whereas that right is only indirectly regulated under Article 6(1) of the ECHR. However, the purpose of this contribution to the *Liber Amicorum* is not to fall down legal rabbit holes, but to provide certain *ad hoc* reflections to a recent decision of the General Court. I shall come to those promptly after introducing the case giving rise thereto.

3 Outline of Case T-486/18 RENV, *Danske Slagtermestre v Commission*

Reading someone else's case digest can be a loathsome affair, so I shall keep the facts as brief as possible, contributing however with bits of local knowledge which hopefully may be of use. Avid readers are, however, advised to read the judgment itself, for which there is no authentic substitute (nor indeed a press release).

3.1 Background to the Dispute

In the political programme for the Thorning Schmidt Government in February 2013,[13] the Danish government set out its intention to submit to the Danish Parliament (*Folketing*) a bill reforming the charges for waste water management applicable to large undertakings. According to the government's political programme, undertakings with large water usage paid more for the drainage of waste water than the actual costs. All things being equal, the government asserted, small undertakings paid less than the actual costs. The government therefore proposed to reduce the waste water charges applicable to heavy water users, including large undertakings exposed to competition, by 700 million Danish kroner annually (approx. 94 million euro annually) over a five year period. It was further asserted that the reform would provide greater cohesion between the costs of waste water management and user payment. The relief provided to the large water-consuming undertakings would also provide a reduction in their costs and support their ability to compete.

On 28 May 2013, the acting Minister for the Environment therefore submitted a bill to the *Folketing* setting out the reform of the rules on waste water charges.

[12] For instance, in Denmark, the rules applicable, although similar, are not the same. See Sections 60–61 of the Danish Administration of Justice Act, which applies to judicial officers, and Section 3 of the Public Administration Act, which applies to administrative staff.

[13] Vækstplan DK, February 2013. Available on line (last accessed on 29 December 2024).

According to the *travaux préparatoires*,[14] the legislative proposal did not contain any aspects pertaining to EU law. During the legislative process, after concerns raised by the Association of Danish Butchers (*Danske Slagtermestre*), the minister subsequently stated that the bill had been submitted to the government's State aid committee (*regeringens statsstøtteudvalg*) for consideration, and the minister affirmed that the bill was compliant with EU State aid rules.[15] Still, compliance with those rules did trigger the adoption of a minor amendment to the bill relating to dual use properties.[16] The bill was not notified to the Commission under State aid rules and was passed into law as Act No. 902 of 4 July 2013 ("Act No. 902/2013").

Around that time, Commissioner X was a member of the Danish cabinet, being the Deputy Prime Minister and Minister for the Economy and the Interior. She was the leader of her political party, a party that was one of the junior members of the coalition government. In that capacity, she was a member of one of the key standing cabinet committees (in Danish "*K-udvalget*", short for "*Koordinationsudvalget*"; other standing committees of the cabinet also exist), which ensures the coordination of policy between the various departments and political parties and is presided over by the prime minister. That aspect is of particular importance to coalition governments (which are very frequent in Denmark).

The rules which govern the functioning of standing cabinet committees in Denmark are unwritten and have mainly evolved out of custom and practice. Those "rules" may thus be subject to variation depending on the government in question and the recollections of senior civil servants. Typically, however, participation in a select committee is restricted to ministers—either as permanent members or as *ad hoc* members invited to the discussions—flanked by their permanent secretaries. Ministers will present for discussion political initiatives or matters falling within their field of responsibility, and other ministers may comment on the items discussed. Inherently, the committee's decision-making is of a consensual nature, gravitating around the signals emitted by the committee chair (typically the prime minister). If a measure is not rejected outright or sent back to the drawing-board for further reflection and adjustment, it receives government mandate and thus becomes applicable government policy at the internal level.

Reverting back to the facts of the dispute, following the adoption of Act No. 902/2013, on 26 September 2013, the Association of Danish Butchers lodged a complaint with the Commission concerning the reform of the waste water charges.

On 31 August 2014, the Danish Prime Minister announced that the deputy Prime Minister and Minister for the Economy and the Interior would be nominated to become European commissioner, which she became on 1 November 2014.

Following several rounds of administrative dialogue between the Commission and the Danish authorities from 26 February 2014 to 12 September 2017, the

[14] Bill No. L 222 of 28 May 2013, Folketingstidende 2012 (1. Saml.), at point 7.

[15] See the minister's answer to Question No. 20 of the Standing Committee for the Environment.

[16] See the Standing Committee Report of 20 June 2013 on Bill No. L 222.

Commission finally adopted, on 19 April 2018, its decision in the State aid matter.[17] In its decision, the Commission concluded that the charges introduced by Act No. 902/2013 did not confer an advantage to certain undertakings and therefore did not constitute State aid within the meaning of Article 107(1) of the Treaty on the Functioning of the European Union. The decision was signed by Commissioner X, who was the commissioner in charge of competition.

3.2 Proceedings Before the EU Courts

An action for annulment was brought by the Association of Danish Butchers before the General Court. Denmark intervened in support of the Commission's plea to dismiss the application as inadmissible.

By order of 1 December 2020, the General Court, sitting in a chamber of three judges, dismissed the case as inadmissible, at it considered that the applicant did not have standing to bring an action for annulment against the measure at issue.[18]

On appeal, the Court of Justice, sitting in a chamber of five judges and following the delivery of a concurrent opinion by the Advocate General, in its judgment of 30 June 2022 set aside the order of the General Court. The Court of Justice considered, *inter alia*, that the General Court had erred in law as to whether the applicant had standing to challenge the Commission decision.[19]

On referral back to the General Court, Denmark intervened in support of the Commission's plea to dismiss the action as ill-founded. Following a hearing held on 26 September 2023, the General Court delivered its judgment on 10 April 2024, whereby it upheld the applicant's line of argument according to which the contested decision was adopted in breach of the duty of impartiality. Consequently, the General Court quashed the contested decision.[20]

In its judgment, the General Court noted that it was the Minister for the Environment, and not Commissioner X in her previous capacity as a member of the Danish cabinet, who was responsible for the submission of the bill before the *Folketing*. However, the General Court also noted that Commissioner X was, at the time, Minister for the Economy and the Interior, Deputy Prime Minister and member of the standing cabinet committee on coordination (*Koordinationsudvalget*). The General Court inferred from this that she had a "particularly important role in the Danish government".[21]

---

[17] Case State aid SA.37433 (2017/FC) – Denmark – Alleged State aid through discounts on waste water charges, C(2018) 2259 final.

[18] Order in *Danske Slagtermestre v Commission*, T-486/18, EU:T:2020:576.

[19] Judgment in *Danske Slagtermestre v Commission*, C-99/21 P, EU:C:2022:510.

[20] The General Court also held that the Commission infringed the market economy investor principle when assessing whether the waste water reform conferred an advantage, but that aspect will not be explored further.

[21] Para. 33 of the judgment.

The General Court then went on to assert that, as the reform of the waste water charges contained measures which could affect the costs applicable to private individuals and undertakings, it was "fair to assume" that such measures could only be proposed with the consent of the minister in charge of the economy, that is to say, Commissioner X (at the time). The General Court also noted that the Act was included in the Government political programme "*Vækstplan DK*".[22]

Finally, the General Court referred to a press article, according to which on 26 February 2013, Commissioner X had participated in a press conference alongside the Prime Minister, the Minister for Finances and the Minister for Taxation announcing the aforementioned political programme "*Vækstplan DK*", during which Commissioner X was reputed to have stated that "*the Government [sent] a very clear message to undertakings*", that it "*[would] not impose the trade and industry new general increases in taxes and duties*", and moreover that "*[besides] corporate tax relief [...] there would be number of reductions in duties, including [...] lower charges on waste water*". The General Court thus concluded that Commissioner X had publicly and explicitly stated her position in favour of lower contribution to waste water management. The General Court therefore held that it was "reasonable to assume" that Commissioner X had an interest in ensuring that Act No. 902/2013 and the reform of the waste water management rules was not called into question by State aid rules.[23]

The General Court then went on to consider whether the Commission's decision-making procedure contained sufficient guarantees to rule out that Commissioner X's own interest rendered that procedure flawed. The General Court held, in particular, that although, under Article 250 of the Treaty on the Functioning of the European Union, the Commission shall act by a majority of its members, and that Commissioner X therefore did not have a casting vote in the adoption of the contested decision, Commissioner X, as commissioner in charge of competition, was nevertheless responsible for the preparation of the contested decision, an important part of the decision which the Commission finally takes. The General Court also referred to the fact that only Commissioner X signed the contested decision, and what this could signify from an outsider's perspective.[24]

The General Court held that, from the point of view of appearances, such a situation could create reasonable doubt in the mind of a third party as to Commissioner X's possible bias, irrespective of her conduct. It therefore concluded that the Commission's decision-making procedure did not contain sufficient guarantees relating to "objective impartiality".[25]

At the time of writing, no notice of appeal has been published, and it can therefore safely be assumed that the judgment of the General Court is final. It follows therefore that the Commission must draw all the necessary consequences to comply

[22] Para. 34 of the judgment.

[23] Paras 35–37 of the judgment.

[24] Paras 39–42 of the judgment.

[25] Para. 44 of the judgment.

with the judgment in accordance with Article 266 of the Treaty on the Functioning of the European Union.

4 Reflections on the Judgment and the Principle of Impartiality

From the outset, I wish to make clear that it is not for me to be an "arbiter of judgments", commenting on whether this judgment or that is "good" or "bad"—I leave that to more professional commentators. The judgment has not been appealed, which in one sense puts an end to the discussion.

However, it is fair to reflect on the judgment and its implications for the principle of impartiality. It would, moreover, make for a poor contribution to this particular *Liber Amicorum* and, in particular, its recipient to be overly diplomatic!

The judgment of the General Court in *Danske Slagtermestre* on referral back from the Court of Justice, is, in my view, defendable.[26] On its face, it seems to embrace whole-heartedly the adage that "*justice must be not only be done, it must also be seen to be done*"—also known as the "appearance aspect"—at least in the context of EU administrative law. Clearly that is a tenable position to take, but it is also not the only position which may validly be affirmed.

That maxim, "*justice must be not only be done, it must also be seen to be done*", while in and of itself aspirational and perhaps grandiose, is also lofty and rather "fluffy". Appearances belong to the realm of illusions, and over-emphasising their importance amounts to living in a "make-believe" world. From my own experience, the "appearance aspect" gives rise, on a day-to-day basis, to a certain amount of hesitation for judges and other decision-makers to whom the duty of impartiality applies. It may even lead to recusal "just to be on the safe side", even though there might not be a legal obligation to do so.[27] That, in turn, can lead to justice being delayed—and thus denied—and a waste of public money. Evidently, the proper balance must be struck.

The judgment of the General Court also gives rise to certain practical difficulties: it may make it more difficult for politicians who are interested in branching out to European politics to do so. It promotes the fostering of poorly known technocrats as commissioners rather than politicians with a popular mandate who have already demonstrated political experience. That is not necessarily ideal if European politics

[26] Professor of administrative law at Ålborg University, S. Bønsing, reacting on the judgment, is quoted as having stated, "*it is a very particular situation, because I have never heard that the EU Court has declared a commissioner as lacking impartiality before. But it is clear that it had been better had she left the handling of that case to another commissioner from the beginning*" (own translation). In Politiken, Wednesday 17 April 2024.

[27] This aspect has, in a Nordic perspective, already been addressed by the former president of the Danish Supreme Court B. Dahl, "*Dommerinhabilitet – strikte jura og fornuftig forsigtighed*", in *Festskrift til Mads Bryde Andersen*, 2018, DJØF Publishing, p. 163.

are to resemble domestic politics more closely. Moreover, when it comes to smaller Member States in particular (or Member States where governments act as a collective), the pool of potential candidates who might both be viable as national ministers and as European commissioners may be quite small. A rigid application of the "appearance aspect" may, therefore, be of particular disadvantage to those Member States.

On a more critical note of the General Court's reasoning, the judgment in my view misunderstands the role that Commissioner X played in the Thorning Schmidt government, at least as regards the impugned measure. At the time that measure was proposed in Denmark, the government consisted of a tripartite coalition, and the Minister for the Environment—whose portfolio the measure belonged to—was a member of the *other* junior government party (the Socialist People's Party) and was therefore neither a Social Democrat nor a member of the Social Liberal Party. Moreover, in my view, the General Court erred when holding that it was "fair to assume" that the waste water reform could only be proposed with Commissioner X's consent in her capacity as Minister for the Economy—that is a misunderstanding of the role of the Danish Minister for the Economy. Such a statement might, at most, be true had she been Minister for Finance or Minister for Taxation (traditionally in charge of public spending and of generating income respectively).

To my mind, and leaving her statements made at the press conference mentally to one side, there is nothing to suggest that Commissioner X had the role or say in the matter of the adoption of the waste water reform which the General Court attributes to her.

Evidently, in hindsight, the statements made at the press conference are unfortunate and can be taken as evidence of a "smoking gun". It is, however, also the only element which arguably does point to the presence of some bias. Be that as it may, they were the only statements that Commissioner X was reported to have made on the issue, they were fairly nondescript, seemingly more a show of support of the government's overall policy ideas, and they were given more than five years before the contested decision was adopted.

What is more, there is, bluntly put, no clear evidence to support the idea that Commissioner X stood to gain anything from approving the measure in question as commissioner. To hold such a view clearly overestimates Commissioner X's influence in domestic Danish politics once she had taken up office in the *Berlaymont*.[28] As a matter of domestic policy, she became a "lame duck" the very day the Prime Minister announced her nomination to the position. The fact that she, in her capacity as minister, supported a proposed measure, does not mean that one can take it for granted that she would also be sympathetic towards that measure as commissioner. In fact, given the change in government in Denmark on 28 June 2015 from a centre-left to a centre-right government, there was no real need for Commissioner X to show political fidelity towards the Danish government. In fact, from an institutional point of view, it is disheartening that no part of the judgment—neither the argu-

[28] The saying, *"In Brussels, no one can hear you scream"*, was not coined out of coincidence.

ments of the parties or the assessment of the General Court—makes reference to the fact that as a European commissioner, Commissioner X was under an *obligation* to act independently of the Danish government and her former role as Danish minister.[29] In that sense, the judgment can be interpreted as meaning that Commissioner X—wilfully or not—breached her treaty obligations.

As to the issue of safeguards, the General Court emphasised the role of Commissioner X in the preparation of the decision. However, again this does not paint an adequate picture of the factual circumstances. The Commission's decision-making process commenced on 26 September 2013 with the lodging of the complaint, and several initial steps were taken after that.[30] Crucially, Commissioner X did not become commissioner in charge of competition before 31 August 2014. It is therefore clear that Commissioner X was not and could not be involved in the initial preparation of the case. The General Court, in merely stating that she was "responsible for the preparation of the contested decision in preparing the case", does not mention that fact. It is not entirely inconceivable that the preliminary assessment taken by DG Competition might just have had the same essential outcome as the final decision.[31]

Last but not least, when referring to how things might be perceived by a third party, as the General Court did, it is wise to exercise caution and restraint. That is especially the case where the court deciding on whether the duty of impartiality has been breached is remotely situated from the factual and legal circumstances applicable to the case brought before it and risks censuring local traditions and sensibilities. Indeed, one cannot but wonder whether the General Court was well-placed to undertake—in a chamber of three—a, perhaps inevitably, speculative assessment, given the different political cultures in a Union currently comprised of 27 Member States, as to the political leverage which a particular commissioner may or may not have wielded in a "previous life" as member of a national government. I am not necessarily convinced that the "appearance argument" must be assessed under an approach essentially consisting of "one size fits all".

Moreover, what lies in the "perception" of a third party? That is, at the very least, an arbitrary assessment and therefore not objective—even though, ironically, it is tied to the criterion of "objective independence". On that point, both the ECtHR and the Court of Justice have stressed that only *legitimate* doubts as concerns impartiality are relevant, implying some sort of lower threshold. The General Court,

[29] I would call to mind that the independence of the European Commission and its commissioners is a matter of primary EU law: see Article 17(3) TEU and Article 245 TFEU.

[30] On 26 February 2014, the Commission services forwarded the complaint to and requested some information from the Danish authorities. By letter of 26 May 2014, the Danish authorities submitted information to the Commission. On 23 July 2014, the Commission services sent a preliminary assessment letter to the complainant. See Case State aid SA.37433 (2017/FC) – Denmark – Alleged State aid through discounts on waste water charges, C(2018) 2259 final, at paragraph 2.

[31] Admittedly, one would have expected the Commission legal service to raise this argument, at least at the hearing. However, it transpires from [41] of the judgment that the Commission representative rather stated at the hearing that Commissioner X had the "overall responsibility for the preparation of the judgment".

however, does not devote much ink to that aspect, and the judgment, in the way it was drafted, seems set on making it somehow appear obvious that an external third party would be appalled at the manifest bias. However, regardless of the specific insight available to the Association of Danish Butchers and its own motives for bringing the action, in the terms used by the General Court, it is "fair to assume"—for this commentator at least—that the public at large in 2018 would have had little to no recollection of any statements made by Commissioner X in 2013 at a press conference or her subsequent involvement in the Commission's handling of the waste water reform, and that only few persons would have made some sort of link between the two.

Be that as it may, I would still tend to consider that, even from a more restrained use of the "appearance aspect", the fact that Commissioner X did make those particular statements during the press conference in 2013 ought, as a matter of propriety, to have led her to ask a colleague to take over that *dossier*, rather than signing the decision in her own name on behalf of the Commission. Even if she might not have remembered having made those declarations in the first place, it would have been fairly easy for her to "bow out" before the decision was taken—not least from the point of view of good administration. That might be more a question of common sense rather than perceptions or appearances at law, though admittedly the lines can be blurred. Ultimately however, I am unwilling to criticise the General Court for reaching the result it did, only perhaps (some of) the reasoning leading it there.

But my thoughts on these matters do not stop there quite yet—what kind of contribution would this be otherwise!

Learned readers will know that, following a long-held practice (or custom?) of the Court of Justice, a reporting judge must not hold the same nationality as the Member State from which a request for a preliminary ruling originates. The same practice applies to a designated advocate general. The "appearance aspect", which concerns not only impartiality but also independence—those two concepts after all being intertwined—may lie at the root of that practice. However, it is of interest to this piece that that practice does not exclude a judge of the same nationality as the Member State from which a request for a preliminary ruling originates from hearing that request as assessor judge. Even more interesting is the fact that, on occasion, it does happen that the practice of the Court of Justice is, for reasons unknown, not observed,[32] without that calling into question the validity of the procedure before the

[32] See, e.g., judgments in *Société Technique Minière*, C-56/65, EU:C:1966:38; and *Colditz*, C-9/67, EU:C:1967:30, where judge Lecourt was reporting judge in both cases referred by French courts, and judgments in *Steenhorst-Neerings*, C-338/91, EU:C:1993:857; and *Van Gemert-Derks*, Case C-337/91, EU:C:1993:856, in which cases hailing from the Netherlands judge Kapteyn was reporting judge. As for Advocates General, see, e.g., Opinions in *Boehringer Ingelheim and Others*, C-348/04, EU:C:2006:235; *Intel Corporation*, Case C-252/07, EU:C:2008:370; *J D Wetherspoon*, C-302/07, EU:C:2008:644; and *East Sussex County Council*, C-71/14, EU:C:2015:234, all cases referred by British courts in which Advocate General Sharpston issued an Opinion. Other examples include the Opinions in *Ikegami*, C-467/03, EU:C:2005:182; *Collée*, C-146/05, EU:C:2007:12; and *Turbon international*, C-250/05, EU:C:2006:384, where Advocate General Kokott gave her Opinion in cases referred by German courts; and the Opinion in *Roda Golf & Beach Resort*,

Court of Justice.[33] From this it could be inferred that the practice is "nice to have", not "need to have".

Moreover, even if that practice might originally have been intended to protect the independence of a Member of the Court of Justice of the European Union from political pressure from the government that appointed that Member—many Members having served their Member State in some political capacity—it is of little use when considering whether that Member of the Court of Justice of the European Union might in fact be biased, as this can only be determined following an individual examination of the circumstances, in line with Article 4(2) of the Code of Conduct for Members and former Members of the Court of Justice of the European Union.[34] To me, that underlines the idea that a broad understanding of the "appearance aspect" works better with the notion of formal independence (or independence "*stricto sensu*"), whereas impartiality—or lack thereof—is best ascertained individually on a case-by-case basis, without the need for far-reaching inferences. Admittedly though, relevant case-law does not always distinguish to a satisfactory degree between the two prongs, presumably because of their mutual interdependence.[35]

Evidently there are good reasons why judges and decision-makers must be impartial, but first and foremost there is a need for them to be independent.[36] Judges and decision-makers come in all shapes and sizes with varying views on different issues, which they invariably bring to the adjudication table. Particularly when it comes to judges, that may be part of the reason why they were appointed in the first place. That means that a complete lack of bias is probably—humanly—impossible. Without wanting to downplay the idea that lack of bias does contribute to the appearance of independence, clearly it is structural and economic separation (independence "*stricto sensu*") that is of primary importance when considering whether a judge or decision-maker is sufficiently divorced from governments and/or "special

---

C-14/08, EU:C:2009:134, a case hailing from Spain in which Advocate General Ruiz-Jarabo Colomer issued an Opinion. This list is in no way exhaustive.

[33] Under the rules applicable to the ECtHR, the judge elected in respect of the Contracting Party concerned is an *ex officio* member of the Grand Chamber. See the Rules of Court (March 2024), rule 24(2)(b).

[34] OJ 2021 C 397, p. 1.

[35] Compare, in that regard, with ECtHR, judgments in *Campbell and Fell v United Kingdom*, CE:ECHR:1992:0325JUD001359088, §§81 and 85; and *Tsfayo v United Kingdom*, *supra*, §§40 and 47, regarding the lack of structural independence of the Hammersmith and Fulham Council Housing Benefit and Council Tax Benefit Review Board, which the subsequent judicial review proceedings did not cure. See also in particular ECtHR, judgment in *Kingsley v United Kingdom*, *supra*, §§ 34 and 41–43, which by using terms such as "objective impartiality", "apparent (objective) bias", "real (subjective) bias" and "objective or structural independence and impartiality", seems to blur all the concepts together.

[36] The Court of Justice has thus held that "*[t]he concept of independence, which is inherent in the task of adjudication, involves primarily an authority acting as a third party in relation to the authority which adopted the contested decision*", see judgment in *Wilson*, C-506/04, EU:C:2006:587, para. 4 and the cases cited. For a recent contribution on this matter, see Opinion of Advocate General Emiliou in Gekus, C-748/23, points 62–65.

interests". I therefore do not fear that a pragmatic stance regarding the principle of impartiality, based on reasonableness, might foster the rise of a new "Polish judges"-situation.

I surmise that some will already be in agreement with me on this proposition, and hope that in time, others might be too.[37]

5 Conclusion

In "*Keeping Up Appeances*", Hyacinth Bucket, the protagonist, brought ridicule unto herself with her eccentric and snobbish airs of grandeur, being terrified that her true background might be revealed. A similar tale can be told in *Danske Slagtermestre*: the General Court valiantly uncovered the dark motives of Commissioner X. However, it can also be argued that the General Court simply raised the bar as to the appearance of impartiality without much thought given to the consequences thereof, and that commissioners henceforth must be more aware of fleeting statements made several years ago in their former incarnations as national politicians, irrespective of whether those statements fell within their portfolio. The General Court's decision has become final, and since the Commission in any event was set for a reshuffle, the decision not to lodge an appeal with the Court of Justice was presumably a "no-brainer". The Commission will have to take a new decision under a newly appointed commissioner, thus solving part of the problem in the specific case, but seemingly leaving the greater issue unresolved.

The saying, "*justice must not only be done, it must also be seen to be done*", ambitious as it is, is notoriously unwieldly. As others have stated many years before me, "*regard for the 'appearance of independence' is often overemphasised and gives rise to problems and practical difficulties of demarcation.*"[38] An overly cautious or rigid stance as to the requirement of impartiality, mainly based on appearances and perceptions, is unnecessary and does not grant greater independence from those who wish to exert undue influence. It can, at worst, lead to justice being delayed—and thus denied—and a waste of public money. Some have even argued that it can have a chilling effect: namely to impair the effective functioning of courts and decision-making bodies and thus, in the long term, their reputation and

[37] I observe that, at para. 29 of his Opinion in *Torresi, supra*, Advocate General Wahl stated that "*I am not convinced that … the criterion of independence … has developed — or, in any event, should develop — in the direction of greater stringency.*" Moreover, at para. 50 of the Opinion, he went on to state that, "*I am not suggesting that the Court should adopt a lax attitude towards the criterion of independence (or, for that matter, towards any other criterion)*", and furthermore, at para. 52, "*I do, however, warn against treating* Wilson *as a precedent which, by grafting an innovation on to previous case-law, would now impose on the Court an in-depth analysis of all the possible grounds which might give rise to some suspicion about the impartiality (or the independence* stricto sensu*) of the referring body.*"

[38] See O. Bisgaard, "*Dommeres inhabilitet*", in *Ugeskrift for Retsvæsen* [1998], section B, p. 360.

integrity.[39] This contribution is therefore a humble plea for a pragmatic stance based on reasonableness when considering the question of impartiality. Ultimately, it is for the Court of Justice and/or the ECtHR, rather than the General Court, to provide proper guidance on how to tackle the "appearance aspect" as it applies to the duty of impartiality.

[39] See E. Smith, "*Habilitetshysteriet*", in *Ugeskrift for Retsvæsen* [1998], section B, p. 375. After the submission of this article to editorial review, the Danish Supreme Court has, in a judgment of 24 June 2025 in case 90/2024, published in *Ugeskrift for Retsvæsen* [2025] p. 3710, issued a decision of relevance to this article, in which the Supreme Court has considered that a judge presiding over criminal proceedings against an accused individual ought to have recused herself, owing to the fact that a civil action for damages had been brought by the accused individual's mother against the judge's sister before the court in which that judge held office (for context: the largest first-tier court of Denmark with over 40 judges). On final appeal against the criminal conviction to the Supreme Court, the judge concerned gave evidence that she had had no knowledge of the prior civil action brought against her sister when issuing her decision. Even though the Supreme Court was satisfied that no actial bias had motivated the conviction of the accused individual, four out of five Supreme Court Justices voted in favour of overturning the appealed judgments for breach of the "appearance aspect" of the principle of impartiality and, more specifically, considerations relating to public confidence in the judiciary. The consequences of that judgment, which may potentially be far-reaching, remain to be analysed by the Danish Court Administration Service.

EU's Technical Standards and Rule of Law

Björn Lundqvist

1 Introduction

Part of my research activities has been dedicated to technical standard-setting and specifically the issue whether technical standards set and published by private standard-setting organisations (SSOs) and referred to in European regulations, directives or in European Union (EU) law generally should be regarded as 'law', that *inter alia* must be accessible to the public. Or, could these standards still be private goods, licensed for royalties and, indeed, only accessible to a few? Interestingly, Judge Nils Wahl has together with his colleagues at the Court of Justice of the European Union (CJEU) provided parts of the answer to this question.

The stated issue might—at a first glance—be regarded as rather unimportant, but it is a substantial legal issue for several reasons. Firstly, it triggers fundamental values in reference to EU Constitutional law, in reference to how we view what "law" is and how law should be treated under the notion of rule of law. Secondly, the method of creating laws by referring to standards have risen in popularity with the legislator, and the legislator now not only utilize the method for technical issues, the method is also used for creating technical-behavioural rules based on the evaluation of ethical matters and values.[1] A recent example being how rules for trustworthy and human centric AI should be developed under the recently enacted AI Act. Finally,

[1] See for example IEEE standards for AI Ethics and Governance Standards (avaiable on IEEE Xplorer website).

B. Lundqvist (✉)
Stockholm University, Stockholm, Sweden
e-mail: Bjorn.Lundqvist@juridicum.su.se

L. Prete, L. Rezki (eds.), *Judging & (Re)Thinking European Union Law*,
https://doi.org/10.1007/978-3-032-13473-8_33

the industries now encompassed by rule-making through standard-setting are valued to billions and billions of Euro, much more than ever expected when the so-called 'New Approach' from the 1980s. The New Approach being the a sui generis intertwined procedure where the European Commission plays a role, but where the technical standards are de facto drawn up through collaborative self-regulation by firms under the supervision of a European standard-setting body, was enacted.[2]

The standard-setting procedure described above has come under fire in the courts in recent years due mainly to two issues, firstly, whether, the European Commission has delegated legislative power to private standard-setting bodies in accordance with EU law and, second, whether the standard-setting bodies can claim copyright and charge royalties for accessing the material rules of a standard referred to by EU law.

Many in the standard-setting industry have awaited a definitive ruling on these issues because they will determine how popular and efficient the model will become; and the European courts have delivered several cases where they slowly but steadily map out the interface between constitutional principles about what constitutes EU law in reference to self-regulation of technical standards, and, where Judge Nils Wahl was part of the Grand Chamber, in the most recent case *Public.Resource.Org*.

The background in reference to the copyright issue is that some, but not all, SSOs charge firms or third persons to access and make use of the technical standards produced, as a way to finance their activities. Such charges are based on the copyright protection of said standards and may range in size depending on the SSO and the market penetration of the standards in question.[3] However, with legislators increasingly referring to standards in legal acts, the question is whether claiming copyright and charging for access to them remains feasible. If technical standards which are used to interpret or fill in norms contained in laws and regulations have to be regarded as law, then their contents should—according to several individuals in academia—fall in the public domain. According to several Member States' copyright regimes and general legal thinking, laws and regulations should be publicly accessible free of charge, since only free access complies with the basic standards of democracy, rule of law and transparency.[4] If technical standards are not to be

---

[2] The New Approach was firstly developed by the Council, but has been enacted through legislation, now primarily in Regulation 1025/2012 on European standardisation, amending Council Directives 89/686/EEC and 93/15/EEC and Directives 94/9/EC, 94/25/EC, 95/16/EC, 97/23/EC, 98/34/EC, 2004/22/EC, 2007/23/EC, 2009/23/EC and 2009/105/EC of the European Parliament and of the Council and repealing Council Decision 87/95/EEC and Decision No 1673/2006/EC of the European Parliament and of the Council.

[3] Whether SSOs charge monopoly prices is a somewhat disputed issue, cf. P. L. Strauss, 'Private Standards Organizations and Public Law' 22 Wm. & Mary Bill Rts. J. (2013) 497, 509 et seq. Compare E. S. Bremer 'On the Cost of Private Standards in Public Law' 63 Kan. L. Rev. (2015) 279, 317 et seq.

[4] See, generally, H-W. Micklitz, R. Van Gestel, 'European Integration Through Standardization: How Judicial Review is Breaking Down the Club House of Private Standardization Bodies' 50 CML Rev (2013), 145–181. Indeed, the issue of whether standards have copyright protection has been discussed in several high profile cases originating from EU Member State cases, and also in

regarded as law, but instead as products of private intellectual, creative production, access may come only at the cost of a licence or other price for the product of the standardisation effort.[5]

So, in these situations, can technical standards be copyright-protected? The question is perhaps even wider: Is the issue whether the standard-setting process is a legislative procedure creating laws, or, whether is it something else—a private procedure? And what consequences can this have, first for the CJEU's capacity to review and interpret standards and second for the copyright protection of standards for the benefit of the SSOs? These are the questions that the CJEU has been pondering in a string of cases the last years, and these are the questions that this article addresses.

First, the chapter provides a short general background to the EU system of creating European standards and the practice of referencing standards in legislative acts. Second, the legal and copyright-related problems connected to these standards are discussed. Various cases will be analysed. Lastly, I present my view on the New Approach, whether it is a legislative procedure, private procedure, or both, while concluding that here is perhaps a well-balanced solution where the positive effects of both private and public governance can be harnessed.

2 The Origins of the European System of Standards[6]

The New Approach originating from 1980s established the following principles for creating norms with the use of standards. Legislative harmonisation in the EU is limited to the "essential requirements" that products and services placed on the Community market must meet if they are to benefit from free movement within the Community. No detailed manufacturing specifications are included in the essential requirements and the degree of detail differs between the legislative acts. The technical specifications or the methods for testing the specifications in reference to the essential requirements are laid down in standards drafted and produced by organisations competent in standard-setting. In essence, the three large European standard setting organisations, CEN, CENELEC and ETSI are the competent organisations for standard-setting under the New Approach. Application of harmonised or other standards remains voluntary, and the manufacturer may apply other technical specifications to meet the requirements. However, products and services in compliance with harmonised standards benefit from a presumption of conformity with the

the US. See for example *Knooble*, The Hague District Court Decision of 31 Dec. 2008, LJN:BG8465; and DIN, BVerfGE, 29 July 1998, ZUM 1998, cited in Van Gestel and Micklitz, also making reference to a German Constitutional Court case from 1983.

[5] See, generally, Van Gestel, Micklitz, *op. cit.*, 145–181.

[6] For a lengthier presentation, cf. B. Lundqvist, *Standardization under EU Competition Rules and US Antitrust Laws: The Rise and Limits of Self-Regulation*, Edward Elgar Publishing, 2014, chapters 2 and 3.

corresponding essential requirements, and thus have the right to be freely circulated in the EU.[7] The connection to free movement rights and the inclusion of technical standards referred to in legislative acts for procurement procedures often create the effect that initially non-binding standards become de facto binding when transposed in the Member States. The New Approach was updated with a number of regulations in 2008 and 2012, but without the basic premises being altered, and is up for renewal in 2025.[8]

Other standards adopted outside the New Approach on the initiative of private firms or other stakeholders can also be referred to in EU legislative acts directly and this method of "direct legislation" has increased in popularity.[9]

It is the responsibility of the national members of European standard-setting organisations (ESOs) to implement European standards as national standards. The national standard-setting bodies (NSBs) distribute the implemented European standards for remuneration (license/sell), and generally claim copyright protection for the implemented standards. The NSBs thus claim that the representatives who participated in the technical committee or working group that prepared the standard are the authors of a collective copyright-protected work and that the NSBs have contractually obtained the exclusive and permanent right to utilise the so-called financial rights connected to said work.[10] Indeed, since most standards take the form of written documents, it is generally understood that they are considered copyrightable works of authorship and protected by copyright law, though this can be disputed.[11] Generally, under the Member States' Copyright regimes, there are exemptions from copyright for legal and administrative acts, while a narrower exemption can be found in the EU InfoSoc Directive.[12]

---

[7] EU Commission, 'Guide to the Implementation of Directives based on the New Approach and the Global Approach 2000' p. 27 et seq.

[8] The New Approach was firstly developed by the Council, but it has then been enacted through legislation, now primarily in Regulation 1025/2012 on European standardisation, amending Council Directives 89/686/EEC and 93/15/EEC and Directives 94/9/EC, 94/25/EC, 95/16/EC, 97/23/EC, 98/34/EC, 2004/22/EC, 2007/23/EC, 2009/23/EC and 2009/105/EC of the European Parliament and of the Council and repealing Council Decision 87/95/EEC and Decision No 1673/2006/EC of the European Parliament and of the Council; Regulation 764/2008 of 9 July 2008 'Laying down Procedures Relating to the Application of Certain National Technical Rules to Products Lawfully Marketed in Another Member State' (OJ 2013 L 218, p. 21); Regulation No 765/2008 of 9 July 2008 setting out the requirements for accreditation and market surveillance relating to the marketing of products, (OJ 2008 L 218, p. 30); and Decision 768/2008 of 9 July 2008 on a 'Common Framework for the Marketing of Products' (OJ 2008 L 218, p. 82).

[9] See reference to that effect in for example Article 56 Health Data Space Regulation, see also common specifications in for example Articles 33–36, 41 AI Act.

[10] Cf, for example, the Swedish Standards Institute's explanation of copyright (available on sis.se), accessed 6 July 2024.

[11] On the contrary, see P. Samuelson, 'Questioning Copyrights in Standards', 48 B.C. L. Rev. (2007) 193.

[12] See Article 5s (e) and (o) and 9 InfoSoc, i.e., Directive 2001/29/EC of the European Parliament and of the Council of 22 May 2001 on the harmonisation of certain aspects of copyright and related rights in the information society. For the copyright background, cf. Art. 2 Section 4 of the Berne

The issue of copyright protection of technical standards will be discussed below, starting with the fundamental question of establishing whether the CJEU could address and interpret standards at al.

3 Testing the Boundaries of the EU Standardisation Process

First, we had the *James Elliot* case[13] in 2016, where the critical issue was whether the CJEU could accept a request for preliminary ruling under Art. 267 TFEU for interpreting a European harmonised standard, while the 'sticking point' was whether a harmonised standard was an act that the CJEU could interpret under Art. 267 TFEU. Indeed, the CJEU, by accepting the case, implicitly acknowledged that harmonised standards had some kind of legal standing within the EU legal order.[14]

The case arose from a contractual dispute regarding whether a breach of contract could be established. James Elliott Construction was to construct a youth facility in Dublin (Ireland), where the specifications given required that the internal floors of the building be built *inter alia* in accordance with a harmonised standard. For that purpose, Irish Asphalt supplied James Elliott Construction with a product (concrete) in accordance with that standard. When the floor eventually collapsed, the issue was whether Irish Asphalt had breached the contract by not supplying concrete with the right content, in accordance with the technical standard. The Irish Supreme Court eventually heard the case and requested a preliminary ruling from the CJEU to ask, *inter alia*, whether the interpretation of a harmonised standard is a matter upon which a preliminary ruling may be sought from the CJEU, pursuant to Article 267 TFEU.

The CJEU confirmed that it has jurisdiction to interpret non-binding EU acts, while also clarifying that acts adopted by bodies that cannot be described as 'institutions, bodies, offices or agencies of the Union' might still be within the Court's reach under Art. 267 TFEU. Indeed, harmonised standards created through European Standardisation Organisations (ESOs), while not considered institutions, bodies, offices or agencies of the Union, might now, according to *James Elliot,* be reviewable under Art. 267 TFEU. According to the CJEU, such jurisdiction was justified by the objective of Article 267 TFEU, which is to ensure the uniform application

Convention for the Protection of Literary and Artistic Works, giving the signing parties a right to exclude official text from the copyright protection. See also the WIPO, Guide to the Copyright and Related Rights Treaties, p. 30. Under UK Copyright rules, legal acts are not exempted, but the Crown Copyright is not enforced in reference to official text. For Germany cf. infra.

[13] Judgment in *James Elliott Construction*, C-613/14, EU:C:2016:821 (hereinafter *James Elliot*). See my earlier discussion of the case in B. Lundqvist, 'European Harmonized Standards as 'Part of EU Law': The Implications of the James Elliott Case for Copyright Protection and, Possibly, for EU Competition Law', 44 LIEI 4 (2017) 421–435.

[14] *James Elliott*, paras. 32 et seq.

and interpretation,[15] throughout the EU, of all provisions forming part of the EU legal system.[16] Moreover, the fact that the measure of EU law has no binding effect does not preclude the Court from ruling on its interpretation in proceedings for a preliminary ruling under Article 267 TFEU.[17]

The CJEU stated that while the development of a harmonised standard is indeed entrusted to an organisation governed by private law and is non-binding, it is nevertheless a necessary implementation measure. As such, it is strictly governed by the essential requirements defined by the relevant directive, initiated, managed and monitored by the Commission, and its legal effects are subject to prior publication by the Commission of its references in the 'C' series of the Official Journal of the European Union (OJ). The Court also specifically stated that a harmonised standard forms part of EU law, since it is by reference to the provisions of such a standard that it is established whether or not the presumption of conformity with the EU directive applies to a given product.[18]

The CJEU clarified that the presumption created through conformity with the essential requirements of EU directive and the 'CE' marking is for the ability to freely circulate and market products within the EU. The objective of a harmonised standard is thus limited to the removal of obstacles to trade. In *James Elliot*, the standard did not extend to harmonising the specific conditions and rules for the use of construction products at the time of their incorporation in construction and engineering works, the rules did only govern market access in respect of such products. Indeed, the CJEU was careful to state that the material technical specifications of the standard created a presumption for free circulation of goods in the EU which could not bind a Member State court when establishing what constitutes 'merchantable quality' and 'fit for purpose' under the Sale of Goods Act of that Member State.

The Court largely followed Advocate General (AG) Campos Sánchez-Bordona's Opinion, establishing that European standards adopted under the New Approach could fall under the CJEU's jurisdiction. However, the CJEU did not, like AG Campos Sánchez-Bordona, submerge itself in the issue of lawful or non-lawful delegation of power under the *Meroni* doctrine. Moreover, the Court did not follow the AG's opinion in reference to the origin of the standards. While AG Campos Sánchez-Bordona argued in favour of equating harmonised standards to 'acts of the institutions, bodies, offices or agencies' under Article 267 TFEU,[19] the Court based its ability to give a preliminary ruling on the interpretation of harmonised standards on the established case law relating to Article 267 TFEU, which allows for the

[15] Judgments in *Sevince*, C-192/89, EU:C:1990:322, para. 10; and *Deutsche Shell*, C-188/91, EU:C:1993:24, para. 17.

[16] Judgment in *Sevince, supra*, para. 11.

[17] Judgments in *James Elliott*, paras 34 et seq; and *Deutsche Shell, supra*, para. 18.

[18] *James Elliott*, paras. 38, 40, and 43.

[19] Opinion by the Advocate General in *James Elliott Construction*, C-613/14, EU:C:2016:63, para. 40.

interpretation of measures other than those listed in the Treaty or from other sources.[20] This is a material difference. Indeed, the Court seemed to imply that the standards are created under private law by SSOs, while the Commission has an oversight and control function over the standards. The Court left unanswered the question of whether standards should be considered as originating from the Commission, with the ESO only serving as a preparatory organ.

The major recent case, the *Public.Resource.Org,*[21] finally decided in March 2024 originated from the inside of the EU bureaucracy and raised parallel if not similar issues as the *James Elliot* case. It was also decided by the European General Court (EGC) before the *Richter* case discussed infra. In the *Public.Resource.Org* case, the applicants had requested access to a harmonised standard under a regulation for public access to public documents (Public Access Regulation).[22] The Commission refused, and the applicants appealed the decision to the EGC and submitted that since the requested harmonised standards formed part of 'EU law', they should be accessible freely and without charge, meaning that no exception to the right of access could apply to them. According to the applicants, private rights cannot be granted with respect to a 'text of the law', which must be freely accessible and, accordingly, those standards could not be protected by copyright. In support of their line of argument, they relied on the *James Elliott* case.

The EGC in its decision from 2021 refused this line of argument, stating that the CJEU in *James Elliott* held only that a harmonised standard such as that at issue in the main proceedings—adopted on the basis of secondary legislation and the references to which have been published in the OJ—forms part of EU law. According to the EGC, the applicants had not, on the basis of constitutional principles and rules, shown that there was a requirement for free access, even if the standard formed part of EU law. Copyright on the text could thus be claimed even though the text was encompassed by the notion of "EU law". The applicants were therefore wrong to claim that harmonised standards should be freely accessible.[23]

However, in a somewhat concurrent case from 2022, the CJEU took the plunge and stated that directly referred to standards could not bind the public if they were not published in their entirety, in accordance with how laws are published in the EU. In the *Richter* case[24] of 22 February 2022, the Grand Chamber established a fundamental milestone on the legal status and consequences of incorporating standards in EU legislation. The case concerned the validity and interpretation of Article

[20] A. Volpato, 'A. Court of Justice The Harmonized Standards Before the CJEU: *James Elliott Construction*' 54 CML Rev. (2017) 591, 600 et seq., with reference.

[21] Judgments in *Public.Resource.Org and Right to Know v Commission and Others*, C-588/21 P, EU:C:2024:201; and *Public.Resource.Org and Right to Know v.* Commission, T-185/19, EU:T:2021:445.

[22] Regulation (EC) No 1049/2001 of the European Parliament and of the Council of 30 May 2001 regarding public access to European Parliament, Council and Commission documents.

[23] Judgment in *Public.Resource.Org and Right to Know v.* Commission, T-185/19, *supra*, paras. 52 et seq.

[24] Judgment in *Stichting Rookpreventie Jeugd and Others*, C-160/20, EU:C:2022:101.

4(1) of Directive 2014/40/EU on the manufacture, presentation and sale of tobacco in the EU internal market. The article referred directly to three specified ISO standards as the required methods for the measurement of tar, nicotine and carbon monoxide emissions, respectively, from cigarettes, i.e. the directive made use of direct legislation method (cf. above) The claimants contested the application of those methods by the Netherlands Food and Consumer Product Safety Authority, because they were based on machine smoking and did not take into account the way in which a cigarette filter is actually used, namely that the smoker's fingers and lips block the small holes in the filter. Their application resulted in the marketing of filter cigarettes resulting in inhalation of quantities of tar, nicotine and carbon monoxide significantly above the maximum emission levels prescribed in the directive. Indeed, the main issue of the case was whether the standard was fit for purpose, while the first question to the CJEU was, in essence, whether Article 4(1) of Directive 2014/40 was valid with regard to the principle of transparency, Article 297(1) TFEU (stating that legislative acts shall be published in the OJ) and the regulation concerning publication in the OJ, read in the light of legal certainty.

After some discussion, the CJEU stated clearly that legislative acts can enter into force and accordingly have legal effect only after they have been published in the OJ.[25] According to the Court, the publication requirement flows from the principle of legal certainty, which requires that EU rules enable those concerned to know precisely the extent of the obligations which are imposed on them. Individuals must be able to ascertain unequivocally what their rights and obligations are.[26] According to the CJEU, technical standards determined by a standards body, such as the ISO in this case, and made mandatory in a legislative act, are binding to the public only if they have been published in the OJ. However, the Court put forward one important caveat: Though standards are not binding to the public save if they have been published in the OJ,[27] account must be taken of the specific features of the system established by the ISO, which consists of a network of national standards bodies. Therefore, those national bodies are able to grant access, upon request, to the official and authentic version of the standards determined by ISO. Accordingly, 'where undertakings have access to the official and authentic version of the standards referred to in Article 4(1) of Directive 2014/40, those standards and, therefore, the reference made thereto by that provision are binding on them.'[28]

Given the general language used by the CJEU, there should be as little difference as possible in the legal treatment between harmonised European standards and directly referred to standards, such as ISO standards, as long as the standard has been made mandatory by a legislative act.[29] Although the Court could have elaborated and broadened its analysis to also include the more common method under the

---

[25] Ibid, paras. 40 et seq.

[26] Ibid, para 42, making reference to the judgment in *Heinrich*, C-345/06, EU:C:2009:140, para 44.

[27] Ibid. para 48.

[28] Ibid, para. 52.

[29] Ibid. para. 48.

New Approach, where the technical standard is not de jure required to adhere to, and the reasoning of the Court appears purposefully elusive on the core issues of the case and the concrete application of the ruling, it may hold an interesting solution. Perhaps the CJEU is telling us that the standard should be available to the public by accessing the OJ, or otherwise, while the SSO may still charge undertakings and others for using the copyright-protected text. The CJEU implies that the undertakings and other that commercial use the standards should still take out a license from the relevant NSB. If so, the decision not only implies improvement for those who advocated for an application of the general principles of EU law and fundamental guarantees of legitimacy and democracy in the context of technical standardisation. The solutions also provides revenue to NSBs. However, the issue is whether copyright may work in that manner and the NSB moreover need to approach the relevant undertakings to enter into license agreements.

4 The Issue of Delegation and Copyright Protection Revisited

The CJEU in both *James Elliot* and *Richter* refused to discuss (i) whether there is a formal delegation of power to SSOs when establishing harmonised standards or whether standards should be considered to have been adopted by the Commission when they are referred to in a legislative act; and (ii) whether the standards should be considered to be copyright-protected. The EGC's judgment in *Public.Resource.Org* implied that standards have copyright protection, while—as discussed below—the CJEU was silent in this regard when addressing the *Public.Resource.Org*. However, in accordance with *Richter,* if a standard is made binding by a legislative act, it must to be published in the OJ or risk not applying to the general public and potentially being overruled by a national judge as inadequate in satisfying the essential requirements stipulated in the legislative act.

The AGs in both *James Elliot* and *Richter* took more bold approaches and at least acknowledged the copyright issue. AG Campos Sánchez-Bordona in *James Elliot* emphasised that the Commission exercised significant control over establishment of harmonised standards and that creating harmonised standards could be viewed as a delegation of power under the *Meroni* doctrine. However, the AG refused to take a stand in reference to the copyright issue, stating:

> [N]ational bodies hold the intellectual property rights in the respective national versions of harmonised technical standards and charge for their distribution, a fact which has led to varying case-law in certain Member States on the necessity of official publication of technical national standards when legislatures make a reference to those standards. For the purposes of this reference for a preliminary ruling, I do not consider it essential to examine in more detail the important question of whether the complete official publication of harmonised technical standards is necessary in order for those standards to have legal effect and for the principle of the publication of legislation to be observed. That requirement would have a very significant impact on the European standardisation system, and in particular on the

sale of harmonised technical standards by national standardisation bodies. [footnotes omitted][30]

AG Campos Sánchez-Bordona noted that the Commission, the European Parliament and the Member States have the option to object to standards set by CEN, and that the Commission is obliged to do this *ex ante*, i.e., before the standard is published. Moreover, decisions relating to the publication of harmonised technical standards and decisions adopted by the Commission concerning formal objections to harmonised technical standards raised by the Member States or the European Parliament are legal acts against which an action for annulment could be brought. Based on this, the AG concluded that harmonised standards should be regarded as drafted under a controlled delegation of legislative power.[31]

The AG made reference to Member State case law regarding copyright protection. In the famous *Knooble* case from the Netherlands, the Dutch Supreme Court seemed to argue that reference to standards in a relevant legal document pulls them into the public domain and makes them generally applicable, but does not turn them into law. According to the Supreme Court, an essential condition for this is missing: standards are not based on delegation of law-making powers by a public authority, but rely on private agreements.[32] In Germany, the highest civil court (*Bundesgerichtshof*) has held that standards should not be copyright-protected because they are produced pursuant to delegation, have external effect and are not only for internal use within the Government. A requirement for this finding is that governmental organisations accept and incorporate the contents of the standards into their decision-making.[33] This notwithstanding, AG Campos Sánchez-Bordona in *James Elliot* refused to take a stand in reference to the copyright issue.

In *Richter*, AG Saugmandsgaard ØE took a diametrically different stand. While reaching the conclusion that there were no constitutional or legal requirements to make public a standard referred to in a legislative act, the issue of copyright was decided based on the need of *inter alia* the members of ISO (that is to say, the national standardisation bodies) to be able to sell those standards—since they keep a significant part of the profits made on such sales. According to AG Saugmandsgaard

[30] Opinion in *James Elliott Construction*, *supra*, para. 51. The footnotes make reference to the German Bundesgerichtshof (BGH, 30 June 1983, GRUG 1984, pp. 117 to 119) and the Bundesverfassungsgericht (BVerfGE, 29 July 1998, ZUM 1998, p. 926) which held that technical standards adopted by the German standards institute (Deutsches Institut für Normung, 'DIN') were not protected by intellectual property rights and should be published. The Netherlands Hoge Raad (Hoge Raad, 22 June 2012, LNJ:BW0393) held in *Knooble* that technical standards adopted by the Dutch standards institute (Nederlands Normalisatie Instituut, 'NEN') were protected by intellectual property rights and it was not compulsory to publish them officially. See the analysis of Micklitz, Van Gestel, *op. cit.*, 145–181.

[31] Opinion in *James Elliott Construction*, *supra*, paras. 47–55.

[32] Cf. M. Medzmariashvili, *Regulating European Standardisation through Law: The Interplay between Harmonised European Standards and EU Law,* thesis, Lund University, Lund, 2019, pp. 59–61. *Knooble*, The Hague District Court decision of 31 Dec. 2008, LJN:BG8465. Later, the case went to the Dutch Supreme Court (Hogee Raad), 22 June 2012, LJN:BW0393.

[33] M. Medzmariashvili, *op. cit.*, pp. 59–61.

ØE, in the light of those factors, it is clear that making standards available free of charge—which would be the result if the EU institutions were under an obligation to provide direct access to them by the public—would have the consequence of reducing investment by those standardisation bodies in the research and development of standards.[34] Therefore, should they *inter alia* potentially be protected under Copyright regimes.

The CJEU took a different route in *Richter* and *James Elliot*. It acknowledged the principles of right to access, legal transparency and legal certainty, to the extent that standard texts need to be accessible to the public, and that the national judge should retain the right to judge and analyse whether a standard in a specific case was set in an appropriate manner or reached the level of the essential requirements stipulated in the legislative act. This was confirmed in *Public.Resource.Org*.

Public.Resource.Org was appealed by the applicants to the CJEU, and they were more successful in their line of argument in reference to the Opinion by the Advocate General. Advocate General Laila Medina took a fundamental different stand than the General Court and concluded firstly that standards cannot be protected by copyright and secondly that there is a public interest, i.e. the requirement of upholding rule of law, to be able to access the material text of the harmonised standards that has be granted the status of 'EU law'.[35] In reference to the issue whether standards can reach the level of copyright protection, AG Medina grapple with the issue, while the CJEU's choose not to address the issue in a meaningful way. The key question being, can standards qualify for copyright protection.

Copyright protection is not limited to specific types or categories subject-matter, and both national legal systems and EU law rather extends protection to a diverse array of literary and artistic expression ("works") including content of a technical (as opposed to an aesthetic) nature such as computer programs, technical drawings and databases.[36]

All EU Member States except for Ireland have legal provisions that exclude laws, official decrees and official texts from the scope of copyright protection, while the Berne Convention allows members the freedom to grant copyright protection to legal texts.[37] However, there is no EU law principle that explicitly excludes official texts or laws from the scope of copyright protection (cf. InfoSoc). Moreover, some member states have addressed the issue of technical standards referred to in law, lex specialise, giving standards (limited) copyright protection.[38] Notwithstanding the

[34] Opinion in *Stichting Rookpreventie Jeugd and Others*, C-160/20, EU:C:2021:618, paras. 74 et seq.

[35] Opinion in *Public.Resource.Org and Right to Know v Commission and Others,* C-588/21 P, EU:C:2023:509.

[36] S. Mendis, O. Kanevskaia, 'Harmonized technical standards under EU copyright: the Public. Resource.Org judgment', in E. Rosati (ed.), *The IPKat Monday*, July 22, 2024, (available on line on ipkitten.blogspot.com).

[37] Cf. Opinion of AG Medina, at para 62.

[38] In Belgium for example, there is a proposal implying that national standards referred to by law need to be freely accessible on the website of the national standardisation body, but there is no

contested status of harmonised standard as "law" or an "official text", the ability to exclude these from the scope of copyright protection can be difficult.[39]

The Grand Chamber of the CJEU pondered the case for a rather long time before delivering the decision, and when it finally arrived, the Court only addressed the second claim without mentioning the issue of copyright. The CJEU relied on the Advocate General, stating there is an overriding public interest justifying the disclosure of the harmonised standards. The CJEU stated, Article 2 TEU provides that the European Union is based on the principle of rule of law, which requires free access to EU law for all natural or legal persons of the European Union, and that individuals must be able to ascertain unequivocally what their rights and obligations are, while citing *Stichting*. The right of access to documents is then ensured under the first subparagraph of Article 15(3) TFEU and enshrined in Article 42 of the Charter. The Court thereby hold that there was an overriding public interest, within the meaning of Article 4(2) Public Access Regulation, justifying the disclosure of the requested harmonised standards. The reference to Article 4(2) is interesting. Article 4(2) fin can be read as stipulating an exemption to an exemption under the Public Access Regulation. Indeed, copyright protected material can be excluded from the general access rule due to commercial interest, while the exemption is not available should access to the material still be considered to be in the public interest. By using Article 4(2), has the CJEU thereby confirmed that harmonized standard are of commercial interest, hence copyright protected? Probably not. It depends on the interpretation of Article 4(2) and the wording of the second claim of the appellant, making special reference to Article 4(2).[40]

However, more importantly, it should be noted that the CJEU consistently in the cases referred to identified that the problematic issue lies in the fact that the

requirement that they can be downloaded or printed. So, the NSB can still require payment for a download or a printed copy, when the standard is included in the law by means of a reference. If international standards are included in law, the body producing the law has to take action to make them available for free while respecting copyright. See also C. Cauffman, M. Gérardy, 'Competition law as a tool to ensure the legitimacy of standard-setting by European standardisation organisations?', in M. Eliantonio, C. Cauffman (eds), *The legitimacy of standardisation as a regulatory technique: A cross-disciplinary and multi-level analysis,* Edward Elgar Publishing, 2020, pp. 64–90.

[39] It should be noted that under EU copyright law qualifying for copyright protection if it can fulfil the two requisite criteria for copyright protection. Firstly, whether the literary or artistic expression is identifiable with sufficient precision and objectivity; and secondly that original in the sense that it qualifies as its author's own intellectual creation can be identified. According the AG Medina, the second prone is nor fulfilled since there is limited creative freedom in the process of drafting an HS: "as regards the content of [technical standards] and the layout, these are constrained by the [...] secondary legislation from which the HTS are derived and by the Commission's mandate. In principle, the above heavily restricts room for creativity and originality." [para. 94 of the Opinion]. AG Medina continued and stated: "the vague reliance on the length of a document is not sufficient in order to prove that [a technical standard is] the result of genuine creative choices [...]" (para 94 of the Opinion). S. Mendis, O. Kanevskaia, *op. cit.*

[40] O. Kanevskaia, 'Is it really all about the money? The future of European standardization after PublicResourceOrg' (2024) European Journal of Risk Regulation 1–8.

standards are confidential, and that Judges and parties cannot access the text to understand the enacted obligations and rights.[41] Indeed, it is only the right to hold something confidential, i.e. included in the right to deny reproduction and distribution, in the bundle of rights under the notion of copyright that the Court is wrestling with. Indeed, the right to deny reproduction and distribution in these circumstances has now been overridden by the principle of rule of law, while other rights within the bundle may be intact.

The CJEU thereby grant access to the document—stating that referred to standards are EU law—without mentioning whether the standard-setting bodies can still claim copyright. The ruling may still suggest that the standard-setting bodies need to change their business model to a certain extent. Members of the standard-setting bodies and other users of the standard should pay a fee, cf. Article 16 of the Access Regulation to this effect, while the standards as such should be freely available and free of charge, at least via the Public Access Regulation, but better by being published in its entire in the OJ.[42]

On a grander scale, the CJEU clearly finds that the right to access to documents is an important corner stone of the rule of law, while notably, the CJEU did not kill off the New Approach. The New Approach is not dead, it needs to be redrafted for future processes to develop new harmonised standards. The difficult issue will be how to handle all the current harmonised standards still in force.

The solution given by the Court is that standards that were referred to in legislative acts should have a privileged status. The standards could still be protected under national copyright laws, but the SSOs could not use confidentiality to boost sales. Indeed, since the texts are freely available, they must seek out the undertakings that use the standards to sell the licenses.

5 Conclusions and some further development

It is obvious that the CJEU and the EU legislature want to obtain the benefits of self-regulation, while still upholding the possibility of judicial review of standards and standard-setting from constitutional, trade and competition law perspectives.

The CJEU in *Richter*, *James Elliot* and now in *Public.Resource.Org* acknowledged the principles of right to access, legal transparency and legal certainty to the extent that standard texts need to be public, and that the national judge should still retain the right to judge and analyse whether a standard in a specific case has been

---

[41] Cf. Judgment in *Public.Resource.Org and Right to Know v Commission and Others*, *supra*, paras. 81–84.

[42] When reading the judgments in *Stichter* and *PublicResource.Org* together. However, the judgment in *Public.Resource.Org* interestingly also opens up for a business model where the Commission pays (royalty) fees, or more remuneration for the preparator work conducted by standard-setting bodies, with the right for the Commission to make the harmonised standard available to any comers.

set in an appropriate manner and achieves the level of the essential requirements stipulated in the relevant legislative act.

Elegantly, the CJEU did not scrap the New Approach. Standards that are referred to in legislative acts will still have a privileged status. The standards may be protected under national copyright laws, but SSOs may not use confidentiality to boost sales. Indeed, since the texts are freely available, they will need to seek out undertakings that use the standards to sell their licenses. Though the Court could have elaborated and broadened its analyses, the gist of the cases in reference to copyright is that the Court has found a solution that meets the need of both constitutional rigour and commercial realities. I would like to say well done CJEU. However, on December 6, 2024, ISO and IEC initiated proceedings against the European Commission before the General Court (case T-631/24 ICO/IEC ECLI:EU:T:2025:1079). The case follows the now landmark case *Public.Resource.Org* judgment discussed in this paper, where the CJEU ruled that harmonized standards are part of EU law and must be publicly accessible. What ISO and IEC Are arguing before the General Court, is that *Public.Resource.Org* applies only to EU harmonized standards and not to international texts still protected by copyright. In short, ISO and IEC claim that the Commission took the judgment too far. The bodies argue that the disclosure will seriously undermine their commercial interests and valuable intellectual property. Case T-631/24 is still pending. No statements of defense or interim measures have been made public, and the Court registry lists it as in progress. Until legal clarity is restored, OJEU publications are expected to remain limited to European-only EN standards, with ISO and IEC-based standards remaining on hold. The last publication of EN ISO/IEC standards was in October 2024. The April 2025 and October 2025 publications only included "pure-EU" standards. This creates significant uncertainty for European manufacturers who rely on harmonized standards for presumption of conformity with EU regulations. The question is still thereby whether the intellectual property of ISO/IEC will be protected, or not. More to come.

Spyware and National Security: Who Is Afraid of EU Law?—A Fresh Overview of the EU Law Protection of Individuals Against Spyware

Luigi Malferrari

1 Introduction

The intrusive and sophisticated surreptitiously-operating software usually termed "spyware" has been widely used by Member State authorities in the EU, including against lawyers, journalists, NGO activists and opposition politicians. The spyware matter has been brought to the attention of public opinion, inter alia, through several scandals.[1] Several opinions, reports, debates, studies and recommendations have followed.[2] Despite the controversiality and sensitiveness of the issue and notwithstanding the public uproars, no case has so far reached the CJEU regarding the

The author thanks J. Baquero Cruz, M. Gerhold, T. Giegerich, H. Kranenborg, H. Mildebrath and D. Voorhoof for precious input. Any error of fact or law is attributable to the author only. The present article partly relies on the author's article "New and reinforced rights for media service providers under Art. 4 European Media Freedom Act", Rivista Italiana di Informatica e Diritto, 2025.

[1] Including the so-called Pegasus scandal from 2021, referring to the notorious software "Pegasus" produced by the Israel-based NSO group. See H. Mildebrath, European Parliamentary Research Service (ed.), Europe's PegasusGate – Countering spyware abuse, European parliament, 2022, page 41; J. E. Kermer, "How far does Article 4 of the European Media Freedom Act go in banning state surveillance of journalists?" (available on line on cmpf.eui.eu). See also Reuters (ed.), "Italian government under pressure in Paragon spyware row", 7 February 2025, available on line

[2] For a list see Venice Commission, Report on a rule of law and human rights compliant regulation of spyware, 13 December 2024, CDL-AD(2024)043, §§ 31–33. See also N. Vidal Marti, The Key

L. Malferrari (✉)
European Commission, Brussels, Belgium
e-mail: Luigi.MALFERRARI@ec.europa.eu

L. Prete, L. Rezki (eds.), *Judging & (Re)Thinking European Union Law*,
https://doi.org/10.1007/978-3-032-13473-8_34

guarantees for individuals against spyware, while complaints have been filed with the ECtHR.[3] Does that suggest that EU law does not offer any protection against spyware? Is EU law "blocked" by Article 4(2) TEU related to the essential State functions, including national security? Or is it rather the fear and awe instilled by secret services?

The present essay argues that the EU Treaties do not contain a "national security exception" taking the national security domain *en bloc* out of the scope of Union law; it further illustrates that EU law, including through the fundamental freedoms, offers protection against the Member States' use of spyware. The essay then focuses on Article 4 of the European Media Freedom Act (EMFA) prohibiting in principle the Member States' use of spyware against media service providers including journalists: its entry into application on 8 August 2025 is likely to give rise to judicial cases and to increase the visibility of the protection of EU law against spyware.

2 What Is Spyware?

A definition of spyware can be found in EMFA, which uses the term "intrusive surveillance software", defined as "any product with digital elements specially designed to exploit vulnerabilities in other products with digital elements that enables the covert surveillance of natural or legal persons by monitoring, extracting, collecting or analyzing data from such products or from the natural or legal persons using such products, including in an indiscriminate manner" (Article 4 n° 20 EMFA).

There are two extraordinary things about spyware. First, its pervasiveness and sophistication: as Bill Marczak of Citizens Lab recalled during his testimony at the Pega Committee of the European Parliament, spyware is not only a tool for listening in and extracting data, but is also capable of doctoring documents, changing preferences of the device and activating tools of the targeted device such as the camera or other apps. Second, spyware's ease of use is remarkable: Bill Marczak explained that, once you buy a license to use Pegasus for a specific country, you merely need to enter the telephone number you want to target, and that is sufficient to put it under surveillance (so-called "zero-click spyware").[4] Thus, thanks to its technological power, spyware yields an unprecedented level of intrusion into an individual's rights. Spyware such as Pegasus should not be equated with "traditional" law enforcement interception tools; rather, it appears to be more similar to "government Trojan" or "online searches" solutions that had in the past raised serious legal

to Ensure Media Pluralism in the EU? A Unified Framework, in Verfassungsblog, 12 June 2023 (available on line).

[3] Judgment in *M.N.*, C-670/22, EU:C:2024:372, concerning evidence obtained through the use of spyware: it raised questions regarding the conditions for use of a European Investigation Order under Directive 2014/41/EU regarding the European Investigation Order in criminal matters; the case did not raise questions regarding the protection of individuals.

[4] See also Venice Commission, cit., § 14.

concerns.[5] It has even been compared—not without ground—to a weapon.[6] Once the device is infected, it can be difficult to find or remove the software, as many of such surveillance technologies market themselves as "untraceable".

The seriousness of the intrusion by spyware is underpinned by the fact that the use of spyware has enormous chilling effects: due to the uncertainty, professionals such as journalists and lawyers refrain from exercising their freedoms in order to avoid the risk of becoming the subject of such measures; by the same token, suspects (both guilty and innocent) no longer dare to seek lawyer advice, whistleblowers no longer step up and seek help, confidants no longer entrust their sources to journalists. According to the Venice Commission, "[t]he Pegasus scandal showed that journalists were apparently being targeted simply because they are journalists, which is unacceptable in a democratic society."[7] Substantial forensic reporting by civil society organizations—such as Citizen Lab, Amnesty Tech, and AccessNow—has identified significant evidence of abusive surveillance using spyware technologies.[8] That is particularly true for the media.[9] Accordingly, Spyware constitutes a major challenge to the rule of law, fundamental rights and values of the EU, which "define the very identity of the European Union as a common legal order".[10]

That said, we live in a world where criminal threats are widespread and increasingly sophisticated. Spyware can be used by law enforcement authorities to put nefarious and technically adept criminals under surveillance. This can be done also cross-border through the cooperation of authorities from different Member States: an example thereof can be drawn from the Case C-670/22, *Staatsanwaltschaft Berlin v M.N.*[11] Thus, spyware can also be used to benefit legitimate societal goals. Indeed, Member States have a national security responsibility under Article 4(2) TEU and a competence for the maintenance of law and order (cf. Article 72 TFEU). The question of how to find an adequate balance between these conflicting needs will be analyzed below in chapters 4 et seq.

[5] European Data Protection Supervisor, *Preliminary Remarks on Modern Spyware*, 15 February 2022, page. 4.

[6] R. Phillips, "The Efficacy of European Union Spyware Regulations", Student Occasional Paper, vol. 5, 2023, pages 1–13 (5).

[7] Venice Commission, cit., § 96.

[8] Venice Commission, cit., § 12.

[9] See recital 25 EMFA.

[10] Judgment in *Hungary v. EP and Council (Conditionality Reg.)*, C-156/21, EU:C:2022:97, § 127.

[11] When the EncroChat case was ongoing in December 2022, the French authorities had still classified the interception tool as a national defense secret, so there was little information on it (see H. Mildebrath, European Parliamentary Research Service, EncroChat's path to Europe's highest courts, available on line).

3 Does Article 4(2) TEU Lay Down a General Exception for Essential State Functions, Including National Security?

Beforehand, as a preliminary point, it needs to be ascertained whether there is any legal obstacle of a horizontal nature to the applicability of the EU rights and freedoms to spyware. Several Member States as well as some commentators consider that Article 4(2) TEU constitutes such an obstacle.[12] That reading is unfounded.[13]

A similar objection based on Article 4(2) TEU had been put forward by the French government in *La Quadrature du Net I*. The CJEU rejected it.[14] In another case the CJEU also held that it cannot be inferred that the FEU Treaty contains an inherent general exception excluding all measures taken for reasons of law and order or public security from the scope of European Union law.[15] The CJEU's position is in line with other case law[16] and is convincing. The wording, purpose and context of the provision indicate that Article 4(2) TEU has a framing function and does not entail an exception to the application of EU law.[17]

---

[12] Cf. O. Rüß, "The national security assumption under Art. 4 TEU and its interdependence with secondary legislation requirements and limits for the Member States' intelligence agencies", in J.-H. Dietrich and A. Pilniok (eds.), *European Security Union*, 2024, pp. 101 et seq.

[13] Cf. O. Lynksey, "General Report Topic 2: The New EU Data Protection Regime", in *The New EU Data Protection Regime: Setting Global Standards for the Right to Personal Data Protection*, The XXIX FIDE Congress in The Hague, 2020 Congress Publications, Vol. 2, pp. 23 et seq. (76).

[14] Judgment in *La Quadrature du Net I*, C-511/18, C-512/18 and C-520/18, EU:C:2020:791, § 99. See also judgments in *ZZ*, C-300/11, EU:C:2013:363, § 38; *Affatato*, C-3/10, EU:C:2010:574, § 41; *O'Brien*, C-393/10, EU:C:2012:110, § 49. See thereon G. Di Federico, "The Potential of Article 4(2) TEU in the Solution of Constitutional Clashes Based on Alleged Violations of National Identity and the Quest for Adequate (Judicial) Standards", European Public Law, 2019, pp. 347 et seq. (361–363).

[15] Judgment in *Commission v Hungary (reception of applicants for international protection)*, C-808/18, EU:C:2020:1029, § 214.

[16] See, for example, judgments in *Commission v France (Spanish strawberries)*, C-265/95, EU:C:1997:595, §§ 33 to 35; *Kreil*, C-285/98, EU:C:2000:2, §§ 16 to17; *Dory*, C-186/01, EU:C:2003:146, § 30; *Commission v Italy (helicopters)*, C-337/05, EU:C:2008:203, §§ 42–43; *Commission v Austria (State printing office)*, C-187/16, EU:C:2018:194, §§ 75 to 78; and *B.K.*, C-742/19, EU:C:2021:597, § 40. See also the Committee of Inquiry to investigate the use of Pegasus and equivalent surveillance spyware Report of the Investigation of alleged contraventions and maladministration in the application of Union law in relation to the use of Pegasus and equivalent surveillance spyware (Europe's PegasusGate – Countering spyware abuse, cit., page 41).

[17] See, to this effect, Opinion of Advocate General Spielmann in *Commission v Poland (judgments of the Polish Constitutional Court)*, C-448/23, EU:C:2025:165, §§ 67–69 and 85–88. Cf. also P. Leino-Sandberg, "The non-integrable core area of national security? On the function and scope of Art. 4(2) sent. 3 TEU", in J.-H. Dietrich and A. Pilniok (eds.), *European Security Union*, 2024, pp. 119 et seq. and 126 et seq.

Indeed, first, the verb "to respect" means to consider worthy of high regard, or to honour.[18] Another possible meaning would be "to refrain from interfering with", but that meaning cannot be reconciled with the fact that several Treaty provisions apply to national measures taken to preserve essential State functions.[19] To interpret "respect" to the effect of "avoid to interfere with" would also contradict settled case law whereby the EU fundamental freedoms are applicable to national measures aiming at safeguarding law and order.[20] There is no trace that the objective of that provision was to reverse such long-standing case law, which has been confirmed after the entry into force of the Lisbon Treaty.

Second, as regards the objective of Article 4(2) TEU, taking Member States' essential functions outside the ambit of application of EU law would run counter to the Treaty drafters' intention to continue the process of creating an ever closer union among the peoples of Europe,[21] and to facilitate the free movement of persons, while ensuring the safety and security of their peoples, by establishing an area of freedom, security and justice.[22] If the Treaty drafters had wanted to take the Member States's essential functions outside the ambit of application of EU law, they would have chosen a different wording for Article 4(2) TEU. This finds a confirmation in the drafting history of Article 4(2) TEU. The competent working group of the Constitutional Convention rejected a listing of Member State competences, by holding that "cette disposition *ne constituait pas une clause dérogatoire*. Les États membres *demeurent tenus de respecter les dispositions des traités*."[23]

Third, as regards the context, the respect for the Member States' essential functions needs to be reconciled with the equality of the Member States before the Treaty, set out at the very beginning of Article 4(2) TEU. If Member States' rules and actions regarding their essential functions completely escaped from any EU law application, it would be very easy for them to deprive the need for equality among

---

[18] A. Buchta, H. Kranenborg, "General Report Topic 2: The New EU Data Protection Regime", cit., page 100.

[19] For ex., the provisions in Title V of the TFEU regarding an area of freedom, security and justice (including border checks, judicial cooperation in criminal matters and police cooperation), ii) Articles 42 TEU et seq. laying down a common security policy (including with regard to international security), iii) Article 346(1)(a) TFEU regarding information the disclosure of which a Member State considers contrary to the essential interests of its security, iv) Article 346(1)(b) TFEU regarding the protection of the essential interests of a Member State's security which are connected with the production of or trade in arms (see judgment in *Commission v Austria*, C-187/16, EU:C:2018:194, § 78), and v) Article 348 TFEU on the coordination regarding essential interests of security of Member States and the possibility of bringing the matter before the CJEU to tackle cases of abuse thereof.

[20] See ex multis judgments in *Commission v France ("Spanish strawberries")*, cit.; and *Calfa*, C-348/96, EU:C:1999:6. See also the case law cited in S. Sule, 'National Security and Sovereignty of Member States – An Introduction', in J.-H. Dietrich and A. Pilniok (eds.), op. cit., pp. 81 et seq. (85).

[21] Preamble to the TEU, 13th passage.

[22] Preamble to the TEU, 12th passage.

[23] Final report of the working group V "Complementary competences" (4 November 2002), European Convention, p. 12 (available on line). See Leino-Sandberg, cit., pp. 123–124.

Member States before the Treaty of any practical effect in many areas of EU law. That would run counter to the effectiveness of EU law and moreover would logically be in tension with the prominence that the Treaty framers have given to the equality of Member States before the Treaty in the same provision.

Fourth, again from a systemic viewpoint, Article 4(2) TEU must be read together i) with Article 2 TEU, which codifies the constitutional identity of the European Union, ii) with Article 6 TEU, which recalls the primary law status of the Charter of Fundamental Rights of the EU, iii) with Article 4(1) TEU, which implies that the Union's competences must be respected, and iv) with Article 4(3) TEU, which lays down the principle of sincere cooperation. In particular, from a systemic viewpoint, Article 4 TEU comes after Article 2 TEU, which sets out the values that are an integral part of the very identity of the European Union as a common legal order.[24] Therefore, Article 4 TEU is not intended to derogate from Article 2 TEU. Accordingly, a concomitant and coherent reading of all the provisions militate against the interpretation of Article 4(2) TEFU as a massive carve-out from the ambit of application of the Treaties, which would create major loopholes to the effective application of Union law.[25]

Furthermore, the Treaty drafters have confirmed, in the Declaration on Article 16 TFEU attached to the TFEU, that the EU privacy acquis can have direct implications for national security.[26] In fact, the possibility of direct implications for national security entails that that matter is as such not subtracted from the ambit of application of Union law. In addition, the EMFA legislator's conception of Article 4(2) TEU is not to the effect that it would exclude domains from the ambit of application of EU law.[27] Indeed, Article 4 EMFA, laying down the guarantees against the national authorities' use of spyware against media service providers, applies horizontally, including where the State exercises essential State functions such as law enforcement, fight against crime and national security.

It follows from the foregoing considerations that the mere fact that a Member State is (genuinely or not) exercising an exclusive competence such as national security does not entail that the acts it takes do not need to comply with the applicable Union law. The fact that a matter is the sole responsibility of Member States may limit the EU's legislative and executive competences in a given field, but does not exclude that, when exercising that sole responsibility, Member States must

[24] Judgment in *Hungary v European Parliament and Council*, cit., §§ 127 and 232.

[25] Opinion of AG Emiliou in *Boriss Cilevičs*, C-391/20, EU:C:2022:166, § 87.

[26] "The Conference declares that, whenever rules on protection of personal data to be adopted on the basis of Article 16 could have direct implications for national security, due account will have to be taken of the specific characteristics of the matter. It recalls that the legislation presently applicable (see in particular Directive 95/46/EC) includes specific derogations in this regard."

[27] A similar approach is also followed in the NIS2 Directive: see Art. 2(6) of Directive (EU) 2022/2555 of the European Parliament and of the Council of 14 December 2022 on measures for a high common level of cybersecurity across the Union, amending Regulation (EU) No 910/2014 and Directive (EU) 2018/1972, and repealing Directive (EU) 2016/1148 (OJ 2022 L 333, p. 80).

comply with EU law.[28] Even commentators who are sympathetic to the Member States' positions consider that the Union is allowed to exercise its competences in a way that has consequences on the national security of Member States.[29] Thus, national security or law and order are not a blank cheque that can be invoked by Member States to escape from their obligations under EU law, including the EU rules on internal market, those on fundamental rights and a fortiori the values laid down in Article 2 TEU. Even if Member States can define what counts as an essential function and enjoy a margin of appreciation in the exercise thereof, that definition and that margin of appreciation must be exercised in compliance with Union law.

What is then the normative meaning of Article 4(2) TEU? Given the elements illustrated above (including its legislative history), this provision entails that national authorities and EU institutions, including the CJEU, have to balance any applicable rule of primary or secondary Union law with the Member States' interest in maintaining essential State functions such as national security.[30] They are also obliged to respect the Member States' essential State functions when applying a provision of EU law to them, thus requiring a balancing exercise. An example thereof is the judgment in B. K., where the CJEU had to rule on whether the Directive concerning the organization of working time[31] precluded the absence of additional remuneration for overtime carried out by a member of the Slovenian army.[32] The CJEU held that Article 4(2) TEU does not have the effect of excluding the organisation of the working time of all military personnel from the scope of EU law.[33] It specified that Article 4(2) TEU requires that the application to military personnel of the rules of EU law relating to the organization of working time is not such as to hinder the proper performance of those essential functions; therefore, those rules cannot be interpreted in such a way as to prevent the armed forces from fulfilling their tasks and, consequently, so as adversely to affect the essential functions of the State, namely the preservation of its territorial integrity and the safeguarding of national security.[34] After having carried out a detailed and multi-sided balancing exercise, the CJEU came to the conclusion that the relevant provision of the working time Directive, read in the light of Article 4(2) TEU, must be interpreted as meaning that a security

[28] Judgment in *Commission v France (Spanish strawberries)*, cit., §§ 33–35. See also, by analogy, judgments in Cilevičs, C-391/20, EU:C:2022:638, § 59; *Commission v Poland (Independence of the Supreme Court)*, C-619/18, EU:C:2019:531, § 52 and the case-law cited; and *Commission v Poland (Independence of the ordinary courts)*, C-192/18, EU:C:2019:924, § 102. See also K. Lenaerts, "Constitutionalism and the Many Faces of Federalism", The American Journal of Comparative Law, 1990, pages 205 et seq. (220).

[29] U. Karpenstein, R. Sangi, "Nationale Sicherheit im Unionsrecht: Zur Bedeutung von Art. 4 II 3 EUV", Zeitschrift für das gesamte Sicherheitsrecht, 2020, pp. 162 et seq. (166).

[30] See, to this effect, also Leino-Sandberg, cit., p. 125 and literature cited therein.

[31] Directive 2003/88/EC of the European Parliament and of the Council of 4 November 2003 concerning certain aspects of the organisation of working time (OJ 2003 L 299, p. 9).

[32] Judgment in *B. K.*, cit.

[33] Ibid., § 46.

[34] Ibid., § 43.

activity performed by a member of military personnel is excluded from the scope of that directive, however only where one of a number of conditions is fulfilled.[35]

4 Are the GDPR, E-privacy Directive and Law Enforcement Directive Applicable and Violated?

The issue of essential State functions leads us to the question of whether the EU privacy acquis is applicable and, if so, what protection it offers to individuals against spyware. The matter is not uncontroversial because the result of the above-mentioned interpretation of primary law has in substance been reflected in some of the articles of the EU privacy acquis, while other articles and/or the corresponding recitals are construed by some Member States to the effect that national security would lie outside the scope of Union law.

As regards the relevant data protection legislation, Article 2(3) LED[36] provides that the Directive does not apply to the processing of data "in the course of an activity which falls outside the scope of Union law". This provision (like analogue ones in the e-privacy Directive[37] and the GDPR[38]) states the obvious and therefore is of purely declaratory nature. Recital 14 LED affirms that "activities concerning national security, activities of agencies or units dealing with national security issues and the processing of personal data by the Member States when carrying out activities which fall within the scope of Chapter 2 of Title V of the TEU should not be considered to be activities falling within the scope of this Directive."

Similar provisions are laid down in the GDPR. Under Article 2(2)(a), this Regulation does not apply to the processing of personal data "in the course of an activity which falls outside the scope of Union law". The difference is that this provision is accompanied by Article 2(2)(d) GDPR, which adds that the Regulation does not apply to the processing of personal data by competent authorities "for the purposes of the prevention, investigation, detection or prosecution of criminal offences or the execution of criminal penalties, including the safeguarding against and the prevention of threats to public security". Recital 16 asserts that the GDPR

---

[35] Ibid., § 88.

[36] Directive (EU) 2016/680 of the European Parliament and of the Council of 27 April 2016 on the protection of natural persons with regard to the processing of personal data by competent authorities for the purposes of the prevention, investigation, detection or prosecution of criminal offences or the execution of criminal penalties, and on the free movement of such data, and repealing Council Framework Decision 2008/977/JHA (OJ 2016 L 119, p. 89).

[37] Directive 2002/58/EC of the European Parliament and of the Council of 12 July 2002 concerning the processing of personal data and the protection of privacy in the electronic communications sector (OJ 2002 L 201, p. 37).

[38] Regulation (EU) 2016/679 of the European Parliament and of the Council of 27 April 2016 on the protection of natural persons with regard to the processing of personal data and on the free movement of such data, and repealing Directive 95/46/EC (OJ 2016 L 119, p. 1).

"does not apply to issues of protection of fundamental rights and freedoms or the free flow of personal data related to activities which fall outside the scope of Union law, such as activities concerning national security."

Then, Article 1(3) of the ePrivacy Directive provides that the Directive does not apply to activities that "fall outside the scope of the Treaty, establishing the European Community, such as those covered by Titles V and VI of the Treaty on European Union, and in any case to activities concerning public security, defence, State security". Recital 11 of the e-privacy Directive states that "this Directive does not affect the ability of Member States to carry out lawful interception of electronic communications, or take other measures, if necessary for any of these purposes" and in accordance with the ECHR.

The exclusion at issue in the LED and in the GDPR is formulated in the sense of carving out processing carried out in the course of an activity which falls outside the scope of Union law or the Treaty.[39] The problem stems from the accompanying recitals which indicate in substance that activities such as those concerning national security should be outside the scope because they do not fall into the ambit of application of Union law.[40] From a methodological viewpoint, the question of what falls into the ambit of application of Union law is to be determined on the basis of primary and secondary law. As illustrated above, national security or law enforcement do not fall outside of the scope of primary Union law. As regards secondary law, the role of recitals is to clarify what articles say, but cannot change or *a fortiori* overrule them: a recital lacks *per se* binding force altogether.

Apart from these recitals, the question remains how to construe the abovementioned carve-outs laid down in the articles of the privacy acquis. Since the legislation lists national security and law enforcement as one of the reasons for justifying a restriction to privacy, it must logically be considered to be in principle within the ambit of application of the EU privacy acquis. It will be taken out of the ambit of application only where it is clear that it falls outside the scope of application of the Treaty. Moreover, the carve-out being an exception to privacy protection, it needs to be interpreted narrowly. The extent of the carve-out is a matter of EU law, thus to be adjudicated by the CJEU. So, the CJEU will have to verify for example whether a carve-out applies or not.

The CJEU has been confronted a number of times with this or analogous issues and has analysed the matter in a circumspect manner, by taking into account in particular the subject matter, the content of the activity, the actor carrying out the activity and the purpose thereof. In Tele 2 and Watson the CJEU was asked to clarify the relationship between the exclusion clause laid down in Article 1(3) of the e-privacy Directive and the derogation clause laid down in Article 15(1) of the same Directive. It set out a detailed and convincing argumentation, in which, by relying notably on

---

[39] See Article 2(3)(a) LED; Article 2(2)(a) GDPR.

[40] Article 15(1) e-privacy Directive; Article 15(1) LED; Article 23(1)(a) GDPR. Cf. M. Brewczyńska, "A critical reflection on the material scope of the application of the Law Enforcement Directive and its boundaries with the General Data Protection Regulation", in E. Kosta, R. Leenes, and I. Kamara (eds.), *Research Handbook on EU Data Protection Law*, 2022, pp. 91 et seq.

the system and the general structure of the Directive, it considered the matter to fall within the scope of the Directive.[41] A further example consists in the activities by a committee of inquiry set up by the parliament of a Member State in the exercise of its power of scrutiny over the executive, the purpose of which is to investigate the activities of a police State-protection authority on account of a suspicion of political influence over that authority: the CJEU clarified that these activities do not fall outside the scope of Union law under the GDPR.[42] The mere circumstance that the controller is an official authority which is tasked with safeguarding national security is insufficient to exclude from the scope of the GDPR the processing of personal data by that authority in the course of other activities that it carries out.[43] Further cases concern national measure adopted by the supervisory authorities which limits or, where appropriate, prohibits the video recording of the vote count at polling stations,[44] and national legislation providing for public access to personal data relating to penalty points imposed for road traffic offences.[45]

The net result is a granular approach that leads to different outcomes on the basis of the legal and factual circumstances of each case.[46] This approach has the advantage of recognizing an ambit of application to any provision at issue. The CJEU verifies first whether the facts of the case fall outside the scope of Union law; if that is not the case, it examines whether any prohibition or obligation under EU law is triggered, whether a valid justification is present and whether the general principles of EU law and the fundamental rights are complied with. The criticism whereby the CJEU would have failed to follow the legislator's will is unfounded because if the CJEU had taken the recitals on their face value, it would have given to recitals autonomous binding force which they do not possess. Moreover, interpreting the carve-outs broadly would have contradicted the content and structure of articles of the EU privacy acquis and primary law. Indeed, the exegesis needs to preserve the coherence and effectiveness of the provisions.[47]

The matter however remains controversial. National governments and judges sometimes construe the provisions in a superficial manner. For example, the German Federal Administrative Court judge has held that "[t]he GDPR does not apply to data processing by the Federal Intelligence Service pursuant to Article 2(2)(a) and

---

[41] Judgment in *Tele 2 and Watson*, C-203/15 and C-698/15EU:C:2016:970, §§ 67 et seq. See also judgments in *Ministerio Fiscal*, C-207/16, EU:C:2018:788, §§ 29 et seq.; *Privacy International*, C-623/17, EU:C:2020:790, §§ 34 et seq.; and *La Qudrature du net I*, cit., §§ 91–104.

[42] Judgment in *Österreichische Datenschutzbehörde*, C-33/22, EU:C:2024:46, §§ 52–57.

[43] Ibid., §§ 41, 42 and 51.

[44] Judgment in *Komisia za zashtita na lichnite danni*, C-306/21, EU:C:2022:813.

[45] Judgment in *Latvijas Republikas Saeima (penalty points)*, C-439/19, EU:C:2021:504.

[46] Cf. also European Union Agency for Fundamental Rights, *Surveillance by Intelligence services: fundamental rights safeguards and remedies in the EU – Volume II: field perspectives and legal update*, 2017, p. 22.

[47] A reference should be added in this regard to part 5 below.

Recital 16 in conjunction with Art. 4 para. 2 sentence 3 TEU."[48] This statement, made without further explanation, is overly broad and could be interpreted as suggesting that any data processing by the intelligence services is automatically exempt from EU law, which is unfounded. A similar attitude was taken by the German Constitutional Court in an order from 2024.[49]

For those matters that fall into their ambit of application, the GDPR, the LED and the e-privacy Directive provide a comprehensive framework for the rights of individuals and how these rights can be exercised, including their right to information, to access, to rectify or erase their personal data.[50] The guarantees laid down in the LED apply to the processing of personal data by competent public authorities for the purposes of the prevention, investigation, detection or prosecution of criminal offences or the execution of criminal penalties, including the safeguarding against and the prevention of threats to public security. Accordingly, the LED applies where criminal law enforcement authorities use intrusive surveillance for these purposes, i.e. for gathering criminal intelligence for preventative purposes, as well as during criminal investigations and proceedings. The LED provides that the personal data, such as those of victims, witnesses and suspects of crime, are duly protected and also lays down a framework for national authorities to process data for law enforcement purposes and for the exchange of such data between public authorities.

The GDPR applies to the processing of personal data by private or public entities, for example in order to retain personal data, to grant access to personal data or to forward such data to State agencies. Importantly, where a spyware is furnished to a Member State by a private service provider—such as the NSO group or Candiru (the producer of the eponymous spyware) or Paragon (the producer of Graphite)—the GDPR comes into play with regard to that provider too. Indeed, the data acquired through the use of spyware are transmitted to the server of the provider. Article 4(7) GDPR defines the concept of "controller" as meaning the person who or which, alone or jointly with others, determines the purposes and means of the processing of personal data; that regulation mentions another party involved in data processing, namely the "processor", which is defined in Article 4(8) GDPR as the person which processes personal data on behalf of the controller.[51] It is true that recital 78 GDPR implies that a producer would usually not come into the ambit of application of this Regulation. However, that does not rule out that it is qualified as data controller or data processor if the relevant legal conditions are fulfilled.[52] It is not so clear whether the spyware provider qualifies as a data controller or data processor. Since it designs the software (thus determining what it can do and how) and has control thereof as

[48] Judgment of 18.09.2019, BVerwG 6 A 7.18, § 43, confirmed by judgment of 25.09.2024 - BVerwG 6 A 3.22, § 44.

[49] Cf. German Constitutional Court's Order of 8 October 2024, 1 BvR 1743/16 and 1 BvR 2539/16, § 77.

[50] See Articles 13, 14 and 16 LED.

[51] Opinion of AG M. Szpunar in *Russmedia*, C-492/23, EU:C:2025:68, § 100.

[52] See, to this effect, judgment in *Gesamtverband Autoteile-Handel*, C-319/22, EU:C:2023:837.

well as of the means, it is plausible that it qualifies as data controller. That is so even if the data acquired are sent immediately to the Member State which has bought the spyware license. On the other hand, where the commercial spyware provider provides and operates a tailor-made service according to the instructions of law enforcement authorities, it may qualify as a processor under theGDPR. The exact qualification depends on the circumstances of the case.[53]

The e-privacy Directive applies only to the processing of personal data in connection with the provision of publicly available electronic communications services in public communications networks in the Union.[54] The Article 29 Data Protection Working Party pointed out in its Opinion 1/200821 that Article 5(3) e-privacy Directive is a general provision, which is applicable not only to electronic communication services but also to any other services when the respective techniques are used; the reformulation of Article 5(3) of the e-privacy Directive in 2009 and the underlying rationale indicate that the Article means to protect information stored on terminal equipment against any type of "third-party" spyware inter alia "involving unwarranted intrusion", irrespective of how the spyware was disseminated (Recitals 65 and 66 Citizen's Rights Directive 2009/136/EC).[55] To the extent that it is applicable, the e-Privacy Directive is relevant because it prohibits—save for the case of consent by the user concerned—any listening, tapping, recording, storage or other interception or surveillance of communications and related traffic data, by either public authorities or private bodies other than the user.[56] However, as already illustrated, restrictions to these rights are permitted for listed legitimate public objectives, such as the prevention, investigation, detection and prosecution of criminal offences, and the protection of public and national security, subject to certain conditions and adequate safeguards.

Spyware entails access to a host of personal data, including sensitive data. As follows from the very terms of Article 10 LED, the requirement that the processing of sensitive data be allowed "only where strictly necessary" must be interpreted as establishing stricter conditions for lawful processing of sensitive data, compared with those which follow from Article 4(1)(b) and (c) and Article 8(1) of that Directive and refer only to the "necessity" of data processing that falls generally, within the Directive's scope.[57] Thus, first, the use of the adverb "only" before the words "where strictly necessary" underlines that the processing of special

---

[53] Judgments in *Wirtschaftsakademie*, C-210/16, EU:C:2018:388; and *Fashion ID*, C-40/17, EU:C:2019:629. See also EDPB, *Guidelines 07/2020 on the concepts of controller and processor in the GDPR* Version 2.1, adopted on 7 July 2021, § 37. Cf. J. Marosi, *(Gem-)Einsame Verantwortlichkeit im Datenschutzrecht - Voraussetzungen, Folgen, Perspektiven*, 2024, pp. 230 and 270.

[54] Article 3(1) e-privacy Directive.

[55] Opinion 2/2010 on online behavioural advertising of 22 June 2010, page 9 (available on line). See also Europe's PegasusGate: Countering spyware abuse, cit., footnotes 593 and 594.

[56] Article 5(1) ePrivacy Directive.

[57] Judgments in *Bezirkshauptmannschaft Landeck*, C-548/21, EU:C:2024:830, § 107; *Ministerstvo na vatreshnite raboti (Recording of biometric and genetic data by the police)*, C-205/21, EU:C:2023:49, §§ 116, 117 and the case-law cited.

categories of data, within the meaning of Article 10 LED, will be capable of being regarded as necessary solely in a limited number of cases. Second, the fact that the necessity for processing of such data is an "absolute" one signifies that that necessity is to be assessed with particular rigour.[58] The same result also flows from the principle of proportionality and thus applies to the GDPR and the e-privacy Directive too.

When a right guaranteed in the EU privacy acquis is limited, individuals can request the competent authorities to review a restriction of the right in question and ask them to verify whether the restriction was carried out in accordance with the rules.[59] The enforcement of the e-privacy Directive provisions at national level is entrusted to a "competent national authority" (Article 15a of the Dir.), without further defining that authority or body. Data protection authorities (DPAs) are often the first point of entry to supervise the processing of personal data when intrusive surveillance software is being used for the prevention, investigation, detection and prosecution of criminal offences and the protection of public security.[60] However, for spyware surveillance by intelligence agencies, DPAs are not always competent.[61] On the other hand, where intelligence agencies overstep their remit (or conduct surveillance under false pretence), it is reasonable to consider that DPAs can supervise them. Relevant national provisions need to be interpreted in conformity with EU law, including the EU fundamental rights and the principle of effectiveness.

In order to validly invoke a justification, Member States must prove in a concrete manner and by reference to the circumstances of the case, that the measure is justified.[62] In particular in order to validly invoke national security, Member States must be able to demonstrate that national security would be compromised in the case at issue,[63] must prove that it is necessary to derogate from EU law in order to safeguard its national security or pursue law enforcement,[64] derogations must be set out in the law, that the public interest could not have been achieved by applying the relevant

[58] Judgment in *Bezirkshauptmannschaft Landeck*, cit., § 108.

[59] Article 17 LED. See also judgment in *Ligue des droits humains*, C-333/22, EU:C:2023:874, §§ 40–41.

[60] Data protection authorities are not competent to supervise the courts acting in their judicial capacity. Member States may also provide that data protection authorities are not competent to supervise other judicial authorities when they are acting in their judicial capacity (see Article 45(2) LED).

[61] Cf. Fundamental Rights Agency's study on Surveillance by intelligence services, pp. 20 et seq.

[62] See, by analogy, judgments in *Commission v Hungary (usufruct)*, C-235/17, EU:C:2020:476, § 77; and *Commission v Hungary (NGOs)*, C-78/18, EU:C:2020:476, § 77.

[63] Judgment in *La Quadrature du Net I*, cit., § 137. See also judgments in *Commission v Poland and Others (temporary mechanism for the relocation of applicants for international protection)*, C-715/17, C-718/17 and 719/17, EU:C:2020:257, §§ 145–146 and 152; and *Commission v Cyprus*, C-515/14, EU:C:2016:30, § 54.

[64] See, by analogy, judgments in *Commission v Poland and Others (temporary mechanism for the relocation of applicants for international protection)*, cit., § 147; and *Commission v Denmark (duty-free imports of military equipment)*, C-461/05, EU:C:2009:783, § 55.

EU law to which they are bound.[65] The scope of the requirements relating to the maintenance of national security or public security or public policy cannot be determined unilaterally by each Member State, "without any control by the institutions of the European Union".[66]

Under the EU case law, the objective of protecting national security corresponds to the essential functions of the State and the fundamental interests of society.[67] This includes the prevention and punishment of activities capable of seriously destabilising the fundamental constitutional, political, economic or social structures of a country, and, in particular, of directly threatening society, the population or the State itself, such as terrorist activities.[68] The ECtHR considered certain activities to constitute a threat to national security as follows: espionage,[69] terrorism,[70] activities of separatist extremist organisations that threaten the unity or security of a State by violent or undemocratic means,[71] activities which threaten the safety or well-being of the State and activities which are intended to undermine or overthrow parliamentary democracy by political, industrial or violent means,[72] and incitement to disaffection of military personnel.[73] The threat to national security must be distinguishable, by its nature, its seriousness, and the specific nature of the circumstances from the general and permanent risk for public security, or from serious criminal offences being committed.[74] Therefore, the threat must be serious, genuine, present or foreseeable.[75] If a journalist, a political opponent or an NGO activist has been subject to spyware in order to spy on him/her because of his/her political colour, that use of spyware will by definition not genuinely correspond to nationality security or the need to fight against crimes; as a result, it cannot be justified.

[65] See, by analogy, judgments in *Commission v Austria ("State printing works")*, cit., §§ 78 to 80; and *Commission v Poland ("State printing office")*, EU:C:2023:629, § 83. See also Opinion of Advocate General S. Øe in Case *B.K.*, C-742/19, EU:C:2021:77.

[66] Judgment in *Commission v Poland and Others (temporary mechanism for the relocation of applicants for international protection)*, cit., § 146. See also judgment in *Zh. and O.*, C-554/13EU:C:2015:377, § 48.

[67] Judgment in *Latvijas Republikas Saeima (penalty points)*, cit., § 67.

[68] Judgments in *La Quadrature du Net I*, cit., § 135; *SpaceNet*, C-793/19 and C 794/19, EU:C:2022:702, § 92.; and *Commission v Poland ("State printing office")*, cit., § 80.

[69] ECtHR, judgments in Roman Zakharov v Russia, CE:ECHR:2006:1005JUD001488103; and Klass v. Germany, CE:ECHR:1978:0906JUD000502971.

[70] ECtHR, judgment in Klass v Germany, cit.; and decision in *Weber and Saravia v Germany*, CE:ECHR:2006:0629DEC005493400.

[71] ECtHR, judgment in United Communist Party of Turkey and Others v Turkey, CE:ECHR:1998:0130JUD001939292.

[72] ECtHR, judgments in Kennedy v the United Kingdom, CE:ECHR:2010:0518JUD002683905, § 159; and Leander v Sweden, CE:ECHR:1987:0326JUD000924881.

[73] ECtHR, decision in Arrowsmith v. United Kingdom, CE:ECHR:1977:0516DEC000705075.

[74] Judgment in *SpaceNet*, cit., §§ 92 to 93.

[75] Judgment in *La Quadrature du Net I*, cit., § 135.

Furthermore, Member States need to prove the proportionality of the measure.[76] In accordance with the principle of proportionality, the surveillance measure, including its duration and scope, shall not exceed what is necessary to achieve the (legitimate) objective pursued.[77] This requires balancing, on the one hand, the need to pursue a legitimate public interest (such as the need to combat a very serious crime) and, on the other hand, the seriousness of the interference with an individual's right to data protection and private life.[78] Recital 26 EMFA, by relying on the case law, explains in detail what the principle of proportionality entails.[79]

Under the CJEU's case law, in compliance with the principles of necessity and proportionality, the seriousness of the intrusion can be justified only by the seriousness of the public interest that is pursued by the public authorities.[80] This corresponds in substance to the ECtHR's case law,[81] whereby the higher the level of interference, the more robust the level of safeguards must be.[82] In *La Quadrature du net II*, the CJEU used the terms "serious and even 'particularly serious' interferences with the fundamental rights concerned" when referring to national measures allowing general access to all retained traffic and location data.[83] As explained above, the interference with fundamental rights by spyware is extremely serious.[84] Therefore, there are doubts that in many instances spyware like Pegasus, Candiru and Graphite,

---

[76] As regards the need for evidence, in the context of the interpretation of LED the CJEU has required that the existence of reasonable suspicions is supported by subjective and sufficient evidence (Judgment in *Bezirkshauptmannschaft Landeck*, cit., § 101).

[77] See also Article 5 of Convention 108 and judgment of the ECtHR of 2 September 2010, Uzun v Germany, CE:ECHR:2010:0902JUD003562305: the ECtHR found that a GPS device for location tracking was a less intrusive measure than the interception of personal communications.

[78] See, by analogy, judgment in *La Quadrature du Net I*, cit., § 131.

[79] It states that "[a]ccording to the principle of proportionality, limitations can be made to an individual's rights and freedoms only if they are necessary and genuinely meet objectives of general interest recognised by the Union. Thus, as regards specifically the deployment of intrusive surveillance software, it is necessary to ascertain whether the offence in question attains a threshold of seriousness as laid down in this Regulation, whether, following an individual assessment of all the relevant circumstances in a given case, the investigation and prosecution of that offence merit the particularly intrusive interference with fundamental rights and economic freedoms consisting in the deployment of intrusive surveillance software, whether there is sufficient evidence that the offence in question has been committed, and whether the deployment of intrusive surveillance software is relevant for the purpose of establishing the facts related to the investigation and prosecution of that offence."

[80] Judgment in *La Quadrature du net II*, C-470/21, EU:C:2024:370, § 95. See also, by analogy, judgment in *Sverige and Watson*, cit., § 102.

[81] See, to this effect, J. Ferreau, "Rechte von Mediendienstanbietern (Art. 4)", in ibid. (ed.), *Das neue EU-Medienfreiheitsgesetz, Nomos*, 2024, p. 47.

[82] Judgments in *Ligue des droits humains*, C-817/19, EU:C:2022:491, §§ 116–117; and *Orde van Vlaamse Balies*, C-694/20, EU:C:2022:963, § 41.

[83] Judgment in *La Quadrature du net II*, § 128.

[84] Venice Commission, cit., § 9. See also European Data Protection Supervisor, cit., page. 8 whereby "[t]he level of interference with the right to privacy is so severe that the individual is in fact deprived of it." Cf. also judgment in *Tele 2 Sverige and Watson*, cit., § 100.

can pass the proportionality test because, given its huge invasiveness and extremely broad reach, its use is likely to go beyond what is necessary and, moreover, because alternative surveillance possibilities are likely to be available. One of the findings in the interesting report published in April 2023 by the UN Human Rights Council and drafted by special rapporteur Prof. Fionnuala Ní Aoláin of the University of Minnesota Law School is that there may well be a category of spyware which, by virtue of its indiscriminate and disproportionate impact, can never be operated in a lawful manner.[85] The implication is also that the safeguards should be built-in, in compliance with the principle of rule of law and the need to ensure the effectiveness of Union law. This in turn raises the issue of the need for further regulation at EU law level, also in view of the regulatory discrepancies in the Internal Market.

5 The Fundamental Freedoms Under the Treaty

Even for those matters that do not fall into the ambit of application of the EU privacy legislation, the applicability of EU law in the context of the use of intrusive surveillance software can be triggered by the fundamental freedoms. The fundamental freedoms guaranteed by the Treaty protect the cross-border provision of services, the free movement of citizens and workers across the Union, the freedom of establishment and the free movement of capital cross-border. All economic activity falls within the scope of the fundamental freedoms.[86] Given the symbiotic relationship between individuals and technological devices such as laptops, smartphones and tablets, the exercise of personal and economic activities relies in many regards on such devices. Surveillance through spyware is liable to have both a disturbance effect and a chilling effect. Therefore, a surveillance intrusion into such devices in a potentially cross-border context is in general liable to affect the rights guaranteed by the Treaties to EU physical and legal persons.

The following scenarios can serve as illustrative examples of situations where the fundamental freedoms apply to Member States using intrusive surveillance: a cross-border active journalist investigating the conduct of a Member State's government; a businessperson working for an EU-foreign undertaking and possessing the formula of a new, not yet patented pharmaceutical product; a scientist moving to a Member State other than the Member State of origin in order to start a salaried work position at a research institute; a human rights organisation receiving funds from a different Member State or from EU-foreigners; an EU-based lawyer active across-border; cross-border policy consulting activities done through video-conferencing services; videos produced for a political party established in another Member State with a view to an upcoming election campaign; a political spin-doctor providing his/her

[85] Fionnuala Ní Aoláin, Human rights implications of the development, use and transfer of new technologies in the context of counter-terrorism and countering and preventing violent extremism - Report of the Special Rapporteur on the promotion and protection of human rights and fundamental freedoms while countering terrorism, UN Human Rights Council, 2023.

[86] Judgment in *Fidium-Finanz*, C-452/04, EU:C:2006:631, § 32.

services electronically to a client established in a different Member State. These situations fall into at least one of the fundamental freedoms guaranteed by the Treaty. In all these situations, the confidentiality of the activity is inherent part thereof, so that spyware is liable to restrict its free exercise and thus constitutes a restriction to free movement: the use of intrusive surveillance software is liable to intrude into and interfere with the way in which individuals and undertakings exercise their right to free movement within the internal market. Thus, for example, the use of intrusive surveillance software is liable to destroy the confidentiality of a journalist's sources, which are tantamount to the raw material for the production of his/her services (see recital 19 EMFA). Similarly, obtaining the formula of a not yet patented pharmaceutical product is liable to frustrate its protection, to the detriment of the business activity of the formula possessor. By the same token, the use of intrusive surveillance software constitutes an intrusion into the scientific research data of a scientist, posing a significant risk of unauthorized disclosure and a potential loss of commercial value. In a similar vein, the possibility to seize information which an NGO is giving to its potential cross-border donors to solicit funding is liable to restrict the free movement of capital within the internal market. Analogue considerations apply to cross-border policy consultant, producers of videos for a political campaign and spin doctors.[87]

Restrictions to free movement are in principle prohibited. They can be accepted only if duly justified and proportionate. The obligation of justification entails that Member State authorities must prove that the use of spyware is justified by an overriding reason of public interest with regard to one of the crimes pursued. The terms "overriding reason of public interest" is an EU law concept, so that Member States authorities cannot define it *ad libitum*: they can invoke it only where the public interest is sufficiently clearly defined and fulfills the criteria set out in the EU case law. The burden of proof for Member States as regards justification and proportionality has been illustrated above.

The importance of the applicability of the fundamental freedoms is not only the protection which they as such afford to individuals, but also lies in the fact that they render the Charter of fundamental Rights applicable (see below).

6 European Media Freedom Act

Article 4 EMFA bestows rights on the media service providers.[88] In particular, Article 4(3) EMFA protects journalistic sources and confidential communications. The term "journalistic sources" comprises any information on facts and opinions

[87] See the concrete case mentioned by M. Szabó, EEP Group Public Hearing of 10 February 2022 on "Pegasus spyware scandal and its impact on democracy in the EU", 53:45-55:05 (available on the EPP Group website).

[88] "Media service provider" is defined as "a natural or legal person whose professional activity is to provide a media service and who has editorial responsibility for the choice of the content of the media service and determines the manner in which it is organized" (Article 2 n° 2 EMFA). "Media service" in turn means "a service as defined by Articles 56 and 57 TFEU, where the principal purpose of the service or a dissociable section thereof consists in providing programmes or press

which can be used by media service providers as the basis for a piece of news or an item of journalism. In light of the case law on freedom of the press and given the objective of Article 4(3) EMFA, the expression "journalistic sources" is to be interpreted broadly.[89] Indeed, in order to take account of the importance of the freedom of the press and the freedom of expression in other media in every democratic society, it is necessary to interpret broadly concepts related to those freedoms.[90]

The term "confidential communications" refers to any communication that because of its content or origin is imparted in a reserved manner and plays a role in the production/distribution of media content. Here again, given the liberal objective of the provision, this term is to be interpreted broadly. Under Article 4(3) EMFA, the protection against State intervention is extended to persons who, because of their regular or professional relationship with a media service provider or its editorial staff, might have relevant information.[91] This category is defined functionally, and, in view of its rationale, it is also to be interpreted broadly.[92]

Recital 19 EMFA explains the economic significance of journalistic sources, which "are tantamount to 'raw material' for journalists: they are the basis for the production of media content by journalists, in particular news and current affairs content." As explained in recital 19 EMFA, "[i]t is therefore crucial that journalists' ability to collect, fact-check and analyse information be protected, in particular information imparted or communicated confidentially, both offline and online, which relates to or is capable of identifying journalistic sources". Journalistic sources are often confidential because, either for ethical or professional reasons, some individuals are willing to give information to journalists only under the condition of anonymity or confidentiality. If the anonymity or confidentiality of sources is destroyed, hampered or made less attractive, confidants will be discouraged from providing information to journalists so that the media service providers will have less "raw material" for producing their services, to the detriment of the free exercise of the media service activity.

The second sentence of Article 4(3) EMFA provides inter alia that Member States shall not deploy intrusive surveillance software on media service providers. Pursuant to Article 4(4) EMFA, State intervention is, however, not prohibited by the EMFA under certain detailed conditions which are set out in the paragraphs 4 and 5. According to Article 4(4) EMFA, one of the national measures listed above is not prohibited only if it is:

a) provided for by Union or national law ("legality principle");
b) in compliance with Article 52(1) of the Charter and other Union law;

publications, under the editorial responsibility of a media service provider, to the general public, by any means, in order to inform, entertain or educate" (Article 2 n° 1 EMFA).

[89] See also Ferreau, cit., page 43.

[90] Judgment in *Autorité des marchés financiers*, C-302/20, EU:C:2022:190, § 66.

[91] See also recital 20 EMFA.

[92] See, to this effect, Ferreau, cit., page 45.

c) justified on a case-by-case basis by an overriding reason of public interest and proportionate;
d) subject to prior authorization by a judicial authority or an independent and impartial decision-making authority or, in duly justified exceptional and urgent cases, is subsequently authorized by such an authority without undue delay.

As regards the deployment of intrusive surveillance software referred to in point c) of Article 4(3) EMFA, two additional conditions for the derogation are laid down in Article 4(5) EMFA as follows:

[1] the measure is carried out for the purpose of investigating one of the persons referred to in paragraph 3, point (c), with regard to:

  (i) offences listed in Article 2(2) of Framework Decision 2002/584/JHA punishable in the Member State concerned by a custodial sentence or a detention order of a maximum period of at least three years; or
  (ii) other serious crimes punishable in the Member State concerned by a custodial sentence or a detention order of a maximum period of at least five years, as determined by the law of that Member State; and

[2] one of the measures mentioned under a) or b) would not be adequate and sufficient ("*ultima ratio*" or "subsidiarity rule").

Exceptions to rules are to be construed narrowly so that general rules are not negated.[93] In addition, according to the settled case-law of the ECtHR, exceptions to the freedom of expression are to be construed strictly and Article 10(2) ECHR leaves little scope for restrictions on freedom of expression in the fields of political speech and matters of public interest.[94] Therefore, all the abovementioned conditions shall be construed rigorously. As remarked by the Venice Commission, "[w]ith particular regard to journalism, it is well-established that surveillance tools may be applied in only the most exceptional circumstances. European and international sources have widely recognized that journalism's watchdog role requires exceptional caution when considering interferences with their functions."[95]

Given the extremely serious interference by spyware with fundamental rights, the public interest that can be invoked to justify the use of spyware must also be very serious i.e. that the seriousness of the offence pursued must be particularly high, accordingly. It follows that the Member States cannot distort the concept of 'serious offence' and, by extension, that of 'serious crime', by including within it, for the purposes of applying the derogation under Article 4(5) EMFA, offences which are manifestly not serious offences, in the light of the societal conditions prevailing in the Member State concerned, even though the legislature of that Member State has provided for such offences to be punishable by a maximum term of imprisonment

[93] Judgment in *HF and Generalstaatsanwaltschaft München*, C-435/22 PPU, EU:C:2022:852, § 120.
[94] Judgment in *Real Madrid v. Le Monde*, C-633/22, EU:C:2024:843, § 53.
[95] Venice Commission, cit., § 93.

of five years.[96] Moreover, the fact that a journalist's conduct falls into the category of the crimes listed in Article 4 EMFA is alone insufficient to justify the deployment of spyware; in fact, the further requirements must be fulfilled, including proportionality in concreto (see below), so that judicial or independent authorities must refuse the authorization of the restrictive measure if the offence at issue is manifestly not serious.[97] That is also in line with the objective of the provision (see recital 25 EMFA).

The obligation of prior authorization under Article 4(4)(c) EMFA, which was introduced during the negotiations of the Regulation, is particularly important because it introduces the verification by an independent organ. The ECtHR has emphasized the importance of prior authorization by an independent organ for interceptions of journalists.[98] The extension of the power of prior authorization to other independent authorities has been criticized on the grounds that they lack the same level of independence as the judicial branch, as they are part of the administrative branch of the executive power.[99] This criticism should be taken seriously.[100] But this criticism needs, at the same time, to be nuanced because (unlike the national rule at issue in the Sanoma case) a sufficient level of independence is required by Article 4(4)(c) EMFA. Indeed, that provision is to be construed in view of its protective objective and in consonance with the fundamental rights. This also finds expression in recital 21 EMFA, whereby "[i]n light thereof, ensuring an adequate level of protection for journalistic sources and confidential communications requires that measures for obtaining such information be authorised by an authority that can independently and impartially assess whether it is justified by an overriding reason of public interest, such as a court, a judge, a prosecutor acting in a judicial capacity, or another such authority with competence to authorise those measures in accordance with national law". The expression "another *such* authority" indicates that the authorities that may authorize the use of the restrictive measures at

---

[96] See, by analogy, judgment in *Procura di Bolzano*, C-178/22, EU:C:2024:371, § 50.

[97] See, by analogy, ibid., § 62. See also, to this effect and by analogy, judgment in *Bezirkshauptmannschaft Landeck*, cit., § 105. See F. Palmiotto, "Criminal investigations, access to data and fundamental rights: The role of judicial review after Procura", Common Market Law Review, vol. 6, 2024, 1633–1644.

[98] ECtHR, judgments of 25 May 2021, Big Brother Watch v UK, CE:ECHR:2021:0525JUD005817013, §§ 351 et seq.; of 28 November 2024, Klaudia Csikós v Hungary, CE:ECHR:2024:1128JUD003109116, §§ 53–54. See D. Voorhoof (2021), Case Law, Strasbourg: Big Brother Watch v United Kingdom, Bulk interception regime violated Articles 8 and 10, 9 June 2021, (available on inform.org); and D. Voorhoof (2025), European Court of Human Rights: Klaudia Csikós v. Hungary, European Audiovisual Observatory, IRIS 2025-1:1/26.

[99] J. Bayer, *Digital Media Regulation within the European Union*, Nomos, 2023, p. 122.

[100] Cf. ECtHR, judgment of 14 September 2014, Sanoma v. Netherlands, CE:ECHR:2010:0914JUD003822403, § 100. See also J. E. Kermer, "Article 4 of the European Media Freedom Act: a missed opportunity?: assessing its shortcomings in protecting journalistic sources", in Simeonov, Yurukova (eds), Papers from the Eleventh International Scientific Conference of the European Studies Department: the agenda of the new EU institutional cycle, Sofia: Minerva, 2024, pages 192–207 (198), available on line.

issue must have a level of independence and impartiality that is analogue to that possessed by a judicial organ. The prior authorization can be dispensed of only "in duly justified exceptional and urgent cases". The urgency must be validly established before that exception can be used.[101] In any event it must remain truly exceptional.

Under Article 4(5)(b) EMFA, the deployment of spyware must be carried out "for the purpose of investigating one of the persons referred to in paragraph 3, point (c)". This wording indicates that spyware can be used against a given journalist only to investigate a crime that has been likely committed by him/her and not by other individuals.[102] This interpretation is also in line with the objective of the provision, which is to offer a "robust harmonized protection in relation to the deployment of intrusive surveillance software in the Union" (recital 19 EMFA), and with the fundamental rights of journalists.

Paragraph 6 of Article 4 EMFA further specifies that the abovementioned measures under b) and c) of Article 4(4) EMFA must be regularly reviewed in order to verify whether the conditions are still being met. This also corresponds in substance to the guarantees existing under the ECHR.[103] Given its purpose, it must be interpreted rigorously. It is an important provision in practice because otherwise the risk of overly long duration of the restrictive measures would be tangible.

Paragraph 8 of Article 4 EMFA, in its first part, is about the remedies for media service providers. It has a declaratory nature, restating what already flows from Article 47 Charter of Fundamental Rights of the EU. Then, the second part of paragraph 8 of Article 4 EMFA provides that "Member States shall entrust an independent authority or body with relevant expertise to provide assistance to the persons referred to in the first subparagraph with regard to the exercise of that right." This authority/body will play an important role in upholding the rights of media service providers, as will be illustrated in detail below.

7 The Charter

Where Member States deploy an intrusive surveillance measure in any of the abovementioned scenarios, without the involvement of private entities, they are considered to be implementing EU law within the meaning of Article 51(1) of the Charter, so that the Charter is applicable. Therefore, in particular Article 7 (respect for private and family life), Article 8 (protection of personal data) and Article 11 (freedom of expression and information) of the Charter are applicable. Freedom of

[101] See also, by analogy, judgment in *Tele 2 Sverige and Watson*, cit., § 120.

[102] Indication given by C. Brill during the EMFA talk "Safeguarding journalistic sources under Article 4 of the European Media Freedom Act", held on 13 January 2025 at the European University Institute.

[103] See, to this effect, ECtHR, judgment in Szabó and Vissy v Hungary, CE:ECHR:2016:0112JUD003713814, § 26.

expression, guaranteed in Article 11 of the Charter, constitutes one of the essential foundations of a pluralistic, democratic society, and is one of the values upon which, under Article 2 TEU, the Union is founded.[104] Spyware interferes with freedom of expression not only of the target, but also of third parties who are subject to communications content. That reinforces the need for a particularly limited use of such measures and the requirement of very precisely developed provisions.[105] The protection of personal data is of fundamental importance to a person's enjoyment of his or her right to respect for private and family life, as guaranteed by Article 8 ECHR.[106] The protection of the fundamental right to respect for private life at EU level requires that derogations and limitations on the protection of personal data are to apply only in so far as is strictly necessary.[107] Special protection is afforded to certain professions such as journalists and lawyers.[108]

Legitimate public interests that can be invoked by public authorities in this context to try to justify the interference caused by spyware comprise the fight against serious forms of crimes such as terrorism and organized crimes, the fight against pedophilia, the protection of public security. Furthermore, Member Sates could try to invoke the protection of further fundamental rights such as the right to human dignity, the right to life, the right to the integrity of the person, the rights of the child.[109]

Given the high seriousness of the interference, the public interest that can be invoked to justify the use of spyware must also be very serious. It is true that the CJEU, when interpreting the LED, held that only combatting serious crime may justify access to data contained in a mobile telephone would limit the investigative power of the competent authorities and that would increase the risk of impunity of such offences.[110] However, that judgment was handed down in a case regarding a "normal" access to a data of a phone that had been physically seized and not an access through spyware, which is much more intrusive. Moreover, the judicial dictum regarding the correspondence between the seriousness of the intrusion and the seriousness of the objective pursued belongs to settled case law of the CJEU.

In its case law, the ECtHR has worked out a number of guarantees to protect individuals from secret surveillance by the State, which pursuant to Article 52(3)

---

[104] See, to this effect, judgment in *La Quadrature du net II*, cit., § 68.

[105] M. Cole and C. Etteldorf, *European Media Freedom Act – Background Analysis*, CULT Committee of the European Parliament, 2023, page 28.

[106] ECtHR, judgment in S. and Marper v. the United Kingdom, CE:ECHR:2008:1204JUD00 3056204, § 103.

[107] Judgments in *Tele 2 Sverige and Watson*, cit., § 96; and *Endemol Shine*, C-740/22, EU:C:2024:216, § 52.

[108] Judgment in *Orde van Vlaamse Balies*, cit., § 27. See also M. Gerhold, "Grundrechtlicher Schutz des anwaltlichen Berufsgeheimnisses als Funktionsprivileg im Mehrebenensystem", Juristenzeitung 2023, pp. 303 et seq.

[109] See, to this effect and by analogy, the arguments put forward by the French government in Case C-188/24, *WebGroup Czech Republic* (pending at the time of writing).

[110] Judgment in *Bezirkshauptmannschaft Landeck*, cit., § 97.

Charter Fundamental Rights constitute the minimum standard of EU fundamental rights, as appropriate. These guarantees include: the State's obligation to set out the circumstances and the conditions upon which public authorities may resort to surveillance measures; the obligation to define the categories of individuals who can be subject to surveillance; the obligation to set a limit on the duration of surveillance; the obligation to determine the procedure that needs to be complied with when examining, using, and storing the data obtained; the obligation to take precautions when communicating the data to other parties; the obligation to specify the circumstances under which the obtained data must be erased or destroyed.[111] Legislation applicable to spyware needs to be particularly detailed, stringent and clear as regards all the aspects underlined above, in particular the conditions for using spyware, the procedures and the modalities of use.

The ECtHR specified that the right to privacy would be "unacceptably weakened if the use of modern technologies in the criminal-justice system were allowed at any cost and without carefully balancing the potential benefits of the extensive use of such technologies against important private-life interests".[112] The particular context in which the interference with fundamental rights takes place, in particular the modalities of the intrusion and the amount of data obtained, cannot be ignored in the analysis.[113] It can be inferred from Article 11 Charter of Fundamental Rights a positive obligation for Member States to avoid lacunae in the security of IT systems, just like Member States are pursuant to Article 10 ECHR under a positive duty to set up a legal framework to ensure effective media pluralism.[114]

It is to be asked whether the interference by spyware does not violate the essence of the fundamental rights concerned. In *Schrems I* the CJEU took issue with European legislation that authorized storage of all the personal data of all the persons whose data has been transferred from the European Union to the United States without any differentiation, limitation or exception being made.[115] It held that "[i]n particular, legislation permitting the public authorities to have access on a generalised basis to the content of electronic communications must be regarded as compromising the essence of the fundamental right to respect for private life, as guaranteed by Article 7 of the Charter".[116] As explained above, Spyware goes well

[111] ECtHR, judgments in Huvig v France, CE:ECHR:1990:0424JUD001110584, § 34; and Association for European Integration and Human Rights and Ekimdzhiev and Others v Bulgaria, CE:ECHR:2007:0628JUD006254000, § 76; and decision in Weber and Saravia v Germany, CE:ECHR:2006:0629DEC005493400, § 95.

[112] ECtHR, judgment in *Podchasov v Russia*, ECHR:2024:0213JUD003369619, § 62.

[113] See, by analogy, judgment in *La Quadrature du net II*, cit., § 107, as regards Article 15(1) of Directive 2002/58.

[114] ECtHR, judgment in Centro Europa 7 v Italy, CE:ECHR:2012:0607JUD003843309, § 134. See also, by analogy, Order by the German Constitutional Court of 8 June 2021, 1 BvR 2771/18, § 32.

[115] Judgment in *Schrems I*, C-362/14, EU:C:2015:650, § 93.

[116] Judgment in *Schrems I*, cit., § 94. See K. Lenaerts, "Limits on Limitations: The Essence of Fundamental Rights in the EU", German Law Journal 2019, 20, pp. 779 et seq. (782).

beyond a traditional wire-tapping tool: it gives access to a truly huge amount of data (including retroactive access to messages, files and passwords and metadata) and moreover it allows to operate the microphone and the camera, to manipulate content and documents on a device as well as to impersonate the individual by accessing their identity and digital credentials. Therefore, unless there are clear, stringent and effective modalities imposed for the design and use of spyware, the fundamental rights under Articles 7, 8 and 11 Charter risk being annihilated and thus their essence being violated, contrary to Article 52(1) Charter.

Furthermore, whereas the secret nature of surveillance serves, to a certain extent, a functional purpose in the investigations, it collides with an individual's rights such as the right of defence. The right for individuals to be notified that they were subject to the use of surveillance is recognized in the case law as being instrumental to enable the affected individuals to exercise their right to the protection of personal data and to privacy as well as their right to an effective judicial remedy.[117] This is also recognized in recital 22 EMFA and the case law.[118] The limitations of the right to notification in due time must be provided for by law, respect the essence of the rights and freedoms at issue and, in compliance with the principle of proportionality, must be necessary and genuinely meet the legitimate objective of general interest or the need to protect rights and freedoms of others.[119] In a case regarding an individual who was considered to constitute a terrorist threat, the CJEU held that the competent authorities (i.e. those that requested the measure) must notify him as soon as the notification no longer jeopardizes the investigation, so that the individual can exercise his rights under Articles 7, 8 and 47 of the Charter.[120] In a similar vein, in a case regarding the use of a surveillance measure, the ECtHR ruled that the notification is to take place once the risk has evaporated.[121]

Under the ECtHR case law, a prior judicial (or quasi-judicial) authorization must be obtained by the authorities in order to subject individuals such as journalists to secret surveillance measures.[122] The requisite review is to be carried out by a body separate from the executive and other interested parties, invested with the power to determine whether a requirement in the public interest overriding the principle of

[117] Judgments in *Tele 2 Sverige and Watson*, cit., § 121; *La Quadrature du Net I*, cit., § 190. See also ECtHR judgments in Roman Zakharov v Russia, cit., § 287; and Klaudia Csikós v Hungary, cit., § 60.

[118] See, by analogy, judgment in *Bezirkshauptmannschaft Landeck*, cit., §§ 117 et seq.

[119] See, by analogy, ibid., § 120.

[120] See, by analogy, ibid., § 120. For example, to request access to their personal data that has been the subject of those measures and, where appropriate, to have the latter rectified or erased and to avail themselves of an effective remedy before a tribunal (judgment in *La Quadrature du Net I*, cit., § 190).

[121] Judgment in Roman Zakharov v Russia, cit., § 287. See also D. Voorhoof, European Court of Human Rights: Klaudia Csikós v. Hungary, cit.

[122] ECtHR, judgment in *Telegraaf Media Nederland Landelijke Media B.V. and Others v. the Netherlands*, E:ECHR:2012:1122JUD003931506, § 101.

protection of journalistic sources exists prior to the handing over of such material and to prevent unnecessary access to information capable of disclosing the sources' identity if it does not.[123] The organ entrusted with carrying out the prior review must have the power to strike a fair balance between, on the one hand, the legitimate interests relating to the needs of the investigation and, on the other hand, the fundamental rights of the persons concerned.[124] If that review is carried out not by a court but by an independent administrative body, that body must have a status that enables it to act objectively and impartially when carrying out its duties and must, for that purpose, be free from any external influence; accordingly, the requirement of independence that has to be satisfied by the body entrusted with carrying out the prior review means that that body must be a third party in relation to the authority which requests access to the data, so that the former is able to carry out the review objectively and impartially and free from any external influence; in particular, in the criminal field, the requirement of independence entails that the body entrusted with the prior review, first, is not to be involved in the conduct of the criminal investigation in question and, secondly, must have a neutral stance vis-à-vis the parties to the criminal proceedings.[125]

The rule of ex ante authorization, however, has a limit: in justified cases, the review can take place after the deployment of the surveillance measures.[126] But this exception, which is to be interpreted very narrowly, comes with two caveats: i) it must take place within a "short time"[127] and ii) there must be sufficient guarantees that the exception is used sparingly and only in duly justified cases.[128] In a case regarding surveillance on a journalist, the ECtHR importantly held that the review is to be done at the latest before the access and use of the obtained materials by the public authorities.[129]

As regards the obligation of recurrent review (which is also laid down in Art. 4(6) EMFA), it is noteworthy that the ECtHR held that an assessment is to be made at each stage of the process of the necessity and proportionality of the surveillance measures, namely not only at the moment of the assessment for authorising the measure but also during its execution and thereafter.[130] When performing the assessment, the competent organ must understand the implications of the surveillance technique used, the nature of the intrusive surveillance

[123] ECtHR, judgment in Sorokin v Russia, CE:ECHR:2009:0730JUD000773906, § 46.

[124] See, by analogy, judgment in *La Quadrature du net II*, cit., § 125 as regards Article 15(1) e-privacy Dir.

[125] See, by analogy, ibid., § 126 as regards Article 15(1) e-privacy Dir.

[126] Judgment in *La Quadrature du Net I*, cit., § 189; see also ECtHR judgment in Szabó and Vissy v Hungary, cit., §§ 76 and 81.

[127] Idem.

[128] Judgment in Roman Zakharov v Russia, cit., § 266.

[129] ECtHR, judgments in Sanoma Uitgevers B.v The Netherlands, cit., § 91; and Big Brothers v UK, cit. See also D. Voorhoof, Case Law, Strasbourg: Big Brother Watch v United Kingdom, Bulk interception regime violated Articles 8 and 10, cit.

[130] Judgment in Klass v. Germany, cit., § 55.

software including its relevant technical features, and consider whether its deployment can be limited to certain individuals or groups of individuals.[131] Furthermore, the competent organ must have full and unfettered access to all necessary information, including confidential materials, and that the officials involved in interception activities have a duty to disclose to it any material it requires.[132]

In the judicial review of the use of intrusive surveillance software, the judge must be able to examine all relevant questions of law and fact for carrying out a proper review of the measure.[133] The individual's right to an effective remedy entails the right to inspect and comment on evidence and observations before the court.[134] This right may be limited by an overriding reason of public interest: the competent organ must verify whether the reasons for the non-disclosure are well-founded.[135] In instances where the ECtHR found the non-disclosure to be justified, and therefore the adversarial principle is limited, it must be counterbalanced by procedural safeguards,[136] ensuring that the essence of the right to a fair trial is not compromised.[137] Moreover, the right of individuals cannot be completely emptied: they must, at the very least, be given the substance of the grounds upon which the decision to use surveillance is based.[138]

In light of the foregoing, it is doubtful whether at least in some Member States the legislation applicable to spyware is compatible with the fundamental rights standards.[139] It is also an open question whether spyware does not violate the essence of the fundamental rights at stake. Moreover, and in any event, in the use of spyware many safeguards need to be taken in compliance with the fundamental rights under Articles 7, 8 and 11 Charter.

[131] See, for example, judgment in Szabó and Vissy v Hungary, cit., § 77.

[132] Judgment in Roman Zakharov v Russia, cit., § 281.

[133] Judgment in *Ligue des droits humains*, cit., §§ 67–69; ECtHR, judgments in Ozdil and Others v the Republic of Moldova, CE:ECHR:2019:0611JUD004230518, § 68; and Chahal v the United Kingdom, CE:ECHR:1996:1115JUD002241493, § 131.

[134] Judgments in *Commission v Ireland and Others*, C-89/08 P, EU:C:2009:742, § 53; *ZZ*, cit., § 55. ECtHR, judgment in Regner v the Czech Republic, CE:ECHR:2015:1126JUD003528911, § 146.

[135] Judgment in *ZZ*, cit., § 60. ECtHR, judgments in Regner v the Czech Republic, cit., §§ 152 to 153; and Jasper v the United Kingdom, CE:ECHR:2000:0216JUD002705295, § 56.

[136] Judgment in *ZZ*, cit., §§ 57–65. ECtHR, judgments in Regner v the Czech Republic, cit., § 148; and Ternovskis v Latvia, CE:ECHR:2014:0429JUD003363702, § 67.

[137] ECtHR judgments in,Regner v the Czech Republic, cit., § 148; and Adomaitis v Lithuania, CE:ECHR:2022:0118JUD001483318, §§ 68–74.

[138] See, by analogy, judgments in *ZZ*, cit., § 65; *Országos Idegenrendézeti Főigazgatóság*, C-159/21, EU:C:2022:708, § 51; and *Bezirkshauptmannschaft Landeck*, cit., § 120. See also judgment in *HYA*, C-349/21, EU:C:2023:102, §§ 46 and 55.

[139] *PegasusGate - Countering spyware abuse*, pages 20 et seq. Cf. also Venice Commission, cit.

8 Other Relevant Legislation

Whereas spyware shows an extraordinary capacity to penetrate any device, it is clear that the greater the cybersecurity arrangements are, the less likely an infection by spyware is. There are three main EU instruments devoted to increase the cybersecurity: i) the cyber-resilience Act,[140] ii) the NIS 2 Directive, iii) the critical infrastructures Directive.[141] The first one aims at increasing the cyber-resilience by design of products and services; the second one is about putting in place the mechanisms to ensure minimum cybersecurity standards in relation to essential and important entities; the third one aims at ensuring the services which are essential for the maintenance of vital societal functions or economic activities and at enhancing the resilience of critical entities.

Spyware is used inter alia by secret services. Moreover, it leaves traces which only forensics experts can recognize. As a result, the cooperation by whistleblowers to uncover unlawful use of spyware is particularly important: sousveillance (undersight) complements oversight. The Whistleblower Directive provides for the Member States' obligation to lay down measures protecting whistleblowers. It applies inter alia to breaches falling within the scope of the Union acts set out in the Annex that concern protection of privacy and personal data and the security of network and information systems and to breaches relating to the internal market.[142] Under Article 3(2) of the Directive, "[t]his Directive shall not affect the responsibility of Member States to ensure national security or their power to protect their essential security interests. The terms "shall not affect" are different from "shall not apply to". They are not a carve-out; they rather entail that an adequate balancing must be found between, on the one hand, the interests protected under Article 3 (such as confidentiality) and, on the other hand, the effectiveness of EU law and the freedom of expression which is granted to the whistleblower.[143] Accordingly, arrangements (for ex. confidentiality clearance to those who need to have access to the information) must be set up in order to preserve the confidentiality and at the same time make the whistleblowing possible even where confidential information is concerned. Moreover, a piece of information cannot be considered to be classified under national security where national security is a mere pretext and the powers of national authorities have been abused.

---

[140] Regulation (EU) 2024/2847 of the European Parliament and of the Council of 23 October 2024 on horizontal cybersecurity requirements for products with digital elements and amending Regulations (EU) No 168/2013 and (EU) 2019/1020 and Directive (EU) 2020/1828 (Cyber Resilience Act) (OJ 2024/2847).

[141] Directive (EU) 2022/2557 of the European Parliament and of the Council of 14 December 2022 on the resilience of critical entities and repealing Council Directive 2008/114/EC (OJ 2022 L 333, p. 164).

[142] Article 2(1)(a)(x) and 2(1)(c) of Directive (EU) 2019/1937 of the European Parliament and of the Council of 23 October 2019 on the protection of persons who report breaches of Union law (OJ 2019 L 305, p. 17).

[143] ECtHR, judgment in Halet v. Lexembourg, CE:ECHR:2023:0214JUD002188418.

The Directive on attacks against information systems[144] obliges Member States to sanction i) illegal access to information systems, ii) illegal system interference and iii) illegal data interference and iv) illegal interception.[145] The Dual-Use Regulation[146] imposes certain requirements with regard to exports of "cyber-surveillance items". A detailed description of these legal instruments would go beyond the scope of this essay.

9 Remedies

The challenges regarding spyware are both legal and practical: in particular, how can it be ensured that the guarantees provided for in EU law are rendered effective in practice? No hard and fast answer can be provided. The following considerations can at least tease out some of the relevant elements.

First, the secrecy of surveillance measures is to be respected (to a certain extent), so that both the authorization of surveillance measures and their execution are carried out without the individual's knowledge. On the other hand, the *effet utile* of EU law requires that measures are taken such as to avoid the guarantees becoming nugatory. In this regard, Article 4(8) EMFA, in its second part, is instructive. Under this provision, Member States shall entrust an independent authority or body with relevant expertise to provide assistance, with regard to the exercise of the right to effective judicial protection, to media service providers, their editorial staff and any persons who, because of their regular or professional relationship with a media service provider or its editorial staff, might have information related to or capable of identifying journalistic sources or confidential communications. Candidates for being the independent authority or body referred to in this provision could be the data protection authority, but it could also be an ad-hoc authority or even a private entity such as a media service provider chamber or journalist association. An important role to be played by this independent authority or body is to supervise the authorization and the execution of surveillance measures (including verifying the duration and ensuring that the conditions are still being met). The need for the abovementioned independent authority or body is indirectly underpinned by the Venice Commission, which recognized that the absence of information for the target of surveillance measures can, to some extent, be compensated by the presence, in the procedure, of bodies acting as "privacy advocates", i.e. legal professionals that represent the interests of targeted persons and

[144] Article 2(a).

[145] Articles 3, 4, 5 and 6 respectively.

[146] Regulation (EU) 2021/821 of the European Parliament and of the Council of 20 May 2021 setting up a Union regime for the control of exports, brokering, technical assistance, transit and transfer of dual-use items (recast), (OJ 2021 L 206, p. 1). See documentation on line on rijksoverheid.nl.

organizations in the authorization procedure.[147] Strict confidentiality obligations can be imposed on the privacy advocates. A security screened advocate does not directly act for the suspect and cannot, obviously, consult with him or her. The advocate may, under certain circumstances, be given only a very short time to familiarize with the particulars of the case, and thus be at a procedural disadvantage compared to the requesting authority; on the other hand, the mechanism can still have some value insofar as it can lead to conditions being imposed to minimize the intrusion into privacy, either for the target, or others affected by the surveillance.[148] Moreover, it can formalize the process of obtaining authorization, making it clearer that it is the requesting authority which has the burden of showing the need for the use of surveillance and that all the conditions for surveillance are fulfilled, including proportionality.[149]

Second, the target still needs to be notified *ex post facto*, so that he/she can exercise his/her right to judicial remedies, including judicial review and damages actions. The confidentiality of national or public security reasons does not entail that the scope of the judicial review must be substantially limited. According to settled case-law, "the very existence of effective judicial review designed to ensure compliance with provisions of EU law is inherent in the existence of the rule of law; thus, legislation not providing for any possibility for an individual to pursue legal remedies in order to have access to personal data relating to him or her, or to obtain the rectification or erasure of such data, does not respect the essence of the fundamental right to effective judicial protection, as enshrined in Article 47 of the Charter."[150] Whereas certain documents will probably need to be redacted or made entirely confidential, this does not rule out the effective review by a judge, who can handle confidentially reports or other documents. Furthermore, there are doubts about the adequacy of the safeguards where the applicant's presumed situation is such that the information on the authorization of covert information gathering remains confidential and therefore inaccessible to the person concerned.[151] There are some, at least, partial solutions that can be envisaged. For example, a complaint mechanism can be set up to make the review effective; access to classified information can be given to remedial bodies.[152] Furthermore, the use of in-camera proceedings may also provide a practical solution.[153] In addition, the independent authority or body referred to in Article 4(8) EMFA could also be given access to confidential

147 Venice Commission, cit., § 113.

148 Venice Commission, cit., § 113.

149 Venice Commission, cit., § 113.

150 Judgment in *Schrems II*, C-311/18, EU:C:2020:559, § 187.

151 ECtHR judgment in Klaudia Csikós v Hungary, cit., § 66.

152 European Union Agency for Fundamental Rights (ed.), *Surveillance by intelligence services: Fundamental rights safeguards and remedies in the EU - 2023 update*, 2023; and Venice Commission, cit., § 123.

153 See by analogy Article 348(2) TFEU.

information, on the basis of which it could protect the interests of the individual concerned.

Third, Prof. Ní Aoláin considers in her abovementioned report that if there is no audit record of the spyware activity on a device, the use of spyware is incompatible with human rights law. That is an important finding: that incompatibility would lead to the impossibility to use the evidence in judicial or administrative proceedings. At the same time, it has a practical limitation with regard to those instances where spyware is used merely to listen in and not to build evidence.[154] Therefore, it is to be asked whether Member States should not set up, in addition to the independent authority/body provided for in Article 4(8) EMFA, an ombudsman-type of organ acting in full confidentiality and with unlimited access to the authorities' surveillance activities. Such an organ would play a complementary and decisive control function, so that there would be an effective check on the use of spyware by public authorities.[155] Where a State has not established a specialised security oversight body, DPAs or other data-related competent authorities may play an important role in the system of oversight of security and intelligence as a whole.[156] Given the quantity of the data accessed, their sensitive nature and the risk of unlawful access, the data obtained through the use of spyware must be retained in the European Union and must be irreversibly destroyed after the end of the authorization period.[157] The Venice Commission "strongly urges States considering the use of spyware to ensure that it has, as a required safeguard, specialised, vetted, professional teams capable of implementing effective information screening as is required with respect to other information-gathering practices. Destruction requirements [related to unlawfully gathered material] should also be in place, backed up by strong, independent and well-resourced external oversight."[158]

Fourth, in case of violation of EU law, an infringement case by the European Commission would be an option. Whereas the absence to date of any case being investigated by the Commission is likely to indicate a lack of political appetite for infringement cases regarding spyware, things might possibly change in the future. There are three types of infringement cases which the Commission could pursue: i) against national legislation where it lacks sufficient safeguards or otherwise breaches EU law; ii) against a practice by the national administration which exists despite the legal safeguards being sufficient; iii) against a single case of violation showing particular seriousness and thus having precedential value. The second and third type of cases would face an arduous path regarding the evidence. At the same time, the Commission may make use of indicia where the Member State fails to provide the

---

[154] See, to this effect, Venice Commission, cit., § 117.

[155] The idea has been given to me by Prof. A. Reichman in a conversation held at the European University Institute in the autumn of 2024. See, to this effect, also Venice Commission, cit., § 117.

[156] Venice Commission, cit., § 118. See also, by analogy, judgment in *Tele 2 Sverige and Watson*, cit., § 123.

[157] See, by analogy, judgment in *Tele 2 Sverige and Watson*, cit., § 122.

[158] Venice Commission, cit., § 85.

necessary information. Moreover, whistleblowers may provide valuable evidence and information.

A Member State's violation of EU law pursued by the Commission could reach the thresholds of systemic nature; that is the case, for example, where it is the reflection of a widespread and coordinated policy; a systemic violation implies a violation that, in its nature or impact, is liable to transcend individual cases, affecting society as a whole.[159] Under those circumstances, the Commission in the infringement procedure could envisage putting forward a violation of Article 2 TEU, besides the violation of other Treaty provisions and/or secondary law. Indeed, if a national government used spyware as part of a widespread and coordinated strategy to systematically surveille political opponents, critical journalists and undomesticated NGOs without objective grounds, that would likely contradict EU values such as the freedom, human rights, rule of law and democracy. Moreover, where the legal conditions are fulfilled, the EU institutions could envisage making use of the conditionality Regulation.[160] This legal instrument concerns violations of the rule of law, including of fundamental rights, where breaches of the principles of the rule of law in a Member State affect or seriously risk affecting the sound financial management of the Union budget or the protection of the financial interests of the Union in a sufficiently direct way.[161] The question of whether the sound financial management of the Union budget or the protection of the financial interests of the Union is affected in a sufficiently direct way depends on the factual and legal context. Finally, the procedure under Article 7 TEU is worth mentioning. Whereas the procedural and substantive thresholds to be met under this procedure are extremely demanding, it is possible that a systemic problem related to spyware would be one of the elements that contribute to the finding of a serious violation of the values under Article 7 TEU.

10 Conclusion

A number of legal instruments are available under EU law to tackle the indiscriminate or arbitrary use of spyware by Member States. Some national authorities under the guise of national security reject the applicability of EU law altogether: that rejection is legally unfounded. Moreover, the surreptitious nature of spyware makes the enforcement of EU law rights for individuals difficult in practice: spyware is a

[159] See the position put forward by the Commission during the oral hearing of 19 Nov. 2024 in Case C-769/22, *Commission v Hungary (values of the EU)*, pending at the time of writing. See L. Kaiser, A. Knecht, L. D. Spieker, "European Society Strikes Back - The Member States Embrace Article 2 TEU in Commission v Hungary", Verfassungsblog of 26 November 2024.

[160] Regulation (EU, Euratom) 2020/2092 of the European Parliament and of the Council of 16 December 2020 on a general regime of conditionality for the protection of the Union budget (OJ 2020 L 433I, p. 1).

[161] Cf. Articles 2 and 4 of the Regulation.

litmus test for the effectiveness and primacy of EU law. Courageous and creative solutions need to be found. At stake are not only the rights of individuals, but also the fabric of the EU as democratic and liberal system based on the rule of law and ultimately the values of the Union.[162] It remains to be seen whether the institutions (both at EU and national level), political parties, civil society and lawyers will be able to give an adequate response.

[162] G. Sartor, A. Loreggia, *The impact of Pegasus on fundamental rights and democratic processes*, study requested by the PEGA Committee of the European Parliament, 2022.

The Budgetary Responsibility of the Legislator and Its Limits in the European Union and in the Member States

Thomas von Danwitz

1 Introduction

The old political adage, according to which the budget is 'politics in the form of figures', still accurately describes the critical importance of the state budget for the exercise of political power. It also illustrates why, besides the right to charge taxes, the approval of public finances was at the heart of the quest for political participation by the young democracy movement in the nineteenth century.[1] The parliamentary decision on the budget is, in the words of the German Federal Constitutional Court, nothing other than the fundamental economic decision for key policy areas.[2] Therefore, the budgetary sovereignty of the German Bundestag is fundamental for democratic self-determination in the constitutional state, and constitutes a central element for its democratic decision-making.[3] Insofar as the German Basic Law

The author thanks Dr Moritz Bleckmann, Legal Secretary at the Court of Justice of the European Union, for his vital support in preparing this contribution.

[1] See, for the historical development in Germany towards a constitutional democracy, for example, Dürig/Herzog/Scholz/Kube, GG, 103rd supplement, January 2024, Art. 110, para. 17 with further references.

[2] See German Federal Constitutional Court, Collection of decisions (BVerfGE) 130, 318 (p. 342 et seq., at para. 105 with further references) – Neuner-Gremium. Previously BVerfGE 79, 311 (p. 329, at para. 55) – Staatsverschuldung and BVerfGE 129, 124 (p. 177 et seq., at paras. 122 and 123) – Europäische Finanzstabilisierungsfazilität.

[3] See, for example, BVerfGE 130, 318 (p. 343, at para. 105 with further references) – Neuner-Gremium.

T. von Danwitz (✉)
Court of Justice of the European Union, Luxembourg, Luxembourg
e-mail: Thomas.Von_Danwitz@curia.europa.eu

L. Prete, L. Rezki (eds.), *Judging & (Re)Thinking European Union Law*,
https://doi.org/10.1007/978-3-032-13473-8_35

draws limits to the parliament's budget sovereignty, the exercise of budgetary powers is subject to a constitutional review taking however into account the margin of appreciation of the budgetary legislator. The actions brought by the respective opposition parties before the German Federal Constitutional Court,[4] have repeatedly focused on questions regarding the constitutional limits of public debt. This thematic focus is hardly surprising, given the fact that the debt burden, which has been approved in a past or contemporary budget law is likely to limit the financial and, thus, political scope for any decision-making of the legislator in the future.[5] The problems that high public debts entail for the future of constitutional democracies are not unknown in the other Member States of the European Union. In Sweden it was, in the absence of a judicial constitutional review, the *Riksdag* itself, which adopted, in a remarkable effort of democratic self-restraint as a reaction to the recession in the 1990s,[6] legally binding limits to its own budgetary sovereignty, by introducing a surplus target[7] for the public sector and an expenditure ceiling[8] as well as a profound reform of the parliamentary decision-making process in order to make it more difficult to increase net spending.[9]

[4] See, for example, the references in footnote n. 2, as well as BVerfGE 167, 86 – Energie- und Klimafonds (English translation available on line, last viewed on 21.02.2025). As regards the Land of North Rhine-Westphalia, VerfGH NRW, NVwZ 2011, p. 805; NVwZ-RR 2013, p. 665.

[5] For this consideration, which is based on the budgetary principle of annuality, see, for example, BVerfGE 167, 86 (p. 142, at para. 162) – Energie- und Klimafonds.

[6] See for an overview and an assessment of these reforms, J. Wehner, 'Budget reform and legislative control in Sweden', *Journal of European Public Policy*, 2007, 14 (2), p. 313. See also OECD (2017), OECD Journal on Budgeting, Vol. 2016 Issue 2, OECD Publishing, Paris, p. 18 to 20 (available on line, last viewed on 21.2.2025).

[7] See chapter 2, paragraph 1 of the Swedish Budget Act. The surplus target obliges the Government to present a budget in surplus. The amount of this surplus target not being specified in the Swedish Budget Act itself, the *Riksdag* has made use of its power, pursuant to chapter 2, paragraph 1a of this Act, to determine this target, which applies until further notice and is reviewed every eight years. It was first set to 2% of GDP in 1997, then adjusted to 1% of GDP in 2007 and finally, in 2019, lowered to the current percentage of 0.33% of GDP. See Swedish Government Communication Ramverket för finanspolitiken (The Swedish fiscal policy framework), skr. 2017/18:207, p. 11 to 12 and 16. Currently, there is a broad political debate on departing from the surplus target and aiming instead for a balanced budget, see Reuters, Sweden to loosen budget rules to boost infrastructure, defence, 17 October 2024 (available on reuters.com, last viewed on 21.02.2025) and SOU 2024:76, Från överskottsmål till balansmål (From surplus target to balance target).

[8] The government must propose an expenditure ceiling for central government expenditure. The proposal relates only to the third year of the medium-term framework, as the expenditure ceilings from the first and second year are carried over automatically from the previous year's budgetary exercise. The Swedish Budget Act is clear that the expenditure ceiling must not be exceeded, and that the government should take action or propose legislation if necessary to avoid this, see chapter 2, paragraphs 2 and 4 of the Swedish Budget Act. Temporarily, this ceiling may be exceeded, but not by more than 10%. Furthermore, under certain circumstances, the *Riksdag* may allow the government to go beyond this percentage, see chapter 3, paragraph 8 of the Swedish Budget Act.

[9] Importantly, as a result of the reform, the Riksdag is required to decide on budget totals before making individual appropriations, see chapter 11, paragraph 18 of the Riksdag Act.

2 The Case-law of the Court: Shaped by the Particular Features of EU Budgetary Law

Questions of this kind have not yet been brought to the attention of the Court of Justice of the European Union. One reason for this may be that any action for annulment brought by political parties and by private individuals against budgetary decisions would have little chance of success, due to the presumable lack of direct and individual concern within the meaning of Article 263(4) TFEU. At a closer look, however, the reasons why the Court of Justice so far has been dealing with other issues in this field are lie in the historical evolution of the financial constitution of the European Union and, in particular, in the specific division of competences in budget matters. Whereas, under the Treaties of Rome, the financial constitution of the European Communities was of a purely intergovernmental nature in terms of decision-making and due to the fact that the Communities' budget was exclusively financed through contributions from the Member States, the development of the European Parliament's legislative powers as a result of successive Treaty reforms is also, and perhaps above all, reflected in the remarkable extension of its budgetary powers (see Sect. 2.1). On the other hand, central decisions in the EU's system of own resources are still largely reserved to the Member States (see Sect. 2.2).

2.1 Division of Competences in EU Budgetary Matters: From an Exclusive Competence of the Council to a Competence Shared with the Parliament

Before 1970, budgetary powers were held exclusively by the Council, while the Parliament had a purely consultative role.

2.1.1 The First Budgetary Treaty in the Case Law of the Court

A first amendment of the European financial constitution was introduced by the Treaty of Luxembourg, signed on 22 April 1970. While confirming the exclusive right of the Council to decide on the compulsory expenditure provided for by the EC Treaty, it granted to the Parliament a real right to say with regard to *non-compulsory expenditure*, albeit those expenses were initially limited to merely 8% of the budget.[10] This amendment of the Treaty led to a first ruling by the Court of Justice in 1986, after the President of the European Parliament had declared the

[10] See, in this regard, the European Parliament's fact sheet on the budgetary procedure of the EU and its historical evolution (available on line, last viewed on 21.02.2025).

budget for that year definitively adopted, despite the fact that the Council and the Parliament had not yet—as provided for in the Treaty[11]—reached an agreement on the maximum rate of non-compulsory expenditure. The Court ruled that the President of the European Parliament had thereby breached the treaty requirements.[12]

The budget for 1986 subsequently led to another judgment of the Court, relating to the distinction between compulsory and non-compulsory expenses. The Court stressed that, in accordance with the provisions of the EC Treaty, it is primarily for the institutions to resolve problems regarding the delimitation of non-compulsory expenditure in relation to compulsory expenditure, through an inter-institutional dialogue characterized by mutual duties of sincere cooperation. In addition, the Court emphasized that the institutions have a margin of discretion in making the said delimitation. With reference to the fact that this discretionary power is limited by the separation of powers, as laid down in the EC Treaty, between the institutions, the Court confined its judicial review to verifying whether, in the context of inter-institutional cooperation, the institutions did not ignore the rules of law and did not exercise their discretionary power in a manifestly wrong or arbitrary way.[13]

2.1.2 Judgments Relating to the Budgetary Procedure Under the Lisbon Treaty

Although a second budgetary treaty, the Treaty of Brussels of 22 July 1975, conferred further budgetary powers to the Parliament in the form of the right to *reject the budget in its entirety for important reasons* and to request the submission of a

---

[11] As regards non-compulsory expenditure, the fifth subparagraph of Article 203(9) of the EC Treaty, as amended by the Treaty of Luxembourg, disposed that if the Council or the Parliament wanted to exceed the maximum rate proposed by the Commission, an agreement had to be reached between the institutions. In the situation leading to the CJEU judgment in *Council v Parliament,* 34/86. EU:C:1986:291, the President of the Parliament did not wait for that agreement before deciding, on the basis of Article 203(7) of this Treaty, that the budget for 1986 had been definitively adopted.

[12] CJEU, judgment in *Council v Parliament*, 34/86, EU:C:1986:291, paras. 34–39. For the same reason the Court annulled, (by judgment in *Council v Parliament*, C-41/95, EU:C:1995:431, para. 37 and number 1 of the operative part), the act of the President of the European Parliament declaring the final adoption of the general budget for the financial year 1995 budget by the President of the European Parliament.

[13] See, to that effect, CJEU, judgment in *Greece v Council*, 204/86, EU:C:1988:450, paras. 14–17 and 22. In the proceedings leading to the judgment in *Council v Parliament*, 34/86, EU:C:1986:291, the Council had also raised the same question. However, since the contested act declaring the final adoption of the general budget for the financial year 1986 had already been annulled for other reasons, the Court decided, in paras. 49 and 50 of the latter judgment, to leave this question unanswered.

new draft,[14] its influence however remained extremely limited with regard to individual budgetary positions. The situation changed substantially only with the Lisbon Treaty. In accordance with Article 314 TFEU, the European Parliament and the Council, acting in accordance with *a special legislative procedure, shall jointly* establish the Union's annual budget, for all Union expenditure. The Parliament's powers are no longer limited either to reject the draft budget in its entirety or to accept it, but it is now empowered to propose amendments without any limits. In case of such amendments, the Treaty provides for a Conciliation Committee having the task to reach an agreement on a so-called "joint text", which is then submitted to the Council and the Parliament for approval.[15] Moreover, the Parliament does not only have a right of participation placing it, in principle, on a level playing field with the Council, but it has, acting by a qualified majority, also the power to enforce that "joint text" against the will of the Council.[16]

As a parliamentary deliberation in plenary sitting is of fundamental importance for the democratic legitimacy of the Union's budgetary procedure, the Court has made clear in two judgments from 2018 and 2020 that the Parliament has to exercise its powers in budget matters in such a sitting. Indeed, it held that the exercise by the Parliament of its budgetary powers in plenary sitting "constitutes a fundamental event in the democratic life of the European Union and requires, inter alia, a public debate in plenary sitting enabling the citizens of the European Union to acquaint themselves with the various political orientations expressed and, as a result, to form a political opinion on the European Union's actions. Furthermore, the transparency afforded by a parliamentary debate in a plenary sitting is likely to strengthen the democratic legitimacy of the budgetary procedure in the eyes of citizens of the European Union and the credibility of the latter's actions." For that reason, the Court judged that not only the examination of the draft budget at first reading requires a public debate and vote in plenary but also, following a conciliation procedure, the so-called "joint text".[17]

---

[14] According to Article 203(8) of the EC Treaty, as amended by the Treaty amending certain financial provisions of the Treaties establishing the European Economic Communities and of the Treaty establishing a single Council and a single Commission of the European Communities (OJ 1977 L 359, p. 1).

[15] See, in that regard, Article 314(4) to (6) TFEU.

[16] See Article 314(7) (d) TFEU. See CJEU, judgment in *France v Parliament (Exercise of budgetary powers)*, C-73/17, EU:C:2018:787, para. 39. Conversely, the Council cannot enforce the "joint text" of the Conciliation Committee against the will of the Parliament. If, by a majority of its members, the Parliament rejects that draft while it is approved by the Council, Article 314(6)(c) TFEU requires the Commission to submit a new draft budget.

[17] See, to that effect, CJEU, judgment in *France v Parliament (Exercise of budgetary powers)*, C-73/17, EU:C:2018:787, paras. 32, 35, 37 and 40, with further references. As the Court made clear in para. 36 of that judgment, the deliberations of the Conciliation Committee cannot itself guarantee the necessary transparency and democratic legitimacy of the budgetary procedure, since its meetings are not public and its composition, though reflecting the majority in the Parliament, does not fully represent the political interests of all the members of that body. See also CJEU, judgment in *France v Parliament (Exercise of budgetary powers II)*, C-92/18, EU:C:2020:506, paras. 19 and 21.

2.1.3 Rare Opportunities to Consider the Substantive Principles of EU Budgetary Law

Against that background, it should be noted that the case-law of the Court of Justice on Article 314 TFEU does not attach less importance to the Parliament's budgetary powers for the democratic legitimacy of the Union budget than does the German constitutional court with regard to the budgetary sovereignty of the German Bundestag. In that regard, it is also interesting to note that the relevant considerations of the Court of Justice relate essentially to budgetary procedural law[18] and that it has so far rather sporadically had the opportunity to consider the substantive principles of EU budgetary law under the Treaty.[19]

2.2 Financing the EU Budget: The Own Resources System

According to Article 311(1) TFEU, the European Union provides itself with the means necessary to attain its objectives and carry through its policies. In that regard, it follows from Article 311(2) TFEU that, without prejudice to "other revenue", the budget of the Union shall be financed wholly from "own resources". Pursuant to the third paragraph of that article, the provisions relating to the system of own resources of the Union are to be laid down by a decision. It follows from the latter provision that the decision is adopted by the Council, acting in accordance with a special legislative procedure, unanimously and after a mere consultation of the Parliament. Furthermore, Article 311(3) TFEU provides that this decision on "own resources" shall not enter into force until it is approved by the Member States in accordance with their respective constitutional requirements. Thus, the funding of the Union remains largely inter-governmental.

2.2.1 EU Own Resources Defined in Secondary Law

The concept of 'own resources' and 'other resources' is not defined in the Treaty. In accordance with the established practice, which is now reflected in Article 1(2)(a)

---

[18] In order to ensure a sufficient preparation for the debate and vote in plenary sitting, the draft budget must be made available to Members of Parliament – not only in English but in all official languages – at least 24 hours before this sitting. See CJEU, judgment in *France v Parliament (Exercise of budgetary powers)*, C-73/17, EU:C:2018:787, paras. 56 to 58.

[19] The *completeness and annuality* of the budget, now enshrined in Article 310(1) TFEU, had already been considered by the Court of Justice in its judgments in *Council v Parliament*, C-284/90, EU:C:1992:154, paras. 24–27, and *Parliament v Council*, C-316/91, EU:C:1994:76, paras. 38 and 39. Similarly, the Court has already held that any significant expenditure presupposes not only an entry in the Union's budget, but also the prior adoption of a basic act authorizing that expenditure (judgment in *United Kingdom v Commission*, C-106/96, EU:C:1998:218, paras. 21 et seq., in particular 26–31). This requirement is now enshrined in Article 310(3) TFEU.

of the 2020 Own Resources Decision,[20] this concept largely covers the so-called classic own resources, which include, inter alia, taxes and duties introduced by EU institutions. Pursuant to Article 2(1)(b) and (d) of that decision, these own resources are completed by VAT revenues at a uniform call rate of 0.30% to the total amount of VAT receipts on all taxable supplies and by revenues from a uniform call rate on the total amount of gross national income (GNI) to be determined in the budgetary procedure.[21]

Moreover, in Article 2(1)(c) of the 2020 Own Resources Decision, the Council for the first time made use of the possibility, now expressly authorised in Article 311 (3) TFEU, of creating a new category of own resources. The newly created category is an environmental packaging tax, which consists of the application of a uniform call rate of EUR 0.80 per kilogram of non-recycled plastic packaging waste generated in each Member State. It is apparent from recitals 4 to 9 of the 2020 Own Resources Decision, that this tax is the first kind of a new category of taxes, which are intended to reduce, in the long term, the importance of own resources based on gross national income (GNI), in other words contributory resources,[22] and thereby to strengthen the financial autonomy of the European Union. Most importantly, this new category of taxes shall establish a more visible link between the financing of the European Union and its politics, while contributing in the form of a steering tax to the achievement of its objectives. Insofar as the question of the correct legal basis has been raised with regard to that purpose,[23] a definitive clarification of EU law is still to be expected.

2.2.2 Capital Market Loans: The Next Generation of Own Resources?

By authorizing the Commission, on the basis of Article 311(3) TFEU, to borrow funds on capital markets on behalf of the Union up to EUR 750 000 million in 2018 prices, the 2020 Own Resources Decision[24] raises another important legal issue

[20] Council Decision (EU, Euratom) 2020/2053 of 14 December 2020 on the system of own resources of the European Union and repealing Decision 2014/335/EU, Euratom (OJ 2020 L 424, p. 1).

[21] For example, C. Waldhoff, in Calliess/Ruffert, *EUV/AEUV*, 6th Edition 2022, Article 311 AEUV, para. 8.

[22] The latter are essentially membership fees, see C. Waldhoff, in Calliess/Ruffert, *EUV/AEUV*, 6th Edition 2022, Article 311 AEUV, para. 8.

[23] For example, J. Hey, `Das Einnahmesystem der Europäischen Union: neue Steuern als neue Eigenmittel?‘, EuZW 2021, p. 277 (282 with further references). In addition to Article 311(3) TFEU, which applies above all to taxes with the primary purpose of financing the Union, Article 192(2)(a) TFEU comes into consideration as an environmental steering tax. Under the latter article, the Council is empowered, acting unanimously in accordance with a special legislative procedure and after consulting the European Parliament, to adopt provisions primarily of a fiscal nature, in environmental policy matters. Critical of the "flat-rate reductions" provided for in the third subparagraph of Article 2(2) of the 2020 Own Resources Decision, C. Waldhoff, i: Calliess/Ruffert, *EUV/AEUV*, 6th Edition 2022, Article 311 AEUV, para. 11.

[24] See Article 5(1) of the Own Resources Decision 2020.

which has not yet been clarified by the Court.[25] Against this background, I would like to limit myself to a few observations in this regard.[26]

European primary law does neither contain any provision expressly providing that the Union borrows funds for the purpose of financing the EU budget, nor does it expressly exclude such a borrowing. Indeed, Article 311(1) TFEU, according to which the Union shall provide itself with the necessary means, is—with regard to the financial instrument to be chosen in that respect—worded as broadly as the concepts of "own resources" and "other resources".[27] The rule laid down in the third subparagraph of Article 310 (1) TFEU, according to which the revenue and expenditure shown in the budget shall be in balance, does not expressly preclude the Union from taking on debt, nor does it implicitly contain such a prohibition. By contrast, the second sentence of Article 318(1) TFEU presupposes the existence of Union debt, as this provision obliges the Commission to transmit an annual statement of the assets and liabilities of the European Union to the Parliament and the Council.[28] This is also in line with the Union's historical practice, which has repeatedly relied on credit-financed funds in order to deal with acute crises.[29]

Insofar as Article 17(2) of the EU Financial Regulation[30] provides that the Union shall not raise loans within the framework of its budget, it is a provision of EU secondary law. In particular, the funds raised by the Commission on the financial markets do not finance the budget in general, but are to be used exclusively under

[25] As for the scope of judicial review of the Own Resources Decision 2020, see J. Dürr, 'Judicial Review of the EU Own Resources Decision by the ECJ' (2024), 52, Intertax, Issue 8, p. 561.

[26] With regard to Article 125 TFEU, the German Federal constitutional Court rightly points out that if, under Article 5 of the Own Resources Decision 2020, the Commission may borrow funds on behalf of the Union on the financial markets, the Union may not be liable or assume the commitments of any Member State. Thus, an infringement of Article 125 TFEU appears in principle, to be excluded [see also BVerfG, judgment of 6 December 2022, 2 BvR 547/21, 2 BvR 798/21, NJW 2023, p. 425 (439, at para. 205) – EU Own Resources Decision 2020 (English translation available on line, last viewed on 21.02.2025)]. Therefore, I will not deal with that provision of the Treaty in the following.

[27] According to A. Steinbach, S. Grund, 'Der EU-Corona-Aufbaufonds – nächste Etappe in die Fiskal- und Transferunion?', NJW 2023, p. 405 (407), Union loans could even be considered as a new category of own resources.

[28] See BVerfG, judgment of 6 December 2022, 2 BvR 547/21, 2 BvR 798/21, NJW 2023, p. 425 (433, at para. 155 with further references).

[29] Similarly, BVerfG, *ibid.* Starting with the so-called oil bond in 1976, this practice continued with the European Financial Stability Mechanism (EFSM) in 2010, the European Financial Stabilisation Mechanism (ESM) in 2012 and, finally, the EU instrument for temporary Support to mitigate Unemployment Risks in an Emergency (SURE) in 2020. See, for an overview, D. Meyer, 'Next Generation EU – Neues Eigenmittelsystem weist in eine Fiskalunion', EuZW 2021, p. 16 (17 et seq. with further references).

[30] Regulation (EU, Euratom) 2024/2509 of the European Parliament and of the Council of 23 September 2024 on the financial rules applicable to the general budget of the Union (recast) (OJ L, 2024/2509, p. 1).

the European Union Recovery Instrument to address the consequences of the COVID-19 crisis.[31]

When it comes to the judicial review of the requirements laid down in Article 311(1) TFEU with regard to the necessity to borrow funds, it follows from the case-law in *Gauweiler* and *Weiss and Others* that the Council has a wide margin of appreciation insofar as it is called to make choices of a technical nature and to undertake complex forecasts and assessments.[32] The Council should also have such a margin of appreciation at its disposal with regard to the assessment of the existence of a severe difficulty, within the meaning of Article 122(1) and (2) TFEU, on the basis of which the EU Recovery Instrument was adopted with the aim to address the consequences of the COVID-19 crisis.[33] However, according to the Court's settled case-law, where an EU institution enjoys a wide discretion, a judicial review of compliance with certain procedural guarantees—in particular the obligation to examine carefully and impartially all the relevant aspects of the individual case and the obligation to give an adequate statement of the reasons—is of fundamental importance.[34]

3 The Protection of the EU's Financial Interests and Its Constitutional Implications

Due to the specific structure of the European Union, the Court of Justice is also dealing with questions relating to the protection of the Union's financial interests, which as such are rather unlikely to be referred to national supreme or constitutional courts. Under Article 325(1) TFEU, Member States are required to take deterrent and effective measures to combat illegal activities affecting the financial interests of the European Union. The activities referred to in this provision are those affecting the collection by the Member States of the Union's own resources, such as value added tax, and preventing them to make the corresponding resources available to the Union budget.[35] If the Court had initially inferred

---

[31] See in this regard Articles 4 and 5(1) of Own Resources Decision 2020 in conjunction with Article 3 of Council Regulation (EU) 2020/2094 of 14 December 2020 establishing a European Union Recovery Instrument to support the recovery in the aftermath of the COVID-19 crisis (OJ 2020 L 433 I, p. 23).

[32] See, by analogy, CJEU, judgments in *Gauweiler and Others*, C-62/14, EU:C:2015:400, para. 68, and *Weiss and Others*, C-493/17, EU:C:2018:1000, para. 73.

[33] See, in the same sens, BverfG, judgment of 6 December 2022, 2 BvR 547/21, 2 BvR 798/21, NJW 2023, p. 425 (437, at para. 183 with further references) – EU Own Resources Decision 2020.

[34] See, by analogy, CJEU, judgments in *Gauweiler and Others*, C-62/14, EU:C:2015:400, para. 69, and *Weiss and Others*, C-493/17, EU:C:2018:1000, para. 30.

[35] CJEU, judgments of 26 February 2013, *Åkerberg Fransson*, C-617/10, EU:C:2013:105, para. 26, and of 8 September 2015, *Taricco and Others*, C-105/14, EU:C:2015:555, para. 38. Similarly, the Member States are required to take effective measures to recover sums wrongly paid to the beneficiary of a subsidy funded in part from the budget of the European Union. See, in that regard, CJUE,

such an obligation from provisions of secondary law in the VAT Directive 2006/112, read in conjunction with Article 4(3) TEU,[36] it based that obligation in the judgment *Taricco* instead directly on the primary law provision of Article 325(1) TFEU. The Court also clarified that while Member States have, in principle, freedom to choose between administrative or criminal penalties, or a combination of the two, the imposition of criminal penalties may nevertheless be essential to combat certain cases of serious VAT evasion in an effective and dissuasive manner.[37]

3.1 *The Judgment* in Taricco*: The Need to Address National Rules on Criminal Procedure*

Already in the *Taricco* case, this clarification of its previous case-law meant that the Court had to address national rules on criminal procedure and their compatibility with EU law. With regard to the rules on the interruption of limitation periods at issue in the main proceedings in that case, the Court found that such rules would be incompatible with Article 325(1) TFEU if their application has the effect that, in a considerable number of cases, the commission of serious fraud will escape criminal punishment, since the offences will usually be time-barred before the criminal penalty laid down by law can be imposed by a final judicial decision.[38] Above all, however, the Court clarified that a national court, in such a case, would be required to disapply national rules incompatible with Article 325(1) TFEU[39] in accordance with the principle of the primacy of EU law. In the case of an infringement of the secondary law provisions of Directive 2006/112, such an application of the principle of primacy to the detriment of the accused would have been excluded according to settled case-law.[40] As the Court based the obligation to impose penalties for the protection of financial interests in the *Taricco* case on the primary law provision of Article 325(1) TFEU, it had, from then on, to deal with difficult fundamental rights issues relating to the principles of legality and

judgment of 21 December 2021, *Euro Box Promotion and Others*, C-357/19, C-379/19, C-547/19, C-811/19 and C-840/19, EU:C:2021:1034, para. 182 with further references.

[36] See CJEU, judgment of 26 February 2013, *Åkerberg Fransson*, C-617/10, EU:C:2013:105, para. 25.

[37] CJEU, judgment of 8 September 2015, *Taricco and Others*, C-105/14, EU:C:2015:555, para. 39.

[38] CJEU, judgment in *Taricco and Others*, C-105/14, EU:C:2015:555, para. 47.

[39] Ibid., para. 49.

[40] According to settled case-law, a directive cannot, of itself and independently of a national law adopted by a Member State for its implementation, have the effect of determining or aggravating the liability in criminal law of persons who act in contravention of the provisions of that directive. See CJEU, judgment in *Berlusconi and Others*, C-387/02, C-391/02 and C-403/02, EU:C:2005:270, para. 74.

proportionality in relation to offences and penalties under Article 49 of the Charter.[41]

3.2 *The* **Eurobox** *Judgment: Clarifications Regarding Judicial Independence and Confirming the Case-law on the Primacy of EU Law*

The *Eurobox* judgment illustrates quite clearly the wide range of fundamental questions of a constitutional nature, that may arise in the context of the protection of the Union's financial interests. In that case, the Court not only held that Article 325(1) TFEU may preclude the application of national constitutional court's case-law relating to the composition of national courts specialized in matters of VAT fraud, where the application of this case-law leads to a modification of the practice as to this composition, which is not required by Article 47 (2) of the Charter, and entails a systemic risk of impunity of acts constituting serious fraud affecting the European Union's financial interests.[42] Furthermore, after having clarified some fundamental questions concerning judicial independence in the context of the case-law of a national constitutional court,[43] the Court also confirmed its settled case-law on the primacy of EU law. It emphasized, in particular, that the "raison d'être" of the principle of primacy, as it always has been, lies in the essential characteristics of the EU legal order established by the Treaties, the autonomy and the unity and effectiveness of EU law, as confirmed most recently by the Treaty of Lisbon.[44] The Court added, that the European Union can only respect the equality of the Member States, as required by Article 4(2) TEU, if the Member States are unable to enforce a unilateral measure against the EU legal order. This is precisely what the principle of primacy ensures.[45]

[41] If, in the first judgment, the Court considered that the non-application of national rules on the interruption of limitation periods would not, in principle, infringe the principles of legality and proportionality in relation to criminal offences and penalties, enshrined in Article 49 of the Charter, on the ground that it would not lead to a conviction for an act or omission which was not punishable at the time when it was committed nor the application of a penalty not provided for at that time (see CJEU, judgment in *Taricco and Others*, C-105/14, EU:C:2015:555, paras. 55–56), it stated in the judgment in *M.A.S. and M.B.*that this would be different if such a disapplication was found to be contrary to the principle that the applicable law must be precise or would lead to the retroactive application of rules of law which impose more stringent conditions of criminal liability than those in force at the time when the offence was committed (see CJEU, judgment in *M.A.S. and M.B.*, C-42/17, EU:C:2017:936, paras. 55 et seq., in particular 59–61).

[42] CJEU, judgment in *Euro Box Promotion and Others*, C-357/19, C-379/19, C-547/19, C-811/19 and C-840/19, EU:C:2021:1034, paras. 203–206 and 213.

[43] See, in this regard, ibid., paras. 215–242.

[44] See, in this regard, ibid., paras. 245–248.

[45] Ibid., para. 249.

3.3 The Rule of Law Conditionality Mechanism Before the Court

The Conditionality Mechanism established by Regulation 2020/2092[46] is a measure of EU law designed to protect, in particular, the financial interests of the Union, which the EU legislature adopted on the correct legal basis of Article 322(1)(a) TFEU. Indeed, Article 310(5) and Article 317 TFEU require that the budget shall be implemented in accordance with the principle of sound financial management and that the Member States shall cooperate with the Union, in particular with the Commission, to ensure that the appropriations entered in the budget are used in accordance with this principle and with the financial regulations made pursuant to Article 322 TFEU.[47] It follows that the financial rules referred to in Article 322(1)(a) TFEU also cover rules intended to ensure observance of the principle of sound financial management, including by the Member States when implementing the EU budget.[48]

According to the Court, the EU legislature adopted the Regulation 2020/2092 properly on the basis of Article 322(1)(a) TFEU, because it made the adoption of 'appropriate measures' to protect the Union budget subject to three conditions. *First,* there must be reasonable grounds for breaches of the principle of the rule of law in a Member State. *Second,* those breaches must affect or seriously risk affecting the sound financial management of the Union budget or the protection of the financial interests of the Union in a sufficiently direct way. *Third,* the 'appropriate measures' are limited to those exhaustively listed in that regulation, all of which relate to the implementation of the Union budget.[49] The link between the respect for the rule of law and the protection of the Union budget, set out by the EU legislature in the Regulation 2020/2092 appears, on a closer look, as a consistent continuation of the classic considerations already underlying the *Taricco* and *Eurobox* case-law.

Against that background, the Court also rejected the alleged circumvention of the rule of law procedure under Article 7 TEU. Indeed, Regulation 2020/2092 does not penalize "as such" potential breaches of the rule of law, but limits the adoption of appropriate measures to situations in which those breaches constitute at least a serious risk for the sound financial management of the Union budget or the protection

[46] Regulation (EU, Euratom) 2020/2092 of the European Parliament and of the Council of 16 December 2020 on a general regime of conditionality for the protection of the Union budget (OJ 2020 L 433I, p. 1).

[47] See CJEU, judgment in *Hungary v Parliament and Council*, C-156/21, EU:C:2022:97, paras. 102 and 104.

[48] See, to that effect, ibid., para. 105.

[49] See, in that regard, the provisions of Article 2(a) and Articles 3 to 6 of Regulation 2020/2092 and CJEU, judgment of 16 February 2022, *Hungary v Parliament and Council*, C-156/21, EU:C:2022:97, paras. 102 et seq. (in particular paras. 102, 104, 105, 111, 112, 121 and 131–139).

of the financial interests of the Union. Thus, the conditionality mechanism does not replace this rule of law procedure, but merely complements it.[50]

4 Conclusion

Due to the structural differences between the European Union and its Member States, the Court of Justice has so far been asked to deal with budgetary constitutional issues other than those raised in the national legal order of the Member States. However, if questions regarding treaty-based limits to permissible public debt are raised before the Court of Justice in the future, it could rely on some valuable insights and principles resulting from its already existing case-law, to which Nils Wahl considerably contributed with outstanding legal expertise and sound economic understanding, first as an Advocate General and later as a Senior Judge.

[50] See, in particular, the considerations in paras. 119, 141–145, 156–165 and 169–178 of the judgment in *Hungary v Parliament and Council*, C-156/21, EU:C:2022:97.

Nils Wahl Biography and Publications

Born: 31 January 1961

Academia

Professor of European Law, Faculty of Law, Stockholm University, November 2001.
Ass. Professor, Faculty of Law, Stockholm University, May 1995.
Juris doctor (European Law), Stockholm University, January 1995.
Juris kandidat (LLM), Stockholm University, September 1987.

Working experience

Senior Of Counsel, Covington & Burling LLP, Brussels, from April 2025.
Visiting Professor of European Law, Faculty of Law, Uppsala University, from January 2025.
Judge, Court of Justice of the European Union, October 2019 – October 2024.
Advocate General, Court of Justice of the European Union, November 2012 – February 2019.
Judge, General Court of the European Union, October 2006 – November 2012.
Professor of European Law, Faculty of Law, Stockholm University, November 2001 – July 2024.
University teacher, Faculty of Law, Stockholm University, July 1994 – October 2001, since July 1995 also holder of the Jean Monnet Chair in European Law, Faculty of Law, Stockholm University.
Managing Director for the foundation *Stiftelsen Fakultetskurser vid Stockholms universitet*, February 1993 – November 2004.
Associate, Advokatfirman Cederquist, Stockholm, October 1987 – June 1989.

L. Prete, L. Rezki (eds.), *Judging & (Re)Thinking European Union Law*,
https://doi.org/10.1007/978-3-032-13473-8

Assignments

Chairman of the Swedish Network for European Legal Studies *Nätverket för europarättsliga studier*, April 2002 – August 2006, member since 1997.

Member of the Council for competition law matters (Sweden) *Rådet för konkurrensfrågor*, July 2001 – August 2006.

Winner of a price for an outstanding academic work *Tore Alméns pris för en framstående rättsvetenskaplig prestation av betydelse för det praktiska rättslivet* (for the book *Konkurrensskada*), Tore Alméns minnesfond, November 2001.

Editor for the Yearbooks from the Swedish Network for European Studies 2002–2005.

Editor for different Liber Amicorums and omnibus books (most recently, co-editor of *Regulation 1/2003 and EU Antitrust Enforcement: A Systematic Guide,* Wolters Kluwer, 2023, with K. Dekeyser, C. Gauer, J. Laitenberger, W. Wils and L. Prete).

Member (during different periods) of the board of editors or the board of directors of Swedish or European law journals.

Faculty opponent or member of the grading board on numerous occasions at Swedish and European universities, both in law and in economics.

Participation in Public Reports

Expert in the public report concerning an overhaul of the Swedish competition law, dir 2004:128, SOU 2006:99 *En ny konkurrenslag.*

Expert in the public report concerning a reform of the Swedish competition law, dir 2003:2 SOU 2003:73 *Reformerad konkurrensövervakning*, SOU 2004:10 *Rätten till skadestånd enligt konkurrenslagen.*

Expert in the public report concerning an effective Swedish competition law, dir 2000:40, inter alia SOU 2001:74 *Kartellbekämpning.*

Expert in the public report concerning national application of the EU competition rules, dir 1998:67, SOU 2000:4 *Svensk tillämpning av EG:s konkurrensregler.*

Expert in the public report concerning small and medium sized companies and competition law, Ds 1998:72 *Små företag och konkurrenslagen.*

Expert in the public report concerning the state of competition within the food industry, dir 1995:137 SOU 1996:144 *Ökad konkurrens i handeln med livsmedel.*

Expert in the public report concerning the applicability of competition rules within the farming industry, dir 1994:59 and 1994:142 SOU 1995:117 *Jordbruk och konkurrens.*

Expert in the public report concerning the Swedish accession to the EU, dir 1993:83 SOU 1994:10 *Anslutning till EU.*

Publications

i) Books

Konkurrensskada. Skadeståndsansvar vid överträdelse av EG:s konkurrensregler och den svenska konkurrenslagen, 436 pages, Stockholm 2000 (second printing 2001).

Märkbara småföretag och konkurrens – fyra uppsatser om små företags samverkansmöjligheter enligt svensk och europeisk konkurrensrätt, 144 pages, Stockholm 2000.

EG-rättsliga frågor och beredskapsplanering, 82 pages, Stockholm 1999.

Konkurrensförhållanden. Om förhållandet mellan EG:s konkurrensrätt och nationell konkurrensrätt, 627 pages, doctoral dissertation, Stockholm 1994.

The Lugano Convention and Legal Integration. The Lugano Convention on Jurisdiction and Enforcement of Judgments in Civil and Commercial Matters and Its Effects on Legal Integration Between the European Community and the EFTA States, 85 pages, Stockholm 1990.

The Free Trade Agreements Between the EC and the EFTA Countries. Their Implementation and Interpretation. A Case Study, 133 pages, Stockholm 1988.

ii) Submissions to Public Reports

Optimala sanktioner inom svensk konkurrensrätt, Expert Opinion commissioned by the Swedish Competition Authority, Konkurrensverkets rapportserie 2006:3, 100 pages.

Expert Opinion to a public report Ds 1998:72 *Små företag och konkurrenslagen* Bilaga, 31 pages.

Gruppundantag för kedjor i detaljhandeln, Expert Opinion commissioned by the Swedish Competition Authority, Konkurrensverkets rapportserie 1997:1, 43 pages.

Expert Opinion to a public report SOU 1996:31 *Attityder och lagstiftning i samverkan*, 33 pages.

Expert Opinion to a public report SOU 1995:117 *Jordbruk och konkurrens*, p. 353–388.

Expert Opinion to a public report (together with Ulf Bernitz), SOU 1991:59 *Konkurrens för ökad välfärd*, Del 1 p. 229–317.

iii) Articles and Contributions

Freedom to Conduct a Business: The Search for a Balance that Avoids Undue Interference, together with Stefano Boni, forthcoming.

Preliminary rulings in EU Antitrust Law – The perspective of a judge of the Court of Justice, together with Leila Rezki, forthcoming.

The Freedom to Conduct a Business: A Right of Fundamental Importance for the Future of the European Union, in The Internal Market and the Future of European Integration: essays in honour of Laurence W. Gormley, 2019.

The gatekeepers of Article 267 TFEU: on jurisdiction and admissibility of references for preliminary rulings, together with Luca Prete, Common Market Law Review, vol. 55, No. 2, 2018.

From Greek Olive Oil to Latvian Music: Is There Any Such Thing as Unfair Prices?, Liber Amicorum Douglas H. Ginsburg, Vol. 1, 2018.

Une même carte de route pour un terrain différent : de quelques propos sur la notion d'avantage sélectif dans la jurisprudence récente de la Cour de justice, in L'Europe au present: liber amicorum Melchior Wathelet, 2018.

Blowin' against the wind: on ACTA, AA, CETA, TTIP and the forgetfulness of David Ricardo, together with Luca Prete, in Journal of World Trade, Vol. 51, Issue 5, 2017.

Näringsfriheten – en rättighet av grundläggande betydelse för EU: framtid, Festskrift till Lars Pehrson, Stockholm, 2016.

Enjeu et limites actuelles de la jurisprudence relative à la compétence de pleine juridiction conférée au juge de l'Union en matière de concurrence, in La Cour de justice de l'Union européenne sous la présidence de Vassilios Skouris (2003–2015): liber amicorum Vassilios Skouris, 2015.

Between certainty, severity and proportionality: some reflections on the nature and functioning of Article 260(3) TFEU, together with Luca Prete, in European Law Reporter No. 6, 2014.

Uncharted waters: reflections on the legal significance of the Charter under EEA law and judicial cross-fertilisation in the field of fundamental rights, in The EEA and the EFTA Court, 2014.

Procedural issues in recent case–law: the EU Courts, 2013 Fordham Comp. l. Inst. 403 (B. Hawk ed.), 2014.

Quelques réflexions sur le rôle du juge, in New frontiers of antitrust, 2012.

Parent company liability – a question of facts or presumption?, 19th St Gallen International Competition Law Forum, 2012.

Antitrust fact finding in judicial and administrative proceedings, 2011 Fordham Comp. L. Inst. 251 (B. Hawk ed.), 2012.

Access to documents in competition cases, 18th St Gallen International Competition Law Forum, 2011.

European Competition law and Fundamental rights post the Lisbon Treaty, GCLC Annual Conference 2010 (M. Merola and J. Derenne eds), Brussels, 2012.

Standard of Review – Comprehensive or Limited?, in European Competition Law Annual 2009 (C-D. Ehlermann and M. Marquis eds), s. 285, Oxford, 2011.

Obsession with Justice – Competition Law Infringements and Their Perpetrators, in EU Competition Law in Context, Essays in honour of Virpi Tiili (H. Kanninen, N. Korjus and A. Rosas eds), Oxford, 2009.

Recent Case–law on Exclusionary Behaviour, 16th St Gallen International Competition Law Forum 2009, Basel, 2010.

Appeals before the Court of First Instance in Competition Cases – A Risk-Free Business? 15th St Gallen International Competition Law Forum 2008, Basel, 2009.

To what extent has the modernisation reform been successful at the national level?, Liber Amicorum Sven Norberg (M. Johansson, N. Wahl, and U. Bernitz eds), Brussels, 2006.

Case annotation: *Vad är oddsen för att det svenska spelmonopolet är förenligt med EG-rätten – Regeringsrättens dom i Wermdö Krog*, ERT 2005 s. 199.

Book review: Mårten P. Broberg, The European Commission's Jurisdiction to Scrutinise Mergers, Second ed., JT 2004–2005 s. 217.

Book review: Lars Henrikssons doktorsavhandling *Rätten till priskonkurrens i marknadsdominans*, JT 2003–2004 s. 675.

Book review: Carl Wetter, mfl., *Konkurrenslagen en handbok*, JT 2002–2003 s. 714.

Book review: Per Norbergs doktorsavhandling, Arbetsrätt och konkurrensrätt en normativ studie av motsättningen mellan marknadsrättsliga och sociala värden, SvJT 2003:402.

Effektivitet och modernisering i europeisk konkurrensrätt, in Europaperspektiv Årsbok 2003, Stockholm, 2002.

Chapter on competition law in *Ekonomirådets rapport 2002* (SNS förlag), Stockholm, 2002.

Skadestånd vid konkurrensbegränsningar, ERT 2001 s. 574.

Kommissionens förslag till modernisering av konkurrensreglerna (eller var det harmonisering?), ERT 2001 s. 227.

Damages for Infringement of Competition Law, 17 Scandinavian Studies in Law, Stockholm, 2001.

Marknadsdominerande företags rätt att prisdifferentiera (together with Lars Pehrson), JT 1998–99 s. 960.

Application of Competition Rules in Sweden, ERT 1998 s. 16.

Systembolaget (together with Lars Pehrson) JT 1997–98 s. 834.

National Report for Sweden, FIDE Congress, Stockholm 1998, p. 245.

Offentlig upphandling och skadestånd – prevention, reparation eller ingendera? JT 1997–98 s. 619.

EG-domstolen tolkar nationell rätt, JT 1997–98 s. 499.

Enforcement of EC Competition Law in National Courts, in EC Shipping Policy, The 17th Nordic Maritime Law Conference, 2–4 September 1996 (H.J. Bull and H. Stemshaug eds), s. 221, Oslo 1997.

Vertikal direkt effekt eller direktivkonform tolkning? JT 1996–97 s. 453.

Recent Developments Regarding Barriers to Trade: A General Shift of Emphasis? in Dealing with Integration. Perspectivs from Seminars on European Law 1995–1996 (I. Cameron, and A. Simoni, eds), s. 123, Uppsala, 1996.

Book review: Carl Michael Quitzow, *Fria varurörelser i den Europeiska gemenskapen* JT 1995–96 s. 889.

Kapitel 18 Konkurrensrätt, i Publica EU (D. Eliasson and N. Wahl eds) Stockholm, 1996.

"Relevanta" avgöranden av EG-domstolen, in EES-avtalet i svensk rätt (Rosén, J., red), Stockholm 1992 s. 181.

Prise de position de la Cour, JT 1991–92 s. 554.
Sweden's "New" Competition Act, EBLR 1992 p. 163.
Judicial Review of Public Procurement Decisions in Sweden, EBLR 1991 p. 77.
National Report for Sweden, FIDE Congress, Madrid 1990, p. 319.
Commentary in EEC – EFTA More than just good friends? (J. Jamar and H. Wallace eds), s. 304, Bruges, 1988.
Book review: Hjalte Rasmussen *On Law and Policy in the European Court of Justice* (together with Ulf Bernitz) SvJT 1988 s. 130.

MIX
Papier aus verantwortungsvollen Quellen
Paper from responsible sources
FSC® C105338

If you have any concerns about our products,
you can contact us on
ProductSafety@springernature.com

In case Publisher is established outside the EU,
the EU authorized representative is:
Springer Nature Customer Service Center GmbH
Europaplatz 3, 69115 Heidelberg, Germany

Printed by Libri Plureos GmbH
in Hamburg, Germany